Table of Atomic Masses*

Element	Symbol	Atomic Number	Atomic Mass	Element	Symbol	Atomic Number	Atomic Mass	Element	Symbol	Atomic Number	Atomic Mass
Actinium	Ac	89	[227]§	Hafnium	Hf	72	178.5	Promethium	Pm	61	[145]
Aluminum	Al	13	26.98	Helium	He	2	4.003	Protactinium	Pa	91	[231]
Americium	Am	95	[243]	Holmium	Ho	67	164.9	Radium	Ra	88	226
Antimony	Sb	51	121.8	Hydrogen	H	1	1.008	Radon	Rn	86	[222]
Argon	Ar	18	39.95	Indium	In	49	114.8	Rhenium	Re	75	186.2
Arsenic	As	33	74.92	Iodine	I	53	126.9	Rhodium	Rh	45	102.9
Astatine	At	85	[210]	Iridium	Ir	77	192.2	Rubidium	Rb	37	85.47
Barium	Ba	56	137.3	Iron	Fe	26	55.85	Ruthenium	Ru	44	101.1
Berkelium	Bk	97	[247]	Krypton	Kr	36	83.80	Samarium	Sm	62	150.4
Beryllium	Be	4	9.012	Lanthanum	La	57	138.9	Scandium	Sc	21	44.96
Bismuth	Bi	83	209.0	Lawrencium	Lr	103	[260]	Selenium	Se	34	78.96
Boron	B	5	10.81	Lead	Pb	82	207.2	Silicon	Si	14	28.09
Bromine	Br	35	79.90	Lithium	Li	3	6.941	Silver	Ag	47	107.9
Cadmium	Cd	48	112.4	Lutetium	Lu	71	175.0	Sodium	Na	11	22.99
Calcium	Ca	20	40.08	Magnesium	Mg	12	24.31	Strontium	Sr	38	87.62
Californium	Cf	98	[251]	Manganese	Mn	25	54.94	Sulfur	S	16	32.07
Carbon	C	6	12.01	Mendelevium	Md	101	[258]	Tantalum	Ta	73	180.9
Cerium	Ce	58	140.1	Mercury	Hg	80	200.6	Technetium	Tc	43	[98]
Cesium	Cs	55	132.90	Molybdenum	Mo	42	95.94	Tellurium	Te	52	127.6
Chlorine	Cl	17	35.45	Neodymium	Nd	60	144.2	Terbium	Tb	65	158.9
Chromium	Cr	24	52.00	Neon	Ne	10	20.18	Thallium	Tl	81	204.4
Cobalt	Co	27	58.93	Neptunium	Np	93	[237]	Thorium	Th	90	232.0
Copper	Cu	29	63.55	Nickel	Ni	28	58.69	Thulium	Tm	69	168.9
Curium	Cm	96	[247]	Niobium	Nb	41	92.91	Tin	Sn	50	118.7
Dysprosium	Dy	66	162.5	Nitrogen	N	7	14.01	Titanium	Ti	22	47.88
Einsteinium	Es	99	[252]	Nobelium	No	102	[259]	Tungsten	W	74	183.9
Erbium	Er	68	167.3	Osmium	Os	76	190.2	Uranium	U	92	238.0
Europium	Eu	63	152.0	Oxygen	O	8	16.00	Vanadium	V	23	50.94
Fermium	Fm	100	[257]	Palladium	Pd	46	106.4	Xenon	Xe	54	131.3
Fluorine	F	9	19.00	Phosphorus	P	15	30.97	Ytterbium	Yb	70	173.0
Francium	Fr	87	[223]	Platinum	Pt	78	195.1	Yttrium	Y	39	88.91
Gadolinium	Gd	64	157.3	Plutonium	Pu	94	[244]	Zinc	Zn	30	65.38
Gallium	Ga	31	69.72	Polonium	Po	84	[209]	Zirconium	Zr	40	91.22
Germanium	Ge	32	72.59	Potassium	K	19	39.10				
Gold	Au	79	197.0	Praseodymium	Pr	59	140.9				

*The values given here are to four significant figures.   § A value given in brackets denotes the mass of the longest-lived isotope.

W9-BFW-878

Basic Chemistry

Third Edition

Steven S. Zumdahl

University of Illinois

D. C. HEATH AND COMPANY

Lexington, Massachusetts   Toronto

Address editorial correspondence to

D. C. Heath and Company
125 Spring Street
Lexington, MA 02173

Senior Acquisitions Editor: Richard C. Stratton
Developmental Editor: June Goldstein
Production Editor: Heather Garrison
Designer: Cornelia Boynton
Photo Researcher: Martha Shethar, Derek Wing
Art Editor: Diane Grossman, Prentice Crosier
Production Coordinator: Richard Tonachel
Permissions Editor: Margaret Roll
Cover: (design) Linda Manly Wade, (photo) Deni McIntyre / Photo Researchers Inc.

For permission to use copyrighted materials, grateful acknowledgment is made to the copyright holders listed on pages A9–A10, which are hereby considered an extension of this copyright page.

Copyright © 1996 by D. C. Heath and Company.

Previous editions copyright © 1990, 1993 by D. C. Heath and Company

All rights reserved. No part of this publication may be reproduced or transmitted in any form or by any means, electronic or mechanical, including photocopy, recording, or any informa-tion storage or retrieval system, without permission in writing from the publisher.

Published simultaneously in Canada.

Printed in the United States of America.

International Standard Book Number: 0–669–39760–1

Library of Congress Catalog Number: 95–75240

10 9 8 7 6 5

Preface

The goal of this book is to make chemistry interesting, accessible, and understandable to the beginning student. Learning chemistry can be very rewarding. And even the novice, we believe, can relate the macroscopic world of chemistry—the observation of color changes and precipitate formation—to the microscopic world of ions and molecules. To achieve that goal, instructors are making a sincere attempt to provide more interesting and more effective ways to learn chemistry, and we hope that *Basic Chemistry* will be perceived as a part of that effort. In this text we have presented concepts in a clear and sensible manner using language and analogies that students can relate to. In addition, we have connected chemistry to real-life experience at every opportunity, from chapter opening discussions of chemical applications to "Chemistry in Focus" features throughout the book. We are convinced that this approach will foster enthusiasm and real understanding as the student uses this text.

New to this Edition

We were very pleased with the positive response to the first two editions of this text. To further enhance the text, we have made the following changes in this edition:

- Chapter 1 was rewritten to highlight the importance of chemistry.

- To make the text more flexible, the material on elements and ions was moved from Chapter 5 to Chapter 4. This arrangement allows for a smoother transition from Chapter 4 to Chapter 11 for instructors who prefer to cover all of atomic structure early in the course. Chapter 5 now deals solely with nomenclature.

- We added several new "Chemistry in Focus" boxes. Every chapter now has one or more of these essays.

- We introduced a new feature, Cumulative Review exercises, which appear after every few chapters.

- Self-Check exercises now include cross references to end-of-chapter problems.

- We added many new end-of-chapter questions and problems. Answers to the even-numbered questions and problems are in the back of the text.

- We reworked any text section that required clarification.

- We updated the chemistry discussion and accompanying photos where necessary.

Emphasis on Reaction Chemistry

We continue to emphasize chemical reactions early in the book, leaving the more abstract material on orbitals for later chapters. In a course in which many students encounter chemistry for the first time, it seems especially important that we present the chemical nature of matter before we discuss the theoretical intricacies of atoms and orbitals. Reactions are inherently interesting to students and can help us draw them to chemistry. In particular, reactions can form the basis for fascinating classroom demonstrations and laboratory experiments.

We have therefore chosen to emphasize reactions before going on to the details of atomic structure. Relying only on very simple ideas about the atom, Chapters 6 through 8 represent a thorough treatment of chemical reactions, including how to recognize a chemical change and what a chemical equation means. The properties of aqueous solutions are discussed in detail, and careful attention is given to precipitation and acid-base reactions. In addition, a simple treatment of oxidation-reduction reactions is given. The material on reactions is covered in three short chapters, allowing students to digest it in small doses with lots of end-of-chapter problems. This arrangement also gives instructors considerable flexibility in covering the material. These three chapters should provide a solid foundation, relatively early in the course, for reaction-based laboratory experiments.

For instructors who feel that it is desirable to introduce orbitals early in the course, prior to chemical reactions, the chapters on atomic theory and bonding (Chapters 11 and 12) can be covered directly after Chapter 4. In this edition, Chapters 4 and 5 were reorganized to make this option even easier. The material on elements and ions was moved from Chapter 5 to Chapter 4, making a transition from Chapter 4 to Chapter 11 more natural. Chapter 5 now deals solely with nomenclature.

Development of Problem-Solving Skills

Problem-solving has become a buzzword in chemical education. We all want our students to acquire problem-solving skills. In fact, developing such skills was a central focus of the earlier editions of this text and we have maintained this approach in this edition.

In the first chapters we spend considerable time guiding students to an understanding of the importance of learning chemistry. At the same time, we explain that the complexities that can make chemistry frustrating at times can also provide the opportunity to develop the problem-solving skills that are beneficial in any profession. Learning to think like a chemist is useful to everyone. To emphasize this idea, we apply scientific thinking to some real-life problems in Chapter 1.

One reason chemistry can be challenging for beginning students is that they often do not possess the required mathematical skills. Thus we have paid careful attention to such fundamental mathematical skills as using scientific notation, rounding off to the correct number of significant figures, and rearranging equations to solve for a particular quantity. And we have meticulously followed the rules we have set down, so as not to confuse students.

Attitude plays a crucial role in achieving success in problem solving. Students must learn that a systematic, thoughtful approach to problems is better than brute force memorization. We foster this attitude early in the book, using temperature conversions as a vehicle in Chapter 2. Throughout the book we encourage an approach that starts with trying to represent the essence of the problem using symbols and/or diagrams, and ends with thinking about whether the answer makes sense. We approach new concepts by carefully working through the material before we give mathematical formulas or over-all strategies. We encourage a thoughtful step-by-step approach rather than the premature use of algorithms. Once we have provided the necessary foundation, we highlight important rules and processes in skill development boxes so that students can locate them easily.

Many of the worked examples are followed by Self-Check exercises, which provide additional practice. The Self-Check exercises are keyed to end-of-chapter exercises to offer another opportunity for students to practice a particular problem-solving skill or understand a particular concept.

We have expanded the number of end-of-chapter exercises. As in the first two editions, the end-of-chapter exercises are arranged in "matched pairs," meaning that both problems in the pair explore similar topics. An "Additional Problems" section includes further practice in chapter concepts as well as more challenging problems. Cumulative Reviews, which appear after every few chapters, test concepts from the preceding chapter block. Answers for all even-numbered exercises appear in a special section at the end of the book.

Handling the Language of Chemistry and Applications

We have gone to great lengths to make this book "student friendly" and have received enthusiastic feedback from students who have used it.

As in the earlier editions, we present a systematic and thorough treatment of chemical nomenclature. Once this framework is established, students can progress through the book comfortably.

Along with chemical reactions, applications form an important part of descriptive chemistry. Because students are interested in chemistry's impact on their lives, we have included many new "Chemistry in Focus" boxes, which describe current applications of chemistry. These special interest boxes cover such topics as artificial sweeteners, a beetle that defends itself by shooting a chemical spray, memory metal, foaming chewing gum, fake fats, the disappearance of the dinosaurs, and the greenhouse effect.

Visual Impact of Chemistry

Responding to instructors' requests to include graphic illustrations of chemical reactions, phenomena, and processes, our full-color design enables color to be used functionally, thoughtfully, and consistently to help students understand chemistry and to make the subject more inviting to them. We have included only those photos that illustrate a chemical reaction or phenomenon or that make a connection between chemistry and the real world. About half of the photographs are new to this edition.

Choices of Coverage

For the convenience of instructors, four versions of the third edition are available: two paperback versions and two hardbound versions. *Basic Chemistry,* Third Edition, a paperback text, provides basic coverage of chemical concepts and applications through solution chemistry and has fifteen chapters. *Introductory Chemistry,* Third Edition, available in hardcover and paperback, expands the coverage to nineteen chapters with the addition of equilibrium, acids and bases, oxidation-reduction reactions and electrochemistry, radioactivity, and nuclear energy. Finally, *Introductory Chemistry: A Foundation,* Third Edition, a hardbound text, has twenty-one chapters, with the final two chapters providing a brief introduction to organic and biological chemistry.

Supplements for the Text

A comprehensive teaching and learning package accompanies all versions of the text:

Instructor's Annotated Edition, with annotations by Iris Stovall

Study Guide by Iris Stovall

Solutions Guide by James F. Hall

Complete Solutions Guide by James F. Hall

Introductory Chemistry in the Laboratory by James F. Hall

Instructor's Resource Guide for Introductory Chemistry in the Laboratory by James F. Hall

Test Item File by Steven S. Zumdahl and Anne Kertz Kernion

Computerized Testing

Chemistry Software: Consult your D. C. Heath sales representative for details.

Chemistry in Motion Videotape and Videodisc

D. C. Heath Chemistry Lecture Demonstrations

Transparencies

Another item that may be of interest to you is our microscale lab text, *Chemical Investigations: A Laboratory Test for Introductory Chemistry* by Jerry A. Bell.

We have worked hard to make this book and its supplements clear, interesting, and accurate. We would appreciate any comments that would make the book more useful to students and instructors.

Acknowledgments

This book represents the collaborative efforts of many talented people to whom I owe much. I greatly appreciate the support and friendship of Kent Porter Hamann, former Editorial Director at D. C. Heath, whose consummate professionalism and unerring judgment concerning level and content have proved invaluable in producing this book. I am also grateful to Richard Stratton, Senior Acquisitions Editor, who came to this project at a critical stage and who provided sound judgment and strong support to help bring it to a successful conclusion. I especially appreciate the efforts of June Goldstein, Developmental Editor, who contributed immeasurably to the success of this edition. June did her job with great skill and consistent good humor and was the main driving force in keeping this project moving forward.

My thanks go also to Heather Garrison, Production Editor, who did her usual excellent job. The creative design by Cornelia Boynton gives the text an inviting and non-threatening appearance. Thanks also to Martha Shethar and Derek Wing, Photo Researchers, for the beautiful chapter openers and other in-text photos.

Jim Hall of the University of Lowell contributed in many different ways to the success of this project. In particular, I appreciate his help with the

Cumulative Review and end-of-chapter exercises and his care in getting everything right.

My sincerest appreciation goes to the following reviewers who examined the second edition in preparation for the revision and evaluated the third edition manuscript:

Larry E. Bennett
San Diego State University

Michael E. Brennan
Chattanooga State Technical Community College

Christine Bilicki
Pasadena City College

John Cronin
Arizona State University

Joseph C. Danner
Long Beach City College

Vicky D. Ellis
Gulf Coast Community College

Samuel Foster
Glendale Community College

Robert Fremland
San Diego Mesa College

Stan Grenda
University of Nevada

Jeffrey A. Hurlbut
Metropolitan State College of Denver

Chet Jablonsky
Memorial University of Newfoundland

John J. Keetch
Southwestern College

Roy Kennedy
Massachusetts Bay Community College

Anne Kertz Kernion
Community College of Allegheny County– North Campus

Christine S. Kerr
Montgomery College

Kristen Kirshbaum
University of Toledo

Alfred T. Lee
City College of San Francisco

Wyatt Rorer Murphy, Jr.
Seton Hall University

William Nickels
Schoolcraft College

Dennis Pap
Chaffey College

Barbara Perez
El Camino College

Richard S. Perkins
University of Southwestern Louisiana

Robert Perkins
Kwantlen College

Karen Pressprich Creager
Indiana University

Melissa S. Reeves
Indiana University

Patricia J. Rogers
University of California, Irvine

Al Shina
San Diego City College

Phil Silberman
Scottsdale Community College

Linda Thomas-Glover
Guilford Technical Community College

Calvin D. Tormanen
Central Michigan University

Joseph Vagedes
St. Thomas Aquinas High School

Ron Valcarce
Salt Lake Community College

David L. Winters
Tidewater Community College

In addition, I want to thank the accuracy reviewers for the text and the supplements: John Goodenow of Lawrence Technological College and John J. Keetch of Southwestern College.

S. S. Z.

CHAPTER 3

Matter and Energy

Chapter Opener   *Expanded*

Each chapter begins with an application and a photograph tying the chapter material to an everyday experience.

3.1 **Matter**

3.2 **Physical and Chemical Properties and Changes**

3.3 **Elements and Compounds**

3.4 **Mixtures and Pure Substances**

3.5 **Separation of Mixtures**

3.6 **Energy and Energy Changes**

Hot lava flowing into the ocean in Hawaii (left). Why does soda fizz when you open the bottle (right)?

As you look around you, you must wonder about the properties of matter. How do plants grow and why are they green? Why is the sun hot? Why does a hot dog get hot in a microwave oven? Why does wood burn whereas rocks do not? What is a flame? How does soap work? Why does soda fizz when you open it? When iron rusts, what's happening? And why doesn't aluminum rust? How does a cold pack for an athletic injury, which is stored for weeks or months at room temperature, suddenly get cold when you need it? How does a hair permanent work?

The answers to these and endless other questions lie in the domain of chemistry. In this chapter we begin to explore the nature of matter: how it is organized and how and why it changes. We will also consider the energy that accompanies these changes.

Aim Statements

Aim statements accompany each numbered section and provide learning objectives for students.

Marginal Notes

Marginal notes for students reinforce important points.

Illustrations and Photos

The illustrations and photos provide visual representations of chemical reactions, phenomena, and processes to help students understand chemistry and make it more inviting to them.

4.11 Compounds That Contain Ions

AIM: To learn how ions combine to form neutral compounds.

Chemists have good reasons to believe that many chemical compounds contain ions. For instance, consider some of the properties of common table salt, sodium chloride (NaCl). It must be heated to about 800 °C to melt and to almost 1500 °C to boil (compare to water, which boils at 100 °C). As a solid, salt will not conduct an electric current, but when melted it is a very good conductor. Pure water will not conduct electricity (will not allow an electric current to flow), but when salt is dissolved in water, the resulting solution readily conducts electricity (see Figure 4.20).

Chemists have come to realize that we can best explain these properties of sodium chloride (NaCl) by picturing it as containing Na^+ ions and Cl^- ions packed together as shown in Figure 4.21. Because the positive and negative charges attract each other very strongly, it must be heated to a very high temperature (800 °C) before it melts.

Melting means that the solid, where the ions are locked into place, is changed to a liquid, where the ions can move.

Source of electric power

Pure water   Salt dissolved in water

(a)   (b)

FIGURE 4.20
(a) Pure water does not conduct a current, so the circuit is not complete and the bulb does not light. (b) Water containing a dissolved salt conducts electricity and the bulb lights.

(a)   (b)

Sometimes the relative numbers of moles you get when you calculate an empirical formula will turn out to be nonintegers, as was the case in Example 9.11. When this happens, you must convert to the appropriate whole numbers. This is done by multiplying all the numbers by the same small integer, which can be found by trial and error. The multiplier needed is almost always between 1 and 6. We will now summarize what we have learned about calculating empirical formulas.

Steps for Determining the Empirical Formula of a Compound

STEP 1 Obtain the mass of each element present (in grams).

STEP 2 Determine the number of moles of each type of atom present.

STEP 3 Divide the number of moles of each element by the smallest number of moles to convert the smallest number to 1. If all of the numbers so obtained are integers (whole numbers), these are the subscripts in the empirical formula. If one or more of these numbers are not integers, go on to step 4.

STEP 4 Multiply the numbers you derived in step 3 by the smallest integer that will convert all of them to whole numbers. This set of whole numbers represents the subscripts in the empirical formula.

EXAMPLE 9.12 *Calculating Empirical Formulas for Binary Compounds*

When a 0.3546-g sample of vanadium metal is heated in air, it reacts with oxygen to achieve a final mass of 0.6330 g. Calculate the empirical formula of this vanadium oxide.

Solution

STEP 1 All the vanadium that was originally present will be found in the final compound, so we can calculate the mass of oxygen that reacted by taking the following difference:

Total mass of compound		Mass of vanadium in compound		Mass of oxygen in compound

0.6330 g — 0.3546 g = 0.2784 g

STEP 2 Using the atomic masses (50.94 for V and 16.00 for O), we obtain

$$0.3546 \ \cancel{g \ V} \times \frac{1 \text{ mol V atoms}}{50.94 \ \cancel{g \ V}} = 0.006961 \text{ mol V atoms}$$

Boxed Rules/Steps   *Expanded*

Important rules and processes appear in skill development boxes so that students can locate them easily.

Worked Examples

The text contains many examples, each titled for easy reference. The worked examples model a thoughtful step-by-step approach. We encourage students to represent the essence of the problem by using symbols and/or diagrams and then to determine whether the answer makes sense.

Self-Check Exercises

Many of the examples are followed by self-check exercises, which provide students with additional practice to master concepts.

Cross References   *NEW*

New to this edition, cross references to similar end-of-chapter exercises are provided. Solutions to the self-check exercises are given in the back of the book.

Self-Check Exercise 5.6

Name each of the following compounds.

a. $Ca(OH)_2$

b. Na_3PO_4

c. $KMnO_4$

d. $(NH_4)_2Cr_2O_7$

e. $Co(ClO_4)_2$

f. $KClO_3$

g. $Cu(NO_2)_2$

See Problems 5.35 and 5.36.

Example 5.7 illustrates that when more than one polyatomic ion appears in a chemical formula, parentheses are used to enclose the ion and a subscript is written after the closing parenthesis. Other examples are $(NH_4)_2SO_4$ and $Fe_3(PO_4)_2$.

In naming chemical compounds, use the strategy summarized in Figure 5.2. If the compound being considered is binary, use the procedure summarized in Figure 5.1. If the compound has more than two elements, ask yourself whether it has any polyatomic ions. Use Table 5.4 to help you recognize these ions until you have committed them to memory. If a polyatomic ion is present, name the compound using procedures very similar to those for naming binary ionic compounds.

FIGURE 5.2
Overall strategy for naming chemical compounds.

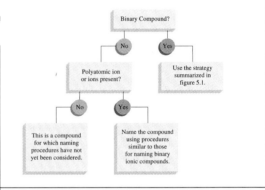

CHEMISTRY IN FOCUS

Metal with a Memory

A distraught mother walks into the optical shop carrying her mangled pair of $400 eyeglasses. Her child had gotten into her purse, found her glasses, and twisted them into a pretzel. She hands them to the optometrist with little hope that they can be salvaged. The optometrist says not to worry and drops the glasses into a dish of warm water where the glasses magically spring back to their original shape. The optometrist hands the restored glasses to the woman and says there is no charge for repairing them.

How can the frames "remember" their original shape when placed in hot water? The answer is a nickel–titanium alloy called Nitinol that was developed in the late 1950s and early 1960s at the Naval Ordnance Laboratory in White Oak, Maryland, by William J. Buehler. (The name Nitinol comes from *Ni*ckel *Ti*tanium *N*aval *O*rdnance *L*aboratory.)

Nitinol has the amazing ability to remember a shape originally impressed in it. For example, note the accompanying photos. What causes Nitinol to behave this way? Although the details are too complicated to describe here, this phenomenon results from two different forms of solid Nitinol. When Nitinol is heated to a sufficiently high temperature, the Ni and Ti atoms arrange themselves in a way that leads to the most compact and regular pattern of the atoms—a form called austenite (A). When the alloy is cooled its atoms rearrange slightly to a form called martensite (M). The shape desired (for example, the word *ICE*) is set into the alloy at a high temperature (A form), then the metal is cooled, causing it to assume the M form. In this process no visible change is noted. Then, if the image is deformed, it will magically return if the alloy is heated (hot water works

fine) to a temperature that changes it back to the A form.

Nitinol has many medical applications, including hooks used by orthopedic surgeons to attach ligaments and tendons to bone, braces to straighten teeth, and "baskets" to catch blood clots. In the latter case a length of Nitinol wire is shaped into a tiny basket and this shape is set at a high temperature. The wires forming the basket are then straightened so they can be inserted as a small bundle through a catheter. When the wires warm up in the blood, the basket shape springs back and acts as a filter to stop blood clots from moving to the heart.

The most promising consumer use of Nitinol is for eyeglasses frames. It's handy to have frames that remember their original shape.

The word ICE is formed from Nitinol wire.

The wire is stretched to obliterate the word ICE.

The wire pops back to ICE when immersed in warm water.

Chemistry in Focus Essays   *Expanded*

The Chemistry in Focus boxes describe current applications of chemistry. These special interest boxes cover such topics as artificial sweeteners, the bombardier beetle, and the greenhouse effect.

Periodic Table Icons

Some of the more common elements are highlighted in periodic table icons to remind students about the position of selected elements and to help them become more familiar with the periodic table.

sider Example 9.15, to obtain the molecular formula we must know the molar mass. In this section we will consider compounds where both the percent composition and the molar mass are known.

 EXAMPLE 9.15

Calculating Molecular Formulas

A white powder is analyzed and found to have an empirical formula of P_2O_5. The compound has a molar mass of 283.88 g. What is the compound's molecular formula?

Solution

To obtain the molecular formula, we must compare the empirical formula mass to the molar mass. The empirical formula mass for P_2O_5 is the mass of 1 mol of P_2O_5 units.

$$\begin{aligned}
&\text{Atomic mass of P} \\
2 \text{ mol P: } &2 \times 30.97 \text{ g} = 61.94 \text{ g} \\
5 \text{ mol O: } &5 \times 16.00 \text{ g} = \underline{80.00 \text{ g}} \\
&\quad\quad\quad\text{Atomic} \quad\quad 141.94 \text{ g} \quad \text{Mass of 1 mol of } P_2O_5 \text{ units} \\
&\quad\quad\quad\text{mass of O}
\end{aligned}$$

Recall that the molecular formula contains a whole number of empirical formula units. That is,

$$\text{Molecular formula} = (\text{empirical formula})_n$$

where n is a small whole number. Now, because

$$\text{Molecular formula} = n \times \text{empirical formula}$$

then

$$\text{Molar mass} = n \times \text{empirical formula mass}$$

Solving for n gives

$$n = \frac{\text{molar mass}}{\text{empirical formula mass}}$$

Thus to determine the molecular formula, we first divide the molar mass by the empirical formula mass. This tells us how many empirical formula masses there are in one molar mass.

$$\frac{\text{Molar mass}}{\text{Empirical formula mass}} = \frac{283.88 \text{ g}}{141.94 \text{ g}} = 2$$

This result means that $n = 2$ for this compound, so the molecular formula consists of two empirical formula units, and the molecular formula is $(P_2O_5)_2$, or P_4O_{10}. The structure of this interesting compound is shown in Figure 9.5.

Self-Check Exercise 9.11

A compound used as an additive for gasoline to help prevent engine knock shows the following percentage composition:

71.65% Cl   24.27% C   4.07% H

of $CaCO_3$ according to the reaction

$$CaCO_3(s) \rightarrow CaO(s) + CO_2(g)$$

Solution

The strategy for solving this problem is summarized by the following schematic:

$$\boxed{\begin{array}{c}\text{Grams}\\\text{of}\\CaCO_3\end{array}} \xrightarrow{1} \boxed{\begin{array}{c}\text{Moles}\\\text{of}\\CaCO_3\end{array}} \xrightarrow{2} \boxed{\begin{array}{c}\text{Moles}\\\text{of}\\CO_2\end{array}} \xrightarrow{3} \boxed{\begin{array}{c}\text{Volume}\\\text{of}\\CO_2\end{array}}$$

STEP 1. Using the molar mass of $CaCO_3$ (100.1 g), we calculate the number of moles of $CaCO_3$.

$$152 \text{ g } CaCO_3 \times \frac{1 \text{ mol } CaCO_3}{100.0 \text{ g } CaCO_3} = 1.52 \text{ mol } CaCO_3$$

STEP 2. Each mole of $CaCO_3$ produces 1 mol of CO_2, so 1.52 mol of CO_2 will be formed.

STEP 3. We can convert the moles of CO_2 to volume by using the molar volume of an ideal gas, because the conditions are STP.

$$1.52 \text{ mol } CO_2 \times \frac{22.4 \text{ L } CO_2}{1 \text{ mol } CO_2} = 34.1 \text{ L } CO_2$$

Thus the decomposition of 152 g of $CaCO_3$ produces 34.1 L of CO_2 at STP.

Remember that the molar volume of an ideal gas is 22.4 L at STP.

Note that the final step in Example 13.17 involves calculating the volume of gas from the number of moles. Because the conditions were specified as STP, we were able to use the molar volume of a gas at STP. If the conditions of a problem are different from STP, we must use the ideal gas law to compute the volume, as we did in Section 13.5.

Chapter Review

Key Terms		Summary
barometer *(13.1)*	ideal gas *(13.5)*	1. Atmospheric pressure is measured with a barometer. The most commonly used units of pressure are mm Hg (torr), atmospheres, and pascals (the SI unit).
mm Hg *(13.1)*	combined gas law *(13.5)*	
torr *(13.1)*	partial pressures *(13.6)*	
standard atmosphere *(13.1)*	Dalton's law of partial	2. Boyle's law states that the volume of a given amount of gas is inversely proportional to its pressure (at constant temperature): $PV = k$ or $P = k/V$. That is, as pressure increases, volume decreases.
pascal *(13.1)*	pressures *(13.6)*	
Boyle's law *(13.2)*	kinetic molecular theory	
absolute zero *(13.2)*	*(13.8)*	
Charles's law *(13.3)*	molar volume *(13.10)*	3. Charles's law states that, for a given amount of gas at constant pressure, the volume is directly proportional to the temperature (in kelvins): $V = bT$. At -273 °C (0 K),
Avogadro's law *(13.4)*	standard temperature and	
universal gas constant *(13.5)*	pressure (STP) *(13.10)*	
ideal gas law *(13.5)*		

Key Terms

Key terms are printed in bold type and are defined where they first appear. They are also grouped at the end of the chapter and in a glossary at the back of the text, for convenient reference.

Chapter Summaries

Each chapter has a summary section to reinforce key concepts in the chapter.

364   12 *Chemical Bonding*

12.9 ■ *Molecular Structure: The VSEPR Model*

QUESTIONS

73. Why is the geometric structure of a molecule important, especially for biological molecules?

74. What general principles determine the molecular structure (shape) of a molecule?

75. How is the structure around a given atom related to repulsion between valence electron pairs on the atom?

76. Why are all diatomic molecules *linear,* regardless of the number of valence electron pairs on the atoms involved?

77. Although the valence electron pairs in ammonia have a tetrahedral arrangement, the overall geometric structure of the ammonia molecule is *not* described as being tetrahedral. Explain.

78. Although both the BF_3 and NF_3 molecules contain the same number of atoms, the BF_3 molecule is flat, whereas the NF_3 molecule is trigonal pyramidal. Explain.

PROBLEMS

79. For the indicated atom in each of the following molecules, give the number and arrangement of the electron pairs around that atom.
    a. C in CH_4
    b. C in CBr_4
    c. each of the carbon atoms in C_2H_6

80. For the indicated atom in each of the following molecules or ions, give the number and arrangement of the electron pairs around that atom.
    a. P in PH_3
    b. Cl in ClO_4^-
    c. O in H_2O

81. Using the VSEPR theory, predict the molecular structure of each of the following molecules.

    b. hydrogen phosphate ion (hydrogen is bonded to oxygen)
    c. sulfite ion

85. For each of the following molecules or ions, indicate the bond angle expected between the central atom and any two adjacent hydrogen atoms.
    a. H_2O c. NH_4^+
    b. NH_3 d. CH_4

86. For each of the following molecules or ions, indicate the bond angle expected between the central atom and any two adjacent chlorine atoms.
    a. Cl_2O c. CCl_4
    b. NCl_3 d. C_2Cl_4

87. Predict the geometric structure of the carbonate ion, CO_3^{2-}. What are the bond angles in this molecule?

88. Predict the geometric structure of the acetylene molecule, C_2H_2. What are the bond angles in this molecule?

Additional Problems

89. What is *resonance?* Give three examples of molecules or ions that exhibit resonance, and draw Lewis structures for each of the possible resonance forms.

90. When two atoms share two pairs of electrons, a _____ bond is said to exist between them.

91. The geometric arrangement of electron pairs around a given atom is determined principally by the tendency to minimize _____ between the electron pairs.

92. In each case, which of the following pairs of bonded elements forms the more polar bond?
    a. S—F or S—Cl
    b. N—O or P—O
    c. C—H or Si—H

93. For each case, which of the following pairs of bonded elements forms the more polar bond?
    a. Br—Cl or Br—F
    b. As—S or As—O
    c. Pb—C or Pb—Si

94. The quantity of energy necessary to _____ a chemical bond is referred to as the bond energy.

95. A _____ chemical bond represents the equal sharing of a pair of electrons between two nuclei.

96. For each of the following pairs of elements, identify which element would be expected to be more electronegative. It should not be necessary to look at a table of actual electronegativity values.

218

Cumulative Review for Chapters 6–8

QUESTIONS

1. What kind of *visual* evidence indicates that a chemical reaction has occurred? Give an example of each type of evidence you have mentioned. Do *all* reactions produce visual evidence that they have taken place?

2. What, in general terms, does a chemical equation indicate? What are the substances indicated to the left of the arrow called in a chemical equation? To the right of the arrow?

3. What does it mean to "balance" an equation? Why is it so important that equations be balanced? What does it mean to say that atoms must be *conserved* in a balanced chemical equation? How are the physical states of reactants and products indicated when writing chemical equations?

4. When balancing a chemical equation, why is it *not* permissible to adjust the subscripts in the formulas of the reactants and products? What would changing the subscripts within a formula do? What do the *coefficients* in a balanced chemical equation represent? Why is it acceptable to adjust a substance's coefficient but not permissible to adjust the subscripts within the substance's formula?

5. What is meant by the *driving force* for a reaction? Give some examples of driving forces that make reactants tend to form products. Write a balanced chemical equation illustrating each type of driving force you have named.

6. What is a *precipitation reaction?* What would you see if a precipitation reaction were to take place in a beaker? Write a balanced chemical equation illustrating a precipitation reaction.

7. Define the term *strong electrolyte*. What types of substances tend to be strong electrolytes? What does a solution of a strong electrolyte contain? Give a way to determine if a substance is a strong electrolyte.

8. Summarize the simple solubility rules for ionic compounds. How do we use these rules in determining the identity of the solid formed in a precipitation reaction? Give examples including balanced complete and net ionic equations.

9. In general terms, what are the *spectator ions* in a precipitation reaction? Why are the spectator ions not included in writing the net ionic equation for a precipitation reaction? Does this mean that the spectator ions do not have to be present in the solution?

10. Describe some physical and chemical properties of *acids* and *bases*. What is meant by a *strong* acid or base? Are strong acids and bases also strong electrolytes? Give several examples of strong acids and strong bases.

11. What is a *salt?* How are salts formed by acid–base reactions? Write chemical equations showing the formation of three different salts. What other product is formed when an aqueous acid reacts with an aqueous base? Write the net ionic equation for the formation of this substance.

12. What is essential in an oxidation–reduction reaction? What is *oxidation?* What is *reduction?* Can an oxidation reaction take place without a reduction reaction also taking place? Why? Write a balanced chemical equation illustrating an oxidation–reduction reaction between a metal and a nonmetal. Indicate which species is oxidized and which is reduced.

13. What is a *combustion* reaction? Are combustion reactions a unique type of reaction, or are they a special case of a more general type of reaction? Write an equation that illustrates a combustion reaction.

14. Give an example of a *synthesis* reaction and of a *decomposition* reaction. Are synthesis and decomposition reactions always also oxidation–reduction reactions? Explain.

15. List and define all the ways of classifying chemical reactions that have been discussed in the text. Give a balanced chemical equation as an example of each type of reaction, and show clearly how your example fits the definition you have given.

PROBLEMS

16. Sodium is a highly reactive metal and calcium is a moderately reactive metal. Write balanced chemical equations for the reaction of each of these metals with the following substances, with the indicated products being produced.
    a. with water, producing aqueous sodium hydroxide or aqueous calcium hydroxide plus hydrogen gas
    b. with liquid bromine, producing solid sodium bromide or solid calcium bromide
    c. with nitrogen gas, producing solid sodium nitride or solid calcium nitride
    d. with oxygen gas, producing solid sodium *peroxide*, Na_2O_2, or solid calcium oxide
    e. with solid sulfur, producing solid sodium sulfide or solid calcium sulfide

(partially obscured center text:)
molecular structure

c. Cl_2O
molecular structure
ions.

molecular structure

molecular structure
ions.

End-of-Chapter Exercises

The end-of-chapter questions and problems are keyed to chapter sections. They are arranged in matched pairs, and the even-numbered exercise is answered in the back of the text. Additional exercises are not keyed to any section or topic and incorporate material from more than one section.

Brief Contents

Contents

12 Chemical Bonding   329

13 Gases   371

Appendix   A1

Basic Chemistry

Chemistry:
An Introduction

Chemistry deals with the natural world (left). *Fireworks are a beautiful illustration of chemistry in action* (right).

Did you ever see a fireworks display on July fourth and wonder how it's possible to produce those beautiful, intricate designs in the air? Have you read about dinosaurs—how they ruled the earth for millions of years and then suddenly disappeared? Although the extinction happened 65 million years ago and may seem unimportant, could the same thing happen to us? Have you ever wondered why an ice cube (pure water) floats in a glass of water (also pure water)? Did you know that the "lead" in your pencil is made of the same substance (carbon) as the diamond in an engagement ring? Did you ever wonder how a corn plant or a palm tree grows seemingly by magic, or why leaves turn beautiful colors in autumn? Do you know how the battery works to start your car or run your calculator? Surely some of these things and many others in the world around you have intrigued you. The fact is that we can explain all of these things in convincing ways using the models of chemistry and the related physical and life sciences.

1.1   Chemistry: An Introduction

AIM: To understand the importance of learning chemistry.

Although chemistry might seem to have little to do with dinosaurs, knowledge of chemistry was the tool that enabled paleontologist Luis W. Alvarez and his co-workers from the University of California at Berkeley to "crack the case" of the disappearing dinosaurs. The key was the relatively high level of iridium found in the sediment that represents the boundary between the earth's Cretaceous (K) and Tertiary (T) periods—the time when the dinosaurs disappeared virtually overnight (on the geological scale). The Berkeley researchers knew that meteorites also have unusually high iridium content (relative to the earth's composition), which led them to suggest that a large meteorite impacted the earth 65 million years ago, causing the climatic changes that wiped out the dinosaurs. We will have more to say about this theory in Chapter 3.

A knowledge of chemistry is useful to almost everyone—chemistry occurs all around us all of the time, and an understanding of chemistry is useful to doctors, lawyers, mechanics, business people, firefighters, and poets among others. Chemistry is important—there is no doubt about that. It lies at the heart of our efforts to produce new materials that make our lives safer and easier, to produce new sources of energy that are abundant and nonpolluting, and to understand and control the many diseases that threaten us and our food supplies. Even if your future career does not require the daily use of chemical principles, your life will be greatly influenced by chemistry.

Although a strong case can be made that the use of chemistry has greatly enriched all of our lives, there is also a dark side to the story. Our society has used its knowledge of chemistry to kill and destroy. It is important to understand that the principles of chemistry are inherently neither good nor bad—it's what we do with this knowledge that really matters. Although humans are clever, resourceful, and concerned about others, they also can be greedy, selfish, and ignorant. In addition, we tend to be shortsighted; we concentrate too much on the present and do not think enough about the long-range implications of our actions. This type of thinking has already caused us a great deal of trouble—severe environmental damage has occurred on many fronts. We cannot place all the responsibility on the chemical companies, because everyone has contributed to these problems. However, it is less important to lay blame than to figure out how to solve these problems. An important part of the answer must rely on chemistry.

One of the "hottest" fields in the chemical sciences is environmental chemistry—an area that involves studying our environmental ills and finding creative ways to address them. For example, meet Bart Eklund, who works in the atmospheric chemistry field for Radian Corporation in Austin, Texas. Bart's interest in a career in environmental science was fostered by two environmental chemistry courses and two ecology courses he took as an undergraduate. His original plan to gain several years of industrial experience and then to return to school for a graduate degree changed when he discovered that professional advancement with a B.S. degree was possible in the environmental research field. The multidisciplinary nature of environmental problems has allowed Bart to pursue his interest in several fields at the same time. You might say that he specializes in being a generalist.

The environmental consulting field appeals to Bart for a number of reasons: the chance to define and solve a number of research problems; the simultaneous work on a number of diverse projects; the mix of desk, field, and laboratory work; the travel; and the opportunity to perform rewarding work that has a positive effect on people's lives.

Among his career highlights are the following:

- Spending a winter month doing air sampling in the Grand Tetons, where he also met his wife and learned to ski;

- Driving sampling pipes by hand into the rocky ground of Death Valley Monument in California;

- Working regularly with experts in their fields and with people who enjoy what they do;

- Doing vigorous work in 100 °F weather while wearing a rubberized suit, double gloves, and a respirator; and

- Getting to work in and see Alaska, Yosemite Park, Niagara Falls, Hong Kong, the People's Republic of China, Mesa Verde, New York City, and dozens of other interesting places.

Bart Eklund checking air quality at a hazardous waste site.

Bart Eklund's career demonstrates how chemists are helping to solve our environmental problems. It is how we use our chemical knowledge that makes all the difference.

An example that shows how technical knowledge can be a "double-edged sword" is the case of chlorofluorocarbons (CFCs). When the compound CCl_2F_2 (originally called Freon-12) was first synthesized, it was hailed as a near-miracle substance. Because of its noncorrosive nature and its unusual ability to resist decomposition, Freon-12 was rapidly applied in refrigeration and air-conditioning systems, cleaning applications, the blowing of foams used for insulation and packing materials, and many other ways. For years everything seemed fine—the CFCs actually replaced more dangerous materials, such as the ammonia formerly used in refrigeration systems. The CFCs were definitely viewed as "good guys." But then a problem was discovered— the ozone in the upper atmosphere that protects us from the high-energy radiation of the sun began to decline. What was happening to cause the destruction of the vital ozone?

Much to everyone's amazement, the culprits turned out to be the seemingly beneficial CFCs. Inevitably, large quantities of CFCs had leaked into the atmosphere but nobody was very worried about this development because these compounds seemed totally benign. In fact, the great stability of the CFCs (a tremendous advantage for their various applications) was in the end a great disadvantage when they were released into the environment. Professor F. S. Rowland and his colleagues at the University of California at Irvine demonstrated that the CFCs eventually drifted to high altitudes in the

A chemist in the laboratory.

atmosphere, where the energy of the sun stripped off chlorine atoms. These chlorine atoms in turn promoted the decomposition of the ozone in the upper atmosphere. (We will discuss this in more detail in Chapter 13.) Thus a substance that possessed many advantages in earth-bound applications turned against us in the atmosphere. Who could have guessed it would turn out this way?

The good news is that the U.S. chemical industry is leading the way to find environmentally safe alternatives to CFCs, which will be banned after 1996 by international agreement. The effort to replace CFCs is now ahead of schedule—the levels of CFCs in the atmosphere are already dropping.

The saga of the CFCs demonstrates that we can respond relatively quickly to a serious environmental problem if we decide to do so. Also, it is important to understand that chemical manufacturers have a new attitude about the environment—they are now among the leaders in finding ways to address our environmental ills. The industries that apply the chemical sciences are now determined to be part of the solution rather than part of the problem.

As you can see, learning chemistry is both interesting and important. A chemistry course can do more than simply help you learn the principles of chemistry, however. A major by-product of your study of chemistry is that you will become a better problem solver. One reason chemistry has the reputation of being "tough" is that it often deals with rather complicated systems that require some effort to figure out. Although this might at first seem like a disadvantage, you can turn it to your advantage if you have the right attitude and skills. Recruiters for companies of all types maintain that one of the first things they look for in a prospective employee is the ability to solve problems. We will spend a good deal of time solving various types of problems in this book by using a systematic, logical approach that will serve you well in solving any kind of problem in any field. Keep this broader goal in mind as you learn to solve the specific problems connected with chemistry.

Although learning chemistry is often not easy, it's never impossible. In fact, anyone who is interested, patient, and willing to work can learn the fundamentals of chemistry. In this book we will try very hard to help you understand what chemistry is and how it works and to point out how chemistry applies to the things going on in your life.

Our sincere hope is that this text will motivate you to learn chemistry, make its concepts understandable to you, and demonstrate how interesting and vital the study of chemistry is.

1.2 What Is Chemistry?

AIM: To define chemistry.

Chemical and physical changes will be discussed in Chapter 3.

Chemistry can be defined as *the science that deals with the materials of the universe and the changes that these materials undergo.* Chemists are involved in activities as diverse as examining the fundamental particles of matter, looking for molecules in space, synthesizing and formulating new materials of all types, using bacteria to produce such chemicals as insulin, and inventing new diagnostic methods for early detection of disease.

Chemistry is often called the central science—and with good reason. Most of the phenomena that occur in the world around us involve chemical changes, changes where one or more substances become different substances. Here are some examples of chemical changes:

Wood burns in air, forming water, carbon dioxide, and other substances.

A plant grows by assembling simple substances into more complex substances.

The steel in a car rusts.

Eggs, flour, sugar, and baking powder are mixed and baked to yield a cake.

The definition of the term *chemistry* is learned and stored in the brain.

Grape juice ferments to form wine.

Emissions from a power plant lead to the formation of acid rain.

As we proceed, you will see how the concepts of chemistry allow us to understand the nature of these and other changes and thus help us manipulate natural materials to our benefit.

The launch of the Space Shuttle Atlantis on November 3, 1994. The evidence is clear that chemical reactions are occurring.

1.3 Solving Problems Using a Scientific Approach

AIM: To understand scientific thinking.

One of the most important things we do in everyday life is solve problems. In fact, most of the decisions you make every day can be described as solving problems.

It's 8:30 A.M. on Friday. Which is the best way to drive to school to avoid traffic congestion?

You have two tests on Monday. Should you divide your study time equally or allot more time to one than to the other?

Your car stalls at a busy intersection and your little brother is with you. What should you do next?

These are everyday problems of the type we all face. What process do we use to solve them? You may not have thought about it before, but there are several steps that almost everyone uses to solve problems:

1. Recognize the problem and state it clearly. Some information becomes known, or something happens that requires action. In science we call this step *making an observation*.

2. Propose *possible* solutions to the problem or *possible* explanations for the observation. In scientific language, suggesting such a possibility is called *formulating a hypothesis*.

A *Mystifying Problem*

To illustrate how science helps us solve problems, consider a true story about two people, David and Susan (not their real names). About fifteen years ago David and Susan were healthy 40-year-olds living in California, where David was serving in the Air Force. Gradually Susan became quite ill, showing flu-like symptoms including nausea and severe muscle pains. Even her personality changed: she became uncharacteristically grumpy. She seemed like a totally different person from the healthy, happy woman of a few months earlier. Following her doctor's orders, she rested and drank a lot of fluids, including large quantities of coffee and orange juice from her favorite mug, part of a 200-piece set of pottery dishes recently purchased in Italy. However, she just got sicker, developing extreme abdominal cramps and severe anemia.

During this time David also became ill and exhibited symptoms much like Susan's: weight loss, excruciating pain in his back and arms, and uncharacteristic fits of temper. The disease became so debilitating that he retired early from the Air Force and

the couple moved to Seattle. For a short time their health improved, but after they unpacked all their belongings (including those pottery dishes), their health began to deteriorate again. Susan's body became so sensitive that she could not tolerate the weight of a blanket. She was near death. What was wrong? The doctors didn't know, but one suggested she might have porphyria, a rare blood disease.

Desperate, David began to search the medical literature himself. One day while he was reading about porphyria, a phrase jumped off the page: "Lead poisoning can sometimes be confused with porphyria." Could the problem be lead poisoning?

We have described a very serious problem with life-or-death implications. What should David do next? Overlooking for a moment the obvious response of calling the couple's doctor immediately to discuss the possibility of lead poisoning, could David solve the problem via scientific thinking? Let's use the three steps described in Section 1.3 to attack the problem one part at a time. This is important: usually we solve complex problems by breaking them down into

manageable parts. We can then assemble the solution to the overall problem from the answers we have found "piecemeal."

In this case there are many parts to the overall problem:
 What is the disease?
 Where is it coming from?
 Can it be cured?
Let's attack "What is the disease?" first.

Observation: David and Susan are ill with the symptoms described. Is the disease lead poisoning?

Hypothesis: The disease is lead poisoning.

Experiment: If the disease is lead poisoning, the symptoms must match those known to characterize lead poisoning. Look up the symptoms of lead poisoning. David did this and found that they matched the couple's symptoms almost exactly.

This discovery points to lead poisoning as the source of their problem, but David needed more evidence.

Observation: Lead poisoning results from high levels of lead in the bloodstream.

3. Decide which of the solutions is the best or decide whether the explanation proposed is reasonable. To do this we search our memory for any pertinent information or we seek new information. In science we call searching for new information *performing an experiment.*

As we will discover in the next section, scientists use these same procedures to study what happens in the world around us. The important point here is that scientific thinking can help you in all parts of your life. It's worthwhile to learn how to think scientifically—whether you want to be a scientist, an auto mechanic, a doctor, a politician, or a poet!

Italian pottery.

Hypothesis: The couple have high levels of lead in their blood.

Experiment: Perform a blood analysis. Susan arranged for such an analysis, and the results showed high lead levels for both David and Susan.

This confirms that lead poisoning is probably the cause of the trouble, but the overall problem is still not solved. David and Susan are likely to die unless they find out where the lead is coming from.

Observation: There is lead in the couple's blood.

Hypothesis: The lead is in their food or drink when they buy it.

Experiment: Find out whether anyone else who shopped at the same store was getting sick (no one was). Also note that moving to a new area did not solve the problem.

Observation: The food they buy is free of lead.

Hypothesis: The dishes they use are the source of the lead poisoning.

Experiment: Find out whether their dishes contain lead. David and Susan learned that lead compounds are often used to put a shiny finish on pottery objects. And laboratory analysis of their Italian pottery dishes showed that lead was present in the glaze.

Observation: Lead is present in their dishes, so the dishes are a possible source of their lead poisoning.

Hypothesis: The lead is leaching into their food.

Experiment: Place a beverage, such as orange juice, in one of the cups and then analyze the beverage for lead. The results showed high levels of lead in drinks that had had contact with the pottery cups.

After many applications of the scientific method, the problem is solved. We can summarize the answer to the problem (David and Susan's illness) as follows: the Italian pottery they used for everyday dishes contained a lead glaze that contaminated their food and drink with lead. This lead accumulated in their bodies to the point where it interfered seriously with normal functions and produced severe symptoms. This overall explanation, which summarizes the hypotheses that agree with the experimental results, is called a *theory* in science. This explanation accounts for the results of all the experiments performed.*

We could continue to use the scientific method to study other aspects of this problem, such as

What types of food or drink leach the most lead from the dishes?

Do all pottery dishes with lead glazes produce lead poisoning?

As we answer questions using the scientific method, other questions naturally arise. By repeating the three steps over and over, we can come to understand a given phenomenon thoroughly.

*"David" and "Susan" recovered from their lead poisoning and are now publicizing the dangers of using lead-glazed pottery. This happy outcome is the answer to the third part of their overall problem, "Can the disease be cured?" They simply stopped eating from that pottery!

1.4   The Scientific Method

AIM: To describe the method scientists use to study nature.

In the last section we began to see how the methods of science are used to solve problems. In this section we will further examine this approach.

Science is a framework for gaining and organizing knowledge. Science is not simply a set of facts but is also a plan of action—a *procedure* for processing and understanding certain types of information. Although scientific thinking is useful in all aspects of life, in this text we will use it to understand how the natural world operates. The process that lies at the center of scientific inquiry is called the **scientific method.** As we saw in the previous section, it consists of the following steps:

Steps in the Scientific Method

1. *State the problem and collect data (make observations).* Observations may be *qualitative* (the sky is blue; water is a liquid) or *quantitative* (water boils at 100 °C; a certain chemistry book weighs 4.5 pounds). A qualitative observation does not involve a number. A quantitative observation is called a **measurement** and does involve a number (and a unit, such as pounds or inches). We will discuss measurements in detail in Chapter 2.

2. *Formulate hypotheses.* A hypothesis is a *possible* explanation for the observation.

3. *Perform experiments.* An experiment is something we do to test the hypothesis. We gather new information that allows us to decide whether the hypothesis is supported by the new information we have learned from the experiment. Experiments always produce new observations, and this brings us back to the beginning of the process again.

Quantitative observations involve a number. Qualitative ones do not.

To explain the behavior of a given part of nature, we repeat these steps many times. Gradually we accumulate the knowledge necessary to understand what is going on.

Once we have a set of hypotheses that agrees with our various observations, we assemble them into a theory that is often called a *model*. A **theory** (model) is a set of tested hypotheses that gives an overall explanation of some part of nature (See Figure 1.1).

It is important to distinguish between observations and theories. An observation is something that is witnessed and can be recorded. A theory is an *interpretation*—a possible explanation of *why* nature behaves in a particular way. Theories inevitably change as more information becomes available. For example, the motions of the sun and stars have remained virtually the same over the thousands of years during which humans have been observing them, but our explanations—our theories—have changed greatly since ancient times.

The point is that we don't stop asking questions just because we have devised a theory that seems to account satisfactorily for some aspect of natural behavior. We continue doing experiments to refine our theories. We generally do this by using the theory to make a prediction and then doing an experiment (making a new observation) to see whether the results bear out this prediction.

Always remember that theories (models) are human inventions. They represent our attempts to explain observed natural behavior in terms of our

FIGURE 1.1
The various parts of the scientific method.

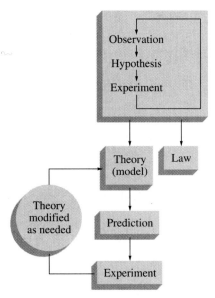

CHEMISTRY IN FOCUS

Observations, Theories, and the Planets

Humans have always been fascinated by the heavens—by the behavior of the sun by day and the stars by night. Although more accurately measured now thanks to precise instruments, our basic *observations* of their behavior have remained the same over the past 4000 years. However, our *interpretations* of these observations have changed dramatically. For example, around 2000 B.C. the Egyptians postulated that the sun was a boat inhabited by the god Ra, who daily sailed across the sky.

Over the years, patterns in the changes in the heavens were recognized and, through marvelous devices such as Stonehenge in England, were connected to the seasons of the year. People also noted that seven objects seemed to move against the background of "fixed stars." These objects (actually the sun, the moon, and the planets Mercury, Venus, Mars, Jupiter, and Saturn) were called the "wanderers." The planets generally seemed to move from west to east, but sometimes they seemed to slow down and even to move backward for a few weeks.

Eudoxus, born in 400 B.C., tried to explain these observations. He imagined the earth as fixed in space and the planets as attached to a set of transparent spheres, each slightly larger than the previous one, that moved at different rates around the earth. The stars were attached to a fixed outermost sphere. This model, although clever, still did not account for the "backward" movement of some of the planets. Five hundred years later Ptolemy, a Greek scholar, worked out a plan more complex than that of Eudoxus, in which the planets were attached to the edges of spheres that "rolled around" the spheres of

The Egyptian sun-god, Ra (drawn on papyrus).

Eudoxus. This model accounted for the observed behavior of all the planets, including the apparent reversals in their motions.

Because of a natural human prejudice that the earth should be the center of the universe, Ptolemy's model was assumed to be correct for more than a thousand years, and its wide acceptance actually inhibited the advancement of astronomy. Finally, in 1543, the Polish cleric Nicholas Copernicus postulated that the earth was only one of the planets, all of which revolved around the sun. This "demotion" of the earth in status produced violent opposition to the new model, and in fact Copernicus's writings were "corrected" by religious officials before scholars were allowed to use them.

The Copernican theory persisted, however, and was finally given a solid mathematical base by Johannes Kepler. Thirty-six years after Kepler's death, his hypotheses were further refined by Isaac Newton, who recognized that the concept of gravity could account for the positions and motions of the planets. However, even the brilliant models of Newton were discovered to be incomplete by Albert Einstein, who showed that Newton's ideas were just a part of a much more general model.

Thus the same basic observations were made for several thousand years, but the explanations—the models—changed remarkably from the Egyptians' boat of Ra to Einstein's relativity.

The lesson is that our models (theories) inevitably change and that we should expect them to do so. They can help us make scientific progress, or they can inhibit our progress if we become too attached to them. Although the fundamental observations of chemistry will remain the same, the models given in a chemistry text written in 2100 will certainly be quite different from the ones presented here.

human experiences. We must continue to do experiments and refine our theories to be consistent with new knowledge if we hope to approach a more nearly complete understanding of nature.

As we observe nature, we often see that the same observation applies to many different systems. For example, studies of innumerable chemical changes have shown that the total mass of the materials involved is the same before and after the change. We often formulate such generally observed behavior into a statement called a **natural law.** The observation that the total mass of materials is not affected by a chemical change in those materials is called the law of conservation of mass.

You must recognize the difference between a law and a theory. A law is a summary of observed (measurable) behavior, whereas a theory is an explanation of behavior. *A law tells what happens; a theory (model) is our attempt to explain why it happens.*

In this section, we have described the scientific method (which is summarized in Figure 1.1) as it might ideally be applied. However, it is important to remember that science does not always progress smoothly and efficiently. Scientists are human. They have prejudices; they misinterpret data; they can become emotionally attached to their theories and thus lose objectivity; and they play politics. Science is affected by profit motives, budgets, fads, wars, and religious beliefs. Galileo, for example, was forced to recant his astronomical observations in the face of strong religious resistance. Lavoisier, the father of modern chemistry, was beheaded because of his political affiliations. And great progress in the chemistry of nitrogen fertilizers resulted from the desire to produce explosives to fight wars. The progress of science is often affected more by the frailties of humans and their institutions than by the limitations of scientific measuring devices. The scientific method is only as effective as the humans using it. It does not automatically lead to progress.

> Law: A summary of observed behavior.
> Theory: An explanation of behavior.

1.5   Learning Chemistry

AIM: To develop successful strategies for learning chemistry.

Chemistry courses have a universal reputation for being difficult. There are some good reasons for this. For one thing, the language of chemistry is unfamiliar in the beginning; many terms and definitions need to be memorized. As with any language, *you must know the vocabulary* before you can communicate effectively. We will try to help here by pointing out those things that it is necessary to memorize.

But memorization is only the beginning. Don't stop there or your experience with chemistry will be frustrating. Be willing to do some thinking, and learn to trust yourself to figure things out. To solve a typical chemistry problem, you must sort through the given information and decide what is really important.

One of the most important things you must realize is that chemical systems tend to be complicated—there are typically many components—and we must make approximations in describing them. Therefore, trial and error play a major role in solving chemical problems. In tackling a complicated system, a practicing chemist really does not expect to be right the first time he or she analyzes the problem. The usual practice is to make several simplifying assumptions and then give it a try. If the answer obtained doesn't make sense, the chemist adjusts the assumptions, using feedback from the first attempt, and tries again. The point is this: in dealing with chemical systems, do not expect to understand immediately everything that is going on. In fact, it is typical (even for an experienced chemist) *not* to understand at first. Make an attempt to solve the problem and then analyze the feedback. *It is no disaster to make a mistake as long as you learn from it.*

CHEMISTRY IN FOCUS

Chemistry: An Important Component of Your Education

What is the purpose of education? Because you are spending considerable time, energy, and money to pursue an education, this is an important question.

Some people seem to equate education with the storage of facts in the brain. These people apparently believe that education simply means memorizing the answers to all of life's present and future problems. Although this is clearly unreasonable, many students seem to behave as though this were their guiding principle. These students want to memorize lists of facts and to reproduce them on tests. They regard as unfair any exam questions that require some original thought or some processing of information. Indeed, it might be tempting to reduce education to a simple filling up with facts, because that approach can produce short-term satisfaction for both student and teacher. And of course, storing facts in the brain *is* important. You cannot function without knowing that red means stop, electricity is hazardous, ice is slippery, and so on.

However, mere recall of abstract information, without the ability to process it, makes you little better than a talking encyclopedia. Former students always seem to bring the same message when they return to campus. The characteristics that are most important to their success are a knowledge of the fundamentals of their fields, the ability to recognize and solve problems, and the ability to communicate effectively. They also emphasize the importance of a high level of motivation.

Students pondering the structure of a molecule.

How does studying chemistry help you achieve these characteristics? The fact that chemical systems are complicated is really a blessing, though one that is well disguised. Studying chemistry will not by itself make you a good problem solver, but it can help you develop a positive, aggressive attitude toward problem solving and can help boost your confidence. Learning to "think like a chemist" can be valuable to anyone in any field. In fact, the chemical industry is heavily populated at all levels and in all areas by chemists and chemical engineers. People who were trained as chemical professionals often excel not only in chemical research and production but also in the areas of personnel, marketing, sales, development, finance, and management. The point is that much of what you learn in this course can be applied to any field of endeavor. So be careful not to take too narrow a view of this course. Try to look beyond short-term frustration to long-term benefits. It may not be easy to learn to be a good problem solver, but it's well worth the effort.

The only way to develop your confidence as a problem solver is to practice solving problems. To help you, this book contains examples worked out in detail. Follow these through carefully, making sure you understand each step. These examples are usually followed by a similar exercise (called a self-check exercise) that you should try on your own (detailed solutions of the self-check exercises are given at the end of each chapter). Use the self-check exercises to test whether you are understanding the material as you go along.

There are questions and problems at the end of each chapter. The questions review the basic concepts of the chapter and give you an opportunity to check whether you properly understand the vocabulary introduced. Some of the problems are really just exercises that are very similar to examples done in the chapter. If you understand the material in the chapter, you should be able to do these exercises in a straightforward way. Other problems require more creativity. These contain a knowledge gap—some unfamiliar territory that you must cross—and call for thought and patience on your part. For this course to be really useful to you, it is important to go beyond the questions and exercises. Life offers us many exercises, routine events that we deal with rather automatically, but the real challenges in life are true problems. This course can help you become a more creative problem solver.

As you do homework, be sure to use the problems correctly. If you cannot do a particular problem, do not immediately look at the solution. Review the relevant material in the text and then try the problem again. Don't be afraid to struggle with a problem. Looking at the solution as soon as you get stuck short-circuits the learning process.

Learning chemistry takes time. Use all the resources available to you and study on a regular basis. Don't expect too much of yourself too soon. You may not understand everything at first, and you may not be able to do many of the problems the first time you try them. This is normal. It doesn't mean you can't learn chemistry. Just remember to keep working and to keep learning from your mistakes, and you will make steady progress.

Chapter Review

Questions and Problems

All even-numbered exercises have answers in the back of this book and solutions in the Solutions Guide.

1.1 ■ *Chemistry: An Introduction*

QUESTIONS

1. The first few paragraphs of this book asked you if you had ever wondered how and why various things in everyday life behave the way they do. Surely there are many other such phenomena that have intrigued you. Make a list of five such things and present them in class for discussion with your instructor and fellow students.

2. Although your own knowledge of chemistry may be limited at this point, you have certainly met many people who make everyday use of chemistry (physicians, nurses, farmers, photographers, and so on). Discuss three specific examples of such persons, and explain how they might make use of chemistry in their professions.

3. This section presents several ways our day-to-day lives have been enriched by chemistry. List three materials or processes involving chemistry that you feel have contributed to such an enrichment, and explain your choices.

4. The text admits that there has also been a "dark side" to our use of chemicals and chemical processes, and uses the example of chlorofluorocarbons (CFCs) to explain this. List three additional improper or unfortunate uses of chemicals or chemical processes, and explain your reasoning.

1.2 ■ *What Is Chemistry?*

QUESTIONS

5. This textbook provides a specific definition of chemistry: the study of the materials of which the universe is made and the transformations that these materials undergo. Obviously, such a general definition has to be very broad and nonspecific. From your point of view at this time, how would *you* define chemistry? In your mind, what are "chemicals"? What do "chemists" do?

6. Several examples of chemical transformations are given in this section. Give five additional examples of chemical changes. Indicate what the chemical is in each of your examples, and how you recognize that a change has taken place.

1.3 ■ *Solving Problems Using a Scientific Approach*

QUESTIONS

7. For the "Chemistry in Focus" discussion of lead poisoning given in this section, discuss how David and Susan analyzed the situation, arriving at the theory that the lead glaze on the pottery was responsible for their symptoms.

8. Discuss several situations in which you have yourself analyzed a problem such as those presented in this section. What hypotheses did you suggest? How did you test those hypotheses?

1.4 ■ *The Scientific Method*

QUESTIONS

9. What are the three operations involved in applying the scientific method? How does the scientific method help us to understand our observations of nature?

10. Which of the following are quantitative observations, and which are qualitative observations?
    a. My waist size is 31 inches.
    b. My eyes are blue.
    c. My right index finger is 1/4 inch longer than my left.
    d. The leaves of most trees are green in summer.
    e. An apple consists of over 95% water.
    f. Chemistry is an easy subject.
    g. I got 90% on my last Chem exam.

11. What is the difference between a *hypothesis* and a *theory?* How are the two similar? How do they differ?

12. What is a *natural law?* Give examples of such laws. How does a law differ from a theory?

13. Discuss several political, social, or personal considerations that might affect a scientist's evaluation of a theory. Give examples of how such external forces have influenced scientists in the past. Discuss methods by which such bias might be excluded from future scientific investigations.

1.5 ■ *Learning Chemistry*

QUESTIONS

14. In some academic subjects, it may be possible to receive a good grade primarily by memorizing facts. Why is chemistry not one of these subjects?

15. Why is the ability to solve problems important in the study of chemistry? Why is it that the *method* used to attack a problem is as important as the answer to the problem itself?

16. Students approaching the study of chemistry must learn certain basic facts (such as the names and symbols of the most common elements), but it is much more important that they learn to think critically and to go beyond the specific examples discussed in class or in the textbook. Explain how learning to do this might be helpful in any career, even one far removed from chemistry.

2

Measurements and Calculations

As we pointed out in Chapter 1, making observations is a key part of the scientific process. Sometimes observations are *qualitative* ("the substance is a yellow solid") and sometimes they are *quantitative* ("the substance weighs 4.3 grams"). A quantitative observation is called a **measurement.** Measurements are very important in our daily lives. For example, we pay for gasoline by the gallon so the gas pump must accurately measure the gas delivered to our fuel tank. The efficiency of the modern automobile engine depends on various measurements including the amount of oxygen in the exhaust gases, the temperature

An Erlenmeyer flask, a Florence flask, and a beaker, each containing the same volume of solution (left). *A gas pump measures the amount of gasoline delivered* (right).

A measurement must always consist of a number *and* a unit.

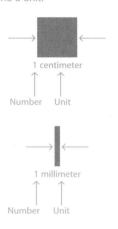

1 centimeter

Number   Unit

1 millimeter

Number   Unit

of the coolant, and the pressure of the lubricating oil. In addition, cars with traction control systems have devices to measure and compare the rates of rotation of all four wheels. As we will see in the "Chemistry in Focus" discussion in this chapter, measuring devices have become very sophisticated in dealing with our fast-moving and complicated society.

As we will discuss in this chapter, a measurement always consists of two parts: a number and a unit. Both parts are necessary to make the measurement meaningful. For example, suppose a friend tells you that she saw a bug 5 long. This statement is meaningless as it stands. Five what? If it's 5 millimeters, the bug is quite small. If it's 5 centimeters, the bug is quite large. If it's 5 meters, run for cover!

The point is that for a measurement to be meaningful, it must consist of both a number and a unit that tells us the scale being used.

In this chapter we will consider the characteristics of measurements and the calculations that involve measurements.

2.1   Scientific Notation

AIM: To show how very large or very small numbers can be expressed as the product of a number between 1 and 10 and a power of 10.

When describing very small distances, such as the diameter of a swine flu virus (shown here magnified 16,537 times), it is convenient to use scientific notation.

The numbers associated with scientific measurements are often very large or very small. For example, the distance from the earth to the sun is approximately 93,000,000 (93 million) miles. Written out, this number is rather bulky. Scientific notation is a method for making very large or very small numbers more compact and easier to write.

To see how this is done, consider the number 125, which can be written as the product

$$125 = 1.25 \times 100$$

Because $100 = 10 \times 10 = 10^2$, we can write

$$125 = 1.25 \times 1\,00 = 1.25 \times 10^2$$

Similarly, the number 1700 can be written

$$1700 = 1.7 \times 1000$$

and because $1000 = 10 \times 10 \times 10 = 10^3$, we can write

$$1700 = 1.7 \times 1000 = 1.7 \times 10^3$$

Scientific notation simply expresses a number as *a product of a number between 1 and 10 and the appropriate power of 10*. For example, the number 93,000,000 can be expressed as

$$93,000,000 = 9.3 \times 10,000,000 = 9.3 \quad \times \quad 10^7$$

Number   Appropriate
between   power of 10
1 and 10   (10,000,000 = 10⁷)

The easiest way to determine the appropriate power of 10 for scientific notation is to start with the number being represented and count the number of places the decimal point must be moved to obtain a number between 1 and 10. For example, for the number

$$9\ 3\ 0\ 0\ 0\ 0\ 0\ 0$$
$$7\ \ 6\ \ 5\ \ 4\ \ 3\ \ 2\ \ 1$$

Keep one digit to the left of the decimal point.

we must move the decimal point seven places to the left to get 9.3 (a number between 1 and 10). To compensate for every move of the decimal point to the left, we must multiply by 10. That is, each time we move the decimal point to the left, we make the number smaller by one power of 10. So for each move of the decimal point to the left, we must multiply by 10 to restore the number to its original magnitude. Thus moving the decimal point seven places to the left means we must multiply 9.3 by 10 seven times, which equals 10^7:

$$93,000,000 = 9.3 \times 10^7$$

We moved the decimal point seven
places to the left, so we need
10^7 to compensate.

Moving the decimal point to the left requires a positive exponent.

Remember: whenever the decimal point is moved to the *left*, the exponent of 10 is *positive*.

We can represent numbers smaller than 1 by using the same convention, but in this case the power of 10 is negative. For example, for the number 0.010 we must move the decimal point two places to the right to obtain a number between 1 and 10:

$$0.0\ 1\ 0$$
$$1\ \ 2$$

Moving the decimal point to the right requires a negative exponent.

This requires an exponent of -2, so $0.010 = 1.0 \times 10^{-2}$. Remember: whenever the decimal point is moved to the *right*, the exponent of 10 is *negative*.

Next consider the number 0.000167. In this case we must move the decimal point four places to the right to obtain 1.67 (a number between 1 and 10):

$$0.0\ 0\ 0\ 1\ \ 6\ \ 7$$
$$1\ \ 2\ \ 3\ \ 4$$

Read Appendix 3 if you need a further discussion of exponents and scientific notation.

Moving the decimal point four places to the right requires an exponent of -4. Therefore,

$$0.000167 = 1.67 \times 10^{-4}$$

We moved the decimal
point four places to the right.

We summarize these procedures on the following page.

$$100 = 1.0 \times 10^2$$
$$.0\hat{1}0 = 1.0 \times 10^{-2}$$

Using Scientific Notation

- Any number can be represented as the product of a number between 1 and 10 and a power of 10 (either positive or negative).

- The power of 10 depends on the number of places the decimal point is moved and in which direction. The *number of places* the decimal point is moved determines the *power of 10*. The *direction* of the move determines whether the power of 10 is *positive* or *negative*. If the decimal point is moved to the left, the power of 10 is positive; if the decimal point is moved to the right, the power of 10 is negative.

Left Is Positive; remember LIP.

EXAMPLE 2.1   *Scientific Notation: Powers of 10 (Positive)*

Represent the following numbers in scientific notation.

a. 238,000
b. 1,500,000

Solution

a. First we move the decimal point until we have a number between 1 and 10, in this case 2.38.

$$2\ 3\ 8\ 0\ 0\ 0$$
   5 4 3 2 1   The decimal point was moved five places to the left.

Because we moved the decimal point five places to the left, the power of 10 is positive 5. Thus $238,000 = 2.38 \times 10^5$.

b. $1\ 5\ 0\ 0\ 0\ 0$
   6 5 4 3 2 1   The decimal point was moved six places to the left, so the power of 10 is 6.

Thus $1,500,000 = 1.5 \times 10^6$.

EXAMPLE 2.2   *Scientific Notation: Powers of 10 (Negative)*

Represent the following numbers in scientific notation.

a. 0.00043
b. 0.089

Solution

a. First we move the decimal point until we have a number between 1 and 10, in this case 4.3.

$$0.0\ 0\ 0\ 4\ 3$$
    1 2 3 4   The decimal point was moved four places to the right.

Because we moved the decimal point four places to the right, the power of 10 is negative 4. Thus $0.00043 = 4.3 \times 10^{-4}$.

b.   0.0 8 9

         1   2   The power of 10 is negative 2 because the decimal point was moved two places to the right.

Thus $0.089 = 8.9 \times 10^{-2}$.

 Self-Check Exercise 2.1

Write the numbers 357 and 0.0055 in scientific notation. If you are having difficulty with scientific notation at this point, reread Appendix 3.

See Problems 2.7 through 2.12.

2.2   Units

AIM: To learn the English, metric, and SI systems of measurement.

The **units** part of a measurement tells us what *scale* or *standard* is being used to represent the results of the measurement. From the earliest days of civilization, trade has required common units. For example, if a farmer from one region wanted to trade some of his grain for the gold of a miner who lived in another region, the two people had to have common standards (units) for measuring the amount of the grain and the weight of the gold.

The need for common units also applies to scientists, who measure quantities such as mass, length, time, and temperature. If every scientist had her or his own personal set of units, complete chaos would result. Unfortunately, although standard systems of units did arise, different systems were adopted in different parts of the world. The two most widely used systems are the **English system** used in the United States and the **metric system** used in most of the rest of the industrialized world.

The metric system has long been preferred for most scientific work. In 1960 an international agreement set up a comprehensive system of units called the **International System** (*le Système Internationale* in French), or **SI.** The SI units are based on the metric system and units derived from the metric system. The most important fundamental SI units are listed in Table 2.1. Later in this chapter we will discuss how to manipulate some of these units.

Because the fundamental units are not always a convenient size, the SI system uses prefixes to change the size of the unit. The most commonly used

TABLE 2.1

Some Fundamental SI Units

Physical Quantity	Name of Unit	Abbreviation
mass	kilogram	kg
length	meter	m
time	second	s
temperature	kelvin	K

TABLE 2.2

The Commonly Used Prefixes in the Metric System

Prefix	Symbol	Meaning	Power of 10 for Scientific Notation
mega	M	1,000,000	10^6
kilo	k	1000	10^3
deci	d	0.1	10^{-1}
centi	c	0.01	10^{-2}
milli	m	0.001	10^{-3}
micro	μ	0.000001	10^{-6}
nano	n	0.000000001	10^{-9}

prefixes are listed in Table 2.2. Although the fundamental unit for length is the meter (m), we can also use the decimeter (dm), which represents one-tenth (0.1) of a meter; the centimeter (cm), which represents one one-hundredth (0.01) of a meter; the millimeter (mm), which represents one one-thousandth (0.001) of a meter; and so on. For example, it's much more convenient to specify the diameter of a certain contact lens as 1.0 cm than as 1.0×10^{-2} m.

2.3   *Measurements of Length, Volume, and Mass*

AIM: To understand the metric system for measuring length, volume, and mass.

The meter was originally defined, in the eighteenth century, as one ten-millionth of the distance from the equator to the North Pole and then, in the late nineteenth century, as the distance between two parallel marks on a special metal bar stored in a vault in Paris. More recently, for accuracy and convenience, a definition expressed in terms of light waves has been adopted.

The fundamental SI unit of length is the meter, which is a little longer than a yard (1 meter = 39.37 inches). In the metric system fractions of a meter or multiples of a meter can be expressed by powers of 10, as summarized in Table 2.3.

The English and metric systems are compared on the ruler shown in Figure 2.1. Note that

> 1 inch = 2.54 centimeters

Other English-metric equivalences are given in Section 2.6.

A quarter is about 2.5 cm across.

TABLE 2.3

The Metric System for Measuring Length

Unit	Symbol	Meter Equivalent
kilometer	km	1000 m or 10^3 m
meter	m	1 m or 1 m
decimeter	dm	0.1 m or 10^{-1} m
centimeter	cm	0.01 m or 10^{-2} m
millimeter	mm	0.001 m or 10^{-3} m
micrometer	μm	0.000001 m or 10^{-6} m
nanometer	nm	0.000000001 m or 10^{-9} m

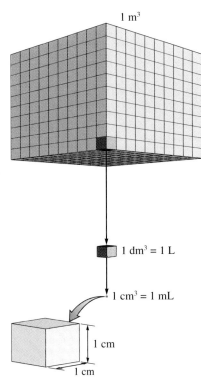

FIGURE 2.2
The largest drawing represents a cube that has sides 1 m in length and a volume of 1 m³. The middle-size cube has sides 1 dm in length and a volume of 1 dm³, or 1 L. The smallest cube has sides 1 cm in length and a volume of 1 cm³, or 1 mL.

FIGURE 2.1
Comparison of English and metric units for length on a ruler.

Volume is the amount of three-dimensional space occupied by a substance. The fundamental unit of volume in the SI system is based on the volume of a cube that measures 1 meter in each of the three directions. That is, each edge of the cube is 1 meter in length. The volume of this cube is

$$1 \text{ m} \times 1 \text{ m} \times 1 \text{ m} = (1 \text{ m})^3 = 1 \text{ m}^3$$

or, in words, one cubic meter.

In Figure 2.2 this cube is divided into 1000 smaller cubes. Each of these small cubes represents a volume of 1 dm³, which is commonly called the **liter** (rhymes with meter and is slightly larger than a quart) and abbreviated L.

The cube with a volume of 1 dm³ (1 liter) can in turn be broken into 1000 smaller cubes each representing a volume of 1 cm³. This means that each liter contains 1000 cm³. One cubic centimeter is called a **milliliter** (abbreviated mL), a unit of volume used very commonly in chemistry. This relationship is summarized in Table 2.4.

The *graduated cylinder* (see Figure 2.3), commonly used in chemical laboratories for measuring the volumes of liquids, is marked off in convenient units of volume (usually milliliters). The graduated cylinder is filled to the desired volume with the liquid, which then can be poured out.

TABLE 2.4

The Relationship of the Liter and Milliliter

Unit	Symbol	Equivalence
liter	L	1 L = 1000 mL
milliliter	mL	$\frac{1}{1000}$ L — 10^{-3} L = 1 mL

FIGURE 2.3
A 100-mL graduated cylinder.

TABLE 2.5

The Most Commonly Used Metric Units for Mass

Unit	Symbol	Gram Equivalent
kilogram	kg	$1000 \text{ g} = 10^3 \text{ g} = 1 \text{ kg}$
gram	g	1 g
milligram	mg	$0.001 \text{ g} = 10^{-3} \text{ g} = 1 \text{ mg}$

TABLE 2.6

Some Examples of Commonly Used Units

length	A dime is 1 mm thick.
	A quarter is 2.5 cm in diameter.
	The average height of adult men is 1.8 m.
mass	A nickel has a mass of about 5 g.
	A 120-lb woman has a mass of about 55 kg.
volume	A 12-oz can of soda has a volume of about 360 mL.
	A half gallon of milk is equal to about 2 L of milk.

Another important measurable quantity is **mass,** which can be defined as the quantity of matter present in an object. The fundamental SI unit of mass is the **kilogram.** Because the metric system, which existed before the SI system, used the gram as the fundamental unit, the prefixes for the various mass units are based on the **gram,** as shown in Table 2.5.

In the laboratory we determine the mass of an object by using a balance. A balance compares the mass of the object to a set of standard masses ("weights"). For example, the mass of an object can be determined by using a single-pan balance (Figure 2.4).

To help you get a feeling for the common units of length, volume, and mass, some familiar objects are described in Table 2.6.

FIGURE 2.4

(a) Actual appearance of a single-pan analytical balance used in chemistry labs. (b) Schematic view showing its principle of operation. An object is placed on the balance pan, and "weights" (masses) are removed from holders above the pan to restore the balance. The mass of the object equals the mass of the removed "weights."

(a)

(b)

Measurement: Past, Present, and Future

Measurement lies at the heart of doing science. We obtain the data for formulating laws and testing theories by doing measurements. Measurements are also of very practical importance; they tell us if our drinking water is safe, whether we are anemic, and the exact amount of gasoline we put in our cars at the filling station.

Although the fundamental measuring devices we consider in this chapter are still widely used, new measuring techniques are being developed everyday to meet the challenges of our increasingly sophisticated world. For example, engines in modern automobiles have oxygen sensors that analyze the oxygen content in the exhaust gases. This information is sent to the computer that controls the engine functions so that instantaneous adjustments can be made in spark timing and air–fuel mixtures to provide efficient power with minimum air pollution.

As another example, consider airline safety: How do we rapidly, conveniently, and accurately determine whether a given piece of baggage contains an explosive device? A thorough hand-search of each piece of luggage is out of the question. Scientists are now developing a screening procedure that bombards the luggage with high-energy particles that cause any substance present to emit radiation characteristic of that substance.

Scientists sampling water to test its purity.

This radiation is monitored to identify luggage with unusually large quantities of nitrogen, because most chemical explosives are based on compounds containing nitrogen.

Scientists are also examining the natural world to find supersensitive detectors because many organisms are sensitive to tiny amounts of chemicals in their environments—recall, for example, the sensitive noses of bloodhounds. One of these natural measuring devices uses the sensory hairs from Hawaiian red swimming crabs, which are connected to electrical analyzers and used to detect hormones down to levels of 10^{-8} g/L. Likewise, tissues from pineapple cores can be

used to detect tiny amounts of hydrogen peroxide.

These types of advances in measuring devices have led to an unexpected problem: detecting all kinds of substances in our food and drinking water scares us. Although these substances were always there, we didn't worry so much when we couldn't detect them. Now that we know they are present what should we do about them? How can we assess whether these trace substances are harmful or benign? Risk assessment has become much more complicated as our sophistication in taking measurements has increased.

2.4   Uncertainty in Measurement

AIMS: To understand how uncertainty in a measurement arises. To learn to indicate a measurement's uncertainty by using significant figures.

Whenever a measurement is made with a device such as a ruler or a graduated cylinder, an estimate is required. We can illustrate this by measuring the pin shown in Figure 2.5(a). We can see from the ruler that the pin is a little longer than 2.8 cm and a little shorter than 2.9 cm. Because there are no graduations on the ruler between 2.8 and 2.9, we must estimate the pin's length

FIGURE 2.5
Measuring a pin. (a) The length is between 2.8 cm and 2.9 cm. (b) Imagine that the distance between 2.8 and 2.9 is divided into 10 equal parts. The end of the pin occurs after about 5 of these divisions.

A student working in a chemistry lab.

Every measurement has some degree of uncertainty.

between 2.8 and 2.9 cm. We do this by *imagining* that the distance between 2.8 and 2.9 is broken into 10 equal divisions (Figure 2.5b) and estimating to which division the end of the pin reaches. The end of the pin appears to come about halfway between 2.8 and 2.9, which corresponds to 5 of our 10 imaginary divisions. So we estimate the pin's length as 2.85 cm. The result of our measurement is that the pin is approximately 2.85 cm in length, but we had to rely on a visual estimate, so it might actually be 2.84 or 2.86 cm.

Because the last number is based on a visual estimate, it may be different when another person makes the same measurement. For example, if five different people measured the pin, the results might be

Person	Result of Measurement
1	2.85 cm
2	2.84 cm
3	2.86 cm
4	2.85 cm
5	2.86 cm

Note that the first two digits in each measurement are the same regardless of who made the measurement; these are called the *certain* numbers of the measurement. However, the third digit is estimated and can vary; it is called an *uncertain* number. When one is making a measurement, the custom is to record all of the certain numbers plus the *first* uncertain number. It would not make any sense to try to measure the pin to the third decimal place (thousandths of a centimeter), because this ruler requires an estimate of even the second decimal place (hundredths of a centimeter).

It is very important to realize that *a measurement always has some degree of uncertainty*. The uncertainty of a measurement depends on the measuring device. For example, if the ruler in Figure 2.5 had marks indicating hundredths of a centimeter, the uncertainty in the measurement of the pin would occur in the thousandths place rather than the hundredths place, but some uncertainty would still exist.

The numbers recorded in a measurement (all the certain numbers plus the first uncertain number) are called **significant figures.** The number of significant figures for a given measurement is determined by the inherent uncertainty of the measuring device. For example, the ruler used to measure the pin can give results only to hundredths of a centimeter. Thus when we record the significant figures for a measurement, we automatically give information about the uncertainty in a measurement. The uncertainty in the last number (the estimated number) is usually assumed to be ± 1 unless otherwise indicated. For example, the measurement 1.86 kilograms can be interpreted as 1.86 ± 0.01 kilograms, where the symbol $\pm$ means plus or minus. That is, it could be 1.86 kg $- 0.01$ kg $= 1.85$ kg or 1.86 kg $+ 0.01$ kg $= 1.87$ kg.

2.5   *Significant Figures*

AIM: To learn to determine the number of significant figures in a calculated result.

We have seen that any measurement involves an estimate and thus is uncertain to some extent. We signify the degree of certainty for a particular measurement by the number of significant figures we record.

Because doing chemistry requires many types of calculations, we must consider what happens when we do arithmetic with numbers that contain uncertainties. It is important that we know the degree of uncertainty in the final result. Although we will not discuss the process here, mathematicians have studied how uncertainty accumulates and have designed a set of rules to determine how many significant figures the result of a calculation should have. You should follow these rules whenever you carry out a calculation. The first thing we need to do is learn how to count the significant figures in a given number. To do this we use the following rules:

Rules for Counting Significant Figures

1. *Nonzero integers.* Nonzero integers *always* count as significant figures. For example, the number 1457 has four nonzero integers, all of which count as significant figures.

2. *Zeros.* There are three classes of zeros:

   Leading zeros are never significant figures.

   a. *Leading zeros* are zeros that *precede* all of the nonzero digits. They *never* count as significant figures. For example, in the number 0.0025, the three zeros simply indicate the position of the decimal point. The number has only two significant figures, the 2 and the 5.

   Captive zeros are always significant figures.

   b. *Captive zeros* are zeros that fall *between* nonzero digits. They *always* count as significant figures. For example, the number 1.008 has four significant figures.

Trailing zeros are sometimes significant figures.

c. *Trailing zeros* are zeros at the *right end* of the number. They are significant only if the number contains a decimal point. The number one hundred written as 100 has only one significant figure, but written as 100., it has three significant figures.

Exact numbers never limit the number of significant figures in a calculation.

3. *Exact numbers.* Often calculations involve numbers that were not obtained using measuring devices but were determined by counting: 10 experiments, 3 apples, 8 molecules. Such numbers are called *exact numbers.* They can be assumed to have an unlimited number of significant figures. Exact numbers can also arise from definitions. For example, 1 inch is defined as *exactly* 2.54 centimeters. Thus in the statement 1 in. = 2.54 cm, neither 2.54 nor 1 limits the number of significant figures when it is used in a calculation.

Significant figures are easily indicated by scientific notation.

Rules for counting significant figures also apply to numbers written in scientific notation. For example, the number 100. can also be written as 1.00×10^2, and both versions have three significant figures. Scientific notation offers two major advantages: the number of significant figures can be indicated easily, and fewer zeros are needed to write a very large or a very small number. For example, the number 0.000060 is much more conveniently represented as 6.0×10^{-5}, and the number has two significant figures, written in either form.

EXAMPLE 2.3   *Counting Significant Figures*

Give the number of significant figures for each of the following measurements.

a. A sample of orange juice contains 0.0108 g of vitamin C.
b. A forensic chemist in a crime lab weighs a hair and records its mass as 0.0050060 g.
c. The distance between two points was found to be 5.030×10^3 ft.
d. In yesterday's bicycle race, 110 riders started but only 60 finished.

Solution

a. The number contains three significant figures. The zeros to the left of the 1 are leading zeros and are not significant, but the remaining zero (a captive zero) is significant.

b. The number contains five significant figures. The leading zeros (to the left of the 5) are not significant. The captive zeros between the 5 and the 6 are significant, and the trailing zero to the right of the 6 is significant because the number contains a decimal point.

c. This number has four significant figures. Both zeros in 5.030 are significant.

d. Both numbers are exact (they were obtained by counting the riders). Thus these numbers have an unlimited number of significant figures.

Self-Check Exercise 2.2

Give the number of significant figures for each of the following measurements.

a. 0.00100 m
b. 2.0800×10^2 L
c. 480 Corvettes

See Problems 2.37 and 2.38.

Rounding Off Numbers

When you perform a calculation on your calculator, the number of digits displayed is usually greater than the number of significant figures that the result should possess. So you must "round off" the number (reduce it to fewer digits). The rules for **rounding off** follow.

Rules for Rounding Off

1. If the digit to be removed
   a. is less than 5, the preceding digit stays the same. For example, 1.33 rounds to 1.3.
   b. is equal to or greater than 5, the preceding digit is increased by 1. For example, 1.36 rounds to 1.4, and 3.15 rounds to 3.2.

2. In a series of calculations, carry the extra digits through to the final result and *then* round off.* This means that you should carry all of the digits that show on your calculator until you arrive at the final number (the answer) and then round off, using the procedures in rule 1.

These rules reflect the way calculators round off.

We need to make one more point about rounding off to the correct number of significant figures. Suppose the number 4.348 needs to be rounded to two significant figures. In doing this, we look *only* at the *first number* to the right of the 3:

> 4.348
> ↑
> Look at this
> number to round off
> to two significant figures.

The number is rounded to 4.3 because 4 is less than 5. It is incorrect to round sequentially. For example, do *not* round the 4 to 5 to give 4.35 and then round the 3 to 4 to give 4.4.

When rounding off, *use only the first number to the right of the last significant figure.*

Do not round off sequentially. The number 6.8347 rounded to three significant figures is 6.83, not 6.84.

---

*This practice will not be followed in the worked-out examples in this text, because we want to show the correct number of significant figures in each step of the example.

Determining Significant Figures in Calculations

Next we will learn how to determine the correct number of significant figures in the result of a calculation. To do this we will use the following rules.

Rules for Using Significant Figures in Calculations

1. For *multiplication or division,* the number of significant figures in the result is the same as that in the measurement with the *smallest number* of significant figures. We say this measurement is *limiting,* because it limits the number of significant figures in the result. For example, consider this calculation:

$$4.56 \times 1.4 = 6.384 \quad \boxed{\text{Round off}} \quad 6.4$$

Three   Limiting (two   Two significant
significant   significant figures)   figures
figures

Because 1.4 has only two significant figures, it limits the result to two significant figures. Thus the product is correctly written as 6.4, which has two significant figures. Consider another example. In the division $\dfrac{8.315}{298}$, how many significant figures should appear in the answer? Because 8.315 has four significant figures, the number 298 (with three significant figures) limits the result. The calculation is correctly represented as

Four
significant
figures

$$\frac{8.315}{298} = 0.0279027 \quad \boxed{\text{Round off}} \quad 2.79 \times 10^{-2}$$

Limiting (three   Result   Three
significant   shown on   significant
figures)   calculator   figures

If you need help in using your calculator, see Appendix 1.

2. For *addition or subtraction,* the limiting term is the one with the smallest number of decimal places. For example, consider the following sum:

$$
\begin{array}{l}
12.11 \\
18.0 \qquad \text{Limiting term (has one decimal place)}\\
\underline{1.013} \\
31.123 \quad \boxed{\text{Round off}} \quad 31.1 \\
\qquad\qquad\qquad\qquad\quad \uparrow \\
\qquad\qquad\qquad \text{One decimal place}
\end{array}
$$

The correct result is 31.1 (it is limited to one decimal place because 18.0 has only one decimal place). Consider another example:

$$
\begin{array}{l}
0.6875 \qquad \text{Limiting term (one decimal place)}\\
\underline{-0.1} \\
0.5875 \quad \boxed{\text{Round off}} \quad 0.6
\end{array}
$$

Note that *for multiplication and division, significant figures are counted. For addition and subtraction, the decimal places are counted.*

Now we will put together the things you have learned about significant figures by considering some mathematical operations in the following examples.

EXAMPLE 2.4   *Counting Significant Figures in Calculations*

Without performing the calculations, tell how many significant figures each answer should contain.

a. 5.19   b. $1081 - 7.25$ c. 2.3×3.14
    1.9
    0.842   d. the total cost of 3 boxes of candy at \$2.50 a box

Solution

a. The answer will have one digit after the decimal place. The limiting number is 1.9, which has one decimal place, so the answer has two significant figures.

b. The answer will have no digits after the decimal point. The number 1081 has no digits to the right of the decimal point and limits the result, so the answer has four significant figures.

c. The answer will have two significant figures because the number 2.3 has only two significant figures (3.14 has three).

d. The answer will have three significant figures. The limiting factor is 2.50 because 3 (boxes of candy) is an exact number.

EXAMPLE 2.5   *Calculations Using Significant Figures*

Carry out the following mathematical operations and give each result to the correct number of significant figures.

a. 5.18×0.0208 d. $116.8 - 0.33$
b. $(3.60 \times 10^{-3}) \times (8.123) \div 4.3$ e. $(1.33 \times 2.8) + 8.41$
c. $21 + 13.8 + 130.36$ 3.7 + 8.41

                                             12.1

Solution

Limiting terms   Round to this digit.
                         ↓
a. $5.18 \times 0.0208 = 0.107744 \Rightarrow 0.108$

The answer should contain three significant figures because each number being multiplied has three significant figures (Rule 1). The 7 is rounded to 8 because the following digit is greater than 5.

$$\text{b.} \quad \frac{(3.60 \times 10^{-3})(8.123)}{4.3} = 6.8006 \times 10^{-3} \Rightarrow 6.8 \times 10^{-3}$$

Round to this digit. ↓
↑
Limiting term

Because 4.3 has the least number of significant figures (two), the result should have two significant figures (Rule 1).

c. 21
    13.8
    130.36
    ‾‾‾‾‾‾
    165.16 ➡ 165

In this case 21 is limiting (there are no digits after the decimal point). Thus the answer must have no digits after the decimal point, in accordance with the rule for addition (Rule 2).

d. 116.8
    − 0.33
    ‾‾‾‾‾‾
    116.47 ➡ 116.5

Because 116.8 has only one decimal place, the answer must have only one decimal place (Rule 2). The 4 is rounded up to 5 because the digit to the right (7) is greater than 5.

e. $1.33 \times 2.8 = 3.724$ ➡ 3.7

    3.7 ⟵ Limiting term
    + 8.41
    ‾‾‾‾‾‾
    12.11 ➡ 12.1

Note that in this case we multiplied and then rounded the result to the correct number of significant figures before we performed the addition so that we would know the correct number of decimal places.

 Self-Check Exercise 2.3

Give the answer for each calculation to the correct number of significant figures.

a. 12.6×0.53
b. $(12.6 \times 0.53) - 4.59$
c. $(25.36 - 4.15) \div 2.317$

See Problems 2.51 through 2.56.

2.6 Problem Solving and Dimensional Analysis

AIM: To learn how dimensional analysis can be used to solve various types of problems.

Suppose that the boss at the store where you work on weekends asks you to pick up 2 dozen doughnuts on the way to work. However, you find that the doughnut shop sells by the doughnut. How many doughnuts do you need?

This "problem" is an example of something you encounter all the time: converting from one unit of measurement to another. Examples of this occur in cooking (The recipe calls for 3 cups of cream, which is sold in pints. How many pints do I buy?); traveling (The purse costs 250 pesos. How much is that in dollars?); sports (A recent Tour de France bicycle race was 3215 kilometers long. How many miles is that?); and many other areas.

How do we convert from one unit of measurement to another? Let's explore this process by using the doughnut problem.

2 dozen doughnuts = ? individual doughnuts

where ? represents a number you don't know yet. The essential information you must have is the definition of a dozen:

1 dozen = 12

You can use this information to make the needed conversion as follows:

$$2 \text{ dozen doughnuts} \times \frac{12}{1 \text{ dozen}} = 24 \text{ doughnuts}$$

You need to buy 24 doughnuts.

Note two important things about this process.

1. The factor $\dfrac{12}{1 \text{ dozen}}$ is a conversion factor based on the definition of the term *dozen*. This conversion factor is a ratio of the two parts of the definition of a dozen given above.

2. The unit dozen itself cancels.

Now let's generalize a bit. To change from one unit to another we will use a conversion factor.

$$\text{Unit}_1 \times \text{conversion factor} = \text{Unit}_2$$

The **conversion factor** is a ratio of the two parts of the statement that relates the two units. We will see this in more detail on the following pages.

Earlier in this chapter we considered a pin that measured 2.85 cm in length. What is the length of the pin in inches? We can represent this problem as

$$2.85 \text{ cm} \rightarrow ? \text{ in.}$$

The question mark stands for the number we want to find. To solve this problem, we must know the relationship between inches and centimeters. In Table 2.7, which gives several equivalents between the English and metric systems, we find the relationship

$$\boxed{2.54 \text{ cm} = 1 \text{ in.}}$$

This is called an **equivalence statement.** In other words, 2.54 cm and 1 in. stand for *exactly the same distance.* (See Figure 2.1.) The respective numbers are different because they refer to different *scales* (*units*) of distance.

The equivalence statement 2.54 cm = 1 in. can lead to either of two conversion factors:

$$\frac{2.54 \text{ cm}}{1 \text{ in.}} \quad \text{or} \quad \frac{1 \text{ in.}}{2.54 \text{ cm}}$$

Note that these *conversion factors* are *ratios of the two parts of the equivalence statement* that relates the two units. Which of the two possible conversion factors do we need? Recall our problem:

$$2.85 \text{ cm} = ? \text{ in.}$$

That is, we want to convert from units of centimeters to inches:

$$2.85 \text{ cm} \times \text{conversion factor} = ? \text{ in.}$$

We choose a conversion factor that cancels the units we want to discard and leaves the units we want in the result. Thus we do the conversion as follows:

$$2.85 \text{ cm} \times \frac{1 \text{ in.}}{2.54 \text{ cm}} = \frac{2.85 \text{ in.}}{2.54} = 1.12 \text{ in.}$$

TABLE 2.7

English–Metric and English–English Equivalents

Length	1 m = 1.094 yd
	2.54 cm = 1 in
	1 mi = 5280. ft
	1 mi = 1760. yd
Mass	1 kg = 2.205 lb
	453.6 g = 1 lb
Volume	1 L = 1.06 qt
	1 ft^3 = 28.32 L

Units cancel just as numbers do.

Note two important facts about this conversion.

1. The centimeter units cancel to give inches for the result. This is exactly what we had wanted to accomplish. Using the other conversion factor $\left(2.85 \text{ cm} \times \dfrac{2.54 \text{ cm}}{1 \text{ in.}}\right)$ would not work because the units would not cancel to give inches in the result.

When you finish a calculation, always check to make sure that the answer makes sense.

2. As the units changed from centimeters to inches, the number changed from 2.85 to 1.12. Thus 2.85 cm has exactly the same value (is the same length) as 1.12 in. Notice that in this conversion, the number decreased from 2.85 to 1.12. This makes sense because the inch is a larger unit of length than the centimeter is. That is, it takes fewer inches to make the same length in centimeters.

The result in the foregoing conversion has three significant figures as required. Caution: Noting that the term 1 appears in the conversion, you might think that because this number appears to have only one significant figure, the result should have only one significant figure. That is, the answer should be given as 1 in. rather than 1.12 in. However, in the equivalence statement 1 in. = 2.54 cm, the 1 is an exact number (by definition). In other words, exactly 1 in. equals 2.54 cm. Therefore, the 1 does not limit the number of significant digits in the result.

When exact numbers are used in a calculation, they never limit the number of significant digits.

We have seen how to convert from centimeters to inches. What about the reverse conversion? For example, if a pencil is 7.00 in. long, what is its length in centimeters? In this case, the conversion we want to make is

$$7.00 \text{ in.} \rightarrow \text{? cm}$$

What conversion factor do we need to make this conversion?

Remember that two conversion factors can be derived from each equivalence statement. In this case, the equivalence statement 2.54 cm = 1 in. gives

$$\frac{2.54 \text{ cm}}{1 \text{ in.}} \quad \text{or} \quad \frac{1 \text{ in.}}{2.54 \text{ cm}}$$

Again, we choose which to use by looking at the *direction* of the required change. For us to change from inches to centimeters, the inches must cancel. Thus the factor

$$\frac{2.54 \text{ cm}}{1 \text{ in.}}$$

is used, and the conversion is done as follows:

$$7.00 \text{ in.} \times \frac{2.54 \text{ cm}}{1 \text{ in.}} = (7.00)(2.54) \text{ cm} = 17.8 \text{ cm}$$

Here the inch units cancel, leaving centimeters as required.

Consider the direction of the required change in order to select the correct conversion factor.

Note that in this conversion, the number increased (from 7.00 to 17.8). This makes sense because the centimeter is a smaller unit of length than the inch. That is, it takes more centimeters to make the same length in inches. *Always take a moment to think about whether your answer makes sense.* This will help you avoid errors.

Changing from one unit to another via conversion factors (based on the equivalence statements between the units) is often called **dimensional analysis.** We will use this method throughout our study of chemistry.

We can now state some general steps for doing conversions by dimensional analysis.

Converting from One Unit to Another

STEP 1   To convert from one unit to another, use the equivalence statement that relates the two units. The conversion factor needed is a ratio of the two parts of the equivalence statement.

STEP 2   Choose the appropriate conversion factor by looking at the direction of the required change (make sure the unwanted units cancel).

STEP 3   Multiply the quantity to be converted by the conversion factor to give the quantity with the desired units.

STEP 4   Check that you have the correct number of significant figures.

STEP 5   Ask whether your answer makes sense.

We will now illustrate this procedure in Example 2.6.

EXAMPLE 2.6   *Conversion Factors: One-Step Problems*

An Italian bicycle has its frame size given as 62 cm. What is the frame size in inches?

Solution

We can represent the problem as

$$62 \text{ cm} = ? \text{ in.}$$

In this problem we want to convert from centimeters to inches.

$$62 \text{ cm} \times \text{conversion factor} = ? \text{ in.}$$

STEP 1   To convert from centimeters to inches, we need the equivalence statement 1 in. = 2.54 cm. This leads to two conversion factors:

$$\frac{1 \text{ in.}}{2.54 \text{ cm}} \quad \text{and} \quad \frac{2.54 \text{ cm}}{1 \text{ in.}}$$

STEP 2   In this case, the direction we want is

$$\text{Centimeters} \rightarrow \text{inches}$$

so we need the conversion factor $\dfrac{1 \text{ in.}}{2.54 \text{ cm}}$. We know this is the one we want because using it will make the units of centimeters cancel, leaving units of inches.

STEP 3   The conversion is carried out as follows:

$$62 \text{ cm} \times \frac{1 \text{ in.}}{2.54 \text{ cm}} = 24 \text{ in.}$$

STEP 4   The result is limited to two significant figures by the number 62. The centimeters cancel, leaving inches as required.

STEP 5   Note that the number decreased in this conversion. This makes sense; the inch is a larger unit of length than the centimeter.

 Self-Check Exercise 2.4

Wine is often bottled in 0.750-L containers. Using the appropriate equivalence statement from Table 2.7, calculate the volume of such a wine bottle in quarts.

See Problems 2.63 and 2.64.

Next we will consider a conversion that requires several steps.

EXAMPLE 2.7   *Conversion Factors: Multiple-Step Problems*

The length of the marathon race is approximately 26.2 mi. What is this distance in kilometers?

Solution

The problem before us can be represented as follows:

$$26.2 \text{ mi} = ? \text{ km}$$

We could accomplish this conversion in several different ways, but because Table 2.7 gives the equivalence statements 1 mi = 1760 yd and 1 m = 1.094 yd, we will proceed as follows:

$$\text{Miles} \rightarrow \text{yards} \rightarrow \text{meters} \rightarrow \text{kilometers}$$

This process will be carried out one conversion at a time to make sure everything is clear.

Miles → Yards   We convert from miles to yards using the conversion factor $\frac{1760 \text{ yd}}{1 \text{ mi}}$.

26.2 mi → $\frac{1760 \text{ yd}}{1 \text{ mi}}$ → 4.61×10^4 yd

$$26.2 \text{ mi} \times \frac{1760 \text{ yd}}{1 \text{ mi}} = 46,112 \text{ yd}$$

Result shown
on calculator

46,112 yd → Round off → 46,100 yd = 4.61×10^4 yd

We can summarize what we learned in Example 2.8 as follows: to convert from the Celsius to the Kelvin scale, we can use the formula

$$T_{°C} \quad + \quad 273 \; = \; T_K$$

Temperature
in Celsius
degrees

Temperature
in kelvins

EXAMPLE 2.9   *Temperature Conversion: Kelvin to Celsius*

Liquid nitrogen boils at 77 K. What is the boiling point of nitrogen on the Celsius scale?

Solution

The problem to be solved here is 77 K = ? °C. Let's explore this question by examining the picture to the left representing the two temperature scales. One key point is to recognize that 0 °C = 273 K. Also note that the difference between 273 K and 77 K is 196 kelvins (273 − 77 = 196). That is, 77 K is 196 kelvins below 273 K. The degree size is the same on these two temperature scales, so 77 K must correspond to 196 Celsius degrees below zero or −196 °C. Thus 77 K = ? °C = −196 °C.

We can also solve this problem by using the formula

$$T_{°C} \; + \; 273 \; = \; T_K$$

However, in this case we want to solve for the Celsius temperature $T_{°C}$. That is, we want to isolate $T_{°C}$ on one side of the equals sign. To do this we use an important general principle: doing *the same thing on both sides of the equals sign* preserves the equality. In other words, it's always okay to perform the same operation on both sides of the equals sign.

To isolate $T_{°C}$ we need to subtract 273 from both sides:

$$T_{°C} + 273 - 273 \; = \; T_K - 273$$

↑   ↑
Sum is zero

to give

$$T_{°C} \; = \; T_K - 273$$

Using this equation to solve the problem, we have

$$T_{°C} \; = \; T_K - 273 \; = \; 77 - 273 \; = \; -196$$

So, as before, we have shown that

$$77 \text{ K} \; = \; -196 \text{ °C}$$

 Self-Check Exercise 2.6
Which temperature is colder, 172 K or −75 °C?

See Problems 2.77 and 2.78.

In summary, because the Kelvin and Celsius scales have the same size unit, to switch from one scale to the other we must simply account for the different zero points. We must add 273 to the Celsius temperature to obtain the temperature on the Kelvin scale:

$$T_K = \boxed{T_{°C} + 273}$$

To convert from the Kelvin scale to the Celsius scale, we must subtract 273 from the Kelvin temperature:

$$\boxed{T_{°C}} = \boxed{T_K - 273}$$

Converting Between the Fahrenheit and Celsius Scales

The conversion between the Fahrenheit and Celsius temperature scales requires two adjustments:

1. For the different size units
2. For the different zero points

To see how to adjust for the different unit sizes, consider the diagram in Figure 2.9. Note that because 212 °F = 100 °C and 32 °F = 0 °C,

$$212 - 32 = 180 \text{ Fahrenheit degrees} = 100 - 0 = 100 \text{ Celsius degrees}$$

Thus

$$180. \text{ Fahrenheit degrees} = 100. \text{ Celsius degrees}$$

Remember, it's okay to do the same thing to both sides of the equation.

FIGURE 2.9
Comparison of the Celsius and Fahrenheit scales.

Dividing both sides of this equation by 100. gives

$$\frac{180.}{100.} \text{ Fahrenheit degrees} = \frac{\cancel{100.}}{\cancel{100.}} \text{ Celsius degrees}$$

or

$$1.80 \text{ Fahrenheit degrees} = 1.00 \text{ Celsius degree}$$

The factor 1.80 is used to convert from one degree size to the other.

Next we have to account for the fact that 0 °C is *not* the same as 0 °F. In fact, 32 °F = 0 °C. Although we will not show how to derive it, the equation to convert a temperature in Celsius degrees to the Fahrenheit scale is

$$T_{°F} = 1.80(T_{°C}) + 32$$

Temperature in °F   Temperature in °C

In this equation the term $1.80(T_{°C})$ adjusts for the difference in degree size between the two scales. The 32 in the equation accounts for the different zero points. We will now show how to use this equation.

EXAMPLE 2.10 *Temperature Conversion: Celsius to Fahrenheit*

On a summer day the temperature in the laboratory, as measured on a lab thermometer, is 28 °C. Express this temperature on the Fahrenheit scale.

Solution

This problem can be represented as 28 °C = ? °F. We will solve it using the formula

$$T_{°F} = 1.80(T_{°C}) + 32$$

In this case,

$T_{°C}$
$\downarrow$

$$T_{°F} = ? \text{ °F} = 1.80(28) + 32 = 50.4 + 32$$

Rounds off to 50

$$= 50. + 32 = 82$$

Note that 28 °C is approximately equal to 82 °F. Because the numbers are just reversed, this is an easy reference point to remember for the two scales.

Thus 28 °C = 82 °F.

EXAMPLE 2.11 *Temperature Conversion: Celsius to Fahrenheit*

Express the temperature −40. °C on the Fahrenheit scale.

Solution

We can express this problem as −40. °C = ? °F. To solve it we will use the formula

$$T_{°F} = 1.80(T_{°C}) + 32$$

In this case,

$$T_{°F} = ? °F = \overset{\overset{T_{°C}}{\downarrow}}{1.80(-40.)} + 32$$
$$= -72 + 32 = -40$$

So $-40 °C = -40 °F$. This is a very interesting result and is another useful reference point.

Self-Check Exercise 2.7

Hot tubs are often maintained at 41 °C. What is this temperature in Fahrenheit degrees?

See Problems 2.79 through 2.82.

To convert from Celsius to Fahrenheit, we have used the equation

$$T_{°F} = 1.80(T_{°C}) + 32$$

To convert a Fahrenheit temperature to Celsius, we need to rearrange this equation to isolate Celsius degrees ($T_{°C}$). Remember we can always do the same operation to both sides of the equation. First subtract 32 from each side:

$$T_{°F} - 32 = 1.80(T_{°C}) + \underset{\underset{\text{Sum is zero}}{\uparrow}}{32} - \underset{\uparrow}{32}$$

to give

$$T_{°F} - 32 = 1.80(T_{°C})$$

Next divide both sides by 1.80:

$$\frac{T_{°F} - 32}{1.80} = \frac{\cancel{1.80}(T_{°C})}{\cancel{1.80}}$$

to give

$$\frac{T_{°F} - 32}{1.80} = T_{°C}$$

or

$$\underset{\substack{\text{Temperature} \\ \text{in °C}}}{T_{°C}} = \frac{\overset{\substack{\text{Temperature} \\ \text{in °F}}}{T_{°F} - 32}}{1.80}$$

$$T_{°C} = \frac{T_{°F} - 32}{1.80}$$

EXAMPLE 2.12 *Temperature Conversion: Fahrenheit to Celsius*

One of the body's responses to an infection or injury is to elevate its temperature. A certain flu victim has a body temperature of 101 °F. What is this temperature on the Celsius scale?

Solution

The problem is 101 °F = ? °C. Using the formula

$$T_{°C} = \frac{T_{°F} - 32}{1.80}$$

yields

$$T_{°C} = \text{? °C} = \frac{\overset{T_{°F}}{101} - 32}{1.80} = \frac{69}{1.80} = 38$$

That is, 101 °F = 38 °C.

Self-Check Exercise 2.8

An antifreeze solution in a car's radiator boils at 239 °F. What is this temperature on the Celsius scale?

See Problems 2.79 through 2.82.

In doing temperature conversions, you will need the following formulas.

Temperature Conversion Formulas

• Celsius to Kelvin	$T_K = T_{°C} + 273$
• Kelvin to Celsius	$T_{°C} = T_K - 273$
• Celsius to Fahrenheit	$T_{°F} = 1.80(T_{°C}) + 32$
• Fahrenheit to Celsius	$T_{°C} = \dfrac{T_{°F} - 32}{1.80}$

2.8   Density

AIM: To define density and its units.

When you were in elementary school, you may have been embarrassed by your answer to the question "Which is heavier, a pound of lead or a pound of feathers?" If you said lead, you were undoubtedly thinking about density, not mass. **Density** can be defined as the amount of matter present *in a given*

Lead has a greater density than feathers.

volume of substance. That is, density is mass per unit volume, the ratio of the mass of an object to its volume:

$$\text{Density} = \frac{\text{mass}}{\text{volume}}$$

It takes a much bigger volume to make a pound of feathers than to make a pound of lead. This is because lead has a much greater mass per unit volume—a greater density.

The density of a liquid can be determined easily by weighing a known volume of the substance as illustrated in Example 2.13.

EXAMPLE 2.13 *Calculating Density*

Suppose a student finds that 23.50 mL of a certain liquid weigh 35.062 g. What is the density of this liquid?

Solution

We can calculate the density of this liquid simply by applying the definition

$$\text{Density} = \frac{\text{mass}}{\text{volume}} = \frac{35.062 \text{ g}}{23.50 \text{ mL}} = 1.492 \text{ g/mL}$$

This result could also be expressed as 1.492 g/cm³ because 1 mL = 1 cm³.

The volume of a solid object is often determined indirectly by submerging it in water and measuring the volume of water displaced. In fact, this is the most accurate method for measuring a person's percent body fat. The person is submerged momentarily in a tank of water, and the increase in volume is measured (see Figure 2.10). It is possible to calculate the body density by using the person's weight (mass) and the volume of the person's body

FIGURE 2.10
(a) Tank of water. (b) Person submerged in the tank, raising the level of the water.

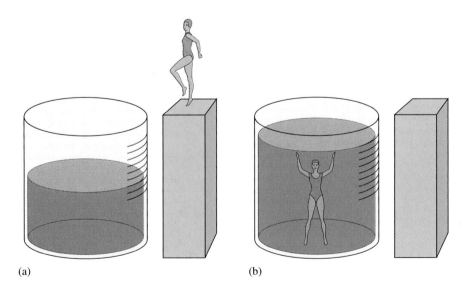

(a)   (b)

determined by submersion. Fat, muscle, and bone have different densities (fat is less dense than muscle tissue, for example), so the fraction of the person's body that is fat can be calculated. The more muscle and the less fat a person has, the higher his or her body density. For example, a muscular person weighing 150 lb has a smaller body volume (and thus a higher density) than a fat person weighing 150 lb.

EXAMPLE 2.14   *Determining Density*

At a local pawn shop a student finds a medallion that the shop owner insists is pure platinum. However, the student suspects that the medallion may actually be silver and thus much less valuable. The student buys the medallion only after the shop owner agrees to refund the price if the medallion is returned within two days. The student, a chemistry major, then takes the medallion to her lab and measures its density as follows. She first weighs the medallion and finds its mass to be 55.64 g. She then places some water in a graduated cylinder and reads the volume as 75.2 mL. Next she drops the medallion into the cylinder and reads the new volume as 77.8 mL. Is the medallion platinum (density = 21.4 g/cm³) or silver (density = 10.5 g/cm³)?

The most common units for density are g/mL = g/cm³.

Solution

The densities of platinum and silver differ so much that the measured density of the medallion will show which metal is present. Because by definition

$$\text{Density} = \frac{\text{mass}}{\text{volume}}$$

to calculate the density of the medallion, we need its mass and its volume. The mass of the medallion is 55.64 g. The volume of the medallion can be obtained by taking the difference between the volume readings of the water in the graduated cylinder before and after the medallion was added.

$$\text{Volume of medallion} = 77.8 \text{ mL} - 75.2 \text{ mL} = 2.6 \text{ mL}$$

The volume appeared to increase by 2.6 mL when the medallion was added, so 2.6 mL represents the volume of the medallion. Now we can use the measured mass and volume of the medallion to determine its density:

$$\text{Density of medallion} = \frac{\text{mass}}{\text{volume}} = \frac{55.64}{2.6 \text{ mL}} = 21 \text{ g/mL}$$

$$\text{or}$$

$$= 21 \text{ g/cm}^3$$

The medallion is really platinum.

 Self-Check Exercise 2.9

A student wants to identify the main component in a commercial liquid cleaner. He finds that 35.8 mL of the cleaner weighs 28.1 g. Of the following possibilities, which is the main component of the cleaner?

Substance	Density, g/cm³
chloroform	1.483
diethyl ether	0.714
isopropyl alcohol	0.785
toluene	0.867

See Problems 2.93 and 2.94.

EXAMPLE 2.15   *Using Density in Calculations*

Mercury has a density of 13.6 g/mL. What volume of mercury must be taken to obtain 225 g of the metal?

Solution

To solve this problem, start with the definition of density:

$$\text{Density} = \frac{\text{mass}}{\text{volume}}$$

and then rearrange this equation to isolate the required quantity. In this case we want to find the volume. Remember that we maintain an equality when we do the same thing to both sides. For example, if we multiply *both sides* of the density definition by volume:

$$\text{volume} \times \text{density} = \frac{\text{mass}}{\cancel{\text{volume}}} \times \cancel{\text{volume}}$$

volume cancels on the right, leaving

$$\text{volume} \times \text{density} = \text{mass}$$

We want the volume, so we now divide both sides by density:

$$\frac{\text{volume} \times \cancel{\text{density}}}{\cancel{\text{Density}}} = \frac{\text{mass}}{\text{density}}$$

to give

$$\text{volume} = \frac{\text{mass}}{\text{density}}$$

Now we can solve the problem by substituting the given numbers:

$$\text{volume} = \frac{225 \text{ g}}{13.6 \text{ g/mL}} = 16.5 \text{ mL}$$

We must take 16.5 mL of mercury to obtain an amount that has a mass of 225 g.

Spherical droplets of mercury, a very dense liquid.

The densities of various common substances are given in Table 2.8.

Besides being a tool for the identification of substances, density has many other uses. For example, the liquid in your car's lead storage battery (a solution of sulfuric acid) changes density because the sulfuric acid is consumed

FIGURE 2.11
A hydrometer being used to determine the density of the antifreeze solution in a car's radiator.

TABLE 2.8
Densities of Various Common Substances at 20 °C

Substance	Physical State	Density (g/cm³)
oxygen	gas	0.00133*
hydrogen	gas	0.000084*
ethanol	liquid	0.785
benzene	liquid	0.880
water	liquid	1.000
magnesium	solid	1.74
salt (sodium chloride)	solid	2.16
aluminum	solid	2.70
iron	solid	7.87
copper	solid	8.96
silver	solid	10.5
lead	solid	11.34
mercury	liquid	13.6
gold	solid	19.32

*At 1 atmosphere pressure

as the battery discharges. In a fully charged battery, the density of the solution is about 1.30 g/cm³. When the density falls below 1.20 g/cm³, the battery has to be recharged. Density measurement is also used to determine the amount of antifreeze, and thus the level of protection against freezing, in the cooling system of a car. Water and antifreeze have different densities, so the measured density of the mixture tells us how much of each is present. The device used to test the density of the solution—a hydrometer—is shown in Figure 2.11.

In certain situations, the term *specific gravity* is used to describe the density of a liquid. **Specific gravity** is defined as the ratio of the density of a given liquid to the density of water at 4 °C. Because it is a ratio of densities, specific gravity has no units.

Chapter Review

Key Terms

measurement *(p. 15)*
scientific notation *(2.1)*
units *(2.2)*
English system *(2.2)*
metric system *(2.2)*
SI units *(2.2)*
mass *(2.3)*
significant figures *(2.4)*

rounding off *(2.5)*
conversion factor *(2.6)*
equivalence statement *(2.6)*
dimensional analysis *(2.6)*
Fahrenheit scale *(2.7)*
Celsius scale *(2.7)*
Kelvin (absolute) scale *(2.7)*
density *(2.8)*

Summary

1. A quantitative observation is called a measurement and always consists of a number and a unit.

2. We can conveniently express very large or very small numbers using scientific notation, which represents the number as a number between 1 and 10 multiplied by 10 raised to a power.

3. Units give a scale on which to represent the results of a measurement. The three systems discussed are the English,

metric, and SI systems. The metric and SI systems use prefixes (Table 2.2) to change the size of the units.

4. The mass of an object represents the quantity of matter in that object.

5. All measurements have a degree of uncertainty, which is reflected in the number of significant figures used to express them. Various rules are used to round off to the correct number of significant figures in a calculated result.

6. We can convert from one system of units to another by a method called dimensional analysis, in which conversion factors are used.

7. Temperature can be measured on three different scales: Fahrenheit, Celsius, and Kelvin. We can readily convert among these scales.

8. Density is the amount of matter present in a given volume (mass per unit volume). That is,

$$\text{Density} = \frac{\text{mass}}{\text{volume}}$$

Questions and Problems

All even-numbered exercises have answers in the back of this book and solutions in the Solutions Guide.

2.1 ■ *Scientific Notation*

QUESTIONS

1. When the number 7312 is expressed in standard scientific notation, it is written as _____ $\times 10^3$.

2. When 3314 is written in scientific notation, the exponent indicating the power of ten will be _____.

3. When the number 4.512×10^3 is written in ordinary decimal notation, it is expressed as _____.

4. When 0.0021 is written in scientific notation, the exponent is (positive/negative), whereas when 4540 is written in scientific notation, the exponent is (positive/negative).

PROBLEMS

5. For each of the following numbers expressed in standard scientific notation, write the number as an "ordinary" decimal number.
   a. 7.214×10^{-4} c. 4.299×10^3
   b. 6.015×10^5 d. 9.089×10^{-6}

6. For each of the following numbers, if the number is rewritten in standard scientific notation, what will be the value of the exponent (for the power of ten)?
   a. 0.000067   c. 1/10,000
   b. 9,331,442   d. 163.1×10^2

7. Express each of the following numbers in scientific (exponential) notation.
   a. 12,500
   b. 37,400,000
   c. 602,300,000,000,000,000,000,000
   d. 375
   e. 0.0202
   f. 0.1550
   g. 0.0000104
   h. 0.00000000000000000000129

8. Express each of the following numbers in *standard* scientific notation.
   a. 0.04731
   b. 4284
   c. 4.201
   d. 0.000000000141
   e. 52.3
   f. 0.04909
   g. 54,331,000
   h. 0.981

9. Express each of the following as an "ordinary" decimal number.
   a. 4.215×10^3 g. 1.9912×10^{-1}
   b. 7.228×10^{-5} h. 1.801×10^4
   c. 9.012×10^{-2} i. 6.9193901×10^7
   d. 1.024×10^5 j. 8.114×10^{-3}
   e. 7.091×10^{-7} k. 1.000×10^2
   f. 6.921×10^2 l. 8.023×10^{-6}

10. Express each of the following as "ordinary" decimal numbers.
    a. 4.83×10^2 g. 9.999×10^3
    b. 7.221×10^{-4} h. 1.016×10^{-5}
    c. 6.1×10^0 i. 1.016×10^5
    d. 9.11×10^{-8} j. 4.11×10^{-1}
    e. 4.221×10^6 k. 9.71×10^4
    f. 1.22×10^{-3} l. 9.71×10^{-4}

11. Write each of the following numbers in *standard* scientific notation.
    a. 0.0102×10^{-3} e. $6,503,300 \times 10^{-5}$
    b. 4551×10^4 f. 0.08178×10^{-3}
    c. 6023×10^{20} g. 27.21×10^{-4}
    d. 0.009921×10^4 h. 8.214×10^{-6}

12. Write each of the following numbers in *standard* scientific notation.
    a. 131.2×10^{-3} e. 0.00721×10^3
    b. 14.72×10^2 f. 0.0914×10^{-4}
    c. 1201×10^{-6} g. 0.000129×10^5
    d. 44.3×10^4 h. $0.00001901 \times 10^{-6}$

13. Write each of the following numbers in *standard* scientific notation.
    a. 1/1033
    b. $1/10^5$
    c. $1/10^{-7}$
    d. 1/0.0002
    e. 1/3,093,000
    f. $1/10^{-4}$
    g. $1/10^9$
    h. 1/0.000015

14. Write each of the following numbers in *standard* scientific notation.
    a. 1/0.00032
    b. $10^3/10^{-3}$
    c. $10^3/10^3$
    d. 1/55,000
    e. $(10^5)(10^4)(10^{-4})/(10^{-2})$
    f. $43.2/(4.32 \times 10^{-5})$
    g. $(4.32 \times 10^{-5})/432$
    h. $1/(10^5)(10^{-6})$

2.2 ■ Units

QUESTIONS

15. The international system of measurement that has the meter, kilogram, and second as its fundamental units is called the _____.

16. Although the standard of mass is, strictly speaking, the kilogram, in chemistry we more commonly make measurements of mass in terms of how many _____ a sample weighs.

17. Indicate the meaning (as a power of 10) for each of the following metric prefixes.
    a. kilo
    b. centi
    c. milli
    d. deci
    e. nano
    f. micro

18. Give the metric prefix that corresponds to each of the following:
    a. 1,000,000
    b. 10^{-3}
    c. 10^{-9}
    d. 10^6
    e. 10^{-2}
    f. 0.000001

2.3 ■ Measurements of Length, Volume, and Mass

QUESTIONS

19. The basic SI unit of length is the _____, which is equivalent to slightly more than a yard.

20. Which distance is farther, 100 mi or 100 km?

21. As a measure of volume, 1 liter is equivalent to 1 cubic _____.

22. One liter of volume in the metric system is approximately equivalent to one _____ in the English system.

23. Which is the greater distance, 50 miles or 100 kilometers?

24. Which weighs more, a pound of hamburger or a kilogram of hamburger?

25. The length 10.0 cm can also be expressed as _____ mm.

26. Which person is taller, a man who is 1.75 m tall or a woman who is 5 ft 2 in. tall?

27. A 1-kg package of hamburger has a mass closest to which of the following?
    a. 8 oz
    b. 1 lb
    c. 2 lb
    d. 10 lb

28. A 2-L bottle of soda contains a volume closest to which of the following?
    a. 5 gal
    b 1 qt
    c. 2 pt
    d. 2 qt

29. A recipe written in metric units calls for 250 mL of milk. Which of the following best approximates this amount?
    a. 1 qt
    b. 1 gal
    c. 1 cup
    d. 1 pt

30. Which metric system unit is most appropriate for measuring the distance between two cities?
    a. meters
    b. millimeters
    c. centimeters
    d. kilometers

For exercises 31 and 32 some examples of simple approximate metric–English equivalents are given in Table 2.6.

31. What is the value in dollars of a stack of dimes that is 10 cm high?

32. How many quarters would have to be lined up in a row to reach a length of 1 meter?

2.4 ■ Uncertainty in Measurement

QUESTIONS

33. When a measuring scale is used properly to the limit of precision, the last significant digit recorded for the measurement is said to be *uncertain*. Explain.

34. No matter how careful an experimenter may be, a measurement always has some degree of _____.

35. For the pin shown in Figure 2.5, why is the third figure determined for the length of the pin uncertain? Considering that the third figure is uncertain, explain why the length of the pin is indicated as 2.85 cm rather than, for example, 2.83 or 2.87 cm.

36. Why can the length of the pin shown in Figure 2.5 not be recorded as 2.850 cm?

2.5 ■ Significant Figures

QUESTIONS

37. Indicate the number of significant figures in each of the following:
    a. 12
    b. 1098
    c. 2001
    d. 2.001×10^3
    e. 0.0000101
    f. 1.01×10^{-5}
    g. 1,000.
    h. 22.0403

38. Indicate the number of significant figures implied in each of the following statements:
    a. One foot is equivalent to 12 inches.
    b. The continental United States is over 3000 miles wide.
    c. There are 60 seconds in one minute.
    d. The population of Massachusetts is 5 million.
    e. One liter contains 1000 mL.

Rounding Off Numbers

QUESTIONS

39. When we are rounding a number off, if the number to the right of the digit to be rounded is less than 5, the digit should _____.

40. When performing a chain of several calculations, we round off the (final/intermediate) answer(s).

41. Round off each of the following numbers to three significant digits.
    a. 1,566,311
    b. 2.7651×10^{-3}
    c. 84,592
    d. 0.0011672
    e. 0.07759

42. Round off each of the following numbers to three significant digits and write the answer in standard scientific notation.
    a. 312.54
    b. 0.00031254
    c. 31,254,000
    d. 0.31254
    e. 31.254×10^{-3}

43. Round off each of the following numbers to the indicated number of significant digits.
    a. 102.4005 to five digits
    b. 15.9995 to three digits
    c. 1.6385 to four digits
    d. 7.355 to three digits

44. Round off each of the following numbers to the indicated number of significant digits and write the answer in standard scientific notation.
    a. 0.00034159 to three digits
    b. 103.351×10^2 to four digits
    c. 17.9915 to five digits
    d. 3.365×10^5 to three digits

Determining Significant Figures in Calculations

QUESTIONS

45. When numbers are multiplied, the answer should contain the same number of significant figures as the multiplier with the _____ number of significant figures.

46. When numbers are added or subtracted, the limiting term is the one with the smallest number of _____ places.

47. When the calculation $(0.0043)(0.0821)(298)$ is performed, the answer should be reported to _____ significant figures.

48. The quotient $(2.3733 \times 10^2)/(343)$ should be written with _____ significant figures.

49. How many digits after the decimal point should be reported when the calculation $(199.0354 + 43.09 + 121.2)$ is performed?

50. How many digits after the decimal point should be reported when the calculation $(10{,}434 - 9.3344)$ is performed?

PROBLEMS

Note: See Appendix 3 for help in doing mathematical operations with numbers that contain exponents.

51. Evaluate each of the following, and write the answer to the correct number of significant figures.
    a. $97.381 + 4.2502 + 0.99195$
    b. $171.5 + 72.915 - 8.23$
    c. $1.00914 + 0.87104 + 1.2012$
    d. $21.901 - 13.21 - 4.0215$

52. Evaluate each of the following and write the answer to the appropriate number of significant figures.
    a. $212.2 + 26.7 + 402.09$
    b. $1.0028 + 0.221 + 0.10337$
    c. $52.331 + 26.01 - 0.9981$
    d. $2.01 \times 10^2 + 3.014 \times 10^3$

53. Evaluate each of the following, and write the answer to the appropriate number of significant figures.
    a. $(0.102)(0.0821)(273)/(1.01)$
    b. $(0.14)(6.022 \times 10^{23})$
    c. $(4.0 \times 10^4)(5.021 \times 10^{-3})(7.34993 \times 10^2)$
    d. $(2.00 \times 10^6)/(3.00 \times 10^{-7})$

54. Evaluate each of the following and write the answer to the appropriate number of significant figures.
    a. $(4.031)(0.08206)(373.1)/(0.995)$
    b. $(12.011)/(6.022 \times 10^{23})$
    c. $(0.500)/(44.02)$
    d. $(0.15)/(280.62)$

55. Evaluate each of the following, and write the answer to the appropriate number of significant figures.
    a. $(2.3232 + 0.2034 - 0.16) \times (4.0 \times 10^3)$
    b. $(1.34 \times 10^2 + 3.2 \times 10^1)/(3.32 \times 10^{-6})$
    c. $(4.3 \times 10^6)/(4.334 + 44.0002 - 0.9820)$
    d. $(2.043 \times 10^{-2})^3$

56. Evaluate each of the following and write the answer to the appropriate number of significant figures.
    a. $(2.0944 + 0.0003233 + 12.22)/(7.001)$
    b. $(1.42 \times 10^2 + 1.021 \times 10^3)/(3.1 \times 10^{-1})$
    c. $(9.762 \times 10^{-3})/(1.43 \times 10^2 + 4.51 \times 10^1)$
    d. $(6.1982 \times 10^{-4})^2$

2.6 ■ Problem Solving and Dimensional Analysis

QUESTIONS

57. A _____ represents a ratio based on an equivalence statement between two measurements.

58. How many significant figures are understood for the numbers in the following definition: 1 mi = 5280 ft?

59. Given that 3 ft = 1 yd, determine what conversion factor is appropriate to convert 35 ft to yards; to convert 2.89 yd to feet.

60. Given that 12 in. = 1 ft, determine what conversion factor is appropriate to convert 72 in. to feet; to convert 3.5 ft to inches.

For exercises 61 and 62 apples cost $0.79 per pound.

61. What conversion factor is appropriate to express the cost of 5.3 lb of apples?

62. What conversion factor could be used to determine how many pounds of apples could be bought for $2.00?

PROBLEMS

Note: Appropriate equivalence statements for various units are found inside the back cover of this book.

63. Perform each of the following conversions, being sure to set up clearly the appropriate conversion factor in each case.
    a. 62.1 ft to yards
    b. 62.1 ft to inches
    c. 62.1 ft to meters
    d. 4.5 gal to quarts
    e. 4.5 gal to liters
    f. 458 g to kilograms
    g. 2.5 lb to ounces
    h. 3.5 hr to minutes

64. Perform each of the following conversions, being sure to set up clearly the appropriate conversion factor in each case.
    a. 2.23 m to yards
    b. 46.2 yd to meters
    c. 292 cm to inches
    d. 881.2 in. to centimeters
    e. 1043 km to miles
    f. 445.5 mi to kilometers
    g. 36.2 m to kilometers
    h. 0.501 km to centimeters

65. Perform each of the following conversions, being sure to set up clearly the appropriate conversion factor in each case.
    a. 62.5 cm to inches
    b. 2.68 in. to centimeters
    c. 3.25 yd to meters
    d. 4.95 m to yards
    e. 62.5 cm to yards
    f. 2.45 mi to kilometers
    g. 4.42 m to inches
    h. 5.01 kg to ounces

66. Perform each of the following conversions, being sure to set up clearly the appropriate conversion factor in each case.
    a. 254.3 g to kilograms
    b. 2.75 kg to grams
    c. 2.75 kg to pounds
    d. 2.75 kg to ounces
    e. 534.1 g to pounds
    f. 1.75 lb to grams
    g. 8.7 oz to grams
    h. 45.9 g to ounces

67. If $1.00 is equivalent to 1.74 German marks, what is $20.00 worth in marks? What is the value in dollars of a 100-mark bill?

68. Boston and New York City are 190 miles apart. What is this distance in kilometers? in meters? in feet?

69. In the United Kingdom, British Rail runs two types of modern high-speed passenger trains, the Intercity-125 and the Intercity-225. The Intercity-125 has a top speed of 125 mi/hr, whereas the newer Intercity-225 has a top speed of 225 km/hr. Which train is faster?

70. The radius of an atom is on the order of 10^{-10} m. What is this radius in centimeters? in inches? in nanometers?

2.7 ■ Temperature Conversions

QUESTIONS

71. The temperature scale in everyday use in the United States is the _____ scale.

72. The _____ temperature scale uses 0° to represent the normal freezing point of water.

73. The boiling point of water is _____ °F, or _____ °C.

74. The freezing point of water is _____ K.

75. On both the Celsius and Kelvin temperature scales, there are _____ degrees between the normal freezing and boiling points of water.

76. On which temperature scale (°F, °C, or K) does 1 degree represent the smallest change in temperature?

PROBLEMS

77. Convert the following temperatures to kelvins.
    a. −200 °C
    b. 150 °C
    c. −40 °C
    d. 23 °C
    e. −100 °C
    f. −196 °C

78. Convert the following Kelvin temperatures to Celsius degrees.
    a. 275 K
    b. 445 K
    c. 0 K
    d. 77 K
    e. 10,000. K
    f. 2 K

79. Convert the following Fahrenheit temperatures to Celsius degrees.
    a. a beautiful spring day, 68 °F
    b. a hot, humid August day, 86 °F
    c. a warm day in Minnesota in January, −10 °F
    d. the surface of a star, 10,000 °F

80. Convert the following Celsius temperatures to Fahrenheit degrees.
    a. the boiling temperature of ethyl alcohol, 78.1 °C
    b. a hot day at the beach on a Greek isle, 40. °C
    c. the lowest possible temperature, −273 °C
    d. the body temperature of a person with hypothermia, 32 °C

81. Carry out the indicated temperature conversions.
    a. −40 °C to Fahrenheit degrees
    b. −40 °F to Celsius degrees
    c. 232 K to Celsius degrees
    d. 232 K to Fahrenheit degrees

82. Carry out the indicated temperature conversions.
    a. −185 °F to Celsius degrees
    b. 255 K to Fahrenheit degrees
    c. 400. °C to kelvins
    d. exactly 0 °F to kelvins

2.8 ■ *Density*

QUESTIONS

83. The ratio of an object's mass to its volume is called the _____ of the object.

84. The most common units for density are _____.

85. A kilogram of lead occupies a much smaller volume than a kilogram of water, because _____ has a much higher density.

86. The _____ of an insoluble object (such as a person; see Figure 2.10) can be determined indirectly by measuring how much water the object displaces.

87. Typically, gases have very (high/low) densities compared to solids and liquids (see Table 2.8).

88. Density may be used as an aid in identifying substances, because every sample of a pure substance always has the _____ density.

89. Referring to Table 2.8, determine whether air, water, alcohol, or aluminum is the most dense.

90. Referring to Table 2.8, determine whether copper, silver, lead, or mercury is the least dense.

PROBLEMS

91. For the masses and volumes indicated, calculate the density in grams per cubic centimeter.
    a. mass = 44.3 g; volume = 22.1 cm^3
    b. mass = 1.23 kg; volume = 0.253 m^3
    c. mass = 4.2 lb; volume = 1.23 ft^3
    d. mass = 234 mg; volume = 2.2×10^{-3} cm^3

92. For the masses and volumes indicated, calculate the density in grams per cubic centimeter.
    a. mass = 122.4 g; volume = 5.5 cm^3
    b. mass = 19,302 g; volume = 0.57 m^3
    c. mass = 0.0175 kg; volume = 18.2 mL
    d. mass = 2.49 g; volume = 0.12 m^3

93. If 100.0 mL of a liquid weigh 81.23 g, calculate the liquid's density.

94. If 67.1 mL of a liquid weigh 55.221 g, calculate the density of the liquid.

95. A cube of metal weighs 1.45 kg and displaces 542 mL of water when immersed. Calculate the density of the metal.

96. A material will float on the surface of a liquid if the material has a density less than that of the liquid. Given that the density of water is approximately 1.0 g/mL under many conditions, will a block of material having a

volume of 1.2×10^4 in.^{3} and weighing 3.5 lb float or sink when placed in a reservoir of water?

97. A particular metal has a density of 4.51 g/cm^3. If 95.7 g of the metal is added to 145 mL of water in a graduated cylinder, to what volume reading will the water level rise?

98. The density of pure silver is 10.5 g/cm^3 at 20 °C. If 5.25 g of pure silver pellets are added to a graduated cylinder containing 11.2 mL of water, to what volume level will the water in the cylinder rise?

99. Use the information given in Table 2.8 to calculate the volume of 1.00 kg of each of the following substances.
   a. ethanol
   b. copper
   c. gold
   d. magnesium

100. Use the information given in Table 2.8 to calculate the mass of 1.00×10^3 cm^3 and 1.00 m^3 of each of the following substances.
   a. lead
   b. sodium chloride
   c. benzene
   d. iron

Additional Problems

101. Write each of the following numbers in standard scientific notation.
   a. 522.3×10^3
   b. 0.000003491
   c. 102,300
   d. 0.08210
   e. $444,000 \times 10^{-6}$
   f. 9.234×10^{-7}

102. Express each of the following as an "ordinary" decimal number.
   a. 3.011×10^{23}
   b. 5.091×10^9
   c. 7.2×10^2
   d. 1.234×10^5
   e. 4.32002×10^{-4}
   f. 3.001×10^{-2}
   g. 2.9901×10^{-7}
   h. 4.2×10^{-1}

103. Write each of the following numbers in standard scientific notation, rounding the numbers to three significant digits.
   a. 34.000434
   b. 0.00098012
   c. 29,000,000
   d. 0.07305
   e. 552.043×10^4

104. Which unit of length in the metric system would be most appropriate in size for measuring each of the following items?
   a. this book's thickness
   b. the distance from New York to Los Angeles
   c. the length of a bacterium
   d. the diameter of a piece of thread

105. Make the following conversions.
   a. 1.25 in. to feet and to centimeters
   b. 2.12 qt to gallons and to liters
   c. 2640 ft to miles and to kilometers
   d. 1.254 kg lead to its volume in cubic centimeters
   e. 250. mL ethanol to its mass in grams
   f. 3.5 in.^{3} of mercury to its volume in milliliters and its mass in kilograms

106. On the planet Xgnu, the most common units of length are the blim (for long distances) and the kryll (for shorter distances). Because the Xgnuese have 14 fingers, it is not perhaps surprising that 1400 kryll = 1 blim.
   a. Two cities on Xgnu are 36.2 blim apart. What is this distance in kryll?
   b. The average Xgnuese is 170 kryll tall. What is this height in blims?
   c. This book is presently being used at Xgnu University. The area of the cover of this book is 72.5 square krylls. What is its area in square blims?

107. You pass a road sign saying "New York 110 km." If you drive at a constant speed of 100. km/hr, how long should it take you to reach New York?

108. At the mall, you decide to try on a pair of French jeans. Naturally, the waist size of the jeans is given in centimeters. What does a waist measurement of 52 cm correspond to in inches?

109. Suppose your car is rated at 45 mi/gal for highway use and 38 mi/gal for city driving. If you wanted to write your friend in Spain about your car's mileage, what ratings in kilometers per liter would you report?

110. You are in Paris, and you want to buy some peaches for lunch. The sign in the fruit stand indicates that peaches are 11.5 francs per kilogram. Given that there are approximately 5 francs to the dollar, calculate what a pound of peaches will cost in dollars.

111. For a pharmacist dispensing pills or capsules, it is often easier to weigh the medication to be dispensed rather than to count the individual pills. If a single antibiotic capsule weighs 0.65 g, and a pharmacist weighs out 15.6 g of capsules, how many capsules have been dispensed?

112. On the planet Xgnu, the natives have 14 fingers. On the official Xgnuese temperature scale (°X), the boiling point of water (under an atmospheric pressure similar to Earth's) is 140 °X, whereas it freezes at 14 °X. Derive the relationship between °X and °C.

113. For a material to float on the surface of water, the material must have a density less than that of water (1.0 g/mL) and must not react with the water or dissolve in it. A spherical ball has a radius of 0.50 cm and weighs 2.0 g. Will this ball float or sink when placed in water? (Note: Volume of a sphere $= \frac{4}{3}\pi r^3$.)

114. A gas cylinder having a volume of 10.5 L contains 36.8 g of gas. What is the density of the gas?

115. Using Table 2.8, calculate the volume of 100. g of each of the following:
    a. oxygen gas (at 1 atmosphere pressure)
    b. benzene
    c. magnesium
    d. copper

116. Ethanol and benzene dissolve in each other. When 100. mL of ethanol is dissolved in 1.00 L of benzene, what is the mass of the mixture? (See Table 2.8.)

117. When 2891 is written in scientific notation, the exponent indicating the power of 10 is _____.

118. For each of the following numbers, if the number is rewritten in scientific notation, will the exponent be positive, negative, or zero?
    a. 0.0421
    b. 2.04
    c. 389
    d. 0.00912

119. For each of the following numbers, if the number is rewritten in scientific notation, will the exponent be positive, negative, or zero?
    a. 4,915,442
    b. 1/1000
    c. 0.001
    d. 3.75

120. For each of the following numbers, by how many places does the decimal point have to be moved to express the number in standard scientific notation? In each case, is the exponent positive or negative?
    a. 102
    b. 0.00000000003489
    c. 2500
    d. 0.00003489
    e. 398,000
    f. 1
    g. 0.3489
    h. 0.0000003489

121. For each of the following numbers, by how many places does the decimal point have to be moved to express the number in standard scientific (exponential) notation? In each case, is the exponent positive or negative?
    a. 0.003901
    b. 0.0034002
    c. 199,000,000
    d. 0.000001024
    e. 652
    f. 92,033
    g. 53
    h. 0.000193

122. For each of the following numbers, by how many places does the decimal point have to be moved to express the number in standard scientific (exponential) notation? In each case, is the exponent positive or negative?
    a. 341
    b. 0.00341
    c. 34.1
    d. 0.0000000341
    e. 42,250
    f. 42.25
    g. 0.000004225
    h. 0.4225

123. Express each of the following numbers in scientific (exponential) notation.
    a. 529
    b. 240,000,000
    c. 301,000,000,000,000,000
    d. 78,444
    e. 0.0003442
    f. 0.000000000902
    g. 0.043
    h. 0.0821

124. Express each of the following as an "ordinary" decimal number.
    a. 2.98×10^{-5}
    b. 4.358×10^{9}
    c. 1.9928×10^{-6}
    d. 6.02×10^{23}
    e. 1.01×10^{-1}
    f. 7.87×10^{-3}
    g. 9.87×10^{7}
    h. 3.7899×10^{2}
    i. 1.093×10^{-1}
    j. 2.9004×10^{0}
    k. 3.9×10^{-4}
    l. 1.904×10^{-8}

125. Write each of the following numbers in *standard* scientific notation.
    a. 102.3×10^{-5}
    b. 32.03×10^{-3}
    c. 59933×10^{2}
    d. 599.33×10^{4}
    e. 5993.3×10^{3}
    f. 2054×10^{-1}
    g. $32,000,000 \times 10^{-6}$
    h. 59.933×10^{5}

126. Write each of the following numbers in *standard* scientific notation. See Appendix 3 if you need help multiplying or dividing numbers with exponents.
    a. $1/10^{2}$
    b. $1/10^{-2}$
    c. $55/10^{3}$
    d. $(3.1 \times 10^{6})/10^{-3}$
    e. $(10^{6})^{1/2}$
    f. $(10^{6})(10^{4})/(10^{2})$
    g. $1/0.0034$
    h. $3.453/10^{-4}$

127. The fundamental unit of length or distance in the metric system is the _____.

128. The SI unit of temperature is the _____.

129. Which distance is farther, 100 km or 50 mi?

130. The unit of volume corresponding to 1/1000 of a liter is referred to as 1 milliliter, or 1 cubic _____.

131. The volume 0.250 L could also be expressed as _____ mL.

132. The distance 10.5 cm could also be expressed as _____ m.

133. Would an automobile moving at a constant speed of 100 km/hr violate a 65-mph speed limit?

134. Which weighs more, 100 g of water or 1 kg of water?

135. Which weighs more, 4.25 grams of gold or 425 milligrams of gold?

136. The length 100 mm can also be expressed as _____ cm.

137. When a measurement is made, the certain numbers plus the first uncertain number are called the _____ of the measurement.

138. In the measurement of the length of the pin indicated in Figure 2.5, what are the *certain* numbers in the measurement shown?

139. Indicate the number of significant figures in each of the following:
    a. This book contains over 500 pages.
    b. A mile is just over 5000 ft.
    c. A liter is equivalent to 1.059 qt.
    d. The population of the United States is approaching 250 million.
    e. A kilogram is 1000 m.
    f. The Boeing 747 cruises at around 600 mi/hr.

140. Round off each of the following numbers to three significant digits.
    a. 0.000032421
    b. 7,212,992
    c. 2.098988×10^{-7}
    d. 550,092
    e. 199.99

141. Round off each of the following numbers to the indicated number of significant digits.
    a. 0.50045 to four digits
    b. 126.5 to three digits
    c. 15.395 to four digits
    d. 23.0975 to five digits

142. Evaluate each of the following, and write the answer to the appropriate number of significant figures.
    a. $149.2 + 0.034 + 2000.34$
    b. $1.0322 \times 10^3 + 4.34 \times 10^3$
    c. $4.03 \times 10^{-2} - 2.044 \times 10^{-3}$
    d. $2.094 \times 10^5 - 1.073 \times 10^6$

143. Evaluate each of the following, and write the answer to the appropriate number of significant figures.
    a. $(0.0432)(2.909)(4.43 \times 10^8)$
    b. $(0.8922)/[(0.00932)(4.03 \times 10^2)]$
    c. $(3.923 \times 10^2)(2.94)(4.093 \times 10^{-3})$
    d. $(4.9211)(0.04434)/[(0.000934)(2.892 \times 10^{-7})]$

144. Evaluate each of the following, and write the answer to the appropriate number of significant figures.
    a. $(2.9932 \times 10^4)[2.4443 \times 10^2 + 1.0032 \times 10^1]$
    b. $[2.34 \times 10^2 + 2.443 \times 10^{-1}]/(0.0323)$
    c. $(4.38 \times 10^{-3})^2$
    d. $(5.9938 \times 10^{-6})^{1/2}$

145. Given that 1 L = 1000 cm³, determine what conversion factor is appropriate to convert 350 cm³ to liters; to convert 0.200 L to cubic centimeters.

146. Given that 12 months = 1 year, determine what conversion factor is appropriate to convert 72 months to years; to convert 3.5 years to months.

147. Perform each of the following conversions, being sure to set up clearly the appropriate conversion factor in each case.
    a. 8.43 cm to millimeters
    b. 2.41×10^2 cm to meters
    c. 294.5 nm to centimeters
    d. 404.5 m to kilometers
    e. 1.445×10^4 m to kilometers
    f. 42.2 mm to centimeters
    g. 235.3 m to millimeters
    h. 903.3 nm to micrometers

148. Perform each of the following conversions, being sure to set up clearly the appropriate conversion factor(s) in each case.
    a. 908 oz to kilograms
    b. 12.8 L to gallons
    c. 125 mL to quarts
    d. 2.89 gal to milliliters
    e. 4.48 lb to grams
    f. 550 mL to quarts

149. The mean distance from the earth to the sun is 9.3×10^7 mi. What is this distance in kilometers? in centimeters?

150. Given that one gross = 144 items, how many pencils are contained in 6 gross?

151. Convert the following temperatures to kelvins.
    a. 0 °C
    b. 25 °C
    c. 37 °C
    d. 100 °C
    e. −175 °C
    f. 212 °C

152. Carry out the indicated temperature conversions.
    a. 175 °F to kelvins
    b. 255 K to Celsius degrees
    c. −45 °F to Celsius degrees
    d. 125 °C to Fahrenheit degrees

153. For the masses and volumes indicated, calculate the density in grams per cubic centimeter.
    a. mass = 234 g; volume = 2.2 cm³
    b. mass = 2.34 kg; volume = 2.2 m³
    c. mass = 1.2 lb; volume = 2.1 ft³
    d. mass = 4.3 tons; volume = 54.2 yd³

154. A sample of alcohol has density 0.82 g/mL. What do 55 mL of the alcohol weigh?

155. A sample of organic liquid has density 1.54 g/mL. What do 75.0 mL of the liquid weigh?

156. A solid metal sphere has a volume of 4.2 ft³. The mass of the sphere is 155 lb. Find the density of the metal sphere in grams per cubic centimeter.

157. A sample containing 33.42 g of metal pellets is poured into a graduated cylinder initially containing 12.7 mL of water, causing the water level in the cylinder to rise to 21.6 mL. Calculate the density of the metal.

158. Convert the following temperatures to Fahrenheit degrees.
    a. −5 °C
    b. 273 K
    c. −196 °C
    d. 0 K
    e. 86 °C
    f. −273 °C

$$D = \frac{m}{v}$$

$$55mL\ 82 = m$$

Matter and Energy

As you look around you, you must wonder about the properties of matter. How do plants grow and why are they green? Why is the sun hot? Why does a hot dog get hot in a microwave oven? Why does wood burn whereas rocks do not? What is a flame? How does soap work? Why does soda fizz when you open it? When iron rusts, what's happening? And why doesn't aluminum rust? How does a cold pack for an athletic injury, which is stored for weeks or months at room temperature, suddenly get cold when you need it? How does a hair permanent work?

The answers to these and endless other questions lie in the domain of chemistry. In this chapter we begin to explore the nature of matter: how it is organized and how and why it changes. We will also consider the energy that accompanies these changes.

Hot lava flowing into the ocean in Hawaii (left). Why does soda fizz when you open the bottle (right)?

The importance of understanding matter sometimes appears in very surprising places. For example, who would have thought that unusual deposits of iridium metal in the sediments of the earth's crust could help explain why the dinosaurs disappeared 65 million years ago? In this chapter we will see how that happened.

3.1   Matter

AIM: To learn about matter and its three states.

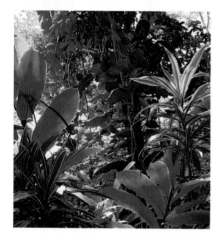

How does this lush vegetation grow in a tropical rain forest, and why is it green?

Matter, the "stuff" of which the universe is composed, has two characteristics: it has mass and it occupies space. Matter comes in a great variety of forms: the stars, the air that you are breathing, the gasoline that you put in your car, the chair on which you are sitting, the turkey in the sandwich you may have had for lunch, the tissues in your brain that enable you to read and comprehend this sentence, and so on.

To try to understand the nature of matter, we classify it in various ways. For example, wood, bone, and steel share certain characteristics. These things are all rigid; they have definite shapes that are difficult to change. On the other hand, water and gasoline, for example, take the shape of any container into which they are poured (see Figure 3.1). Even so, 1 L of water has a volume of 1 L whether it is in a pail or a beaker. In contrast, air takes the shape of its container and fills any container uniformly.

The substances we have just described illustrate the three **states of matter: solid, liquid,** and **gas.** These are defined and illustrated in Table 3.1. The state of a given sample of matter depends on the strength of the forces among the particles contained in the matter; the stronger these forces, the more rigid the matter. We will discuss this in more detail in the next section.

FIGURE 3.1
Liquid water takes the shape of its container.

TABLE 3.1

The Three States of Matter

State	Definition	Examples
solid	rigid; has a fixed shape and volume	ice cube, diamond, iron bar
liquid	has a definite volume but takes the shape of its container	gasoline, water, alcohol, blood
gas	has no fixed volume or shape; takes the shape and volume of its container	air, helium, oxygen

3.2 Physical and Chemical Properties and Changes

AIMS: To learn to distinguish between physical and chemical properties. To learn to distinguish between physical and chemical changes.

A mixed crystal of colorless calcite (composed of calcium carbonate) and green malachite. The color of a substance is an example of a physical property.

When you see a friend, you immediately respond and call him or her by name. We recognize a friend because each person has unique characteristics or properties. The person may be thin and tall, may have blonde hair and blue eyes, and so on. The characteristics just mentioned are examples of **physical properties.** Substances also have physical properties. Typical physical properties of a substance include odor, color, volume, state (gas, liquid, or solid), density, melting point, and boiling point. Another set of properties that we ascribe to a pure substance are its **chemical properties,** which refer to its ability to form new substances. An example of a chemical change is wood burning in a fireplace giving off heat and gases and leaving a residue of ashes. In this process, the wood is changed to several new substances. Other examples of chemical changes include the rusting of the steel in our cars, the digestion of food in our stomachs, and the growth of grass in our yards. In a chemical change a given substance changes to a fundamentally different substance or substances.

EXAMPLE 3.1 *Identifying Physical and Chemical Properties*

Classify each of the following as a physical or a chemical property.

a. The boiling point of a certain alcohol is 78 °C.

b. Diamond is very hard.

c. Sugar ferments to form alcohol.

d. A metal wire conducts an electric current.

Solution

Items (a), (b), and (d) are physical properties; they describe inherent characteristics of each substance, and no change in composition occurs. A metal wire has the same composition before and after an electric current has passed through it. Item (c) is a chemical property of sugar. Fermentation of sugars involves the formation of a new substance (alcohol).

✓ Self-Check Exercise 3.1

Which of the following are physical properties and which are chemical properties?

a. Gallium metal melts in your hand.
b. Platinum does not react with oxygen at room temperature.
c. This page is white.
d. The copper sheets that form the "skin" of the Statue of Liberty have acquired a greenish coating over the years.

See Problems 3.11 through 3.14.

Gallium metal has such a low melting point (30°C) that it melts from the heat of a hand.

Matter can undergo changes in both its physical and its chemical properties. To illustrate the fundamental differences between physical and chemical changes, we will consider water. As we will see in much more detail in later chapters, a sample of water contains a very large number of individual units (called molecules), each made up of two atoms of hydrogen and one atom of oxygen—the familiar H_2O. This molecule can be represented as

where the letters stand for atoms and the lines show attachments (called bonds) between atoms, and the molecular model (on the right) represents water in a more three-dimensional fashion.

What is really occurring when water undergoes the following changes?

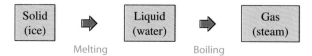

We will describe these changes of state precisely in Chapter 14, but you already know something about these processes because you have observed them many times.

When ice melts, the rigid solid becomes a mobile liquid that takes the shape of its container. Continued heating brings the liquid to a boil, and the water becomes a gas or vapor that seems to disappear into "thin air." The changes that occur as the substance goes from solid to liquid to gas are represented in Figure 3.2. In ice the water molecules are locked into fixed

The purpose here is to give an overview. Don't worry about the precise definitions of *atom* and *molecule* now. We will explore these concepts more fully in Chapter 4.

The letters indicate atoms and the lines indicate attachments (bonds) between atoms.

FIGURE 3.2
The three states of water (where pink spheres represent oxygen atoms and blue spheres represent hydrogen atoms). (a) Solid: The water molecules are locked into rigid positions and are close together. (b) Liquid: The water molecules are still close together but can move around to some extent. (c) Gas: The water molecules are far apart and move randomly.

(a) Solid (Ice)   (b) Liquid (Water)   (c) Gas (Steam)

FIGURE 3.3
Electrolysis, the decomposition of water by an electric current, is a chemical process.

positions. In the liquid the molecules are still very close together, but some motion is occurring; the positions of the molecules are no longer fixed as they are in ice. In the gaseous state the molecules are much farther apart and move randomly, hitting each other and the walls of the container.

The most important thing about all these changes is that the water molecules are still intact. The motions of individual molecules and the distances between them change, but *H_2O molecules are still present.* These changes of state are **physical changes** because they do not affect the composition of the substance. In each state we still have water (H_2O), not some other substance.

Now suppose we run an electric current through water as illustrated in Figure 3.3. Something very different happens. The water disappears and is replaced by two new gaseous substances, hydrogen and oxygen. An electric current actually causes the water molecules to come apart—the water *decomposes* to hydrogen and oxygen. As we will see in Chapter 18 we can represent this process as follows:

$$
\begin{array}{ccc}
\text{H} & \text{H} & \text{H—H} \\
\diagdown & \diagdown & \\
\quad \text{O} & \quad \text{O} \Rightarrow & \text{O—O} \\
\diagup & \diagup & \\
\text{H} & \text{H} \quad \text{Electric current} & \text{H—H}
\end{array}
$$

This is a **chemical change** because water (consisting of H_2O molecules) has changed into different substances: hydrogen (containing H_2 molecules) and oxygen (containing O_2 molecules). Thus in this process, the H_2O molecules have been replaced by O_2 and H_2 molecules. Let us summarize:

Physical and Chemical Changes

1. A *physical change* involves a change in one or more physical properties, but no change in the fundamental components that make up the substance. The most common physical changes are changes of state: solid ⇔ liquid ⇔ gas.

2. A *chemical change* involves a change in the fundamental components of the substance; a given substance changes into a different substance or substances. Chemical changes are called **reactions:** silver tarnishes by reacting with substances in the air; a plant forms a leaf by combining various substances from the air and soil; and so on.

EXAMPLE 3.2 *Identifying Physical and Chemical Changes*

Classify each of the following as a physical or a chemical change.

a. Iron metal is melted.
b. Iron combines with oxygen to form rust.
c. Wood burns in air.
d. A rock is broken into small pieces.

Oxygen combines with the chemicals in wood to produce flames. Is a physical or chemical change taking place?

Solution

a. Melted iron is just liquid iron and could cool again to the solid state. This is a physical change.
b. When iron combines with oxygen, it forms a different substance (rust) that contains iron and oxygen. This is a chemical change because a different substance forms.
c. Wood burns to form different substances (as we will see later, they include carbon dioxide and water). After the fire, the wood is no longer in its original form. This is a chemical change.
d. When the rock is broken up, all the smaller pieces have the same composition as the whole rock. Each new piece differs from the original only in size and shape. This is a physical change.

 Self-Check Exercise 3.2

Classify each of the following as a chemical change, a physical change, or a combination of the two.

a. Milk turns sour.
b. Wax is melted over a flame and then catches fire and burns.

See Problems 3.17 and 3.18.

3.3 Elements and Compounds

AIM: To understand the definitions of elements and compounds.

Element: A substance that cannot be broken down into other substances by chemical methods.

As we examine the chemical changes of matter, we encounter a series of fundamental substances called **elements.** Elements cannot be broken down into other substances by chemical means. Examples of elements are iron, aluminum, oxygen, and hydrogen. All of the matter in the world around us contains elements. The elements sometimes are found in an isolated state, but more often they are combined with other elements. Most substances contain several elements combined together.

Compound: A substance composed of a given combination of elements that can be broken down into those elements by chemical methods.

The atoms of certain elements have special affinities for each other. They bind together in special ways to form **compounds,** substances that have the same composition no matter where we find them. Because compounds are made of elements, they can be broken down into elements through chemical changes:

Compounds   Elements

Chemical changes

Water is an example of a compound. Pure water always has the same composition (the same relative amounts of hydrogen and oxygen) and can be broken down into the elements hydrogen and oxygen by chemical means, such as by the use of an electric current (see Figure 3.3).

CHEMISTRY IN FOCUS

*E*lements in the Dinosaur Puzzle

Dinosaurs in amazing variety ruled the earth for over 150 million years! This surely represents one of the most astonishing success stories of any group of organisms to date. However, 65 million years ago the dinosaurs suddenly disappeared, and their demise was almost instantaneous on the geological time scale. What happened? How could a group of animals that dominated the earth for so long suddenly disappear?

Although many theories have been suggested to explain the extinction of the dinosaurs, none has seemed very convincing until recently. Geologists, examining samples of rocks containing material that was on the earth's surface when the dinosaurs died, have found unusual amounts of the elements iridium and niobium. Because these metals are often found in relatively large amounts in extraterrestrial objects such as meteorites and comets, it has been suggested that a large object may have collided with the earth. Geologists propose that this happened about 65 million years ago.

It is believed that the tremendous explosion resulting from such an impact would throw millions of tons of fine dust into the atmosphere, blocking much of the sunlight that would normally reach the earth's surface. Presumably this would lead to the

A paleontologist cleans sandstone away from the bones of diplodocus, the longest of the ancient dinosaurs, at Dinosaur National Monument in Colorado.

disappearance of many plants, because plants depend on the sun's energy to grow. The animals on earth would in turn find their food supply greatly diminished and might well die off.

The critics of this theory had a legitimate question: "Where's the crater?" Such a large impact should leave a massive depression on the earth's surface. In 1991 this objection was answered when a gigantic impact crater at least 280 kilometers in diameter was discovered beneath the northern tip of Mexico's Yucután Peninsula. Most scientists now agree that a very large object hit the earth at this point 65 million years ago.

However, disagreement remains about how this event led to the extinction of the dinosaurs and possibly 70 percent of all of the other species living on the earth at that time. One suggestion is that the sulfur-rich soil of the Yucután Peninsula could have released as much as a trillion tons of sulfur dioxide gas after the impact, leading to the formation of sulfuric acid droplets. These droplets could have blocked the sunlight to such an extent that the earth cooled up to an average of 10 °C for a decade—an incredible cooling when compared to the 4 °C cooling that occurred during the last ice age.

As we will discuss in more detail in Chapter 4, each element is made up of a particular kind of atom: a pure sample of the element aluminum contains only aluminum atoms, elemental copper contains only copper atoms, and so on. Thus an element contains only one kind of atom; a sample of iron contains many atoms, but they are all iron atoms. Samples of certain pure elements do contain molecules; for example, hydrogen gas contains H—H (usually written H_2) molecules, and oxygen gas contains O—O (O_2) molecules.

However, any pure sample of an element contains only atoms of that element, *never* any atoms of any other element.

A compound *always* contains atoms of *different* elements. For example, water contains hydrogen atoms and oxygen atoms, and there are always exactly twice as many hydrogen atoms as oxygen atoms because water consists of H—O—H molecules. A different compound, carbon dioxide, consists of CO_2 molecules and so contains carbon atoms and oxygen atoms (always in the ratio 1:2).

A compound, although it contains more than one type of atom, *always has the same composition*—that is, the same combination of atoms. The properties of a compound are typically very different from those of the elements it contains. For example, the properties of water are quite different from the properties of pure hydrogen and pure oxygen.

3.4   Mixtures and Pure Substances

AIM: To learn to distinguish between mixtures and pure substances.

Virtually all of the matter around us consists of mixtures of substances. For example, if you closely observe a sample of soil, you will see that it has many types of components, including tiny grains of sand and remnants of plants. The air we breathe is a complex mixture of such gases as oxygen, nitrogen, carbon dioxide, and water vapor. Even the sparkling water from a drinking fountain contains many substances besides water.

A **mixture** can be defined as something that has variable composition. For example, wood is a mixture (its composition varies greatly depending on the tree from which it originates); wine is a mixture (it can be red or pale yellow, sweet or dry); coffee is a mixture (it can be strong, weak, or bitter); and, although it looks very pure, water pumped from deep in the earth is a mixture (it contains dissolved minerals and gases).

A **pure substance,** on the other hand, will always have the same composition. Pure substances are either elements or compounds. For example, pure water is a compound containing individual H_2O molecules. However, as we find it in nature, liquid water always contains other substances in addition to pure water—it is a mixture. This is obvious from the different tastes, smells, and colors of water samples obtained from various locations. However, if we take great pains to purify samples of water from various sources (such as oceans, lakes, rivers, and the earth's interior), we always end up with the same pure substance—water, which is made up only of H_2O molecules. Pure water always has the same physical and chemical properties and is always made of molecules containing hydrogen and oxygen in exactly the same proportions, regardless of the original source of the water. The properties of a pure substance make it possible to identify that substance conclusively.

Mixtures can be separated into pure substances: elements and/or compounds.

The earth's atmosphere is a mixture containing many gases and water that condenses to form clouds.

Although we say we can separate mixtures into pure substances, it is virtually impossible to separate mixtures into totally pure substances. No matter how hard we try, some impurities (components of the original mixture) remain in each of the "pure substances."

For example, the mixture known as air can be separated into oxygen (element), nitrogen (element), water (compound), carbon dioxide (compound), argon (element), and other pure substances.

A solution is a homogeneous mixture.

Mixtures can be classified as either homogeneous or heterogeneous. A **homogeneous mixture** is *the same throughout.* For example, when we dissolve some salt in water and stir well, all regions of the resulting mixture have the same properties. A homogeneous mixture is also called a **solution.** Of course, different amounts of salt and water can be mixed to form various solutions, but a homogeneous mixture (a solution) does not vary in composition from one region to another (see Figure 3.4).

The air around you is a solution—it is a homogeneous mixture of gases. Solid solutions also exist. Brass is a homogeneous mixture of the metals copper and zinc.

Coffee is a solution that has variable composition. It can be strong or weak.

A **heterogeneous mixture** contains regions that have different properties from those of other regions. For example, when we pour sand into water, the resulting mixture has one region containing water and another, very different region containing mostly sand (see Figure 3.5).

FIGURE 3.4
When table salt is stirred into water (left), a homogeneous mixture called a solution is formed (right).

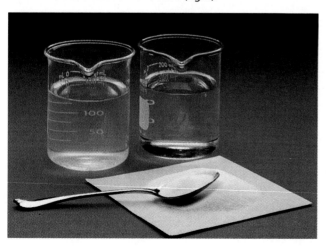

FIGURE 3.5
Sand and water do not mix to form a uniform mixture. After stirring, the sand settles back to the bottom.

EXAMPLE 3.3   *Distinguishing Between Mixtures and Pure Substances*

Identify each of the following as a pure substance, a homogeneous mixture, or a heterogeneous mixture.

a. gasoline
b. a stream with gravel at the bottom
c. air

d. brass
e. copper metal

Solution

a. Gasoline is a homogeneous mixture containing many compounds.

b. A stream with gravel on the bottom is a heterogeneous mixture.

c. Air is a homogeneous mixture of elements and compounds.

d. Brass is a homogeneous mixture containing the elements copper and zinc. Brass is not a pure substance because the relative amounts of copper and zinc are different in different brass samples.

e. Copper metal is a pure substance (an element).

Self-Check Exercise 3.3

Classify each of the following as a pure substance, a homogeneous mixture, or a heterogeneous mixture.

a. wine
b. the oxygen and helium in a scuba tank
c. oil and vinegar salad dressing
d. common salt (sodium chloride)

See Problems 3.29 through 3.32.

3.5   *Separation of Mixtures*

AIM: To learn two methods of separating mixtures.

The separation of a mixture sometimes occurs in the natural environment and can be to our benefit (see photo on p. 68).

We have seen that the matter found in nature is typically a mixture of pure substances. For example, seawater is water containing dissolved minerals. We can separate the water from the minerals by boiling, which changes the water to steam (gaseous water) and leaves the minerals behind as solids. If we collect and cool the steam, it condenses to pure water. This separation process, called **distillation,** is shown in Figure 3.6.

When we carry out the distillation of salt water, water is changed from the liquid state to the gaseous state and then back to the liquid state. These changes of state are examples of physical changes. We are separating a mixture of substances, but we are not changing the composition of the individual substances. We can represent this as shown in Figure 3.7.

FIGURE 3.6

Distillation of a solution consisting of salt dissolved in water. (a) When the solution is boiled, steam (gaseous water) is driven off. If this steam is collected and cooled, it condenses to form pure water, which drips into the collection flask as shown. (b) After all of the water has been boiled off, the salt remains in the original flask and the water is in the collection flask.

Suppose we scooped up some sand with our sample of seawater. This sample is a heterogeneous mixture, because it contains an undissolved solid as well as the saltwater solution. We can separate out the sand by simple **filtration.** We pour the mixture onto a mesh, such as a filter paper, which allows the liquid to pass through and leaves the solid behind (see Figure 3.8). The salt can then be separated from the water by distillation. The total separation process is represented in Figure 3.9. All the changes involved are physical changes.

FIGURE 3.7

No chemical change occurs when salt water is distilled.

Saltwater solution
(homogeneous mixture)

Distillation
(physical method)

Salt   +   Pure water

FIGURE 3.8

Filtration separates a liquid from a solid. The liquid passes through the filter paper, but the solid particles are trapped.

FIGURE 3.9
Separation of a sand–saltwater mixture.

When water from the Great Salt Lake evaporates (changes to a gas and escapes), the salt is left behind. This is one commercial source of salt.

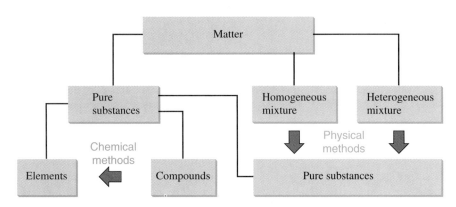

FIGURE 3.10
The organization of matter.

We can summarize the description of matter given in this chapter with the diagram shown in Figure 3.10. Note that a given sample of matter can be a pure substance (either an element or a compound) or, more commonly, a mixture (homogeneous or heterogeneous). We have seen that all matter exists as elements or can be broken down into elements, the most fundamental substances we have encountered up to this point. We will have more to say about the nature of elements in the next chapter.

3.6   *Energy and Energy Changes*

AIM: To understand energy and its effect on matter.

Energy is a familiar term. We speak of solar energy, nuclear energy, and energy from coal and gasoline, and when we're tired, we say that we have run out of energy. Energy allows us to "do things"—to work, to drive to school, and to cook eggs. A common definition of **energy** is the capacity to do work.

FIGURE 3.11
In ice, the water molecules vibrate randomly about their positions in the solid. Their motions are represented by arrows.

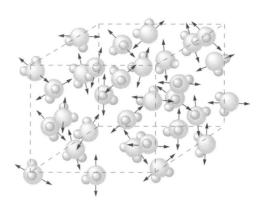

One way we use energy is to change the temperature of a substance. For example, we often heat water using the energy provided by a stove or Bunsen burner. As we will see in more detail later, the temperature of a substance reflects the random motions of the components of that substance. For example, in ice the components are water molecules that vibrate randomly about their fixed positions in the solid, as represented in Figure 3.11. When the solid is heated to higher temperatures, the random vibrations become more energetic. Finally, at the melting point of ice, the molecules are vibrating energetically enough to break loose from their positions, and rigid ice changes to liquid water.

We have seen that the motions of molecules in a substance increase as we raise the temperature of that substance. *The amount of energy (heat) required to raise the temperature of one gram of water by one Celsius degree* is called a **calorie** in the metric system of units. The unit of energy in the SI system is called the **joule** (pronounced "jewel"). We can convert between joules and calories by using the definition that exactly 1 calorie = 4.184 joules, which leads to the equivalence statement

$$1 \text{ cal} = 4.184 \text{ J}$$

Gases will be discussed fully in Chapter 13.

calorie: The energy (heat) required to raise the temperature of 1 g of water by 1 °C.

The abbreviations for calorie and joule are cal and J.

EXAMPLE 3.4

Converting Calories to Joules

Express 60.1 cal of energy in units of joules.

Solution

By definition 1 cal = 4.184 J, so the conversion factor needed is $\dfrac{4.184 \text{ J}}{1 \text{ cal}}$, and the result is

$$60.1 \text{ cal} \times \frac{4.184 \text{ J}}{1 \text{ cal}} = 251 \text{ J}$$

Note that the 1 in the denominator is an exact number by definition and so does not limit the number of significant figures.

 Self-Check Exercise 3.4

How many calories of energy correspond to 28.4 J?

See Problems 3.45 and 3.46.

Now think about heating a substance from one temperature to another. How does the amount of substance heated affect the energy required? In 2 g of water there are twice as many molecules as in 1 g of water. It takes twice as much energy to change the temperature of 2 g of water by 1 °C, because we must change the motions of twice as many molecules in a 2-g sample as in a 1-g sample. Also, as we would expect, it takes twice as much energy to raise the temperature of a given sample of water by 2 degrees as it does to raise the temperature by 1 degree.

EXAMPLE 3.5   *Calculating Energy Requirements*

Determine the amount of energy (heat) in joules required to raise the temperature of 7.40 g water from 29.0 °C to 46.0 °C.

Solution

In solving any kind of problem, it is often useful to draw a diagram that represents the situation. In this case, we have 7.40 g of water that are to be heated from 29.0 °C to 46.0 °C.

| 7.40 g water
$T = 29.0$ °C | ⇨ | 7.40 g water
$T = 46.0$ °C |

? energy

Our task is to determine how much energy is required to accomplish this.

From the discussion in the text, we know that 4.184 J of energy are required to raise the temperature of *one* gram of water by *one* Celsius degree.

| 1.00 g water
$T = 29.0$ °C | ⇨ | 1.00 g water
$T = 30.0$ °C |

4.184 J

Because in our case we have 7.40 g of water instead of 1.00 g, it will take 7.40×4.184 J to raise the temperature by one degree.

| 7.40 g water
$T = 29.0$ °C | ⇨ | 7.40 g water
$T = 30.0$ °C |

7.40×4.184 J

However, we want to raise the temperature of our sample of water by more than 1 °C. In fact, the temperature change required is from 29.0 °C to 46.0 °C. This is a change of 17.0 °C (46.0 °C − 29.0 °C = 17.0 °C). Thus we will have to supply 17.0 times the energy necessary to raise the temperature of 7.40 g of water by 1 °C.

$17.0 \times 7.40 \times 4.184$ J

CHEMISTRY IN FOCUS

Nature Has Hot Plants

The voodoo lily is a beautiful and seductive plant. The exotic-looking lily features an elaborate reproductive mechanism—a purple spike that can reach nearly 3 feet in length and is cloaked by a hoodlike leaf. But approach to the plant reveals bad news—it smells terrible!

Despite its antisocial odor, this putrid plant has fascinated biologists for many years because of its ability to generate heat. At the peak of its metabolic activity, the plant's blossom can be as much as 15 °C above its surrounding temperature. To generate this much heat, the metabolic rate of the plant must be close to that of a flying hummingbird!

What's the purpose of this intense heat production? For a plant faced with limited food supplies in the very competitive tropical climate where it grows, heat production seems like a great waste of energy. The answer to this mystery is that the voodoo lily is pollinated mainly by carrion-loving insects. Thus the lily prepares a malodorous mixture of chemicals characteristic of rotting meat, which it then "cooks" off into the surrounding air to attract flesh-feeding beetles and flies. Then, once the insects enter the pollination chamber, the high temperatures there (as high as 110 °F) cause the insects to remain very active to better carry out their pollination duties.

The voodoo lily is only one of many thermogenic (heat-producing) plants. These plants are of special interest to biologists because they provide opportunities to study metabolic reactions that are quite subtle in "normal" plants.

A voodoo lily.

This calculation is summarized as follows:

The result you will get on your calculator is 4.184 × 7.40 × 17.0 = 526.3472, which rounds off to 526.

$$4.184\,\frac{J}{g\,°C}\ \times\ 7.40\text{ g}\ \times\ 17.0\ °C\ =\ 526\text{ J}$$

$$\underset{\substack{\text{Energy per gram}\\\text{of water per degree}\\\text{of temperature}}}{} \times \underset{\substack{\text{Actual}\\\text{grams}\\\text{of water}}}{} \times \underset{\substack{\text{Actual}\\\text{temperature}\\\text{change}}}{} = \underset{\substack{\text{Energy}\\\text{required}}}{}$$

We have shown that 526 J of energy (as heat) are required to raise the temperature of 7.40 g of water from 29.0 °C to 46.0 °C. Note that because 4.184 J of energy are required to heat 1 g of water by 1 °C, the units are J/g °C (joules per gram per Celsius degree).

 Self-Check Exercise 3.5

Calculate the joules of energy required to heat 454 g of water from 5.4 °C to 98.6 °C.

See Problems 3.51 and 3.52.

TABLE 3.2

The Specific Heat Capacities
of Some Common Substances

Substance	Specific Heat Capacity (J/g °C)
water (*l*)* (liquid)	4.184
water (*s*) (ice)	2.03
water (*g*) (steam)	2.0
aluminum (*s*)	0.89
iron (*s*)	0.45
mercury (*l*)	0.14
carbon (*s*)	0.71
silver (*s*)	0.24
gold (*s*)	0.13

*The symbols (*s*), (*l*), and (*g*) indicate the solid, liquid, and gaseous states, respectively.

So far we have seen that the energy (heat) required to change the temperature of a substance depends on

1. The amount of substance being heated (number of grams)
2. The temperature change (number of degrees)

There is another important factor: the identity of the substance.

Different substances respond differently to being heated. We have seen that 4.184 J of energy raises the temperature of 1 g of water 1 °C. In contrast, this same amount of energy applied to 1 g of gold raises its temperature by approximately 32 °C! The point is that some substances require relatively large amounts of energy to change their temperatures, whereas others require relatively little. Chemists describe this difference by saying that substances have different heat capacities. *The amount of energy required to change the temperature of one gram of a substance by one Celsius degree* is called its **specific heat capacity** or, more commonly, its **specific heat.** The specific heat capacities for several substances are listed in Table 3.2. You can see from the table that the specific heat capacity for water is very high compared to those of the other substances listed. This is why lakes and seas are much slower to respond to cooling or heating than are the surrounding land masses.

EXAMPLE 3.6   *Calculations Involving Specific Heat Capacity*

a. What quantity of energy (in joules) is required to heat a piece of iron weighing 1.3 g from 25 °C to 46 °C?

b. What is the answer in calories?

Solution

a. It is helpful to draw the following diagram to represent the problem.

1.3 g iron		1.3 g iron
T = 25 °C		*T* = 46 °C

? joules

From Table 3.2 we see that the specific heat capacity of iron is 0.45 J/g °C. That is, it takes 0.45 J to raise the temperature of a 1-g piece of iron by 1 °C.

In this case our sample is 1.3 g, so 1.3 × 0.45 J is required for *each* degree of temperature increase.

| 1.3 g iron
T = 25 °C | ⇨ | 1.3 g iron
T = 26 °C |

1.3 × 0.45 J

The result you will get on your calculator is: 0.45 × 1.3 × 21 = 12.285, which rounds off to 12.

Because the temperature increase is 21 °C (46 °C − 25 °C = 21 °C), the total amount of energy required is

$$0.45 \ \frac{J}{g \ °C} \ \times \ 1.3 \ g \ \times \ 21 \ °C \ = \ 12 \ J$$

| 1.3 g iron
T = 25 °C | ⇨ | 1.3 g iron
T = 46 °C |

21 × 1.3 × 0.45 J

Note that the final units are joules, as they should be.

b. To calculate this energy in calories, we can use the definition 1 cal = 4.184 J to construct the appropriate conversion factor. We want to change from joules to calories, so cal must be in the numerator and J in the denominator where it cancels:

$$12 \ \cancel{J} \ \times \ \frac{1 \ cal}{4.184 \ \cancel{J}} \ = \ 2.9 \ cal$$

Remember that 1 in this case is an exact number by definition and therefore does not limit the number of significant figures (the number 12 is limiting here).

 Self-Check Exercise 3.6

A 5.63-g sample of solid gold is heated from 21 °C to 32 °C. How much energy (in joules and calories) is required?

See Problems 3.53 through 3.60.

Note that in Example 3.6, to calculate the energy (heat) required, we took the product of the specific heat capacity, the sample size in grams, and the change in temperature in Celsius degrees.

| Energy (heat)
required (Q) | = | Specific heat
capacity (s) | × | Mass (m)
in grams
of sample | × | Change in
temperature
(ΔT) in °C |

CHEMISTRY IN FOCUS

Firewalking: Magic or Science?

For millennia people have been amazed at the ability of Eastern mystics to walk across beds of glowing coals without any apparent discomfort. Even in the United States, thousands of people have performed feats of firewalking as part of motivational seminars. How can this be possible? Do firewalkers have supernatural powers?

Actually, there are good scientific explanations of why firewalking is possible. First, human tissue is mainly composed of water, which has a relatively large specific heat capacity. This means that a large amount of energy must be transferred from the coals to change significantly the temperature of the feet. During the brief contact between feet and coals involved in firewalking, there is relatively little time for energy flow, so the feet do not reach a high enough temperature to cause damage.

Second, although the surface of the coals has a very high temperature, the red-hot layer is very thin. Therefore, the quantity of energy available to heat the feet is smaller than might be expected.

A third factor that aids firewalkers is the so-called Leidenfrost effect, the phenomenon that allows water droplets to skate around on a hot griddle for a surprisingly long time. The part of the droplet in contact with the hot surface vaporizes first, providing a gaseous layer that both allows the droplet to skate around and acts as a barrier through which energy does not readily flow to the rest of the droplet. The perspiration on the feet of the presumably tense firewalker would have the same effect. And because firewalking is often done at night when moist grass surrounds the bed of coals, the firewalker's feet are probably damp before the walk, providing ample moisture for the Leidenfrost effect to occur.

Thus, although firewalking is impressive, there are several scientific reasons why anyone with the proper training should be able to do it on a properly prepared bed of coals. (Don't try this on your own!)

A Hindu firewalking ceremony in the Fiji Islands.

The symbol Δ (the Greek letter delta) is shorthand for "change in."

We can represent this by the following equation:

$$Q = s \times m \times \Delta T$$

where

Q = energy (heat) required
s = specific heat capacity
m = mass of the sample in grams
ΔT = change in temperature in Celsius degrees

This equation always applies when a substance is being heated (or cooled) and no change of state occurs. Before you begin to use this equation, however, make sure you understand where it comes from.

EXAMPLE 3.7   *Specific Heat Capacity Calculations: Using the Equation*

A 1.6-g sample of a metal that has the appearance of gold requires 5.8 J of energy to change its temperature from 23 °C to 41 °C. Is the metal pure gold?

Solution

We can represent the data given in this problem by the following diagram:

| 1.6 g metal | | 1.6 g metal |
| *T* = 23 °C | ⟹ | *T* = 41 °C |

5.8 J

$$\Delta T = 41\ °C - 23\ °C = 18\ °C$$

Using the data given, we can calculate the value of the specific heat capacity for the metal and compare this value to the one for gold given in Table 3.2. We know that

$$Q = s \times m \times \Delta T$$

or, pictorially,

| 1.6 g metal | | 1.6 g metal |
| *T* = 23 °C | ⟹ | *T* = 41 °C |

5.8 J = ? × 1.6 × 18

When we divide both sides of the equation

$$Q = s \times m \times \Delta T$$

by $m \times \Delta T$, we get

$$\frac{Q}{m \times \Delta T} = s$$

Thus using the data given, we can calculate the value of *s*. In this case,

$$Q = \text{energy (heat) required} = 5.8\ \text{J}$$
$$m = \text{mass of the sample} = 1.6\ \text{g}$$
$$\Delta T = \text{change in temperature} = 18\ °C\ (41\ °C - 23\ °C = 18\ °C)$$

Thus

$$s = \frac{Q}{m \times \Delta T} = \frac{5.8\ \text{J}}{(1.6\ \text{g})\ (18\ °C)} = 0.20\ \text{J/g °C}$$

The result you will get on your calculator is: 5.8/(1.6)(18) = 0.2013889, which rounds off to 0.20.

From Table 3.2, the specific heat capacity for gold is 0.13 J/g °C. Thus the metal must not be pure gold.

Self-Check Exercise 3.7

A 2.8-g sample of pure metal requires 10.1 J of energy to change its temperature from 21 °C to 36 °C. What is this metal? (Use Table 3.2.)

See Problems 3.61 and 3.62.

Chapter Review

Key Terms

matter *(3.1)*

states of matter *(3.1)*

solid *(3.1)*

liquid *(3.1)*

gas *(3.1)*

physical properties *(3.2)*

chemical properties *(3.2)*

physical change *(3.2)*

chemical change *(3.2)*

element *(3.3)*

compound *(3.3)*

mixture *(3.4)*

pure substance *(3.4)*

homogeneous mixture *(3.4)*

solution *(3.4)*

heterogeneous mixture *(3.4)*

distillation *(3.5)*

filtration *(3.5)*

energy *(3.6)*

calorie *(3.6)*

joule *(3.6)*

specific heat capacity *(3.6)*

Summary

1. Matter can exist in three states—solid, liquid, and gas—and can be described in terms of its physical and chemical properties. Chemical properties describe a substance's ability to undergo a change to a different substance. Physical properties are the characteristics a substance exhibits as long as no chemical change occurs.

2. A physical change involves a change in one or more physical properties, but no change in composition. A chemical change transforms a substance into a new substance or substances.

3. A mixture has variable composition. A homogeneous mixture has the same properties throughout; a heterogeneous mixture does not. A pure substance always has the same composition. We can physically separate mixtures of pure substances by distillation and filtration.

4. Pure substances are of two types: elements, which cannot be broken down chemically into simpler substances, and compounds, which can be broken down chemically into elements.

5. Energy can be defined as the capacity to do work.

6. Specific heat capacity is the amount of energy required to change the temperature of one gram of a substance by one Celsius degree. Each substance has a characteristic specific heat capacity. The energy (heat) required to change the temperature of a substance depends on three factors: the amount of substance, the temperature change, and the specific heat capacity of the substance.

Questions and Problems

All even-numbered exercises have answers in the back of this book and solutions in the Solutions Guide.

3.1 ■ *Matter*

QUESTIONS

1. Matter is anything that has _____ and occupies space.

2. The three physical _____ of matter are solid, liquid, and gas.

3. Solids and liquids are virtually incompressible; they have _____ volumes.

4. Liquids have definite volumes but are able to take on the shape of their _____.

5. In liquid substances, the molecules are very close to each other but are still able to _____ fairly freely.

6. Matter in the _____ state has no shape and fills completely whatever container holds it.

7. Discuss the similarities and differences between a liquid and a solid.

8. The _____ the forces among the particles in a sample of matter, the more rigid the matter will be.

9. Consider three 10-g samples of water: one as ice, one as a liquid, and one as vapor. How do the volumes of these three samples compare with one another? How is this difference in volume related to the physical state involved?

10. In a sample of a gaseous substance, more than 99% of the overall volume of the sample is empty space. How is this fact reflected in the properties of a gaseous substance, compared with the properties of a liquid or solid substance?

3.2 ■ *Physical and Chemical Properties and Changes*

QUESTIONS

11. Acetone, a solvent widely used in industry, boils at 65 °C; this is an example of a _____ property of acetone.

12. Acetone is highly flammable because it reacts easily with oxygen gas in the atmosphere; this is an example of a _____ property of acetone.

(For Exercises 13–14) Aqueous solutions of potassium permanganate have an intense deep purple color. When aqueous potassium permanganate is added to iron(II) sulfate, the purple color of the potassium permanganate disappears as it is converted to almost colorless manganese(II) ion.

13. The fact that potassium permanganate solutions are deep purple in color is an example of a _____ property.

14. The change that occurs when potassium permanganate and iron(II) sulfate are combined is an example of a _____ property.

15. Describe, on a microscopic basis, the physical changes that take place when an ice cube is heated strongly until it melts and the water vaporizes. Why are these changes *physical* and not chemical in nature?

16. Describe, on a microscopic basis, what happens when a strong electric current is passed through water, and why the resulting changes are *chemical* changes.

17. Classify the following as *physical* or as *chemical* changes.
    a. Mothballs gradually vaporize in a closet.
    b. A French chef making a sauce with brandy is able to burn off the alcohol from the brandy, leaving just the brandy flavoring.

c. Hydrofluoric acid attacks glass, and is used to etch calibration marks on glass laboratory utensils.
d. Calcium chloride lowers the temperature at which water freezes, and can be used to melt ice on city sidewalks and roadways.
e. An antacid tablet fizzes and releases carbon dioxide gas when it comes in contact with hydrochloric acid in the stomach.
f. A flashlight battery corrodes and leaks on prolonged storage.
g. Chemistry majors usually get holes in the cotton jeans they wear to lab because of the acids used in many experiments.
h. Whole milk curdles if vinegar is added to it.
i. A piece of rubber stretches when you pull on it.
j. Rubbing alcohol evaporates quickly from the skin.
k. Acetone is used to dissolve and remove nail polish.

18. Classify the following as *physical* or *chemical* changes/properties.
    a. A copper pan acquires a blue-green coating (patina) with use.
    b. Drain cleaner dissolves a hair clog in a bathroom drain.
    c. Hydrogen peroxide fizzes when applied to a wound.
    d. Acids produced by bacteria in plaque cause teeth to decay.
    e. Marble statues deteriorate when attacked by acid rain.
    f. Grape juice ferments when yeast is added.
    g. Mothballs vaporize in a cedar closet.
    h. Alcohol feels cool as it evaporates from the skin.
    i. Your car battery will run down if you leave the lights on.
    j. Soap lathers when you wash your hands.
    k. The sulfur in eggs will turn a silver spoon black.

3.3 ■ *Elements and Compounds*

QUESTIONS

19. _____ cannot be broken down into simpler substances by chemical means.

20. A pure sample of a(n) _____ contains only one kind of atom.

21. Certain elements have special affinities for other elements. This causes them to bind together in special ways to form _____.

22. Compounds can be broken down into _____ by chemical changes.

23. What does it mean to say that a given compound always has the same composition?

24. The properties of a compound are usually very (different from/similar to) those of the elements it contains.

3.4 ■ *Mixtures and Pure Substances*

QUESTIONS

25. A pure substance always has (a variable/the same) composition.

26. A mixture can be defined as something that has (a variable/the same) composition.

27. A homogeneous mixture is more commonly referred to as a _____.

28. A mixture of salt and sand would be an example of a _____ mixture.

29. Identify the following as *mixtures* or as *pure substances*.
    a. milk
    b. the paper this book is printed on
    c. a teaspoon of sugar
    d. a teaspoon of sugar dissolved in a glass of water
    e. steel

30. Classify the following as *mixtures* or as *pure substances*.
    a. a white cotton handkerchief
    b. distilled water
    c. water scooped from a pond
    d. the mercury used in a thermometer

31. Classify the following mixtures as *homogeneous* or *heterogeneous*.
    a. a bag of various colored marbles
    b. beach sand
    c. a sample of sodium chloride dissolved in water
    d. a sample of table salt dissolved in water
    e. air

32. Classify the following mixtures as *homogeneous* or *heterogeneous*.
    a. gasoline
    b. a jar of jelly beans
    c. chunky peanut butter
    d. margarine
    e. the paper this question is printed on

3.5 ■ *Separation of Mixtures*

QUESTIONS

33. Water from the sea can be made fit for drinking by boiling the water and then condensing the vapor back to the liquid state. This process is known as _____.

34. An insoluble contaminant may be removed from a liquid medium most simply by the process of _____.

35. In a common laboratory experiment in general chemistry, students are asked to determine the relative amounts of benzoic acid and charcoal in a solid mixture. Benzoic acid is relatively soluble in hot water, but charcoal is not. Devise a method for separating the two components of this mixture.

36. Describe the process of distillation depicted in Figure 3.6. Does the separation of the components of a mixture by distillation represent a chemical or a physical change?

3.6 ■ *Energy and Energy Changes*

QUESTIONS

37. _____ is defined as the capacity to do work.

38. _____ is defined as the amount of energy required to raise the temperature of one gram of water by one degree Celsius.

39. Describe what happens to the molecules in a sample of ice as the sample is slowly heated until it liquefies and then vaporizes.

40. Describe what happens to the molecules in liquid water as it is heated and begins to boil.

41. Metallic substances tend to have (higher/lower) specific heat capacities than nonmetallic substances.

42. The quantity of energy required to change the temperature of a sample is calculated by taking the product of the mass of the sample, the specific heat capacity of the sample, and the _____ change undergone by the sample.

43. If it takes 526 J of energy to warm 7.40 g of water by 17 °C, it will take _____ J to warm 3.20 g of water by the same amount.

44. If it takes 526 J of heat energy to warm 7.40 g of water by 17 °C, then it will require 1.052 kJ of heat energy to warm _____ g of water by 17 °C.

45. Convert the following numbers of calories into joules.
    a. 5562 cal
    b. 2.25×10^3 cal
    c. 4.184 cal
    d. 85,550 cal

46. Convert the following numbers of kilojoules into kilocalories. (Remember: kilo means 1000.)
    a. 462.4 kJ
    b. 18.28 kJ
    c. 1.014 kJ
    d. 190.5 kJ

47. Convert the following numbers of calories into kilocalories. (Remember: kilo means 1000.)
    a. 850 cal
    b. 1530 cal
    c. 227,200 cal
    d. 0.00289 cal

48. Convert the following numbers of kilocalories into calories.
    a. 12.30 kcal
    b. 290.4 kcal
    c. 940,000 kcal
    d. 4201 kcal

49. Convert the following numbers of joules (J) into kilojoules (kJ). (Remember: kilo means 1000.)
    a. 243,000 J
    b. 4.184 J
    c. 0.251 J
    d. 450.3 J

50. Perform the following conversions.
    a. 75.25 kJ into calories
    b. 133,200 cal into kilojoules
    c. 232.4 kcal into joules
    d. 645,200 J into kilocalories

51. Calculate the amount of energy required (in calories) to heat 145 g of water from 22.3 °C to 75.0 °C.

52. If 52.5 kJ of heat is added to a 1.02-kg block of metal, the temperature of the metal increases by 11.2 °C. Calculate the specific heat capacity of the metal in J/g °C.

53. Calculate the energy required (in joules) to heat 25.0 g of gold from 120. °C to 155 °C. (See Table 3.2.)

54. It takes 1.25 kJ of energy to heat a certain sample of pure silver from 12.0 °C to 15.2 °C. Calculate the mass of the sample of silver.

55. If 50. J of heat are applied to 10. g of iron, by how much will the temperature of the iron increase? (See Table 3.2.)

56. If 4.524×10^3 J of heat is applied to a 742.1-g sample of iron, by how many degrees Celsius will the temperature of the iron sample increase?

57. The specific heat capacity of silver is 0.24 J/g °C. Express this in terms of calories per gram per Celsius degree.

58. The specific heat capacity of gold is 0.13 J/g °C. Calculate the specific heat capacity of gold in cal/g °C. Calculate the specific heat capacity of gold in J/mol °C.

59. Three separate 50.0-g samples of aluminum, iron, and silver are available. Each of these samples is initially at 20.0 °C, and then 1.00 kJ of heat is applied to each

sample. What final temperature will each of the samples reach?

60. If the temperatures of separate 25.0-g samples of gold, mercury, and carbon are to be raised by 20. °C, how much heat (in joules) must be applied to each substance?

61. A 22.5-g sample of metal X requires 540. J of energy to heat it from 10. °C to 92 °C. Calculate the specific heat capacity of metal X.

62. A 35.2 g sample of metal Z requires 1251 J of energy to heat the sample by 25.0 °C. Calculate the specific heat capacity of metal Z.

Additional Problems

63. If solid iron pellets and sulfur powder are poured into a container at room temperature, a simple _____ has been made. If the iron and sulfur are heated until a chemical reaction takes place between them, a(n) _____ will form.

64. Pure substance X is melted, and the liquid is placed in an electrolysis apparatus such as that shown in Figure 3.3. When an electric current is passed through the liquid, a brown solid forms in one chamber and a white solid forms in the other chamber. Is substance X a compound or an element?

65. When a 1.00-g sample of baking soda is heated, a gas is formed. The solid that remains weighs less than 1.00 g and does not have the same properties as the original sample. Is baking soda an element or a compound?

66. During a very cold winter, the temperature may remain below freezing for extended periods. However, fallen snow can still disappear, even though it cannot melt. This is possible because a solid can vaporize directly, without passing through the liquid state. Is this process (sublimation) a physical or a chemical change?

67. Perform the indicated conversions.
    a. 750,900 cal to kilojoules
    b. 9.985 kJ to kilocalories
    c. 7.899 kcal to joules
    d. 900.4 kcal to kilojoules
    e. 89,930 J to kilocalories
    f. 5.901 kJ to calories

68. Calculate the amount of energy required (in joules) to heat 2.5 kg of water from 18.5 °C to 55.0 °C.

69. If 10. J of heat is applied to 5.0-g samples of each of the substances listed in Table 3.2, which substance's temperature will increase the most? Which substance's temperature will increase the least?

70. A 5-g sample of aluminum and a 5-g sample of iron are heated in a boiling water bath in separate test tubes. The test tubes are then placed together into a beaker containing ice. Which metal will lose the most heat in cooling down?

71. Hydrogen gives off 120. J/g of energy when burned in oxygen, and methane gives off 50. J/g under the same circumstances. If a mixture of 5.0 g of hydrogen and 10. g of methane is burned, and the heat released is transferred to 500. g of water at 25 °C, what final temperature will be reached by the water?

72. A 5.00-g sample of aluminum pellets and a 10.00-g sample of iron pellets are placed together in a dry test tube, and the test tube is heated in a boiling water bath to 100. °C. The mixture of hot iron and aluminum is then poured into 97.3 g of water at 22.5 °C. To what final temperature is the water heated by the metals?

73. A 50.0-g sample of water at 100. °C is poured into a 50.0-g sample of water at 25 °C. What will be the final temperature of the water?

74. A 25.0-g sample of pure iron at 85 °C is dropped into 75 g of water at 20. °C. What is the final temperature of the water–iron mixture?

75. Discuss the similarities and differences between a liquid and a gas.

76. In gaseous substances, the individual molecules are relatively (close/far apart) and are moving freely, rapidly, and randomly.

77. The fact that the chemical substance sodium chromate is bright yellow is an example of a _____ property.

78. The fact that the chemical substance sodium chromate reacts in solution with lead compounds is an example of a _____ property.

(For Exercises 79–80) Solutions containing copper(II) ions are bright blue in color. When sodium hydroxide is added to such a solution, a precipitate is formed that is a much lighter blue.

79. The fact that a solution containing copper(II) ions is bright blue is a _____ property.

80. The fact that a reaction takes place when sodium hydroxide is added to a solution of copper(II) ions is a _____ property.

81. The processes of melting and evaporation involve changes in the _____ of a substance.

82. _____ is the process of making a chemical reaction take place by passage of an electric current through a substance or solution.

83. Classify the following as *physical* or *chemical* properties/changes.
    a. Milk curdles if a few drops of vinegar are added.
    b. Butter turns rancid if left exposed at room temperature.
    c. Salad dressing separates into layers after standing.
    d. Milk of magnesia neutralizes stomach acid.
    e. The steel in a car has rust spots.
    f. A person is asphyxiated by breathing carbon monoxide.
    g. Spilled acid burns a hole in cotton jeans.
    h. Sweat cools the body as it evaporates from the skin.
    i. Aspirin reduces fever.
    j. Oil feels slippery.
    k. Alcohol burns, forming carbon dioxide and water.

84. Identify the following as *mixtures* or as *pure substances*.
    a. wood
    b. aluminum foil
    c. salad dressing
    d. wine
    e. a vitamin tablet

85. Classify the following mixtures as *homogeneous* or *heterogeneous*.
    a. blood
    b. rust as scraped from an automobile bumper
    c. salad dressing
    d. window glass
    e. pond water

86. If it takes 4.5 J of energy to warm 5.0 g of aluminum from 25 °C to a certain higher temperature, then it will take _____ J to warm 10. g of aluminum over the same temperature interval.

87. If it takes 103 J of energy to warm a certain mass of iron from 25 °C to 50. °C, then it will take _____ J to warm the same mass of iron from 25 °C to 75 °C.

88. Convert the following numbers of calories into joules (J).
    a. 150.0 cal
    b. 4462 cal
    c. 10.0 cal
    d. 4.184 cal

89. Convert the following numbers of joules (J) into calories.
    a. 4.184 J
    b. 1520 J
    c. 8.02 J
    d. 23.29 J

90. Perform the following conversions.
    a. 1.25×10^4 J to kilojoules
    b. 1.25×10^4 J to kilocalories
    c. 512.2 cal to kilojoules
    d. 14.2 kJ to kilocalories

91. Calculate the energy required (in calories) to heat 10.4 g of mercury from 37.0 °C to 42.0 °C.

92. Calculate the energy required (in joules) to heat 75 g of water from 25 °C to 39 °C.

93. If 50. J of heat are applied to 10. g of aluminum, by how much will the temperature of the aluminum increase? (See Table 3.2.)

94. For each of the substances listed in Table 3.2, calculate the quantity of heat required to heat 150. g of the substance by 11.2 °C.

95. Suppose you had 10.0-g samples of each of the substances listed in Table 3.2 and that 1.00 kJ of heat is applied to each of these samples. By what amount would the temperature of each sample be raised?

96. A 55.0-g sample of metal Z requires 675 J of energy to heat it from 25 °C to 118 °C. Calculate the specific heat capacity of metal Z.

Cumulative Review for Chapters 1–3

QUESTIONS

1. In the exercises for Chapter 1 of this text, you were asked to give your *own* definition of what chemistry represents. After having completed a few more chapters in this book, has your definition changed? Do you have a better appreciation for what chemists do? Explain.

2. Early on in this text, some aspects of the best way to go about learning chemistry were presented. In *beginning* your study of chemistry, you may initially have approached studying chemistry as you would any of your other academic subjects (taking notes in class, reading the text, memorizing facts, and so on). Discuss why the ability to sort through and analyze facts and the ability to propose and solve problems are so much more important in learning chemistry.

3. You have learned the basic way in which scientists analyze problems, propose models to explain the systems under consideration, and then experiment to test their models. Suppose you have a sample of a liquid material. You are not sure whether the liquid is a pure *compound* (for example, water or alcohol) or a *solution*. How could you apply the scientific method to study the liquid and to determine which type of material the liquid is?

4. Many college students would not choose to take a chemistry course if it were not required for their major. Do you have a better appreciation of *why* chemistry is a required course for your own particular major or career choice? Discuss.

5. In Chapter 2 of this text, you were introduced to the International System *(SI)* of measurements. What are the basic units of this system for mass, distance, time, and temperature? What are some of the common multiples and subdivisions of these basic units? Why do you suppose this system is used practically everywhere in the world except the United States? Why do you suppose the United States is reluctant to adopt this system? Do you think the United States *should* adopt this system? Why or why not?

6. Most people think of science as being a specific, exact discipline, with a "correct" answer for every problem. Yet you were introduced to the concept of *uncertainty* in scientific measurements. What is meant by "uncertainty"? How does uncertainty creep into measurements? How is uncertainty *indicated* in scientific measurements? Can uncertainty ever be completely eliminated in experiments? Explain.

7. After studying a few chapters of this text, and perhaps having done a few lab experiments and taken a few quizzes in chemistry, you are probably sick of hearing the term *significant figures*. Most chemistry teachers make a big deal about significant figures. Why is reporting the correct number of significant figures so important in science? Summarize the rules for deciding whether or not a figure in a calculation is "significant." Summarize the rules for rounding off numbers. Summarize the rules for doing arithmetic with the correct number of significant figures.

8. This chemistry course may have been the first time you have encountered the method of *dimensional analysis* in problem solving. Explain what are meant by a *conversion factor* and an *equivalence statement*. Give an everyday example of how you might use dimensional analysis to solve a simple problem.

9. You have learned about several temperature scales so far in this text. Describe the Fahrenheit, Celsius, and Kelvin temperature scales. How are these scales defined? Why were they defined this way? Which of these temperature scales is the most fundamental? Why?

10. What is *matter?* What is matter composed of? What are some of the different types of matter? How do these types of matter differ and how are they the same?

11. What is the difference between a chemical property and a physical property? Give examples of each. What is the difference between a chemical change and a physical change? Give examples of each.

12. What is an *element* and what is a *compound?* Give examples of each. What does it mean to say that a compound has a *constant composition?* Would samples of a particular compound here and in another part of the world have the same composition and properties?

13. What is a mixture? What is a solution? How do mixtures differ from pure substances? What are some of the techniques by which mixtures can be resolved into their components?

14. How is the concept of *energy* defined? What are some common *units* of energy, and how are these units defined? What is meant by the *specific heat capacity* of a material? How is specific heat capacity used to measure energy changes in processes?

PROBLEMS

15. For each of the following, make the indicated conversion.
    a. 1.14×10^{-4} to standard scientific notation
    b. 1.73×10^{-3} to ordinary decimal notation
    c. 721.6×10^{3} to standard scientific notation
    d. 4.71×10^{3} to ordinary decimal notation
    e. 0.000142 to standard scientific notation
    f. 4431 to standard scientific notation

16. For each of the following, make the indicated conversion.
    a. 7.50 mi to kilometers
    b. 6.91 kg to pounds
    c. 5550 mL to liters
    d. 2.10 L to quarts
    e. 2.10 L to gallons
    f. 1.315 m to millimeters
    g. 12.5 in. to meters
    h. 16 fl. oz. to liters
    i. 2.04 m to yards
    j. 8.11 pt to liters

17. Evaluate each of the following mathematical expressions, being sure to express the answer to the correct number of significant figures.
    a. $10.20 + 4.1 + 26.001 + 2.4$
    b. $(1.091 - 0.991) + 1.2$
    c. $(4.06 + 5.1)(2.032 - 1.02)$
    d. $(67.21)(1.003)(2.4)$
    e. $[(7.815 + 2.01)(4.5)]/(1.9001)$
    f. $(1.67 \times 10^{-9})(1.1 \times 10^{-4})$
    g. $(4.02 \times 10^{-4})(2.91 \times 10^{3})/(9.102 \times 10^{-1})$
    h. $(1.04 \times 10^{2} + 2.1 \times 10^{1})/(4.51 \times 10^{3})$
    i. $(1.51 \times 10^{-3})^{2}/(1.074 \times 10^{-7})$
    j. $(1.89 \times 10^{2})/[(7.01 \times 10^{-3})(4.1433 \times 10^{4})]$

18. Make the indicated temperature conversions.
    a. $-50.1\ °C$ to Fahrenheit degrees
    b. $-30.7\ °F$ to Celsius degrees
    c. 541 K to Celsius degrees
    d. 221 °C to kelvins
    e. 351 K to Fahrenheit degrees
    f. 72 °F to kelvins

19. Given the following mass, volume, and density information, calculate the missing quantity.
    a. mass = 121.4 g; volume = 42.4 cm^3; density = ? g/cm^3
    b. mass = 0.721 lb; volume = 241 cm^3; density = ? g/cm^3
    c. mass = ? g; volume = 124.1 mL; density = 0.821 g/mL
    d. mass = ? g; volume = 4.51 L; density = 1.15 g/cm^3
    e. mass = 142.4 g; volume = ?; density = 0.915 g/mL
    f. mass = 4.2 lb; volume = ?; density = 3.75 g/cm^3

20. For each of the following amounts of energy, perform the indicated conversion of units.
    a. 459 J to calories
    b. 7031 cal to kilojoules
    c. 55.31 kJ to joules
    d. 78.3 kcal to kilojoules
    e. 4541 cal to kilocalories
    f. 84.1 kJ to kilocalories

21. Calculate the quantity of energy, in joules, required to warm each of the following samples over the indicated temperature range.
    a. 5.01 g of water from 10 °C to 55 °C
    b. 5.2 g of iron from 15 °C to 43 °C
    c. 62.1 g of gold from $-11\ °F$ to 45 °F
    d. 4.1 g of ice from 5 °F to 31 °F
    e. 4.21 lb of aluminum from 21 °C to 37 °C
    f. 5.04 kg of carbon from 31 °F to 78 °F

Chemical Foundations: Elements, Atoms, and Ions

The chemical elements are very important to each of us in our daily lives. Although certain elements are present in our bodies in tiny amounts, they can have a profound impact on our health and behavior. As we will see in this chapter, lithium can be a miracle treatment for someone with manic-depressive disease and our cobalt levels can have a remarkable impact on whether we behave violently.

Since ancient times, humans have used chemical changes to their advantage. The processing of ores to produce metals for ornaments and tools and the use of embalming fluids are two applications of chemistry that were used before 1000 B.C.

The Greeks were the first to try to explain why chemical changes occur. By about 400 B.C. they had proposed that all matter was composed of four fundamental substances: fire, earth, water, and air.

Gold, an element prized for its ability to resist tarnishing, is used for jewelry and to honor athletic prowess (left). *Lithium is administered in the form of lithium carbonate pills* (right).

Robert Boyle at 62 years of age.

The next 2000 years of chemical history were dominated by alchemy. Alchemists were often mystics and fakes who were obsessed with the idea of turning cheap metals into gold. However, this period also saw important events: the elements mercury, sulfur, and antimony were discovered, and alchemists learned how to prepare acids.

The first scientist to recognize the importance of careful measurements was the Irishman Robert Boyle (1627–1691). Boyle is best known for his pioneering work on the properties of gases, but his most important contribution to science was probably his insistence that science should be firmly grounded in experiments. For example, Boyle held no preconceived notions about how many elements there might be. His definition of the term *element* was based on experiments: a substance was an element unless it could be broken down into two or more simpler substances. For example, air could not be an element as the Greeks believed, because it could be broken down into many pure substances.

As Boyle's experimental definition of an element became generally accepted, the list of known elements grew, and the Greek system of four elements died. But although Boyle was an excellent scientist, he was not always right. For some reason he ignored his own definition of an element and clung to the alchemists' views that metals were not true elements and that a way would be found eventually to change one metal into another.

4.1 The Elements

AIMS: To learn about the relative abundances of the elements. To learn the names of some elements.

In studying the materials of the earth (and other parts of the universe), scientists have found that all matter can be broken down chemically into about one hundred different elements. At first it might seem amazing that the millions of known substances are composed of so few fundamental elements. Fortunately for those trying to understand and systematize it, nature often uses a relatively small number of fundamental units to assemble even extremely complex materials. For example, proteins, a group of substances that serve the human body in almost uncountable ways, are all made by linking together a few fundamental units to form huge molecules. A nonchemical example is the English language, where hundreds of thousands of words are constructed from only 26 letters. If you take apart the thousands of words in an English dictionary, you will find only these 26 fundamental components. In much the same way, when we take apart all of the substances in the world around us, we find only about one hundred fundamental building blocks— the elements. Compounds are made by combining atoms of the various elements, just as words are constructed from the 26 letters of the alphabet. And just as you had to learn the letters of the alphabet before you learned to read and write, you need to learn the names and symbols of the chemical elements before you can read and write chemistry.

Presently 110 different elements are known, 88 of which occur naturally. (The rest have been made in laboratories.) The elements vary tremendously individual atoms as the fundamental components. For example, chemists know that oxygen gas consists of molecules with two oxygen atoms connected together (represented as O—O or more commonly as O_2). Thus when we refer to the element oxygen we might mean a single atom of oxygen, a single O_2 molecule, or a macroscopic sample containing many O_2 molecules. Finally, we often use the term *element* in a generic fashion. When we say the human body contains the elements sodium or lithium, we do not mean that free elemental sodium or lithium is present. Rather, we mean that atoms of these elements are present in some form. In this text we will try to make clear what we mean when we use the term *element* in a particular case.

4.2 Symbols for the Elements

AIM: To learn the symbols of some elements

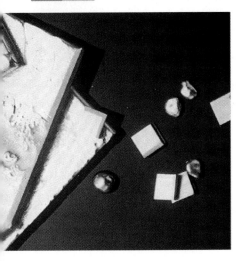

Various forms of the element gold.

In the symbol for an element, only the first letter is capitalized

The names of the chemical elements have come from many sources. Often an element's name is derived from a Greek, Latin, or German word that describes some property of the element. For example, gold was originally called *aurum,* a Latin word meaning "shining dawn," and lead was known as *plumbum,* which means "heavy." The names for chlorine and iodine come from Greek words describing their colors, and the name for bromine comes from a Greek word meaning "stench." In addition, it is very common for an element to be named for the place where it was discovered. You can guess where the elements francium, germanium, californium*, and americium* were first found. Some of the heaviest elements are named after famous scientists, for example, einsteinium* and nobelium*.

We often use abbreviations to simplify the written word. For example, it is much easier to put MA on an envelope than to write out Massachusetts, and we often write USA instead of United States of America. Likewise, chemists have invented a set of abbreviations or **element symbols** for the chemical elements. These symbols usually consist of the first letter or the first two letters of the element names. The first letter is always capitalized, and the second is not. Examples include:

fluorine	F	neon	Ne
oxygen	O	silicon	Si
carbon	C		

Sometimes, however, the two letters used are not the first two letters in the name. For example,

| zinc | Zn | cadmium | Cd |
| chlorine | Cl | platinum | Pt |

The symbols for some other elements are based on the original Latin or Greek name.

---

*These elements are made artificially. They do not occur naturally.

TABLE 4.3

The Names and Symbols of the Most Common Elements

Element	Symbol	Element	Symbol
aluminum	Al	lithium	Li
antimony (stibium)*	Sb	magnesium	Mg
argon	Ar	manganese	Mn
arsenic	As	mercury (hydrargyrum)	Hg
barium	Ba	neon	Ne
bismuth	Bi	nickel	Ni
boron	B	nitrogen	N
bromine	Br	oxygen	O
cadmium	Cd	phosphorus	P
calcium	Ca	platinum	Pt
carbon	C	potassium (kalium)	K
chlorine	Cl	radium	Ra
chromium	Cr	silicon	Si
cobalt	Co	silver (argentium)	Ag
copper (cuprum)	Cu	sodium (natrium)	Na
fluorine	F	strontium	Sr
gold (aurum)	Au	sulfur	S
helium	He	tin (stannum)	Sn
hydrogen	H	titanium	Ti
iodine	I	tungsten (wolfram)	W
iron (ferrum)	Fe	uranium	U
lead (plumbum)	Pb	zinc	Zn

*Where appropriate, the original name is shown in parentheses so that you can see where some of the symbols came from.

Current Name	*Original Name*	*Symbol*
gold	aurum	Au
lead	plumbum	Pb
sodium	natrium	Na
iron	ferrum	Fe

A list of the most common elements and their symbols is given in Table 4.3. You can also see the elements represented on a table in the inside front cover of this text. We will explain the form of this table (which is called the periodic table) in later chapters.

4.3   Dalton's Atomic Theory

AIMS: To learn about Dalton's theory of atoms. To understand and illustrate the law of constant composition.

As scientists of the eighteenth century studied the nature of materials, several things became clear:

1. Most natural materials are mixtures of pure substances.

2. Pure substances are either elements or combinations of elements called compounds.

3. A given compound always contains the same proportions (by mass) of the elements. For example, water *always* contains 8 g of oxygen for every 1 g of hydrogen, and carbon dioxide *always* contains 2.7 g of oxygen for every 1 g of carbon. This principle became known as the **law of constant composition.** It means that a given compound always has the same composition, regardless of where it comes from.

John Dalton (Figure 4.1), an English scientist and teacher, was aware of these observations, and in about 1808 he offered an explanation for them that became known as **Dalton's atomic theory.** The main ideas of this theory (model) can be stated as follows:

Dalton's Atomic Theory

1. Elements are made of tiny particles called atoms.

2. All atoms of a given element are identical.

3. The atoms of a given element are different from those of any other element.

4. Atoms of one element can combine with atoms of other elements to form compounds. A given compound always has the same relative numbers and types of atoms.

5. Atoms are indivisible in chemical processes. That is, atoms are not created or destroyed in chemical reactions. A chemical reaction simply changes the way the atoms are grouped together.

FIGURE 4.1
John Dalton (1766–1844) was an English scientist who made his living as a teacher in Manchester. Although Dalton is best known for his atomic theory, he made contributions in many other areas, including meteorology (he recorded daily weather conditions for 46 years, producing a total of 200,000 data entries). A rather shy man, Dalton was colorblind to red (a special handicap for a chemist) and suffered from lead poisoning contracted from drinking stout (strong beer or ale) that had been drawn through lead pipes.

FIGURE 4.2
Dalton pictured compounds as collections of atoms. Here NO, NO_2, and N_2O are represented. Note that the number of atoms of each type in a molecule is given by a subscript, except that the number 1 is always assumed and never written.

Dalton's model successfully explained important observations such as the law of constant composition. This law makes sense because if a compound always contains the same relative numbers of atoms, it will always contain the same proportions by mass of the various elements.

Like most new ideas, Dalton's model was not accepted immediately. However, Dalton was convinced he was right and *used his model to predict* how a given pair of elements might combine to form more than one compound. For example, nitrogen and oxygen might form a compound containing one atom of nitrogen and one atom of oxygen (written NO), a compound containing two atoms of nitrogen and one atom of oxygen (written N_2O), a compound containing one atom of nitrogen and two atoms of oxygen (written NO_2), and so on (Figure 4.2). When the existence of these substances was verified, it was a triumph for Dalton's model. Because Dalton was able to predict correctly the formation of multiple compounds between two elements, his atomic theory became widely accepted.

4.4   Formulas of Compounds

AIM: To learn how a formula describes a compound's composition.

Here, relative refers to ratios.

A **compound** is a distinct substance that is composed of the atoms of two or more elements and always contains exactly the same relative masses of those elements. In light of Dalton's atomic theory, this simply means that a compound always contains the same relative *numbers* of atoms of each element. For example, water always contains two hydrogen atoms for each oxygen atom.

The types of atoms and the number of each type in each unit (molecule) of a given compound are conveniently expressed by a **chemical formula.** In a chemical formula the atoms are indicated by the element symbols, and the number of each type of atom is indicated by a subscript, a number that appears to the right of and below the symbol for the element. The formula for water is written H_2O, indicating that each molecule of water contains two atoms of hydrogen and one atom of oxygen (the subscript 1 is always understood and not written). Following are some general rules for writing formulas:

Rules for Writing Formulas

1. Each atom present is represented by its element symbol.

2. The number of each type of atom is indicated by a subscript written to the right of the element symbol.

3. When only one atom of a given type is present, the subscript 1 is not written.

EXAMPLE 4.1   *Writing Formulas of Compounds*

Write the formula for each of the following compounds, listing the elements in the order given.

a. Each molecule of a compound that has been implicated in the formation of acid rain contains one atom of sulfur and three atoms of oxygen.

b. Each molecule of a certain compound contains two atoms of nitrogen and five atoms of oxygen.

c. Each molecule of glucose, a type of sugar, contains six atoms of carbon, twelve atoms of hydrogen, and six atoms of oxygen.

Solution

a. Symbol for sulfur ——————   —— Symbol for oxygen

SO_3

One atom of sulfur ——————   —— Three atoms of oxygen

b.

Symbol for nitrogen ———→↓ ↓⌐——— Symbol for oxygen

$$N_2O_5$$

Two atoms ————↑ ↑——— Five atoms
of nitrogen   of oxygen

c.

Symbol for
hydrogen

Symbol for carbon ———→↓ ↓ ⌐——— Symbol for oxygen

$$C_6H_{12}O_6$$

Six atoms ——↑ ↑ ↑—— Six atoms
of carbon   of oxygen
Twelve atoms
of hydrogen

 Self-Check Exercise 4.1

Write the formula for each of the following compounds, listing the elements in the order given.

a. A molecule contains four phosphorus atoms and ten oxygen atoms.

b. A molecule contains one uranium atom and six fluorine atoms.

c. A molecule contains one aluminum atom and three chlorine atoms.

See Problems 4.19 and 4.20.

4.5 The Structure of the Atom

AIMS: To learn about the internal parts of an atom. To understand Rutherford's experiment to characterize the atom's structure.

Dalton's atomic theory, proposed in about 1808, provided such a convincing explanation for the composition of compounds that it became generally accepted. Scientists came to believe that *elements consist of atoms* and that *compounds are a specific collection of atoms* bound together in some way. But what is an atom like? It might be a tiny ball of matter that is the same throughout with no internal structure—like a ball bearing. Or the atom might be composed of parts—it might be made up of a number of subatomic particles. But if the atom contains parts, there should be some way to break up the atom into its components.

Many scientists pondered the nature of the atom during the 1800s, but it was not until almost 1900 that convincing evidence became available that the atom has a number of different parts.

A physicist in England named J. J. Thomson showed in the late 1890s that the atoms of any element can be made to emit tiny negative particles. (He knew they had a negative charge because he could show that they were repelled by the negative part of an electric field.) Thus he concluded that all types of atoms must contain these negative particles, which are now called **electrons.**

On the basis of his results, Thomson wondered what an atom must be like. Although atoms contain these tiny negative particles, he also knew that

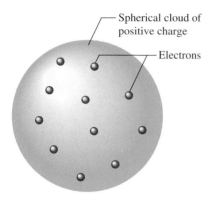

— Spherical cloud of positive charge

— Electrons

FIGURE 4.3
One of the early models of the atom was the plum pudding model, in which the electrons were pictured as embedded in a positively charged spherical cloud, much as raisins are distributed in an old-fashioned plum pudding.

FIGURE 4.4
Ernest Rutherford (1871–1937) was born on a farm in New Zealand. In 1895 he placed second in a scholarship competition to attend Cambridge University but was awarded the scholarship when the winner decided to stay home and get married. Rutherford was an intense, hard-driving person who became a master at designing just the right experiment to test a given idea. He was awarded the Nobel Prize in chemistry in 1908.

Some historians credit J. J. Thomson for the plum pudding model.

One of Rutherford's co-workers in this experiment was an undergraduate named Ernest Marsden who, like Rutherford, was from New Zealand.

whole atoms are not negatively *or* positively charged. Thus he concluded that the atom must also contain positive particles that balance exactly the negative charge carried by the electrons, giving the atom a zero overall charge.

Another scientist pondering the structure of the atom was William Thomson (better known as Lord Kelvin and no relation to J. J. Thomson). Lord Kelvin got the idea (which might have occurred to him during dinner) that the atom might be something like plum pudding (a pudding with raisins randomly distributed throughout). Kelvin reasoned that the atom might be thought of as a uniform "pudding" of positive charge with enough negative electrons scattered within to counterbalance that positive charge (see Figure 4.3). Thus the plum pudding model of the atom came into being.

If you had taken this course in 1910, the plum pudding model would have been the only picture of the atom described. However, our ideas about the atom were changed dramatically in 1911 by a physicist named Ernest Rutherford (Figure 4.4), who learned physics in J. J. Thomson's laboratory in the late 1890s. By 1911 Rutherford had become a distinguished scientist with many important discoveries to his credit. One of his main areas of interest involved alpha particles (α particles), positively charged particles with a mass approximately 7500 times that of an electron. In studying the flight of these particles through air, Rutherford found that some of the α particles were deflected by something in the air. Puzzled by this, he designed an experiment that involved directing α particles toward a thin metal foil. Surrounding the foil was a detector coated with a substance that produced tiny flashes wherever it was hit by an α particle (Figure 4.5). The results of the experiment were very different from those Rutherford anticipated. Although most of the α particles passed straight through the foil, some of the particles were deflected at large angles, as shown in Figure 4.5, and some were reflected backward.

FIGURE 4.5
Rutherford's experiment on α-particle bombardment of metal foil.

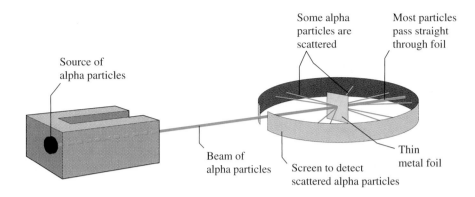

This outcome was a great surprise to Rutherford. (He described this result as comparable to shooting a gun at a piece of paper and having the bullet bounce back.) Rutherford knew that if the plum pudding model of the atom was correct, the massive α particles would crash through the thin foil like cannonballs through paper (as shown in Figure 4.6a). So he expected the α particles to travel through the foil experiencing, at most, very minor deflections of their paths.

Rutherford concluded from these results that the plum pudding model for the atom could not be correct. The large deflections of the α particles could be caused only by a center of concentrated positive charge that would repel the positively charged α particles, as illustrated in Figure 4.6(b). Most of the α particles passed directly through the foil because the atom is mostly open space. The deflected α particles were those that had a "close encounter" with the positive center of the atom, and the few reflected α particles were those that scored a "direct hit" on the positive center. In Rutherford's mind these results could be explained only in terms of a **nuclear atom**—an atom with a dense center of positive charge (the **nucleus**) around which tiny electrons moved in a space that was otherwise empty.

He concluded that the nucleus must have a positive charge to balance the negative charge of the electrons and that it must be small and dense. What was it made of? By 1919 Rutherford concluded that the nucleus of an atom

FIGURE 4.6
(a) The results that the metal foil experiment would have yielded if the plum pudding model had been correct.
(b) Actual results.

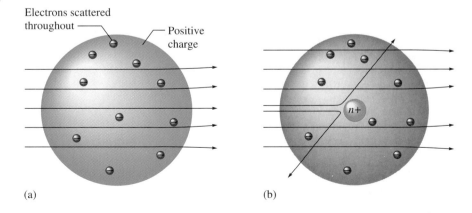

If the atom were expanded to the size of a huge stadium like the Astrodome, the nucleus would be only about as big as a fly at the center.

contained what he called protons. A **proton** has the same magnitude (size) of charge as the electron, but its charge is *positive*. We say that the proton has a charge of 1+ and the electron a charge of 1−.

Rutherford reasoned that the hydrogen atom has a single proton at its center and one electron moving through space at a relatively large distance from the proton (the hydrogen nucleus). He also reasoned that other atoms must have nuclei (the plural of *nucleus*) composed of many protons bound together somehow. In addition, Rutherford and a co-worker, James Chadwick, were able to show in 1932 that most nuclei also contain a neutral particle that they named the **neutron.** A neutron is slightly more massive than a proton but has no charge.

CHEMISTRY IN FOCUS

Glowing Tubes for Signs, Television Sets, and Computers

J. J. Thomson discovered that atoms contain electrons by using a device called a cathode ray tube (often abbreviated CRT today). When he did these experiments, he could not have imagined that he was making television sets and computer monitors possible. A cathode ray tube is a sealed glass tube that contains a gas and has separated metal plates connected to external wires (Figure 4.7). When a source of electrical energy is applied to the metal plates, a glowing beam is produced (Figure 4.8). Thomson became convinced that the glowing gas was caused by a stream of negatively charged particles coming from the metal plate. In addition, because Thomson always got the same kind of negative particles no matter what metal he used, he concluded that all types of atoms must contain these same negative particles (we now call them electrons).

Thomson's cathode ray tube has many modern applications. For example, "neon" signs consist of small-diameter cathode ray tubes containing different kinds of gases to produce various colors. For example, if the gas in the tube is neon, the tube glows with a red–orange color; if

argon is present, a blue glow appears. The presence of krypton gives an intense white light.

A television picture tube or computer monitor is also fundamentally a cathode ray tube. In this case the electrons are directed onto a screen

containing chemical compounds that glow when struck by fast-moving electrons. The use of various compounds that emit different colors when they are struck by the electrons makes color pictures possible on the screens of these CRTs.

FIGURE 4.7
Schematic of a cathode ray tube. A stream of electrons passes between the electrodes. The fast-moving particles excite the gas in the tube, causing a glow between the plates.

FIGURE 4.8
A CRT being used to display computer graphics.

4.6 Introduction to the Modern Concept of Atomic Structure

AIM: To understand some important features of subatomic particles.

In the years since Thomson and Rutherford, a great deal has been learned about atomic structure. The simplest view of the atom is that it consists of a tiny nucleus (about 10^{-13} cm in diameter) and electrons that move about the nucleus at an average distance of about 10^{-8} cm from it (Figure 4.9). To visualize how small the nucleus is compared with the size of the atom, consider that if the nucleus were the size of a grape, the electrons would be about one *mile* away on average. The nucleus contains protons, which have a positive charge equal in magnitude to the electron's negative charge, and neutrons, which have almost the same mass as a proton but no charge. The neutrons' function in the nucleus is not obvious. They may help hold the protons (which repel each other) together to form the nucleus, but we will not be concerned with that here. The relative masses and charges of the electron, proton, and neutron are shown in Table 4.4.

An important question arises at this point: *"If all atoms are composed of these same components, why do different atoms have different chemical properties?"* The answer lies in the number and arrangement of the electrons. The space in which the electrons move accounts for most of the atomic volume. The electrons are the parts of atoms that "intermingle" when atoms combine to form molecules. Therefore, the number of electrons a given atom possesses greatly affects the way it can interact with other atoms. As a result, atoms of different elements, which have different numbers of electrons, show different chemical behavior. Although the atoms of different elements also differ in their numbers of protons, it is the number of electrons that really determines chemical behavior. We will discuss how this happens in later chapters.

In this model the atom is called a nuclear atom because the positive charge is localized in a small, compact structure (the nucleus) and not spread out uniformly, as in the plum pudding view.

The *chemistry* of an atom arises from its electrons.

Nucleus

$\sim 10^{-13}$cm

FIGURE 4.9
A nuclear atom viewed in cross section. (The symbol $\sim$ means approximately.) This drawing does not show the actual scale. The nucleus is actually *much* smaller compared with the size of an atom.

TABLE 4.4

The Mass and Charge of the Electron, Proton, and Neutron

Particle	Relative Mass*	Relative Charge
electron	1	1−
proton	1836	1+
neutron	1839	none

*The electron is arbitrarily assigned a mass of 1 for comparison.

4.7 Isotopes

AIMS: To learn about the terms isotope, atomic number, and mass number.
To understand the use of the symbol $^A_Z X$ to describe a given atom.

We have seen that an atom has a nucleus with a positive charge due to its protons and has electrons in the space surrounding the nucleus at relatively large distances from it.

As an example, consider a sodium atom, which has 11 protons in its nucleus. Because an atom has no overall charge, the number of electrons must equal the number of protons. Therefore, a sodium atom has 11 electrons in the space around its nucleus. It is *always* true that a sodium atom has 11 protons and 11 electrons. However, each sodium atom also has neutrons in its nucleus, and different types of sodium atoms exist that have different numbers of neutrons.

When Dalton stated his atomic theory in the early 1800s, he assumed all of the atoms of a given element were identical. This idea persisted for over a hundred years, until James Chadwick discovered that the nuclei of most atoms contain neutrons as well as protons. (This is a good example of how a theory changes as new observations are made.) After the discovery of the neutron, Dalton's statement that all atoms of a given element are identical had to be changed to "All atoms of the same element contain the same number of protons and electrons, but atoms of a given element may have different numbers of neutrons."

To illustrate this idea, consider the sodium atoms represented in Figure 4.10. These atoms are **isotopes,** or *atoms with the same number of protons but different numbers of neutrons.* The number of protons in a nucleus is called the atom's **atomic number.** The *sum* of the number of neutrons and the number of protons in a given nucleus is called the atom's **mass number.** To specify which of the isotopes of an element we are talking about, we use the symbol

$$^A_Z X$$

All atoms of the same element have the same number of protons (the element's atomic number) and the same number of electrons.

In a free atom, the positive and negative charges always balance to yield a net zero charge.

Atomic number: the number of protons.
Mass number: the sum of protons and neutrons.

FIGURE 4.10
Two isotopes of sodium. Both have 11 protons and 11 electrons, but they differ in the number of neutrons in their nuclei.

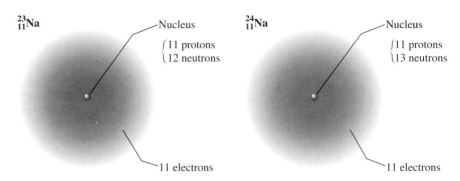

$^{23}_{11}$Na

Nucleus
{ 11 protons
12 neutrons

$^{24}_{11}$Na

Nucleus
{ 11 protons
13 neutrons

11 electrons

11 electrons

where

X = the symbol of the element

A = the mass number (number of protons and neutrons)

Z = the atomic number (number of protons)

For example, the symbol for one particular type of sodium atom is written

The particular atom represented here is called sodium-23, because it has a mass number of 23. Let's specify the number of each type of subatomic particle. From the atomic number 11 we know that the nucleus contains 11 protons. And because the number of electrons is equal to the number of protons, we know that this atom contains 11 electrons. How many neutrons are present? We can calculate the number of neutrons from the definition of the mass number

Mass number = number of protons + number of neutrons

or, in symbols,

$$A = Z + \text{number of neutrons}$$

We can isolate (solve for) the number of neutrons by subtracting Z from both sides of the equation

$$A - Z = Z - Z + \text{number of neutrons}$$

$$A - Z = \text{number of neutrons}$$

This is a general result. You can always determine the number of neutrons present in a given atom by subtracting the atomic number from the mass number. In this case ($^{23}_{11}\text{Na}$), we know that $A = 23$ and $Z = 11$. Thus

$$A - Z = 23 - 11 = 12 = \text{number of neutrons}$$

In summary, sodium-23 has 11 electrons, 11 protons, and 12 neutrons.

EXAMPLE 4.2   *Interpreting Symbols for Isotopes*

In nature, elements are usually found as a mixture of isotopes. Three isotopes of elemental carbon are $^{12}_{6}\text{C}$ (carbon-12), $^{13}_{6}\text{C}$ (carbon-13), and $^{14}_{6}\text{C}$ (carbon-14). Determine the number of each of the three types of subatomic particles in each of these carbon atoms.

Solution

The number of protons and electrons is the same in each of the isotopes and is given by the atomic number of carbon, 6. The number of neutrons can be determined by subtracting the atomic number (Z) from the mass number:

$$A - Z = \text{number of neutrons}$$

The numbers of neutrons in the three isotopes of carbon are

$^{12}_{6}\text{C}$: number of neutrons $= A - Z = 12 - 6 = 6$

$^{13}_{6}\text{C}$: number of neutrons $= 13 - 6 = 7$

$^{14}_{6}\text{C}$: number of neutrons $= 14 - 6 = 8$

In summary,

Symbol	Number of Protons	Number of Electrons	Number of Neutrons
$^{12}_{6}\text{C}$	6	6	6
$^{13}_{6}\text{C}$	6	6	7
$^{14}_{6}\text{C}$	6	6	8

 Self-Check Exercise 4.2

Give the number of protons, neutrons, and electrons in the atom symbolized by $^{90}_{38}$ Sr. Strontium-90 occurs in fallout from nuclear testing. It can accumulate in bone marrow and may cause leukemia and bone cancer.

See Problems 4.39 and 4.40.

 Self-Check Exercise 4.3

Give the number of protons, neutrons, and electrons in the atom symbolized by $^{201}_{80}$Hg.

See Problems 4.39 and 4.40.

Magnesium burns in air to give a bright white flame.

EXAMPLE 4.3   *Writing Symbols for Isotopes*

Write the symbol for the magnesium atom (atomic number 12) with a mass number of 24. How many electrons and how many neutrons does this atom have?

Solution

The atomic number 12 means the atom has 12 protons. The element magnesium is symbolized by Mg. The atom is represented as

$$^{24}_{12}\text{Mg}$$

and is called magnesium-24. Because the atom has 12 protons, it must also have 12 electrons. The mass number gives the total number of protons and neutrons, which means that this atom has 12 neutrons ($24 - 12 = 12$).

EXAMPLE 4.4   *Calculating Mass Number*

Write the symbol for the silver atom ($Z = 47$) that has 61 neutrons.

Solution

The element symbol is ^A_ZAg, where we know that $Z = 47$. We can find A from its definition, $A = Z +$ number of neutrons. In this case,

$$A = 47 + 61 = 108$$

The complete symbol for this atom is $^{108}_{47}\text{Ag}$.

 Self-Check Exercise 4.4

Give the symbol for the phosphorus atom ($Z = 15$) that contains 17 neutrons.

See Problems 4.41 and 4.42.

4.8   Introduction to the Periodic Table

AIMS: To learn about various features of the periodic table. To learn some of the properties of metals, nonmetals, and metalloids.

In any room where chemistry is taught or practiced, you are almost certain to find a chart called the **periodic table** hanging on the wall. This chart shows all of the known elements and gives a good deal of information about each. As our study of chemistry progresses, the usefulness of the periodic table will become more obvious. This section will simply introduce it.

A simple version of the periodic table is shown in Figure 4.11. Note that each box of this table contains a number written over one or two letters. The letters are the symbols for the elements. The number shown above each symbol is the atomic number (the number of protons and also the number of electrons) for that element. For example, carbon (C) has atomic number 6:

```
┌──────┐
│  6   │
│  C   │
└──────┘
```

and lead (Pb) has atomic number 82:

```
┌──────┐
│  82  │
│  Pb  │
└──────┘
```

Notice that elements 104 through 111 have unusual three-letter designations beginning with U. These are abbreviations for the systematic names of the atomic numbers of these elements. Alternative names for elements 104 through 109 have been suggested by various groups in the scientific community. They are listed on page 102.

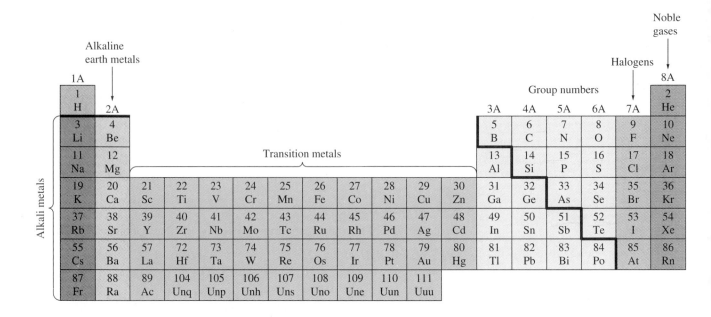

FIGURE 4.11
The periodic table.

Element	Suggested Names	Suggested Symbols
104	rutherfordium or dubnium	Rf or Db
105	hahnium or joliotium	Ha or Jl
106	seaborgium or rutherfordium	Sg or Rf
107	nielsbohrium or bohrium	Ns or Bh
108	hassium or hahnium	Hs or Hn
109	meitnerium	Mt

Mendeleev actually arranged the elements in order of increasing atomic weight rather than atomic number.

These names are now being considered for approval in the scientific community. Elements 110 and 111 have not yet been named.

Note that the elements are listed on the periodic table in order of increasing atomic number. They are also arranged in specific horizontal rows and vertical columns. The elements were first arranged in this way in 1869 by Dmitri Mendeleev, a Russian scientist. Mendeleev arranged the elements in this way because of similarities in the chemical properties of various "families" of elements. For example, fluorine and chlorine are reactive gases that form similar compounds. It was also known that sodium and potassium behave very similarly. Thus the name *periodic table* refers to the fact that as we increase the atomic numbers, every so often an element occurs with properties similar to those of an earlier (lower-atomic-number) element. For example, the elements

9 F
17 Cl
35 Br
53 I
85 At

all show similar chemical behavior and so are listed vertically, as a "family" of elements.

These families of elements with similar chemical properties that lie in the same vertical column on the periodic table are called **groups.** Groups are often referred to by the number over the column (see Figure 4.11). Note that the group numbers are accompanied by the letter A on the periodic table in Figure 4.11 and the one inside the front cover of the text. For simplicity we will delete the As when we refer to groups in the text. Many of the groups have special names. For example, the first column of elements (Group 1) has the name **alkali metals.** The Group 2 elements are called **alkaline earth metals,** the Group 7 elements are the **halogens,** and the elements in Group 8 are called the **noble gases.** A large collection of elements that spans many vertical columns consists of the **transition metals.**

Most of the elements are **metals.** Metals have the following characteristic physical properties:

Physical Properties of Metals

1. Efficient conduction of heat and electricity

2. Malleability (they can be hammered into thin sheets)

3. Ductility (they can be pulled into wires)

4. A lustrous (shiny) appearance

For example, copper is a typical metal. It is lustrous (although it tarnishes readily); it is an excellent conductor of electricity (it is widely used in electrical wires); and it is readily formed into various shapes, such as pipes for water systems. Copper is one of the transition metals—the metals shown in

Throughout the text, we will highlight the location of various elements by presenting a small version of the periodic table.

There's another convention recommended by the International Union of Pure and Applied Chemistry for group designations that uses numbers 1 through 18 and includes the transition metals. Do not confuse that system with the one used in this text, where only the representative elements have group numbers (1 through 8).

Rolls of copper pipe for use in plumbing systems. Copper is a transition metal.

FIGURE 4.12
The elements classified as metals and as nonmetals.

Nonmetals sometimes have one or more metallic properties. For example, solid iodine is lustrous, and graphite (a form of pure carbon) conducts electricity.

Elemental sulfur occurs in large deposits in the southern United States.

the center of the periodic table. Iron, aluminum, and gold are other familiar elements that have metallic properties. All of the elements shown to the left and below of the heavy "stair-step" black line in Figure 4.11 are classified as metals, except for hydrogen (Figure 4.12).

The relatively small number of elements that appear in the upper right-hand corner of the periodic table (to the right of the heavy line in Figures 4.11 and 4.12) are called **nonmetals.** Nonmetals generally lack those properties that characterize metals and show much more variation in their properties than metals do. Whereas almost all metals are solids at normal temperatures, many nonmetals (such as nitrogen, oxygen, chlorine, and neon) are gaseous and one (bromine) is a liquid. Several nonmetals (such as carbon, phosphorus, and sulfur) are also solids.

The elements that lie close to the "stair-step" line in Figure 4.11 often show a mixture of metallic and nonmetallic properties. These elements, which are called **metalloids** or **semimetals,** include boron, silicon, germanium, arsenic, antimony, and tellurium.

As we continue our study of chemistry, we will see that the periodic table is a valuable tool for organizing accumulated knowledge and that it helps us predict the properties we expect a given element to exhibit. We will also develop a model for atomic structure that will explain why there are groups of elements with similar chemical properties.

EXAMPLE 4.5 *Interpreting the Periodic Table*

For each of the following elements, use the periodic table in the front of the book to give the symbol and atomic number and to specify whether the element is a metal or a nonmetal. Also give the named family to which the element belongs (if any).

a. iodine

b. magnesium

c. gold

d. lithium

Solution

a. Iodine (symbol I) is element 53 (its atomic number is 53). Iodine lies to the right of the stair-step line in Figure 4.12 and thus is a nonmetal. Iodine is a member of Group 7, the family of halogens.

b. Magnesium (symbol Mg) is element 12 (atomic number 12). Magnesium is a metal and is a member of the alkaline earth metal family (Group 2).

c. Gold (symbol Au) is element 79 (atomic number 79). Gold is a metal and is not a member of a named vertical family. It is classed as a transition metal.

d. Lithium (symbol Li) is element 3 (atomic number 3). Lithium is a metal in the alkali metal family (Group 1).

 Self-Check Exercise 4.5

Give the symbol and atomic number for each of the following elements. Also indicate whether each element is a metal or a nonmetal and whether it is a member of a named family.

a. argon   c. barium
b. chlorine   d. cesium

See Problems 4.53 and 4.54.

4.9   Natural States of the Elements

AIM: To learn the natures of the common elements.

A gold nugget weighing 13 lb, 7 oz, that came to be called Tom's Baby, was found by Tom Grove near Breckenridge, Colorado, on July 23, 1887.

Group 8
| He |
| Ne |
| Ar |
| Kr |
| Xe |
| Rn |

Recall that a molecule is a collection of atoms that behaves as a unit. Molecules are always electrically neutral (zero charge).

As we have noted, the matter around us consists mainly of mixtures. Most often these mixtures contain compounds, in which atoms from different elements are bound together. Most elements are quite reactive: their atoms tend to combine with those of other elements to form compounds. Thus we do not often find elements in nature in pure form—uncombined with other elements. However, there are notable exceptions. The gold nuggets found at Sutter's Mill in California that launched the Gold Rush in 1849 are virtually pure elemental gold. And platinum and silver are often found in nearly pure form.

Gold, silver, and platinum are members of a class of metals called *noble metals* because they are relatively unreactive. (The term *noble* implies a class set apart.)

Other elements that appear in nature in the uncombined state are the elements in Group 8: helium, neon, argon, krypton, xenon, and radon. Because the atoms of these elements do not combine readily with those of other elements, we call them the **noble gases.** For example, helium gas is found in uncombined form in underground deposits with natural gas.

When we take a sample of air (the mixture of gases that constitute the earth's atmosphere) and separate it into its components, we find several pure elements present. One of these is argon. Argon gas consists of a collection of separate argon atoms, as shown in Figure 4.13.

Air also contains nitrogen gas and oxygen gas. When we examine these two gases, however, we find that they do not contain single atoms, as argon does, but instead contain **diatomic molecules:** molecules made up of *two atoms,* as represented in Figure 4.14. In fact, any sample of elemental oxygen

FIGURE 4.13
Argon gas consists of a collection of separate argon atoms.

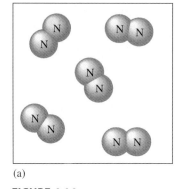

(a)   (b)

FIGURE 4.14
Gaseous nitrogen and oxygen contain diatomic (two-atom) molecules. (a) Nitrogen gas contains N—N (N_2) molecules. (b) Oxygen gas contains O—O (O_2) molecules.

gas at normal temperatures contains O_2 molecules. Likewise, nitrogen gas contains N_2 molecules.

Hydrogen is another element that forms diatomic molecules. Though virtually all of the hydrogen found on earth is present in compounds with other elements (such as with oxygen in water), when hydrogen is prepared as a free element it contains diatomic H_2 molecules. For example, an electric current can be used to decompose water (see Figure 4.15 below and Figure 3.3 on p. 61) into elemental hydrogen and oxygen containing H_2 and O_2 molecules, respectively.

Several other elements, in addition to hydrogen, nitrogen, and oxygen, exist as diatomic molecules. For example, when sodium chloride is melted and subjected to an electric current, chlorine gas is produced (along with sodium metal). This chemical change is represented in Figure 4.16. Chlorine gas is a pale green gas that contains Cl_2 molecules.

Chlorine is a member of Group 7, the halogen family. All the elemental forms of the Group 7 elements contain diatomic molecules. Fluorine is a pale yellow gas containing F_2 molecules. Bromine is a brown liquid made up of Br_2 molecules. Iodine is a lustrous, purple solid that contains I_2 molecules.

The only elemental hydrogen found naturally on earth occurs in the exhaust gases of volcanoes.

Water molecules ⟶ Diatomic hydrogen molecules + Diatomic oxygen molecule

FIGURE 4.15
The decomposition of two water molecules (H_2O) to form two hydrogen molecules (H_2) and an oxygen molecule (O_2). Note that only the grouping of the atoms changes in this process; no atoms are created or destroyed. There must be the same number of H atoms and O atoms before and after the process. Thus the decomposition of two H_2O molecules (containing four H atoms and two O atoms) yields one O_2 molecule (containing two O atoms) and two H_2 molecules (containing a total of four H atoms).

(a)

(b)

(c)

FIGURE 4.16

(a) Sodium chloride (common table salt) can be decomposed by an electric current to give (b) chlorine gas and (c) sodium metal, shown here being cut by a knife.

~ means "approximately."

Platinum is a noble metal used in jewelry and in many industrial processes.

Liquid bromine in a flask with bromine vapor.

Table 4.5 lists the elements that contain diatomic molecules in their pure, elemental forms.

So far we have seen that several elements are gaseous in their elemental forms at normal temperatures (~25 °C). The noble gases (the Group 8 elements) contain individual atoms, whereas several other gaseous elements contain diatomic molecules (H_2, N_2, O_2, F_2, and Cl_2).

Only two elements are liquids in their elemental forms at 25 °C: the non-metal bromine (containing Br_2 molecules) and the metal mercury. The metals gallium and cesium almost qualify in this category; they are solids at 25 °C, but both melt at ~30 °C.

The other elements are solids in their elemental forms at 25 °C. For metals these solids contain large numbers of atoms packed together much like marbles in a jar (see Figure 4.17).

The structures of solid nonmetallic elements are more varied than those of metals. In fact, different forms of the same element often occur. For example, solid carbon occurs in three forms. Different forms of a given element are called *allotropes*. The three allotropes of carbon are the familiar diamond

TABLE 4.5

Elements That Exist as Diatomic Molecules in Their Elemental Forms

Element Present	Elemental State at 25 °C	Molecule
hydrogen	colorless gas	H_2
nitrogen	colorless gas	N_2
oxygen	pale blue gas	O_2
fluorine	pale yellow gas	F_2
chlorine	pale green gas	Cl_2
bromine	reddish-brown liquid	Br_2
iodine	lustrous, dark purple solid	I_2

FIGURE 4.17
In solid metals, the spherical atoms are packed closely together.

Graphite and diamond, two forms of carbon.

and graphite forms plus a form that has only recently been discovered called *buckminsterfullerene.* These elemental forms have very different properties because of their different structures (see Figure 4.18). Diamond is the hardest natural substance known and is often used for industrial cutting tools. Diamonds are also valued as gemstones. Graphite, on the other hand, is a rather soft material useful for writing (pencil "lead" is really graphite) and (in the form of a powder) for lubricating locks. The rather odd name given to buckminsterfullerene comes from the structure of the C_{60} molecules that comprise it. The soccer-ball-like structure contains 5- and 6-member rings reminiscent of the structure of geodesic domes suggested by the late industrial designer Buckminster Fuller. Other "fullerenes" containing molecules with more than 60 carbon atoms have also recently been discovered, leading to a new area of chemistry.

FIGURE 4.18
The three solid elemental (allotropes) forms of carbon: (a) diamond, (b) graphite, and (c) buckminsterfullerene. The representation of diamond and graphite are just fragments of much larger structures that extend in all directions from the parts shown here. Buckminsterfullerene contains C_{60} molecules, of which one is shown.

(a) Diamond

(b) Graphite

(c) Buckminsterfullerene

Miracle Coatings

Imagine a pair of plastic-lens sunglasses that are unscratchable, even if you drop them on concrete or rub them with sandpaper. Research may make such glasses possible, along with cutting tools that never need sharpening, special glass for windshields and buildings that cannot be scratched by wind-blown sand, and speakers that reproduce sound with a crispness unimagined until now. The secret of all these marvels is a thin diamond coating. Diamond is so hard that virtually nothing can scratch it. A thin diamond coating on a speaker cone limits resonance and gives a remarkably pure tone.

But how do you coat something with a diamond? It is nearly impossi-ble to melt diamond (melting point, 3500 °C). And even if diamond were melted, the object being coated would itself melt immediately at this temperature. Surprisingly, a diamond

coating can be applied quite easily to something even as fragile as plastic. First the surface is bathed with a mixture of gaseous methane (CH_4) and hydrogen (H_2). Next the methane is broken apart into its component elements by an energy source similar to that used in microwave ovens. The carbon atoms freed from the methane then form a thin diamond coating on the surface being treated.

The coating of soft, scratchable materials with a super-tough diamond layer should improve many types of consumer products in the near future.

Sunglasses would be unscratchable with a diamond coating.

4.10 Ions

AIMS: To understand the formation of ions from their parent atoms, and learn to name them. To learn how the periodic table can help predict which ion a given element forms.

We have seen that an atom has a certain number of protons in its nucleus and an equal number of electrons in the space around the nucleus. This results in an exact balance of positive and negative charges. We say that an atom is a neutral entity—it has *zero net charge.*

We can produce a charged entity, called an **ion,** by taking a neutral atom and adding or removing one or more electrons. For example, a sodium atom ($Z = 11$) has eleven protons in its nucleus and eleven electrons outside its nucleus.

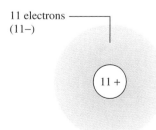

11 electrons
(11−)

11 +

Neutral sodium
atom (Na)

An ion has a net positive or negative charge.

If one of the electrons is lost, there will be eleven positive charges but only ten negative charges. This gives an ion with a net positive one (1+) charge: $(11+) + (10-) = 1+$. We can represent this process as follows:

Neutral sodium
atom (Na)

Sodium ion
(Na$^+$)

or, in shorthand form, as

$$Na \rightarrow Na^+ + e^-$$

where Na represents the neutral sodium atom, Na$^+$ represents the 1+ ion formed, and e$^-$ represents an electron.

A positive ion, called a **cation** (pronounced *cat' eye on*), is produced when one or more electrons are *lost* from a neutral atom. We have seen that sodium loses one electron to become a 1+ cation. Some atoms lose more than one electron. For example, a magnesium atom typically loses two electrons to form a 2+ cation:

Neutral magnesium
atom (Mg)

Magnesium ion
(Mg^{2+})

We usually represent this process as follows:

$$Mg \rightarrow Mg^{2+} + 2e^-$$

Aluminum forms a 3+ cation by losing three electrons:

Neutral aluminum
atom (Al)

Aluminum ion
(Al^{3+})

or

$$Al \rightarrow Al^{3+} + 3e^-$$

A cation is named using the name of the parent atom. Thus Na^+ is called the sodium ion (or sodium cation), Mg^{2+} is called the magnesium ion (or magnesium cation), and Al^{3+} is called the aluminum ion (or aluminum cation).

When electrons are *gained* by a neutral atom, an ion with a negative charge is formed. A negatively charged ion is called an **anion** (pronounced *an' ion*). An atom that gains one extra electron forms an anion with a $1-$ charge. An example of an atom that forms a $1-$ anion is the chlorine atom, which has seventeen protons and seventeen electrons:

Neutral chlorine atom (Cl)	$1-$ ion chloride (Cl^-)

or

$$Cl + e^- \rightarrow Cl^-$$

Note that the anion formed by chlorine has eighteen electrons but only seventeen protons, so the net charge is $(18-) + (17+) = 1-$. Unlike a cation, which is named for the parent atom, an anion is named by taking the root name of the atom and changing the ending. For example, the Cl^- anion produced from the Cl (chlorine) atom is called the *chloride* ion (or chloride anion). Notice that the word *chloride* is obtained from the root of the atom name (*chlor-*) plus the suffix *-ide*. Other atoms that add one electron to form $1-$ ions include

The name of an anion is obtained by adding *-ide* to the root of the atom name.

fluorine	$F + e^- \rightarrow F^-$	(*fluor*ide ion)
bromine	$Br + e^- \rightarrow Br^-$	(*brom*ide ion)
iodine	$I + e^- \rightarrow I^-$	(*iod*ide ion)

Note that the name of each of these anions is obtained by adding *-ide* to the root of the atom name.

Some atoms can add two electrons to form $2-$ anions. Examples include

oxygen	$O + 2e^- \rightarrow O^{2-}$	(*ox*ide ion)
sulfur	$S + 2e^- \rightarrow S^{2-}$	(*sulf*ide ion)

Note that the names for these anions are derived in the same way as those for the $1-$ anions.

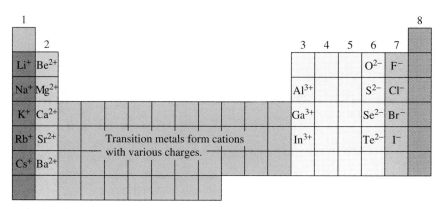

FIGURE 4.19
The ions formed by selected members of Groups 1, 2, 3, 6, and 7.

It is important to recognize that ions are always formed by removing electrons from an atom (to form cations) or adding electrons to an atom (to form anions). *Ions are never formed by changing the number of protons* in an atom's nucleus.

It is essential to understand that isolated atoms do not form ions on their own. Most commonly, ions are formed when metallic elements combine with nonmetallic elements. As we will discuss in detail in Chapter 8, when metals and nonmetals react, the metal atoms tend to lose one or more electrons, which are in turn gained by the atoms of the nonmetal. Thus reactions between metals and nonmetals tend to form compounds that contain metal cations and nonmetal anions. We will have more to say about these compounds in Section 4.11.

Ion Charges and the Periodic Table

We find the periodic table very useful when we want to know what type of ion is formed by a given atom. Figure 4.19 shows the types of ions formed by atoms in several of the groups on the periodic table. Note that the Group 1 metals all form $1+$ ions (M^+), the Group 2 metals all form 2^+ ions (M^{2+}), and the Group 3 metals form 3^+ ions (M^{3+}). Thus for groups 1 through 3 the charges of the cations formed are identical to the group numbers.

In contrast to the Group 1, 2, and 3 metals, most of the many *transition metals* form cations with various positive charges. For these elements there is no easy way to predict the charge of the cation that will be formed.

Note that metals always form positive ions. This tendency to lose electrons is a fundamental characteristic of metals. Nonmetals, on the other hand, form negative ions by gaining electrons. Note that the Group 7 atoms all gain one electron to form $1-$ ions and that all the nonmetals in Group 6 gain two electrons to form $2-$ ions.

At this point you should memorize the relationships between the group number and the type of ion formed, as shown in Figure 4.19. You will understand why these relationships exist after we further discuss the theory of the atom in Chapter 11.

For Groups 1, 2, and 3, the charges of the cations equal the group numbers.

4.11 Compounds That Contain Ions

AIM: To learn how ions combine to form neutral compounds.

Melting means that the solid, where the ions are locked into place, is changed to a liquid, where the ions can move.

Chemists have good reasons to believe that many chemical compounds contain ions. For instance, consider some of the properties of common table salt, sodium chloride (NaCl). It must be heated to about 800 °C to melt and to almost 1500 °C to boil (compare to water, which boils at 100 °C). As a solid, salt will not conduct an electric current, but when melted it is a very good conductor. Pure water will not conduct electricity (will not allow an electric current to flow), but when salt is dissolved in water, the resulting solution readily conducts electricity (see Figure 4.20).

Chemists have come to realize that we can best explain these properties of sodium chloride (NaCl) by picturing it as containing Na^+ ions and Cl^- ions packed together as shown in Figure 4.21. Because the positive and negative charges attract each other very strongly, it must be heated to a very high temperature (800 °C) before it melts.

FIGURE 4.20
(a) Pure water does not conduct a current, so the circuit is not complete and the bulb does not light. (b) Water containing a dissolved salt conducts electricity and the bulb lights.

FIGURE 4.21
(a) The arrangement of sodium ions (Na^+) and chloride ions (Cl^-) in the ionic compound sodium chloride.
(b) Solid sodium chloride highly magnified.

A substance containing ions that can move can conduct an electric current.

To explore further the significance of the electrical conductivity results, we need to discuss briefly the nature of electric currents. An electric current can travel along a metal wire because *electrons are free to move* through the wire; the moving electrons carry the current. In ionic substances the ions carry the current. Thus substances that contain ions can conduct an electric current *only if the ions can move*—the current travels by the movement of the charged ions. In solid NaCl the ions are tightly held and cannot move, but when the solid is melted and changed to a liquid, the structure is disrupted and the ions can move. As a result, an electric current can travel through the melted salt.

Dissolving NaCl causes the ions to be randomly dispersed in the water, allowing them to move freely. Dissolving is not the same as melting, but both processes free the ions to move.

The same reasoning applies to NaCl dissolved in water. When the solid dissolves, the ions are dispersed throughout the water and can move around in the water, allowing it to conduct a current.

Thus, we recognize substances that contain ions by their characteristic properties. They often have very high melting points, and they conduct an electric current when melted or when dissolved in water.

Many substances contain ions. In fact, whenever a compound forms between a metal and a nonmetal, it can be expected to contain ions. We call these substances **ionic compounds.**

An ionic compound cannot contain only anions or only cations, because the net charge of a compound must be zero.

One fact very important to remember is that *a chemical compound must have a net charge of zero.* This means that if a compound contains ions, then

1. There must be both positive ions (cations) and negative ions (anions) present.

2. The numbers of cations and anions must be such that the net charge is zero.

The net charge of a compound (zero) is the sum of the positive and negative charges.

For example, note that the formula for sodium chloride is written NaCl, indicating one of each type of these elements. This makes sense because sodium chloride contains Na^+ ions and Cl^- ions. Each sodium ion has a $1+$ charge and each chloride ion has a $1-$ charge, so they must occur in equal numbers to give a net charge of zero.

And for *any* ionic compound,

$$\begin{array}{c}\text{Total charge}\\ \text{of cations}\end{array} + \begin{array}{c}\text{Total charge}\\ \text{of anions}\end{array} = \begin{array}{c}\text{Zero}\\ \text{net charge}\end{array}$$

Consider an ionic compound that contains the ions Mg^{2+} and Cl^-. What combination of these ions will give a net charge of zero? To balance the $2+$ charge on Mg^{2+}, we will need two Cl^- ions to give a net charge of zero.

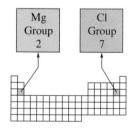

The subscript 1 in a formula is not written.

This means that the formula of the compound must be $MgCl_2$. Remember that subscripts are used to give the relative numbers of atoms (or ions).

Now consider an ionic compound that contains the ions Ba^{2+} and O^{2-}. What is the correct formula? These ions have charges of the same size (but opposite sign), so they must occur in equal numbers to give a net charge of zero. The formula of the compound is BaO, because $(2+) + (2-) = 0$.

Similarly, the formula of a compound that contains the ions Li^+ and N^{3-} is Li_3N, because three Li^+ cations are needed to balance the charge of the N^{3-} anion.

EXAMPLE 4.6 *Writing Formulas for Ionic Compounds*

The pairs of ions contained in several ionic compounds are listed below. Give the formula for each compound.

a. Ca^{2+} and Cl^- b. Na^+ and S^{2-} c. Ca^{2+} and P^{3-}

Solution

a. Ca^{2+} has a 2+ charge, so two Cl^- ions (each with the charge 1−) will be needed.

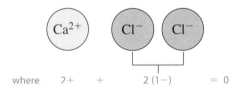

The formula is $CaCl_2$.

b. In this case S^{2-}, with its 2− charge, requires two Na^+ ions to produce a zero net charge.

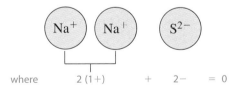

The formula is Na_2S.

c. We have the ions Ca^{2+} (charge 2+) and P^{3-} (charge 3−). We must figure out how many of each are needed to balance exactly the positive and negative charges. Let's try two Ca^{2+} and one P^{3-}.

The resulting net charge is $2(2+) + (3-) = (4+) + (3-) = 1-$. This doesn't work because the net charge is not zero. We can obtain the same total positive and total negative charges by having three Ca^{2+} ions and two P^{3-} ions.

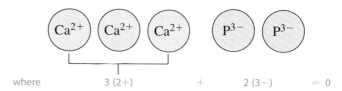

Thus the formula must be Ca_3P_2.

Self-Check Exercise 4.6

Give the formulas for the compounds that contain the following pairs of ions.

a. K^+ and I^- b. Mg^{2+} and N^{3-} c. Al^{3+} and O^{2-}

See Problems 4.83 and 4.84.

Chapter Review

Key Terms

element symbols *(4.2)*
law of constant composition *(4.3)*
Dalton's atomic theory *(4.3)*
atom *(4.3)*
compound *(4.4)*
chemical formula *(4.4)*
electron *(4.5)*
nuclear atom *(4.5)*
nucleus *(4.5)*
proton *(4.5)*
neutron *(4.5)*
isotopes *(4.7)*
atomic number, Z *(4.7)*
mass number, A *(4.7)*

periodic table *(4.8)*
groups *(4.8)*
alkali metals *(4.8)*
alkaline earth metals *(4.8)*
halogens *(4.8)*
noble gases *(4.8)*
transition metals *(4.8)*
metals *(4.8)*
nonmetals *(4.8)*
metalloids (semimetals) *(4.8)*
diatomic molecule *(4.9)*
ion *(4.10)*
cation *(4.10)*
anion *(4.10)*
ionic compound *(4.11)*

Summary

1. Of the 111 different elements now known, only 9 account for about 98% of the total mass of the earth's crust, oceans, and atmosphere. In the human body, oxygen, carbon, hydrogen, and nitrogen are the most abundant elements.

2. Elements are represented by symbols that usually consist of the first one or two letters of the element's name. Sometimes, however, the symbol is taken from the element's original Latin or Greek name.

3. The law of constant composition states that a given compound always contains the same proportions by mass of the elements of which it is composed.

4. Dalton accounted for this law with his atomic theory. He postulated that all elements are composed of atoms; that all atoms of a given element are identical, but that atoms of different elements are different; that chemical compounds are formed when atoms combine; and that atoms are not created or destroyed in chemical reactions.

5. A compound can be represented by a chemical formula that uses the symbol for each type of atom and gives the number of each type of atom that appears in a molecule of the compound.

6. Atoms consist of a nucleus containing protons and neutrons, surrounded by electrons that occupy a large volume relative to the size of the nucleus. Electrons have a relatively small mass (1/1836 of the proton mass) and a

negative charge. Protons have a positive charge equal in magnitude (but opposite in sign) to that of the electron. A neutron has a slightly greater mass than the proton but no charge.

7. Isotopes are atoms with the same number of protons but different numbers of neutrons.

8. The periodic table displays the elements in rows and columns in order of increasing atomic number. Elements that have similar chemical properties fall into vertical columns called groups. Most of the elements are metals. These occur on the left-hand side of the periodic table; the nonmetals appear on the right-hand side.

9. Each chemical element is composed of a given type of atom. These elements may exist as individual atoms or as groups of like atoms. For example, the noble gases contain single, separated atoms. However, elements such as oxygen, nitrogen, and chlorine exist as diatomic (two-atom) molecules.

10. When an atom loses one or more electrons, it forms a positive ion called a cation. This behavior is characteristic of metals. When an atom gains one or more electrons, it becomes a negatively charged ion called an anion. This behavior is characteristic of nonmetals. Oppositely charged ions form ionic compounds. A compound is always neutral overall—it has zero net charge.

11. The elements in Groups 1 and 2 on the periodic table form 1+ and 2+ cations, respectively. Group 7 atoms can gain one electron to form 1− ions. Group 6 atoms form 2− ions.

Questions and Problems

All even-numbered exercises have answers in the back of this book and solutions in the Solutions Guide.

4.1 ■ The Elements

QUESTIONS

1. The ancient Greeks believed that all matter was composed of four fundamental substances: earth, air, fire, and water. How does this early conception of matter compare with our modern theories about matter?

2. Although they were not able to transform base metals into gold, what contributions did the alchemists make to the development of chemistry?

3. In addition to his important work on the properties of gases, what other valuable contributions did Robert Boyle make to the development of the study of chemistry?

4. How many elements are presently known? How many of these elements occur naturally, and how many are synthesized artificially? What are the most common elements present on the earth?

5. Oxygen, the most abundant element on the earth, makes up a large percentage of the atmosphere. Where else is oxygen found? Is oxygen found more commonly as an element or in compounds?

6. What are the most abundant elements found in living creatures? Are these elements also the most abundant elements found in the nonliving world?

4.2 ■ Symbols for the Elements

Note: Refer to the tables on the inside front cover when appropriate.

QUESTIONS

7. Give the symbols and names for the elements whose chemical symbols consist of only one letter.

8. In some cases, the symbol of an element does not seem to bear any relationship to the name we use for the element. Generally, the symbol for such an element is based on its name in another language. Give the symbols and names for five examples of such elements.

9. Give the chemical symbol for each of the following elements.
   a. tin
   b. lead
   c. carbon
   d. lithium
   e. cobalt
   f. copper

10. Give the chemical symbol for each of the following elements.
   a. hydrogen
   b. iron
   c. magnesium
   d. calcium
   e. gold
   f. helium

11. Give the chemical symbol for each of the following elements.
   a. aluminum
   b. arsenic
   c. argon
   d. antimony
   e. fluorine

12. Use the periodic table inside the front cover of this book to look up the symbol or name for each of the following less common elements.

Symbol	Name
Ir	————
————	tantalum
————	bismuth
Pu	————
Fr	————
————	astatine

13. For each of the following chemical symbols, give the name of the corresponding element.
    a. U
    b. Fe
    c. Au
    d. Sn
    e. Sb
    f. Si
    g. Sr
    h. S

14. For each of the following chemical symbols, give the name of the corresponding element.
    a. Co
    b. Ag
    c. Cl
    d. Al
    e. Zn
    f. Pt
    g. Cr
    h. Na

4.3 ■ *Dalton's Atomic Theory*

QUESTIONS

15. Indicate whether each of the following statements is true or false. If a statement is false, correct the statement so that it becomes true.
    a. Most materials occur in nature as pure substances.
    b. A given compound usually contains the same relative number of atoms of its various elements.
    c. Atoms are made up of tiny particles called molecules.

16. What does the "law of constant composition" tell us? How did Dalton's atomic theory help to explain this law? Give examples.

4.4 ■ *Formulas of Compounds*

QUESTIONS

17. What is a compound?

18. A given compound always contains the same relative masses of its constituent elements. How is this related to the relative numbers of each kind of atom present?

19. Write the formula for each of the following substances, listing the elements in the order given.
    a. a molecule containing one phosphorus atom and three chlorine atoms
    b. a molecule containing two boron atoms and six hydrogen atoms
    c. a compound containing one calcium atom for every two chlorine atoms
    d. a molecule containing one carbon atom and four bromine atoms
    e. a compound containing two iron atoms for every three oxygen atoms
    f. a molecule containing three hydrogen atoms, one phosphorus atom, and four oxygen atoms.

20. Using pens having different color inks, and using circles of different colors to represent different atoms, write "formulas" for each of the following "substances." (A chemical example for each type of formula is given in parentheses.)
    a. a molecule containing two blue atoms and one red atom (H_2O)
    b. a molecule containing two blue atoms, one red atom, and four green atoms (H_2SO_4)
    c. a substance containing one blue atom, one red atom, and three green atoms ($NaNO_3$)
    d. a molecule containing three red atoms for every two blue atoms (Ca_3P_2)
    e. a molecule such as acetylene (C_2H_2), which contains two atoms of one type (red) and two atoms of another type (blue)
    f. a substance such as $Ca_3(PO_4)_2$, containing three atoms of one type (red), two atoms of a second type (blue), and eight atoms of a third type (green)

4.5 ■ *The Structure of the Atom*

QUESTIONS

21. Indicate whether each of the following statements is true or false. If a statement is false, correct the statement so that it becomes true.
    a. In his cathode ray tube experiments, J. J. Thomson obtained beams of different types of particles whose nature depended on which gas was contained in the tube.
    b. Thomson assumed that there must be positively charged particles in the atom, since isolated atoms have no overall charge.
    c. In the plum pudding model of the atom, the atom was envisioned as a sphere of negative charge in which positively charged electrons were randomly distributed.

22. Indicate whether each of the following statements is true or false. If false, correct the statement so that it becomes true.
    a. Rutherford's bombardment experiments with metal foil suggested that the alpha particles were being deflected by coming near a large, negatively charged atomic nucleus.
    b. The proton and the electron have similar masses but opposite electrical charges.
    c. Most atoms also contain neutrons, which are slightly heavier than protons but carry no charge.

4.6 ■ *Introduction to the Modern Concept of Atomic Structure*

QUESTIONS

23. The nucleus of an atom contains ————, which are positively charged.

24. The nucleus of an atom may also contain ————, which are uncharged.

25. How do the masses of the subatomic particles compare on a relative basis? Do the proton and neutron have exactly the same mass?

26. The proton and the (electron/neutron) have almost equal masses. The proton and the (electron/neutron) have charges that are equal in magnitude but opposite in nature.

27. An average atomic nucleus has a diameter of about ———— m.

28. Although the nucleus of an atom is very important, it is the ———— of the atom that determine its chemical properties.

4.7 ■ *Isotopes*

QUESTIONS

29. True or false? Atoms that have the same number of neutrons but different numbers of protons are called isotopes.

30. True or false? The mass number of a nucleus represents the number of protons in the nucleus.

31. For an atom, the number of protons and electrons is (different/the same).

32. The ———— number represents the sum of the number of protons and neutrons in a nucleus.

33. How did Dalton's atomic theory have to be modified after the discovery that several isotopes of an element may exist?

34. Are all atoms of the same element identical? If not, how can they differ?

35. For each of the following atomic numbers, write the name and chemical symbol of the corresponding element. (Refer to Figure 4.11.)
    a. 46
    b. 78
    c. 15
    d. 94
    e. 5
    f. 4
    g. 56
    h. 83

36. For each of the following elements, use the periodic table on the inside cover of this book to write the element's atomic number.

    a. Rb, rubidium
    b. V, vanadium
    c. Pd, palladium
    d. Zn, zinc
    e. I, iodine
    f. Am, americium
    g. Bi, bismuth
    h. Mo, molybdenum

37. Write the atomic symbol ($_Z^A X$) for each of the isotopes described below.
    a. $Z = 8$, number of neutrons = 9
    b. the isotope of chlorine in which $A = 37$
    c. $Z = 27$, $A = 60$
    d. number of protons = 26, number of neutrons = 31
    e. the isotope of I with a mass number of 131
    f. $Z = 3$, number of neutrons = 4

38. Write the atomic symbol for each of the atoms described below.
    a. $Z = 25$, $A = 55$
    b. atomic number = 12, number of neutrons = 13
    c. the isotope with 20 protons and 21 neutrons in its nucleus
    d. the isotope of iron with 30 neutrons in its nucleus
    e. $Z = 92$, number of neutrons = 146
    f. mass number = 244, number of protons = 94

39. How many protons and neutrons are contained in the nucleus of each of the following atoms. Assuming each atom is unchanged, how many electrons are present?
    a. $_{94}^{244}Pu$
    b. $_{95}^{241}Am$
    c. $_{89}^{227}Ac$
    d. $_{55}^{132}Cs$
    e. $_{77}^{193}Ir$
    f. $_{25}^{56}Mn$

40. How many protons and neutrons are contained in the nucleus of each of the following atoms? In an uncharged atom of each element, how many electrons are present?
    a. $_{27}^{60}Co$
    b. $_{16}^{33}S$
    c. $_{4}^{10}Be$
    d. $_{18}^{40}Ar$
    e. $_{11}^{23}Na$
    f. $_{36}^{84}Kr$

41. Complete the following table.

Name	Symbol	Atomic Number	Mass Number	Neutrons
sodium	——	11	23	——
nitrogen	$_7^{15}N$	——	——	——
——	$_{56}^{136}Ba$	——	——	——
lithium	——	——	——	6
boron	——	5	11	——

42. Complete the following table.

Name	Neutrons	Atomic Number	Mass Number	Symbol
nitrogen	6	——	14	——
——	——	7	——	——
lead	——	——	206	——
——	31	26	——	——
——	——	——	——	$_{36}^{84}Kr$

4.8 ■ *Introduction to the Periodic Table*

QUESTIONS

43. How are the elements ordered in the periodic table?

44. True or false? The horizontal rows in the periodic table are referred to as "groups" or "families" because these elements have similar chemical properties.

45. List the characteristic physical properties that distinguish the metallic elements from the nonmetallic elements.

46. Where are the metallic elements found on the periodic table? Are there more metallic elements or nonmetallic elements?

47. Under ordinary conditions, what physical state is most common for the metallic elements? Are there any common exceptions?

48. Give several examples of nonmetallic elements that occur in the gaseous state under ordinary conditions.

49. Under ordinary conditions, only a few pure elements occur as liquids. Give an example of a metallic and a nonmetallic element that ordinarily occur as liquids.

50. Where are the metalloids found on the periodic table? Give two examples of elements that are metalloids.

51. Write the number and name (if any) of the group (family) to which each of the following elements belongs.
    a. cesium   e. strontium
    b. Ra   f. Xe
    c. Rn   g. Rb
    d. chlorine

52. Write the number and name (if any) of the group (family) to which each of the following elements belongs.
    a. krypton   e. Na
    b. bromine   f. barium
    c. K   g. Ne
    d. aluminum   h. fluorine

53. For each of the following elements, use the table on the inside front cover of the book to give the chemical symbol and atomic number and to specify whether the element is a metal or a nonmetal. Also give the named family to which the element belongs (if any).
    a. rubidium   c. tellurium
    b. magnesium   d. astatine

54. For each of the following elements, use the tables on the inside cover of the book to give the chemical symbol, atomic number, and group number of each element, and to specify whether each element is a metal, metalloid, or nonmetal.

a. rubidium   d. titanium
b. germanium   e. iodine
c. magnesium

4.9 ■ *Natural States of the Elements*

QUESTIONS

55. Most substances contain _____ rather than elemental substances.

56. Are most of the chemical elements found in nature in the elemental form or combined in compounds? Why?

57. The noble gas present in relatively large concentrations in the atmosphere is _____.

58. Why are the elements of Group 8 referred to as the noble or inert gas elements?

59. Molecules of nitrogen gas and oxygen gas are said to be _____, which means they consist of pairs of atoms.

60. Give three examples of gaseous elements that exist as diatomic molecules. Give three examples of gaseous elements that exist as monatomic species.

61. A simple way to generate elemental hydrogen gas is to pass _____ through water.

62. If sodium chloride (table salt) is melted and then subjected to an electric current, elemental _____ gas is produced, along with sodium metal.

63. What four elemental substances exist in the liquid state at or near room temperature?

64. The two most common elemental forms of carbon are graphite and _____.

4.10 ■ *Ions*

QUESTIONS

65. An isolated atom has a net charge of _____.

66. Ions are formed when an atom gains or loses _____; they never involve a change in the atom's nucleus.

67. When an atom loses one electron, the ion formed has a charge of _____.

68. An ion with two more protons than electrons has a charge of _____.

69. Positive ions are called _____, whereas negative ions are called _____.

70. Simple negative ions formed from single atoms are given names that end in _____.

71. The tendency to *lose* electrons is a fundamental property of the _____ elements.

72. The tendency to *gain* electrons is a fundamental property of the _____ elements.

73. For each of the positive ions listed in column 1, use the periodic table to find in column 2 the total number of electrons that ion contains. The same answer may be used more than once.

Column 1	Column 2
[1] Al^{3+}	[a] 2
[2] Fe^{3+}	[b] 10
[3] Mg^{2+}	[c] 21
[4] Sn^{2+}	[d] 23
[5] Co^{2+}	[e] 24
[6] Co^{3+}	[f] 25
[7] Li^+	[g] 36
[8] Cr^{3+}	[h] 48
[9] Rb^+	[i] 76
[10] Pt^{2+}	[j] 81

74. For each of the following ions, indicate the total number of protons and electrons in the ion. For the positive ions in the list, predict the formula of the simplest compound formed between each positive ion and the chloride ion, Cl^-. For the negative ions in the list, predict the formula of the simplest compound formed between each negative ion and the sodium ion, Na^+.
    a. Fe^{2+}
    b. Fe^{3+}
    c. Ba^{2+}
    d. Cs^+
    e. S^{2-}
    f. P^{3-}
    g. Br^-
    h. O^{2-}

75. For the following processes that show the formation of ions, use the periodic table to indicate the number of electrons and protons present in both the *ion* and the *neutral atom* from which it is made.
    a. $K \rightarrow K^+ + e^-$
    b. $Ba \rightarrow Ba^{2+} + 2e^-$
    c. $C + 4e^- \rightarrow C^{4-}$
    d. $Sr \rightarrow Sr^{2+} + 2e^-$
    e. $O + 2e^- \rightarrow O^{2-}$
    f. $I + e^- \rightarrow I^-$

76. For the following processes that show the formation of ions, fill in the number of electrons that must be lost or gained to complete the process.
    a. $Sr \rightarrow Sr^{2+} +$ _____ e^-
    b. $Se +$ _____ $e^- \rightarrow Se^{2-}$
    c. $Fe \rightarrow Fe^{2+} +$ _____ e^-
    d. $P +$ _____ $e^- \rightarrow P^{3-}$
    e. $Br +$ _____ $e^- \rightarrow Br^-$
    f. $Au \rightarrow Au^{3+} +$ _____ e^-

77. For each of the following atomic numbers, use the periodic table to write the formula (including the charge) for the simple *ion* that the element is most likely to form.

    a. 85
    b. 88
    c. 34
    d. 56
    e. 13
    f. 38

78. On the basis of its location on the periodic table, indicate what simple ion each of the following elements is most likely to form.
    a. Ra ($Z = 88$)
    b. Te ($Z = 52$)
    c. I ($Z = 53$)
    d. Fr ($Z = 87$)
    e. At ($Z = 85$)
    f. Rn ($Z = 86$)

4.11 ■ Compounds That Contain Ions

QUESTIONS

79. List some properties of a substance that would lead you to believe it consists of ions. How do these properties differ from those of nonionic compounds?

80. Why does a solution of sodium chloride in water conduct an electric current, whereas a solution of sugar in water does not?

81. Why does an ionic compound conduct an electric current when the compound is melted but not when it is in the solid state?

82. Why must the total number of positive charges in an ionic compound equal the total number of negative charges?

83. For the following pairs of ions, use the principle of electrical neutrality to predict the formula of the binary compound that the ions are most likely to form.
    a. Mg^{2+} and I^-
    b. Ti^{4+} and O^{2-}
    c. Cr^{3+} and O^{2-}
    d. Rb^+ and N^{3-}
    e. Fe^{3+} and O^{2-}
    f. Fe^{2+} and O^{2-}
    g. Ba^{2+} and Se^{2-}
    h. K^+ and P^{3-}

84. For the following pairs of ions, use the principle of electrical neutrality to predict the formula of the binary compound that the ions will form.
    a. Ba^{2+} and Se^{2-}
    b. Ca^{2+} and I^-
    c. K^+ and S^{2-}
    d. Sn^{4+} and O^{2-}
    e. Sn^{2+} and O^{2-}
    f. Pb^{4+} and P^{3-}
    g. Pb^{2+} and N^{3-}
    h. Al^{3+} and I^-

Additional Problems

85. For each of the following elements, give the chemical symbol and the atomic number.
    a. sulfur
    b. sodium
    c. silver
    d. strontium
    e. zinc
    f. mercury
    g. neon
    h. radium

86. Give the group number (if any) in the periodic table for the elements listed in problem 85. If the group has a family name, give that name.

87. List the names, symbols, and atomic numbers of the top four elements in Groups 1, 2, 6, and 7.

88. List the names, symbols, and atomic numbers of the top four elements in Groups 3, 5, and 8.

89. What is the difference between the atomic number and the mass number of an element? Can atoms of two different elements have the same atomic number? Could they have the same mass number? Why or why not?

90. Which subatomic particles contribute most to the atom's mass? Which subatomic particles determine the atom's chemical properties?

91. Is it possible for the same two elements to form more than one compound? Is this consistent with Dalton's atomic theory? Give an example.

92. Carbohydrates, a class of compounds containing the elements carbon, hydrogen, and oxygen, were originally thought to contain one water molecule (H_2O) for each carbon atom present. The carbohydrate glucose contains six carbon atoms. Write a general formula showing the relative numbers of each type of atom present in glucose.

93. When iron rusts in moist air, the product is typically a mixture of two iron–oxygen compounds. In one compound, there is an equal number of iron and oxygen atoms. In the other compound, there are three oxygen atoms for every two iron atoms. Write the formulas for the two iron oxides.

94. How many protons and neutrons are contained in the nucleus of each of the following atoms? For an atom of the element, how many electrons are present?
    a. $_{29}^{63}Cu$ b. $_{35}^{80}Br$ c. $_{12}^{24}Mg$

95. Though the common isotope of aluminum has a mass number of 27, isotopes of aluminum have been isolated (or prepared in nuclear reactors) with mass numbers of 24, 25, 26, 28, 29, and 30. How many neutrons are present in each of these isotopes? Why are they all considered aluminum atoms, even though they differ greatly in mass? Write the atomic symbol for each isotope.

96. The principal goal of alchemists was to convert cheaper, more common metals into gold. Considering that gold had no particular practical uses (for example, it was too soft to be used for weapons), why do you think early civilizations placed such emphasis on the value of gold?

97. How did Robert Boyle define an element?

98. Give the chemical symbol for each of the following elements.
    a. barium   c. bismuth   e. potassium
    b. bromine   d. boron   f. phosphorus

99. Give the chemical symbol for each of the following elements.
    a. chromium   c. iodine   e. platinum
    b. cadmium   d. chlorine

100. Give the chemical symbol for each of the following elements.
    a. zinc   c. tungsten
    b. uranium

101. Give the chemical symbol for each of the following elements.
    a. strontium   b. sodium   c. silver

102. For each of the following chemical symbols, give the name of the corresponding element.
    a. B   d. Ca   g. F
    b. Ra   e. Hg   h. P
    c. As   f. Br

103. For each of the following chemical symbols, give the name of the corresponding element.
    a. Ba   d. Li   g. Cu
    b. K   e. I   h. O
    c. Cd   f. N

104. Write the simplest formula for each of the following substances, listing the elements in the order given.
    a. a molecule containing one carbon atom and two oxygen atoms
    b. a compound containing one aluminum atom for every three chlorine atoms
    c. perchloric acid, which contains one hydrogen atom, one chlorine atom, and four oxygen atoms
    d. a molecule containing one sulfur atom and six chlorine atoms

105. For each of the following atomic numbers, write the name and chemical symbol of the corresponding element. (Refer to Figure 4.11.)
    a. 7   d. 28   g. 36
    b. 10   e. 22   h. 54
    c. 11   f. 18

106. Write the atomic symbol ($_Z^A X$) for each of the isotopes described below.
    a. $Z = 6$, number of neutrons $= 7$
    b. the isotope of carbon with a mass number of 13
    c. $Z = 6$, $A = 13$
    d. $Z = 19$, $A = 44$
    e. the isotope of calcium with a mass number of 41
    f. the isotope with 19 protons and 16 neutrons

107. How many protons and neutrons are contained in the nucleus of each of the following atoms? In an atom of each element, how many electrons are present?

    a. $^{41}_{22}$Ti   c. $^{76}_{32}$Ge   e. $^{75}_{33}$As

    b. $^{64}_{30}$Zn   d. $^{86}_{36}$Kr   f. $^{41}_{19}$K

108. Complete the following table.

Symbol	Protons	Neutrons	Mass Number
$^{41}_{20}$Ca	___	___	___
___	25	30	___
___	47	___	109
$^{45}_{21}$Sc	___	___	___

109. For each of the following elements, use the table on the inside front cover of the book to give the chemical symbol and atomic number and to specify whether the element is a metal or a nonmetal. Also give the named family to which the element belongs (if any).

    a. carbon   c. radon

    b. selenium   d. beryllium

5 Nomenclature

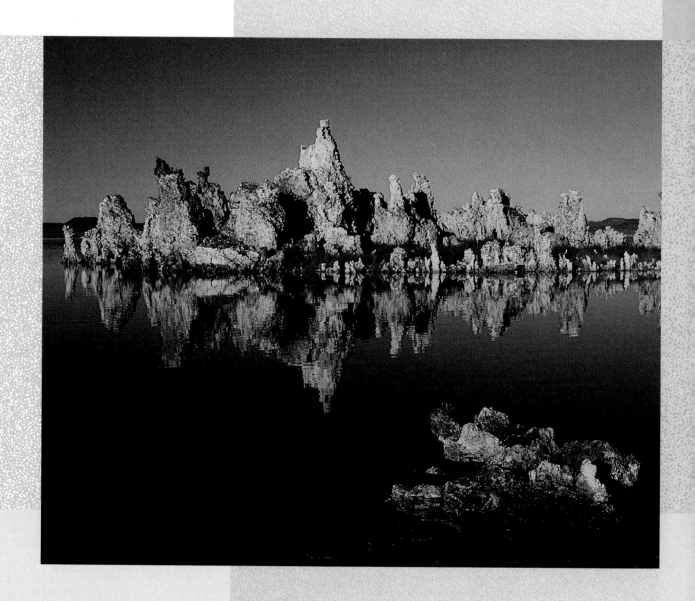

When chemistry was an infant science, there was no system for naming compounds. Names such as sugar of lead, blue vitriol, quicklime, Epsom salts, milk of magnesia, gypsum, and laughing gas were coined by early chemists. Such names are called *common names*. As our knowledge of chemistry grew, it became clear that using common names for compounds was not practical. More than four million chemical compounds are currently known. Memorizing common names for all these compounds would be impossible.

The solution, of course, is a *system* for naming compounds in which the name tells something about the composition of the compound. After learning the system, you should be able to name a compound when you are given its formula. And, vice versa, you should be able to construct a compound's formula, given its name. In the next few sections we will specify the most important rules for naming compounds other than organic compounds (those based on chains of carbon atoms).

Mineral towers in Mono Lake, California (left). *An artist using plaster of Paris a gypsum plaster* (right).

125

5.1 Naming Compounds

AIM: To understand why it is necessary to have a system for naming compounds.

We will begin by discussing the system for naming **binary compounds**—compounds composed of two elements. We can divide binary compounds into two broad classes:

1. Compounds that contain a metal and a nonmetal

2. Compounds that contain two nonmetals

We will describe how to name compounds in each of these classes in the next several sections. Then, in succeeding sections, we will describe the systems used for naming more complex compounds.

CHEMISTRY IN FOCUS

Sugar of Lead

In ancient Roman society it was common to boil wine in a lead vessel, driving off much of the water to produce a very sweet, viscous syrup called *sapa*. This syrup was commonly used as a sweetener for many types of food and drink.

We now realize that a major component of this syrup was lead acetate, $Pb(C_2H_3O_2)_2$. This compound has a very sweet taste—hence its original name, sugar of lead.

Many historians believe that the fall of the Roman Empire was due at least in part to lead poisoning, which causes lethargy and mental malfunctions. One major source of this lead was the sapa syrup. In addition, the Romans' highly advanced plumbing system employed lead water pipes, which allowed lead to be leached into their drinking water.

Sadly, this story is more relevant to today's society than you might think. Lead-based solder has been widely used for many years to connect the copper pipes in water systems in homes and commercial buildings. There is evidence that dangerous amounts of lead can be leached from these soldered joints into drinking water. In fact, large quantities of lead have been found in the water that some drinking fountains and water coolers dispense. In response to these problems, the U.S. Congress has passed a law banning lead from the solder used in plumbing systems for drinking water.

An ancient painting showing Romans drinking wine.

5.2   Naming Compounds That Contain a Metal and a Nonmetal

AIM: To learn to name binary compounds of a metal and a nonmetal.

As we saw in Section 4.11, when a metal such as sodium combines with a nonmetal such as chlorine, the resulting compound contains ions. The metal loses one or more electrons to become a cation, and the nonmetal gains one or more electrons to form an anion. The resulting substance is called a **binary ionic compound.** Binary ionic compounds contain a positive ion (cation), which is always written first in the formula, and a negative ion (anion). *To name these compounds we simply name the ions.*

In this section we will consider binary ionic compounds of two types based on the cations they contain. Certain metal atoms form only one cation. For example, the Na atom always forms Na^+, *never* Na^{2+} or Na^{3+}. Likewise, Cs always forms Cs^+, Ca always forms Ca^{2+}, and Al always forms Al^{3+}. We will call compounds that contain this type of metal atom Type I binary compounds and the cations they contain Type I cations. Examples of Type I cations are Na^+, Ca^{2+}, Cs^+, and Al^{3+}.

Other metal atoms can form two or more cations. For example, Cr can form Cr^{2+} and Cr^{3+} and Cu can form Cu^+ and Cu^{2+}. We will call such ions Type II cations and their compounds Type II binary compounds.

In summary:

Type I compounds: The metal present forms only one type of cation.

Type II compounds: The metal present can form two (or more) cations that have different charges.

Some common cations and anions and their names are listed in Table 5.1. You should memorize these. They are an essential part of your chemical vocabulary.

TABLE 5.1

Common Simple Cations and Anions

Cation	Name	Anion	Name*
H^+	hydrogen	H^-	hydride
Li^+	lithium	F^-	fluoride
Na^+	sodium	Cl^-	chloride
K^+	potassium	Br^-	bromide
Cs^+	cesium	I^-	iodide
Be^{2+}	beryllium	O^{2-}	oxide
Mg^{2+}	magnesium	S^{2-}	sulfide
Ca^{2+}	calcium		
Ba^{2+}	barium		
Al^{3+}	aluminum		
Ag^+	silver		

*The root is given in color.

Type I Binary Ionic Compounds

The following rules apply for Type I ionic compounds:

Rules for Naming Type I Ionic Compounds

1. The cation is always named first and the anion second.

2. A simple cation (obtained from a single atom) takes its name from the name of the element. For example, Na^+ is called sodium in the names of compounds containing this ion.

3. A simple anion (obtained from a single atom) is named by taking the first part of the element name (the root) and adding *-ide*. Thus the Cl^- ion is called chloride.

A simple cation has the same name as its parent element.

We will illustrate these rules by naming a few compounds. For example, the compound NaI is called sodium iodide. It contains Na^+ (the sodium cation, named for the parent metal) and I^- (iodide: the root of iodine plus *-ide*). Similarly, the compound CaO is called calcium oxide because it contains Ca^{2+} (the calcium cation) and O^{2-} (the oxide anion).

The rules for naming binary compounds are also illustrated by the following examples:

Compound	*Ions Present*	*Name*
NaCl	Na^+, Cl^-	sodium chloride
KI	K^+, I^-	potassium iodide
CaS	Ca^{2+}, S^{2-}	calcium sulfide
CsBr	Cs^+, Br^-	cesium bromide
MgO	Mg^{2+}, O^{2-}	magnesium oxide

It is important to note that in the *formulas* of ionic compounds, simple ions are represented by the element symbol: Cl means Cl^-, Na means Na^+, etc. However, when *individual ions* are shown, the charge is always included. Thus the formula of potassium bromide is written KBr, but when the potassium and bromide ions are shown individually, they are written K^+ and Br^-.

EXAMPLE 5.1 *Naming Type I Binary Compounds*

Name each binary compound.

a. CsF   b. $AlCl_3$ c. MgI_2

Solution

We will name these compounds by systematically following the rules given above.

a. CsF

STEP 1 Identify the cation and anion. Cs is in Group 1, so we know it will form the 1+ ion Cs^+. Because F is in Group 7, it forms the 1− ion F^-.

STEP 2 Name the cation. Cs^+ is simply called cesium, the same as the element name.

STEP 3 Name the anion. F^- is called fluoride: we use the root name of the element plus -*ide*.

STEP 4 Name the compound by combining the names of the individual ions. The name for CsF is cesium fluoride. (Remember that the name of the cation is always given first.)

b.

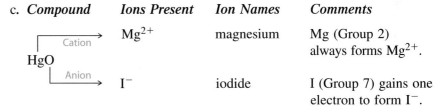

Compound	Ions Present	Ion Names	Comments
	Al^{3+}	aluminum	Al (Group 3) always forms Al^{3+}.
	Cl^-	chloride	Cl (Group 7) always forms Cl^-.

The name of $AlCl_3$ is aluminum chloride.

c.

Compound	Ions Present	Ion Names	Comments
	Mg^{2+}	magnesium	Mg (Group 2) always forms Mg^{2+}.
	I^-	iodide	I (Group 7) gains one electron to form I^-.

The name of MgI_2 is magnesium iodide.

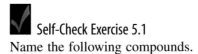 **Self-Check Exercise 5.1**

Name the following compounds.

a. Rb_2O b. SrI_2 c. K_2S

See Problems 5.9 and 5.10.

Example 5.1 reminds us of three things:

1. Compounds formed from metals and nonmetals are ionic.

2. In an ionic compound the cation is always named first.

3. The *net* charge on an ionic compound is always zero. Thus in CsF, one of each type of ion (Cs^+ and F^-) is required: (1+) + (1−) = 0 charge. In $AlCl_3$, however, three Cl^- ions are needed to balance the charge of Al^{3+}: (3+) + 3 (1−) = 0 charge. In MgI_2, two I^- ions are needed for each Mg^{2+} ion: (2+) + 2 (1−) = 0 charge.

Type II Binary Ionic Compounds

So far we have considered binary ionic compounds (Type I) containing metals that always give the same cation. For example, sodium always forms the Na^+ ion, calcium always forms the Ca^{2+} ion, and aluminum always forms the Al^{3+} ion. As we said in the previous section, we can predict with certainty that each Group 1 metal will give a 1+ cation and each Group 2 metal will give a 2+ cation. And aluminum always forms Al^{3+}.

However, there are many metals that can form more than one type of cation. For example, lead (Pb) can form Pb^{2+} or Pb^{4+} in ionic compounds. Also, iron (Fe) can produce Fe^{2+} or Fe^{3+}, chromium (Cr) can produce Cr^{2+} or Cr^{3+}, gold (Au) can produce Au^+ or Au^{3+}, and so on. This means that if we saw the name gold chloride, we wouldn't know whether it referred to the compound AuCl (containing Au^+ and Cl^-) or the compound $AuCl_3$ (containing Au^{3+} and three Cl^- ions). Therefore, we need a way of specifying which cation is present in compounds containing metals that can form more than one type of cation.

Chemists have decided to deal with this situation by using a Roman numeral to specify the charge on the cation. To see how this works, consider the compound $FeCl_2$. Iron can form Fe^{2+} or Fe^{3+}, so we must first decide which of these cations is present. We can determine the charge on the iron cation, because we know it must just balance the charge on the two 1− anions (the chloride ions). Thus if we represent the charges as

$$\underset{\substack{\uparrow \\ \text{Charge} \\ \text{on iron} \\ \text{cation}}}{\textcircled{?+}} + 2\ \underset{\substack{\uparrow \\ \text{Charge} \\ \text{on Cl}^-}}{\textcircled{1−}} = \underset{\substack{\uparrow \\ \text{Net} \\ \text{charge}}}{0}$$

we know that ? must represent 2 because

$$(2+) + 2(1−) = 0$$

The compound $FeCl_2$, then, contains one Fe^{2+} ion and two Cl^- ions. We call this compound iron(II) chloride, where the II tells the charge of the iron cation. That is, Fe^{2+} is called iron(II). Likewise, Fe^{3+} is called iron(III). And $FeCl_3$, which contains one Fe^{3+} ion and three Cl^- ions, is called iron(III) chloride.

Note that in the above examples the Roman numeral for the cation turned out to be the same as the subscript needed for the anion (to balance the charge). This is often not the case. For example, consider the compound PbO_2. Since the oxide ion is O^{2-}, for PbO_2 we have:

$$\underset{\substack{\uparrow \\ \text{Charge on} \\ \text{lead ion}}}{\textcircled{?+}} + \underset{\substack{\uparrow \\ (4-) \\ \text{the charge on} \\ \text{two } O^{2-} \text{ ions}}}{2\ \textcircled{2−}} = \underset{\uparrow}{0}$$

Thus the charge on the lead ion must be 4+ to balance the 4− charge of the two oxide ions. The name of PbO_2 is therefore lead(IV) oxide, where the IV indicates the presence of the Pb^{4+} cation.

Type II binary ionic compounds contain a metal that can form more than one type of cation.

$FeCl_3$ must contain Fe^{3+} to balance the charge of three Cl^- ions.

Copper (II) sulfate crystals.

TABLE 5.2
Common Type II Cations

Ion	Systematic Name	Older Name
Fe^{3+}	iron(III)	ferric
Fe^{2+}	iron(II)	ferrous
Cu^{2+}	copper(II)	cupric
Cu^+	copper(I)	cuprous
Co^{3+}	cobalt(III)	cobaltic
Co^{2+}	cobalt(II)	cobaltous
Sn^{4+}	tin(IV)	stannic
Sn^{2+}	tin(II)	stannous
Pb^{4+}	lead(IV)	plumbic
Pb^{2+}	lead(II)	plumbous
Hg^{2+}	mercury(II)	mercuric
Hg_2^{2+}*	mercury(I)	mercurous

*Mercury(I) ions always occur bound together in pairs to form Hg_2^{2+}.

There is another system for naming ionic compounds containing metals that form two cations. *The ion with the higher charge has a name ending in* -ic, *and the one with the lower charge has a name ending in* -ous. In this system, for example, Fe^{3+} is called the ferric ion, and Fe^{2+} is called the ferrous ion. The names for $FeCl_3$ and $FeCl_2$, in this system, are ferric chloride and ferrous chloride, respectively.

Table 5.2 gives both names for many Type II cations. We will use the system of Roman numerals exclusively in this text; the other system is falling into disuse.

EXAMPLE 5.2

Naming Type II Binary Compounds

Give the systematic name of each of the following compounds.

a. CuCl   c. Fe_2O_3 e. $PbCl_4$

b. HgO   d. MnO_2

Solution

All these compounds include a metal that can form more than one type of cation; thus we must first determine the charge on each cation. We do this by recognizing that a compound must be electrically neutral; that is, the positive and negative charges must balance exactly. We will use the known charge on the anion to determine the charge of the cation.

a. In CuCl we recognize the anion as Cl^-. To determine the charge on the copper cation, we invoke the principle of charge balance.

$$\underset{\substack{\uparrow \\ \text{Charge} \\ \text{on copper} \\ \text{ion}}}{\text{?}+} \quad + \quad \underset{\substack{\uparrow \\ \text{Charge} \\ \text{on } Cl^-}}{\text{1}-} \quad = \quad \underset{\substack{\uparrow \\ \text{Net charge} \\ \text{(must be zero)}}}{0}$$

In this case, ?+ must be 1+ because $(1+) + (1-) = 0$. Thus the copper cation must be Cu^+. Now we can name the compound by using the regular steps.

Compound	Ions Present	Ion Names	Comments
CuCl (Cation)	Cu^+	copper(I)	Copper forms other cations (it is a transition metal), so we must include the I to specify its charge.
(Anion)	Cl^- chloride		

The name of CuCl is copper(I) chloride.

b. In HgO we recognize the O^{2-} anion. To yield zero net charge, the cation must be Hg^{2+}.

Compound	Ions Present	Ion Names	Comments
HgO (Cation)	Hg^{2+}	mercury(II)	The II is necessary to specify the charge.
(Anion)	O^{2-}	oxide	

The name of HgO is mercury(II) oxide.

c. Because Fe_2O_3 contains three O^{2-} anions, the charge on the iron cation must be 3+.

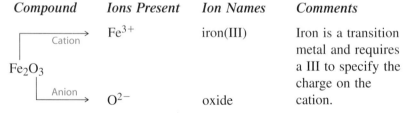

$$2(3+) + 3(2-) = 0$$

Fe³⁺   O²⁻   Net charge

Compound	Ions Present	Ion Names	Comments
Fe_2O_3 (Cation)	Fe^{3+}	iron(III)	Iron is a transition metal and requires a III to specify the charge on the cation.
(Anion)	O^{2-}	oxide	

The name of Fe_2O_3 is iron(III) oxide.

d. MnO_2 contains two O^{2-} anions, so the charge on the manganese cation is 4+.

$$(4+) + 2(2-) = 0$$

Mn⁴⁺   O²⁻   Net charge

Compound	Ions Present	Ion Names	Comments
MnO_2 (Cation)	Mn^{4+}	manganese(IV)	Manganese is a transition metal and requires a IV to specify the charge on the cation.
(Anion)	O^{2-}	oxide	

The name of MnO_2 is manganese(IV) oxide.

e. Because $PbCl_4$ contains four Cl^- anions, the charge on the lead cation is 4+.

$$(4+) + 4(1-) = 0$$

↑	↑	↑
Pb^{4+}	Cl^-	Net charge

Compound	Ions Present	Ion Names	Comments
$PbCl_4$ → Cation → Pb^{4+}		lead(IV)	Lead forms both Pb^{2+} and Pb^{4+}, so a Roman numeral is required.
$PbCl_4$ → Anion → Cl^-		chloride	

The name for $PbCl_4$ is lead(IV) chloride.

Sometimes transition metals form only one ion, such as silver, which forms Ag^+; zinc, which forms Zn^{2+}; and cadmium, which forms Cd^{2+}. In these cases, chemists do not use a Roman numeral, although it is not "wrong" to do so.

The use of a Roman numeral in a systematic name for a compound is required only in cases where more than one ionic compound forms between a given pair of elements. This occurs most often for compounds that contain transition metals, which frequently form more than one cation. *Metals that form only one cation do not need to be identified by a Roman numeral.* Common metals that do not require Roman numerals are the Group 1 elements, which form only 1+ ions; the Group 2 elements, which form only 2+ ions; and such Group 3 metals as aluminum and gallium, which form only 3+ ions.

As shown in Example 5.2, when a metal ion that forms more than one type of cation is present, the charge on the metal ion must be determined by balancing the positive and negative charges of the compound. To do this, you must be able to recognize the common anions and you must know their charges (see Table 5.1).

EXAMPLE 5.3

Naming Binary Ionic Compounds: Summary

Give the systematic name of each of the following compounds.

a. $CoBr_2$

c. Al_2O_3

b. $CaCl_2$

d. $CrCl_3$

Solution

Compound	Ions and Names	Compound Name	Comments
a. $CoBr_2$ → Co^{2+} cobalt(II) → Br^- bromide		cobalt(II) bromide	Cobalt is a transition metal; the name of the compound must have a Roman numeral. The two Br^- ions must be balanced by a Co^{2+} cation.

b. $CaCl_2$ → Ca^{2+} calcium — calcium chloride — Calcium, an alkaline earth metal, forms only the Ca^{2+} ion. A Roman numeral is not necessary.

→ Cl^- chloride

c. Al_2O_3 → Al^{3+} aluminum — aluminum oxide — Aluminum forms only Al^{3+}. A Roman numeral is not necessary.

→ O^{2-} oxide

d. $CrCl_3$ → Cr^{3+} chromium(III) — chromiumIII chloride — Chromium is a transition metal. The name of the compound must have a Roman numeral. $CrCl_3$ contains Cr^{3+}.

→ Cl^- chloride

✔ **Self-Check Exercise 5.2**

Give the names of the following compounds.

a. $PbBr_2$ and $PbBr_4$ d. Na_2S

b. FeS and Fe_2S_3 e. $CoCl_3$

c. $AlBr_3$

See Problems 5.9, 5.10, and 5.13 through 5.16.

The following flow chart is useful when you are naming binary ionic compounds:

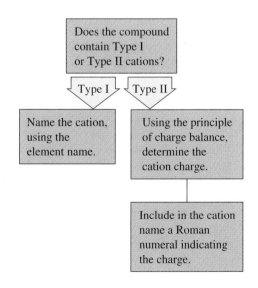

Does the compound contain Type I or Type II cations?

Type I → Name the cation, using the element name.

Type II → Using the principle of charge balance, determine the cation charge.

Include in the cation name a Roman numeral indicating the charge.

5.3 Naming Binary Compounds That Contain Only Nonmetals (Type III)

AIM: To learn how to name binary compounds containing only nonmetals.

Binary compounds that contain only nonmetals are named in accordance with a system similar in some ways to the rules for naming binary ionic compounds, but there are important differences. *Type III binary compounds contain only nonmetals.* The following rules cover the naming of these compounds.

TABLE 5.3

Prefixes Used to Indicate Numbers in Chemical Names

Prefix	Number Indicated
mono-	1
di-	2
tri-	3
tetra-	4
penta-	5
hexa-	6
hepta-	7
octa-	8

Rules for Naming Type III Binary Compounds

1. The first element in the formula is named first, and the full element name is used.

2. The second element is named as though it were an anion.

3. Prefixes are used to denote the numbers of atoms present. These prefixes are given in Table 5.3.

4. The prefix *mono-* is never used for naming the first element. For example, CO is called carbon monoxide, *not* monocarbon monoxide.

We will illustrate the application of these rules in Example 5.4.

EXAMPLE 5.4   *Naming Type III Binary Compounds*

Name the following binary compounds, which contain two nonmetals (Type III).

a. BF_3 b. NO   c. N_2O_5

Solution

a. BF_3

RULE 1   Name the first element, using the full element name: boron.

RULE 2   Name the second element as though it were an anion: fluoride.

RULES 3 AND 4   Use prefixes to denote numbers of atoms. One boron atom; do not use *mono-* in first position. Three fluorine atoms: use the prefix *tri-*.

The name of BF_3 is boron trifluoride.

b. *Compound*	*Individual Names*	*Prefixes*	*Comments*
NO	nitrogen	none	*Mono-* is not used
	oxide	*mono-*	for the first element.

A piece of copper metal about to be placed in nitric acid (left). Copper reacts with nitric acid to produce colorless NO, which immediately reacts with the oxygen in the air to form reddish-brown NO2 gas (right).

The name for NO is nitrogen monoxide. Note that the second *o* in *mono-* has been dropped for easier pronunciation. The *common* name for NO, which is often used by chemists, is nitric oxide.

c.

Compound	Individual Names	Prefixes	Comments
N_2O_5	nitrogen	*di-*	two N atoms
	oxide	*penta-*	five O atoms

The name for N_2O_5 is dinitrogen pentoxide. The *a* in *penta-* has been dropped for easier pronunciation.

✓ Self-Check Exercise 5.3

Name the following compounds.

a. CCl_4 b. NO_2 c. IF_5

See Problems 5.17 and 5.18.

The previous examples illustrate that, to avoid awkward pronunciation, we often drop the final *o* or *a* of the prefix when the second element is oxygen. For example, N_2O_4 is called dinitrogen tetroxide, *not* dinitrogen tetr*a*oxide, and CO is called carbon monoxide, *not* carbon mon*o*oxide.

Some compounds are always referred to by their common names. The two best examples are water and ammonia. The systematic names for H_2O and NH_3 are never used.

To make sure you understand the procedures for naming binary non-metallic compounds (Type III), study Example 5.5 and then do Self-Check Exercise 5.4.

Water and ammonia are always referred to by their common names.

EXAMPLE 5.5 *Naming Type III Binary Compounds: Summary*

Name each of the following compounds.

a. PCl_5 c. SF_6 e. SO_2

b. P_4O_6 d. SO_3 f. N_2O_3

Solution

	Compound	*Name*
a.	PCl_5	phosphorus pentachloride
b.	P_4O_6	tetraphosphorus hexoxide
c.	SF_6	sulfur hexafluoride
d.	SO_3	sulfur trioxide
e.	SO_2	sulfur dioxide
f.	N_2O_3	dinitrogen trioxide

 Self-Check Exercise 5.4

Name the following compounds.

a. SiO_2

b. O_2F_2

c. XeF_6

See Problems 5.17 and 5.18.

5.4   Naming Binary Compounds: A Review

AIM: To review the naming of Type I, Type II, and Type III binary compounds.

Because different rules apply for naming various types of binary compounds, we will now consider an overall strategy to use for these compounds. We have considered three types of binary compounds, and naming each of them requires different procedures.

Type I: Ionic compounds with metals that always form a cation with the same charge

Type II: Ionic compounds with metals (usually transition metals) that form cations with various charges

Type III: Compounds that contain only nonmetals

In trying to determine which type of compound you are naming, use the periodic table to help you identify metals and nonmetals and to determine which elements are transition metals.

FIGURE 5.1
A flow chart for naming binary compounds.

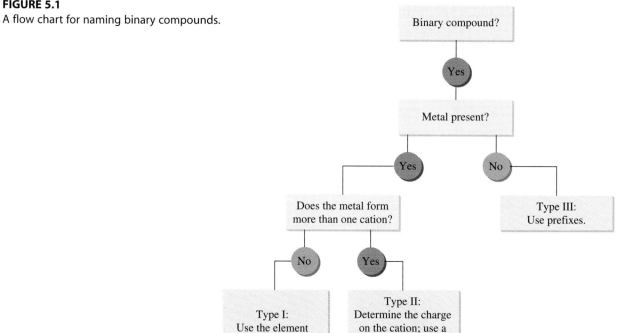

The flow chart given in Figure 5.1 should help you as you name binary compounds of the various types.

EXAMPLE 5.6 *Naming Binary Compounds: Summary*

Name the following binary compounds.

a. CuO

b. SrO

c. B_2O_3

d. $TiCl_4$

e. K_2S

f. OF_2

g. NH_3

Solution

a.

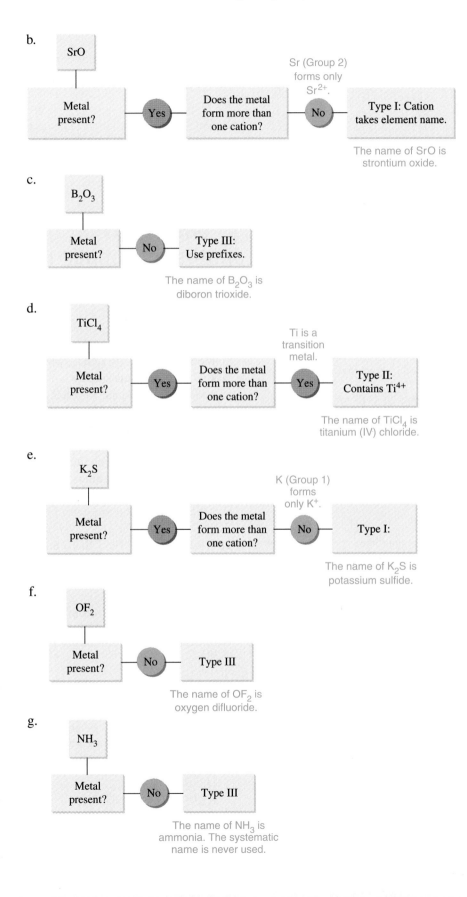

b.

SrO

Metal present? —Yes— Does the metal form more than one cation? —No— Type I: Cation takes element name.

Sr (Group 2) forms only Sr^{2+}.

The name of SrO is strontium oxide.

c.

B$_2$O$_3$

Metal present? —No— Type III: Use prefixes.

The name of B$_2$O$_3$ is diboron trioxide.

d.

TiCl$_4$

Metal present? —Yes— Does the metal form more than one cation? —Yes— Type II: Contains Ti^{4+}

Ti is a transition metal.

The name of TiCl$_4$ is titanium (IV) chloride.

e.

K$_2$S

Metal present? —Yes— Does the metal form more than one cation? —No— Type I:

K (Group 1) forms only K$^+$.

The name of K$_2$S is potassium sulfide.

f.

OF$_2$

Metal present? —No— Type III

The name of OF$_2$ is oxygen difluoride.

g.

NH$_3$

Metal present? —No— Type III

The name of NH$_3$ is ammonia. The systematic name is never used.

Self-Check Exercise 5.5

Name the following binary compounds.

a. ClF_3 d. MnO_2

b. VF_5 e. MgO

c. $CuCl$ f. H_2O

See Problems 5.19 and 5.20.

5.5   Naming Compounds That Contain Polyatomic Ions

AIM: To learn the names of common polyatomic ions and how to use them in naming compounds.

Ionic compounds containing polyatomic ions are not binary compounds, because they contain more than two elements.

The names and charges of polyatomic ions must be memorized. They are an important part of the vocabulary of chemistry.

Note that the SO_3^{2-} anion has very different properties from SO_3 (sulfur trioxide), a pungent, toxic gas.

A type of ionic compound that we have not yet considered is exemplified by ammonium nitrate, NH_4NO_3, which contains the **polyatomic ions** NH_4^+ and NO_3^-. As their name suggests, polyatomic ions are charged entities composed of several atoms bound together. Polyatomic ions are assigned special names that you *must memorize* in order to name the compounds containing them. The most important polyatomic ions and their names are listed in Table 5.4.

Note in Table 5.4 that several series of polyatomic anions exist that contain an atom of a given element and different numbers of oxygen atoms. These anions are called **oxyanions.** When there are two members in such a series, the name of the one with the smaller number of oxygen atoms ends in *-ite,* and the name of the one with the larger number ends in *-ate.* For example, SO_3^{2-} is sulfite and SO_4^{2-} is sulfate. When more than two oxyanions make up a series, *hypo-* (less than) and *per-* (more than) are used as prefixes to

TABLE 5.4

Names of Common Polyatomic Ions

Ion	Name	Ion	Name
NH_4^+	ammonium	CO_3^{2-}	carbonate
NO_2^-	nitrite	HCO_3^-	hydrogen carbonate
NO_3^-	nitrate		(bicarbonate is a widely
SO_3^{2-}	sulfite		used common name)
SO_4^{2-}	sulfate	ClO^-	hypochlorite
HSO_4^-	hydrogen sulfate	ClO_2^-	chlorite
	(bisulfate is a widely	ClO_3^-	chlorate
	used common name)	ClO_4^-	perchlorate
OH^-	hydroxide	$C_2H_3O_2^-$	acetate
CN^-	cyanide	MnO_4^-	permanganate
PO_4^{3-}	phosphate	$Cr_2O_7^{2-}$	dichromate
HPO_4^{2-}	hydrogen phosphate	CrO_4^{2-}	chromate
$H_2PO_4^-$	dihydrogen phosphate	O_2^{2-}	peroxide

name the members of the series with the fewest and the most oxygen atoms, respectively. The best example involves the oxyanions containing chlorine:

ClO^- *hypo*chlor*ite*
ClO_2^- chlor*ite*
ClO_3^- chlor*ate*
ClO_4^- *per*chlor*ate*

Naming ionic compounds that contain polyatomic ions is very similar to naming binary ionic compounds. For example, the compound NaOH is called sodium hydroxide, because it contains the Na^+ (sodium) cation and the OH^- (hydroxide) anion. To name these compounds, *you must learn to recognize the common polyatomic ions.* That is, you must learn the *composition* and *charge* of each of the ions in Table 5.4. Then when you see the formula $NH_4C_2H_3O_2$, you should immediately recognize its two "parts":

The correct name is ammonium acetate.

Remember that when a metal is present that forms more than one cation, a Roman numeral is required to specify the cation charge, just as in naming Type II binary ionic compounds. For example, the compound $FeSO_4$ is called iron(II) sulfate, because it contains Fe^{2+} (to balance the $2-$ charge on SO_4^{2-}). Note that to determine the charge on the iron cation, you must know that sulfate has a $2-$ charge.

Except for hydroxide and cyanide, the names of polyatomic ions do not have an *-ide* ending.

EXAMPLE 5.7   *Naming Compounds That Contain Polyatomic Ions*

Give the systematic name of each of the following compounds.

a. Na_2SO_4 c. $Fe(NO_3)_3$ e. Na_2SO_3

b. KH_2PO_4 d. $Mn(OH)_2$

Solution

Compound	Ions Present	Ion Names	Compound Name
a. Na_2SO_4	two Na^+ SO_4^{2-}	sodium sulfate	sodium sulfate
b. KH_2PO_4	K^+ $H_2PO_4^-$	potassium dihydrogen phosphate	potassium dihydrogen phosphate
c. $Fe(NO_3)_3$	Fe^{3+} three NO_3^-	iron(III) nitrate	iron(III) nitrate
d. $Mn(OH)_2$	Mn^{2+} two OH^-	manganese(II) hydroxide	manganese(II) hydroxide
e. Na_2SO_3	two Na^+ SO_3^{2-}	sodium sulfite	sodium sulfite

Self-Check Exercise 5.6

Name each of the following compounds.

a. $Ca(OH)_2$

b. Na_3PO_4

c. $KMnO_4$

d. $(NH_4)_2Cr_2O_7$

e. $Co(ClO_4)_2$

f. $KClO_3$

g. $Cu(NO_2)_2$

See Problems 5.35 and 5.36.

Example 5.7 illustrates that when more than one polyatomic ion appears in a chemical formula, parentheses are used to enclose the ion and a subscript is written after the closing parenthesis. Other examples are $(NH_4)_2SO_4$ and $Fe_3(PO_4)_2$.

In naming chemical compounds, use the strategy summarized in Figure 5.2. If the compound being considered is binary, use the procedure summarized in Figure 5.1. If the compound has more than two elements, ask yourself whether it has any polyatomic ions. Use Table 5.4 to help you recognize these ions until you have committed them to memory. If a polyatomic ion is present, name the compound using procedures very similar to those for naming binary ionic compounds.

FIGURE 5.2
Overall strategy for naming chemical compounds.

EXAMPLE 5.8   *Summary of Naming Binary Compounds and Compounds That Contain Polyatomic Ions*

Name the following compounds.

a. Na_2CO_3

b. $FeBr_3$

c. $CsClO_4$

d. PCl_3

e. $CuSO_4$

Solution

Compound	Name	Comments
a. Na_2CO_3	sodium carbonate	Contains $2Na^+$ and CO_3^{2-}.
b. $FeBr_3$	iron(III) bromide	Contains Fe^{3+} and $3Br^-$.
c. $CsClO_4$	cesium perchlorate	Contains Cs^+ and ClO_4^-.
d. PCl_3	phosphorus trichloride	Type III binary compound (both P and Cl are nonmetals).
e. $CuSO_4$	copper(II) sulfate	Contains Cu^{2+} and SO_4^{2-}.

 Self-Check Exercise 5.7

Name the following compounds.

Although the rules state that a Roman numeral is required in the name of a compound that contains a transition metal ion, certain transition metals form only one ion. Common examples are zinc (forms only Zn^{2+}) and silver (forms only Ag^+). For these cases the Roman numeral is often omitted from the name.

a. $NaHCO_3$

b. $BaSO_4$

c. $CsClO_4$

d. BrF_5

e. $NaBr$

f. $KOCl$

g. $Zn_3(PO_4)_2$

See Problems 5.29 through 5.36.

5.6 Naming Acids

AIMS: To learn how the anion composition determines the acid's name. To learn names for common acids.

Acids

When dissolved in water, certain molecules produce H^+ ions (protons). These substances, which are called **acids,** were first recognized by the sour taste of their solutions. For example, citric acid is responsible for the tartness of lemons and limes. Acids will be discussed in detail later. Here we simply present the rules for naming acids.

An acid can be viewed as a molecule with one or more H^+ ions attached to an anion. The rules for naming acids depend on whether the anion contains oxygen.

Rules for Naming Acids

1. If the *anion does not contain oxygen,* the acid is named with the prefix *hydro-* and the suffix *-ic* attached to the root name for the element. For example, when gaseous HCl (hydrogen chloride) is dissolved in water, it forms hydrochloric acid. Similarly, hydrogen cyanide (HCN) and dihydrogen sulfide (H_2S) dissolved in water are called hydrocyanic acid and hydrosulfuric acid, respectively.

2. When the *anion contains oxygen,* the acid name is formed from the root name of the central element of the anion or the anion name, with a suffix of *ic,* or *-ous.* When the anion name ends in *-ate,* the suffix *-ic* is used.

For example,

Acid	Anion	Name
H_2SO_4	SO_4^{2-} (sulfate)	sulfuric acid
H_3PO_4	PO_4^{3-} (phosphate)	phosphoric acid
$HC_2H_3O_2$	$C_2H_3O_2^-$ (acetate)	acetic acid

When the anion name ends in *-ite,* the suffix *-ous* is used in the acid name.

For example,

Acid	Anion	Name
H_2SO_3	SO_3^{2-} (sulfite)	sulfurous acid
HNO_2	NO_2^- (nitrite)	nitrous acid

TABLE 5.5

Names of Acids That Do Not Contain Oxygen

Acid	Name
HF	hydrofluoric acid
HCl	hydrochloric acid
HBr	hydrobromic acid
HI	hydroiodic acid
HCN	hydrocyanic acid
H_2S	hydrosulfuric acid

The application of rule 2 can be seen in the names of the acids of the oxyanions of chlorine, as shown below. The rules for naming acids are given in schematic form in Figure 5.3. The names of the most important acids are given in Table 5.5 and Table 5.6. These should be memorized.

Acid	Anion	Name
$HClO_4$	perchlor*ate*	perchlor*ic* acid
$HClO_3$	chlor*ate*	chlor*ic* acid
$HClO_2$	chlor*ite*	chlor*ous* acid
$HClO$	hypochlor*ite*	hypochlor*ous* acid

TABLE 5.6

Names of Some Oxygen-Containing Acids

Acid	Name
HNO_3	nitric acid
HNO_2	nitrous acid
H_2SO_4	sulfuric acid
H_2SO_3	sulfurous acid
H_3PO_4	phosphoric acid
$HC_2H_3O_2$	acetic acid

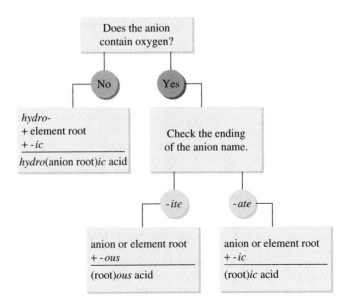

FIGURE 5.3

A flow chart for naming acids. The acid is considered as one or more H^+ ions attached to an anion.

5.7 Writing Formulas from Names

AIM: To learn to write the formula of a compound, given its name.

So far we have started with the chemical formula of a compound and decided on its systematic name. Being able to reverse the process is also important. Often a laboratory procedure describes a compound by name, but the label on the bottle in the lab shows only the formula of the chemical it contains. It is essential that you are able to get the formula of a compound from its name. In fact, you already know enough about compounds to do this. For example, given the name calcium hydroxide, you can write the formula as $Ca(OH)_2$ because you know that calcium forms only Ca^{2+} ions and that, since hydroxide is OH^-, two of these anions are required to give a neutral compound. Similarly, the name iron(II) oxide implies the formula FeO, because the Roman numeral II indicates the presence of the cation Fe^{2+} and the oxide ion is O^{2-}.

We emphasize at this point that it is essential to learn the name, composition, and charge of each of the common polyatomic anions (and the NH_4^+ cation). If you do not recognize these ions by formula and by name, you will not be able to write the compound's name given its formula or the compound's formula given its name. You must also learn the names of the common acids.

EXAMPLE 5.9   *Writing Formulas from Names*

Give the formula for each of the following compounds.

a. potassium hydroxide

b. sodium carbonate

c. nitric acid

d. cobalt(III) nitrate

e. calcium chloride

f. lead(IV) oxide

g. dinitrogen pentoxide

h. ammonium perchlorate

Solution

Name	Formula	Comments
a. potassium hydroxide	KOH	Contains K^+ and OH^-.
b. sodium carbonate	Na_2CO_3	We need two Na^+ to balance CO_3^{2-}.
c. nitric acid	HNO_3	Common strong acid; memorize.
d. cobalt(III) nitrate	$Co(NO_3)_3$	Cobalt(III) means Co^{3+}; we need three NO_3^- to balance Co^{3+}.
e. calcium chloride	$CaCl_2$	We need two Cl^- to balance Ca^{2+}; Ca (Group 2) always forms Ca^{2+}.
f. lead(IV) oxide	PbO_2	Lead(IV) means Pb^{4+}; we need two O^{2-} to balance Pb^{4+}.
g. dinitrogen pentoxide	N_2O_5	*di-* means two; *pent(a)-* means five.
h. ammonium perchlorate	NH_4ClO_4	Contains NH_4^+ and ClO_4^-.

 Self-Check Exercise 5.8

Write the formula for each of the following compounds.

a. ammonium sulfate

b. vanadium(V) fluoride

c. disulfur dichloride

d. rubidium peroxide

e. aluminum oxide

See Problems 5.41 through 5.46.

Chapter Review

Key Terms

binary compound *(5.1)*
binary ionic compound *(5.2)*
polyatomic ion *(5.5)*

Summary

1. Binary compounds can be named systematically by following a set of relatively simple rules. For compounds containing both a metal and a nonmetal, the metal is always named first, followed by a name derived from the root name for the nonmetal. For compounds containing a metal that can form more than one cation (Type II), we use a Roman numeral to specify the cation's charge. In binary compounds containing only nonmetals (Type III), prefixes are used to specify the numbers of atoms.

2. Polyatomic ions are charged entities composed of several atoms bound together. These have special names that must be memorized. Naming ionic compounds that contain polyatomic ions is very similar to naming binary ionic compounds.

3. The names of acids (molecules with one or more H^+ ions attached to an anion) depend on whether or not the anion contains oxygen.

Questions and Problems

All even-numbered exercises have answers in the back of this book and solutions in the Solutions Guide.

5.1 ■ Naming Compounds

QUESTIONS

1. A compound containing only two elements is called a _____ compound.

2. What are the two major types of binary compounds?

5.2 ■ Naming Compounds That Contain a Metal and a Nonmetal

QUESTIONS

3. In an ionic compound, the positive ion is called the _____ and the negative ion is called the _____.

4. In naming ionic compounds, we always name the _____ first.

5. A simple _____ ion has the same name as its parent element.

6. Although the formula of sodium chloride is written simply as NaCl, the compound actually contains _____ and _____ ions.

7. For a metallic element that forms two stable cations, the ending _____ is sometimes used for the cation with the lower charge.

8. We indicate the charge of a metallic element that forms more than one cation by adding a _____ after the name of the cation.

9. Give the name of each of the following simple binary ionic compounds.
   a. Na_2O
   b. K_2S
   c. $MgCl_2$
   d. $CaBr_2$
   e. BaI_2
   f. Al_2S_3
   g. $CsBr$
   h. AgF

10. Give the name of each of the following simple binary ionic compounds.
   a. Na_3N
   b. K_2O
   c. $AgBr$
   d. MgI_2
   e. SrO
   f. CaH_2
   g. $BaCl_2$
   h. AlI_3

11. Identify each case in which the name is incorrect. Give the correct name.
   a. BaH_2, barium hydroxide
   b. Na_2O, disodium oxide
   c. $SnCl_4$, tin(IV) chloride
   d. SiO_2, silver dioxide
   e. $FeBr_3$, iron(III) bromide

12. In which of the following pairs is the name incorrect?
   a. silver oxide, S_2O
   b. aluminum sulfide, Al_2S_3
   c. trisodium nitride, Na_3N
   d. barium dichloride, $BaCl_2$
   e. strontium hydride, SrH_2

13. Write the name of each of the following ionic substances, using the system that includes a Roman numeral to specify the charge of the cation.
   a. $SnBr_2$
   b. $SnBr_4$
   c. CrO
   d. Cr_2O_3
   e. Hg_2I_2
   f. HgI_2

14. Write the name of each of the following ionic substances, using the system that includes a Roman numeral to specify the charge of the cation.
    a. $PbCl_2$ d. Hg_2O
    b. Fe_2O_3 e. HgS
    c. SnI_2 f. CuI

15. Write the name of each of the following ionic substances, using *-ous* or *-ic* to indicate the charge of the cation.
    a. $CrCl_3$ d. CuI_2
    b. SnO_2 e. CoO
    c. PbO_2 f. Co_2O_3

16. Write the name for each of the following substances using the *-ous/-ic* notation.
    a. PbO_2 d. CuI
    b. $SnBr_2$ e. Hg_2I_2
    c. Cu_2S f. CrF_3

5.3 ■ *Naming Binary Compounds That Contain Only Nonmetals (Type III)*

QUESTIONS

17. Name each of the following binary compounds of nonmetallic elements.

    a. CBr_4 d. ICl
    b. N_2O_3 e. NCl_3
    c. PCl_3 f. SiF_4

18. Write the name for each of the following binary compounds of nonmetallic elements.
    a. GeH_4 d. SeO_2
    b. N_2Br_4 e. NH_3
    c. P_2S_5 f. SiO_2

5.4 ■ *Naming Binary Compounds: A Review*

QUESTIONS

19. Name each of the following binary compounds, using the periodic table to determine whether the compound is likely to be ionic (containing a metal and a nonmetal) or nonionic (containing only nonmetals).
    a. $CoCl_3$ d. Hg_2O
    b. P_2Cl_4 e. $SnCl_4$
    c. BCl_3 f. $SiCl_4$

20. Name each of the following binary compounds, using the periodic table to determine whether the compound is likely to be ionic (containing a metal and a nonmetal) or nonionic (containing only nonmetals).
    a. B_2H_6 d. Ag_2S
    b. Ca_3N_2 e. $CuCl_2$
    c. CBr_4 f. ClF

21. Name each of the following binary compounds, using the periodic table to determine whether the compound is likely to be ionic (containing a metal and a nonmetal) or nonionic (containing only nonmetals).
    a. Mg_2S_3 d. $ClBr$
    b. $AlCl_3$ e. Li_2O
    c. PH_3 f. P_4O_{10}

22. Name each of the following binary compounds, using the periodic table to determine whether the compound is likely to be ionic (containing a metal and a nonmetal) or nonionic (containing only nonmetals).
    a. Al_2O_3 d. Co_2S_3
    b. B_2O_3 e. N_2O_5
    c. N_2O_4 f. Al_2S_3

5.5 ■ *Naming Compounds That Contain Polyatomic Ions*

QUESTIONS

23. A charged entity composed of several atoms bound together is called a _____ ion.

24. An anion containing an element and one or more _____ atoms is called an oxyanion.

25. For the oxyanions of sulfur, the ending *-ite* is used for SO_3^{2-} to indicate that it contains _____ than does SO_4^{2-}.

26. Which oxyanion of chlorine contains the most oxygen atoms: hypochlorite, chlorite, or perchlorate?

27. Complete the following list by filling in the missing names or formulas of the oxyanions of chlorine.

    ClO_4^- _____

    _____   hypochlorite

    ClO_3^- _____

    _____   chlorite

28. Complete the following list by filling in the missing names or formulas of the indicated oxyanions.

    BrO^- _____

    _____   iodate

    IO_4^- _____

    _____   hypoiodide

29. Write the formula for each of the following sulfur-containing polyatomic ions, including the overall charge of the ion.
    a. sulfate   c. bisulfate
    b. sulfite   d. hydrogen sulfate

30. Write the formula for each of the following nitrogen-containing polyatomic ions, including the overall charge of the ion.
    a. nitrate
    b. nitrite
    c. ammonium
    d. cyanide

31. Write the formula for each of the following chlorine-containing ions, including the overall charge of the ion.
    a. chloride
    b. hypochlorite
    c. chlorate
    d. perchlorate

32. Write the formula for each of the following phosphorus-containing anions, including the overall charge of the ion.
    a. phosphate
    b. phosphide
    c. dihydrogen phosphate
    d. hydrogen phosphate

33. Give the name of each of the following polyatomic anions.
    a. MnO_4^-
    b. O_2^{2-}
    c. CrO_4^{2-}
    d. $Cr_2O_7^{2-}$
    e. NO_3^-
    f. SO_3^{2-}

34. Give the name of each of the following polyatomic ions.
    a. HCO_3^-
    b. NO_2^-
    c. HSO_4^-
    d. $H_2PO_4^-$
    e. $C_2H_3O_2^-$
    f. ClO_2^-

35. Name each of the following compounds, which contain polyatomic ions.
    a. $Fe(NO_3)_3$
    b. $Co_3(PO_4)_2$
    c. $Cr(CN)_3$
    d. $Al_2(SO_4)_3$
    e. $Cr(C_2H_3O_2)_2$
    f. $(NH_4)_2SO_3$

36. Name each of the following compounds, which contain polyatomic ions.
    a. NH_4NO_3
    b. $KClO_3$
    c. $PbSO_4$
    d. $Ca_3(PO_4)_2$
    e. $NaClO_4$
    f. $Cu(OH)_2$

5.6 ■ Naming Acids

QUESTIONS

37. Give a simple definition of an *acid*.

38. Many acids contain the element _____ in addition to hydrogen.

39. Name each of the following acids.
    a. HCl
    b. H_2SO_4
    c. HNO_3
    d. HI
    e. HNO_2
    f. $HClO_3$
    g. HBr
    h. HF
    i. $HC_2H_3O_2$

40. Name each of the following acids.
    a. HOBr
    b. HIO_4
    c. H_3PO_3
    d. $HClO_2$
    e. H_2SeO_4
    f. HOI
    g. HIO_2
    h. H_2Te

5.7 ■ Writing Formulas from Names

PROBLEMS

41. Write the formula for each of the following simple binary ionic compounds.
    a. lithium bromide
    b. sodium iodide
    c. silver(I) sulfide (usually called silver sulfide)
    d. cesium oxide
    e. beryllium iodide
    f. barium hydride
    g. aluminum fluoride
    h. potassium oxide

42. Write the formula for each of these ionic substances.
    a. plumbic oxide
    b. stannous bromide
    c. cupric sulfide
    d. cuprous iodide
    e. mercurous chloride
    f. chromic fluoride

43. Write the formula for each of the following binary compounds of nonmetallic elements.
    a. phosphorus triiodide
    b. silicon tetrachloride
    c. dinitrogen pentoxide
    d. iodine monobromide
    e. diboron trioxide
    f. dinitrogen tetroxide
    g. carbon monoxide

44. Write the formula for each of the following binary compounds of nonmetallic elements.
    a. carbon dioxide
    b. sulfur dioxide
    c. dinitrogen tetrachloride
    d. carbon tetraiodide
    e. phosphorus pentafluoride
    f. diphosphorus pentoxide

45. Write the formula for each of the following compounds, which contain polyatomic ions. Be sure to enclose the polyatomic ion in parentheses if more than one such ion is needed to balance the oppositely charged ion(s).
    a. tin(IV) acetate
    b. sodium peroxide
    c. ammonium hydrogen sulfate
    d. potassium sulfite

e. mercury(II) sulfate
f. potassium dihydrogen phosphate
g. sodium hydrogen sulfite
h. ammonium phosphate

46. Write the formula for each of the following compounds that contain polyatomic ions. Be sure to enclose the polyatomic ion in parentheses if more than one such ion is needed.
    a. calcium phosphate
    b. ammonium nitrate
    c. aluminum hydrogen sulfate
    d. barium sulfate
    e. ferric nitrate
    f. copper(I) hydroxide

47. Write the formula for each of the following acids.
    a. nitrous acid   e. periodic acid
    b. acetic acid   f. hydrosulfuric acid
    c. hydroiodic   g. bromous acid
        acid   h. sulfurous acid
    d. perbromic acid

48. Write the formula for each of the following acids.
    a. hydrocyanic acid   e. hypochlorous acid
    b. nitric acid   f. hydrofluoric acid
    c. sulfuric acid   g. bromous acid
    d. phosphoric acid   h. hydrofluoric acid

49. Write the formula for each of the following substances.
    a. lithium chloride
    b. cuprous carbonate
    c. hydrobromic acid
    d. calcium nitrate
    e. sodium perchlorate
    f. aluminum hydroxide
    g. barium hydrogen carbonate
    h. iron(II) sulfate
    i. dinitrogen tetraoxide
    j. phosphorus pentabromide
    k. potassium sulfite
    l. barium acetate

50. Write the formula for each of the following substances.
    a. sodium hydrogen phosphate
    b. magnesium acetate
    c. strontium iodide
    d. hydroselenic acid
    e. calcium phosphide
    f. silver(I) perchlorate (usually called silver perchlorate)
    g. iron(III) hydroxide
    h. stannous fluoride
    i. plumbous oxide
    j. diboron trioxide
    k. sodium dihydrogen phosphate
    l. phosphorous acid

Additional Problems

51. Although sucrose (table sugar) and sodium chloride (table salt) are very similar in appearance, sodium chloride melts at over 800 °C, whereas table sugar melts at around 185 °C. What kinds of forces give an ionic compound such a high resistance to melting?

52. Before an electrocardiogram (ECG) is recorded for a cardiac patient, the ECG leads are usually coated with a moist paste containing sodium chloride. What property of an ionic substance such as NaCl is being made use of here?

53. What is a *binary* compound? What is a *polyatomic* anion? What is an *oxyanion?*

54. On some periodic tables, hydrogen is listed both as a member of Group 1 and as a member of Group 7. Write an equation showing the formation of H^+ ion and an equation showing the formation of H^- ion.

55. In general, oxyacids contain a nonmetal, oxygen, and what other element?

56. Complete the following list by filling in the missing oxyanion or oxyacid for each pair.

    ClO_4^- _____

    _____ HIO_3

    ClO^- _____

    BrO_2^- _____

    _____ $HClO_2$

57. Name the following compounds.
    a. $Mg(OH)_2$ e. $Fe(NH_4)_2(SO_4)_2$
    b. Cr_2O_3 f. $KHCO_3$
    c. P_4O_{10} g. $CuCN$
    d. $Cr_2(CO_3)_3$

58. Name the following compounds.
    a. $AuBr_3$ e. NH_3
    b. $Co(CN)_3$ f. Ag_2SO_4
    c. $MgHPO_4$ g. $Be(OH)_2$
    d. B_2H_6

59. Name the following compounds.
    a. $HClO_3$ e. $HC_2H_3O_2$
    b. $CoCl_3$ f. $Fe(NO_3)_3$
    c. B_2O_3 g. $CuSO_4$
    d. H_2O

60. Name the following compounds.
    a. $(NH_4)_2CO_3$ e. MnO_2
    b. NH_4HCO_3 f. HIO_3
    c. $Ca_3(PO_4)_2$ g. KH
    d. H_2SO_3

61. Most metallic elements form *oxides,* and often the oxide is the most common compound of the element that is found in the earth's crust. Write the formulas for the oxides of the following metallic elements.
    a. potassium
    b. magnesium
    c. iron(II)
    d. iron(III)
    e. zinc(II)
    f. lead(II)
    g. aluminum

62. Consider a hypothetical simple ion M^{4+}. Determine the formula of the compound this ion would form with each of the following anions.
    a. chloride
    b. nitrate
    c. oxide
    d. phosphate
    e. cyanide
    f. sulfate
    g. dichromate

63. Consider a hypothetical element M, which is capable of forming stable simple cations that have charges of $1+$, $2+$, and $3+$, respectively. Write the formulas of the compounds formed by the various M cations with each of the following anions.
    a. chromate
    b. dichromate
    c. sulfide
    d. bromide
    e. bicarbonate
    f. hydrogen phosphate

64. Consider the hypothetical metallic element M, which is capable of forming stable simple cations that have charges of $1+$, $2+$, and $3+$, respectively. Consider also the nonmetallic elements D, E, and F, which form anions that have charges of $1-$, $2-$, and $3-$, respectively. Write the formulas of all possible compounds between metal M and nonmetals D, E, and F.

65. Complete Table 5.A (below) by writing the names and formulas for the ionic compounds formed when the cations listed across the top combine with the anions shown in the left-hand column.

66. Complete Table 5.B (on page 152) by writing the formulas for the ionic compounds formed when the anions listed across the top combine with the cations shown in the left-hand column.

67. The noble metals gold, silver, and platinum are often used in fashioning jewelry because they are relatively _____.

68. The noble gas _____ is frequently found in underground deposits of natural gas.

69. The elements of Group 7 (fluorine, chlorine, bromine, and iodine) consist of molecules containing _____ atom(s).

70. The halogen element that exists in the solid state under normal conditions is _____.

71. When an atom gains two electrons, the ion formed has a charge of _____.

72. An ion with one more electron than it has protons has a _____ charge.

73. An atom that has lost two electrons has a _____ charge.

74. An atom that has gained one electron has a charge of _____ .

TABLE 5.A

Ions	Fe^{2+}	Al^{3+}	Na^+	Ca^{2+}	NH_4^+	Fe^{3+}	Ni^{2+}	Hg_2^{2+}	Hg^{2+}
CO_3^{2-}	___	___	___	___	___	___	___	___	___
BrO_3^-	___	___	___	___	___	___	___	___	___
$C_2H_3O_2^-$	___	___	___	___	___	___	___	___	___
OH^-	___	___	___	___	___	___	___	___	___
HCO_3^-	___	___	___	___	___	___	___	___	___
PO_4^{3-}	___	___	___	___	___	___	___	___	___
SO_3^{2-}	___	___	___	___	___	___	___	___	___
ClO_4^-	___	___	___	___	___	___	___	___	___
SO_4^{2-}	___	___	___	___	___	___	___	___	___
O^{2-}	___	___	___	___	___	___	___	___	___
Cl^-	___	___	___	___	___	___	___	___	___

TABLE 5.B

Ions	bromide	hydrogen carbonate	hydride	acetate	hydrogen sulfate	phosphate
calcium	___	___	___	___	___	___
strontium	___	___	___	___	___	___
ammonium	___	___	___	___	___	___
aluminum	___	___	___	___	___	___
iron(III)	___	___	___	___	___	___
nickel(II)	___	___	___	___	___	___
silver(I)	___	___	___	___	___	___
gold(III)	___	___	___	___	___	___
potassium	___	___	___	___	___	___
mercury(II)	___	___	___	___	___	___
barium	___	___	___	___	___	___

75. For each of the negative ions listed in column 1, use the periodic table to find in column 2 the total number of electrons the ion contains. A given answer may be used more than once.

Column 1	*Column 2*
[1]Se^{2-}	[a] 18
[2]S^{2-}	[b] 35
[3]P^{3-}	[c] 52
[4]O^{2-}	[d] 34
[5]N^{3-}	[e] 36
[6]I^-	[f] 54
[7]F^-	[g] 10
[8]Cl^-	[h] 9
[9]Br^-	[i] 53
[10]At^-	[j] 86

76. For the following processes that show the formation of ions, use the periodic table to determine the number of electrons and protons present in both the *ion* and the *neutral atom* from which it is made.
   a. $Mn \rightarrow Mn^{2+} + 2e^-$ d. $Co \rightarrow Co^{3+} + 3e^-$
   b. $Ni \rightarrow Ni^{2+} + 2e^-$ e. $Fe \rightarrow Fe^{2+} + 2e^-$
   c. $N + 3e^- \rightarrow N^{3-}$ f. $P + 3e^- \rightarrow P^{3-}$

77. For each of the following atomic numbers, use the periodic table to write the formula (including the charge) for the simple *ion* that the element is most likely to form.
   a. 36   d. 81
   b. 31   e. 35
   c. 52   f. 87

78. For the following pairs of ions, use the principle of electrical neutrality to predict the formula of the binary compound that the ions are most likely to form.
   a. Na^+ and S^{2-} e. Cu^{2+} and Br^-
   b. K^+ and Cl^- f. Al^{3+} and I^-
   c. Ba^{2+} and O^{2-} g. Al^{3+} and O^{2-}
   d. Mg^{2+} and Se^{2-} h. Ca^{2+} and N^{3-}

79. Give the name of each of the following simple binary ionic compounds.
   a. BeO e. HCl
   b. MgI_2 f. LiF
   c. Na_2S g. Ag_2S
   d. Al_2O_3 h. CaH_2

80. In which of the following pairs is the name incorrect?
   a. $CaCl_2$, calcium chloride
   b. AlH_3, aluminum trihydride
   c. K_2O, potassium oxide
   d. $Fe(OH)_2$, iron(III) hydroxide
   e. $CoCl_3$, cobalt(II) chloride

81. Write the name of each of the following ionic substances, using the system that includes a Roman numeral to specify the charge of the cation.
   a. $FeBr_2$ d. SnO_2
   b. CoS e. Hg_2Cl_2
   c. Co_2S_3 f. $HgCl_2$

82. Write the name of each of the following ionic substances, using -*ous* or -*ic* to indicate the charge of the cation.

a. $CoBr_3$ d. FeS
b. PbI_4 e. $SnCl_4$
c. Fe_2O_3 f. SnO

83. Name each of the following binary compounds.
    a. XeF_6 d. N_2O_4
    b. OF_2 e. Cl_2O
    c. AsI_3 f. SF_6

84. Name each of the following binary compounds, using the periodic table to determine whether the compound is likely to be ionic (containing a metal and a nonmetal) or nonionic (containing only nonmetals).
    a. Fe_2S_3 d. ClF
    b. $AuCl_3$ e. K_2O
    c. AsH_3 f. CO_2

85. Which oxyanion of nitrogen contains a larger number of oxygen atoms, the nit*rate* ion or the nit*rite* ion?

86. Write the formula for each of the following carbon-containing polyatomic ions, including the overall charge of the ion.
    a. carbonate   c. acetate
    b. hydrogen carbonate   d. cyanide

87. Write the formula for each of the following chromium-containing ions, including the overall charge of the ion.
    a. chromous   c. chromic
    b. chromate   d. dichromate

88. Give the name of each of the following polyatomic anions.
    a. CO_3^{2-} d. PO_4^{3-}
    b. ClO_3^- e. ClO_4^-
    c. SO_4^{2-} f. MnO_4^-

89. Name each of the following compounds, which contain polyatomic ions.
    a. LiH_2PO_4 d. Na_2HPO_4
    b. $Cu(CN)_2$ e. $NaClO_2$
    c. $Pb(NO_3)_2$ f. $Co_2(SO_4)_3$

90. Write the formula for each of the following simple binary ionic compounds.
    a. calcium chloride
    b. silver(I) oxide (usually called silver oxide)
    c. aluminum sulfide
    d. beryllium bromide
    e. hydrogen sulfide
    f. potassium hydride
    g. magnesium iodide
    h. cesium fluoride

91. Write the formula for each of the following binary compounds of nonmetallic elements.
    a. sulfur dioxide
    b. dinitrogen monoxide
    c. xenon tetrafluoride
    d. tetraphosphorus decoxide
    e. phosphorus pentachloride
    f. sulfur hexafluoride
    g. nitrogen dioxide

92. Write the formula for each of the following ionic substances.
    a. magnesium phosphide   d. ferrous iodide
    b. calcium fluoride   e. barium oxide
    c. cobalt(III) bromide   f. potassium sulfide

93. Write the formula for each of the following compounds, which contain polyatomic ions. Be sure to enclose the polyatomic ion in parentheses if more than one such ion is needed to balance the oppositely charged ion(s).
    a. silver(I) perchlorate (usually called silver perchlorate)
    b. cobalt(III) hydroxide
    c. sodium hypochlorite
    d. potassium dichromate
    e. ammonium nitrite
    f. ferric hydroxide
    g. ammonium hydrogen carbonate
    h. potassium perbromate

Cumulative Review for Chapters 4–5

1. What is an element? How many elements are presently known? How many of these occur naturally and how many are man-made? Which elements are most abundant on the earth?

2. Without consulting any reference, write the name and symbol for as many elements as you can. How many could you name? How many symbols did you write correctly?

3. Why do the symbols for some elements seem to bear no relationship to the name for the element? Give several examples and explain.

4. Without consulting your textbook or notes, state as many points as you can of Dalton's atomic theory. Explain in your own words each point of the theory.

5. What is a compound? What is meant by the *law of constant composition* for compounds and why is this law so important to our study of chemistry?

6. What is meant by a *nuclear atom?* Describe the points of Rutherford's model for the nuclear atom and how he tested this model. Based on his experiments, how did Rutherford envision the structure of the atom? How did Rutherford's model of the atom's structure differ from Kelvin's "plum pudding" model?

7. What are the three fundamental particles that compose all atoms? Indicate the electrical charge and relative mass of each of these particles. Where is each type of particle found in the atom? Which of these particles is responsible for the chemical behavior of a given type of atom? Why?

8. What are *isotopes?* To what do the *atomic number* and the *mass number* of an isotope refer? How are specific isotopes indicated symbolically (give an example and explain)? Do the isotopes of a given element have the same chemical and physical properties? Explain.

9. Describe the periodic table of the elements. How are the elements arranged in the table? What significance is there in the way the elements are arranged into vertical groups? Which general area of the periodic table contains the metallic elements? Which general area contains the nonmetallic elements? Give the names of some of the families of elements in the periodic table.

10. Are most elements found in nature in the elemental or in the combined form? Why? Name several elements that are usually found in the elemental form.

11. What are *ions?* How are ions formed from atoms? Do isolated atoms form ions spontaneously? To what do the terms *cation* and *anion* refer? In terms of subatomic particles, how is an ion related to the atom from which it is formed? Does the nucleus of an atom change when the atom is converted into an ion? How can the periodic table be used to predict what ion an element's atoms will form?

12. What are some general physical properties of ionic compounds such as sodium chloride? How do we know that substances such as sodium chloride consist of positively and negatively charged particles? Since ionic compounds are made up of electrically charged particles, why doesn't such a compound have an overall electric charge? Can an ionic compound consist only of cations or anions (but not both)? Why not?

13. What principle do we use in writing the formula of an ionic compound such as NaCl or MgI_2? How do we know that *two* iodide ions are needed for each magnesium ion, whereas only one chloride ion is needed per sodium ion?

14. When writing the name of an ionic compound, which is named first, the anion or the cation? Give an example. What ending is added to the root name of an element to show that it is a simple anion in a Type I ionic compound? Give an example. What *two* systems are used to show the charge of the cation in a Type II ionic compound? Give examples of each system for the same compound. What general type of element is involved in Type II compounds?

15. Describe the system used to name Type III binary compounds (compounds of nonmetallic elements). Give several examples illustrating the method. How does this system differ from that used for ionic compounds? How is the system for Type III compounds similar to those for ionic compounds?

16. What is a *polyatomic* ion? Without consulting a reference, list the formulas and names of at least ten polyatomic ions. When writing the overall formula of an ionic compound involving polyatomic ions, why are parentheses used around the formula of a polyatomic ion when more than one such ion is present? Give an example.

17. What is an *oxyanion?* What special system is used in a series of related oxyanions that indicates the relative number of oxygen atoms in each ion? Give examples.

18. What is an *acid?* How are acids that do *not* contain oxygen named? Give several examples. Describe the naming system for the oxyacids. Give examples of a series of oxyacids illustrating this system.

PROBLEMS

19. Write the *symbol* and *atomic number* for each of the following elements:

    magnesium, tin, lead, sodium, hydrogen, chlorine, silver, potassium, calcium, bromine, neon, aluminum, gold, mercury, and iodine.

20. Write the *name* and *atomic number* for each of the following elements:

    a. He   e. S   i. P
    b. B   f. Ba   j. Si
    c. C   g. Be
    d. F   h. O

21. Write the *name* and *chemical symbol* corresponding to each of the following atomic numbers:

    a. 19   f. 6   k. 29
    b. 12   g. 15   l. 35
    c. 36   h. 20   m. 2
    d. 92   i. 79   n. 8
    e. 1   j. 82

22. Indicate the number of protons, neutrons, and electrons in isolated atoms having the following nuclear symbols:

    a. $^{4}_{2}He$ d. $^{41}_{20}Ca$ g. $^{235}_{92}U$
    b. $^{37}_{17}Cl$ e. $^{40}_{20}Ca$ h. $^{1}_{1}H$
    c. $^{79}_{35}Br$ f. $^{238}_{92}U$

23. What simple ion does each of the following elements most commonly form?

    a. Mg   f. Ba   j. Ca
    b. F   g. Na   k. S
    c. Ag   h. Br   l. Li
    d. Al   i. K   m. Cl
    e. O

24. For each of the following simple ions, indicate the number of protons and electrons the ion contains.

    a. K^+ e. Al^{3+} i. H^-
    b. Ca^{2+} f. Ag^+ j. Na^+
    c. N^{3-} g. Cl^- k. O^{2-}
    d. Br^- h. H^+ l. I^-

25. Using the ions indicated in Question 24, write the formulas and give the names for all possible simple ionic compounds involving these ions.

26. Give the name of each of the following binary ionic compounds.

    a. $FeCl_3$ d. Fe_2O_3 g. MnO_2
    b. Cu_2S e. AuI_3 h. CuO
    c. $CoBr_2$ f. Cr_2S_3 i. NiS

27. Which of the following formulas are incorrect? Correct each incorrect formula.

    a. NaS   d. $CaBr_3$ f. $NaCl_2$
    b. K_2S e. AlI_3 g. Cs_3Cl_2
    c. Rb_3N

28. Give the name of each of the following polyatomic ions:

    a. NH_4^+ e. NO_2^- h. ClO_4^-
    b. SO_3^{2-} f. CN^- i. ClO^-
    c. NO_3^- g. OH^- j. PO_4^{3-}
    d. SO_4^{2-}

29. Using the polyatomic anions in Question 28, write the formulas for each of their sodium, calcium, and aluminum compounds.

30. Give the name of each of the following compounds.

    a. B_2O_3 d. N_2O_4 g. SF_6
    b. NO_2 e. P_2O_5 h. N_2O_3
    c. PCl_5 f. ICl

31. Write formulas for each of the following compounds.

    a. potassium sulfide   i. magnesium perchlorate
    b. sodium hydride   j. diphosphorus pentoxide
    c. hydrochloric acid   k. nitric acid
    d. dinitrogen tetroxide   l. silver sulfite
    e. aluminum nitrate   m. copper(II) bromide
    f. calcium sulfate   n. barium phosphate
    g. hydrosulfuric acid   o. gold(III) chloride
    h. ammonium acetate   p. manganous chloride

Chemical Reactions: An Introduction

Chemistry is about change. Grass grows. Steel rusts. Hair is bleached, dyed, "permed," or straightened. Natural gas burns to heat houses. Nylon is produced for jackets, swimsuits, and pantyhose. Water is decomposed to hydrogen and oxygen gas by an electric current. Grape juice ferments in the production of wine. The bombardier beetle concocts a toxic spray to shoot at its enemies (see "Chemistry in Focus," p. 166).

These are just a few examples of chemical changes that affect each of us. Chemical reactions are the heart and soul of chemistry, and in this chapter we will discuss the fundamental ideas about chemical reactions.

When aluminum and iodine react, the heat of the reaction vaporizes excess iodine producing the purple vapor shown (left). *Nylon jackets are sturdy and dry quickly. These characteristics make them ideal for athletic wear* (right).

157

Production of plastic film for use in containers such as soft drink bottles (*left*). Nylon being drawn from the boundary between two solutions containing different reactants (*right*).

6.1 Evidence for a Chemical Reaction

AIM: To learn the signals that show a chemical reaction has occurred.

How do we know when a chemical reaction has occurred? That is, what are the clues that a chemical change has taken place? A glance back at the processes in the introduction suggests that *chemical reactions often give a visual signal.* Steel changes from a smooth, shiny material to a reddish brown, flaky substance when it rusts. Hair changes color when it is bleached. Solid nylon is formed when two particular liquid solutions are brought into contact. A blue flame appears when natural gas reacts with oxygen. Chemical reactions, then, often give *visual* clues: a color changes, a solid forms, bubbles are produced (see Figure 6.1), a flame occurs, and so on. However, reactions are not always visible. Sometimes the only signal that a reaction is occurring is a change in temperature as heat is produced or absorbed (see Figure 6.2).

Table 6.1 summarizes common clues to the occurrence of a chemical reaction, and Figure 6.3 gives some examples of reactions that show these clues.

Energy and chemical reactions will be discussed in more detail in Chapter 8.

FIGURE 6.1
Bubbles of hydrogen and oxygen gas form when an electric current is used to decompose water.

TABLE 6.1

Some Clues That a Chemical Reaction Has Occurred

1. The color changes.
2. A solid forms.
3. Bubbles form.
4. Heat and/or a flame is produced, or heat is absorbed.

FIGURE 6.2
(a) An athlete wears a cold pack to help prevent swelling of an injury. The pack is activated by breaking an ampule; this initiates a chemical reaction that absorbs heat rapidly, lowering the temperature of the area to which the pack is applied. (b) A hot pack used to warm hands and feet in winter. When the package is opened, oxygen from the air penetrates a bag containing solid chemicals. The resulting reaction produces heat for several hours.

(b)

(a)

(a)　　　　　(b)　　　　　(c)　　　　　(d)

FIGURE 6.3
(a) When colorless hydrochloric acid is added to a red solution of cobalt(II) nitrate, the solution turns blue, a sign that a chemical reaction has taken place. (b) A solid forms when a solution of sodium dichromate is added to a solution of lead nitrate. (c) Bubbles of hydrogen gas form when calcium metal reacts with water. (d) Methane gas reacts with oxygen to produce a flame in a bunsen burner.

6.2　Chemical Equations

AIM: To learn to identify the characteristics of a chemical reaction and the information given by a chemical equation.

Chemists have learned that a chemical change always involves a rearrangement of the ways in which the atoms are grouped. For example, when the methane, CH_4, in natural gas combines with oxygen, O_2, in the air and burns, carbon dioxide, CO_2, and water, H_2O, are formed. A chemical change such as this is called a **chemical reaction.** We represent a chemical reaction by writing a **chemical equation** in which the chemicals present before the reaction (the **reactants**) are shown to the left of an arrow and the chemicals formed by the reaction (the **products**) are shown to the right of an arrow.

The arrow indicates the direction of the change and is read as "yields" or "produces":

Reactants → Products

For the reaction of methane with oxygen, we have

Note from this equation that the products contain the same atoms as the reactants but that the atoms are associated in different ways. That is, a *chemical reaction involves changing the ways the atoms are grouped.*

It is important to recognize that **in a chemical reaction, atoms are neither created nor destroyed.** *All atoms present in the reactants must be accounted for among the products.* In other words, there must be the same number of each type of atom on the product side as on the reactant side of the arrow. Making sure that the equation for a reaction obeys this rule is called **balancing the chemical equation** for a reaction.

The equation that we have shown for the reaction between CH_4 and O_2 is not balanced. We can see that it is not balanced by taking the reactants and products apart.

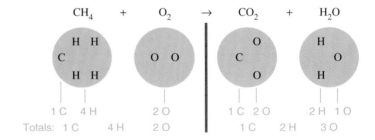

The reaction cannot happen this way because, as it stands, this equation states that one oxygen atom is created and two hydrogen atoms are destroyed. A reaction is only rearrangement of the way the atoms are grouped; atoms are not created or destroyed. The total number of each type of atom must be the same on both sides of the arrow. We can fix the imbalance in this equation by involving one more O_2 molecule on the left and by showing the production of one more H_2O molecule on the right.

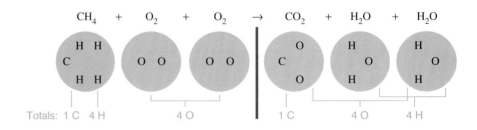

This *balanced chemical equation* shows the actual numbers of molecules involved in this reaction (see Figure 6.4).

When we write the balanced equation for a reaction, we group like molecules together. Thus

$$CH_4 + \boxed{O_2 + O_2} \rightarrow CO_2 + \boxed{H_2O + H_2O}$$

is written

$$CH_4 + \boxed{2O_2} \rightarrow CO_2 + \boxed{2H_2O}$$

The chemical equation for a reaction provides us with two important types of information:

1. The identities of the reactants and products
2. The relative numbers of each

Physical States

Besides specifying the compounds involved in the reaction, we often indicate in the equation the *physical states* of the reactants and products by using the following symbols:

Symbol	*State*
(*s*)	solid
(*l*)	liquid
(*g*)	gas
(*aq*)	dissolved in water (in aqueous solution)

For example, when solid potassium reacts with liquid water, the products are hydrogen gas and potassium hydroxide; the latter remains dissolved in the water. From this information about the reactants and products, we can write the equation for the reaction. Solid potassium is represented by K(*s*); liquid water is written as $H_2O(l)$; hydrogen gas contains diatomic molecules and is represented as $H_2(g)$; potassium hydroxide dissolved in water is written as KOH(*aq*). So the *unbalanced* equation for the reaction is

$$\underset{\substack{\text{Solid} \\ \text{potassium}}}{K(s)} + \underset{\text{Water}}{H_2O(l)} \rightarrow \underset{\substack{\text{Hydrogen} \\ \text{gas}}}{H_2(g)} + \underset{\substack{\text{Potassium hydroxide} \\ \text{dissolved in water}}}{KOH(aq)}$$

This reaction is shown in Figure 6.5.

The hydrogen gas produced in this reaction then reacts with the oxygen gas in the air, producing gaseous water and a flame. The *unbalanced* equation for this second reaction is

$$H_2(g) + O_2(g) \rightarrow H_2O(g)$$

Both of these reactions produce a great deal of heat. In Example 6.1 we will practice writing the unbalanced equations for reactions. Then, in the next section, we will discuss systematic procedures for balancing equations.

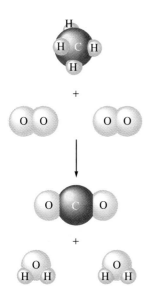

FIGURE 6.4
The reaction between methane and oxygen to give water and carbon dioxide. Note that there are four oxygen atoms in the products *and* in the reactants; none has been gained or lost in the reaction. Similarly, there are four hydrogen atoms and one carbon atom in the reactants *and* in the products. The reaction simply changes the way the atoms are grouped.

(a)

(b)

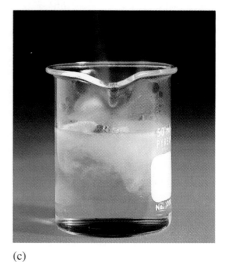
(c)

FIGURE 6.5
The reactants (a) potassium metal (stored in mineral oil to prevent oxidation) and (b) water. (c) The reaction of potassium with water. The flame occurs because the hydrogen gas, $H_2(g)$ produced by the reaction burns in air (reacts with $O_2(g)$)at the high temperatures caused by the reaction.

 EXAMPLE 6.1   *Chemical Equations: Recognizing Reactants and Products*

Write the *unbalanced* chemical equation for each of the following reactions.

a. Solid mercury(II) oxide decomposes to produce liquid mercury metal and gaseous oxygen.

b. Solid carbon reacts with gaseous oxygen to form gaseous carbon dioxide.

Zinc metal reacts with hydrochloric acid to produce bubbles of hydrogen gas.

c. Solid zinc is added to an aqueous solution containing dissolved hydrogen chloride to produce gaseous hydrogen that bubbles out of the solution and zinc(II) chloride that remains dissolved in the water.

Solution

a. In this case we have only one reactant, mercury(II) oxide. The name mercury(II) oxide means that the Hg^{2+} cation is present, so one O^{2-} ion is required for a zero net charge. Thus the formula is HgO, which is written HgO(*s*) in this case because it is given as a solid. The products are liquid mercury, written Hg(*l*), and gaseous oxygen, written $O_2(g)$. (Remember that oxygen exists as a diatomic molecule under normal conditions.) The unbalanced equation is

$$\underset{\text{Reactant}}{HgO(s)} \quad \rightarrow \quad \underset{\text{Products}}{Hg(l) \quad + \quad O_2(g)}$$

b. In this case, solid carbon, written C(*s*), reacts with oxygen gas, $O_2(g)$, to form gaseous carbon dioxide, which is written $CO_2(g)$. The equation (which happens to be balanced) is

$$\underset{\text{Reactants}}{C(s) \ + \ O_2(g)} \ \rightarrow \ \underset{\text{Product}}{CO_2(g)}$$

c. In this reaction solid zinc, Zn(*s*), is added to an aqueous solution of hydrogen chloride, which is written HCl(*aq*) and called hydrochloric acid. These are the reactants. The products of the reaction are gaseous hydrogen, $H_2(g)$, and aqueous zinc(II) chloride. The name zinc(II) chloride means that the Zn^{2+} ion is present, so two Cl^- ions are needed to achieve a zero net charge. Thus zinc(II) chloride dissolved in water is written $ZnCl_2(aq)$. The unbalanced equation for the reaction is

Because Zn only forms the Zn^{2+} ion, a roman numeral is usually not used. Thus $ZnCl_2$ is commonly called zinc chloride.

Reactants   Products

$$Zn(s) \;+\; HCl(aq) \;\rightarrow\; H_2(g) \;+\; ZnCl_2(aq)$$

 Self-Check Exercise 6.1

Identify the reactants and products and write the *unbalanced* equation (including symbols for states) for each of the following chemical reactions.

a. Solid magnesium metal reacts with liquid water to form solid magnesium hydroxide and hydrogen gas.

b. Solid ammonium dichromate (review Table 5.4 if this compound is unfamiliar) decomposes to solid chromium(III) oxide, gaseous nitrogen, and gaseous water.

c. Gaseous ammonia reacts with gaseous oxygen to form gaseous nitrogen monoxide and gaseous water.

See Problems 6.13 through 6.34.

6.3   *Balancing Chemical Equations*

AIM: To learn how to write a balanced equation for a chemical reaction.

As we saw in the previous section, an unbalanced chemical equation is not an accurate representation of the reaction that occurs. Whenever you see an equation for a reaction, you should ask yourself whether it is balanced. The principle that lies at the heart of the balancing process is that **atoms are conserved in a chemical reaction.** That is, atoms are neither created nor destroyed. They are just grouped differently. The same number of each type of atom is found among the reactants and among the products.

Chemists determine the identity of the reactants and products of a reaction by experimental observation. For example, when methane (natural gas) is burned in the presence of sufficient oxygen gas, the products are always carbon dioxide and water. **The identities (formulas) of the compounds must never be changed in balancing a chemical equation.** In other words, the subscripts in a formula cannot be changed, nor can atoms be added to or subtracted from a formula.

Trial and error is often useful for solving problems. It's okay to make a few wrong turns before you get to the right answer.

Most chemical equations can be balanced by trial and error—that is, by inspection. Keep trying until you find the numbers of reactants and products that give the same number of each type of atom on both sides of the arrow. For example, consider the reaction of hydrogen gas and oxygen gas to form

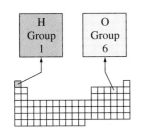

Reactants	Products
2 H	2 H
2 O	1 O

liquid water. First, we write the unbalanced equation from the description of the reaction.

$$H_2(g) + O_2(g) \rightarrow H_2O(l)$$

We can see that this equation is unbalanced by counting the atoms on both sides of the arrow.

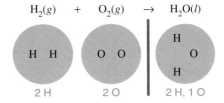

We have one more oxygen atom in the reactants than in the products. Because we cannot create or destroy atoms and because we *cannot change the formulas* of the reactants or products, we must balance the equation by adding more molecules of reactants and/or products. In this case we need one more oxygen atom on the right, so we add another water molecule (which contains one O atom). Then we count all of the atoms again.

Reactants	Products
2 H	4 H
2 O	2 O

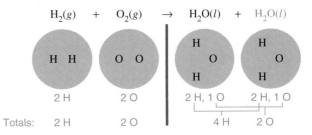

We have balanced the oxygen atoms, but now the hydrogen atoms have become unbalanced. There are more hydrogen atoms on the right than on the left. We can solve this problem by adding another hydrogen molecule (H_2) to the reactant side.

Reactants	Products
4 H	4 H
2 O	2 O

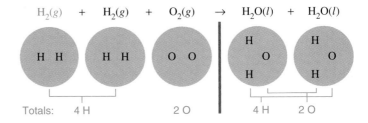

The equation is now balanced. We have the same numbers of hydrogen and oxygen atoms represented on both sides of the arrow. Collecting like molecules, we write the balanced equation as

$$2H_2(g) + O_2(g) \rightarrow 2H_2O(l)$$

Consider next what happens if we multiply every part of this balanced equation by 2:

$$2 \times [2H_2(g) + O_2(g) \rightarrow 2H_2O(l)]$$

to give

$$4H_2(g) + 2O_2(g) \rightarrow 4H_2O(l)$$

This equation is balanced (count the atoms to verify this). In fact, we can multiply or divide *all parts* of the original balanced equation by any number to give a new balanced equation. Thus each chemical reaction has many possible balanced equations. Is one of the many possibilities preferred over the others? Yes.

The accepted convention is that the "best" balanced equation is the one with the *smallest integers (whole numbers)*. These integers are called the **coefficients** for the balanced equation. Therefore, for the reaction of hydrogen and oxygen to form water, the "correct" balanced equation is

$$2H_2(g) + O_2(g) \rightarrow 2H_2O(l)$$

The coefficients 2, 1 (never written), and 2, respectively, are the smallest *integers* that give a balanced equation for this reaction.

Next we will balance the equation for the reaction of liquid ethanol, C_2H_5OH, with oxygen gas to form gaseous carbon dioxide and water. This reaction, among many others, occurs in engines that burn a gasoline–ethanol mixture called gasohol.

The first step in obtaining the balanced equation for a reaction is always to identify the reactants and products from the description given for the reaction. In this case we are told that liquid ethanol, $C_2H_5OH(l)$, reacts with gaseous oxygen, $O_2(g)$, to produce gaseous carbon dioxide, $CO_2(g)$, and gaseous water, $H_2O(g)$. Therefore, the unbalanced equation is

$$C_2H_5OH(l) + O_2(g) \rightarrow CO_2(g) + H_2O(g)$$

| Liquid ethanol | Gaseous oxygen | Gaseous carbon dioxide | Gaseous water |

In balancing equations, start by looking at the most complicated molecule.

When one molecule in an equation is more complicated (contains more elements) than the others, it is best to start with that molecule. The most complicated molecule here is C_2H_5OH, so we begin by considering the products that contain the atoms in C_2H_5OH. We start with carbon. The only product that contains carbon is CO_2. Because C_2H_5OH contains two carbon atoms, we place a 2 before the CO_2 to balance the carbon atoms.

C_2H_5OH

2 C, 6H, 1 O

$$C_2H_5OH(l) + O_2(g) \rightarrow 2CO_2(g) + H_2O(g)$$

2 C atoms   2 C atoms

Remember, we cannot change the formula of any reactant or product when we balance an equation. We can only place coefficients in front of the formulas.

Next we consider hydrogen. The only product containing hydrogen is H_2O. C_2H_5OH contains six hydrogen atoms, so we need six hydrogen atoms on the right. Because each H_2O contains two hydrogen atoms, we need three H_2O molecules to yield six hydrogen atoms. So we place a 3 before the H_2O.

$$C_2H_5OH(l) + O_2(g) \rightarrow 2CO_2(g) + 3H_2O(g)$$

(5 + 1) H   (3 × 2) H
6 H   6 H

CHEMISTRY IN FOCUS

The Beetle That Shoots Straight

If someone said to you, "Name something that protects itself by spraying its enemies," your answer would almost certainly be "a skunk." Of course, you would be correct, but there is another correct answer—the bombadier beetle. When threatened, this beetle shoots a boiling stream of toxic chemicals at its enemy. How does this clever beetle accomplish this? Obviously, the boiling mixture cannot be stored inside the beetle's body all the time. Instead, when endangered, the beetle mixes chemicals that produce the hot spray. The chemicals involved are stored in two compartments. One compartment contains the chemicals hydrogen peroxide (H_2O_2) and methylhydroquinone ($C_7H_8O_2$). The key reaction is the decomposition of hydrogen peroxide to form oxygen gas and water:

$$2H_2O_2(aq) \rightarrow 2H_2O(l) + O_2(g)$$

Hydrogen peroxide also reacts with the hydroquinones to produce other compounds that become part of the toxic spray.

However, none of these reactions occurs very fast unless certain enzymes are present. (Enzymes are natural substances that speed up biological reactions by means we will not discuss here.) When the beetle mixes the hydrogen peroxide and hydroquinones with the enzyme, the decomposition of H_2O_2 occurs rapidly, producing a hot mixture pressurized by the formation of oxygen gas. When the gas pressure becomes high enough, the hot spray is ejected in one long stream or in short bursts. The beetle has highly accurate aim and can shoot several attackers with one batch of spray.

A bombardier beetle.

O—C—O
O—C—O

4 O atoms

H—O—H
H—O—H
H—O—H

3 O atoms

Finally, we count the oxygen atoms. On the left we have three oxygen atoms (one in C_2H_5OH and two in O_2), and on the right we have seven oxygen atoms (four in $2CO_2$ and three in $3H_2O$). We can correct this imbalance if we have three O_2 molecules on the left. That is, we place a coefficient of 3 before the O_2 to produce the balanced equation.

$$C_2H_5OH(l) + 3O_2(g) \rightarrow 2CO_2(g) + 3H_2O(g)$$

1 O   (3 × 2) O   (2 × 2) O   3 O

7 O   7 O

At this point you may have a question: why did we choose O_2 on the left when we balanced the oxygen atoms? Why not use C_2H_5OH, which has an oxygen atom? The answer is that if we had changed the coefficient in front of C_2H_5OH, we would have unbalanced the hydrogen and carbon atoms. Now we count all of the atoms as a check to make sure the equation is balanced.

Reactants	Products
2 C	2 C
6 H	6 H
7 O	7 O

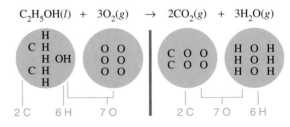

$$C_2H_5OH(l) + 3O_2(g) \rightarrow 2CO_2(g) + 3H_2O(g)$$

Totals: 2 C   6 H   7 O   2 C   7 O   6 H

The equation is now balanced. We have the same numbers of all types of atoms on both sides of the arrow. Notice that these coefficients are the smallest integers that give a balanced equation.

The process of writing and balancing the equation for a chemical reaction consists of several steps:

How to Write and Balance Equations

STEP 1 Read the description of the chemical reaction. What are the reactants, the products, and their states? Write the appropriate formulas.

STEP 2 Write the *unbalanced* equation that summarizes the information from step 1.

STEP 3 Balance the equation by inspection, starting with the most complicated molecule. Proceed element by element to determine what coefficients are necessary so that the same number of each type of atom appears on both the reactant side and the product side. Do not change the identities (formulas) of any of the reactants or products.

STEP 4 Check to see that the coefficients used give the same number of each type of atom on both sides of the arrow. (Note that an "atom" may be present in an element, compound, or ion.) Also check to see that the coefficients used are the smallest integers that give the balanced equation. This can be done by determining whether all coefficients can be divided by the same integer to give a set of smaller *integer* coefficients.

EXAMPLE 6.2 *Balancing Chemical Equations I*

For the following reaction, write the unbalanced equation and then balance the equation: solid potassium reacts with liquid water to form gaseous hydrogen and potassium hydroxide that dissolves in the water.

Solution

STEP 1 From the description given for the reaction, we know that the reactants are solid potassium, $K(s)$, and liquid water, $H_2O(l)$. The products are gaseous hydrogen, $H_2(g)$, and dissolved potassium hydroxide, $KOH(aq)$.

STEP 2 The unbalanced equation for the reaction is

$$K(s) \ + \ H_2O(l) \ \rightarrow \ H_2(g) \ + \ KOH(aq)$$

STEP 3 Although none of the reactants or products is very complicated, we will start with KOH because it contains the most elements (three). We will arbitrarily consider hydrogen first. Note that on the reactant side of the equation in Step 2, there are two hydrogen atoms but on the product side there are three. If we place a coefficient of 2 in front of both H_2O and KOH, we now have four H atoms on each side.

$$K(s) + 2H_2O(l) \rightarrow H_2(g) + 2KOH(aq)$$

4 H	2 H	2 H
atoms	atoms	atoms

Also note that the oxygen atoms balance.

$$K(s) + 2H_2O(l) \rightarrow H_2(g) + 2KOH(aq)$$

2 O	2 O
atoms	atoms

However, the K atoms do not balance; we have one on the left and two on the right. We can fix this easily by placing a coefficient of 2 in front of K(s) to give the balanced equation:

$$2K(s) + 2H_2O(l) \rightarrow H_2(g) + 2KOH(aq)$$

STEP 4
Check: There are 2 K, 4 H, and 2 O on both sides of the arrow, and the co-efficients are the smallest integers that give a balanced equation. We know this because we cannot divide through by a given integer to give a set of smaller *integer* (whole-number) coefficients. For example, if we divide all of the coefficients by 2, we get

$$K(s) + H_2O(l) \rightarrow \tfrac{1}{2}H_2(g) + KOH(aq)$$

This is not acceptable because the coefficient for H_2 is not an integer.

Reactants	Products
2 K	2 K
4 H	4 H
2 O	2 O

EXAMPLE 6.3   *Balancing Chemical Equations II*

Under appropriate conditions at 1000 °C, ammonia gas reacts with oxygen gas to produce gaseous nitrogen monoxide (common name, nitric oxide) and gaseous water. Write the unbalanced and balanced equations for this reaction.

Solution

STEP 1   The reactants are gaseous ammonia, $NH_3(g)$, and gaseous oxygen, $O_2(g)$. The products are gaseous nitrogen monoxide, $NO(g)$, and gaseous water, $H_2O(g)$.

STEP 2   The unbalanced equation for the reaction is

$$NH_3(g) + O_2(g) \rightarrow NO(g) + H_2O(g)$$

STEP 3   In this equation there is no molecule that is obviously the most com-plicated. Three molecules contain two elements, so we arbitrarily start with NH_3. We arbitrarily begin by looking at hydrogen. A coefficient of 2 for NH_3 and a coefficient of 3 for H_2O give six atoms of hydrogen on both sides.

$$2NH_3(g) + O_2(g) \rightarrow NO(g) + 3H_2O(g)$$

| | |
| 6 H | 6 H |

We can balance the nitrogen by giving NO a coefficient of 2.

$$2NH_3(g) + O_2(g) \rightarrow 2NO(g) + 3H_2O(g)$$

| | |
| 2 N | 2 N |

Reactants	Products
1 N	1 N
3 H	2 H
2 O	1 O

$\frac{5}{2} = 2\frac{1}{2}$
O—O $2\frac{1}{2}$ O$_2$
O—O   contains
O—O   5 O atoms

Finally, we note that there are two atoms of oxygen on the left and five on the right. The oxygen can be balanced with a coefficient of $\frac{5}{2}$ for O$_2$, because $\frac{5}{2} \times$ O$_2$ gives five oxygen atoms.

$$2NH_3(g) + \tfrac{5}{2}O_2(g) \rightarrow 2NO(g) + 3H_2O(g)$$

          5 O   2 O   3 O

However, the convention is to have integer (whole-number) coefficients, so we multiply the entire equation by 2.

$$2 \times [2NH_3(g) + \tfrac{5}{2}O_2(g) \rightarrow 2NO(g) + 3H_2O(g)]$$

or

$$2 \times 2NH_3(g) + 2 \times \tfrac{5}{2}O_2(g) \rightarrow 2 \times 2NO(g) + 2 \times 3H_2O(g)$$

$$4NH_3(g) + 5O_2(g) \rightarrow 4NO(g) + 6H_2O(g)$$

STEP 4

Check: There are 4 N, 12 H, and 10 O atoms on both sides, so the equation is balanced. These coefficients are the smallest integers that give a balanced equation. That is, we cannot divide all coefficients by the same integer and obtain a smaller set of *integers*.

Reactants	Products
4 N	4 N
12 H	12 H
10 O	10 O

 Self-Check Exercise 6.2

Propane, C$_3$H$_8$, a liquid at 25 °C under high pressure, is often used for gas grills and as a fuel in rural areas where there is no natural gas pipeline. When liquid propane is released from its storage tank, it changes to propane gas that reacts with oxygen gas (it "burns") to give gaseous carbon dioxide and gaseous water. Write and balance the equation for this reaction.

Hint: This description of a chemical process contains many words, some of which are crucial to solving the problem and some of which are not. First sort out the important information and use symbols to represent it.

See Problems 6.37 through 6.44.

 EXAMPLE 6.4

Decorations on glass are produced by etching with hydrofluoric acid.

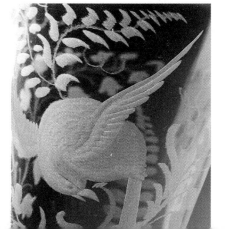

Balancing Chemical Equations III

Glass is sometimes decorated by etching patterns on its surface. Etching occurs when hydrofluoric acid (an aqueous solution of HF) reacts with the silicon dioxide in the glass to form gaseous silicon tetrafluoride and liquid water. Write and balance the equation for this reaction.

Solution

STEP 1   From the description of the reaction we can identify the reactants:

    hydrofluoric acid   HF(*aq*)

    solid silicon dioxide   SiO$_2$(*s*)

and the products:

    gaseous silicon tetrafluoride   SiF$_4$(*g*)

    liquid water   H$_2$O(*l*)

Reactants	Products
1 Si	1 Si
1 H	2 H
1 F	4 F
2 O	1 O

Reactants	Products
1 Si	1 Si
4 H	2 H
4 F	4 F
2 O	1 O

Reactants	Products
1 Si	1 Si
4 H	4 H
4 F	4 F
2 O	2 O

If you are having trouble writing formulas from names, review the appropriate sections of Chapter 5. It is very important that you are able to do this.

STEP 2   The unbalanced equation is

$$SiO_2(s) + HF(aq) \rightarrow SiF_4(g) + H_2O(l)$$

STEP 3   There is no clear choice here for the most complicated molecule. We arbitrarily start with the elements in SiF_4. The silicon is balanced (one atom on each side), but the fluorine is not. To balance the fluorine, we need a coefficient of 4 before the HF.

$$SiO_2(s) + 4HF(aq) \rightarrow SiF_4(g) + H_2O(l)$$

Hydrogen and oxygen are not balanced. Because we have four hydrogen atoms on the left and two on the right, we place a 2 before the H_2O:

$$SiO_2(s) + 4HF(aq) \rightarrow SiF_4(g) + 2H_2O(l)$$

This balances the hydrogen *and* the oxygen (two atoms on each side).

STEP 4
Check: $$SiO_2(s) + 4HF(aq) \rightarrow SiF_4(g) + 2H_2O(l)$$

Totals: 1 Si, 2 O, 4 H, 4 F   →   1 Si, 4 F, 4 H, 2 O

All atoms check, so the equation is balanced.

 Self-Check Exercise 6.3

Give the balanced equation for each of the following reactions.

a. When solid ammonium nitrite is heated, it produces nitrogen gas and water vapor.

b. Gaseous nitrogen monoxide (common name, nitric oxide) decomposes to produce dinitrogen monoxide gas (common name, nitrous oxide) and nitrogen dioxide gas.

c. Liquid nitric acid decomposes to reddish brown nitrogen dioxide gas, liquid water, and oxygen gas. (This is why bottles of nitric acid become yellow upon standing.)

See Problems 6.37 through 6.44.

Chapter Review

Key Terms

chemical reaction *(6.2)*
chemical equation *(6.2)*
reactant *(6.2)*
coefficient *(6.3)*

product *(6.2)*
balancing a chemical
    equation *(6.2)*

Summary

1. Chemical reactions usually give some kind of visual signal—a color changes, a solid forms, bubbles form, heat and/or flame are produced.

2. A chemical equation represents a chemical reaction. Reactants are shown on the left side of an arrow and products on the right. In a chemical reaction, atoms are

neither created nor destroyed; they are merely rearranged. A balanced chemical equation gives the relative numbers of reactant and product molecules.

3. A chemical equation for a reaction can be balanced by using a systematic approach. First identify the reactants and products and write the formulas. Next write the unbalanced equation. Then balance by trial and error, starting with the most complicated molecule(s). Finally, check to be sure the equation is balanced.

Questions and Problems

All even-numbered exercises have answers in the back of this book and solutions in the Solutions Guide.

6.1 ■ *Evidence for a Chemical Reaction*

QUESTIONS

1. List some possible signals that a chemical reaction has occurred. Are these clues always visible? Can you think of any other indications that a chemical reaction has occurred?

2. A solution of hydrogen peroxide, H_2O_2, is often used to clean cuts and scrapes, particularly if it is feared that anerobic bacteria such as *Clostridium* (the microbe that causes tetanus) have been introduced into the wound. What evidence is there for a chemical reaction taking place when hydrogen peroxide is applied to a wound?

3. Sterling silver, as used for fashioning jewelry and dinnerware, tarnishes easily when exposed to air. Is there evidence that products for removing tarnish from silver work by chemical reaction?

4. Oven cleaners typically contain lye (sodium hydroxide), which converts the greases and oils soiling the oven walls into soap, which can then be washed away more easily. What evidence is there that such oven cleaners work by a chemical reaction?

5. Baking powder is used to make certain doughs "rise." Can you think of any evidence that the action of baking powder represents a chemical reaction?

6. When fruit juice is left exposed to the air, it eventually ferments into wine or vinegar. What evidence is there that a chemical reaction is occurring?

6.2 ■ *Chemical Equations*

QUESTIONS

7. The substances present before a chemical reaction takes place are called the _____, and the substances present after the reaction takes place are called the _____.

8. In an ordinary chemical reaction, _____ are neither created nor destroyed.

9. The total number of atoms present before and after a chemical reaction takes place must be _____.

10. Balancing an equation for a reaction ensures that the number of each type of atom is _____ on both sides of the equation.

11. The notation "(g)" after a substance's formula indicates that the substance exists in the _____ state.

12. In a chemical equation for a reaction, the notation "(aq)" after a substance's formula means that the substance is dissolved in _____.

PROBLEMS

Note: In some of the following problems you will need to write a chemical formula from the name of the compound. Review Chapter 5 if you are having trouble with this.

13. When sodium hydrogen carbonate (sodium bicarbonate), $NaHCO_3$, is heated strongly in a test tube, carbon dioxide gas, CO_2, and water vapor, H_2O, are evolved from the test tube, leaving a residue of sodium carbonate, Na_2CO_3. Write the unbalanced chemical equation for this process.

14. When a mixture of powdered gray zinc metal and powdered yellow sulfur is heated strongly, a spectacular chemical reaction occurs, and white zinc sulfide solid is produced. Write the unbalanced chemical equation for this process. (Zinc only forms the Zn^{2+} ion.)

15. If a sample of pure hydrogen gas is ignited very carefully, the hydrogen burns gently, combining with the oxygen gas of the air to form water vapor. Write the unbalanced chemical equation for this reaction.

16. Solid ammonium carbonate, $(NH_4)_2CO_3$, is used as the active ingredient in "smelling salts." When solid ammonium carbonate is heated, it decomposes into ammonia gas and carbon dioxide gas. Write the unbalanced chemical equation for this process.

17. If an iron ore containing iron(II) oxide is heated with carbon in a furnace, the iron(II) oxide is converted to molten iron metal, and the carbon is converted to carbon dioxide gas. Write the unbalanced chemical equation for this process.

18. If elemental chlorine gas is bubbled through a solution of potassium iodide, the iodide ion is converted to elemental iodine, which may be recovered as a gray solid, leaving a solution of potassium chloride. Write the unbalanced chemical equation for this reaction.

19. Elemental boron is produced in one industrial process by heating diboron trioxide with magnesium metal, also producing magnesium oxide as a by-product. Write the unbalanced chemical equation for this process.

20. Calcium metal is moderately reactive. If turnings of calcium are added to water, the metal begins to bubble as hydrogen gas is formed. The water begins to turn cloudy, as relatively insoluble calcium hydroxide begins to form. Write the unbalanced chemical equation for the reaction of calcium metal with water.

21. Boric acid, H_3BO_3, is produced by treating borax ($Na_2B_4O_7$) with aqueous sulfuric acid. Sodium sulfate is a by-product of this process. Write the unbalanced chemical equation for the reaction.

22. Acetylene gas, C_2H_2, is produced by treating calcium carbide, CaC_2, with water. Calcium hydroxide is also produced as a by-product of this reaction. Write the unbalanced chemical equation for this process.

23. Nitrous oxide gas (systematic name: dinitrogen monoxide) is used by some dental practitioners as an anesthetic. Nitrous oxide (and water vapor as by-product) can be produced in small quantities in the laboratory by careful heating of ammonium nitrate. Write the unbalanced chemical equation for this reaction.

24. Hydrogen sulfide gas is responsible for the odor of rotten eggs. Hydrogen sulfide burns in air, producing sulfur dioxide gas and water vapor. Write the unbalanced chemical equation for this process.

25. When sulfuric acid is added to solid sodium chloride and the mixture is heated, hydrogen chloride gas is generated, leaving a solid residue of sodium sulfate. Write an unbalanced chemical equation for this reaction.

26. A process that uses electricity to cause a chemical reaction to occur is called an electrolysis reaction. When an electrical current is passed through a concentrated aqueous sodium chloride solution (brine), several useful products can be isolated: $NaOH(s)$, $Cl_2(g)$, and $H_2(g)$. Write the unbalanced chemical equation for this process.

27. The Group 2 metals (Ba, Ca, Sr) can be produced in the elemental state by the reaction of their oxides with aluminum metal at high temperatures, also producing solid aluminum oxide as a by-product. Write the unbalanced chemical equations for the reactions of barium oxide, calcium oxide, and strontium oxide with aluminum.

28. Ozone gas is a form of elemental oxygen containing molecules with *three* oxygen atoms, O_3. Ozone is produced from atmospheric oxygen gas, O_2, by the high-energy outbursts found in lightning storms. Write the unbalanced equation for the formation of ozone gas from oxygen gas.

29. When sulfuric acid is added to ordinary table sugar (sucrose), $C_{12}H_{22}O_{11}$, a long black "snake" of elemental carbon forms, with the release of a cloud of steam (water vapor). Write the unbalanced chemical equation for this process.

30. Sand consists primarily of silicon dioxide, SiO_2. Pure elemental silicon for use in the semiconductor industry can be produced by reaction of sand with elemental carbon at high temperatures. Carbon monoxide gas is also a product of the reaction. Write the unbalanced chemical equation for the reaction of silicon dioxide with carbon.

31. The principal natural ore of lead is galena, which is primarily lead(II) sulfide. Lead(II) sulfide can be converted to lead(II) oxide by heating strongly in air, with sulfur dioxide gas as a by-product. Lead(II) oxide can then be heated with elemental carbon (coke), producing pure lead metal and carbon dioxide gas. Write unbalanced chemical equations for the reaction of lead(II) sulfide with oxygen gas, and for the reaction of lead(II) oxide with carbon.

32. Although they were formerly called the inert gases, the heavier elements of Group 8 do form relatively stable compounds. For example, at high temperatures in the presence of an appropriate catalyst, xenon gas will combine directly with fluorine gas to produce solid xenon tetrafluoride. Write the unbalanced chemical equation for this process.

33. When bright red mercury(II) oxide is heated in a test tube, oxygen gas is evolved, and droplets of liquid mercury condense at the cooler top of the test tube. Write the unbalanced chemical equation for this process.

34. If ordinary table sugar (sucrose, $C_{12}H_{22}O_{11}$) is heated strongly in pure oxygen gas, it will ignite and burn, producing carbon dioxide gas and water vapor. Write the unbalanced chemical equation for this process.

6.3 ■ Balancing Chemical Equations

QUESTIONS

35. When balancing a chemical equation, one must never change the _____ of any reactant or product.

36. After balancing a chemical equation, we ordinarily make sure that the coefficients are the smallest _____ possible.

PROBLEMS

37. Balance each of the following chemical equations.
    a. $FeCl_3(aq) + KOH(aq) \rightarrow Fe(OH)_3(s) + KCl(aq)$

b. $Pb(C_2H_3O_2)_2(aq) + KI(aq) \rightarrow$
   $PbI_2(s) + KC_2H_3O_2(aq)$
c. $P_4O_{10}(s) + H_2O(l) \rightarrow H_3PO_4(aq)$
d. $Li_2O(s) + H_2O(l) \rightarrow LiOH(aq)$
e. $MnO_2(s) + C(s) \rightarrow Mn(s) + CO_2(g)$
f. $Sb(s) + Cl_2(g) \rightarrow SbCl_3(s)$
g. $CH_4(g) + H_2O(g) \rightarrow CO(g) + H_2(g)$
h. $FeS(s) + HCl(aq) \rightarrow FeCl_2(aq) + H_2S(g)$

38. Balance each of the following chemical equations.
    a. $Br_2(l) + KI(aq) \rightarrow KBr(aq) + I_2(s)$
    b. $Co(s) + O_2(g) \rightarrow Co_2O_3(s)$
    c. $P_4(s) + O_2(g) \rightarrow P_4O_{10}(s)$
    d. $Al(s) + HNO_3(aq) \rightarrow Al(NO_3)_3(aq) + H_2(g)$
    e. $PBr_3(l) + H_2O(l) \rightarrow H_3PO_3(aq) + HBr(aq)$
    f. $NO(g) + O_2(g) \rightarrow NO_2(g)$
    g. $C_2H_6(g) + O_2(g) \rightarrow CO_2(g) + H_2O(g)$
    h. $CuO(s) + H_2SO_4(aq) \rightarrow CuSO_4(aq) + H_2O(l)$

39. Balance each of the following chemical equations.
    a. $C_4H_{10}(g) + O_2(g) \rightarrow CO_2(g) + H_2O(g)$
    b. $C_6H_{14}(g) + O_2(g) \rightarrow CO_2(g) + H_2O(g)$
    c. $B(s) + Cl_2(g) \rightarrow BCl_3(l)$
    d. $NO(g) + O_2(g) \rightarrow NO_2(g)$
    e. $Ti_2O_3(s) + CO_2(g) \rightarrow Ti_2(CO_3)_3(s)$
    f. $OF_2(g) \rightarrow O_2(g) + F_2(g)$
    g. $NaClO_3(s) \rightarrow NaCl(s) + O_2(g)$
    h. $Al(OH)_3(s) \rightarrow Al_2O_3(s) + H_2O(l)$

40. Balance each of the following chemical equations.
    a. $CaF_2(s) + H_2SO_4(l) \rightarrow CaSO_4(s) + HF(g)$
    b. $KBr(s) + H_3PO_4(aq) \rightarrow K_3PO_4(aq) + HBr(g)$
    c. $TiCl_4(l) + Na(s) \rightarrow NaCl(s) + Ti(s)$
    d. $K_2CO_3(s) \rightarrow K_2O(s) + CO_2(g)$
    e. $KO_2(s) + H_2O(l) \rightarrow KOH(aq) + O_2(g)$
    f. $Na_2O_2(s) + H_2O(g) + CO_2(g) \rightarrow NaHCO_3(s) + O_2(g)$
    g. $KNO_2(s) + C(s) \rightarrow K_2CO_3(s) + CO(g) + N_2(g)$
    h. $BaO(s) + Al(s) \rightarrow Al_2O_3(s) + Ba(s)$

41. Balance each of the following chemical equations.
    a. $Li(s) + Cl_2(g) \rightarrow LiCl(s)$
    b. $Ba(s) + N_2(g) \rightarrow Ba_3N_2(s)$
    c. $NaHCO_3(s) \rightarrow Na_2CO_3(s) + CO_2(g) + H_2O(g)$
    d. $Al(s) + HCl(aq) \rightarrow AlCl_3(aq) + H_2(g)$
    e. $NiS(s) + O_2(g) \rightarrow NiO(s) + SO_2(g)$
    f. $CaH_2(s) + H_2O(l) \rightarrow Ca(OH)_2(s) + H_2(g)$
    g. $H_2(g) + CO(g) \rightarrow CH_3OH(l)$
    h. $B_2O_3(s) + C(s) \rightarrow B_4C_3(s) + CO_2(g)$

42. Balance each of the following chemical equations.
    a. $SiI_4(s) + Mg(s) \rightarrow Si(s) + MgI_2(s)$
    b. $MnO_2(s) + Mg(s) \rightarrow Mn(s) + MgO(s)$
    c. $Ba(s) + S_8(s) \rightarrow BaS(s)$
    d. $NH_3(g) + Cl_2(g) \rightarrow NH_4Cl(s) + NCl_3(g)$
    e. $Cu_2S(s) + S_8(s) \rightarrow CuS(s)$
    f. $Al(s) + H_2SO_4(aq) \rightarrow Al_2(SO_4)_3(aq) + H_2(g)$
    g. $NaCl(s) + H_2SO_4(aq) \rightarrow HCl(g) + Na_2SO_4(s)$
    h. $CO(g) + O_2(g) \rightarrow CO_2(g)$

43. Balance each of the following chemical equations.
    a. $TiCl_4(l) + Mg(s) \rightarrow Ti(s) + MgCl_2(s)$
    b. $C_2H_2(g) + Br_2(l) \rightarrow C_2H_2Br_4(l)$
    c. $ZnS(s) + O_2(g) \rightarrow ZnO(s) + SO_2(g)$
    d. $Zn(s) + NaOH(aq) + H_2O(l) \rightarrow Na_2Zn(OH)_4(aq) + H_2(g)$
    e. $C_6H_6(l) + H_2(g) \rightarrow C_6H_{12}(l)$
    f. $C(s) + H_2(g) + O_2(g) \rightarrow C_2H_5OH(l)$
    g. $Hg_2Cl_2(s) \rightarrow Hg(l) + Cl_2(g)$
    h. $Cl_2(g) + H_2O(l) \rightarrow HCl(aq) + HClO(aq)$

44. Balance each of the following chemical equations.
    a. $Ba(NO_3)_2(aq) + Na_2CrO_4(aq) \rightarrow BaCrO_4(s) + NaNO_3(aq)$
    b. $PbCl_2(aq) + K_2SO_4(aq) \rightarrow PbSO_4(s) + KCl(aq)$
    c. $C_2H_5OH(l) + O_2(g) \rightarrow CO_2(g) + H_2O(l)$
    d. $CaC_2(s) + H_2O(l) \rightarrow Ca(OH)_2(s) + C_2H_2(g)$
    e. $Sr(s) + HNO_3(aq) \rightarrow Sr(NO_3)_2(aq) + H_2(g)$
    f. $BaO_2(s) + H_2SO_4(aq) \rightarrow BaSO_4(s) + H_2O_2(aq)$
    g. $AsI_3(s) \rightarrow As(s) + I_2(s)$
    h. $CuSO_4(aq) + KI(s) \rightarrow CuI(s) + I_2(s) + K_2SO_4(aq)$

Additional Problems

45. Sodium hydrogen carbonate, more commonly known as baking soda, can be produced by bubbling carbon dioxide gas through an ice-cold aqueous solution containing large amounts of sodium chloride and ammonia. Because sodium hydrogen carbonate is not very soluble in cold water, it precipitates, whereas the other product of the reaction, ammonium chloride, remains dissolved. Write the unbalanced chemical equation for the process. *Hint:* Water is a reactant.

46. The metallic elements of Group 1 are all very reactive. For example, each of these metals reacts with water, producing hydrogen gas and leaving a solution of the metal's hydroxide compound. Write unbalanced chemical equations for the reactions of the Group 1 metals with water.

47. Crude gunpowders often contain a mixture of potassium nitrate and charcoal (carbon). When such a mixture is heated until reaction occurs, a solid residue of potassium carbonate is produced. The explosive force of the gunpowder comes from the fact that two gases are also produced (carbon monoxide and nitrogen), which increase in volume with great force and speed. Write the unbalanced chemical equation for the process.

48. The sugar sucrose, which is present in many fruits and vegetables, reacts in the presence of certain yeast enzymes to produce ethyl alcohol (ethanol) and carbon dioxide gas. Balance the following equation for this reaction of sucrose.

$$C_{12}H_{22}O_{11}(aq) + H_2O(l) \rightarrow C_2H_5OH(aq) + CO_2(g)$$

49. Methanol (methyl alcohol), CH_3OH, is a very important industrial chemical. Formerly, methanol was prepared by heating wood to high temperatures in the absence of air. The complex compounds present in wood are degraded by this process into a charcoal residue and a volatile portion that is rich in methanol. Today, methanol is instead synthesized from carbon monoxide and elemental hydrogen. Write the balanced chemical equation for this latter process.

50. The Hall process is an important method by which pure aluminum is prepared from its oxide (alumina, Al_2O_3) by indirect reaction with graphite (carbon). Balance the following equation, which is a simplified representation of this process.

$$Al_2O_3(s) + C(s) \rightarrow Al(s) + CO_2(g)$$

51. Iron oxide ores, commonly a mixture of FeO and Fe_2O_3, are given the general formula Fe_3O_4. They yield elemental iron when heated to a very high temperature with either carbon monoxide or elemental hydrogen. Balance the following equations for these processes.

$$Fe_3O_4(s) + H_2(g) \rightarrow Fe(s) + H_2O(g)$$
$$Fe_3O_4(s) + CO(g) \rightarrow Fe(s) + CO_2(g)$$

52. The elements of Group 2 all react with elemental fluorine and chlorine gases to produce the metal fluorides or the metal chlorides. For each of the elements of Group 2, write a balanced chemical equation for its reaction with fluorine gas and for its reaction with chlorine gas.

53. When steel wool (iron) is heated in pure oxygen gas, the steel wool bursts into flame and a fine powder consisting of a mixture of iron oxides (FeO and Fe_2O_3) forms. Write *separate* unbalanced equations for the reaction of iron with oxygen to give each of these products.

54. A common demonstration in introductory chemistry courses is the "volcano" reaction of ammonium dichromate, $(NH_4)_2Cr_2O_7$. When a small pile of the bright orange ammonium dichromate is heated strongly, the compound decomposes with a great deal of sparking into a large volume of green chromium(III) oxide, nitrogen gas, and water vapor. Write the balanced chemical equation for this process.

55. When elemental boron, B, is burned in oxygen gas, the product is diboron trioxide. If the diboron trioxide is then reacted with a measured quantity of water, it reacts with the water to form what is commonly known as boric acid, $B(OH)_3$. Write a balanced chemical equation for each of these processes.

56. A common experiment in introductory chemistry courses involves heating a weighed mixture of potassium chlorate, $KClO_3$, and potassium chloride. Potassium chlorate decomposes when heated, producing potassium chloride and evolving oxygen gas. By measuring the volume of oxygen gas produced in this experiment, students can calculate the relative percentage of $KClO_3$ and KCl in the original mixture. Write the balanced chemical equation for this process.

57. A common demonstration in chemistry courses involves adding a tiny speck of manganese(IV) oxide to a concentrated hydrogen peroxide, H_2O_2, solution. Hydrogen peroxide is unstable, and it decomposes quite spectacularly under these conditions to produce oxygen gas and steam (water vapor). Manganese(IV) oxide is a catalyst for the decomposition of hydrogen peroxide and is not consumed in the reaction. Write the balanced equation for the decomposition reaction of hydrogen peroxide.

58. The benches in many undergraduate chemistry laboratories are often covered by a film of white dust. This may be due to poor housekeeping, but the dust is usually ammonium chloride, produced by the gaseous reaction in the laboratory of hydrogen chloride and ammonia; most labs have aqueous solutions of these common reagents. Write the balanced chemical equation for the reaction of gaseous ammonia and hydrogen chloride to form solid ammonium chloride.

59. Glass is a mixture of several compounds, but a major constituent of most glass is calcium silicate, $CaSiO_3$. Glass can be etched by treatment with hydrogen fluoride: HF attacks the calcium silicate of the glass, producing gaseous and water-soluble products (which can be removed by washing the glass). For example, the volumetric glassware in chemistry laboratories is often graduated by using this process. Balance the following equation for the reaction of hydrogen fluoride with calcium silicate.

$$CaSiO_3(s) + HF(g) \rightarrow CaF_2(aq) + SiF_4(g) + H_2O(l)$$

60. Suppose that you were about to fry some chicken and that you left the oil on to heat for too long and at too high a temperature. What could happen? Is there evidence that a chemical reaction is occurring?

61. If you had a "sour stomach," you might try an over-the-counter antacid tablet to relieve the problem. Can you think of evidence that the action of such an antacid is a chemical reaction?

62. When iron wire is heated in the presence of sulfur the iron soon begins to glow, and a chunky, blue-black mass of iron(II) sulfide is formed. Write the unbalanced chemical equation for this reaction.

63. When finely divided solid sodium is dropped into a flask containing chlorine gas an explosion occurs and a fine powder of sodium chloride is deposited on the walls of the flask. Write the unbalanced chemical equation for this process.

64. Suburban homes sometimes use bottled propane gas, C_3H_8, for cooking purposes. When propane is burned in air, carbon dioxide and water vapor are produced (the presence of water vapor may be demonstrated by holding a cool dish above a burning propane flame, allowing liquid water to form on the cool surface). Write the unbalanced chemical equation for the reaction of gaseous propane with oxygen gas.

65. When hydrogen sulfide, H_2S, gas is bubbled through a solution of lead(II) nitrate, $Pb(NO_3)_2$, a black precipitate of lead(II) sulfide, PbS, forms, and nitric acid, HNO_3, is produced. Write the unbalanced chemical equation for this reaction.

66. When an electric current is passed through an aqueous solution of potassium iodide, hydrogen gas is evolved at one electrode, while elemental iodine, I_2, is produced at the other electrode. If the solution remaining is then evaporated, solid potassium hydroxide is recovered. Write the unbalanced chemical equation for this reaction.

67. When a strip of magnesium metal is heated in oxygen, it bursts into an intensely white flame and produces a finely powdered dust of magnesium oxide. Write the unbalanced chemical equation for this process.

68. Although magnesium metal does not react readily with cold water, magnesium reacts easily with steam, producing magnesium hydroxide and hydrogen gas. Write the unbalanced chemical equation for this process.

69. When solid red phosphorus, P_4, is burned in air, the phosphorus combines with oxygen, producing a choking cloud of tetraphosphorus decoxide. Write the unbalanced chemical equation for this reaction.

70. When copper(II) oxide is boiled in an aqueous solution of sulfuric acid, a strikingly blue solution of copper(II) sulfate forms along with additional water. Write the unbalanced chemical equation for this reaction.

71. When lead(II) sulfide is heated to high temperatures in a stream of pure oxygen gas, solid lead(II) oxide forms with the release of gaseous sulfur dioxide. Write the unbalanced chemical equation for this reaction.

72. When sodium sulfite is boiled with sulfur, the sulfite ions, SO_3^{2-}, are converted to thiosulfate ions, $S_2O_3^{2-}$, resulting in a solution of sodium thiosulfate, $Na_2S_2O_3$. Write the unbalanced chemical equation for this reaction.

73. Balance each of the following chemical equations.
    a. $Cl_2(g) + KBr(aq) \rightarrow Br_2(l) + KCl(aq)$
    b. $Cr(s) + O_2(g) \rightarrow Cr_2O_3(s)$
    c. $P_4(s) + H_2(g) \rightarrow PH_3(g)$
    d. $Al(s) + H_2SO_4(aq) \rightarrow Al_2(SO_4)_3(aq) + H_2(g)$
    e. $PCl_3(l) + H_2O(l) \rightarrow H_3PO_3(aq) + HCl(aq)$
    f. $SO_2(g) + O_2(g) \rightarrow SO_3(g)$
    g. $C_7H_{16}(l) + O_2(g) \rightarrow CO_2(g) + H_2O(g)$
    h. $C_2H_6(g) + O_2(g) \rightarrow CO_2(g) + H_2O(g)$

74. Balance each of the following chemical equations.
    a. $Ba(NO_3)_2(aq) + KF(aq) \rightarrow BaF_2(s) + KNO_3(aq)$
    b. $Zn(s) + HCl(aq) \rightarrow ZnCl_2(aq) + H_2(g)$
    c. $Fe(s) + S(s) \rightarrow Fe_2S_3(s)$
    d. $C_6H_{12}O_6(s) + O_2(g) \rightarrow CO_2(g) + H_2O(g)$
    e. $H_2O(l) + Cl_2(g) \rightarrow HCl(aq) + HOCl(aq)$
    f. $ZnS(s) + O_2(g) \rightarrow ZnO(s) + SO_2(g)$
    g. $PbSO_4(s) + NaCl(aq) \rightarrow$
       $$Na_2SO_4(aq) + Na_2PbCl_4(aq)$$
    h. $Fe_2O_3(s) + C(s) \rightarrow Fe_3O_4(s) + CO(g)$

75. Balance each of the following chemical equations.
    a. $SiCl_4(l) + Mg(s) \rightarrow Si(s) + MgCl_2(s)$
    b. $NO(g) + Cl_2(g) \rightarrow NOCl(g)$
    c. $MnO_2(s) + Al(s) \rightarrow Mn(s) + Al_2O_3(s)$
    d. $Cr(s) + S_8(s) \rightarrow Cr_2S_3(s)$
    e. $NH_3(g) + F_2(g) \rightarrow NH_4F(s) + NF_3(g)$
    f. $Ag_2S(s) + H_2(g) \rightarrow Ag(s) + H_2S(g)$
    g. $O_2(g) \rightarrow O_3(g)$
    h. $Na_2SO_3(aq) + S_8(s) \rightarrow Na_2S_2O_3(aq)$

76. Balance each of the following chemical equations.
    a. $Pb(NO_3)_2(aq) + K_2CrO_4(aq) \rightarrow$
       $$PbCrO_4(s) + KNO_3(aq)$$
    b. $BaCl_2(aq) + Na_2SO_4(aq) \rightarrow BaSO_4(s) + NaCl(aq)$
    c. $CH_3OH(l) + O_2(g) \rightarrow CO_2(g) + H_2O(g)$
    d. $Na_2CO_3(aq) + S(s) + SO_2(g) \rightarrow$
       $$CO_2(g) + Na_2S_2O_3(aq)$$
    e. $Cu(s) + H_2SO_4(aq) \rightarrow$
       $$CuSO_4(aq) + SO_2(g) + H_2O(l)$$
    f. $MnO_2(s) + HCl(aq) \rightarrow$
       $$MnCl_2(aq) + Cl_2(g) + H_2O(l)$$
    g. $As_2O_3(s) + KI(aq) + HCl(aq) \rightarrow$
       $$AsI_3(s) + KCl(aq) + H_2O(l)$$
    h. $Na_2S_2O_3(aq) + I_2(aq) \rightarrow Na_2S_4O_6(aq) + NaI(aq)$

Reactions in Aqueous Solutions

The chemical reactions that are most important to us occur in water—in aqueous solutions. Virtually all of the chemical reactions that keep each of us alive and well take place in the aqueous medium present in our bodies. For example, the oxygen you breathe dissolves in your blood, where it associates with the hemoglobin in the red blood cells. While attached to the hemoglobin it is transported to your cells, where it reacts with fuel (from the food you eat) to provide energy for living. However, the reaction between oxygen and fuel is not direct—the cells are not tiny furnaces. Instead, electrons are transferred from the fuel to a series of molecules that pass them along (this is called the respiratory chain) until they eventually reach oxygen. Many other reactions are also crucial to our health and well-being, including those that involve the dissolving and reforming of tooth enamel (see the "Chemistry in Focus" on p. 184).

Potassium reacts vigorously when it comes into contact with water (left). *Developing a photo involves several aqueous chemical reactions* (right).

In this chapter we will study some common types of reactions that take place in water, and we will become familiar with some of the driving forces that make these reactions occur. We will also learn how to predict the products for these reactions and how to write various equations to describe them.

7.1 Predicting Whether a Reaction Will Occur

AIM: To learn about some of the factors that cause reactions to occur.

In this text we have already seen many chemical reactions. Now let's consider an important question: why does a chemical reaction occur? What causes reactants to "want" to form products? As chemists have studied reactions, they have recognized several "tendencies" in reactants that drive them to form products. That is, there are several "driving forces" that pull reactants toward products—changes that tend to make reactions go in the direction of the arrow. The most common of these driving forces are

1. Formation of a solid
2. Formation of water
3. Transfer of electrons
4. Formation of a gas

When two or more chemicals are brought together, if any of these things can occur, a chemical change (a reaction) is likely to take place. Accordingly, when we are confronted with a set of reactants and want to predict whether a reaction will occur and what products might form, we will consider these driving forces. They will help us organize our thoughts as we encounter new reactions.

In this chapter we consider examples of reactions in aqueous solutions where the first two of these driving forces are operating. In Chapter 8 we will consider reactions that involve electron transfer and formation of gases.

7.2 Reactions in Which a Solid Forms

AIM: To learn to identify the solid that forms in a precipitation reaction.

One driving force for a chemical reaction is the formation of a solid, a process called **precipitation.** The solid that forms is called a **precipitate,** and the reaction is known as a **precipitation reaction.** For example, when an aqueous (water) solution of potassium chromate, $K_2CrO_4(aq)$, which is yellow, is added to a colorless aqueous solution containing barium nitrate, $Ba(NO_3)_2(aq)$, a yellow solid forms (see Figure 7.1). The fact that a solid forms tells us that a reaction—a chemical change—has occurred. That is, we have a situation where

$$\text{Reactants} \rightarrow \text{Products}$$

FIGURE 7.1
The precipitation reaction that occurs when yellow potassium chromate, $K_2CrO_4(aq)$, is mixed with a colorless barium nitrate solution, $Ba(NO_3)_2(aq)$.

What is the equation that describes this chemical change? To write the equation, we must decipher the identities of the reactants and products. The reactants have already been described: $K_2CrO_4(aq)$ and $Ba(NO_3)_2(aq)$. Is there some way in which we can predict the identities of the products? What is the yellow solid? The best way to predict the identity of this solid is to first *consider what products are possible.* To do this we need to know what chemical species are present in the solution that results when the reactant solutions are mixed. First, let's think about the nature of each reactant in an aqueous solution.

What Happens When an Ionic Compound Dissolves in Water?

The designation $Ba(NO_3)_2(aq)$ means that barium nitrate (a white solid) has been dissolved in water. Note from its formula that barium nitrate contains the Ba^{2+} and NO_3^- ions. *In virtually every case when a solid containing ions dissolves in water, the ions separate* and move around independently. That is, $Ba(NO_3)_2(aq)$ does not contain $Ba(NO_3)_2$ units. Rather, it contains separated Ba^{2+} and NO_3^- ions. In the solution there are two NO_3^- ions for every Ba^{2+} ion. Chemists know that separated ions are present in this solution because it is an excellent conductor of electricity (see Figure 7.2). Pure water does not conduct an electric current. Ions must be present in water for a current to flow.

When each unit of a substance that dissolves in water produces separated ions, the substance is called a **strong electrolyte.** Barium nitrate is a strong electrolyte in water, because each $Ba(NO_3)_2$ unit produces the separated ions (Ba^{2+}, NO_3^-, NO_3^-).

Similarly, aqueous K_2CrO_4 also behaves as a strong electrolyte. Potassium chromate contains the K^+ and CrO_4^{2-} ions, so an aqueous solution of potassium chromate (which is prepared by dissolving solid K_2CrO_4 in water) contains these separated ions. That is, $K_2CrO_4(aq)$ does not contain

FIGURE 7.2
Electrical conductivity of aqueous solutions. (a) Pure water does not conduct an electric current. The lamp does not light. (b) When an ionic compound is dissolved in water, current flows and the lamp lights. The result of this experiment is strong evidence that ionic compounds dissolved in water exist in the form of separated ions.

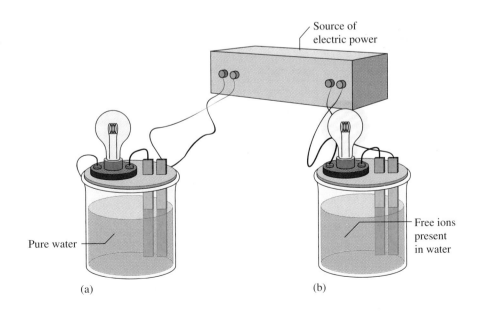

Source of electric power

Pure water

Free ions present in water

(a)   (b)

K_2CrO_4 units but instead contains K^+ cations and CrO_4^{2-} anions, which move around independently. (There are two K^+ ions for each CrO_4^{2-} ion.)

The idea introduced here is very important: when ionic compounds dissolve, the *resulting solution contains the separated ions*. Therefore, we can represent the mixing of $K_2CrO_4(aq)$ and $Ba(NO_3)_2(aq)$ in two ways. We usually write these reactants as

$$K_2CrO_4(aq) \ + \ Ba(NO_3)_2(aq) \ \rightarrow \ Products$$

However, a more accurate representation of the situation is

We can express this information in equation form as follows:

$$2K^+(aq) \ + \ CrO_4^{2-}(aq) \ + \ Ba^{2+}(aq) \ + \ 2NO_3^-(aq) \ \rightarrow \ Products$$

The ions in $K_2CrO_4(aq)$ The ions in $Ba(NO_3)_2(aq)$

Thus the *mixed solution* contains four types of ions: K^+, CrO_4^{2-}, Ba^{2+}, and NO_3^-. Now that we know what the reactants are, we can make some educated guesses about the possible products.

How to Decide What Products Form

Which of these ions combine to form the yellow solid observed when the original solutions are mixed? This is not an easy question to answer. Even an experienced chemist is not sure what will happen in a new reaction. The chemist tries to think of the various possibilities, considers the likelihood of each possibility, and then makes a prediction (an educated guess). Only after identifying each product experimentally can the chemist be sure what reaction actually has taken place. However, an educated guess is very useful because it indicates what kinds of products are most likely. It gives us a place to start. So the best way to proceed is first to think of the various possibilities and then to decide which of them is most likely.

What are the possible products of the reaction between $K_2CrO_4(aq)$ and $Ba(NO_3)_2(aq)$ or, more accurately, what reaction can occur among the ions K^+, CrO_4^{2-}, Ba^{2+}, and NO_3^-? We already know some things that will help us decide. We know that a *solid compound must have a zero net charge*. This means that the product of our reaction must contain *both anions and cations* (negative and positive ions). For example, K^+ and Ba^{2+} could not combine to form the solid because such a solid would have a positive charge. Similarly, CrO_4^{2-} and NO_3^- could not combine to form a solid because that solid would have a negative charge.

Something else that will help us is an observation that chemists have made by examining many compounds: *most ionic materials contain only two types of ions*—one type of cation and one type of anion. This idea is illustrated by the following compounds (among many others):

Compound	Cation	Anion
NaCl	Na^+	Cl^-
KOH	K^+	OH^-
Na_2SO_4	Na^+	SO_4^{2-}
NH_4Cl	NH_4^+	Cl^-
Na_2CO_3	Na^+	CO_3^{2-}

All the possible combinations of a cation and an anion to form uncharged compounds from among the ions K^+, CrO_4^{2-}, Ba^{2+}, and NO_3^- are shown below:

	NO_3^-	CrO_4^{2-}
K^+	KNO_3	K_2CrO_4
Ba^{2+}	$Ba(NO_3)_2$	$BaCrO_4$

So the list of compounds that *might* make up the solid are

K_2CrO_4	$BaCrO_4$
KNO_3	$Ba(NO_3)_2$

Which of these possibilities is most likely to represent the yellow solid? We know it's not K_2CrO_4 or $Ba(NO_3)_2$; these are the reactants. They were present (dissolved) in the separate solutions that were mixed initially. The only real possibilities are KNO_3 and $BaCrO_4$. To decide which of these is more likely to represent the yellow solid, we need more facts. An experienced chemist, for example, knows that KNO_3 is a white solid. On the other hand, the CrO_4^{2-} ion is yellow. Therefore, the yellow solid must be $BaCrO_4$.

We have determined that one product of the reaction between $K_2CrO_4(aq)$ and $Ba(NO_3)_2(aq)$ is $BaCrO_4(s)$, but what happened to the K^+ and NO_3^- ions? The answer is that these ions are left dissolved in the solution. That is, KNO_3 does not form a solid when the K^+ and NO_3^- ions are present in water. In other words, if we took the white solid $KNO_3(s)$ and put it in water, it would totally dissolve (the white solid would "disappear," yielding a colorless solution). So when we mix $K_2CrO_4(aq)$ and $Ba(NO_3)_2(aq)$, $BaCrO_4(s)$ forms but KNO_3 is left behind in solution [we write it as $KNO_3(aq)$]. (If we poured the mixture through a filter to remove the solid $BaCrO_4$ and then evaporated all of the water, we would obtain the white solid KNO_3.)

After all this thinking, we can finally write the unbalanced equation for the precipitation reaction.

$$K_2CrO_4(aq) + Ba(NO_3)_2(aq) \rightarrow BaCrO_4(s) + KNO_3(aq)$$

We can represent this reaction in pictures as follows:

Note that the K^+ and NO_3^- ions are not involved in the chemical change. They remain dispersed in the water before and after the reaction.

Using Solubility Rules

In the example considered above we were finally able to identify the products of the reaction by using two types of chemical knowledge:

1. Knowledge of facts
2. Knowledge of concepts

For example, knowing the colors of the various compounds proved very helpful. This represents factual knowledge. Awareness of the concept that solids always have a net charge of zero was also essential. These two kinds of knowledge allowed us to make a good guess about the identity of the solid that formed. As you continue to study chemistry, you will see that a balance of factual and conceptual knowledge is always required. You must both *memorize* important facts and *understand* crucial concepts in order to succeed.

In the present case we are dealing with a reaction in which an ionic solid forms—that is, a process in which ions that are dissolved in water combine to give a solid. We know that for a solid to form, both positive and negative ions must be present in relative numbers that give zero net charge. However, oppositely charged ions in water do not always react to form a solid, as we have seen for K^+ and NO_3^-. In addition, Na^+ and Cl^- can coexist in water in very large numbers with no formation of solid NaCl. In other words, when solid NaCl (common salt) is placed in water, it dissolves—the white solid "disappears" as the Na^+ and Cl^- ions are dispersed throughout the water. (You probably have observed this phenomenon in preparing salt water to cook food.) The following two statements, then, are really saying the same thing.

1. Solid NaCl is very soluble in water.
2. Solid NaCl does not form when one solution containing Na^+ is mixed with another solution containing Cl^-.

To predict whether a given pair of dissolved ions will form a solid when mixed, we must know some facts about the solubilities of various types of ionic compounds. In this text we will use the term **soluble solid** to mean a solid that readily dissolves in water; the solid "disappears" as the ions are dispersed in the water. The terms **insoluble solid** and **slightly soluble solid** are taken to mean the same thing: a solid where such a tiny amount dissolves in water that it is undetectable with the naked eye. The solubility information about common solids that is summarized in Table 7.1 is based

Solids must contain both anions and cations in the relative numbers necessary to produce zero net charge.

TABLE 7.1
General Rules for Solubility of Ionic Compounds (Salts) in Water at 25 °C

1. Most nitrate (NO_3^-) salts are soluble.
2. Most salts of Na^+, K^+, and NH_4^+ are soluble.
3. Most chloride salts are soluble. Notable exceptions are $AgCl$, $PbCl_2$, and Hg_2Cl_2.
4. Most sulfate salts are soluble. Notable exceptions are $BaSO_4$, $PbSO_4$, and $CaSO_4$.
5. Most hydroxide compounds are only slightly soluble.* The important exceptions are $NaOH$ and KOH. $Ba(OH)_2$ and $Ca(OH)_2$ are only moderately soluble.
6. Most sulfide (S^{2-}), carbonate (CO_3^{2-}), and phosphate (PO_4^{3-}) salts are only slightly soluble.*

*The terms *insoluble* and *slightly soluble* really mean the same thing: such a tiny amount dissolves that it is not possible to detect it with the naked eye.

on observations of the behavior of many compounds. This is factual knowledge that you will need to predict what will happen in chemical reactions where a solid might form. This information is summarized in Figure 7.3.

Notice that in Table 7.1 and Figure 7.3 the term *salt* is used to mean *ionic compound*. Many chemists use the terms *salt* and *ionic compound* interchangeably. In Example 7.1, we will illustrate how to use the solubility rules to predict the products of reactions among ions.

FIGURE 7.3
Solubilities of common compounds.

(a) Soluble compounds

NO_3^- salts

Na^+, K^+, NH_4^+ salts

Cl^-, Br^-, I^- salts	Except for those containing	Ag^+, Hg_2^{2+}, Pb^{2+}

SO_4^{2-} salts	Except for those containing	Ba^{2+}, Pb^{2+}, Ca^{2+}

(b) Insoluble compounds

S^{2-}, CO_3^{2-}, PO_4^{3-} salts

OH^- salts	Except for those containing	Na^+, K^+, Ca^{2+}

CHEMISTRY IN FOCUS

The Chemistry of Teeth

If dental chemistry continues to progress at its present rate, tooth decay may soon be a thing of the past. Cavities are holes that develop in tooth enamel, which is composed of the mineral hydroxyapatite, $Ca_5(PO_4)_3OH$. Recent studies have shown that there is constant dissolving and reforming of the tooth mineral in the saliva at the tooth's surface. Demineralization (dissolving of tooth enamel) is caused mainly by acids in the saliva that are created by bacteria as they digest food.

In the first stages of tooth decay, parts of the tooth surface become porous and spongy and develop Swiss-cheese-like holes that, if untreated, eventually turn into cavities (see the accompanying photograph). However, recent results indicate that

if the affected tooth is bathed in a solution containing appropriate amounts of Ca^{2+}, PO_4^{3-}, and F^-, it remineralizes. In this process, F^- replaces some of the OH^- present in the original tooth mineral. That is, some of the $Ca_5(PO_4)_3OH$ is changed to $Ca_5(PO_4)_3F$. The remineralized area is more resistant to decay in the future, because the fluoride mineral is less soluble than the original tooth enamel. In addition, it has been shown that the presence of Sr^{2+} in the remineralizing fluid significantly increases resistance to decay.

These results suggest that the work of dentists will change dramatically. Dentists most likely will be more involved in preventing damage to teeth than in repairing damage that has already occurred. One can picture

Tooth enamel in early stages of decay.

the routine use of a remineralization rinse that will repair enamel in problem areas before they become cavities. Dental drills could join leeches as a medical anachronism (and patients would probably miss them about as much!).

EXAMPLE 7.1 *Identifying Precipitates in Reactions Where a Solid Forms*

$AgNO_3$ is usually called silver nitrate rather than silver(I) nitrate because silver only forms Ag^+.

When an aqueous solution of silver nitrate is added to an aqueous solution of potassium chloride, a white solid forms. Identify the white solid and write the balanced equation for the reaction that occurs.

Solution

First let's use the description of the reaction to represent what we know:

$$AgNO_3(aq) + KCl(aq) \rightarrow \text{White solid}$$

Remember, try to determine the essential facts from the words and represent these facts by symbols or diagrams. To answer the main question (What is the white solid?) we must establish what ions are present in the mixed solution. That is, we must know what the reactants are really like. Remember that *when ionic substances dissolve in water, the ions separate.* So we can write the equation

$$Ag^+(aq) + NO_3^-(aq) + K^+(aq) + Cl^-(aq) \rightarrow \text{Products}$$

Ions in
$AgNO_3(aq)$

Ions in
$KCl(aq)$

or use pictures

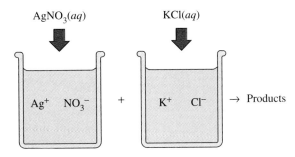

to represent the ions present in the mixed solution before any reaction occurs. In summary:

Now we will consider what solid *might* form from this collection of ions. Because the solid must contain both positive and negative ions, the possible compounds that can be assembled from this collection of ions are

$AgNO_3$ $AgCl$

KNO_3 KCl

$AgNO_3$ and KCl are the substances already dissolved in the reactant solutions, so we know that they do not represent the white solid product. We are left with two possibilities:

$AgCl$

KNO_3

Another way to obtain these two possibilities is by *ion interchange*. This means that in the reaction of $AgNO_3(aq)$ and $KCl(aq)$, we take the cation from one reactant and combine it with the anion of the other reactant.

$$Ag^+ + NO_3^- + K^+ + Cl^- \rightarrow \text{Products}$$

Possible solid products

Ion interchange leads to the following possible solids:

$AgCl$ or KNO_3

To decide whether $AgCl$ or KNO_3 is the white solid, we need the solubility rules (Table 7.1). Rule 2 states that most salts containing K^+ are soluble in water. Rule 1 says that most nitrate salts (those containing NO_3^-) are soluble. So the salt KNO_3 is water-soluble. That is, when K^+ and NO_3^- are mixed in water, a solid (KNO_3) does *not* form.

On the other hand, rule 3 states that although most chloride salts (salts that contain Cl^-) are soluble, $AgCl$ is an exception. That is, $AgCl(s)$ is insoluble in

	NO_3^-	Cl^-
Ag+	AgNO₃	AgCl
K+	KNO₃	KCl

FIGURE 7.4
Precipitation of silver chloride occurs when solutions of silver nitrate and potassium chloride are mixed. The K^+ and NO_3^- ions remain in solution.

water. Thus the white solid must be AgCl. Now we can write

$$AgNO_3(aq) + KCl(aq) \rightarrow AgCl(s) + ?$$

What is the other product?

To form $AgCl(s)$, we have used the Ag^+ and Cl^- ions:

$$Ag^+(aq) + NO_3^-(aq) + K^+(aq) + Cl^-(aq) \rightarrow AgCl(s)$$

This leaves the K^+ and NO_3^- ions. What do they do? Nothing. Because KNO_3 is very soluble in water (rules 1 and 2), the K^+ and NO_3^- ions remain separate in the water; the KNO_3 remains dissolved and we represent it as $KNO_3(aq)$. We can now write the full equation:

$$AgNO_3(aq) + KCl(aq) \rightarrow AgCl(s) + KNO_3(aq)$$

Figure 7.4 shows the precipitation of $AgCl(s)$ that occurs when this reaction takes place. In graphic form, the reaction is

The following strategy is useful for predicting what will occur when two solutions containing dissolved salts are mixed.

How to Predict Precipitates When Solutions of Two Ionic Compounds Are Mixed

STEP 1 Write the reactants as they actually exist before any reaction occurs. Remember that when a salt dissolves, its ions separate.

STEP 2 Consider the various solids that could form. To do this, simply *exchange the anions* of the added salts.

STEP 3 Use the solubility rules (Table 7.1) to decide whether a solid forms and, if so, to predict the identity of the solid.

EXAMPLE 7.2 *Using Solubility Rules to Predict the Products of Reactions*

Using the solubility rules in Table 7.1, predict what will happen when the following solutions are mixed. Write the balanced equation for any reaction that occurs.

a. $KNO_3(aq)$ and $BaCl_2(aq)$

b. $Na_2SO_4(aq)$ and $Pb(NO_3)_2(aq)$

c. $KOH(aq)$ and $Fe(NO_3)_3(aq)$

Solution (a)

STEP 1 $KNO_3(aq)$ represents an aqueous solution obtained by dissolving solid KNO_3 in water to give the ions $K^+(aq)$ and $NO_3^-(aq)$. Likewise, $BaCl_2(aq)$ is a solution formed by dissolving solid $BaCl_2$ in water to produce $Ba^{2+}(aq)$ and $Cl^-(aq)$. When these two solutions are mixed, the following ions will be present:

$$K^+, \quad NO_3^-, \quad Ba^{2+}, \quad Cl^-$$

From $KNO_3(aq)$ From $BaCl_2(aq)$

STEP 2 To get the possible products, we exchange the anions.

$$K^+ \quad NO_3^- \quad Ba^{2+} \quad Cl^-$$

This yields the possibilities KCl and $Ba(NO_3)_2$. These are the solids that *might* form. Notice that two NO_3^- ions are needed to balance the 2+ charge on Ba^{2+}.

STEP 3 The rules listed in Table 7.1 indicate that both KCl and $Ba(NO_3)_2$ are soluble in water. So no precipitate forms when $KNO_3(aq)$ and $BaCl_2(aq)$ are mixed. All of the ions remain dissolved in the solution. This means that no reaction takes place. That is, no chemical change occurs.

Solution (b)

STEP 1 The following ions are present in the mixed solution before any reaction occurs:

$$Na^+, \quad SO_4^{2-}, \quad Pb^{2+}, \quad NO_3^-$$

From
$Na_2SO_4(aq)$ From
$Pb(NO_3)_2(aq)$

STEP 2 Exchanging anions as follows:

$$Na^+ \quad SO_4^{2-} \quad Pb^{2+} \quad NO_3^-$$

yields the *possible* solid products $PbSO_4$ and $NaNO_3$.

STEP 3 Using Table 7.1, we see that $NaNO_3$ is soluble in water (rules 1 and 2) but that $PbSO_4$ is only slightly soluble (rule 4). Thus when these solutions are mixed, solid $PbSO_4$ forms. The balanced reaction is

$$Na_2SO_4(aq) + Pb(NO_3)_2(aq) \rightarrow PbSO_4(s) + 2NaNO_3(aq)$$

Remains dissolved

which can be represented as

Solution (c)

STEP 1 The ions present in the mixed solution before any reaction occurs are

$$K^+, \quad OH^-, \quad Fe^{3+}, \quad NO_3^-$$

From $KOH(aq)$ From $Fe(NO_3)_3(aq)$

STEP 2 Exchanging anions as follows:

$$K^+ \quad OH^- \quad Fe^{3+} \quad NO_3^-$$

yields the possible solid products KNO_3 and $Fe(OH)_3$.

STEP 3 Rules 1 and 2 (Table 7.1) state that KNO_3 is soluble, whereas $Fe(OH)_3$ is only slightly soluble (rule 5). Thus when these solutions are mixed, solid $Fe(OH)_3$ forms. The balanced equation for the reaction is

$$3KOH(aq) + Fe(NO_3)_3(aq) \rightarrow Fe(OH)_3(s) + 3KNO_3(aq)$$

which can be represented as

 Self-Check Exercise 7.1

Predict whether a solid will form when the following pairs of solutions are mixed. If so, identify the solid and write the balanced equation for the reaction.

a. $Ba(NO_3)_2(aq)$ and $NaCl(aq)$

b. $Na_2S(aq)$ and $Cu(NO_3)_2(aq)$

c. $NH_4Cl(aq)$ and $Pb(NO_3)_2(aq)$

See Problems 7.17 and 7.18.

7.3 Describing Reactions in Aqueous Solutions

AIM: To learn to describe reactions in solutions by writing molecular, complete ionic, and net ionic equations.

Much important chemistry, including virtually all of the reactions that make life possible, occurs in aqueous solutions. We will now consider the types of equations used to represent reactions that occur in water. For example, as we saw earlier, when we mix aqueous potassium chromate with aqueous barium nitrate, a reaction occurs to form solid barium chromate and dissolved potassium nitrate. One way to represent this reaction is by the equation

$$K_2CrO_4(aq) + Ba(NO_3)_2(aq) \rightarrow BaCrO_4(s) + 2KNO_3(aq)$$

This is called the **molecular equation** for the reaction; it shows the complete formulas of all reactants and products. However, although this equation shows the reactants and products of the reaction, it does not give a very clear picture of what actually occurs in solution. As we have seen, aqueous solutions of potassium chromate, barium nitrate, and potassium nitrate contain the individual ions, not molecules as is implied by the molecular equation. Thus the **complete ionic equation,**

Ions from K_2CrO_4 Ions from $Ba(NO_3)_2$

$$2K^+(aq) + CrO_4^{2-}(aq) + Ba^{2+}(aq) + 2NO_3^-(aq) \rightarrow$$
$$BaCrO_4(s) + 2K^+(aq) + 2NO_3^-(aq)$$

better represents the actual forms of the reactants and products in solution. *In a complete ionic equation, all substances that are strong electrolytes are represented as ions.* Notice that $BaCrO_4$ is not written as the separate ions, because it is present as a solid; it is not dissolved.

A strong electrolyte is a substance that completely breaks apart into ions when dissolved in water. The resulting solution readily conducts an electric current.

The complete ionic equation reveals that only some of the ions participate in the reaction. Notice that the K^+ and NO_3^- ions are present in solution both before and after the reaction. Ions such as these, which do not participate directly in a reaction in solution, are called **spectator ions.** The ions that participate in this reaction are the Ba^{2+} and CrO_4^{2-} ions, which combine to form solid $BaCrO_4$:

$$Ba^{2+}(aq) + CrO_4^{2-}(aq) \rightarrow BaCrO_4(s)$$

The net ionic equation includes only those components that undergo a change in the reaction.

This equation, called the **net ionic equation,** includes only those components that are directly involved in the reaction. Chemists usually write the net ionic equation for a reaction in solution, because it gives the actual forms of the reactants and products and includes only the species that undergo a change.

Types of Equations for Reactions in Aqueous Solutions

Three types of equations are used to describe reactions in solutions.

1. The *molecular equation* shows the overall reaction but not necessarily the actual forms of the reactants and products in solution.

2. The *complete ionic equation* represents all reactants and products that are strong electrolytes as ions. All reactants and products are included.

3. The *net ionic equation* includes only those components that undergo a change. Spectator ions are not included.

To make sure these ideas are clear, we will do another example. In Example 7.2 we considered the reaction between aqueous solutions of lead nitrate and sodium sulfate. The molecular equation for this reaction is

$$Pb(NO_3)_2(aq) + Na_2SO_4(aq) \rightarrow PbSO_4(s) + 2NaNO_3(aq)$$

Because any ionic compound that is dissolved in water is present as the separated ions, we can write the complete ionic equation as follows:

$$Pb^{2+}(aq) + 2NO_3^-(aq) + 2Na^+(aq) + SO_4^{2-}(aq) \rightarrow$$
$$PbSO_4(s) + 2Na^+(aq) + 2NO_3^-(aq)$$

The $PbSO_4$ is not written as separate ions because it is present as a solid. The ions that take part in the chemical change are the Pb^{2+} and the SO_4^{2-} ions, which combine to form solid $PbSO_4$. Thus the net ionic equation is

$$Pb^{2+}(aq) + SO_4^{2-}(aq) \rightarrow PbSO_4(s)$$

The Na^+ and NO_3^- ions do not undergo any chemical change; they are spectator ions.

EXAMPLE 7.3   *Writing Equations for Reactions*

For each of the following reactions, write the molecular equation, the complete ionic equation, and the net ionic equation.

Because silver is present as Ag^+ in all of its common ionic compounds, we usually delete the (I) when naming silver compounds.

a. Aqueous sodium chloride is added to aqueous silver nitrate to form solid silver chloride plus aqueous sodium nitrate.

b. Aqueous potassium hydroxide is mixed with aqueous iron(III) nitrate to form solid iron(III) hydroxide and aqueous potassium nitrate.

Solution

a. *Molecular equation:*

$$NaCl(aq) + AgNO_3(aq) \rightarrow AgCl(s) + NaNO_3(aq)$$

Complete ionic equation:

$$Na^+(aq) + Cl^-(aq) + Ag^+(aq) + NO_3^-(aq) \rightarrow$$
$$AgCl(s) + Na^+(aq) + NO_3^-(aq)$$

Net ionic equation:

$$Cl^-(aq) + Ag^+(aq) \rightarrow AgCl(s)$$

b. *Molecular equation:*

$$3KOH(aq) + Fe(NO_3)_3(aq) \rightarrow Fe(OH)_3(s) + 3KNO_3(aq)$$

Complete ionic equation:

$$3K^+(aq) + 3OH^-(aq) + Fe^{3+}(aq) + 3NO_3^-(aq) \rightarrow$$
$$Fe(OH)_3(s) + 3K^+(aq) + 3NO_3^-(aq)$$

Net ionic equation:

$$3OH^-(aq) + Fe^{3+}(aq) \rightarrow Fe(OH)_3(s)$$

 Self-Check Exercise 7.2

For each of the following reactions, write the molecular equation, the complete ionic equation, and the net ionic equation.

a. Aqueous sodium sulfide is mixed with aqueous copper(II) nitrate to produce solid copper(II) sulfide and aqueous sodium nitrate.

b. Aqueous ammonium chloride and aqueous lead(II) nitrate react to form solid lead(II) chloride and aqueous ammonium nitrate.

See Problems 7.25 through 7.30.

7.4 Reactions That Form Water: Acids and Bases

AIM: To learn the key characteristics of the reactions between strong acids and strong bases.

Don't taste chemicals!

In this section we encounter two very important classes of compounds: acids and bases. Acids were first associated with the sour taste of citrus fruits. In fact, the word *acid* comes from the Latin word *acidus*, which means "sour." Vinegar tastes sour because it is a dilute solution of acetic acid; citric acid is responsible for the sour taste of a lemon. Bases, sometimes called *alkalis*, are characterized by their bitter taste and slippery feel, like wet soap. Most commercial preparations for unclogging drains are highly basic.

Acids have been known for hundreds of years. For example, the *mineral acids* sulfuric acid, H_2SO_4, and nitric acid, HNO_3, so named because they were originally obtained by the treatment of minerals, were discovered around 1300. However, it was not until the late 1800s that the essential nature of acids was discovered by Svante Arrhenius, then a Swedish graduate student in physics.

The Nobel Prize in chemistry was awarded to Arrhenius in 1903 for his studies of solution conductivity.

Arrhenius, who was trying to discover why only certain solutions could conduct an electric current, found that conductivity arose from the presence of ions. In his studies of solutions, Arrhenius observed that when the substances HCl, HNO_3, and H_2SO_4 were dissolved in water, they behaved as strong electrolytes. He suggested that this was the result of ionization reactions in water.

$$HCl \xrightarrow{H_2O} H^+(aq) + Cl^-(aq)$$

$$HNO_3 \xrightarrow{H_2O} H^+(aq) + NO_3^-(aq)$$

$$H_2SO_4 \xrightarrow{H_2O} H^+(aq) + HSO_4^-(aq)$$

FIGURE 7.5
When gaseous HCl is dissolved in water, each molecule dissociates to produce H^+ and Cl^- ions. That is, HCl behaves as a strong electrolyte.

The Arrhenius definition of an acid: a substance that produces H^+ ions in aqueous solution.

A lemon tastes sour because it contains citric acid in its juice.

Arrhenius proposed that an **acid** *is a substance that produces H^+ ions (protons) when it is dissolved in water.*

Studies show that when HCl, HNO_3, and H_2SO_4 are placed in water, *virtually every molecule* dissociates to give ions. This means that when 100 molecules of HCl are dissolved in water, 100 H^+ ions and 100 Cl^- ions are produced. Virtually no HCl molecules exist in aqueous solution (see Figure 7.5). Because these substances are strong electrolytes that produce H^+ ions, they are called **strong acids.**

Arrhenius also found that *aqueous solutions that exhibit basic behavior* always contain hydroxide ions. He defined a **base** as a *substance that produces hydroxide ions (OH^-) in water.* The base most commonly used in the chemical laboratory is sodium hydroxide, NaOH, which contains Na^+ and OH^- ions and is very soluble in water. Sodium hydroxide, like all ionic substances, produces separated cations and anions when it is dissolved in water.

$$NaOH(s) \xrightarrow{H_2O} Na^+(aq) + OH^-(aq)$$

Although dissolved sodium hydroxide is usually represented as NaOH(*aq*), you should remember that the solution really contains separated Na^+ and OH^- ions. In fact, for every 100 units of NaOH dissolved in water, 100 Na^+ and 100 OH^- ions are produced.

Potassium hydroxide (KOH) has properties markedly similar to those of sodium hydroxide. It is very soluble in water and produces separated ions.

$$KOH(s) \xrightarrow{H_2O} K^+(aq) + OH^-(aq)$$

Because these hydroxide compounds are strong electrolytes that contain OH^- ions, they are called **strong bases.**

When strong acids and strong bases (hydroxides) are mixed, the fundamental chemical change that always occurs is that *H^+ ions react with OH^- ions to form water.*

$$H^+(aq) + OH^-(aq) \rightarrow H_2O(l)$$

Water is a very stable compound, as evidenced by the abundance of it on the earth's surface. Therefore, when substances that can form water are mixed, there is a strong tendency for the reaction to occur. In particular, the hydroxide ion OH^- has a high affinity for H^+ ions, because water is produced in the reaction between these ions.

The tendency to form water is the second of the driving forces for reactions that we mentioned in Section 7.1. Any compound that produces OH^- ions in water reacts vigorously to form H_2O with any compound that can furnish H^+ ions. For example, the reaction between hydrochloric acid and aqueous sodium hydroxide is represented by the following molecular equation:

$$HCl(aq) + NaOH(aq) \rightarrow H_2O(l) + NaCl(aq)$$

Because HCl, NaOH, and NaCl exist as completely separated ions in water, the complete ionic equation for this reaction is

$$H^+(aq) + Cl^-(aq) + Na^+(aq) + OH^-(aq) \rightarrow$$
$$H_2O(l) + Na^+(aq) + Cl^-(aq)$$

Notice that the Cl^- and Na^+ are spectator ions (they undergo no changes), so the net ionic equation is

$$H^+(aq) + OH^-(aq) \rightarrow H_2O(l)$$

Thus the only chemical change that occurs when these solutions are mixed is that water is formed from H^+ and OH^- ions.

Hydrochloric acid is an aqueous solution that contains dissolved hydrogen chloride. It is a strong electrolyte.

EXAMPLE 7.4 *Writing Equations for Acid–Base Reactions*

Nitric acid is a strong acid. Write the molecular, complete ionic, and net ionic equations for the reaction of aqueous nitric acid and aqueous potassium hydroxide.

Solution

Molecular equation:
$$HNO_3(aq) + KOH(aq) \rightarrow H_2O(l) + KNO_3(aq)$$

Complete ionic equation:
$$H^+(aq) + NO_3^-(aq) + K^+(aq) + OH^-(aq) \rightarrow$$
$$H_2O(l) + K^+(aq) + NO_3^-(aq)$$

Net ionic equation:
$$H^+(aq) + OH^-(aq) \rightarrow H_2O(l)$$

Note that K^+ and NO_3^- are spectator ions and that the formation of water is the driving force for this reaction.

Hydrochloric acid is an aqueous solution of HCl.

There are two important things to note as we examine the reaction of hydrochloric acid with aqueous sodium hydroxide and the reaction of nitric acid with aqueous potassium hydroxide.

1. The net ionic equation is the same in both cases; water is formed.
$$H^+(aq) + OH^-(aq) \rightarrow H_2O(l)$$

2. Besides water, which is *always a product* of the reaction of an acid with OH^-, the second product is an ionic compound, which might precipitate or remain dissolved, depending on its solubility.

$$HCl(aq) + NaOH(aq) \rightarrow H_2O(l) + NaCl(aq)$$

$$HNO_3(aq) + KOH(aq) \rightarrow H_2O(l) + KNO_3(aq)$$

Dissolved ionic compounds

This ionic compound is called a **salt.** In the first case the salt is sodium chloride, and in the second case the salt is potassium nitrate. We can obtain these soluble salts in solid form (both are white solids) by evaporating the water.

Summary of Strong Acids and Bases

Both strong acids and strong bases are strong electrolytes.

The following points about strong acids and bases are particularly important.

1. The common strong acids are aqueous solutions of HCl, HNO$_3$, and H$_2$SO$_4$.

2. A strong acid is a substance that completely dissociates in water. (Each molecule breaks up into an H$^+$ ion plus an anion.)

3. A strong base is a metal hydroxide compound that is very soluble in water. The most common strong bases are NaOH and KOH, which completely break up into separated ions (Na$^+$ and OH$^-$ or K$^+$ and OH$^-$) when they are dissolved in water.

4. The net ionic equation for the reaction of a strong acid and a strong base is always the same: it shows the production of water.

   $$H^+(aq) + OH^-(aq) \rightarrow H_2O(l)$$

5. In the reaction of a strong acid and a strong base, one product is always water and the other is always an ionic compound called a salt, which remains dissolved in the water. This salt can be obtained as a solid by evaporating the water.

6. The reaction of H$^+$ and OH$^-$ is often called an acid–base reaction, where H$^+$ is the acidic ion and OH$^-$ is the basic ion.

Drano contains a strong base.

Chapter Review

Key Terms

precipitation reaction *(7.2)*
strong electrolyte *(7.2)*
soluble solid *(7.2)*
insoluble (slightly soluble) solid *(7.2)*
molecular equation *(7.3)*
complete ionic equation *(7.3)*
spectator ions *(7.3)*

net ionic equation *(7.3)*
acid *(7.4)*
strong acid *(7.4)*
base *(7.4)*
strong base *(7.4)*
salt *(7.4)*

Summary

1. Four driving forces that favor chemical change (chemical reaction) are formation of a solid, formation of water, transfer of electrons, and formation of a gas.

2. A reaction where a solid forms is called a precipitation reaction. General rules on solubility help predict whether a solid—and what solid—will form when two solutions are mixed.

3. Three types of equations are used to describe reactions in solution: (1) the molecular equation, which shows the complete formulas of all reactants and products; (2) the complete ionic equation, in which all reactants and products that are strong electrolytes are shown as ions; and (3) the net ionic equation, which includes only those components of the solution that undergo a change. Spectator ions (those ions that remain unchanged in a reaction) are not included in a net ionic equation.

4. A strong acid is a compound in which virtually every molecule dissociates in water to give an H^+ ion and an anion. Similarly, a strong base is a metal hydroxide compound that is soluble in water, giving OH^- ions and cations. The products of the reaction of a strong acid and a strong base are water and a salt.

Questions and Problems

All even-numbered exercises have answers in the back of this book and solutions in the Solutions Guide.

7.1 ■ *Predicting Whether a Reaction Will Occur*

QUESTIONS

1. Why is water an important solvent? Although you have not yet studied water in detail, can you think of some properties of water that make it so important?

2. What is a "driving force"? What are some of the driving forces discussed in this section that tend to make reactions likely to occur? Can you think of any other possible driving forces?

7.2 ■ *Reactions in Which a Solid Forms*

QUESTIONS

3. What is a *precipitate?* What is a reaction called in which a precipitate is formed?

4. When two solutions of ionic substances are mixed and a precipitate forms, what is the net charge of the precipitate? Why?

5. What does it mean to say that the ions of an electrolyte behave independently of one another when the electrolyte is dissolved in water?

6. When an ionic substance dissolves, the resulting solution contains the separated _____.

7. What does it mean to say that an electrolyte is a strong electrolyte?

8. What information is used to determine what products are formed when two solutions of ionic substances are mixed to form a precipitate? Is there a way to determine, merely by inspection, what the products are?

9. When aqueous solutions of potassium chloride, KCl, and silver nitrate, $AgNO_3$, are mixed, a precipitate forms, but the precipitate is *not* potassium chloride. What does this tell you about the solubility of KCl in water?

10. What do we mean when we say that a solid is "slightly" soluble in water? Is there a practical difference between *slightly* soluble and *in*soluble?

11. On the basis of the general solubility rules given in Table 7.1, predict which of the following substances are likely to be soluble in water.
    a. sodium bromide
    b. magnesium sulfate
    c. potassium sulfate
    d. nickel(II) hydroxide
    e. sodium phosphate
    f. silver(I) chloride (usually called silver chloride)
    g. iron(II) carbonate

12. On the basis of the general solubility rules given in Table 7.1, predict which of the following substances are likely to be soluble in water.
    a. barium nitrate
    b. potassium carbonate
    c. sodium sulfate
    d. copper(II) hydroxide
    e. mercury(I) chloride
    f. ammonium phosphate
    g. chromium(III) sulfide
    h. lead sulfate

13. On the basis of the general solubility rules given in Table 7.1, explain why the following compounds are not likely to be soluble in water. That is, indicate *which* of the solubility rules covers each substance's particular situation.
    a. iron(III) sulfide, Fe_2S_3
    b. silver hydroxide, AgOH
    c. cobalt(II) carbonate, $CoCO_3$
    d. copper(I) phosphate, Cu_3PO_4

14. On the basis of the general solubility rules given in Table 7.1, for each of the following compounds indicate *which* of the solubility rules reveals that the substance is expected to be insoluble.
    a. mercury(II) sulfide, HgS
    b. nickel(II) hydroxide, $Ni(OH)_2$
    c. barium sulfate, $BaSO_4$
    d. zirconium carbonate, $ZrCO_3$

15. On the basis of the general solubility rules given in Table 7.1, predict the identity of the precipitate that forms when

aqueous solutions of the following substances are mixed. If no precipitate is likely, indicate why (which rules apply).

a. iron(III) chloride, $FeCl_3$, and phosphoric acid, H_3PO_4
b. barium nitrate, $Ba(NO_3)_2$, and sodium sulfate, Na_2SO_4
c. potassium chloride, KCl, and iron(II) sulfate, $FeSO_4$
d. lead(II) nitrate, $Pb(NO_3)_2$, and hydrochloric acid, HCl
e. calcium nitrate, $Ca(NO_3)_2$, and sodium chloride, NaCl
f. ammonium sulfide, $(NH_4)_2S$, and copper(II) chloride, $CuCl_2$

16. On the basis of the general solubility rules given in Table 7.1, predict the identity of the precipitate that forms when aqueous solutions of the following substances are mixed. If no precipitate is likely, indicate which rules apply.

a. mercury(II) nitrate, $Hg(NO_3)_2$, and sodium sulfide, Na_2S
b. sulfuric acid, H_2SO_4, and calcium nitrate, $Ca(NO_3)_2$
c. ammonium chloride, NH_4Cl, and silver nitrate, $AgNO_3$
d. barium nitrate, $Ba(NO_3)_2$, and potassium carbonate, K_2CO_3
e. phosphoric acid, H_3PO_4, and nickel(II) chloride, $NiCl_2$
f. potassium carbonate, K_2CO_3, and copper(II) sulfate, $CuSO_4$

PROBLEMS

17. On the basis of the general solubility rules given in Table 7.1, write a balanced molecular equation for the precipitation reactions that take place when the following aqueous solutions are mixed. Circle the formula of the precipitate (solid) that forms. If no precipitation reaction is likely for the reactants given, so indicate.

a. hydrochloric acid, HCl, and silver nitrate, $AgNO_3$
b. nitric acid, HNO_3, and ammonium chloride, NH_4Cl
c. sulfuric acid, H_2SO_4, and barium nitrate, $Ba(NO_3)_2$
d. hydrochloric acid, HCl, and lead acetate, $Pb(C_2H_3O_2)_2$
e. lead acetate, $Pb(C_2H_3O_2)_2$, and sodium chloride, NaCl
f. barium chloride, $BaCl_2$, and sodium carbonate, Na_2CO_3

18. On the basis of the general solubility rules given in Table 7.1, write a balanced molecular equation for the precipitation reactions that take place when the following aqueous solutions are mixed. Circle the formula of the precipitate (solid) that forms. If no precipitation reaction is likely for the solutes given, so indicate.
a. nitric acid, HNO_3, and barium chloride, $BaCl_2$
b. ammonium sulfide, $(NH_4)_2S$, and cobalt(II) chloride, $CoCl_2$
c. sulfuric acid, H_2SO_4, and lead(II) nitrate, $Pb(NO_3)_2$
d. calcium chloride, $CaCl_2$, and carbonic acid, H_2CO_3

e. sodium acetate, $NaC_2H_3O_2$, and ammonium nitrate, NH_4NO_3
f. sodium phosphate, Na_3PO_4, and chromium(III) chloride, $CrCl_3$

19. Balance each of the following equations that describe precipitation reactions.
a. $(NH_4)_2S(aq) + CoCl_3(aq) \rightarrow Co_2S_3(s) + NH_4Cl(aq)$
b. $Ba(NO_3)_2(aq) + (NH_4)_2CO_3(aq) \rightarrow BaCO_3(s) + NH_4NO_3(aq)$
c. $Na_3PO_4(aq) + NiCl_2(aq) \rightarrow Ni_3(PO_4)_2(s) + NaCl(aq)$

20. Balance each of the following equations that describe precipitation reactions.
a. $AgNO_3(aq) + H_2SO_4(aq) \rightarrow Ag_2SO_4(s) + HNO_3(aq)$
b. $Ca(NO_3)_2(aq) + H_2SO_4(aq) \rightarrow CaSO_4(s) + HNO_3(aq)$
c. $Pb(NO_3)_2(aq) + H_2SO_4(aq) \rightarrow PbSO_4(s) + HNO_3(aq)$

21. For each of the following precipitation reactions, complete and balance the equation, indicating clearly which product is the precipitate.
a. $Na_2SO_4(aq) + BaCl_2(aq) \rightarrow$
b. $H_3PO_4(aq) + CuSO_4(aq) \rightarrow$
c. $AgNO_3(aq) + NiCl_2(aq) \rightarrow$

22. For each of the following precipitation reactions, complete and balance the equation, indicating clearly which product is the precipitate.
a. $NiCl_2(aq) + H_2S(aq) \rightarrow$
b. $CuSO_4(aq) + NaOH(aq) \rightarrow$
c. $Ba(NO_3)_2(aq) + Na_2CO_3(aq) \rightarrow$

7.3 ■ Describing Reactions in Aqueous Solutions

QUESTIONS

23. What is a net ionic equation? What species are shown in such an equation, and which species are not shown?

24. Ions that do not directly participate in a reaction in solution are called _____ ions.

PROBLEMS

25. Write balanced net ionic equations for the reactions that occur when the following aqueous solutions are mixed. If no reaction is likely to occur, so indicate.
a. silver nitrate, $AgNO_3$, and potassium chloride, KCl
b. nickel(II) sulfate, $NiSO_4$, and barium chloride, $BaCl_2$
c. ammonium phosphate, $(NH_4)_3PO_4$, and calcium chloride, $CaCl_2$
d. hydrofluoric acid, HF, and potassium sulfate, K_2SO_4

e. calcium chloride, $CaCl_2$, and ammonium sulfate, $(NH_4)_2SO_4$

f. lead(II) nitrate, $Pb(NO_3)_2$, and barium chloride, $BaCl_2$

26. Write balanced net ionic equations for the reactions that occur when the following aqueous solutions are mixed. If no reaction is likely to occur, so indicate.
a. iron(III) nitrate and potassium hydroxide
b. nickel(II) chloride and potassium sulfide
c. silver nitrate and ammonium chloride
d. sodium sulfate and barium chloride
e. potassium bromide and mercury(I) nitrate
f. barium nitrate and potassium sulfate

27. A common analysis for the quantity of halide ions (Cl^-, Br^-, and I^-) in a sample is to precipitate and weigh the halide ions as their silver salts. For example, a given sample of seawater can be treated with dilute silver nitrate, $AgNO_3$, solution to precipitate the halides. The mixture of precipitated silver halides can then be filtered from the solution, dried, and weighed as an indication of the halide content of the original sample. Write the net ionic equations showing the precipitation of halide ions from seawater with silver nitrate.

28. The procedures and principles of qualitative analysis are covered in many introductory chemistry laboratory courses. In qualitative analysis, students learn to analyze mixtures of the common positive and negative ions, separating and confirming the presence of the particular ions in the mixture. One of the first steps in such an analysis is to treat the mixture with hydrochloric acid, which precipitates and removes silver ion, lead(II) ion, and mercury(I) ion from the aqueous mixture as the insoluble chloride salts. Write balanced net ionic equations for the precipitation reactions of these three cations with chloride ion.

29. Many plants are poisonous because their stems and leaves contain oxalic acid, $H_2C_2O_4$, or sodium oxalate, $Na_2C_2O_4$; when ingested, these substances cause swelling of the respiratory tract and suffocation. A standard analysis for determining the amount of oxalate ion, $C_2O_4^{2-}$, in a sample is to precipitate this species as calcium oxalate, which is insoluble in water. Write the net ionic equation for the reaction between sodium oxalate and calcium chloride, $CaCl_2$ in aqueous solution.

30. Another step in the qualitative analysis of cations (see Question 28) involves precipitating some of the metal ions as the insoluble sulfides (followed by subsequent treatment of the mixed sulfide precipitate to separate the individual ions). Write balanced net ionic equations for the reactions of Co(II), Co(III), Fe(II), and Fe(III) ions with sulfide ion, S^{2-}.

7.4 ■ *Reactions That Form Water: Acids and Bases*

QUESTIONS

31. When an acid like HCl is placed in water, virtually _____ percent of the molecules ionize.

32. What are some of the general physical and chemical properties that historically have led chemists to classify particular substances as acids or as bases?

33. The fundamental net ionic process that occurs when a strong acid reacts with a strong base is _____.

34. The common strong acids are H_2SO_4, HNO_3, and _____.

35. If 1000 NaOH units were dissolved in a sample of water, the NaOH would produce _____ Na^+ ions and _____ OH^- ions.

36. The ionic compound produced when a strong acid and a strong base react is called a(n) _____.

PROBLEMS

37. In addition to the three strong acids emphasized in the chapter (HCl, HNO_3, and H_2SO_4), hydrobromic acid, HBr, and perchloric acid, $HClO_4$, are also strong acids. Write equations for the dissociation of each of these additional strong acids in water.

38. In addition to the strong bases NaOH and KOH discussed in this chapter, the hydroxide compounds of other Group 1 elements also behave as strong bases when dissolved in water. Write equations for RbOH and CsOH that show what ions form when they dissolve in water.

39. Complete and balance each of the following molecular equations for strong acid/strong base reactions; circle the formula of the salt produced in each.
a. $HCl(aq) + RbOH(aq) \rightarrow$
b. $HClO_4(aq) + NaOH(aq) \rightarrow$
c. $HBr(aq) + NaOH(aq) \rightarrow$
d. $H_2SO_4(aq) + CsOH(aq) \rightarrow$

40. Below are the formulas of some salts. Such salts could be formed by the reaction of the appropriate strong acid and strong base (with the other product of the reaction, of course, being water). For each salt, indicate which strong acid and which strong base would be needed to produce the salt.
a. $NaNO_3$
b. K_2SO_4
c. RbCl
d. $NaClO_4$

Additional Problems

41. Complete and balance each of the following precipitation reactions; circle the formula of the solid that precipitates.
    a. $CaCl_2(aq) + K_2SO_4(aq) \rightarrow$
    b. $KOH(aq) + Fe(NO_3)_3(aq) \rightarrow$
    c. $Na_2SO_4(aq) + Pb(C_2H_3O_2)_2(aq) \rightarrow$
    d. $FeCl_3(aq) + H_2S(aq) \rightarrow$
    e. $CuSO_4(aq) + NaOH(aq) \rightarrow$

42. Distinguish between the *molecular* equation, the *complete ionic* equation, and the *net ionic* equation for a reaction in solution. Which type of equation most clearly shows the species that actually react with one another?

43. Write balanced net ionic equations for the reactions that occur when the following aqueous solutions are mixed. If no reaction is likely to occur, so indicate.
    a. silver nitrate and calcium nitrate
    b. nickel(II) chloride and lead(II) acetate
    c. silver nitrate and ammonium carbonate
    d. sodium sulfate and calcium chloride
    e. mercury(I) nitrate and copper(II) chloride
    f. calcium nitrate and sulfuric acid

44. In the subfield of chemistry called *qualitative analysis,* precipitation reactions are used as a means of identifying the ions present in a sample. For example, lead ions in solution precipitate when hydrochloric acid is added. If the precipitate of lead chloride is dissolved by heating it in boiling water, the lead may be reprecipitated as a bright yellow solid with potassium chromate. Lead ion is the only metal ion that behaves this way. Write net ionic equations for both of these precipitation reactions.

45. Using the general solubility rules given in Table 7.1, name three reactants that would form precipitates with each of the following ions in aqueous solution. Write the net ionic equation for each of your suggestions.
    a. chloride ion   d. sulfate ion
    b. calcium ion   e. mercury(I) ion, Hg_2^{2+}
    c. iron(III) ion   f. silver ion

46. Without first writing a full molecular or ionic equation, write the net ionic equations for any precipitation reactions that occur when aqueous solutions of the following compounds are mixed. If no reaction occurs, so indicate.
    a. cobalt(III) chloride and sodium hydroxide
    b. silver nitrate and ammonium carbonate
    c. barium nitrate and hydrochloric acid
    d. barium chloride and sulfuric acid
    e. copper(II) sulfate and nickel(II) chloride
    f. calcium chloride and sodium phosphate
    g. aluminum chloride and potassium hydroxide

47. List the formulas of four strong acids and four strong bases. What do we mean when we say that these acids and bases are *strong?* Write a full molecular equation for the reaction of each of the four acids you have chosen with each of the four bases.

48. The hydroxide compounds of the common Group 2 elements—$Ca(OH)_2$, $Mg(OH)_2$, $Sr(OH)_2$, and $Ba(OH)_2$—are not very soluble in water. However, the small amount of the compound that does dissolve produces ions. Therefore, these hydroxide compounds are sometimes considered strong bases. Write an equation for each of these bases, showing the ions produced when they dissolve in water.

49. Complete and balance each of the following molecular equations for strong acid/strong base reactions; circle the formula of the salt produced in each.
    a. $HCl(aq) + Ca(OH)_2(aq) \rightarrow$
    b. $H_2SO_4(aq) + Sr(OH)_2(aq) \rightarrow$
    c. $HNO_3(aq) + Ba(OH)_2(aq) \rightarrow$
    d. $HClO_4(aq) + Mg(OH)_2(aq) \rightarrow$

50. One important measurement for a chemical reaction is the quantity of heat energy liberated or absorbed when the reaction takes place. It has been found that when any strong acid is reacted with an excess amount of any strong base, exactly the same amount of heat energy is liberated per unit amount of strong acid. Explain this observation. *Hint:* Think of the net ionic equation.

51. For the cations listed in the left-hand column, give the formulas of the precipitates that would form with each of the anions in the right-hand column. If no precipitate is expected for a particular combination, so indicate.

Cations	*Anions*
Ag^+	$C_2H_3O_2^-$
Ba^{2+}	Cl^-
Ca^{2+}	CO_3^{2-}
Fe^{3+}	NO_3^-
Hg_2^{2+}	OH^-
Na^+	PO_4^{3-}
Ni^{2+}	S^{2-}
Pb^{2+}	SO_4^{2-}

52. On the basis of the general solubility rules given in Table 7.1, predict which of the following substances are likely to be soluble in water.
    a. potassium hexacyanoferrate(III), $K_3Fe(CN)_6$
    b. ammonium molybdate, $(NH_4)_2MoO_4$
    c. osmium(II) carbonate, $OsCO_3$
    d. gold phosphate, $AuPO_4$
    e. sodium hexanitrocobaltate(III), $Na_3Co(NO_2)_6$
    f. barium carbonate, $BaCO_3$
    g. iron(III) chloride, $FeCl_3$

53. On the basis of the general solubility rules given in Table 7.1, explain *why* the following compounds are *not* likely to be soluble in water. That is, indicate *which* of the solubility rules covers each substance's particular situation.
    a. iron(III) sulfide
    b. chromium(III) hydroxide
    c. nickel(II) carbonate
    d. aluminum phosphate

54. On the basis of the general solubility rules given in Table 7.1, predict the identity of the precipitate that forms when aqueous solutions of the following substances are mixed. If no precipitate is likely, indicate why (which rules apply).
    a. iron(III) chloride and sodium hydroxide
    b. nickel(II) nitrate and ammonium sulfide
    c. silver nitrate and potassium chloride
    d. sodium carbonate and barium nitrate
    e. potassium chloride and mercury(I) nitrate
    f. barium nitrate and sulfuric acid

55. On the basis of the general solubility rules given in Table 7.1, write a balanced molecular equation for the precipitation reactions that take place when the following aqueous solutions are mixed. Circle the formula of the precipitate (solid) that forms. If no precipitation reaction is likely for the reactants given, so indicate.
    a. silver nitrate and barium nitrate
    b. nickel(II) chloride and silver acetate
    c. lead nitrate and ammonium carbonate
    d. sodium sulfate and calcium acetate
    e. nickel(II) chloride and mercury(I) nitrate
    f. calcium nitrate and sulfuric acid

56. Balance each of the following equations that describe precipitation reactions.
    a. $Co(NO_3)_2(aq) + (NH_4)_2S(aq) \rightarrow$
       $$CoS(s) + NH_4NO_3(aq)$$
    b. $CaCl_2(aq) + H_2SO_4(aq) \rightarrow CaSO_4(s) + HCl(aq)$
    c. $FeCl_3(aq) + Na_3PO_4(aq) \rightarrow FePO_4(s) + NaCl(aq)$

57. For each of the following precipitation reactions, complete and balance the equation, indicating clearly which product is the precipitate.
    a. $Pb(NO_3)_2(aq) + Na_2CO_3(aq) \rightarrow$
    b. $K_2SO_4(aq) + CaCl_2(aq) \rightarrow$
    c. $Ni(C_2H_3O_2)_2(aq) + Na_2S(aq) \rightarrow$

58. For each of the following *un*balanced molecular equations, write the corresponding *balanced net ionic equation* for the reaction.
    a. $HCl(aq) + AgNO_3(aq) \rightarrow AgCl(s) + HNO_3(aq)$
    b. $CaCl_2(aq) + Na_3PO_4(aq) \rightarrow$
       $$Ca_3(PO_4)_2(s) + NaCl(aq)$$
    c. $Pb(NO_3)_2(aq) + BaCl_2(aq) \rightarrow$
       $$PbCl_2(s) + Ba(NO_3)_2(aq)$$
    d. $FeCl_3(aq) + NaOH(aq) \rightarrow Fe(OH)_3(s) + NaCl(aq)$

59. For each of the following *un*balanced molecular equations, write the corresponding *balanced net ionic equation* for the reaction.
    a. $Ca(NO_3)_2(aq) + H_2SO_4(aq) \rightarrow$
       $$CaSO_4(s) + HNO_3(aq)$$
    b. $Na_2CO_3(aq) + CoCl_2(aq) \rightarrow CoCO_3(s) + NaCl(aq)$
    c. $NiCl_2(aq) + Na_2S(aq) \rightarrow NiS(s) + NaCl(aq)$
    d. $Hg_2(NO_3)_2(aq) + NaCl(aq) \rightarrow$
       $$Hg_2Cl_2(s) + NaNO_3(aq)$$

60. Most sulfide compounds of the transition metals are insoluble in water. Many of these metal sulfides have striking and characteristic colors by which we can identify them. Therefore, in the analysis of mixtures of metal ions, it is very common to precipitate the metal ions by using dihydrogen sulfide (commonly called hydrogen sulfide), H_2S. Suppose you had a mixture of Fe^{2+}, Cr^{3+}, and Ni^{2+}. Write net ionic equations for the precipitation of these metal ions by the use of H_2S.

61. _____ and nitric acids are sometimes referred to as the "mineral" acids.

62. The strong bases considered in this chapter are the _____ compounds of the Group 1 elements.

63. When substances that can react to form water are mixed, there is a (strong/weak) tendency for the reaction to occur readily.

64. Complete and balance each of the following molecular equations for strong acid/strong base reactions; circle the formula of the salt produced in each.
    a. $HClO_4(aq) + RbOH(aq) \rightarrow$
    b. $HNO_3(aq) + KOH(aq) \rightarrow$
    c. $H_2SO_4(aq) + NaOH(aq) \rightarrow$
    d. $HBr(aq) + CsOH(aq) \rightarrow$

65. What strong acid and what strong base would react in aqueous solution to produce the salts listed below?
    a. potassium sulfate, K_2SO_4
    b. sodium nitrate, $NaNO_3$
    c. cesium bromide, $CsBr$
    d. sodium perchlorate, $NaClO_4$

66. Using the general solubility rules given in Table 7.1, name three reactants that would form precipitates with each of the following ions in aqueous solutions. Write the balanced molecular equation for each of your suggested reactants.
    a. sulfide ion
    b. carbonate ion
    c. hydroxide ion
    d. phosphate ion

Classifying Chemical Reactions

A car runs, a fire burns, and the space shuttle is launched by a very important class of reactions that we will study in this chapter: oxidation–reduction reactions.

In Chapter 7 we explored two important driving forces for reactions that occur in aqueous solutions. Precipitation reactions are driven by the formation of an insoluble solid, whereas acid–base reactions are driven by the formation of that very stable substance, water. A third driving force for chemical reactions is the transfer of electrons from one substance to another, a process called oxidation–reduction. A good example of this process occurs when a metal, which tends to lose one or more electrons, reacts with a nonmetal, which tends to gain one or more electrons. This is the type of reaction that occurs when steel rusts in the air. Interestingly, these reactions also have been implicated as important reasons why our body "wears out." As we show in the "Chemistry in Focus" on p. 206, oxidation–reduction reactions seem to contribute significantly to the aging process in humans and other organisms.

The power to launch the Space Shuttle (left) *and rusting* (right) *involve oxidation–reduction reactions.*

201

Because there are so many different chemical reactions, it is helpful to classify them in various ways. This makes it easier to remember the reactions that we have studied and helps us understand the new reactions that we encounter. The following diagram gives an overview of the classes of reactions we have mentioned up to this point. The driving force for each type of reaction is given in parentheses.

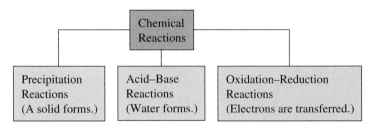

As we explore oxidation–reduction reactions in this chapter, we will see that there are several subclasses of this type of process.

8.1 Reactions of Metals with Nonmetals (Oxidation–Reduction)

AIMS: To learn the general characteristics of a reaction between a metal and a nonmetal. To understand electron transfer as a driving force for a chemical reaction.

In Chapter 4 we spent considerable time discussing ionic compounds—compounds formed in the reaction of a metal and a nonmetal. A typical example is sodium chloride, formed by the reaction of sodium metal and chlorine gas:

$$2Na(s) + Cl_2(g) \rightarrow 2NaCl(s)$$

Let's examine what happens in this reaction. Sodium metal is composed of sodium atoms, each of which has a net charge of zero. (The positive charges of the eleven protons in its nucleus are exactly balanced by the negative charges on the eleven electrons.) Similarly, the chlorine molecule consists of two uncharged chlorine atoms (each has seventeen protons and seventeen electrons). However, in the product (sodium chloride), the sodium is present as Na^+ and the chlorine as Cl^-. By what process do the neutral atoms become ions? The answer is that one electron is transferred from each sodium atom to each chlorine atom.

$$Na + Cl \rightarrow Na^+ + Cl^-$$

After the electron transfer, each sodium has ten electrons and eleven protons (a net charge of $1+$), and each chlorine has eighteen electrons and seventeen protons (a net charge of $1-$).

Thus the reaction of a metal with a nonmetal to form an ionic compound involves the transfer of one or more electrons from the metal (which forms a cation) to the nonmetal (which forms an anion). This tendency to transfer electrons from metals to nonmetals is the third driving force for reactions that we listed in Section 7.1. A reaction that *involves a transfer of electrons* is called an **oxidation–reduction reaction.**

There are many examples of oxidation–reduction reactions in which a metal reacts with a nonmetal to form an ionic compound. Consider the reaction of magnesium metal with oxygen,

$$2Mg(s) + O_2(g) \rightarrow 2MgO(s)$$

which produces a bright, white light useful in camera flash units. Note that the reactants contain uncharged atoms, but the product contains ions:

MgO

Contains Mg^{2+}, O^{2-}

Therefore, in this reaction, each magnesium atom loses two electrons ($Mg \rightarrow Mg^{2+} + 2e^-$) and each oxygen atom gains two electrons ($O + 2e^- \rightarrow O^{2-}$). We might represent this reaction as follows:

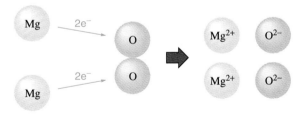

Another example is

$$2Al(s) + Fe_2O_3(s) \rightarrow 2Fe(s) + Al_2O_3(s)$$

which is a reaction (called the thermite reaction) that produces so much energy (heat) that the iron is initially formed as a liquid (see Figure 8.1). In this case the aluminum is originally present as the elemental metal (which contains uncharged Al atoms) and ends up in Al_2O_3, where it is present as Al^{3+} cations (the $2Al^{3+}$ ions just balance the charge of the $3O^{2-}$ ions). Therefore, in the reaction each aluminum atom loses three electrons.

$$Al \rightarrow Al^{3+} + 3e^-$$

The opposite process occurs with the iron, which is initially present as Fe^{3+} ions in Fe_2O_3 and ends up as uncharged atoms in the elemental iron. Thus

FIGURE 8.1
The thermite reaction gives off so much heat that the iron formed is molten.

This equation is read, "An aluminum atom yields an aluminum ion with a 3+ charge and three electrons."

each iron cation gains three electrons to form an uncharged atom:

$$Fe^{3+} + 3e^- \rightarrow Fe$$

We can represent this reaction in schematic form as follows:

FIGURE 8.2
When powdered aluminum and iodine react, the heat given off changes some of the solid iodine to a purple cloud of vapor.

EXAMPLE 8.1   *Identifying Electron Transfer in Oxidation–Reduction Reactions*

For each of the following reactions, show how electrons are gained and lost.

a. $2Al(s) + 3I_2(s) \rightarrow 2AlI_3(s)$

(This reaction is shown in Figure 8.2. Note the flame plus the purple "smoke," which is excess I_2 being driven off by the heat.)

b. $2Cs(s) + F_2(g) \rightarrow 2CsF(s)$

Solution

a. In AlI_3 the ions are Al^{3+} and I^- (aluminum always forms Al^{3+}, and iodine always forms I^-). In $Al(s)$ the aluminum is present as uncharged atoms. Thus aluminum goes from Al to Al^{3+} by losing three electrons $(Al \rightarrow Al^{3+} + 3e^-)$. In I_2 each iodine atom is uncharged. Thus each iodine atom goes from I to I^- by gaining one electron $(I + e^- \rightarrow I^-)$. A schematic for this reaction is

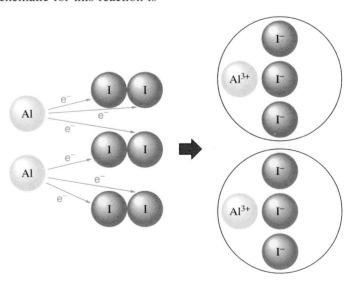

b. In CsF the ions present are Cs^+ and F^-. Cesium metal, $Cs(s)$, contains uncharged cesium atoms; and fluorine gas, $F_2(g)$, contains uncharged fluorine atoms. Thus in the reaction each cesium atom loses one electron

$(Cs \rightarrow Cs^+ + e^-)$ and each fluorine atom gains one electron $(F + e^- \rightarrow F^-)$. The schematic for this reaction is

 Self-Check Exercise 8.1

For each reaction, show how electrons are gained and lost.

a. $2Na(s) + Br_2(l) \rightarrow 2NaBr(s)$
b. $2Ca(s) + O_2(g) \rightarrow 2CaO(s)$

See Problems 8.7 and 8.8

So far we have emphasized electron transfer (oxidation–reduction) reactions that involve a metal and a nonmetal. Electron transfer reactions can also take place between two nonmetals. We will not discuss these reactions in detail here. All we will say at this point is that one sure sign of an oxidation–reduction reaction between nonmetals is the presence of oxygen, $O_2(g)$, as a reactant or product. In fact, oxidation got its name from oxygen. Thus the reactions

$$CH_4(g) + 2O_2(g) \rightarrow CO_2(g) + 2H_2O(g)$$

and

$$2SO_2(g) + O_2(g) \rightarrow 2SO_3(g)$$

are electron transfer reactions, even though it is not obvious at this point.

We can summarize what we have learned about oxidation–reduction reactions as follows:

Characteristics of Oxidation–Reduction Reactions

1. When a metal reacts with a nonmetal, an ionic compound is formed. The ions are formed when the metal transfers one or more electrons to the nonmetal, the metal atom becoming a cation and the nonmetal

atom becoming an anion. *Therefore, a metal–nonmetal reaction can always be assumed to be an oxidation–reduction reaction, which involves electron transfer.*

2. Two nonmetals can also undergo an oxidation–reduction reaction. At this point we can recognize these cases only by looking for O_2 as a reactant or product. When two nonmetals react, the compound formed is not ionic. More will be said about these reactions in Chapter 18.

CHEMISTRY IN FOCUS

Do We Age by Oxidation?

People (especially those over age 30) seem obsessed about staying young, but the fountain of youth sought since the days of Ponce de Leon has proved elusive. The body inevitably seems to wear out after 70 or 80 years. Is this our destiny or can we find ways to combat aging?

Why do we age? No one knows for certain, but many scientists think that oxidation plays a major role. Although oxygen is essential for life, it can also have a detrimental effect. The oxygen molecule and other oxidizing substances in the body can extract single electrons from the large molecules that make up cell membranes (walls), thus causing them to become very reactive. In fact, these activated molecules can react with each other to change the properties of the cell membranes. If enough of these changes accumulate, the body's immune system comes to view the changed cell as "foreign" and destroys it. This action is particularly harmful to the organism if the cells involved are irreplaceable, such as nerve cells.

Because the human body is so complex, it is very difficult to pin-point the cause or causes of aging. Scientists are therefore studying simpler life forms. For example, Rajundar Sohal and his co-workers at Southern Methodist University in Dallas are examining aging in common houseflies. Their work indicates that the accumulated damage from oxidation is linked to both the fly's vitality and its life expectancy. One study showed that flies that were forced to be sedentary (couldn't fly

Foods that contain natural antioxidants.

around) showed much less damage from oxidation (because of their lower oxygen consumption) and lived twice as long as flies that had normal activities.

Accumulated knowledge from various studies indicates that oxidation is probably a major cause of aging. If this is true, how can we protect ourselves? The best way to approach the answer to this question is to study the body's natural defenses against oxidation. A recent study by Russel J. Reiter of the Texas Health Science Center at San Antonio has shown that melatonin—a chemical secreted by the pineal gland in the brain (but only at night)—protects against oxidation. In addition, it has long been shown that vitamin E is an antioxidant. Studies have shown that red blood cells deficient in vitamin E age much faster than cells with normal vitamin E levels. On the basis of this type of evidence many people take daily doses of vitamin E to ward off the effects of aging.

Oxidation is only one possible cause of aging. Research continues on many fronts to find out why we get "older" as time passes.

8.2 Ways to Classify Reactions

AIM: To learn various classification schemes for reactions.

So far in our study of chemistry we have seen many, many chemical reactions—and this is just Chapter 8. In the world around us and in our bodies, literally millions of chemical reactions are taking place. Obviously, we need a system for putting reactions into meaningful classes that will make them easier to remember and easier to understand.

In Chapters 7 and 8 we have so far considered the following "driving forces" for chemical reactions:

- Formation of a solid
- Formation of water
- Transfer of electrons

We will now discuss how to classify reactions involving these processes. For example, in the reaction

$$K_2CrO_4(aq) \ + \ Ba(NO_3)_2(aq) \ \rightarrow \ BaCrO_4(s) \ + \ 2KNO_3(aq)$$

Solution   Solution   Solid   Solution
                                formed

solid $BaCrO_4$ (a precipitate) is formed. Because the *formation of a solid when two solutions are mixed* is called *precipitation,* we call this a **precipitation reaction.**

Notice in this reaction that two anions (NO_3^- and CrO_4^{2-}) are simply exchanged. Note that CrO_4^{2-} was originally associated with K^+ in K_2CrO_4 and that NO_3^- was associated with Ba^{2+} in $Ba(NO_3)_2$. In the products these associations are reversed. Because of this double exchange, we sometimes call this reaction a double-exchange reaction or **double-displacement reaction.** We might represent such a reaction as

$$AB + CD \ \rightarrow \ AD + CB$$

So we can classify a reaction such as the one above as a precipitation reaction or as a double-displacement reaction. Either name is correct, but the former is more commonly used by chemists.

In Chapter 7 we also considered reactions in which water is formed when a strong acid is mixed with a strong base. All of these reactions had the same net ionic equation:

$$H^+ (aq) + OH^-(aq) \ \rightarrow \ H_2O(l)$$

The H^+ ion comes from a strong acid, such as $HCl(aq)$ or $HNO_3(aq)$, and the origin of the OH^- ion is from a strong base, such as $NaOH(aq)$ or $KOH(aq)$. An example is

$$HCl(aq) \ + \ KOH(aq) \ \rightarrow \ H_2O(l) \ + \ KCl(aq)$$

We classify these reactions as **acid–base reactions.** You can recognize this as an acid–base reaction because it *involves an H^+ ion that ends up in the product water.*

CHEMISTRY IN FOCUS

*O*xidation–Reduction Reactions Launch the Space Shuttle

Launching into space a vehicle that weighs millions of pounds requires unimaginable quantities of energy—all furnished by oxidation–reduction reactions.

Notice from Figure 8.3 that three cylindrical objects are attached to the shuttle orbiter. In the center is a tank 28 feet in diameter and 154 feet long that contains liquid oxygen and liquid hydrogen (in separate compartments). These fuels are fed to the orbiter's rocket engines, where they react to form water and release a huge quantity of energy.

$$2H_2 + O_2 \rightarrow 2H_2O + \text{energy}$$

Note that we can recognize this reaction as an oxidation–reduction reaction because O_2 is a reactant.

Two solid-fuel rockets 12 feet in diameter and 150 feet long are also attached to the orbiter. Each rocket contains 1.1 million pounds fuel: ammonium perchlorate (NH_4ClO_4) and powdered aluminum mixed with a binder ("glue"). Because the rockets are so large, they are built in segments and assembled at the launch site as shown in Figure 8.4. Each segment is filled with the syrupy propellant (Figure 8.5), which then solidifies to a consistency much like that of a hard rubber eraser.

The oxidation–reduction reaction between the ammonium perchlorate and the aluminum is represented as follows:
$$3NH_4ClO_4(s) + 3Al(s)$$
$$\rightarrow Al_2O_3(s) + AlCl_3(s)$$
$$+ 3NO(g) + 6H_2O(g) + \text{energy}$$
It produces temperatures of about 5700 °F and 3.3 million pounds of thrust in each rocket.

Thus we can see that oxidation–reduction reactions furnish the energy to launch the space shuttle.

External fuel tank
(153.8 feet long,
27.5 feet in diameter)

Left solid rocket booster

Right solid rocket booster

Orbiter vehicle

Space shuttle main engines

|← 78.06 feet →|

Space shuttle *Discovery* stacked for launch

FIGURE 8.3
For launch, the space shuttle orbiter is attached to two solid-fuel rockets (left and right) and a fuel tank (center) that supplies hydrogen and oxygen to the orbiter's engines. *(Adapted with permission from* Chemical and Engineering News, *September 19, 1988, Volume 66, Number 33, p. 9. Copyright 1988, American Chemical Society.)*

Solid booster

Aft field joint
(point of failure in
Challenger's right booster)

Solid propellant

149.16 feet long,
12.17 feet in diameter

FIGURE 8.4
The solid-fuel rockets are assembled from segments to make loading the fuel more convenient. *(Adapted with permission from* Chemical and Engineering News, *September 19, 1988, Volume 66, Number 33, p. 9. Copyright 1988, American Chemical Society.)*

FIGURE 8.5
A rocket segment being filled with the propellant mixture.

The third driving force—the one we are considering in the present chapter—is electron transfer. We see evidence of this driving force particularly in the "desire" of a metal to donate electrons to nonmetals. An example is

$$2Li(s) + F_2(g) \rightarrow 2LiF(s)$$

where each lithium atom loses one electron to form Li^+, and each fluorine atom gains one electron to form the F^- ion. The process of electron transfer is also called oxidation–reduction. Thus we classify the above reaction as an **oxidation–reduction reaction.**

An additional driving force for chemical reactions that we have not yet discussed is *formation of a gas*. A reaction in aqueous solution that forms a gas (which escapes as bubbles) is pulled toward the products by this event. An example is the reaction

$$2HCl(aq) + Na_2CO_3(aq) \rightarrow CO_2(g) + H_2O(l) + NaCl(aq)$$

for which the net ionic equation is

$$2H^+(aq) + CO_3^{2-}(aq) \rightarrow CO_2(g) + H_2O(l)$$

Note that this reaction forms carbon dioxide gas as well as water, so it illustrates two of the driving forces that we have considered. Because this reaction involves H^+ that ends up in the product water, we classify it as an acid–base reaction.

Consider another reaction that forms a gas:

$$Zn(s) + 2HCl(aq) \rightarrow H_2(g) + ZnCl_2(aq)$$

How might we classify this reaction? A careful look at the reactants and products shows the following:

Note that in the reactant zinc metal, Zn exists as uncharged atoms, whereas in the product it exists as Zn^{2+}. Thus each Zn atom loses two electrons. Where have these electrons gone? They have been transferred to two H^+ ions to form H_2. The schematic for this reaction is

Zn metal   Solution of HCl H_2 molecule   Solution of $ZnCl_2$

This is an electron transfer process, so the reaction can be classified as an oxidation–reduction reaction.

Another way this reaction is sometimes classified is based on the fact that a *single* type of anion (Cl^-) has been exchanged between H^+ and Zn^{2+}. That is, Cl^- is originally associated with H^+ in HCl and ends up associated with Zn^{2+} in the product $ZnCl_2$. We can call this a *single-replacement reaction* in contrast to double-displacement reactions, in which two types of anions are exchanged. We can represent a single replacement as

$$A + BC \rightarrow B + AC$$

8.3   *Other Ways to Classify Reactions*

AIM: To consider additional classes of chemical reactions.

So far in this chapter we have classified chemical reactions in several ways. The most commonly used of these classifications are

- Precipitation reactions
- Acid–base reactions
- Oxidation–reduction reactions

However, there are still other ways to classify reactions that you may encounter in your future studies of chemistry. We will consider several of these in this section.

Combustion Reactions

Many chemical reactions that involve oxygen produce energy (heat) so rapidly that a flame results. Such reactions are called **combustion reactions.** We have considered some of these reactions previously. For example, the methane in natural gas reacts with oxygen according to the following balanced equation:

$$CH_4(g) \; + \; 2O_2(g) \; \rightarrow \; CO_2(g) \; + \; 2H_2O(g)$$

This reaction produces the flame of the common laboratory burner and is used to heat most homes in the United States. Recall that we originally classified this reaction as an oxidation–reduction reaction in Section 8.1. Thus we can say that the reaction of methane with oxygen is both an oxidation–reduction reaction and a combustion reaction. Combustion reactions, in fact, are a special class of oxidation–reduction reactions (see Figure 8.6).

FIGURE 8.6

Classes of reactions. Combustion reactions are a special type of oxidation–reduction reaction.

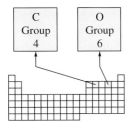

There are many combustion reactions, most of which are used to provide heat or electricity for homes or businesses or energy for transportation. Some examples are

- Combustion of propane (used to heat some rural homes)

$$C_3H_8(g) \; + \; 5O_2(g) \; \rightarrow \; 3CO_2(g) \; + \; 4H_2O(g)$$

- Combustion of gasoline* (used to power cars and trucks)

$$2C_8H_{18}(l) \; + \; 25O_2(g) \; \rightarrow \; 16CO_2(g) \; + \; 18H_2O(g)$$

- Combustion of coal* (used to generate electricity)

$$C(s) + O_2(g) \rightarrow CO_2(g)$$

Synthesis (Combination) Reactions

One of the most important activities in chemistry is the synthesis of new compounds. Each of our lives has been greatly affected by synthetic compounds such as plastic, polyester, and aspirin. When a given compound is formed from simpler materials, we call this a **synthesis** (or **combination**) **reaction.**

In many cases synthesis reactions start with elements, as shown by the following examples:

- Synthesis of water $\qquad\qquad$ $2H_2(g) \; + \; O_2(g) \; \rightarrow \; 2H_2O(l)$

- Synthesis of carbon dioxide $\qquad$ $C(s) \; + \; O_2(g) \; \rightarrow \; CO_2(g)$

- Synthesis of nitrogen monoxide $\quad$ $N_2(g) \; + \; O_2(g) \; \rightarrow \; 2NO(g)$

Production of Mylar film is an example of a synthesis reaction.

Notice that each of these reactions involves oxygen, so each can be classified as an oxidation–reduction reaction. The first two reactions are also commonly called combustion reactions because they produce flames. The reaction of hydrogen with oxygen to produce water, then, can be classified three ways: as an oxidation–reduction reaction, as a combustion reaction, and as a synthesis reaction.

There are also many synthesis reactions that do not involve oxygen:

- Synthesis of sodium chloride $\qquad$ $2Na(s) \; + \; Cl_2(g) \; \rightarrow \; 2NaCl(s)$

- Synthesis of magnesium fluoride $\quad$ $Mg(s) \; + \; F_2(g) \; \rightarrow \; MgF_2(s)$

We have discussed the formation of sodium chloride before and have noted that it is an oxidation–reduction reaction; uncharged sodium atoms lose electrons to form Na^+ ions, and uncharged chlorine atoms gain electrons to form Cl^- ions. The synthesis of magnesium fluoride is also an oxidation–reduction reaction because Mg^{2+} and F^- ions are produced from the uncharged atoms.

We have seen that synthesis reactions in which the reactants are elements are oxidation–reduction reactions as well. In fact, we can think of these synthesis reactions as another subclass of the oxidation–reduction class of reactions.

---

*This substance is really a complex mixture of compounds, but the reaction shown is representative of what takes place.

Decomposition Reactions

In many cases a compound can be broken down into simpler compounds or all the way to the component elements. This is usually accomplished by heating or by the application of an electric current. Such reactions are called **decomposition reactions.** We have discussed decomposition reactions before, including

- Decomposition of water

$$2H_2O(l) \xrightarrow[\text{current}]{\text{Electric}} 2H_2(g) + O_2(g)$$

- Decomposition of mercury(II) oxide

$$2HgO(s) \xrightarrow{\text{Heat}} 2Hg(l) + O_2(g)$$

Because O_2 is involved in the first reaction, we recognize it as an oxidation–reduction reaction. In the second reaction, HgO, which contains Hg^{2+} and O^{2-} ions, is decomposed to the elements, which contain uncharged atoms. In this process each Hg^{2+} gains two electrons and each O^{2-} loses two electrons, so this is both a decomposition reaction and an oxidation–reduction reaction.

A decomposition reaction, in which a compound is broken down into its elements, is just the opposite of the synthesis (combination) reaction, in which elements combine to form the compound. For example, we have just discussed the synthesis of sodium chloride from its elements. Sodium chloride can be decomposed into its elements by melting it and passing an electric current through it:

$$2NaCl(l) \xrightarrow[\text{current}]{\text{Electric}} 2Na(l) + Cl_2(g)$$

There are other schemes for classifying reactions that we have not considered. However, we have covered many of the classifications that are commonly used by chemists as they pursue their science in laboratories and industrial plants.

It should be apparent that many important reactions can be classified as oxidation–reduction reactions. As shown in Figure 8.7, various types of reactions can be viewed as subclasses of the overall oxidation–reduction category.

Hg	O
Transition Metal	Group 6

EXAMPLE 8.2   *Classifying Reactions*

Classify each of the following reactions in as many ways as possible.

a. $2K(s) + Cl_2(g) \rightarrow 2KCl(s)$

b. $Fe_2O_3(s) + 2Al(s) \rightarrow Al_2O_3(s) + 2Fe(s)$

c. $2Mg(s) + O_2(g) \rightarrow 2MgO(s)$

FIGURE 8.7
Summary of classes of reactions.

d. $HNO_3(aq) + NaOH(aq) \rightarrow H_2O(l) + NaNO_3(aq)$

e. $KBr(aq) + AgNO_3(aq) \rightarrow AgBr(s) + KNO_3(aq)$

f. $PbO_2(s) \rightarrow Pb(s) + O_2(g)$

Solution

a. This is both a synthesis reaction (elements combine to form a compound) and an oxidation–reduction reaction (uncharged potassium and chlorine atoms are changed to K^+ and Cl^- ions in KCl).

b. This is an oxidation–reduction reaction. Iron is present in $Fe_2O_3(s)$ as Fe^{3+} ions and in elemental iron, $Fe(s)$, as uncharged atoms. So each Fe^{3+} must gain three electrons to form Fe. The reverse happens to aluminum, which is present initially as uncharged aluminum atoms, each of which loses three electrons to give Al^{3+} ions in Al_2O_3. Note that this reaction might also be called a single-replacement reaction because O is switched from Fe to Al.

c. This is both a synthesis reaction (elements combine to form a compound) and an oxidation–reduction reaction (each magnesium atom loses two electrons to give Mg^{2+} ions in MgO, and each oxygen atom gains two electrons to give O^{2-} in MgO).

d. This is an acid–base reaction. It might also be called a double-displacement reaction because NO_3^- and OH^- "switch partners."

e. This is a precipitation reaction that might also be called a double-displacement reaction in which the anions Br^- and NO_3^- are exchanged.

f. This is a decomposition reaction (a compound breaks down into elements). It also is an oxidation–reduction reaction, because the ions in PbO_2 (Pb^{4+} and O^{2-}) are changed to uncharged atoms in the elements $Pb(s)$ and $O_2(g)$. That is, electrons are transferred from O^{2-} to Pb^{4+} in the reaction.

Self-Check Exercise 8.2

Classify each of the following reactions in as many ways as possible.

a. $4NH_3(g) + 5O_2(g) \rightarrow 4NO(g) + 6H_2O(g)$

b. $S_8(s) + 8O_2(g) \rightarrow 8SO_2(g)$

c. $2Al(s) + 3Cl_2(g) \rightarrow 2AlCl_3(s)$

d. $2AlN(s) \rightarrow 2Al(s) + N_2(g)$

e. $BaCl_2(aq) + Na_2SO_4(aq) \rightarrow BaSO_4(s) + 2NaCl(aq)$

f. $2Cs(s) + Br_2(l) \rightarrow 2CsBr(s)$

g. $KOH(aq) + HCl(aq) \rightarrow H_2O(l) + KCl(aq)$

h. $2C_2H_2(g) + 5O_2(g) \rightarrow 4CO_2(g) + 2H_2O(l)$

See Problems 8.13 and 8.14.

Chapter Review

Key Terms

oxidation–reduction reaction *(8.1)*
combustion reaction *(8.3)*
synthesis (combination) reaction *(8.3)*
decomposition reaction *(8.3)*

Summary

1. Reactions of metals and nonmetals involve a transfer of electrons and are called oxidation–reduction reactions. A reaction between a nonmetal and oxygen is also an oxidation–reduction reaction. Combustion reactions involve oxygen and are a subgroup of oxidation–reduction reactions.

2. When a given compound is formed from simpler materials, such as elements, the reaction is called a synthesis or combination reaction. The reverse process, which occurs when a compound is broken down into its component elements, is called a decomposition reaction. These reactions are also subgroups of oxidation–reduction reactions.

Questions and Problems

All even-numbered exercises have answers in the back of this book and solutions in the Solutions Guide.

8.1 ■ Reactions of Metals with Nonmetals (Oxidation–Reduction)

QUESTIONS

1. What is an oxidation–reduction reaction? What is transferred during such a reaction?

2. The reaction $2Na + Cl_2 \rightarrow 2NaCl$, like any reaction between a metal and a nonmetal, involves the _____ of electrons.

3. What do we mean when we say that the transfer of electrons can be the "driving force" for a reaction? Give an example of a reaction where this happens.

4. When a metal reacts with a nonmetal, which atoms form the cations of the ionic product? Which atoms form the negative ions? Which atoms lose electrons, and which gain them?

5. If potassium atoms were to react with atoms of the nonmetal sulfur, how many electrons would each potassium atom lose? How many electrons would each sulfur atom gain? How many potassium atoms would have to react to provide enough electrons for one sulfur atom? What charges would the resulting potassium and sulfur ions have?

6. If a bromine molecule, Br_2, were to react with a metal such as sodium, what charge would the resulting bromide ions have? How many electrons would be gained by each bromine atom? How many electrons would be gained by each Br_2 molecule?

PROBLEMS

7. For the reaction $Ca(s) + F_2(g) \rightarrow CaF_2(s)$, illustrate how electrons are gained and lost by the atoms during the reaction.

8. For the reaction $2Al(s) + 3Br_2(l) \rightarrow 2AlBr_3(s)$, show how electrons are gained and lost by the atoms.

9. Balance each of the following oxidation–reduction chemical reactions.
   a. $K(s) + F_2(g) \rightarrow KF(s)$
   b. $K(s) + O_2(g) \rightarrow K_2O(s)$
   c. $K(s) + N_2(g) \rightarrow K_3N(s)$
   d. $K(s) + C(s) \rightarrow K_4C(s)$

10. Balance each of the following oxidation–reduction chemical reactions.
   a. $Na(s) + S(s) \rightarrow Na_2S(s)$
   b. $Cu(s) + AgNO_3(aq) \rightarrow Cu(NO_3)_2(aq) + Ag(s)$
   c. $Mg(s) + HCl(aq) \rightarrow MgCl_2(aq) + H_2(g)$
   d. $Pb(s) + S(s) \rightarrow PbS_2(s)$
   e. $Li(s) + H_2O(l) \rightarrow LiOH(aq) + H_2(g)$

8.2 ■ *Ways to Classify Reactions*

QUESTIONS

11. What is a *double*-displacement reaction? What is a *single*-displacement reaction? Write balanced chemical equations showing two examples of each type.

12. Two "driving forces" for reactions discussed in this section are the formation of water in an acid–base reaction and the formation of a gaseous product. Write balanced chemical equations showing two examples of each type.

13. Identify each of the following unbalanced reaction equations as belonging to one or more of the following categories: precipitation, acid–base, or oxidation–reduction.
   a. $Na_2SO_4(aq) + BaCl_2(aq) \rightarrow BaSO_4(s) + NaCl(aq)$
   b. $H_3PO_4(aq) + Ca(OH)_2(aq) \rightarrow$
      $Ca_3(PO_4)_2(s) + H_2O(l)$
   c. $H_3PO_4(aq) + CuSO_4(aq) \rightarrow$
      $Cu_3(PO_4)_2(s) + H_2SO_4(aq)$
   d. $H_3PO_4(aq) + Mg(s) \rightarrow Mg_3(PO_4)_2(s) + H_2(g)$
   e. $Mg(s) + CuCl_2(aq) \rightarrow MgCl_2(aq) + Cu(s)$
   f. $AgNO_3(aq) + NiCl_2(aq) \rightarrow AgCl(s) + Ni(NO_3)_2(aq)$
   g. $NaHSO_3(aq) + NaOH(aq) \rightarrow$
      $Na_2SO_3(aq) + H_2O(l)$
   h. $KHCO_3(aq) + HCl(aq) \rightarrow$
      $KCl(aq) + H_2O(l) + CO_2(g)$
   i. $AlCl_3(aq) + Mg(s) \rightarrow MgCl_2(aq) + Al(s)$

14. Identify each of the following unbalanced reaction equations as belonging to one or more of the following categories: precipitation, acid–base, or oxidation–reduction.
   a. $H_2O_2(aq) \rightarrow H_2O(l) + O_2(g)$
   b. $H_2SO_4(aq) + Cu(s) \rightarrow CuSO_4(aq) + H_2(g)$
   c. $H_2SO_4(aq) + NaOH(aq) \rightarrow Na_2SO_4(aq) + H_2O(l)$
   d. $H_2SO_4(aq) + Ba(OH)_2(aq) \rightarrow BaSO_4(s) + H_2O(l)$
   e. $AgNO_3(aq) + CuCl_2(aq) \rightarrow$
      $Cu(NO_3)_2(aq) + AgCl(s)$
   f. $KOH(aq) + CuSO_4(aq) \rightarrow$
      $Cu(OH)_2(s) + K_2SO_4(aq)$
   g. $Cl_2(g) + F_2(g) \rightarrow ClF(g)$
   h. $NO(g) + O_2(g) \rightarrow NO_2(g)$
   i. $Ca(OH)_2(s) + HNO_3(aq) \rightarrow Ca(NO_3)_2(aq) + H_2O(l)$

8.3 ■ *Other Ways to Classify Reactions*

QUESTIONS

15. A reaction in which a compound reacts rapidly with elemental oxygen, usually with the release of heat or light, is referred to as a _____ reaction.

16. Reactions involving the combustion of fuel substances make up a subclass of _____ reactions.

17. What is a *synthesis* or *combination* reaction? Give an example. Can such reactions also be classified in other ways? Give an example of a synthesis reaction that is also a *combustion* reaction. Give an example of a synthesis reaction that is also an *oxidation–reduction* reaction, but which does not involve combustion.

18. What is a *decomposition* reaction? Give an example. Can such reactions also be classified in other ways?

PROBLEMS

19. Balance each of the following equations that describe combustion reactions.
   a. $C_2H_6(g) + O_2(g) \rightarrow CO_2(g) + H_2O(g)$
   b. $C_4H_{10}(g) + O_2(g) \rightarrow CO_2(g) + H_2O(g)$
   c. $C_6H_{14}(l) + O_2(g) \rightarrow CO_2(g) + H_2O(g)$

20. Balance each of the following equations that describe combustion reactions.
   a. $C_3H_8(g) + O_2(g) \rightarrow CO_2(g) + H_2O(g)$
   b. $C_4H_{10}(g) + O_2(g) \rightarrow CO_2(g) + H_2O(g)$
   c. $C_5H_{12}(l) + O_2(g) \rightarrow CO_2(g) + H_2O(g)$

21. Complete and balance each of the following equations that describe combustion reactions.
   a. $C_2H_2(g) + O_2(g) \rightarrow$
   b. $C_3H_8(g) + O_2(g) \rightarrow$
   c. $C_2H_4O_2(l) + O_2(g) \rightarrow$

22. Complete and balance each of the following equations that describe combustion reactions.
   a. $C_{19}H_{40}(s) + O_2(g) \rightarrow$
   b. $C_6H_{12}O_6(s) + O_2(g) \rightarrow$
   c. $C_{12}H_{22}O_{11}(s) + O_2(g) \rightarrow$

23. Balance each of the following equations that describe synthesis reactions.
    a. $Cu(s) + S(s) \rightarrow Cu_2S(s)$
    b. $Cu_2O(s) + O_2(g) \rightarrow CuO(s)$
    c. $B(s) + O_2(g) \rightarrow B_2O_3(s)$
    d. $Na(s) + N_2(g) \rightarrow Na_3N(s)$
    e. $Fe(s) + Cl_2(g) \rightarrow FeCl_3(s)$

24. Balance each of the following equations that describe synthesis reactions.
    a. $Co(s) + S(s) \rightarrow Co_2S_3(s)$
    b. $NO(g) + O_2(g) \rightarrow NO_2(g)$
    c. $FeO(s) + CO_2(g) \rightarrow FeCO_3(s)$
    d. $Al(s) + F_2(g) \rightarrow AlF_3(s)$
    e. $NH_3(g) + H_2CO_3(aq) \rightarrow (NH_4)_2CO_3(s)$

25. Balance each of the following equations that describe decomposition reactions.
    a. $NH_4NO_3(s) \rightarrow N_2O(g) + H_2O(g)$
    b. $N_2H_4(l) \rightarrow N_2(g) + H_2(g)$
    c. $Ca(HSO_3)_2(s) \rightarrow CaO(s) + H_2O(g) + SO_2(g)$
    d. $NH_4NO_3(s) \rightarrow N_2(g) + O_2(g) + H_2O(g)$
    e. $Ni(CO)_4(g) \rightarrow Ni(s) + CO(g)$

26. Balance each of the following equations that describe decomposition reactions.
    a. $NI_3(s) \rightarrow N_2(g) + I_2(s)$
    b. $BaCO_3(s) \rightarrow BaO(s) + CO_2(g)$
    c. $C_6H_{12}O_6(s) \rightarrow C(s) + H_2O(g)$
    d. $Cu(NH_3)_4SO_4(s) \rightarrow CuSO_4(s) + NH_3(g)$
    e. $NaN_3(s) \rightarrow Na_3N(s) + N_2(g)$

Additional Problems

27. For each of the following metals, how many electrons will the metal atoms lose when the metal reacts with a nonmetal?
    a. sodium
    b. potassium
    c. magnesium
    d. barium
    e. aluminum

28. For each of the following nonmetals, how many electrons will each atom of the nonmetal gain in reacting with a metal?
    a. oxygen
    b. fluorine
    c. nitrogen
    d. chlorine
    e. sulfur
    f. bromine
    g. iodine

29. There is much overlapping of the classification schemes for reactions discussed in this chapter. Give an example of a reaction that is, at the same time, an oxidation–reduction reaction, a combustion reaction, and a synthesis reaction.

30. Most substances used as fuels are compounds that contain carbon and hydrogen; oxygen also occurs in some of these compounds. When these compounds react with oxygen, what are the most common products of the reaction?

31. Classify the reactions represented by the following unbalanced equations by as many methods as possible. Use both the classifications developed in this chapter and those discussed in Chapter 7. Balance the equations.
    a. $I_4O_9(s) \rightarrow I_2O_6(s) + I_2(s) + O_2(g)$
    b. $Mg(s) + AgNO_3(aq) \rightarrow Mg(NO_3)_2(aq) + Ag(s)$
    c. $SiCl_4(l) + Mg(s) \rightarrow MgCl_2(s) + Si(s)$
    d. $CuCl_2(aq) + AgNO_3(aq)$
       $\rightarrow Cu(NO_3)_2(aq) + AgCl(s)$
    e. $Al(s) + Br_2(l) \rightarrow AlBr_3(s)$

32. Classify the reactions represented by the following unbalanced equations by as many methods as possible. Use both the classifications developed in this chapter and those discussed in Chapter 7. Balance the equations.
    a. $C_3H_8O(l) + O_2(g) \rightarrow CO_2(g) + H_2O(g)$
    b. $HCl(aq) + AgC_2H_3O_2(aq)$
       $\rightarrow AgCl(s) + HC_2H_3O_2(aq)$
    c. $HCl(aq) + Al(OH)_3(s) \rightarrow AlCl_3(aq) + H_2O(l)$
    d. $H_2O_2(aq) \rightarrow H_2O(l) + O_2(g)$
    e. $N_2H_4(l) + O_2(g) \rightarrow N_2(g) + H_2O(g)$

33. The metals of Group 1 of the periodic table are very reactive. When reacted with virtually any nonmetallic element, these metals all easily lose one electron to form unipositive (1+) ions. Write and balance the reactions the Group 1 metals sodium, potassium, and cesium would be expected to undergo with the nonmetallic elements chlorine, sulfur, bromine, and oxygen.

34. Corrosion of metals costs us billions of dollars annually, slowly destroying cars, bridges, and buildings. Corrosion of a metal involves the oxidation of the metal by the oxygen in the air, typically in the presence of moisture. Write a balanced equation for the reaction of each of the following metals with O_2: Zn, Al, Fe, Cr, and Ni.

35. Elemental chlorine, Cl_2, is very reactive, combining with most metallic substances. Write a balanced equation for the reaction of each of the following metals with Cl_2: Na, Al, Zn, Ca, and Fe.

36. For each of the elements listed in the next column, choose the *charge* of the ion each element would form in undergoing a simple oxidation–reduction reaction from the list below.

Charges

1+	2+	3+
1−	2−	3−

Elements

Al	Li
Br	Mg
Ca	Na
Cl	O
Cs	Rb
I	S
K	Sr

37. If a chlorine molecule were to react with a metal such as sodium, what charge would the resulting chloride ions have? If a sulfur molecule were to react with sodium, what charge would the resulting sulfide ions have?

38. If a potassium atom were to react with a nonmetal, what charge would the resulting potassium ion have? If a calcium atom were to react with the same nonmetal, what charge would the resulting calcium ion have?

39. For the reaction $16Fe(s) + 3S_8(s) \rightarrow 8Fe_2S_3(s)$, show how electrons are gained and lost by the atoms.

40. Balance the equation for each of the following oxidation–reduction chemical reactions.
    a. $Na(s) + O_2(g) \rightarrow Na_2O_2(s)$
    b. $Fe(s) + H_2SO_4(aq) \rightarrow FeSO_4(aq) + H_2(g)$
    c. $Al_2O_3(s) \rightarrow Al(s) + O_2(g)$
    d. $Fe(s) + Br_2(l) \rightarrow FeBr_3(s)$
    e. $Zn(s) + HNO_3(aq) \rightarrow Zn(NO_3)_2(aq) + H_2(g)$

41. Identify each of the following unbalanced reaction equations as belonging to one or more of the following categories: precipitation, acid–base, or oxidation–reduction.
    a. $Fe(s) + H_2SO_4(aq) \rightarrow Fe_3(SO_4)_2(aq) + H_2(g)$
    b. $HClO_4(aq) + RbOH(aq) \rightarrow RbClO_4(aq) + H_2O(l)$
    c. $Ca(s) + O_2(g) \rightarrow CaO(s)$
    d. $H_2SO_4(aq) + NaOH(aq) \rightarrow Na_2SO_4(aq) + H_2O(l)$
    e. $Pb(NO_3)_2(aq) + Na_2CO_3(aq) \rightarrow$
       $ PbCO_3(s) + NaNO_3(aq)$
    f. $K_2SO_4(aq) + CaCl_2(aq) \rightarrow KCl(aq) + CaSO_4(s)$
    g. $HNO_3(aq) + KOH(aq) \rightarrow KNO_3(aq) + H_2O(l)$
    h. $Ni(C_2H_3O_2)_2(aq) + Na_2S(aq) \rightarrow$
       $ NiS(s) + NaC_2H_3O_2(aq)$
    i. $Ni(s) + Cl_2(g) \rightarrow NiCl_2(s)$

42. Balance each of the following equations that describe combustion reactions.
    a. $C_5H_{12}(l) + O_2(g) \rightarrow CO_2(g) + H_2O(g)$
    b. $C_2H_6O(l) + O_2(g) \rightarrow CO_2(g) + H_2O(g)$
    c. $C_6H_6(l) + O_2(g) \rightarrow CO_2(g) + H_2O(g)$

43. Complete and balance each of the following equations that describe combustion reactions.
    a. $C_2H_4(g) + O_2(g) \rightarrow$
    b. $C_8H_{18}(l) + O_2(g) \rightarrow$
    c. $C_{30}H_{62}(s) + O_2(g) \rightarrow$

44. Balance each of the following equations that describe synthesis reactions.
    a. $FeO(s) + O_2(g) \rightarrow Fe_2O_3(s)$
    b. $CO(g) + O_2(g) \rightarrow CO_2(g)$
    c. $H_2(g) + Cl_2(g) \rightarrow HCl(g)$
    d. $K(s) + S_8(s) \rightarrow K_2S(s)$
    e. $Na(s) + N_2(g) \rightarrow Na_3N(s)$

45. Balance each of the following equations that describe decomposition reactions.
    a. $NaHCO_3(s) \rightarrow Na_2CO_3(s) + H_2O(g) + CO_2(g)$
    b. $NaClO_3(s) \rightarrow NaCl(s) + O_2(g)$
    c. $HgO(s) \rightarrow Hg(l) + O_2(g)$
    d. $C_{12}H_{22}O_{11}(s) \rightarrow C(s) + H_2O(g)$
    e. $H_2O_2(l) \rightarrow H_2O(l) + O_2(g)$

46. Write a balanced oxidation–reduction equation for the reaction of each of the metals in the left-hand column with each of the nonmetals in the right-hand column.

Ba	O_2
K	S
Mg	Cl_2
Rb	N_2
Ca	Br_2
Li	

47. Fluorine gas, F_2, is so reactive that it attacks the other halogen elements (Cl_2, Br_2, I_2), forming *inter*halogen compounds (for example, ClF, BrF, IF). Write the balanced oxidation–reduction equations for the reactions of fluorine gas with each of the other elemental halogens to form ClF, BrF, and IF.

48. Sulfuric acid, H_2SO_4, oxidizes many metallic elements. One of the effects of acid rain is that it produces sulfuric acid in the atmosphere which then reacts with metals used in construction. Write balanced oxidation–reduction equations for the reaction of sulfuric acid with Fe, Zn, Mg, Co, and Ni.

49. Although the metals of Group 2 of the periodic table are not nearly as reactive as those of Group 1, many of the Group 2 metals will combine with common nonmetals, especially at elevated temperatures. Write balanced chemical equations for the reactions of Mg, Ca, Sr, and Ba with Cl_2, Br_2, and O_2.

50. Elemental sulfur (S_8) combines with many metals, especially at higher temperatures. Write balanced chemical equations for the reaction of sulfur (S_8) with each of the following metals: Na, Ba, Al, Fe, K, Ca, Mg.

Cumulative Review for Chapters 6–8

QUESTIONS

1. What kind of *visual* evidence indicates that a chemical reaction has occurred? Give an example of each type of evidence you have mentioned. Do *all* reactions produce visual evidence that they have taken place?

2. What, in general terms, does a chemical equation indicate? What are the substances indicated to the left of the arrow called in a chemical equation? To the right of the arrow?

3. What does it mean to "balance" an equation? Why is it so important that equations be balanced? What does it mean to say that atoms must be *conserved* in a balanced chemical equation? How are the physical states of reactants and products indicated when writing chemical equations?

4. When balancing a chemical equation, why is it *not* permissible to adjust the subscripts in the formulas of the reactants and products? What would changing the subscripts within a formula do? What do the *coefficients* in a balanced chemical equation represent? Why is it acceptable to adjust a substance's coefficient but not permissible to adjust the subscripts within the substance's formula?

5. What is meant by the *driving force* for a reaction? Give some examples of driving forces that make reactants tend to form products. Write a balanced chemical equation illustrating each type of driving force you have named.

6. What is a *precipitation reaction?* What would you see if a precipitation reaction were to take place in a beaker? Write a balanced chemical equation illustrating a precipitation reaction.

7. Define the term *strong electrolyte.* What types of substances tend to be strong electrolytes? What does a solution of a strong electrolyte contain? Give a way to determine if a substance is a strong electrolyte.

8. Summarize the simple solubility rules for ionic compounds. How do we use these rules in determining the identity of the solid formed in a precipitation reaction? Give examples including balanced complete and net ionic equations.

9. In general terms, what are the *spectator ions* in a precipitation reaction? Why are the spectator ions not included in writing the net ionic equation for a precipitation reaction? Does this mean that the spectator ions do not have to be present in the solution?

10. Describe some physical and chemical properties of *acids* and *bases.* What is meant by a *strong* acid or base? Are strong acids and bases also strong electrolytes? Give several examples of strong acids and strong bases.

11. What is a *salt?* How are salts formed by acid–base reactions? Write chemical equations showing the formation of three different salts. What other product is formed when an aqueous acid reacts with an aqueous base? Write the net ionic equation for the formation of this substance.

12. What is essential in an oxidation–reduction reaction? What is *oxidation?* What is *reduction?* Can an oxidation reaction take place without a reduction reaction also taking place? Why? Write a balanced chemical equation illustrating an oxidation–reduction reaction between a metal and a nonmetal. Indicate which species is oxidized and which is reduced.

13. What is a *combustion* reaction? Are combustion reactions a unique type of reaction, or are they a special case of a more general type of reaction? Write an equation that illustrates a combustion reaction.

14. Give an example of a *synthesis* reaction and of a *decomposition* reaction. Are synthesis and decomposition reactions always also oxidation–reduction reactions? Explain.

15. List and define all the ways of classifying chemical reactions that have been discussed in the text. Give a balanced chemical equation as an example of each type of reaction, and show clearly how your example fits the definition you have given.

PROBLEMS

16. Sodium is a highly reactive metal and calcium is a moderately reactive metal. Write balanced chemical equations for the reaction of each of these metals with the following substances, with the indicated products being produced.
   a. with water, producing aqueous sodium hydroxide or aqueous calcium hydroxide plus hydrogen gas
   b. with liquid bromine, producing solid sodium bromide or solid calcium bromide
   c. with nitrogen gas, producing solid sodium nitride or solid calcium nitride
   d. with oxygen gas, producing solid sodium *per*oxide, Na_2O_2, or solid calcium oxide
   e. with solid sulfur, producing solid sodium sulfide or solid calcium sulfide

17. Balance the following chemical equations:
    a. $AlCl_3(aq) + KOH(aq) \rightarrow Al(OH)_3(s) + KCl(aq)$
    b. $Pb(C_2H_3O_2)_2(aq) + KCl(aq) \rightarrow$
    $$PbCl_2(s) + KC_2H_3O_2(aq)$$
    c. $Rb_2O(s) + H_2O(l) \rightarrow RbOH(aq)$
    d. $SnO(s) + C(s) \rightarrow Sn(s) + CO_2(g)$
    e. $Al(s) + Cl_2(g) \rightarrow AlCl_3(s)$
    f. $Fe_2S_3(s) + HCl(aq) \rightarrow FeCl_3(aq) + H_2S(g)$
    g. $CaCl_2(s) + H_2SO_4(l) \rightarrow CaSO_4(s) + HCl(g)$
    h. $SiCl_4(l) + Na(s) \rightarrow NaCl(s) + Si(s)$
    i. $Na_2O_2(s) + H_2O(l) + CO_2(g) \rightarrow$
    $$NaHCO_3(s) + O_2(g)$$

18. The reagent shelf in a general chemistry lab contains aqueous solutions of the following substances: silver nitrate, sodium chloride, acetic acid, nitric acid, sulfuric acid, potassium chromate, barium nitrate, phosphoric acid, hydrochloric acid, lead nitrate, sodium hydroxide, and sodium carbonate. Suggest how you might prepare the following pure substances using these reagents and any normal laboratory equipment. If it is *not* possible to prepare a substance using these reagents, indicate why.
    a. $BaCrO_4(s)$
    b. $NaC_2H_3O_2(s)$
    c. $AgCl(s)$
    d. $PbSO_4(s)$
    e. $Na_2SO_4(s)$
    f. $BaCO_3(s)$

19. The common strong acids are HCl, HNO_3, and H_2SO_4, whereas $NaOH$ and KOH are the common strong bases. Write the neutralization reaction equations for each of these strong acids with each of these strong bases in aqueous solution.

20. Classify each of the following chemical equations in as *many* ways as possible based on what you have learned. Balance each equation.
    a. $FeO(s) + HNO_3(aq) \rightarrow Fe(NO_3)_2(aq) + H_2O(l)$
    b. $Mg(s) + CO_2(g) + O_2(g) \rightarrow MgCO_3(s)$
    c. $NaOH(s) + CuSO_4(aq)$
    $$\rightarrow Cu(OH)_2(s) + Na_2SO_4(aq)$$
    d. $HI(aq) + KOH(aq) \rightarrow KI(aq) + H_2O(l)$
    e. $C_3H_8(g) + O_2(g) \rightarrow CO_2(g) + H_2O(g)$
    f. $Co(NH_3)_6Cl_2(s) \rightarrow CoCl_2(s) + NH_3(g)$
    g. $HCl(aq) + Pb(C_2H_3O_2)_2(aq)$
    $$\rightarrow HC_2H_3O_2(aq) + PbCl_2(s)$$
    h. $C_{12}H_{22}O_{11}(s) \rightarrow C(s) + H_2O(g)$
    i. $Al(s) + HNO_3(aq) \rightarrow Al(NO_3)_3(aq) + H_2(g)$
    j. $B(s) + O_2(g) \rightarrow B_2O_3(s)$

9

Chemical Composition

One very important chemical activity is the synthesis of new substances. Nylon, the artificial sweetener aspartame (Nutra-Sweet®), Kevlar used in bulletproof vests and the body parts of exotic cars, polyvinyl chloride (PVC) for plastic water pipes, Teflon, Nitinol—the alloy that remembers its shape even after being severely distorted—and so many other materials that make our lives easier—all originated in some chemist's laboratory. Some of the new materials have truly amazing properties such as the plastic that listens and talks, described in the "Chemistry in Focus" on page 224. When a chemist makes a new substance, the first order of business is to identify it. What is its composition? What is its chemical formula?

In this chapter we will learn to determine a compound's formula. Before we can do that, however, we need to think about counting atoms. How do we determine the number of each type of atom in a substance so that we can write its formula? Of course atoms are too small to count individually. As we will see in this chapter, we typically count atoms by weighing them. So let us first consider the general principle of counting by weighing.

A sample of mints and a sample of jelly beans, each having a mass of 50 grams (left). A Ferrari F-40 has composite body parts (right).

221

9.1   *Counting by Weighing*

AIM: To understand the concept of average mass and explore how counting can be done by weighing.

A synthetic polymer leg brace.

Suppose you work in a candy store that sells gourmet jelly beans by the bean. People come in and ask for 50 beans, 100 beans, 1000 beans, and so on, and you have to count them out—a tedious process at best. As a good problem solver, you try to come up with a better system. It occurs to you that it might be far more efficient to buy a scale and count the jelly beans by weighing them. How can you count jelly beans by weighing them? What information about the individual beans do you need to know?

Assume that all of the jelly beans are identical and that each has a mass of 5 g. If a customer asks for 1000 jelly beans, what mass of jelly beans would be required? Each bean has a mass of 5 g, so you would need 1000 beans × 5 g/bean, or 5000 g (5 kg). It takes just a few seconds to weigh out 5 kg of jelly beans. It would take much longer to count out 1000 of them.

In reality, jelly beans are not identical. For example, let's assume that you weigh 10 beans individually and get the following results:

Bean	Mass
1	5.1 g
2	5.2 g
3	5.0 g
4	4.8 g
5	4.9 g
6	5.0 g
7	5.0 g
8	5.1 g
9	4.9 g
10	5.0 g

Can we count these nonidentical beans by weighing? Yes. The key piece of information we need is the *average mass* of the jelly beans. Let's compute the average mass for our 10-bean sample.

$$\text{Average mass} = \frac{\text{total mass of beans}}{\text{number of beans}}$$

$$= \frac{5.1\text{ g} + 5.2\text{ g} + 5.0\text{ g} + 4.8\text{ g} + 4.9\text{ g} + 5.0\text{ g} + 5.0\text{ g} + 5.1\text{ g} + 4.9\text{ g} + 5.0\text{ g}}{10}$$

$$= \frac{50.0}{10} = 5.0\text{ g}$$

The average mass of a jelly bean is 5.0 g. Thus to count out 1000 beans, we need to weigh out 5000 g of beans. This sample of beans, in which the beans have an average mass of 5.0 g, can be treated exactly like a sample where all of the beans are identical. Objects do not need to have identical masses in order to be counted by weighing. We simply need to know the average mass of the objects. For purposes of counting, the objects *behave as though they were all identical,* as though they each actually had the average mass.

Suppose a customer comes into the store and says, "I want to buy a bag of candy for each of my kids. One of them likes jelly beans and the other one likes mints. Please put a scoopful of jelly beans in a bag and a scoopful of mints in another bag." Then the customer recognizes a problem. "Wait! My kids will fight unless I bring home exactly the same number of candies for each one. Both bags must have the same number of pieces because they'll definitely count them and compare. But I'm really in a hurry, so we don't have time to count them here. Is there a simple way you can be sure the bags will contain the same number of candies?"

You need to solve this problem quickly. Suppose you know the average masses of the two kinds of candy:

Jelly beans: average mass = 5 g

Mints: average mass = 15 g

You fill the scoop with jelly beans and dump them onto the scale, which reads 500 g. Now the key question: what mass of mints do you need to give the same number of mints as there are jelly beans in 500 g of jelly beans? Comparing the average masses of the jelly beans (5 g) and mints (15 g), you realize that each mint has three times the mass of each jelly bean:

$$\frac{15 \text{ g}}{5 \text{ g}} = 3$$

This means that you must weigh out an amount of mints that is three times the mass of the jelly beans:

$$3 \times 500 \text{ g} = 1500 \text{ g}$$

You weigh out 1500 g of mints and put them in a bag. The customer leaves with your assurance that both the bag containing 500 g of jelly beans and the bag containing 1500 g of mints contain the same number of candies.

In solving this problem, you have discovered a principle that is very important in chemistry: two samples containing different types of components, A and B, both contain the same number of components if the ratio of the sample masses is the same as the ratio of the masses of the individual components of A and B.

Let's illustrate this rather intimidating statement by using the example we just discussed. The individual components have the masses 5 g (jelly beans) and 15 g (mints). Consider several cases.

• Each sample contains 1 component:

Mass of mint = 15 g
Mass of jelly bean = 5 g

• Each sample contains 10 components:

$$10 \text{ mints} \times \frac{15 \text{ g}}{\text{mint}} = 150 \text{ g of mints}$$

$$10 \text{ jelly beans} \times \frac{5 \text{ g}}{\text{jelly bean}} = 50 \text{ g of jelly beans}$$

CHEMISTRY IN FOCUS

*P*lastic That Talks and Listens

Imagine a plastic so "smart" that it can be used to sense a baby's breath, measure the force of a karate punch, sense the presence of a person 100 ft away, or make a balloon that sings. There is a plastic film capable of doing all these things. It's called **polyvinylidene difluoride (PVDF),** which has the structure

When this polymer is processed in a particular way, it becomes piezoelectric and pyroelectric. A *piezoelectric* substance produces an electric current when it is physically deformed or, alternately, undergoes a deformation when a current is applied. A *pyroelectric* material is one that develops an electrical potential in response to a change in its temperature.

Because PVDF is piezoelectric, it can be used to construct a paper-thin microphone; it responds to sound by producing a current proportional to the deformation caused by the sound waves. A ribbon of PVDF plastic one quarter of an inch wide could be strung along a hallway and used to listen to all the conversations going on as people walk through. On the other hand, electric pulses can be applied to the PVDF film to produce a speaker. A strip of PVDF film glued to the inside of a balloon can play any song stored on a microchip attached to the film—hence a balloon that can sing happy birthday at a party. The PVDF film also can be used to construct a sleep apnea monitor, which, when placed beside the mouth of a sleeping infant, will set off an alarm if the breathing stops, thus helping to prevent sudden infant death syndrome (SIDS). The same type of film is used by the U.S. Olympic karate team to measure the force of kicks and punches as the team trains. Also, gluing two strips of film together gives a material that curls in response to a current, creating an artificial muscle. In addition, because the PVDF film is pyroelectric, it responds to the infrared (heat) radiation emitted by a human as far away as 100 ft, making it useful for burglar alarm systems. Making the PVDF polymer piezoelectric and pyroelectric requires some very special processing, which makes it costly ($10 per square foot), but this seems a small price to pay for its near-magical properties.

Each child's bag of candy contained 100 pieces of candy.

- Each sample contains 100 components:

$$100 \text{ mints} \times \frac{15 \text{ g}}{\text{mint}} = 1500 \text{ g of mints}$$

$$100 \text{ jelly beans} \times \frac{5 \text{ g}}{\text{jelly bean}} = 500 \text{ g of jelly beans}$$

Note in each case that the ratio of the masses is always 3 to 1:

$$\frac{1500}{500} = \frac{150}{50} = \frac{15}{5} = \frac{3}{1}$$

which is the ratio of the masses of the individual components:

$$\frac{\text{Mass of mint}}{\text{Mass of jelly bean}} = \frac{15}{5} = \frac{3}{1}$$

Any two samples, one of mints and one of jelly beans, that have a *mass ratio* of 15/5 = 3/1 will contain the same number of components. And these same ideas apply also to atoms, as we will see in the next section.

9.2 *Atomic Masses: Counting Atoms by Weighing*

AIM: To understand atomic mass and its experimental determination.

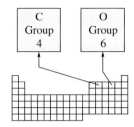

In Chapter 6 we considered the balanced equation for the reaction of solid carbon and gaseous oxygen to form gaseous carbon dioxide:

$$C(s) + O_2(g) \rightarrow CO_2(g)$$

Now suppose you have a small pile of solid carbon and want to know how many oxygen molecules are required to convert all of this carbon into carbon dioxide. The balanced equation tells us that one oxygen molecule is required for each carbon atom.

$$C(s) \quad + \quad O_2(g) \quad \rightarrow \quad CO_2(g)$$
1 atom reacts with 1 molecule to yield 1 molecule

To determine the number of oxygen molecules required, we must know how many carbon atoms are present in the pile of carbon. But individual atoms are far too small to see. We must learn to count atoms by weighing samples containing large numbers of them.

In the last section we saw that we can easily count things like jelly beans and mints by weighing. Exactly the same principles can be applied to counting atoms.

Because atoms are so tiny, the normal units of mass—the gram and the kilogram—are much too large to be convenient. For example, the mass of a single carbon atom is 1.99×10^{-23} g. To avoid using terms like 10^{-23} when describing the mass of an atom, scientists have defined a much smaller unit of mass called the **atomic mass unit,** which is abbreviated **amu.** In terms of grams,

$$1 \text{ amu} = 1.66 \times 10^{-24} \text{ g}$$

Now let's return to our problem of counting carbon atoms. To count carbon atoms by weighing, we need to know the mass of individual atoms, just as we needed to know the mass of the individual jelly beans. Recall from Chapter 4 that the atoms of a given element exist as isotopes. The isotopes of carbon are $^{12}_{6}C$, $^{13}_{6}C$, and $^{14}_{6}C$. Any sample of carbon contains a mixture of these isotopes, always in the same proportions. Each of these isotopes has a slightly different mass. Therefore, just like the nonidentical jelly beans, we need to use an average mass for the carbon atoms. The **average atomic mass** for carbon atoms is 12.01 amu. This means that any sample of carbon from nature *can be treated as though it were composed of identical carbon atoms,* each with a mass of 12.01 amu. Now that we know the average mass of the carbon atom, we can count carbon atoms by weighing samples of natural carbon. For example, what mass of natural carbon must we take to have 1000 carbon atoms present? Because 12.01 amu is the average mass,

Remember that 1000 is an exact number here.

$$\text{Mass of 1000 natural carbon atoms} = (1000 \text{ atoms}) (12.01 \frac{\text{amu}}{\text{atom}})$$

$$= 12{,}010 \text{ amu} = 1.201 \times 10^4 \text{ amu}$$

Now let's assume that when we weigh the pile of natural carbon mentioned earlier, the result is 3.00×10^{20} amu. How many carbon atoms are present in this sample? We know that an average carbon atom has the mass 12.01 amu, so we can compute the number of carbon atoms by using the equivalence statement

$$1 \text{ carbon atom } = 12.01 \text{ amu}$$

to construct the appropriate conversion factor,

$$\frac{1 \text{ carbon atom}}{12.01 \text{ amu}}$$

The calculation is carried out as follows:

$$3.00 \times 10^{20} \text{ amu} \times \frac{1 \text{ carbon atom}}{12.01 \text{ amu}} = 2.50 \times 10^{19} \text{ carbon atoms}$$

The principles we have just discussed for carbon apply to all the other elements as well. All the elements as found in nature typically consist of a mixture of various isotopes. So to count the atoms in a sample of a given element by weighing, we must know the mass of the sample and the average mass for that element. Some average masses for common elements are listed in Table 9.1.

TABLE 9.1

Average Atomic Mass Values for Some Common Elements

Element	Average Atomic Mass (amu)
Hydrogen	1.008
Carbon	12.01
Nitrogen	14.01
Oxygen	16.00
Sodium	22.99
Aluminum	26.98

EXAMPLE 9.1 *Calculating Mass Using Atomic Mass Units (amu)*

Calculate the mass, in amu, of a sample of aluminum that contains 75 atoms.

Solution

To solve this problem we use the average mass for an aluminum atom: 26.98 amu. We set up the equivalence statement:

$$1 \text{ Al atom } = 26.98 \text{ amu}$$

which gives the conversion factor we need:

$$75 \text{ Al atoms } \times \frac{26.98 \text{ amu}}{\text{Al atom}} = 2024 \text{ amu}$$

The 75 in this problem is an exact number—the number of atoms.

 Self-Check Exercise 9.1

Calculate the mass of a sample that contains 23 nitrogen atoms.

See Problems 9.5 and 9.8.

The opposite calculation can also be carried out. That is, if we know the mass of a sample, we can determine the number of atoms present. This procedure is illustrated in Example 9.2.

EXAMPLE 9.2 *Calculating the Number of Atoms from the Mass*

Calculate the number of sodium atoms present in a sample that has a mass of 1172.49 amu.

Solution

We can solve this problem by using the average atomic mass for sodium (see Table 9.1) of 22.99 amu. The appropriate equivalence statement is

$$1 \text{ Na atom} = 22.99 \text{ amu}$$

which gives the conversion factor we need:

$$1172.49 \ \cancel{\text{amu}} \times \frac{1 \text{ Na atom}}{22.99 \ \cancel{\text{amu}}} = 51.00 \text{ Na atoms}$$

 Self-Check Exercise 9.2

Calculate the number of oxygen atoms in a sample that has a mass of 288 amu.

See Problems 9.6 and 9.7

   To summarize, we have seen that we can count atoms by weighing if we know the average atomic mass for that type of atom. This is one of the fundamental operations in chemistry, as we will see in the next section.

   The average atomic mass for each element is listed in tables found inside the front cover of this book. Chemists often call these values the *atomic weights* for the elements, although this terminology is slowly passing out of use.

9.3   *The Mole*

AIMS: To understand the mole concept and Avogadro's number. To learn to convert among moles, mass, and number of atoms in a given sample.

In the previous section we used atomic mass units for mass, but these are extremely small units. In the laboratory a much larger unit, the gram, is the convenient unit for mass. In this section we will learn to count atoms in samples with masses given in grams.

   Let's assume we have a sample of aluminum that has a mass of 26.98 g. What mass of copper contains exactly the same number of atoms as this sample of aluminum?

26.98 g aluminum	←——————→ Contains the same number of atoms	? grams copper

To answer this question, we need to know the average atomic masses for aluminum (26.98 amu) and copper (63.55 amu). Which atom has the greater atomic mass, aluminum or copper? The answer is copper. If we have 26.98 g of aluminum, do we need more or less than 26.98 g of copper to have the same number of copper atoms as aluminum atoms? We need more than 26.98 g of copper because each copper atom has a greater mass than each aluminum atom. Therefore, a given number of copper atoms will weigh more than an equal number of aluminum atoms. How much copper do we need? Because the average masses of aluminum and copper atoms are 26.98 amu and 63.55 amu, respectively, 26.98 g of aluminum and 63.55 g of copper contain exactly the same number of atoms. So we need 63.55 g of copper. As we saw in the first section when we were discussing candy, *samples in which the ratio of the masses is the same as the ratio of the masses of the individual atoms always contain the same number of atoms.* In the case just considered, the ratios are

$$\underbrace{\frac{26.98 \text{ g}}{63.55 \text{ g}}}_{\substack{\text{Ratio of} \\ \text{sample} \\ \text{masses}}} = \underbrace{\frac{26.98 \text{ amu}}{63.55 \text{ amu}}}_{\substack{\text{Ratio of} \\ \text{atomic} \\ \text{masses}}}$$

Therefore, 26.98 g of aluminum contains the same number of aluminum atoms as 63.55 g of copper contains copper atoms.

Now compare carbon (average atomic mass, 12.01 amu) and helium (average atomic mass, 4.003 amu). A sample of 12.01 g of carbon contains the same number of atoms as 4.003 g of helium. In fact, if we weigh out samples of all the elements such that each sample has a mass equal to that element's average atomic mass in grams, these samples all contain the same number of atoms (Figure 9.1). This number (the number of atoms present in all of these samples) assumes special importance in chemistry. It is called the mole, the unit all chemists use in describing numbers of atoms. The **mole** (abbreviated mol) can be defined as *the number equal to the number of carbon atoms in 12.01 grams of carbon.* Techniques for counting atoms very precisely have been used to determine this number to be 6.022×10^{23}. This number is called **Avogadro's number.** *One mole of something consists of 6.022×10^{23} units of that substance.* Just as a dozen eggs is 12 eggs, a mole of eggs is 6.022×10^{23} eggs. And a mole of water contains 6.022×10^{23} H_2O molecules.

The magnitude of the number 6.022×10^{23} is very difficult to imagine. To give you some idea, 1 mol of seconds represents a span of time 4 million times as long as the earth has already existed! One mole of marbles is enough to cover the entire earth to a depth of 50 miles! However, because atoms are

This definition of the mole is slightly different from the SI definition but is used because it is easier to understand at this point.

Avogadro's number (to four significant figures) is 6.022×10^{23}. One mole of *anything* is 6.022×10^{23} units of that substance.

FIGURE 9.1
All these samples of pure elements contain the *same number* (a mole) of atoms: 6.022×10^{23} atoms.

Lead bar
207.2 g

Silver bars
107.9 g

Pile of copper
63.55 g

FIGURE 9.2
One mole samples of iron (nails), iodine crystals, liquid mercury, and powdered sulfur.

TABLE 9.2

Comparison of 1-Mol Samples of Various Elements

Element	Number of Atoms Present	Mass of Sample (g)
Aluminum	6.022×10^{23}	26.98
Gold	6.022×10^{23}	196.97
Iron	6.022×10^{23}	55.85
Sulfur	6.022×10^{23}	32.07
Boron	6.022×10^{23}	10.81
Xenon	6.022×10^{23}	131.3

so tiny, a mole of atoms or molecules is a perfectly manageable quantity to use in a reaction (Figure 9.2).

How do we use the mole in chemical calculations? Recall that Avogadro's number is defined such that a 12.01-g sample of carbon contains 6.022×10^{23} atoms. By the same token, because the average atomic mass of hydrogen is 1.008 amu (Table 9.1), 1.008 g of hydrogen contains 6.022×10^{23} hydrogen atoms. Similarly, 26.98 g of aluminum contains 6.022×10^{23} aluminum atoms. The point is that a sample of *any* element that weighs a number of grams equal to the average atomic mass of that element contains 6.022×10^{23} atoms (1 mol) of that element.

The mass of 1 mol of an element is equal to its average atomic mass in grams.

Table 9.2 shows the masses of several elements that contain 1 mol of atoms.

In summary, *a sample of an element with a mass equal to that element's average atomic mass expressed in grams contains 1 mol of atoms.*

To do chemical calculations, you *must* understand what the mole means and how to determine the number of moles in a given mass of a substance. However, before we do any calculations, let's be sure that the process of counting by weighing is clear. Consider the following "bag" of H atoms (symbolized by dots), which contains 1 mol (6.022×10^{23}) of H atoms and has a mass of 1.008 g. Assume the bag itself has no mass.

A 1 mol sample of graphite (a form of carbon) weighs 12.01 g.

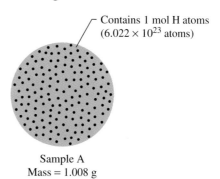

Contains 1 mol H atoms
(6.022×10^{23} atoms)

Sample A
Mass = 1.008 g

Now consider another "bag" of hydrogen atoms in which the number of hydrogen atoms is unknown.

Sample B

We want to find out how many H atoms are present in sample ("bag") B. How can we do that? We can do it by weighing the sample. We find the mass of sample B to be 0.500 g.

How does this measured mass help us determine the number of atoms in sample B? We know that 1 mol of H atoms has a mass of 1.008 g. Sample B has a mass of 0.500 g, which is approximately half the mass of a mole of H atoms.

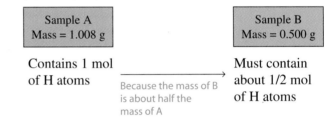

We carry out the actual calculation by using the equivalence statement

1 mol H atoms = 1.008 g H

to construct the conversion factor we need:

$$0.500 \; \cancel{g \, H} \times \frac{1 \; mol \; H}{1.008 \; \cancel{g \, H}} = 0.496 \; mol \; H \; in \; sample \; B$$

Let's summarize. We know the mass of 1 mol of H atoms, so we can determine the number of moles of H atoms in any other sample of pure hydrogen by weighing the sample and *comparing* its mass to 1.008 g (the mass of 1 mol of H atoms). We can follow this same process for any element, because we know the mass of 1 mol for each of the elements.

Also, because we know that 1 mol is 6.022×10^{23} units, once we know the *moles* of atoms present, we can easily determine the *number* of atoms present. In the case considered above, we have approximately 0.5 mol of H atoms in sample B. This means that about 1/2 of 6×10^{23}, or 3×10^{23}, H atoms are present. We carry out the actual calculation by using the equivalence statement

1 mol = 6.022×10^{23}

to determine the conversion factor we need:

$$0.496 \text{ mol H atoms} \times \frac{6.022 \times 10^{23} \text{ H atoms}}{1 \text{ mol H atoms}} =$$

$$2.99 \times 10^{23} \text{ H atoms in sample B}$$

These procedures are illustrated in Example 9.3.

EXAMPLE 9.3

Calculating Moles and Number of Atoms

Aluminum (Al), a metal with a high strength-to-weight ratio and a high resistance to corrosion, is often used for structures such as high-quality bicycle frames. Compute both the number of moles of atoms and the number of atoms in a 10.0-g sample of aluminum.

A bicycle with an aluminum frame.

Solution

In this case we want to change from mass to moles of atoms:

| 10.0 g Al | ➡ | ? moles of Al atoms |

The mass of 1 mol (6.022×10^{23} atoms) of aluminum is 26.98 g. The sample we are considering has a mass of 10.0 g. Its mass is less than 26.98 g, so this sample contains less than 1 mol of aluminum atoms. We calculate the number of moles of aluminum atoms in 10.0 g by using the equivalence statement

$$1 \text{ mol Al} = 26.98 \text{ g Al}$$

to construct the appropriate conversion factor:

$$10.0 \text{ g Al} \times \frac{1 \text{ mol Al}}{26.98 \text{ g Al}} = 0.371 \text{ mol Al}$$

Next we convert from moles of atoms to the number of atoms, using the equivalence statement

$$6.022 \times 10^{23} \text{ Al atoms} = 1 \text{ mol Al atoms}$$

We have

$$0.371 \text{ mol Al} \times \frac{6.022 \times 10^{23} \text{ Al atoms}}{1 \text{ mol Al}} = 2.23 \times 10^{23} \text{ Al atoms}$$

We can summarize this calculation as follows:

| 10.0 g Al | $\times \frac{1 \text{ mol}}{26.98 \text{ g}}$ ➡ | 0.371 mol Al |

| 0.371 mol Al atoms | $\times \frac{6.022 \times 10^{23} \text{ Al atoms}}{\text{mol}}$ ➡ | 2.23 x 10^{23} Al atoms |

A silicon chip of the type used in electronic equipment.

EXAMPLE 9.4

Calculating the Number of Atoms

A silicon chip used in an integrated circuit of a microcomputer has a mass of 5.68 mg. How many silicon (Si) atoms are present in this chip? The average atomic mass for silicon is 28.09 amu.

Solution

Our strategy for doing this problem is to convert from milligrams of silicon to grams of silicon, then to moles of silicon, and finally to atoms of silicon:

where each arrow in the schematic represents a conversion factor. Because 1 g = 1000 mg, we have

$$5.68 \text{ mg Si} \times \frac{1 \text{ g Si}}{1000 \text{ mg Si}} = 5.68 \times 10^{-3} \text{ g Si}$$

Next, because the average mass of silicon is 28.09 amu, we know that 1 mol of Si atoms weighs 28.09g. This leads to the equivalence statement

$$1 \text{ mol Si atoms} = 28.09 \text{ g Si}$$

Thus,

$$5.68 \times 10^{-3} \text{ g Si} \times \frac{1 \text{ mol Si}}{28.09 \text{ g Si}} = 2.02 \times 10^{-4} \text{ mol Si}$$

Using the definition of a mole (1 mol = 6.022×10^{23}), we have

$$2.02 \times 10^{-4} \text{ mol Si} \times \frac{6.022 \times 10^{23} \text{ atoms}}{1 \text{ mol Si}} = 1.22 \times 10^{20} \text{ Si atoms}$$

We can summarize this calculation as follows:

$$5.68 \text{ mg Si} \times \frac{1 \text{ g}}{1000 \text{ mg}} \Rightarrow 5.68 \times 10^{-3} \text{ g Si}$$

$$5.68 \times 10^{-3} \text{ g Si} \times \frac{1 \text{ mol}}{28.09 \text{ g}} \Rightarrow 2.02 \times 10^{-4} \text{ mol Si}$$

$$2.02 \times 10^{-4} \text{ mol Si} \times \frac{6.022 \times 10^{23} \text{ Si atoms}}{\text{mol}} \Rightarrow 1.22 \times 10^{20} \text{ Si atoms}$$

Problem Solving: Does the Answer Make Sense?

When you finish a problem, always think about the "reasonableness" of your answers. In Example 9.4, 5.68 mg of silicon is clearly much less than 1 mol of silicon (which has a mass of 28.09 g), so the final answer of 1.22×10^{20} atoms (compared to 6.022×10^{23} atoms in a mole) at least lies in the right direction. That is, 1.22×10^{20} atoms is a smaller number than 6.022×10^{23}. Also, always include the units as you perform calculations and make sure the correct units are obtained at the end. Paying careful attention to units and making this type of general check can help you detect errors such as an inverted conversion factor or a number that was incorrectly entered into your calculator.

 Self-Check Exercise 9.3

The values for the average masses of the atoms of the elements are listed inside the front cover of this book.

Chromium (Cr) is a metal that is added to steel to improve its resistance to corrosion (for example, to make stainless steel). Calculate both the number of moles in a sample of chromium containing 5.00×10^{20} atoms and the mass of the sample.

See Problems 9.19 through 9.24.

9.4   *Molar Mass*

AIMS: To understand the definition of molar mass. To learn to convert between moles and mass of a given sample of a chemical compound.

Note that when we say 1 mol of methane, we mean 1 mol of methane molecules.

A chemical compound is, fundamentally, a collection of atoms. For example, methane (the major component of natural gas) consists of molecules each containing one carbon atom and four hydrogen atoms (CH_4). How can we calculate the mass of 1 mol of methane; that is, what is the mass of 6.022×10^{23} CH_4 molecules? Because each CH_4 molecule contains one carbon atom and four hydrogen atoms, 1 mol of CH_4 molecules consists of 1 mol of carbon atoms and 4 mol of hydrogen atoms (Figure 9.3). The mass of 1 mol of

FIGURE 9.3
Various numbers of methane molecules showing their constituent atoms.

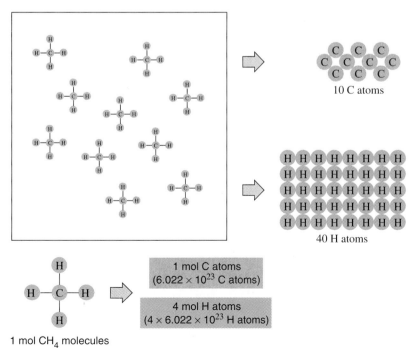

methane can be found by summing the masses of carbon and hydrogen present:

Remember that the least number of decimal places limits the number of significant figures in addition.

$$\begin{aligned}
\text{Mass of 1 mol of C} &= 1 \times 12.01 \text{ g} = 12.01 \text{ g} \\
\text{Mass of 4 mol of H} &= 4 \times 1.008 \text{ g} = \underline{4.032 \text{ g}} \\
\text{Mass of 1 mol of CH}_4 & \qquad\qquad\qquad = 16.04 \text{ g}
\end{aligned}$$

The quantity 16.04 g is called the molar mass for methane: the mass of 1 mol of CH_4 molecules. The **molar mass*** of any substance is the *mass (in grams) of 1 mol of the substance*. The molar mass is obtained by summing the masses of the component atoms.

A substance's molar mass (in grams) is the mass of 1 mol of that substance.

EXAMPLE 9.5 *Calculating Molar Mass*

Calculate the molar mass of sulfur dioxide, a gas produced when sulfur-containing fuels are burned. Unless "scrubbed" from the exhaust, sulfur dioxide can react with moisture in the atmosphere to produce acid rain.

Solution

The formula for sulfur dioxide is SO_2. We need to compute the mass of 1 mol of SO_2 molecules—the molar mass for sulfur dioxide. We know that 1 mol of SO_2 molecules contains 1 mol of sulfur atoms and 2 mol of oxygen atoms:

$$\begin{aligned}
\text{Mass of 1 mol of S} &= 1 \times 32.07 = 32.07 \text{ g} \\
\text{Mass of 2 mol of O} &= 2 \times 16.00 = \underline{32.00 \text{ g}} \\
\text{Mass of 1 mol of SO}_2 & \qquad\qquad = 64.07 \text{ g} = \text{molar mass}
\end{aligned}$$

The molar mass of SO_2 is 64.07 g. It represents the mass of 1 mol of SO_2 molecules.

 Self-Check Exercise 9.4

Polyvinyl chloride (called PVC), which is widely used for floor coverings ("vinyl") and for plastic pipes in plumbing systems, is made from a molecule with the formula C_2H_3Cl. Calculate the molar mass of this substance.

See Problems 9.27 through 9.30.

---

*The term *molecular weight* was traditionally used instead of *molar mass*. The terms *molecular weight* and *molar mass* mean exactly the same thing. Because the term *molar mass* more accurately describes the concept, it will be used in this text.

Some substances exist as a collection of ions rather than as separate molecules. For example, ordinary table salt, sodium chloride (NaCl), is composed of an array of Na^+ and Cl^- ions. There are no NaCl molecules present. In some books the term **formula weight** is used instead of molar mass for ionic compounds. However, in this book we will apply the term *molar mass* to both ionic and molecular substances.

To calculate the molar mass for sodium chloride, we must realize that 1 mol of NaCl contains 1 mol of Na^+ ions and 1 mol of Cl^- ions.

1 mol Na^+

Na^+

Cl^-

1 mol Cl^-

1 mol NaCl

The mass of the electron is so small that Na^+ and Na have the same mass for our purposes, even though Na^+ has one electron less than Na. Also the mass of Cl virtually equals the mass of Cl^- even though it has one more electron than Cl.

Therefore, the molar mass (in grams) for sodium chloride represents the sum of the mass of 1 mol of sodium ions and the mass of 1 mol of chloride ions.

$$\begin{array}{ll} \text{Mass of 1 mol of } Na^+ & = 22.99 \text{ g} \\ \text{Mass of 1 mol of } Cl^- & = \underline{35.45 \text{ g}} \\ \text{Mass of 1 mol of NaCl} & = 58.44 \text{ g} = \text{molar mass} \end{array}$$

The molar mass of NaCl is 58.44 g. It represents the mass of 1 mol of sodium chloride.

EXAMPLE 9.6

Calculating Mass from Moles

Calcium carbonate, $CaCO_3$ (also called calcite), is the principal mineral found in limestone, marble, chalk, pearls, and the shells of marine animals such as clams.

a. Calculate the molar mass of calcium carbonate.

b. A certain sample of calcium carbonate contains 4.86 mol. What is the mass in grams of this sample?

Solution

An abalone shell consists mainly of the mineral calcium carbonate, $CaCO_3$.

a. Calcium carbonate is an ionic compound composed of Ca^{2+} and CO_3^{2-} ions. One mole of calcium carbonate contains 1 mol of Ca^{2+} and 1 mol of CO_3^{2-} ions. We calculate the molar mass by summing the masses of the components.

$$\begin{array}{ll} \text{Mass of 1 mol of } Ca^{2+} = 1 \times 40.08 \text{ g} = 40.08 \text{ g} \\ \text{Mass of 1 mol of } CO_3^{2-} \text{ (contains 1 mol of C and 3 mol of O):} \\ \quad 1 \text{ mol of C} = 1 \times 12.01 \text{ g} = 12.01 \text{ g} \\ \quad 3 \text{ mol of O} = 3 \times 16.00 \text{ g} = \underline{48.00 \text{ g}} \\ \qquad \text{Mass of 1 mol of } CaCO_3 = 100.09 \text{ g} = \text{molar mass} \end{array}$$

b. We determine the mass of 4.86 mol of $CaCO_3$ by using the molar mass.

$$4.86 \text{ mol } CaCO_3 \times \frac{100.09 \text{ g } CaCO_3}{1 \text{ mol } CaCO_3} = 486 \text{ g } CaCO_3$$

which can be diagrammed as follows:

$$\boxed{4.86 \text{ mol CaCO}_3} \times \frac{100.09 \text{ g}}{\text{mol}} \quad \blacktriangleright \quad \boxed{486 \text{ g CaCO}_3}$$

Note that the sample under consideration contains nearly 5 mol and thus should have a mass of nearly 500 g, so our answer makes sense.

 Self-Check Exercise 9.5

For average atomic masses, look inside the front cover of this book.

Calculate the molar mass for sodium sulfate, Na_2SO_4. A sample of sodium sulfate with a mass of 300.0 g represents what number of moles of sodium sulfate?

See Problems 9.35 through 9.38

In summary, the molar mass of a substance can be obtained by summing the masses of the component atoms. The molar mass (in grams) represents the mass of 1 mol of the substance. Once we know the molar mass of a compound, we can compute the number of moles present in a sample of known mass. The reverse, of course, is also true as illustrated in Example 9.7.

EXAMPLE 9.7   *Calculating Moles from Mass*

Juglone, a dye known for centuries, is produced from the husks of black walnuts. It is also a natural herbicide (weed killer) that kills off competitive plants around the black walnut tree but does not affect grass and other noncompetitive plants. The formula for juglone is $C_{10}H_6O_3$.

a. Calculate the molar mass of juglone.

b. A sample of 1.56 g of pure juglone was extracted from black walnut husks. How many moles of juglone does this sample represent?

Solution

a. The molar mass is obtained by summing the masses of the component atoms. In 1 mol of juglone there are 10 mol of carbon atoms, 6 mol of hydrogen atoms, and 3 mol of oxygen atoms.

$$
\begin{aligned}
\text{Mass of 10 mol of C} &= 10 \times 12.01 \text{ g} = 120.1 \text{ g} \\
\text{Mass of 6 mol of H} &= 6 \times 1.008 \text{ g} = 6.048 \text{ g} \\
\text{Mass of 3 mol of O} &= 3 \times 16.00 \text{ g} = \underline{48.00 \text{ g}} \\
\text{Mass of 1 mol of } C_{10}H_6O_3 &= 174.1 \text{ g} \quad = \quad \text{molar mass}
\end{aligned}
$$

b. The mass of 1 mol of this compound is 174.1 g, so 1.56 g is much less than a mole. We can determine the exact fraction of a mole by using the equivalence statement

$$1 \text{ mol} = 174.1 \text{ g juglone}$$

to derive the appropriate conversion factor:

$$1.56 \text{ g juglone} \times \frac{1 \text{ mol juglone}}{174.1 \text{ g juglone}} = 0.00896 \text{ mol juglone}$$

$$= 8.96 \times 10^{-3} \text{ mol juglone}$$

$$\boxed{1.56 \text{ g juglone}} \times \frac{1 \text{ mol}}{174.1 \text{ g}} \implies \boxed{8.96 \times 10^{-3} \text{ mol juglone}}$$

EXAMPLE 9.8 *Calculating Number of Molecules*

Isopentyl acetate, $C_7H_{14}O_2$, the compound responsible for the scent of bananas, can be produced commercially. Interestingly, bees release about 1 μg (1×10^{-6} g) of this compound when they sting. This attracts other bees, which then join the attack. How many moles and how many molecules of isopentyl acetate are released in a typical bee sting?

Solution

We are given a mass of isopentyl acetate and want the number of molecules, so we must first compute the molar mass.

$$7 \text{ mol C} \times 12.01 \frac{\text{g}}{\text{mol}} = 84.07 \text{ g C}$$

$$14 \text{ mol H} \times 1.008 \frac{\text{g}}{\text{mol}} = 14.11 \text{ g H}$$

$$2 \text{ mol O} \times 16.00 \frac{\text{g}}{\text{mol}} = \frac{32.00 \text{ g O}}{130.18 \text{ g}}$$

This means that 1 mol of isopentyl acetate (6.022×10^{23} molecules) has a mass of 130.18 g.

Next we determine the number of moles of isopentyl acetate in 1 μg, which is 1×10^{-6} g. To do this, we use the equivalence statement

1 mol isopentyl acetate = 130.18 g isopentyl acetate

which yields the conversion factor we need:

$$1 \times 10^{-6} \text{ g } C_7H_{14}O_2 \times \frac{1 \text{ mol } C_7H_{14}O_2}{130.18 \text{ g } C_7H_{14}O_2} = 8 \times 10^{-9} \text{ mol } C_7H_{14}O_2$$

Using the equivalence statement 1 mol = 6.022×10^{23} units, we can determine the number of molecules:

$$8 \times 10^{-9} \text{ mol } C_7H_{14}O_2 \times \frac{6.022 \times 10^{23} \text{ molecules}}{1 \text{ mol } C_7H_{14}O_2} = 5 \times 10^{15} \text{ molecules}$$

This very large number of molecules is released in each bee sting.

Self-Check Exercise 9.6

The substance Teflon, the slippery coating on many frying pans, is made from the C_2F_4 molecule. Calculate the number of C_2F_4 units present in 135 g of Teflon.

See Problems 9.39 and 9.40.

9.5   Percent Composition of Compounds

AIM: To learn to find the mass percent of an element in a given compound.

So far we have discussed the composition of compounds in terms of the numbers of constituent atoms. It is often useful to know a compound's composition in terms of the *masses* of its elements. We can obtain this information from the formula of the compound by comparing the mass of each element present in 1 mol of the compound to the total mass of 1 mol of the compound. The mass fraction for each element is calculated as follows:

$$\text{Mass fraction for a given element} = \frac{\text{mass of the element present in 1 mol of compound}}{\text{mass of 1 mol of compound}}$$

The mass fraction is converted to *mass percent* by multiplying by 100%.

We will illustrate this concept using the compound ethanol, an alcohol obtained by fermenting the sugar in grapes, corn, and other fruits and grains. Ethanol is often added to gasoline as an octane enhancer to form a fuel called gasohol. The added ethanol has the effect of increasing the octane of the gasoline and also lowering the carbon monoxide in automobile exhaust.

Note from its formula that each molecule of ethanol contains two carbon atoms, six hydrogen atoms, and one oxygen atom. This means that each mole of ethanol contains 2 mol of carbon atoms, 6 mol of hydrogen atoms, and 1 mol of oxygen atoms. We calculate the mass of each element present and the molecular weight for ethanol as follows:

The formula for ethanol is written C_2H_5OH, although you might expect it to be written simply as C_2H_6O.

$$\text{Mass of C} = 2\ \text{mol} \times 12.01\ \frac{\text{g}}{\text{mol}} = 24.02\ \text{g}$$

$$\text{Mass of H} = 6\ \text{mol} \times 1.008\ \frac{\text{g}}{\text{mol}} = 6.048\ \text{g}$$

$$\text{Mass of O} = 1\ \text{mol} \times 16.00\ \frac{\text{g}}{\text{mol}} = 16.00\ \text{g}$$

$$\text{Mass of 1 mol of C}_2\text{H}_5\text{OH} = 46.07\ \text{g} = \text{molar mass}$$

The **mass percent** (sometimes called the weight percent) of carbon in ethanol can be computed by comparing the mass of carbon in 1 mol of ethanol with the total mass of 1 mol of ethanol and multiplying the result by 100%.

$$\text{Mass percent of C} = \frac{\text{mass of C in 1 mol C}_2\text{H}_5\text{OH}}{\text{mass of 1 mol C}_2\text{H}_5\text{OH}} \times 100\%$$

$$= \frac{24.02 \text{ g}}{46.07 \text{ g}} \times 100\% = 52.14\%$$

That is, ethanol contains 52.14% by mass of carbon. The mass percents of hydrogen and oxygen in ethanol are obtained in a similar manner.

$$\text{Mass percent of H} = \frac{\text{mass of H in 1 mol C}_2\text{H}_5\text{OH}}{\text{mass of 1 mol C}_2\text{H}_5\text{OH}} \times 100\%$$

$$= \frac{6.048 \text{ g}}{46.07 \text{ g}} \times 100\% = 13.13\%$$

$$\text{Mass percent of O} = \frac{\text{mass of O in 1 mol C}_2\text{H}_5\text{OH}}{\text{mass of 1 mol C}_2\text{H}_5\text{OH}} \times 100\%$$

$$= \frac{16.00 \text{ g}}{46.07 \text{ g}} \times 100\% = 34.73\%$$

Sometimes, because of rounding-off effects, the sum of the mass percents in a compound is not exactly 100%.

The mass percentages of all the elements in a compound add up to 100%, although rounding-off effects may produce a small deviation. Adding up the percentages is a good way to check the calculations. In this case, the sum of the mass percents is 52.14% + 13.13% + 34.73% = 100.00%.

EXAMPLE 9.9   *Calculating Mass Percent*

Carvone is a substance that occurs in two forms, both of which have the same molecular formula ($C_{10}H_{14}O$) and molar mass. One type of carvone gives caraway seeds their characteristic smell; the other is responsible for the smell of spearmint oil. Compute the mass percent of each element in carvone.

Solution

Because the formula for carvone is $C_{10}H_{14}O$, the masses of the various elements in 1 mol of carvone are

$$\text{Mass of C in 1 mol} = 10 \text{ mol} \times 12.01 \frac{\text{g}}{\text{mol}} = 120.1 \text{ g}$$

$$\text{Mass of H in 1 mol} = 14 \text{ mol} \times 1.008 \frac{\text{g}}{\text{mol}} = 14.11 \text{ g}$$

$$\text{Mass of O in 1 mol} = 1 \text{ mol} \times 16.00 \frac{\text{g}}{\text{mol}} = \underline{16.00 \text{ g}}$$

$$\text{Mass of 1 mol of C}_{10}\text{H}_{14}\text{O} = 150.21 \text{ g}$$

$$\text{Molar mass} = 150.2 \text{ g}$$

The 120.1 limits the sum to one decimal place.

(rounding to the correct number of significant figures)

Next we find the fraction of the total mass contributed by each element and convert it to a percentage.

$$\text{Mass percent of C} = \frac{120.1 \text{ g C}}{150.2 \text{ g C}_{10}\text{H}_{14}\text{O}} \times 100\% = 79.96\%$$

$$\text{Mass percent of H} = \frac{14.11 \text{ g H}}{150.2 \text{ g C}_{10}\text{H}_{14}\text{O}} \times 100\% = 9.394\%$$

$$\text{Mass percent of O} = \frac{16.00 \text{ g O}}{150.2 \text{ g C}_{10}\text{H}_{14}\text{O}} \times 100\% = 10.65\%$$

Check: Add the individual mass percent values—they should total 100% within a small range due to rounding off. In this case, the percentages add up to 100.00%.

Self-Check Exercise 9.7

Penicillin, an important antibiotic (antibacterial agent), was discovered accidentally by the Scottish bacteriologist Alexander Fleming in 1928, although he was never able to isolate it as a pure compound. This and similar antibiotics have saved millions of lives that would otherwise have been lost to infections. Penicillin, like many of the molecules produced by living systems, is a large molecule containing many atoms. One type of penicillin, penicillin F, has the formula $C_{14}H_{20}N_2SO_4$. Compute the mass percent of each element in this compound.

See Problems 9.45 through 9.50.

9.6 *Formulas of Compounds*

AIM: To understand the meaning of empirical formulas of compounds.

Assume that you have mixed two solutions and a solid product (a precipitate) forms. How can you find out what the solid is? What is its formula? There are several possible approaches you can take to answering these questions. For example, we saw in Chapter 7 that we can usually predict the identity of a precipitate formed when two solutions are mixed in a reaction of this type if we know some facts about the solubilities of ionic compounds.

However, although an experienced chemist can often predict the product expected in a chemical reaction, the only sure way to identify the product is to perform experiments. Usually we compare the physical properties of the product to the properties of known compounds.

Sometimes a chemical reaction gives a product that has never been obtained before. In such a case, a chemist determines what compound has been formed by determining which elements are present and how much of each. These data can be used to obtain the formula of the compound. In Section 9.5 we used the formula of the compound to determine the mass of each element present in a mole of the compound. To obtain the formula of an unknown compound, we do the opposite. That is, we use the measured masses of the elements present to determine the formula.

Recall that the formula of a compound represents the relative numbers of the various types of atoms present. For example, the molecular formula CO_2 tells us that for each carbon atom there are two oxygen atoms in each molecule of carbon dioxide. So to determine the formula of a substance we need to count the atoms. As we have seen in this chapter, we can do this by weighing. Suppose we know that a compound contains only the elements carbon, hydrogen, and oxygen, and we weigh out a 0.2015-g sample for analysis. Using methods we will not discuss here, we find that this 0.2015-g sample of compound contains 0.0806 g of carbon, 0.01353 g of hydrogen, and 0.1074 g of oxygen. We have just learned how to convert these masses to numbers of atoms by using the atomic mass of each element. We begin by converting to moles.

Carbon

$$(0.0806 \text{ g C}) \times \frac{1 \text{ mol C atoms}}{12.01 \text{ g C}} = 0.00671 \text{ mol C atoms}$$

Hydrogen

$$(0.01353 \text{ g H}) \times \frac{1 \text{ mol H atoms}}{1.008 \text{ g H}} = 0.01342 \text{ mol H atoms}$$

Oxygen

$$(0.1074 \text{ g O}) \times \frac{1 \text{ mol O atoms}}{16.00 \text{ g O}} = 0.006713 \text{ mol O atoms}$$

Let's review what we have established. We now know that 0.2015 g of the compound contains 0.00671 mol of C atoms, 0.01342 mol of H atoms, and 0.006713 mol of O atoms. Because 1 mol is 6.022×10^{23}, these quantities can be converted to actual numbers of atoms.

Carbon

$$(0.00671 \text{ mol C atoms}) \frac{(6.022 \times 10^{23} \text{ C atoms})}{1 \text{ mol C atoms}} = 4.04 \times 10^{21} \text{ C atoms}$$

Hydrogen

$$(0.01342 \text{ mol H atoms}) \frac{(6.022 \times 10^{23} \text{ H atoms})}{1 \text{ mol H atoms}} = 8.08 \times 10^{21} \text{ H atoms}$$

Oxygen

$$(0.006713 \text{ mol O atoms}) \frac{(6.022 \times 10^{23} \text{ O atoms})}{1 \text{ mol O atoms}} = 4.043 \times 10^{21} \text{ O atoms}$$

These are the numbers of the various types of atoms *in 0.2015 g of compound*. What do these numbers tell us about the formula of the compound? Note the following:

1. The compound contains the same number of C and O atoms.

2. There are twice as many H atoms as C atoms or O atoms.

We can represent this information by the formula CH_2O, which expresses the *relative* numbers of C, H, and O atoms present. Is this the true formula for the compound? In other words, is the compound made up of CH_2O molecules? It may be. However, it might also be made up of $C_2H_4O_2$ molecules,

FIGURE 9.4
The glucose molecule. The molecular formula is $C_6H_{12}O_6$, as can be verified by counting the atoms. The empirical formula for glucose is CH_2O.

$C_3H_6O_3$ molecules, $C_4H_8O_4$ molecules, $C_5H_{10}O_5$ molecules, $C_6H_{12}O_6$ molecules, and so on. Note that each of these molecules has the required 1:2:1 ratio of carbon to hydrogen to oxygen atoms (the ratio shown by experiment to be present in the compound).

When we break a compound down into its separate elements and "count" the atoms present, we learn only the ratio of atoms—we get only the *relative* numbers of atoms. The formula of a compound that expresses the smallest whole-number ratio of the atoms present is called the **empirical formula** or *simplest formula*. A compound that contains the molecules $C_4H_8O_4$ has the same empirical formula as a compound that contains $C_6H_{12}O_6$ molecules. The empirical formula for both is CH_2O. The actual formula of a compound—the one that gives the composition of the molecules that are present—is called the **molecular formula**. The sugar called glucose is made of molecules with the molecular formula $C_6H_{12}O_6$ (Figure 9.4). Note from the molecular formula for glucose that the empirical formula is CH_2O. We can represent the molecular formula as a multiple (by 6) of the empirical formula:

$$C_6H_{12}O_6 = (CH_2O)_6$$

In the next section, we will explore in more detail how to calculate the empirical formula for a compound from the relative masses of the elements present. As we will see in Sections 9.8 and 9.9, we must know the molar mass of a compound to determine its molecular formula.

EXAMPLE 9.10 *Determining Empirical Formulas*

In each case below, the molecular formula for a compound is given. Determine the empirical formula for each compound.

a. C_6H_6. This is the molecular formula for benzene, a liquid commonly used in industry as a starting material for many important products.

b. $C_{12}H_4Cl_4O_2$. This is the molecular formula for a substance commonly called dioxin, a powerful poison that sometimes occurs as a by-product in the production of other chemicals.

c. $C_6H_{16}N_2$. This is the molecular formula for one of the reactants used to produce nylon.

Solution

a. $C_6H_6 = (CH)_6$; CH is the empirical formula. Each subscript in the empirical formula is multiplied by 6 to obtain the molecular formula.

b. $C_{12}H_4Cl_4O_2$; $C_{12}H_4Cl_4O_2 = (C_6H_2Cl_2O)_2$; $C_6H_2Cl_2O$ is the empirical formula. Each subscript in the empirical formula is multiplied by 2 to obtain the molecular formula.

c. $C_6H_{16}N_2 = (C_3H_8N)_2$; C_3H_8N is the empirical formula. Each subscript in the empirical formula is multiplied by 2 to obtain the molecular formula.

9.7   *Calculation of Empirical Formulas*

AIM: To learn to calculate empirical formulas.

As we said in the previous section, one of the most important things we can learn about a new compound is its chemical formula. To calculate the empirical formula of a compound, we first determine the relative masses of the various elements that are present.

One way to do this is to measure the masses of elements that react to form the compound. For example, suppose we weigh out 0.2636 g of pure nickel metal into a crucible and heat this metal in the air so that the nickel can react with oxygen to form a nickel oxide compound. After the sample has cooled, we weigh it again and find its mass to be 0.3354 g. The gain in mass is due to the oxygen that reacts with the nickel to form the oxide. Therefore, the mass of oxygen present in the compound is the total mass of the product minus the mass of the nickel:

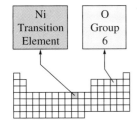

Total mass of nickel oxide	−	Mass of nickel originally present	=	Mass of oxygen that reacted with the nickel

or

$$0.3354 \text{ g} \ - \ 0.2636 \text{ g} \ = \ 0.0718 \text{ g}$$

Note that the mass of nickel present in the compound is the nickel metal originally weighed out. So we know that the nickel oxide contains 0.2636 g of nickel and 0.0718 g of oxygen. What is the empirical formula of this compound?

To answer this question we must convert the masses to numbers of atoms, using atomic masses:

Four significant figures allowed.

$$0.2636 \text{ g Ni} \times \frac{1 \text{ mol Ni atoms}}{58.69 \text{ g Ni}} = 0.004491 \text{ mol Ni atoms}$$

Three significant figures allowed.

$$0.0718 \text{ g O} \times \frac{1 \text{ mol O atoms}}{16.00 \text{ g O}} = 0.00449 \text{ mol O atoms}$$

These mole quantities represent numbers of atoms (remember that a mole of atoms is 6.022×10^{23} atoms). It is clear from the moles of atoms that the compound contains an equal number of Ni and O atoms, so the formula is NiO. This is the *empirical formula;* it expresses the smallest whole-number (integer) ratio of atoms:

$$\frac{0.004491 \text{ mol Ni atoms}}{0.00449 \text{ mol O atoms}} = \frac{1 \text{ Ni}}{1 \text{ O}}$$

That is, this compound contains equal numbers of nickel atoms and oxygen atoms. We say the ratio of nickel atoms to oxygen atoms is 1:1 (1 to 1).

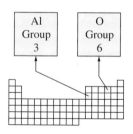

EXAMPLE 9.11   *Calculating Empirical Formulas*

An oxide of aluminum is formed by the reaction of 4.151 g of aluminum with 3.692 g of oxygen. Calculate the empirical formula for this compound.

Solution

We know that the compound contains 4.151 g of aluminum and 3.692 g of oxygen. But we need to know the relative numbers of each type of atom to write the formula, so we must convert these masses to moles of atoms to get the empirical formula. We carry out the conversion by using the atomic masses of the elements.

$$4.151 \text{ g Al} \times \frac{1 \text{ mol Al}}{26.98 \text{ g Al}} = 0.1539 \text{ mol Al atoms}$$

$$3.692 \text{ g O} \times \frac{1 \text{ mol O}}{16.00 \text{ g O}} = 0.2308 \text{ mol O atoms}$$

Because chemical formulas use only whole numbers, we next find the integer (whole-number) ratio of the atoms. To do this we start by dividing both numbers by the smallest of the two. This converts the smallest number to 1.

$$\frac{0.1539 \text{ mol Al}}{0.1539} = 1.000 \text{ mol Al atoms}$$

$$\frac{0.2308 \text{ mol O}}{0.1539} = 1.500 \text{ mol O atoms}$$

Note that dividing both numbers of moles of atoms by the *same* number does not change the *relative* numbers of oxygen and aluminum atoms. That is,

$$\frac{0.2308 \text{ mol O}}{0.1539 \text{ mol Al}} = \frac{1.500 \text{ mol O}}{1.000 \text{ mol Al}}$$

Thus we know that the compound contains 1.500 mol of O atoms for every 1.000 mol of Al atoms, or, in terms of individual atoms, we could say that the compound contains 1.500 O atoms for every 1.000 Al atom. However, because only *whole* atoms combine to form compounds, we must find a set of *whole numbers* to express the empirical formula. When we multiply both 1.000 and 1.500 by 2, we get the integers we need.

$$1.500 \text{ O} \times 2 = 3.000 = 3 \text{ O atoms}$$

$$1.000 \text{ Al} \times 2 = 2.000 = 2 \text{ Al atoms}$$

Therefore, this compound contains two Al atoms for every three O atoms, and the empirical formula is Al_2O_3. Note that the *ratio* of atoms in this compound is given by each of the following fractions:

$$\frac{0.2308 \text{ O}}{0.1539 \text{ Al}} = \frac{1.500 \text{ O}}{1.000 \text{ Al}} = \frac{\frac{3}{2} \text{ O}}{1 \text{ Al}} = \frac{3 \text{ O}}{2 \text{ Al}}$$

The smallest whole-number ratio corresponds to the subscripts of the empirical formula, Al_2O_3.

Sometimes the relative numbers of moles you get when you calculate an empirical formula will turn out to be nonintegers, as was the case in Example 9.11. When this happens, you must convert to the appropriate whole numbers. This is done by multiplying all the numbers by the same small integer, which can be found by trial and error. The multiplier needed is almost always between 1 and 6. We will now summarize what we have learned about calculating empirical formulas.

Steps for Determining the Empirical Formula of a Compound

STEP 1 Obtain the mass of each element present (in grams).

STEP 2 Determine the number of moles of each type of atom present.

STEP 3 Divide the number of moles of each element by the smallest number of moles to convert the smallest number to 1. If all of the numbers so obtained are integers (whole numbers), these are the subscripts in the empirical formula. If one or more of these numbers are not integers, go on to step 4.

STEP 4 Multiply the numbers you derived in step 3 by the smallest integer that will convert all of them to whole numbers. This set of whole numbers represents the subscripts in the empirical formula.

EXAMPLE 9.12 *Calculating Empirical Formulas for Binary Compounds*

When a 0.3546-g sample of vanadium metal is heated in air, it reacts with oxygen to achieve a final mass of 0.6330 g. Calculate the empirical formula of this vanadium oxide.

Solution

STEP 1 All the vanadium that was originally present will be found in the final compound, so we can calculate the mass of oxygen that reacted by taking the following difference:

$$\begin{bmatrix} \text{Total mass} \\ \text{of compound} \end{bmatrix} - \begin{bmatrix} \text{Mass of} \\ \text{vanadium} \\ \text{in compound} \end{bmatrix} = \begin{bmatrix} \text{Mass of} \\ \text{oxygen} \\ \text{in compound} \end{bmatrix}$$

$$0.6330 \text{ g} \quad - \quad 0.3546 \text{ g} \quad = \quad 0.2784 \text{ g}$$

STEP 2 Using the atomic masses (50.94 for V and 16.00 for O), we obtain

$$0.3546 \text{ g V} \times \frac{1 \text{ mol V atoms}}{50.94 \text{ g V}} = 0.006961 \text{ mol V atoms}$$

$$0.2784 \text{ g O} \times \frac{1 \text{ mol O atoms}}{16.00 \text{ g O}} = 0.01740 \text{ mol O atoms}$$

STEP 3   Then we divide both numbers of moles by the smaller, 0.006961.

$$\frac{0.006961 \text{ mol V atoms}}{0.006961} = 1.000 \text{ mol V atoms}$$

$$\frac{0.01740 \text{ mol O atoms}}{0.006961} = 2.500 \text{ mol O atoms}$$

Because one of these numbers (2.500) is not an integer, we go on to step 4.

STEP 4   We note that $2 \times 2.500 = 5.000$ and $2 \times 1.000 = 2.000$, so we multiply both numbers by 2 to get integers.

$$2 \times 1.000 \text{ V} = 2.000 \text{ V} = 2 \text{ V}$$
$$2 \times 2.500 \text{ O} = 5.000 \text{ O} = 5 \text{ O}$$

This compound contains 2 V atoms for every 5 O atoms, and the empirical formula is V_2O_5.

 Self-Check Exercise 9.8

In a lab experiment it was observed that 0.6884 g of lead combines with 0.2356 g of chlorine to form a binary compound. Calculate the empirical formula of this compound.

See Problems 9.58, 9.61, 9.63, 9.65, and 9.66.

The same procedures we have used for binary compounds also apply to compounds containing three or more elements, as Example 9.13 illustrates.

 EXAMPLE 9.13   *Calculating Empirical Formulas for Compounds Containing Three or More Elements*

A sample of lead arsenate, an insecticide used against the potato beetle, contains 1.3813 g of lead, 0.00672 g of hydrogen, 0.4995 g of arsenic, and 0.4267 g of oxygen. Calculate the empirical formula for lead arsenate.

Solution

STEP 1   The compound contains 1.3813 g Pb, 0.00672 g H, 0.4995 g As, and 0.4267 g O.

STEP 2   We use the atomic masses of the elements present to calculate the moles of each.

$$1.3813 \text{ g Pb} \times \frac{1 \text{ mol Pb}}{207.2 \text{ g Pb}} = 0.006667 \text{ mol Pb}$$

Only three significant figures allowed.

$$0.00672 \text{ g H} \times \frac{1 \text{ mol H}}{1.008 \text{ g H}} = 0.00667 \text{ mol H}$$

$$0.4995 \text{ g As} \times \frac{1 \text{ mol As}}{74.92 \text{ g As}} = 0.006667 \text{ mol As}$$

$$0.4267 \text{ g O} \times \frac{1 \text{ mol O}}{16.00 \text{ g O}} = 0.02667 \text{ mol O}$$

STEP 3 Now we divide by the smallest number of moles.

$$\frac{0.006667 \text{ mol Pb}}{0.006667} = 1.000 \text{ mol Pb}$$

$$\frac{0.00667 \text{ mol H}}{0.006667} = 1.00 \text{ mol H}$$

$$\frac{0.006667 \text{ mol As}}{0.006667} = 1.000 \text{ mol As}$$

$$\frac{0.02667 \text{ mol O}}{0.006667} = 4.000 \text{ mol O}$$

The numbers of moles are all whole numbers, so the empirical formula is $PbHAsO_4$.

 Self-Check Exercise 9.9

Sevin, the commercial name for an insecticide used to protect crops such as cotton, vegetables, and fruit, is made from carbamic acid. A chemist analyzing a sample of carbamic acid finds 0.8007 g of carbon, 0.9333 g of nitrogen, 0.2016 g of hydrogen, and 2.133 g of oxygen. Determine the empirical formula for carbamic acid.

See Problems 9.57 and 9.59.

When a compound is analyzed to determine the relative amounts of the elements present, the results are usually given in terms of percentages by masses of the various elements. In Section 9.5 we learned to calculate the percent composition of a compound from its formula. Now we will do the opposite. Given the percent composition, we will calculate the empirical formula.

Percent by mass for a given element means the grams of that element in 100 g of the compound.

To understand this procedure, you must understand the meaning of *percent*. Remember that percent means parts of a given component per 100 parts of the total mixture. For example, if a given compound is 15% carbon (by mass), the compound contains 15 g of carbon per 100 g of compound.

Calculation of the empirical formula of a compound when one is given its percent composition is illustrated in Example 9.14.

 EXAMPLE 9.14 *Calculating Empirical Formulas from Percent Composition*

Cisplatin, the common name for a platinum compound that is used to treat cancerous tumors, has the composition (mass percent) 65.02% platinum, 9.34% nitrogen, 2.02% hydrogen, and 23.63% chlorine. Calculate the empirical formula for cisplatin.

Solution

STEP 1 Determine how many grams of each element are present in 100 g of compound. Cisplatin is 65.02% platinum (by mass), which means there are 65.02 g of platinum (Pt) per 100.00 g of compound. Similarly, a 100.00-g sample of cisplatin contains 9.34 g of nitrogen (N), 2.02 g of hydrogen (H), and 26.63 g of chlorine (Cl).

If we have a 100.00-g sample of cisplatin, we have 65.02 g Pt, 9.34 g N, 2.02 g H, and 23.63 g Cl.

STEP 2 Determine the number of moles of each type of atom. We use the atomic masses to calculate moles.

$$65.02 \text{ g Pt} \times \frac{1 \text{ mol Pt}}{195.1 \text{ g Pt}} = 0.3333 \text{ mol Pt}$$

$$9.34 \text{ g N} \times \frac{1 \text{ mol N}}{14.01 \text{ g N}} = 0.667 \text{ mol N}$$

$$2.02 \text{ g H} \times \frac{1 \text{ mol H}}{1.008 \text{ g H}} = 2.00 \text{ mol H}$$

$$23.63 \text{ g Cl} \times \frac{1 \text{ mol Cl}}{35.45 \text{ g Cl}} = 0.6666 \text{ mol Cl}$$

STEP 3 Divide through by the smallest number of moles.

$$\frac{0.3333 \text{ mol Pt}}{0.3333} = 1.000 \text{ mol Pt}$$

$$\frac{0.667 \text{ mol N}}{0.3333} = 2.00 \text{ mol N}$$

$$\frac{2.00 \text{ mol H}}{0.3333} = 6.01 \text{ mol H}$$

$$\frac{0.6666 \text{ mol Cl}}{0.3333} = 2.000 \text{ mol Cl}$$

The empirical formula for cisplatin is $PtN_2H_6Cl_2$. Note that the number for hydrogen is slightly greater than 6 because of rounding-off effects.

 Self-Check Exercise 9.10

The most common form of nylon (Nylon-6) is 63.68% carbon, 12.38% nitrogen, 9.80% hydrogen, and 14.14% oxygen. Calculate the empirical formula for Nylon-6.

See Problems 9.67 through 9.74.

Note from Example 9.14 that once the percentages are converted to masses, this example is the same as earlier examples in which the masses were given directly.

9.8   *Calculation of Molecular Formulas*

AIM: To learn to calculate the molecular formula of a compound, given its empirical formula and molar mass.

If we know the composition of a compound in terms of the masses (or mass percentages) of the elements present, we can calculate the empirical formula but not the molecular formula. For reasons that will become clear as we consider Example 9.15, to obtain the molecular formula we must know the molar mass. In this section we will consider compounds where both the percent composition and the molar mass are known.

EXAMPLE 9.15 *Calculating Molecular Formulas*

A white powder is analyzed and found to have an empirical formula of P_2O_5. The compound has a molar mass of 283.88 g. What is the compound's molecular formula?

Solution

To obtain the molecular formula, we must compare the empirical formula mass to the molar mass. The empirical formula mass for P_2O_5 is the mass of 1 mol of P_2O_5 units.

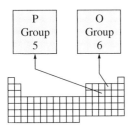

Atomic
mass of P

2 mol P: 2×30.97 g $= 61.94$ g
5 mol O: 5×16.00 g $= \underline{80.00}$ g

Atomic
mass of O   141.94 g   Mass of 1 mol of P_2O_5 units

Recall that the molecular formula contains a whole number of empirical formula units. That is,

$$\text{Molecular formula} = (\text{empirical formula})_n$$

where n is a small whole number. Now, because

$$\text{Molecular formula} = n \times \text{empirical formula}$$

then

$$\text{Molar mass} = n \times \text{empirical formula mass}$$

Solving for n gives

$$n = \frac{\text{molar mass}}{\text{empirical formula mass}}$$

Thus to determine the molecular formula, we first divide the molar mass by the empirical formula mass. This tells us how many empirical formula masses there are in one molar mass.

$$\frac{\text{Molar mass}}{\text{Empirical formula mass}} = \frac{283.88 \text{ g}}{141.94 \text{ g}} = 2$$

This result means that $n = 2$ for this compound, so the molecular formula consists of two empirical formula units, and the molecular formula is $(P_2O_5)_2$, or P_4O_{10}. The structure of this interesting compound is shown in Figure 9.5.

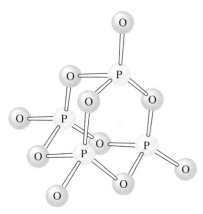

FIGURE 9.5
The structure of P_4O_{10} as a "ball-and-stick" model. This compound has a great affinity for water and is often used as a desiccant, or drying agent.

 Self-Check Exercise 9.11

A compound used as an additive for gasoline to help prevent engine knock shows the following percentage composition:

71.65% Cl   24.27% C   4.07% H

The molar mass is known to be 98.96 g. Determine the empirical formula and the molecular formula for this compound.

See Problems 9.81 through 9.82.

It is important to realize that the molecular formula is always an integer multiple of the empirical formula. For example, the sugar glucose (see Figure 9.4) has the empirical formula CH_2O and the molecular formula $C_6H_{12}O_6$. In this case there are six empirical formula units in each glucose molecule:

$$(CH_2O)_6 = C_6H_{12}O_6$$

In general, we can represent the molecular formula in terms of the empirical formula as follows:

Molecular formula = (empirical formula)$_n$, where n is an integer.

$$(\text{Empirical formula})_n = \text{molecular formula}$$

where n is an integer. If $n = 1$, the molecular formula is the same as the empirical formula. For example, for carbon dioxide the empirical formula (CO_2) and the molecular formula (CO_2) are the same, so $n = 1$. On the other hand, for tetraphosphorus decoxide the empirical formula is P_2O_5 and the molecular formula is $P_4O_{10} = (P_2O_5)_2$. In this case $n = 2$.

Chapter Review

Key Terms

atomic mass unit *(9.2)*

average atomic mass *(9.2)*

mole *(9.3)*

Avogadro's number *(9.3)*

molar mass *(9.4)*

mass percent *(9.5)*

empirical formula *(9.6)*

molecular formula *(9.6)*

Summary

1. We can count individual units by weighing if we know the average mass of the units. Thus when we know the average mass of the atoms of an element as that element occurs in nature, we can calculate the number of atoms in any given sample of that element by weighing the sample.

2. A mole is a unit of measure equal to 6.022×10^{23}, which is called Avogadro's number. One mole of any substance contains 6.022×10^{23} units.

3. One mole of an element has a mass equal to the element's atomic mass expressed in grams. The molar mass of any compound is the mass (in grams) of 1 mol of the compound and is the sum of the masses of the component atoms.

4. Percent composition consists of the mass percent of each element in a compound:

Mass percent =
$$\frac{\text{mass of a given element in 1 mol of compound}}{\text{mass of 1 mol of compound}} \times 100\%$$

5. The empirical formula of a compound is the simplest whole-number ratio of the atoms present in the compound; it can be derived from the percent composition of the compound. The molecular formula is the exact formula of the molecules present; it is always an integer multiple of the empirical formula. The following diagram summarizes these different ways of expressing the same information.

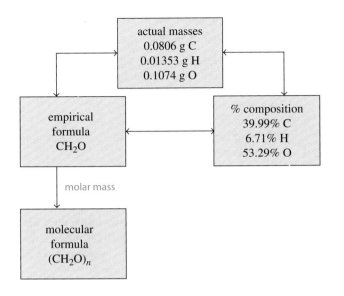

Questions and Problems*

All even-numbered exercises have answers in the back of this book and solutions in the Solutions Guide.

9.1 ■ Counting by Weighing

PROBLEMS

1. Merchants usually sell small nuts, washers, and bolts by weight (like jelly beans!) rather than by individually counting the items. Suppose a particular type of washer weighs 0.110 g on the average. What would 100 such washers weigh? How many washers would there be in 100. g of washers?

2. A particular small laboratory cork weighs 1.63 g, whereas a rubber lab stopper of the same size weighs 4.31 g. How many corks would there be in 500. g of such corks? How many rubber stoppers would there be in 500. g of similar stoppers? How many grams of rubber stoppers would be needed to contain the same number of stoppers as there are corks in 1.00 kg of corks?

9.2 ■ Atomic Masses: Counting Atoms by Weighing

QUESTIONS

3. Define the *amu*. What is one amu equivalent to in grams?

*The element symbols and formulas are given in some problems but not in others to help you learn this necessary "vocabulary."

4. When using the average atomic mass of an element for calculations, we pretend that all atoms of the element are _____.

PROBLEMS

5. Using the average atomic masses given in Table 9.1, calculate the mass, in amu, of each of the following samples.
   a. 455 atoms of hydrogen
   b. 455 atoms of carbon
   c. 455 atoms of aluminum
   d. 1.255×10^4 atoms of nitrogen
   e. 1.255×10^4 atoms of sodium

6. Using the average atomic masses given in Table 9.2, calculate the number of atoms present in each of the following samples.
   a. 10.81 amu of boron
   b. 320.7 amu of sulfur
   c. 19,697 amu of gold
   d. 19,695 amu of xenon
   e. 3588.3 amu of aluminum

7. If an average atom of calcium weighs 40.08 amu, how many calcium atoms are contained in a sample with mass 1002 amu? What is the mass of 4.654×10^{21} calcium atoms?

8. If an average gold atom weighs 196.97 amu, what does a sample containing 1.00×10^4 gold atoms weigh? How many gold atoms are contained in a sample of gold that has a mass of 2.955×10^5 amu?

9.3 ■ The Mole

QUESTIONS

9. 6.022×10^{23} atoms of carbon weigh _____ grams.

10. A sample equal to the atomic mass of an element in grams contains _____ atoms.

PROBLEMS

11. What mass of calcium metal contains the same number of atoms as 12.16 g of magnesium? What mass of calcium metal contains the same number of atoms as 24.31 g of magnesium?

12. What mass of carbon contains the same number of atoms as 1.008 g of hydrogen?

13. What mass of hydrogen contains the same number of atoms as 7.00 g of nitrogen?

14. What mass of nitrogen contains the same number of atoms as 48 g of oxygen?

15. If an average sodium atom has the mass 3.817×10^{-23} g, what is the mass of an average magnesium atom in grams? What is the average mass of a potassium atom in grams?

16. Calculate the average mass in grams of 1 atom of oxygen.

17. Which has the smaller mass, 1 mol of He atoms or 4 mol of H atoms?

18. Which weighs more, 0.50 mol of oxygen atoms or 4 mol of hydrogen atoms?

19. Using the average masses given inside the front cover of the text, calculate the number of *moles* of each element represented in the following masses.
    a. 2.411 g of helium, He
    b. 62.55 kg of iron, Fe
    c. 4.474 mg of fluorine, F
    d. 3.000 lb of lithium, Li
    e. 65.45 μg of potassium, K
    f. 1.245×10^4 g of chromium, Cr
    g. 7.214 g of iridium, Ir

20. Using the average atomic masses given inside the front cover of the text, calculate the number of *moles* of each element in samples with the following masses.
    a. 26.2 g of gold
    b. 41.5 g of calcium
    c. 335 mg of barium
    d. 1.42×10^{-3} g of palladium
    e. 3.05×10^{-5} μg of nickel
    f. 1.00 lb of iron
    g. 12.01 g of carbon

21. Using the average atomic masses given inside the front cover of the text, calculate the *mass in grams* of each of the following samples.
    a. 2.71×10^{-4} mol of platinum, Pt
    b. 4.35 mol of uranium, U
    c. 56.2 mol of hydrogen, H
    d. 0.00371 mol of chromium, Cr
    e. 0.256 mol of iron, Fe
    f. 2.61×10^3 mol of tungsten, W
    g. 0.00000113 mol of cobalt, Co

22. Using the average atomic masses given inside the front cover of the text, calculate the *mass in grams* of each of the following samples.
    a. 2.00 mol of iron
    b. 0.521 mol of nickel
    c. 1.23×10^{-3} mol of platinum
    d. 72.5 mol of lead
    e. 0.00102 mol of magnesium
    f. 4.87×10^3 mol of aluminum

g. 211.5 mol of lithium
h. 1.72×10^{-6} mol of sodium

23. Using the average atomic masses given inside the front cover of the text, calculate the number of *atoms* present in each of the following samples.
    a. 1.50 g of silver, Ag
    b. 0.0015 mol of copper, Cu
    c. 0.0015 g of copper, Cu
    d. 2.00 kg of magnesium, Mg
    e. 2.34 oz of calcium, Ca
    f. 2.34 g of calcium, Ca
    g. 2.34 mol of calcium, Ca

24. Using the average atomic masses given inside the front cover of the text, calculate the indicated quantity.
    a. the mass of a sample of lithium containing 6.42×10^{22} atoms
    b. the mass of 0.551 mol of Li
    c. the number of lithium atoms in 0.00103 mol of Li
    d. the mass of one lithium atom
    e. the number of moles of lithium in 0.500 g of Li
    f. the number of lithium atoms in 5.22 g of Li
    g. the number of moles of lithium in 4.75×10^{24} atoms of Li

9.4 ■ Molar Mass

QUESTIONS

25. The _____ of a substance is the mass (in grams) of 1 mol of the substance.

26. The molar mass of a substance can be obtained by _____ the atomic weights of the component atoms.

PROBLEMS

27. Calculate the molar mass for each of the following substances.
    a. methane, CH_4
    b. sodium nitrate, $NaNO_3$
    c. carbon monoxide, CO
    d. carbon dioxide, CO_2
    e. ammonium fluoride, NH_4F
    f. potassium chlorate, $KClO_3$

28. Calculate the molar mass for each of the following substances.
    a. sodium nitride, Na_3N
    b. carbon disulfide, CS_2
    c. ammonium bromide, NH_4Br
    d. ethyl alcohol, C_2H_5OH
    e. sulfurous acid, H_2SO_3
    f. sulfuric acid, H_2SO_4

29. Calculate the molar mass for each of the following substances.
    a. silver(I) oxide (silver oxide)
    b. iron(II) sulfate
    c. ammonium nitrate
    d. methyl alcohol, CH_3OH
    e. chlorine dioxide
    f. strontium chloride

30. Calculate the molar mass for each of the following substances.
    a. ammonium sulfide, $(NH_4)_2S$
    b. dichlorophenol, $C_6H_4OCl_2$
    c. barium hydride, BaH_2
    d. potassium dihydrogen phosphate, KH_2PO_4
    e. potassium hydrogen phosphate, K_2HPO_4
    f. potassium phosphate, K_3PO_4

31. Calculate the number of *moles* of the indicated substance in each of the following samples.
    a. 4.25 g of phenol, C_6H_6O
    b. 63.7 mg of potassium cyanide, KCN
    c. 49.3 kg of calcium chloride, $CaCl_2$
    d. 78.9 μg of ammonium fluoride, NH_4F
    e. 91.3 g of acetylene, C_2H_2

32. Calculate the number of *moles* of the indicated substance in each of the following samples.
    a. 49.2 mg of sulfur trioxide
    b. 7.44×10^4 kg of lead(IV) oxide
    c. 59.1 g of chloroform, $CHCl_3$
    d. 3.27 μg of trichloroethane, $C_2H_3Cl_3$
    e. 4.01 g of lithium hydroxide

33. Calculate the number of *moles* of the indicated substance present in each of the following samples.
    a. 18.0 g of dextrose, $C_6H_{12}O_6$
    b. 21.94 g of nitrous oxide, N_2O
    c. 21.94 g of nitric oxide, NO
    d. 1.24 oz of gold(III) acetate, $Au(C_2H_3O_2)_3$
    e. 44.2 g of ammonium dichromate, $(NH_4)_2Cr_2O_7$

34. Calculate the number of *moles* of the indicated substance present in each of the following samples.
    a. 0.000314 g of aluminum chloride
    b. 1.00 lb of sodium hydroxide
    c. 7.4 μg of arsenic triiodide
    d. 44.2 kg of sodium hydrogen carbonate
    e. 6.21 g of potassium hydrogen phosphate

35. Calculate the mass in grams of each of the following samples.
    a. 0.251 mol of potassium chromate
    b. 1.51 mol of lithium perchlorate
    c. 2.52×10^4 mol of lead(II) oxide

    d. 1.74×10^{-3} mol lead(IV) chloride
    e. 0.00205 mol of tin(II) fluoride

36. Calculate the mass in grams of each of the following samples.
    a. 1.50 mol aluminum iodide
    b. 1.91×10^{-3} mol of benzene, C_6H_6
    c. 4.00 mol of glucose, $C_6H_{12}O_6$
    d. 4.56×10^5 mol of ethanol, C_2H_5OH
    e. 2.27 mol of calcium nitrate

37. Calculate the mass in grams of each of the following samples.
    a. 125 millimol of silver nitrate, $AgNO_3$
    b. 0.138 mol of sucrose, $C_{12}H_{22}O_{11}$
    c. 4.51 mol of tetraphosphorus decoxide, P_4O_{10}
    d. 2.76 millimol of copper(I) oxide, Cu_2O
    e. 0.00475 mol of cobalt(III) chloride, $CoCl_3$

38. Calculate the mass in grams in the following samples.
    a. 1.27 millimol of carbon dioxide
    b. 4.12×10^3 mol of nitrogen trichloride
    c. 0.00451 mol of ammonium nitrate
    d. 18.0 mol of water
    e. 62.7 mol of copper(II) sulfate

39. Calculate the number of *molecules* in each of the following samples.
    a. 4.75 millimol of phosphine, PH_3
    b. 4.75 g of phosphine, PH_3
    c. 1.25×10^{-2} g of lead(II) acetate, $Pb(CH_3CO_2)_2$
    d. 1.25×10^{-2} mol of lead(II) acetate, $Pb(CH_3CO_2)_2$
    e. a sample of benzene, C_6H_6, which contains a total of 5.40 mol of carbon

40. Calculate the number of *molecules* present in each of the following samples.
    a. 4.29 mol of nitrogen dioxide
    b. 4.29 g of nitrogen dioxide
    c. 1.95×10^{-10} mol of hydrogen fluoride
    d. 1.95×10^{-10} g of hydrogen fluoride
    e. 4.61 g of ammonia

41. Calculate the number of *moles* of carbon atoms present in each of the following samples.
    a. 1.271 g of ethanol, C_2H_5OH
    b. 3.982 g of 1,4-dichlorobenzene, $C_6H_4Cl_2$
    c. 0.4438 g of carbon suboxide, C_3O_2
    d. 2.910 g of methylene chloride, CH_2Cl_2

42. Calculate the number of *moles* of sulfur atoms present in each of the following samples.
    a. 2.01 g of sodium sulfate
    b. 2.01 g of sodium sulfite
    c. 2.01 g of sodium sulfide
    d. 2.01 g of sodium thiosulfate, $Na_2S_2O_3$

9.5 ■ *Percent Composition of Compounds*

QUESTIONS

43. The mass fraction of an element present in a compound can be obtained by comparing the mass of the particular element present in 1 mol of the compound to the _____ mass of the compound.

44. The mass percentage of a given element in a compound must always be (greater/less) than 100%.

PROBLEMS

45. Calculate the percent by mass of each element in the following compounds.
    a. methane, CH_4
    b. chloromethane, CH_3Cl
    c. dichloromethane, CH_2Cl_2
    d. trichloromethane (chloroform), $CHCl_3$
    e. tetrachloromethane (carbon tetrachloride), CCl_4
    f. dichlorodifluoromethane, CCl_2F_2
    g. chlorotrifluoromethane, $CClF_3$
    h. tetrafluoromethane, CF_4

46. Calculate the percent by mass of each element in the following compounds.
    a. sodium sulfate
    b. sodium sulfite
    c. sodium sulfide
    d. sodium thiosulfate, $Na_2S_2O_3$
    e. potassium phosphate
    f. potassium hydrogen phosphate
    g. potassium dihydrogen phosphate
    h. potassium phosphide

47. Calculate the percent by mass of the element mentioned *first* in the formulas for each of the following compounds.
    a. methane, CH_4
    b. sodium nitrate
    c. carbon monoxide, CO
    d. nitrogen dioxide
    e. 1-octanol, $C_8H_{18}O$
    f. calcium phosphate
    g. 3-phenylphenol, $C_{12}H_{10}O$
    h. aluminum acetate, $Al(C_2H_3O_2)_3$

48. Calculate the percent by mass of the element listed *first* in the formulas for each of the following compounds.
    a. calcium nitride, Ca_3N_2
    b. potassium permanganate, $KMnO_4$
    c. tin(II) bromide, $SnBr_2$
    d. aluminum sulfide, Al_2S_3
    e. acetylene, C_2H_2
    f. ammonium phosphide, $(NH_4)_3P$
    g. iron(III) iodide, FeI_3
    h. tetraphosphorus decoxide, P_4O_{10}

49. Calculate the percent by mass of the element mentioned *first* in the formulas for each of the following compounds.
    a. adipic acid, $C_6H_{10}O_4$
    b. ammonium nitrate, NH_4NO_3
    c. caffeine, $C_8H_{10}N_4O_2$
    d. chlorine dioxide, ClO_2
    e. cyclohexanol, $C_6H_{11}OH$
    f. dextrose, $C_6H_{12}O_6$
    g. eicosane, $C_{20}H_{42}$
    h. ethanol, C_2H_5OH

50. Calculate the percent by mass of the element mentioned *first* in the formulas for each of the following compounds.
    a. iron(III) chloride
    b. oxygen difluoride, OF_2
    c. benzene, C_6H_6
    d. ammonium perchlorate, NH_4ClO_4
    e. silver oxide
    f. cobalt(II) chloride
    g. dinitrogen tetroxide
    h. manganese(II) chloride

51. For each of the following samples of ionic substances, calculate the number of moles and mass of the positive ions present in each sample.
    a. 4.25 g of ammonium iodide, NH_4I
    b. 6.31 mol of ammonium sulfide, $(NH_4)_2S$
    c. 9.71 g of barium phosphide, Ba_3P_2
    d. 7.63 mol of calcium phosphate, $Ca_3(PO_4)_2$

52. For each of the following ionic substances, calculate the *percentage* of the overall molar mass of the compound that is represented by the *negative ions* the compound contains.
    a. calcium phosphate
    b. cadmium sulfate
    c. iron(III) sulfate
    d. manganese(II) chloride

9.6 ■ *Formulas of Compounds*

QUESTIONS

53. What experimental evidence about a new compound must be known before its formula can be determined?

54. What does the *empirical* formula of a compound represent? How does the *molecular* formula differ from the empirical formula?

55. Give the empirical formula that corresponds to each of the following molecular formulas.
    a. sodium peroxide, Na_2O_2
    b. terephthalic acid, $C_8H_6O_4$
    c. phenobarbital, $C_{12}H_{12}N_2O_3$
    d. 1,4-dichloro-2-butene, $C_4H_6Cl_2$

56. Which of the following pairs of compounds have the same *empirical* formula?
    a. acetylene, C_2H_2, and benzene, C_6H_6
    b. ethane, C_2H_6, and butane, C_4H_{10}
    c. nitrogen dioxide, NO_2, and dinitrogen tetroxide, N_2O_4
    d. diphenyl ether, $C_{12}H_{10}O$, and phenol, C_6H_5OH

9.7 ■ Calculation of Empirical Formulas

PROBLEMS

57. A new compound has been prepared. A 0.4791-g sample was analyzed and was found to contain the following masses of elements: carbon, 0.1929 g; hydrogen, 0.01079 g; oxygen, 0.08566 g; chlorine, 0.1898 g. Determine the empirical formula of the new compound.

58. If 1.000 g of barium metal is heated in a stream of pure oxygen gas, 1.117 g of an oxide is produced. Calculate the empirical formula of the oxide.

59. A 0.5998-g sample of a new compound has been analyzed and found to contain the following masses of elements: carbon, 0.2322 g; hydrogen, 0.05848 g; oxygen, 0.3091 g. Calculate the empirical formula of the compound.

60. A compound has the following percentages by mass: barium, 58.84%; sulfur, 13.74%; oxygen, 27.43%. Determine the empirical formula of the compound.

61. When 4.008 g of calcium metal is heated in air, the sample gains 1.600 g of oxygen in forming calcium oxide. Calculate the empirical formula of calcium oxide.

62. Analysis of a certain compound yielded the following percentages of the elements by mass: nitrogen, 29.16%; hydrogen, 8.392%; carbon, 12.50%; oxygen, 49.95%. Determine the empirical formula of the compound.

63. When 3.269 g of zinc is heated in pure oxygen, the sample gains 0.800 g of oxygen in forming the oxide. Calculate the empirical formula of zinc oxide.

64. If cobalt metal is mixed with excess sulfur and heated strongly, a sulfide is produced that contains 55.06% cobalt by mass. Calculate the empirical formula of the sulfide.

65. When 1.916 g of titanium is strongly heated in a stream of pure oxygen, an oxide sample weighing 3.196 g results. Calculate the empirical formula of the oxide.

66. If 10.00 g of copper metal is heated strongly in the air, the sample gains 2.52 g of oxygen in forming an oxide. Determine the empirical formula of this oxide.

67. A compound used in the nuclear industry has the following composition: uranium, 67.61%; fluorine, 32.39%. Determine the empirical formula of the compound.

68. A compound has the following percentages by mass: aluminum, 32.13%; fluorine, 67.87%. Calculate the empirical formula of the compound.

69. A compound has the following percentage composition by mass: copper, 33.88%; nitrogen, 14.94%; oxygen, 51.18%. Determine the empirical formula of the compound.

70. When lithium metal is heated strongly in an atmosphere of pure nitrogen, the product contains 59.78% Li and 40.22% N on a mass basis. Determine the empirical formula of the compound.

71. A compound has been analyzed and has been found to have the following composition: copper, 66.75%; phosphorus, 10.84%; oxygen, 22.41%. Determine the empirical formula of the compound.

72. A compound was analyzed and found to have the following percentage composition: aluminum, 15.77%; sulfur, 28.11%; oxygen, 56.12%. Calculate the empirical formula of the compound.

73. A mercury(I) salt has the following composition by mass: mercury, 80.69%; sulfur, 6.436%; oxygen, 12.87%. Determine the empirical formula of the salt.

74. A compound consists of 21.60% Na, 33.31% Cl, and 45.09% O on a mass basis. Determine the empirical formula of the compound.

9.8 ■ Calculation of Molecular Formulas

QUESTIONS

75. How does the *molecular* formula of a compound differ from the empirical formula? Can a compound's empirical and molecular formulas be the same? Explain.

76. What information do we need to determine the molecular formula of a compound if we know only the empirical formula?

PROBLEMS

77. A compound with the empirical formula CH_2O was found to have a molar mass between 89 and 91 g. What is the molecular formula of the compound?

78. A compound with empirical formula CH was found by experiment to have a molar mass of approximately 78. What is the molecular formula of the compound?

79. A compound with the empirical formula CH_2 was found to have a molar mass of approximately 84 g. What is the molecular formula of the compound?

80. A compound with the empirical formula NO_2 was found to have a molar mass of 92 g. What is the molecular formula of the compound?

81. A compound having an approximate molar mass of 165–170 g has the following percentage composition by mass: carbon, 42.87%; hydrogen, 3.598%; oxygen, 28.55%; nitrogen, 25.00%. Determine the empirical and molecular formulas of the compound.

82. A compound consists of 65.45% C, 5.492% H, and 29.06% O on a mass basis and has a molar mass of approximately 110. Determine the molecular formula of the compound.

Additional Problems

83. Use the periodic table inside the front cover of this text to determine the atomic mass (per mole) or molar mass of each of the substances in column 1, and find that mass in column 2.

Column 1	Column 2
(1) molybdenum	(a) 33.99g
(2) lanthanum	(b) 79.9 g
(3) carbon tetrabromide	(c) 95.94 g
(4) mercury(II) oxide	(d) 125.84 g
(5) titanium(IV) oxide	(e) 138.9 g
(6) manganese(II) chloride	(f) 143.1 g
(7) phosphine, PH_3	(g) 156.7 g
(8) tin(II) fluoride	(h) 216.6 g
(9) lead(II) sulfide	(i) 239.3 g
(10) copper(I) oxide	(j) 331.6 g

84. Complete the following table.

Mass of sample	Moles of sample	Atoms in sample
5.00 g Al	_____	_____
_____	0.00250 mol Fe	_____
_____	_____	2.6×10^{24} atoms Cu
0.00250 g Mg	_____	_____
_____	2.7×10^{-3} mol Na	_____
_____	_____	1.00×10^4 atoms U

85. Complete the following table.

Mass of sample	Moles of sample	Molecules in sample
2.98 g N_2O_4	_____	_____
_____	0.050 mol CO_2	_____
0.3049 g $C_6H_5O_4$	_____	4.8×10^{25} molecules $SiCl_4$
_____	2.1×10^{-2} mol C_2F_4	_____
_____	_____	1 million molecules C_2H_5OH

86. Consider a hypothetical compound composed of elements X, Y, and Z with the empirical formula X_2YZ_3. Given that the atomic masses of X, Y, and Z are 41.2, 57.7, and 63.9, respectively, calculate the percentage composition by mass of the compound. If the molecular formula of the compound is found by molar mass determination to be actually $X_4Y_2Z_6$, what is the percentage of each element present? Explain your results.

87. A binary compound of magnesium and nitrogen is analyzed, and 1.2791 g of the compound is found to contain 0.9240 g of magnesium. When a second sample of this compound is treated with water and heated, the nitrogen is driven off as ammonia, leaving a compound that contains 60.31% magnesium and 39.69% oxygen by mass. Calculate the empirical formulas of the two magnesium compounds.

88. When a 2.118-g sample of copper is heated in an atmosphere in which the amount of oxygen present is restricted, the sample gains 0.2666 g of oxygen in forming a reddish brown oxide. However, when 2.118 g of copper is heated in a stream of pure oxygen, the sample gains 0.5332 g of oxygen. Calculate the empirical formulas of the two oxides of copper.

89. Nitrogen and oxygen combine under different conditions to give a series of binary compounds: N_2O, NO, NO_2, N_2O_4. Calculate the percent by mass of nitrogen in each.

90. Calculate the number of atoms of each element present in each of the following samples.
    a. 2.37 g of lead(II) nitrate
    b. 22.4 g of elemental oxygen
    c. 101.9 mg of elemental sulfur, S_8
    d. 43.7 μg of uranium(VI) fluoride

91. Calculate the mass in grams of each of the following samples.
    a. 10,000,000,000 nitrogen molecules
    b. 2.49×10^{20} carbon dioxide molecules
    c. 7.0983 mol of sodium chloride
    d. 9.012×10^{-6} mol of 1,2-dichloroethane, $C_2H_4Cl_2$

92. Calculate the mass of carbon in grams, the percent carbon by mass, and the number of individual carbon atoms present in each of the following samples.

a. 7.819 g of carbon suboxide, C_3O_2
b. 1.53×10^{21} molecules of carbon monoxide
c. 0.200 mol of phenol, C_6H_6O

93. Find the item in column 2 that best explains or completes the statement or question in column 1.

Column 1
(1) 1 amu
(2) 1008 amu
(3) mass of the "average" atom of an element
(4) number of carbon atoms in 12.01 g of carbon
(5) 6.022×10^{23} molecules
(6) total mass of all atoms in 1 mol of a compound
(7) smallest whole-number ratio of atoms present in a molecule
(8) formula showing actual number of atoms present in a molecule
(9) product formed when any carbon-containing compound is burned in O_2
(10) have the same empirical formulas, but different molecular formulas

Column 2
(a) 6.022×10^{23}
(b) atomic mass
(c) mass of 1000 hydrogen atoms
(d) benzene, C_6H_6, and acetylene, C_2H_2
(e) carbon dioxide
(f) empirical formula
(g) 1.66×10^{-24} g
(h) molecular formula
(i) molar mass
(j) 1 mol

94. Calculate the number of grams of lead that contain the same number of atoms as 1.00 g of neon.

95. Calculate the number of grams of uranium that contain the same number of atoms as 1.00 g of sodium

96. Calculate the number of grams of mercury that contain the same number of atoms as 5.00 g of tellurium.

97. Calculate the number of grams of lithium that contain the same number of atoms as 1.00 kg of zirconium.

98. Given that the molar mass of carbon tetrachloride, CCl_4, is 153.8 g, calculate the mass in grams of 1 molecule of CCl_4.

99. Calculate the mass in grams of oxygen present in 1.000 g of each of the following compounds.
a. formaldehyde, CH_2O
b. barium peroxide
c. calcium carbonate
d. serine, $C_3H_7O_3N$

100. Calculate the mass in grams of nitrogen present in 5.000 g of each of the following compounds.
a. glycine, $C_2H_5O_2N$
b. magnesium nitride, Mg_3N_2
c. calcium nitrate
d. dinitrogen tetroxide

101. A strikingly beautiful copper compound with the common name "blue vitriol" has the following elemental composition: 25.45% Cu, 12.84% S, 4.036% H, 57.67% O. Determine the empirical formula of the compound.

102. A magnesium salt has the following elemental composition: 16.39% Mg, 18.89% N, 64.72% O. Determine the empirical formula of the salt.

103. The mass 1.66×10^{-24} g is equivalent to 1 _____.

104. Even though most elements consist of several isotopes, we use the _____ mass of the isotopes in most chemical calculations.

105. Using the average atomic masses given in Table 9.1, calculate the number of atoms present in each of the following samples.
a. 160,000 amu of oxygen
b. 8139.81 amu of nitrogen
c. 13,490 amu of aluminum
d. 5040 amu of hydrogen
e. 367,495.15 amu of sodium

106. If an average sodium atom weighs 22.99 amu, how many sodium atoms are contained in 1.98×10^{13} amu of sodium? What will 3.01×10^{23} sodium atoms weigh?

107. Using the average atomic masses given inside the front cover of this text, calculate how many *moles* of each element the following *masses* represent.
a. 1.5 mg of chromium
b. 2.0×10^{-3} g of strontium
c. 4.84×10^4 g of boron
d. 3.6×10^{-6} μg of californium
e. 1.0 ton (2000 lb) of iron
f. 20.4 g of barium
g. 62.8 g of cobalt

108. Using the average atomic masses given inside the front cover of this text, calculate the *mass in grams* of each of the following samples.
a. 5.0 mol of potassium
b. 0.000305 mol of mercury
c. 2.31×10^{-5} mol of manganese
d. 10.5 mol of phosphorus
e. 4.9×10^4 mol of iron
f. 125 mol of lithium
g. 0.01205 mol of fluorine

109. Using the average atomic masses given inside the front cover of this text, calculate the number of *atoms* present in each of the following samples.
    a. 2.89 g of gold
    b. 0.000259 mol of platinum
    c. 0.000259 g of platinum
    d. 2.0 lb of magnesium
    e. 1.90 mL of liquid mercury (density = 13.6 g/mL)
    f. 4.30 mol of tungsten
    g. 4.30 g of tungsten

110. Calculate the molar mass for each of the following substances.
    a. propane, C_3H_8
    b. iron(III) sulfate
    c. dinitrogen pentoxide
    d. sucrose, $C_{12}H_{22}O_{11}$
    e. ammonium carbonate
    f. barium chloride

111. Calculate the molar mass for each of the following substances.
    a. adipic acid, $C_6H_{10}O_4$
    b. caffeine, $C_8H_{10}N_4O_2$
    c. eicosane, $C_{20}H_{42}$
    d. cyclohexanol, $C_6H_{11}OH$
    e. vinyl acetate, $C_4H_6O_2$
    f. dextrose, $C_6H_{12}O_6$

112. Calculate the number of *moles* of the indicated substance present in each of the following samples.
    a. 21.2 g of ammonium sulfide
    b. 44.3 g of calcium nitrate
    c. 4.35 g of dichlorine monoxide
    d. 1.0 lb of ferric chloride
    e. 1.0 kg of ferric chloride

113. Calculate the number of *moles* of the indicated substance present in each of the following samples.
    a. 0.00056 g of potassium cyanide
    b. 1.90 mg of mescaline, $C_{11}H_{17}O_3N$
    c. 23.09 g of calcium phosphate
    d. 2.6×10^{-3} mg of rubidium oxide
    e. 6.0 μg of ammonium nitrate

114. Calculate the mass in grams of each of the following samples.
    a. 2.6×10^{-2} mol of copper(II) sulfate, $CuSO_4$
    b. 3.05×10^3 mol of tetrafluoroethylene, C_2F_4
    c. 7.83 millimol (1 millimol = 0.001 mol) of 1,4-pentadiene, C_5H_8
    d. 6.30 mol of bismuth trichloride, $BiCl_3$
    e. 12.2 mol of sucrose, $C_{12}H_{22}O_{11}$

115. Calculate the mass in grams of each of the following samples.
    a. 3.09 mol of ammonium carbonate
    b. 4.01×10^{-6} mol of sodium hydrogen carbonate
    c. 88.02 mol of carbon dioxide
    d. 1.29 millimol of silver nitrate
    e. 0.0024 mol of chromium(III) chloride

116. Calculate the number of *molecules* present in each of the following samples.
    a. 3.45 g of $C_6H_{12}O_6$
    b. 3.45 mol of $C_6H_{12}O_6$
    c. 25.0 g of ICl_5
    d. 1.00 g of B_2H_6
    e. 1.05 millimol of $Al(NO_3)_3$

117. Calculate the number of moles of oxygen atoms present in each of the following samples.
    a. 1.002 g of phenol, C_6H_6O
    b. 4.901 g of sodium peroxide
    c. 124.5 mg of *p*-aminobenzoic acid, $C_7H_7O_2N$
    d. 9.821 g of aluminum nitrate

118. Calculate the percent by mass of each element in the following compounds.
    a. calcium phosphate
    b. cadmium sulfate
    c. iron(III) sulfate
    d. manganese(II) chloride
    e. ammonium carbonate
    f. sodium hydrogen carbonate
    g. carbon dioxide
    h. silver(I) nitrate

119. Calculate the percent by mass of the element mentioned *first* in the formulas for each of the following compounds.
    a. propane, C_3H_8
    b. potassium chlorate, $KClO_3$
    c. dinitrogen pentoxide, N_2O_5
    d. sucrose, $C_{12}H_{22}O_{11}$
    e. ammonium fluoride, NH_4F
    f. sodium perchlorate, $NaClO_4$
    g. ammonium carbonate, $(NH_4)_2CO_3$
    h. barium chloride, $BaCl_2$

120. Calculate the percent by mass of the element mentioned *first* in the formulas for each of the following compounds.
    a. iron(II) sulfate
    b. silver(I) oxide
    c. strontium chloride
    d. vinyl acetate, $C_4H_6O_2$
    e. methanol, CH_3OH
    f. aluminum oxide
    g. potassium chlorite
    h. potassium chloride

121. A 1.2569-g sample of a new compound has been analyzed and found to contain the following masses of elements: carbon, 0.7238 g; hydrogen, 0.07088 g; nitrogen, 0.1407 g; oxygen, 0.3214 g. Calculate the empirical formula of the compound.

122. A 0.7221-g sample of a new compound has been analyzed and found to contain the following masses of elements: carbon, 0.2990 g; hydrogen, 0.05849 g; nitrogen, 0.2318 g; oxygen, 0.1328 g. Calculate the empirical formula of the compound.

123. When 2.004 g of calcium is heated in pure nitrogen gas, the sample gains 0.4670 g of nitrogen. Calculate the empirical formula of the calcium nitride formed.

124. When 4.01 g of mercury is strongly heated in air, the resulting oxide weighs 4.33 g. Calculate the empirical formula of the oxide.

125. When 1.00 g of metallic chromium is heated with elemental chlorine gas, 3.045 g of a chromium chloride salt results. Calculate the empirical formula of the compound.

126. When barium metal is heated in chlorine gas, a binary compound forms that consists of 65.95% Ba and 34.05% Cl by mass. Calculate the empirical formula of the compound.

Chemical Quantities

Suppose you work for a consumer advocate organization and you want to test a company's advertising claims about the effectiveness of its antacid. The company claims that its product neutralizes 10 times as much stomach acid per tablet as its nearest competitor. How would you test the validity of this claim?

Or suppose that after graduation you go to work for a chemical company that makes methanol (methyl alcohol), a substance used as a starting material for the manufacture of products such as antifreeze and aviation fuels and as a fuel in the cars that race in the Indianapolis 500 (see "Chemistry in Focus" on p. 272). You are working with an experienced chemist who is trying to improve the company's process for making methanol from the reaction of gaseous hydrogen with carbon

The ammonium dichromate decomposition looks like a volcano erupting (left). *Methanol is a starting material for some jet fuels* (right).

More than 10 *billion* pounds of methanol are produced annually.

monoxide gas. The first day on the job, you are instructed to order enough hydrogen and carbon monoxide to produce 6.0 kg of methanol in a test run. How would you determine how much carbon monoxide and hydrogen you should order?

After you study this chapter, you will be able to answer these questions.

10.1 Information Given by Chemical Equations

AIM: To understand the molecular and mass information given in a balanced equation.

Reactions are what chemistry is really all about. Recall that chemical changes are really rearrangements of atom groupings that can be described by chemical equations. In this section we will review the meaning and usefulness of chemical equations by considering one of the process mentioned in the introduction: the reaction between gaseous carbon monoxide and hydrogen to produce liquid methanol, $CH_3OH(l)$. The reactants and products are

$$\text{Unbalanced: } \underset{\text{Reactants}}{CO(g) + H_2(g)} \rightarrow \underset{\text{Product}}{CH_3OH(l)}$$

Because atoms are just rearranged (not gained or lost) in a chemical reaction, we must always balance a chemical equation. That is, we must choose coefficients that give the same number of each type of atom on both sides. Using the smallest set of integers that satisfies this condition gives the balanced equation

$$\text{Balanced: } CO(g) + 2H_2(g) \rightarrow CH_3OH(l)$$

Check: Reactants: 1 C, 1 O, 4 H; Products: 1 C, 1 O, 4 H

It is important to recognize that the coefficients in a balanced equation give the *relative* numbers of molecules. That is, we could multiply this balanced equation by any number and still have a balanced equation. For example, we could multiply by 12:

$$12[CO(g) + 2H_2(g) \rightarrow CH_3OH(l)]$$

to obtain

$$12CO(g) + 24H_2(g) \rightarrow 12CH_3OH(l)$$

This is still a balanced equation (check to be sure). Because 12 represents a dozen, we could even describe the reaction in terms of dozens:

$$1 \text{ dozen } CO(g) + 2 \text{ dozen } H_2(g) \rightarrow 1 \text{ dozen } CH_3OH(l)$$

We could also multiply the original equation by a very large number, such as 6.022×10^{23}:

$$6.022 \times 10^{23}[CO(g) + {>}2H_2(g) \rightarrow CH_3OH(l)]$$

TABLE 10.1

Information Conveyed by the Balanced Equation for the Production of Methanol

$CO(g)$	+	$2H_2(g)$	→	$CH_3OH(l)$
1 molecule CO	+	2 molecules H_2	→	1 molecule CH_3OH
1 dozen CO molecules	+	2 dozen H_2 molecules	→	1 dozen CH_3OH molecules
6.022×10^{23} CO molecules	+	$2(6.022 \times 10^{23})$ H_2 molecules	→	6.022×10^{23} CH_3OH molecules
1 mol CO molecules	+	2 mol H_2 molecules	→	1 mol CH_3OH molecules

which leads to the equation

$$6.022 \times 10^{23} \, CO(g) + 2(6.022 \times 10^{23})H_2(g) \rightarrow 6.022 \times 10^{23} \, CH_3OH(l)$$

One mole is 6.022×10^{23} units.

Just as 12 is called a dozen, chemists call 6.022×10^{23} a *mole* (abbreviated mol). Our equation, then, can be written in terms of moles:

$$1 \text{ mol } CO(g) + 2 \text{ mol } H_2(g) \rightarrow 1 \text{ mol } CH_3OH(l)$$

Various ways of interpreting this balanced chemical equation are given in Table 10.1.

EXAMPLE 10.1   *Relating Moles to Molecules in Chemical Equations*

Propane, C_3H_8, is a fuel commonly used for cooking on gas grills and for heating in rural areas where natural gas is unavailable. Propane reacts with oxygen gas to produce heat and the products carbon dioxide and water. This combustion reaction is represented by the unbalanced equation

$$C_3H_8(g) + O_2(g) \rightarrow CO_2(g) + H_2O(g)$$

Give the balanced equation for this reaction, and state the meaning of the equation in terms of numbers of molecules and moles of molecules.

Solution

Using the techniques explained in Chapter 6, we can balance the equation.

$$C_3H_8(g) + 5O_2(g) \rightarrow 3CO_2(g) + 4H_2O(g)$$

Check: 3 C, 8 H, 10 O   → 3 C, 8 H, 10 O

This equation can be interpreted in terms of molecules as follows:

1 molecule of C_3H_8 reacts with 5 molecules of O_2 to give 3 molecules of CO_2 plus 4 molecules of H_2O

or as follows in terms of moles (of molecules):

1 mol of C_3H_8 reacts with 5 mol of O_2 to give 3 mol of CO_2 plus 4 mol of H_2O

Tanks for storing propane, a fuel often used when natural gas is unavailable.

10.2 *Mole–Mole Relationships*

AIM: To learn to use a balanced equation to determine relationships between moles of reactants and moles of products.

Now that we have discussed the meaning of a balanced chemical equation in terms of moles of reactants and products, we can use an equation to predict the moles of products that a given number of moles of reactants will yield. For example, consider the decomposition of water to give hydrogen and oxygen, which is represented by the following balanced equation:

$$2H_2O(l) \rightarrow 2H_2(g) + O_2(g)$$

This equation tells us that 2 mol of H_2O yields 2 mol of H_2 and 1 mol of O_2.

Now suppose that we have 4 mol of water. If we decompose 4 mol of water, how many moles of products do we get?

One way to answer this question is to multiply the entire equation by 2 (that will give us 4 mol of H_2O).

$$2[2H_2O(l) \rightarrow 2H_2(g) + O_2(g)]$$
$$4H_2O(l) \rightarrow 4H_2(g) + 2O_2(g)$$

Now we can state that

4 mol of H_2O yields 4 mol of H_2 plus 2 mol of O_2

which answers the question of how many moles of products we get with 4 mol of H_2O.

Next, suppose we decompose 5.8 mol of water. What numbers of moles of products are formed in this process? We could answer this question by re-balancing the chemical equation as follows: First, we divide *all coefficients* of the balanced equation

$$2H_2O(l) \rightarrow 2H_2(g) + O_2(g)$$

by 2, to give

$$H_2O(l) \rightarrow H_2(g) + \tfrac{1}{2}O_2(g)$$

Now, because we have 5.8 mol of H_2O, we multiply this equation by 5.8.

$$5.8[H_2O(l) \rightarrow H_2(g) + \tfrac{1}{2}O_2(g)]$$

This gives

$$5.8H_2O(l) \rightarrow 5.8H_2(g) + 5.8(\tfrac{1}{2})O_2(g)$$

$$5.8H_2O(l) \rightarrow 5.8H_2(g) + 2.9O_2(g)$$

This equation with noninteger coefficients makes sense only if the equation means moles (of molecules) of the various reactants and products.

(Verify that this is a balanced equation.) Now we can state that

5.8 mol of H_2O yields 5.8 mol of H_2 plus 2.9 mol of O_2

This procedure of rebalancing the equation to obtain the number of moles involved in a particular situation always works, but it can be cumbersome. In Example 10.2 we will develop a more convenient procedure, which uses conversion factors, or **mole ratios,** based on the balanced chemical equation.

EXAMPLE 10.2 *Determining Mole Ratios*

What number of moles of O_2 will be produced by the decomposition of 5.8 mol of water?

Solution

Our problem can be diagrammed as follows:

| 5.8 mol H_2O | yields | ? mol of O_2 |

To answer this question, we need to know the relationship between moles of H_2O and moles of O_2 in the balanced equation (conventional form):

$$2H_2O(l) \rightarrow 2H_2(g) + O_2(g)$$

From this equation we can state that

| 2 mol H_2O | yields | 1 mol O_2 |

which can be represented by the following equivalence statement:

$$2 \text{ mol } H_2O = 1 \text{ mol } O_2$$

The statement 2 mol H_2O = >1 mol O_2 is obviously not true in a literal sense, but it correctly expresses the chemical equivalence between H_2O and O_2.

We now want to use this equivalence statement to obtain the conversion factor (mole ratio) that we need. Because we want to go from moles of H_2O to moles of O_2, we need the mole ratio

$$\frac{1 \text{ mol } O_2}{2 \text{ mol } H_2O}$$

so that mol H_2O will cancel in the conversion from moles of H_2O to moles of O_2.

$$5.8 \text{ mol } H_2O \times \frac{1 \text{ mol } O_2}{2 \text{ mol } H_2O} = 2.9 \text{ mol } O_2$$

So if we decompose 5.8 mol of H_2O, we will get 2.9 mol of O_2. Note that this is the same answer we obtained above when we rebalanced the equation to give

$$5.8H_2O(l) \rightarrow 5.8H_2(g) + 2.9O_2(g)$$

We saw in Example 10.2 that to determine the moles of a product that can be formed from a specified number of moles of a reactant, we can use the balanced equation to obtain the appropriate mole ratio. We will now extend these ideas in Example 10.3.

EXAMPLE 10.3 *Using Mole Ratios in Calculations*

Calculate the number of moles of oxygen required to react exactly with 4.30 mol of propane, C_3H_8, in the reaction described by the following balanced equation:

$$C_3H_8(g) + 5O_2(g) \rightarrow 3CO_2(g) + 4H_2O(g)$$

Solution

In this case the problem can be stated as follows:

| 4.30 mol of C_3H_8 | requires | ? mol of O_2 |

To solve this problem, we need to consider the relationship between the reactants C_3H_8 and O_2. Using the balanced equation, we find that

1 mol of C_3H_8 requires 5 mol of O_2

which can be represented by the equivalence statement

1 mol C_3H_8 = 5 mol O_2

This leads to the required mole ratio

$$\frac{5 \text{ mol } O_2}{1 \text{ mol } C_3H_8}$$

for converting from moles of C_3H_8 to moles of O_2. We construct the conversion ratio this way so that mol C_3H_8 cancels:

$$4.30 \text{ mol } C_3H_8 \times \frac{5 \text{ mol } O_2}{1 \text{ mol } C_3H_8} = 21.5 \text{ mol } O_2$$

We can now answer the original question:

4.30 mol of C_3H_8 requires 21.5 mol of O_2

 Self-Check Exercise 10.1

Calculate the moles of CO_2 formed when 4.30 mol of C_3H_8 react with the required 21.5 mol of O_2.

Hint: Use the moles of C_3H_8, and obtain the mole ratio between C_3H_8 and CO_2 from the balanced equation.

See Problems 10.15 and 10.16.

10.3 *Mass Calculations*

AIM: To learn to relate masses of reactants and products in a chemical reaction.

In the last section we saw how to use the balanced equation for a reaction to calculate the numbers of moles of reactants and products for a particular case. However, moles represent numbers of molecules, and we cannot count molecules directly. In chemistry we count by weighing. Therefore, in this section we will review the procedures for converting between moles and masses and will see how these procedures are applied to chemical calculations.

To develop these procedures we will consider the reaction between powdered aluminum metal and finely ground iodine to produce aluminum iodide. The balanced equation for this vigorous chemical reaction is

$$2Al(s) + 3I_2(s) \rightarrow 2AlI_3(s)$$

Suppose we have 35.0 g of aluminum. What mass of I_2 should we weigh out to react exactly with this amount of aluminum?

To answer this question we need to think about what the balanced equation tells us. The equation states that

2 mol of Al requires 3 mol of I_2

which leads to the mole ratio

$$\frac{3 \text{ mol } I_2}{2 \text{ mol Al}}$$

We can use this ratio to calculate the moles of I_2 needed:

$$\text{Moles of Al present} \times \frac{3 \text{ mol } I_2}{2 \text{ mol Al}} = \text{moles of } I_2 \text{ required}$$

This leads us to the question: how many moles of Al are present? The problem states that we have 35.0 g of aluminum, so we must convert from grams to moles of aluminum. This is something we already know how to do. Using the table of average atomic masses inside the front cover of this book, we find the atomic mass of aluminum to be 26.98. This means that 1 mol of aluminum has a mass of 26.98 g. We can use the equivalence statement

1 mol Al = 26.98 g

to find the moles of Al in 35.0 g.

$$35.0 \text{ g Al} \times \frac{1 \text{ mol Al}}{26.98 \text{ g Al}} = 1.30 \text{ mol Al}$$

Now that we have moles of Al, we can find the moles of I_2 required.

$$1.30 \text{ mol Al} \times \frac{3 \text{ mol } I_2}{2 \text{ mol Al}} = 1.95 \text{ mol } I_2$$

We now know the *moles* of I_2 required to react with the 1.30 mol of Al (35.0 g). The next step is to convert 1.95 mol of I_2 to grams so we will know how much to weigh out. We do this by using the molar mass of I_2. The atomic mass of iodine is 126.9 g (for 1 mol of I atoms), so the molar mass of I_2 is

$$2 \times 126.9 \text{ g/mol} = 253.8 \text{ g/mol} = \text{mass of 1 mol of } I_2$$

Now we convert the 1.95 mol of I_2 to grams of I_2.

$$1.95 \text{ mol } I_2 \times \frac{253.8 \text{ g } I_2}{\text{mol } I_2} = 495 \text{ g } I_2$$

We have solved the problem. We need to weigh out 495 g of iodine (contains I_2 molecules) to react exactly with the 35.0 g of aluminum. We will further develop procedures for dealing with masses of reactants and products in Example 10.4.

Remember that to show the correct significant figures in each step, we are rounding off after each calculation. In doing problems, you should carry extra numbers, rounding off only at the end.

EXAMPLE 10.4 *Using Mass–Mole Conversions with Mole Ratios*

Propane, C_3H_8, when used as a fuel, reacts with oxygen to produce carbon dioxide and water according to the following unbalanced equation:

$$C_3H_8(g) \; + \; O_2(g) \; \rightarrow \; CO_2(g) \; + \; H_2O(g)$$

What mass of oxygen will be required to react exactly with 96.1 g of propane?

Solution

Always balance the equation for the reaction first.

To deal with the amounts of reactants and products, we first need the balanced equation for this reaction:

$$C_3H_8(g) \; + \; 5O_2(g) \; \rightarrow \; 3CO_2(g) \; + \; 4H_2O(g)$$

Next, let's summarize what we know and what we want to find.

What we know:

- The balanced equation for the reaction
- The mass of propane available (96.1 g)

What we want to calculate:

- The mass of oxygen (O_2) required to react exactly with all the propane

Our problem, in schematic form, is

Using the ideas we developed when we discussed the aluminum–iodine reaction, we will proceed as follows:

1. We are given the number of grams of propane, so we must convert to moles of propane (C_3H_8).

2. Then we can use the coefficients in the balanced equation to determine the moles of oxygen (O_2) required.

3. Finally, we will use the molar mass of O_2 to calculate grams of oxygen.

We can sketch this strategy as follows:

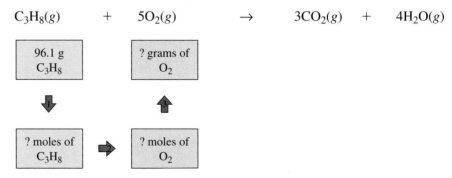

Thus the first question we must answer is *How many moles of propane are present in 96.1 g of propane?* The molar mass of propane is 44.09 g

$(3 \times 12.01 + 8 \times 1.008)$. The moles of propane present can be calculated as follows:

$$96.1 \text{ g } \cancel{C_3H_8} \times \frac{1 \text{ mol } C_3H_8}{44.09 \text{ g } \cancel{C_3H_8}} = 2.18 \text{ mol } C_3H_8$$

➡ Next we recognize that each mole of propane reacts with 5 mol of oxygen. This gives us the equivalence statement

$$1 \text{ mol } C_3H_8 = 5 \text{ mol } O_2$$

from which we construct the mole ratio

$$\frac{5 \text{ mol } O_2}{1 \text{ mol } C_3H_8}$$

that we need to convert from moles of propane molecules to moles of oxygen molecules.

$$2.18 \text{ } \cancel{\text{mol } C_3H_8} \times \frac{5 \text{ mol } O_2}{1 \text{ } \cancel{\text{mol } C_3H_8}} = 10.9 \text{ mol } O_2$$

Notice that the mole ratio is set up so that the moles of C_3H_8 cancel and the resulting units are moles of O_2.

➡ Because the original question asked for the *mass* of oxygen needed to react with 96.1 g of propane, we must convert the 10.9 mol of O_2 to grams, using the molar mass of O_2 ($32.00 = 2 \times 16.00$).

$$10.9 \text{ } \cancel{\text{mol } O_2} \times \frac{32.0 \text{ g } O_2}{1 \text{ } \cancel{\text{mol } O_2}} = 349 \text{ g } O_2$$

Therefore, 349 g of oxygen is required to burn 96.1 g of propane. We can summarize this problem by writing out a "conversion string" that shows how the problem was done.

$$96.1 \text{ g } C_3H_8 \times \frac{1 \text{ } \cancel{\text{mol } C_3H_8}}{44.09 \text{ g } \cancel{C_3H_8}} \times \frac{5 \text{ } \cancel{\text{mol } O_2}}{1 \text{ } \cancel{\text{mol } C_3H_8}} \times \frac{32.0 \text{ g } O_2}{1 \text{ mol } O_2} = 349 \text{ g } O_2$$

This is a convenient way to make sure the final units are correct. The procedure we have followed is summarized below.

Use units as a check to see that you have used the correct conversion factors (mole ratios).

$$C_3H_8(g) \quad + \quad 5O_2(g) \rightarrow 3CO_2(g) + H_2O(g)$$

| 96.1 g C_3H_8 | 349 g O_2 |

Use molar mass of C_3H_8 (44.09 g)   Use molar mass of O_2 (32.0 g)

| 2.18 mol C_3H_8 | Use mole ratio: $\dfrac{5 \text{ mol } O_2}{1 \text{ mol } C_3H_8}$ | 10.9 mol O_2 |

Self-Check Exercise 10.2

What mass of carbon dioxide is produced when 96.1 g of propane react with sufficient oxygen?

See Problems 10.23 through 10.26.

 Self-Check Exercise 10.3

Calculate the mass of water formed by the complete reaction of 96.1 g of propane with oxygen.

See Problems 10.23 through 10.26.

So far in this chapter, we have spent considerable time "thinking through" the procedures for calculating the masses of reactants and products in chemical reactions. We can summarize these procedures in the following steps:

Steps for Calculating the Masses of Reactants and Products in Chemical Reactions

STEP 1 Balance the equation for the reaction.

STEP 2 If amounts are given as masses, convert the known masses of reactants or products to moles.

STEP 3 Use the balanced equation to set up the appropriate mole ratio(s).

STEP 4 Use the mole ratio(s) to calculate the number of moles of the desired reactant or product.

STEP 5 Convert from moles back to mass, if this is required by the problem.

The process of using a chemical equation to calculate the relative masses of reactants and products involved in a reaction is called **stoichiometry** (pronounced stoý·kē·oḿ·ĕtry). Chemists say that the balanced equation for a chemical reaction describes the stoichiometry of the reaction.

We will now consider a few more examples that involve chemical stoichiometry. Because real-world examples often involve very large or very small masses of chemicals that are most conveniently expressed by using scientific notation, we will deal with such a case in Example 10.5.

 EXAMPLE 10.5   *Stoichiometric Calculations: Using Scientific Notation*

For a review of writing formulas of ionic compounds, see Chapter 5.

Solid lithium hydroxide is used in space vehicles to remove exhaled carbon dioxide from the living environment. The products are solid lithium carbonate and liquid water. What mass of gaseous carbon dioxide can 1.00×10^3 g of lithium hydroxide absorb?

Astronaut Sidney M. Gutierrez changes the lithium hydroxide cannisters on Space Shuttle *Columbia*. The lithium hydroxide is used to purge carbon dioxide from the air in the shuttle's cabin.

Carrying extra significant figures and rounding off only at the end gives an answer of 919 g CO_2.

Solution

STEP 1 Using the description of the reaction, we can write the unbalanced equation

$$LiOH(s) + CO_2(g) \rightarrow Li_2CO_3(s) + H_2O(l)$$

The balanced equation is

$$2LiOH(s) + CO_2(g) \rightarrow Li_2CO_3(s) + H_2O(l)$$

Check this for yourself.

STEP 2 We convert the given mass of LiOH to moles, using the molar mass of LiOH, which is 6.941 g + 16.00 g + 1.008 g = 23.95 g.

$$1.00 \times 10^3 \text{g LiOH} \times \frac{1 \text{ mol LiOH}}{23.95 \text{ g LiOH}} = 41.8 \text{ mol LiOH}$$

STEP 3 The appropriate mole ratio is

$$\frac{1 \text{ mol } CO_2}{2 \text{ mol LiOH}}$$

STEP 4 Using this mole ratio, we calculate the moles of CO_2 needed to react with the given mass of LiOH.

$$41.8 \text{ mol LiOH} \times \frac{1 \text{ mol } CO_2}{2 \text{ mol LiOH}} = 20.9 \text{ mol } CO_2$$

STEP 5 We calculate the mass of CO_2 by using its molar mass (44.01 g).

$$20.9 \text{ mol } CO_2 \times \frac{44.01 \text{ g } CO_2}{1 \text{ mol } CO_2} = 920. \text{ g } CO_2 = 9.20 \times 10^2 \text{ g } CO_2$$

Thus 1.00×10^3 g of LiOH(s) can absorb 920. g of $CO_2(g)$. We can summarize this problem as follows:

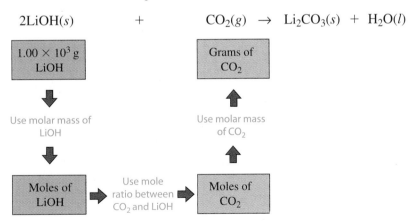

$$2LiOH(s) + CO_2(g) \rightarrow Li_2CO_3(s) + H_2O(l)$$

The conversion string is

$$1.00 \times 10^3 \text{ g LiOH} \times \frac{1 \text{ mol LiOH}}{23.95 \text{ g LiOH}} \times \frac{1 \text{ mol } CO_2}{2 \text{ mol LiOH}} \times \frac{44.01 \text{ g } CO_2}{1 \text{ mol } CO_2}$$

$$= 9.20 \times 10^2 \text{ g } CO_2$$

CHEMISTRY IN FOCUS

Methyl Alcohol: Fuel with a Future?

Southern California is famous for many things, and among them, unfortunately, is smog. Smog is produced when pollutants in the air are trapped near the ground and are caused to react by sunlight. One step being considered by the state of California to help solve the smog problem is to replace gasoline with methyl alcohol (usually called methanol). One advantage of methanol is that it reacts more nearly completely than gasoline with oxygen in a car's engine, thus releasing lower amounts of unburned fuel into the atmosphere. Methanol also produces less carbon monoxide (CO) in the exhaust than does gasoline. Carbon monoxide not only is toxic itself but also encourages the formation of nitrogen dioxide by the reaction

$$CO(g) + O_2(g) + NO(g) \rightarrow$$
$$CO_2(g) + NO_2(g)$$

Nitrogen dioxide is a reddish brown gas that leads to ozone formation and acid rain.

Using methanol as a fuel is not a new idea. For example, it is the only fuel allowed in the open-wheeled race cars used in the Indianapolis 500 and in similar races. Methanol works very well in racing engines because it has outstanding antiknock characteristics, even at the tremendous speeds at which these engines operate (around 11,000 revolutions per minute).

A crewman adds methanol fuel to a race car in the Indianapolis 500 during a pit stop.

The news about methanol is not all good, however. One problem is lower fuel mileage. Because it takes about twice as many gallons of methanol as gasoline to travel a given distance, a methanol-powered car's fuel tank must be twice the usual size. However, although costs vary greatly depending on market conditions, the cost of methanol averages about half that of gasoline, so the net cost is about the same for both fuels.

A second disadvantage of methanol is that its high affinity for water causes condensation from the air, which leads to increased corrosion of the fuel tank and fuel lines. This problem can be solved by using more expensive stainless steel for these parts.

The most serious problem with methanol may be its tendency to form formaldehyde, HCHO, when it is combusted. Formaldehyde has been implicated as a carcinogen (a substance that causes cancer). Formaldehyde can also lead to ozone formation in the air, which causes even more severe smog. Researchers are now working on catalytic converters for exhaust systems to help decompose the formaldehyde.

To test the feasibility of methanol as a motor fuel, California has operated several hundred vehicles on methanol since 1980. Because accessibility to methanol is limited, cars are now being prepared that can run on methanol or gasoline. These vehicles will soon be tested on a large scale in California. So if you live in southern California, in a few years your neighborhood "gas station" may actually be pumping methanol.

 Self-Check Exercise 10.4

Hydrofluoric acid, an aqueous solution containing dissolved hydrogen fluoride, is used to etch glass by reacting with the silica, SiO_2, in the glass to produce gaseous silicon tetrafluoride and liquid water. The unbalanced

equation is

$$HF(aq) + SiO_2(s) \rightarrow SiF_4(g) + H_2O(l)$$

a. Calculate the mass of hydrogen fluoride needed to react with 5.68 g of silica. *Hint:* Think carefully about this problem. What is the balanced equation for the reaction? What is given? What do you need to calculate? Sketch a map of the problem before you do the calculations.

b. Calculate the mass of water produced in the reaction described in part a.

See Problems 10.23 through 10.26.

EXAMPLE 10.6 *Stoichiometric Calculations: Comparing Two Reactions*

Baking soda, $NaHCO_3$, is often used as an antacid. It neutralizes excess hydrochloric acid secreted by the stomach. The balanced equation for the reaction is

$$NaHCO_3(s) + HCl(aq) \rightarrow NaCl(aq) + H_2O(l) + CO_2(g)$$

Milk of magnesia, which is an aqueous suspension of magnesium hydroxide, $Mg(OH)_2$, is also used as an antacid. The balanced equation for the reaction is

$$Mg(OH)_2(s) + 2HCl(aq) \rightarrow 2H_2O(l) + MgCl_2aq)$$

Which antacid can consume the most stomach acid, 1.00 g of $NaHCO_3$ or 1.00 g of $Mg(OH)_2$?

Solution

Before we begin, let's think about the problem to be solved. The question we must ask for each antacid is *How many moles of HCl will react with 1.00 g of each antacid?* The antacid that reacts with the larger number of moles of HCl is more effective because it will neutralize more moles of acid. A schematic for this procedure is

Notice that in this case we do not need to calculate how many grams of HCl react; we can answer the question with moles of HCl. We will now solve this problem for each antacid. Both of the equations are balanced, so we can proceed with the calculations.

Using the molar mass of $NaHCO_3$, which is 22.99 g + 1.008 g + 12.01 g + 3(16.00 g) = 84.01 g, we determine the moles of $NaHCO_3$ in 1.00 g of $NaHCO_3$.

$$1.00 \text{ g NaHCO}_3 \times \frac{1 \text{ mol NaHCO}_3}{84.01 \text{ g NaHCO}_3} = 0.0119 \text{ mol NaHCO}_3$$

$$= 1.19 \times 10^{-2} \text{ mol NaHCO}_3$$

Next we determine the moles of HCl, using the mole ratio $\dfrac{1 \text{ mol HCl}}{1 \text{ mol NaHCO}_3}$.

$$1.19 \times 10^{-2} \text{ mol NaHCO}_3 \times \frac{1 \text{ mol HCl}}{1 \text{ mol NaHCO}_3} = 1.19 \times 10^{-2} \text{ mol HCl}$$

Thus 1.00 g of $NaHCO_3$ neutralizes 1.19×10^{-2} mol of HCl. We need to compare this to the number of moles of HCl that 1.00 g of $Mg(OH)_2$ neutralizes.

Using the molar mass of $Mg(OH)_2$, which is 24.31 g + 2(16.00 g) + 2(1.008 g) = 58.33 g, we determine the moles of $Mg(OH)_2$ in 1.00 g of $Mg(OH)_2$.

$$1.00 \text{ g Mg(OH)}_2 \times \frac{1 \text{ mol Mg(OH)}_2}{58.33 \text{ g Mg(OH)}_2} = 0.0171 \text{ mol Mg(OH)}_2$$

$$= 1.71 \times 10^{-2} \text{ mol Mg(OH)}_2$$

To determine the moles of HCl that react with this amount of $Mg(OH)_2$, we use the mole ratio $\dfrac{2 \text{ mol HCl}}{1 \text{ mol Mg(OH)}_2}$.

$$1.71 \times 10^{-2} \text{ mol Mg(OH)}_2 \times \frac{2 \text{ mol HCl}}{1 \text{ mol Mg(OH)}_2} = 3.42 \times 10^{-2} \text{ mol HCl}$$

Therefore, 1.00 g of $Mg(OH)_2$ neutralizes 3.42×10^{-2} mol of HCl. We have already calculated that 1.00 g of $NaHCO_3$ neutralizes only 1.19×10^{-2} mol of HCl. Therefore, $Mg(OH)_2$ is a more effective antacid than $NaHCO_3$ on a mass basis.

 Self-Check Exercise 10.5

In Example 10.6 we answered one of the questions we posed in the introduction to this chapter. Now let's see if you can answer the other question posed there. Determine what mass of carbon monoxide and what mass of hydrogen are required to form 6.0 kg of methanol by the reaction

$$CO(g) + 2H_2(g) \rightarrow CH_3OH(l)$$

See Problem 10.39.

10.4 Calculations Involving a Limiting Reactant

AIMS: To learn to recognize the limiting reactant in a reaction. To learn to use the limiting reactant to do stoichiometric calculations.

Ammonia being dissolved in irrigation water to provide fertilizer for a field of corn.

Manufacturers of cars, bicycles, and appliances order parts in the same proportion as they are used in their products. For example, auto manufacturers order four times as many wheels as engines and bicycle manufacturers order twice as many pedals as seats. Likewise, when chemicals are mixed together so that they can undergo a reaction, they are often mixed in stoichiometric quantities—that is, in exactly the correct amounts so that all reactants "run out" (are used up) at the same time. To clarify this concept, we will consider the production of hydrogen for use in the manufacture of ammonia. Ammonia, a very important fertilizer itself and a starting material for other fertilizers, is made by combining nitrogen from the air with hydrogen. The hydrogen for this process is produced by the reaction of methane with water according to the balanced equation

$$CH_4(g) + H_2O(g) \rightarrow 3H_2(g) + CO(g)$$

Let's consider the question *What mass of water is required to react exactly with 249 g of methane?* That is, how much water will just use up all of the 249 g of methane, leaving no methane or water remaining?

This problem requires the same strategies we developed in the previous section. Again, drawing a map of the problem is helpful.

We first convert the mass of CH_4 to moles, using the molar mass of CH_4 (16.04 g/mol).

$$249 \text{ g } CH_4 \times \frac{1 \text{ mol } CH_4}{16.04 \text{ g } CH_4} = 15.5 \text{ mol } CH_4$$

Because in the balanced equation 1 mol of CH_4 reacts with 1 mol of H_2O, we have

$$15.5 \text{ mol } CH_4 \times \frac{1 \text{ mol } H_2O}{1 \text{ mol } CH_4} = 15.5 \text{ mol } H_2O$$

FIGURE 10.1

A mixture of 5CH$_4$ and 3H$_2$O molecules undergoes the reaction (CH$_4$(*g*) + H$_2$O(*g*) → 3H$_2$(*g*) 1 >CO(*g*). Note that the H$_2$O molecules are used up first, leaving two CH$_4$ molecules unreacted.

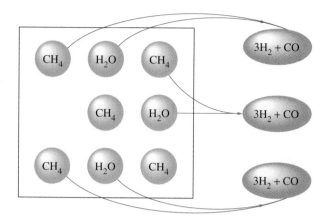

Therefore, 15.5 mol of H$_2$O will react exactly with the given mass of CH$_4$. Converting 15.5 mol of H$_2$O to grams of H$_2$O (molar mass = 18.02 g/mol) gives

$$15.5 \; \cancel{\text{mol H}_2\text{O}} \times \frac{18.02 \text{ g H}_2\text{O}}{1 \; \cancel{\text{mol H}_2\text{O}}} = 279 \text{ g H}_2\text{O}$$

This result means that if 249 g of methane is mixed with 279 g of water, both reactants will "run out" at the same time. The reactants have been mixed in stoichiometric quantities.

If, on the other hand, 249 g of methane is mixed with 300 g of water, the methane will be consumed before the water runs out. The water will be in *excess*. In this case, the quantity of products formed will be determined by the quantity of methane present. Once the methane is consumed, no more products can be formed, even though some water still remains. In this situation, because the amount of methane *limits* the amount of products that can be formed, it is called the **limiting reactant,** or **limiting reagent.** In any stoichiometry problem, where reactants are not mixed in stoichiometric quantities, it is essential to determine which reactant is limiting in order to calculate correctly the amounts of products that will be formed. This concept is illustrated in Figure 10.1. Note from this figure that because there are fewer water molecules than CH$_4$ molecules, the water is consumed first. After the water molecules are gone, no more products can form. So in this case water is the limiting reactant.

You probably have been dealing with limiting-reactant problems for most of your life. For example, suppose a lemonade recipe calls for 1 cup of sugar for every 6 lemons. You have 12 lemons and 3 cups of sugar. Which ingredient is limiting, the lemons or the sugar?*

> The reactant that is consumed first limits the amounts of products that can form.

---

*The ratio of lemons to sugar that the recipe calls for is 6 lemons to 1 cup of sugar. We can calculate the number of lemons required to "react with" the 3 cups of sugar as follows:

$$3 \; \cancel{\text{cups sugar}} \times \frac{6 \text{ lemons}}{1 \; \cancel{\text{cup sugar}}} = 18 \text{ lemons}$$

Thus 18 lemons would be required to use up 3 cups of sugar. However, we have only 12 lemons, so the lemons are limiting.

EXAMPLE 10.7 *Stoichiometric Calculations: Identifying the Limiting Reactant*

Suppose 25.0 kg (2.50×10^4 g) of nitrogen gas and 5.00 kg (5.00×10^3 g) of hydrogen gas are mixed and reacted to form ammonia. Calculate the mass of ammonia produced when this reaction is run to completion.

Solution

The unbalanced equation for this reaction is

$$N_2(g) + H_2(g) \rightarrow NH_3(g)$$

which leads to the balanced equation

$$N_2(g) + 3H_2(g) \rightarrow 2NH_3(g)$$

This problem is different from the others we have done so far in that we are mixing *specified amounts of two reactants* together. To know how much product forms, we must determine which reactant is consumed first. That is, we must determine which is the limiting reactant in this experiment. To do so we must add a step to our normal procedure. We can map this process as follows:

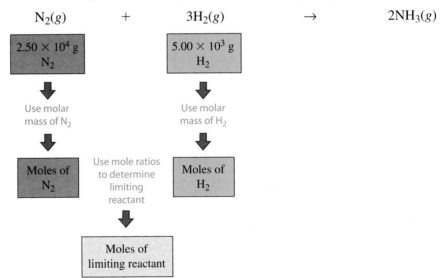

We will use the moles of the limiting reactant to calculate the moles and then the grams of the product.

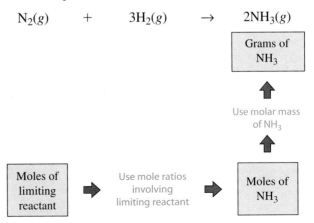

We first calculate the moles of the two reactants present:

$$2.50 \times 10^4 \, \cancel{g \, N_2} \times \frac{1 \, mol \, N_2}{28.02 \, \cancel{g \, N_2}} = 8.92 \times 10^2 \, mol \, N_2$$

$$5.00 \times 10^3 \, \cancel{g \, H_2} \times \frac{1 \, mol \, H_2}{2.016 \, \cancel{g \, H_2}} = 2.48 \times 10^3 \, mol \, H_2$$

Now we must determine which reactant is limiting (will be consumed first). We have 8.92×10^2 mol of N_2. Let's determine *how many moles of H_2 are required to react with this much N_2*. Because 1 mol of N_2 reacts with 3 mol of H_2, the number of moles of H_2 we need to react completely with 8.92×10^2 mol of N_2 is determined as follows:

$$8.92 \times 10^2 \, \cancel{mol \, N_2} \times \frac{3 \, mol \, H_2}{1 \, \cancel{mol \, N_2}} = 2.68 \times 10^3 \, mol \, H_2$$

Is N_2 or H_2 the limiting reactant? The answer comes from the comparison

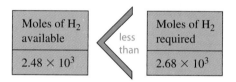

We see that 8.92×10^2 mol of N_2 require 2.68×10^3 mol of H_2 to react completely. However, only 2.48×10^3 mol of H_2 are present. This means that the hydrogen will be consumed before the nitrogen runs out, so hydrogen is the *limiting reactant* in this particular situation.

Note that in our effort to determine the limiting reactant, we could have started instead with the given amount of hydrogen and calculated the moles of nitrogen required.

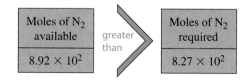

$$2.48 \times 10^3 \, \cancel{mol \, H_2} \times \frac{1 \, mol \, N_2}{3 \, \cancel{mol \, H_2}} = 8.27 \times 10^2 \, mol \, N_2$$

Thus 2.48×10^3 mol of H_2 require 8.27×10^2 mol of N_2. Because 8.92×10^2 mol of N_2 are actually present, the nitrogen is in excess.

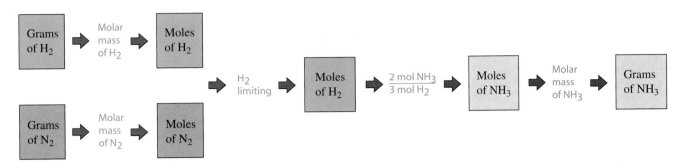

FIGURE 10.2
A map of the procedure used in Example 10.7.

Always check to see which, if any, reactant is limiting when you are given the amounts of two or more reactants.

If nitrogen is in excess, hydrogen will "run out" first; again we find that hydrogen limits the amount of ammonia formed.

Because the moles of H_2 present are limiting, we must use this quantity to determine the moles of NH_3 that can form.

$$2.48 \times 10^3 \, \text{mol } H_2 \times \frac{2 \text{ mol } NH_3}{3 \text{ mol } H_2} = 1.65 \times 10^3 \text{ mol } NH_3$$

Next we convert moles of NH_3 to mass of NH_3.

$$1.65 \times 10^3 \, \text{mol } NH_3 \times \frac{17.03 \text{ g } NH_3}{1 \text{ mol } NH_3} = 2.81 \times 10^4 \text{ g } NH_3 = 28.1 \text{ kg } NH_3$$

Therefore, 25.0 kg of N_2 and 5.00 kg of H_2 can form 28.1 kg of NH_3.

The strategy used in Example 10.7 is summarized in Figure 10.2.

The following list summarizes the steps to take in solving stoichiometry problems in which the amounts of two (or more) reactants are given.

Steps for Solving Stoichiometry Problems Involving Limiting Reactants

STEP 1 Write and balance the equation for the reaction.

STEP 2 Convert known masses of reactants to moles.

STEP 3 Using the numbers of moles of reactants and the appropriate mole ratios, determine which reactant is limiting.

STEP 4 Using the amount of the limiting reactant and the appropriate mole ratios, compute the number of moles of the desired product.

STEP 5 Convert from moles of product to grams of product, using the molar mass (if this is required by the problem).

EXAMPLE 10.8   *Stoichiometric Calculations:*
Reactions Involving the Masses of Two Reactants

Copper(II) oxide reacting with ammonia in a heated tube.

Nitrogen gas can be prepared by passing gaseous ammonia over solid copper(II) oxide at high temperatures. The other products of the reaction are solid copper and water vapor. How many grams of N_2 are formed when 18.1 g of NH_3 are reacted with 90.4 g of CuO?

Solution

STEP 1   From the description of the problem, we obtain the following balanced equation:

$$2NH_3(g) + 3CuO(s) \rightarrow N_2(g) + 3Cu(s) + 3H_2O(g)$$

STEP 2   Next, from the masses of reactants available we must compute the moles of NH_3 (molar mass = 17.03 g) and of CuO (molar mass = 79.55 g).

$$18.1 \text{ g } NH_3 \times \frac{1 \text{ mol } NH_3}{17.03 \text{ g } NH_3} = 1.06 \text{ mol } NH_3$$

$$90.4 \text{ g } CuO \times \frac{1 \text{ mol } CuO}{79.55 \text{ g } CuO} = 1.14 \text{ mol } CuO$$

STEP 3   To determine which reactant is limiting, we use the mole ratio between CuO and NH_3.

$$1.06 \text{ mol } NH_3 \times \frac{3 \text{ mol } CuO}{2 \text{ mol } NH_3} = 1.59 \text{ mol } CuO$$

Then we compare how much CuO we have with how much of it we need.

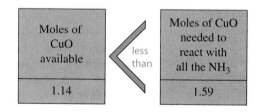

Therefore, 1.59 mol of CuO are required to react with 1.06 mol of NH_3, but only 1.14 mol of CuO are actually present. So the amount of CuO is limiting; CuO will run out before NH_3 does.

STEP 4   CuO is the limiting reactant, so we must use the amount of CuO in calculating the amount of N_2 formed. Using the mole ratio between CuO and N_2 from the balanced equation, we have

$$1.14 \text{ mol } CuO \times \frac{1 \text{ mol } N_2}{3 \text{ mol } CuO} = 0.380 \text{ mol } N_2$$

STEP 5   Using the molar mass of N_2 (28.02), we can now calculate the mass of N_2 produced.

$$0.380 \text{ mol } N_2 \times \frac{28.02 \text{ g } N_2}{1 \text{ mol } N_2} = 10.6 \text{ g } N_2$$

Self-Check Exercise 10.6

Lithium nitride, an ionic compound containing the Li^+ and N^{3-} ions, is prepared by the reaction of lithium metal and nitrogen gas. Calculate the mass of lithium nitride formed from 56.0 g of nitrogen gas and 56.0 g of lithium in the unbalanced reaction

$$Li(s) \ + \ N_2(g) \ \rightarrow \ Li_3N(s)$$

See Problems 10.51 through 10.54.

10.5 Percent Yield

AIM: To learn to calculate actual yield as a percentage of theoretical yield.

In the previous section we learned how to calculate the amount of products formed when specified amounts of reactants are mixed together. In doing these calculations, we used the fact that the amount of product is controlled by the limiting reactant. Products stop forming when one reactant runs out.

The amount of product calculated in this way is called the **theoretical yield** of that product. It is the amount of product predicted from the amounts of reactants used. For instance, in Example 10.8, 10.6 g of nitrogen represents the theoretical yield. This is the *maximum amount* of nitrogen that can be produced from the quantities of reactants used. Actually, however, the amount of product predicted (the theoretical yield) is seldom obtained. One reason for this is the presence of side reactions (other reactions that consume one or more of the reactants or products).

The *actual yield* of product, which is the amount of product *actually obtained,* is often compared to the theoretical yield. This comparison, usually expressed as a percent, is called the **percent yield.**

Percent yield is important as an indicator of the efficiency of a particular reaction.

$$\frac{\text{Actual yield}}{\text{Theoretical yield}} \ \times \ 100\% \ = \ \text{percent yield}$$

For example, *if* the reaction considered in Example 10.8 *actually* gave 6.63 g of nitrogen instead of the *predicted* 10.6 g, the percent yield of nitrogen would be

$$\frac{6.63 \ \text{g } N_2}{10.6 \ \text{g } N_2} \ \times \ 100\% \ = \ 62.5\%$$

 EXAMPLE 10.9   *Stoichiometric Calculations: Determining Percent Yield*

In the "Chemistry in Focus" on page 272, we stated that methanol can be produced by the reaction between carbon monoxide and hydrogen. Let's consider this process again. Suppose 68.5 kg (6.85×10^4 g) of CO(g) is reacted with 8.60 kg (8.60×10^3 g) of $H_2(g)$.

a. Calculate the theoretical yield of methanol.

b. If 3.57×10^4 g of CH_3OH is actually produced, what is the percent yield of methanol?

Solution (a)

STEP 1   The balanced equation is

$$2H_2(g) + CO(g) \rightarrow CH_3OH(l).$$

STEP 2   Next we calculate the moles of reactants.

$$6.85 \times 10^4 \, \text{g CO} \times \frac{1 \, \text{mol CO}}{28.01 \, \text{g CO}} = 2.45 \times 10^3 \, \text{mol CO}$$

$$8.60 \times 10^3 \, \text{g H}_2 \times \frac{1 \, \text{mol H}_2}{2.016 \, \text{g H}_2} = 4.27 \times 10^3 \, \text{mol H}_2$$

STEP 3   Then we determine which reactant is limiting. Using the mole ratio between CO and H_2 from the balanced equation, we have

$$2.45 \times 10^3 \, \text{mol CO} \times \frac{2 \, \text{mol H}_2}{1 \, \text{mol CO}} = 4.90 \times 10^3 \, \text{mol H}_2$$

We see that 2.45×10^3 mol of CO requires 4.90×10^3 mol of H_2. Because only 4.27×10^3 mol of H_2 is actually present, *H_2 is limiting.*

STEP 4   We must therefore use the amount of H_2 and the mole ratio between H_2 and CH_3OH to determine the maximum amount of methanol that can be produced in the reaction.

$$4.27 \times 10^3 \, \text{mol H}_2 \times \frac{1 \, \text{mol CH}_3\text{OH}}{2 \, \text{mol H}_2} = 2.14 \times 10^3 \, \text{mol CH}_3\text{OH}$$

This represents the theoretical yield in moles.

STEP 5   Using the molar mass of CH_3OH (32.04 g), we can calculate the theoretical yield in grams.

$$2.14 \times 10^3 \, \text{mol CH}_3\text{OH} \times \frac{32.04 \, \text{g CH}_3\text{OH}}{1 \, \text{mol CH}_3\text{OH}} = 6.86 \times 10^4 \, \text{g CH}_3\text{OH}$$

So, from the amounts of reactants given, the maximum amount of CH_3OH that can be formed is 6.85×10^4 g. This is the *theoretical yield.*

Solution (b)

The percent yield is

$$\frac{\text{Actual yield (grams)}}{\text{Theoretical yield (grams)}} \times 100\% = \frac{3.57 \times 10^4 \, \text{g CH}_3\text{OH}}{6.86 \times 10^4 \, \text{g CH}_3\text{OH}} \times 100\%$$

$$= 52.0\%$$

✓ Self-Check Exercise 10.7

Titanium(IV) oxide is a white compound used as a coloring pigment. In fact, the page you are now reading is white because of the presence of this compound in the paper. Solid titanium(IV) oxide can be prepared by reacting gaseous titanium(IV) chloride with oxygen gas. A second product of this reaction is chlorine gas.

$$TiCl_4(g) + O_2(g) \rightarrow TiO_2(s) + Cl_2(g)$$

a. Suppose 6.71×10^3 g of titanium(IV) chloride is reacted with 2.45×10^3 g of oxygen. Calculate the maximum mass of titanium(IV) oxide that can form.

b. If the percent yield of TiO_2 is 75%, what mass is actually formed?

See Problems 10.63 and 10.64.

Chapter Review

Key Terms

mole ratio *(10.2)*
stoichiometry *(10.3)*
stoichiometric quantities *(10.4)*
limiting reactant (limiting reagent) *(10.4)*
theoretical yield *(10.5)*
percent yield *(10.5)*

Summary

1. A balanced equation relates the numbers of molecules of reactants and products. It can also be expressed in terms of the numbers of moles of reactants and products.

2. The process of using a chemical equation to calculate the relative amounts of reactants and products involved in the reaction is called doing stoichiometric calculations. To convert between moles of reactants and moles of products, we use mole ratios derived from the balanced equation.

3. Often reactants are not mixed in stoichiometric quantities (they do not "run out" at the same time). In that case, we must use the limiting reactant to calculate the amounts of products formed.

4. The actual yield of a reaction is usually less than its theoretical yield. The actual yield is often expressed as a percentage of the theoretical yield, which is called the percent yield.

Questions and Problems

All even-numbered exercises have answers in the back of this book and solutions in the Solutions Guide.

10.1 ■ *Information Given by Chemical Equations*

QUESTIONS

1. What do the coefficients of a balanced chemical equation tell us about the proportions in which atoms and molecules react on an individual (microscopic) basis?

2. What do the coefficients of a balanced chemical equation tell us about the proportions in which substances react on a macroscopic (mole) basis?

3. Explain why the coefficients of a balanced chemical equation are interpreted on a mole basis, rather than directly on the basis of mass.

4. Explain why, in the balanced chemical equation $C + O_2 \rightarrow CO_2$, we know that 1 g of C will *not* react exactly with 1 g of O_2.

PROBLEMS

5. For each of the following reactions, give the balanced equation for the reaction and state the meaning of the equation in terms of numbers of *individual molecules* and in terms of *moles* of molecules.
   a. $NO(g) + O_2(g) \rightarrow NO_2(g)$

b. $AgC_2H_3O_2(aq) + CuSO_4(aq) \rightarrow Ag_2SO_4(s) + Cu(C_2H_3O_2)_2(aq)$

c. $PCl_3(l) + H_2O(l) \rightarrow H_3PO_3(l) + HCl(g)$

d. $C_2H_6(g) + Cl_2(g) \rightarrow C_2H_5Cl(g) + HCl(g)$

6. For each of the following reactions, give the balanced chemical equation for the reaction and state the meaning of the equation in terms of *individual molecules* and in terms of *moles* of molecules.

a. $MnO_2(s) + Al(s) \rightarrow Mn(s) + Al_2O_3(s)$

b. $B_2O_3(s) + CaF_2(s) \rightarrow BF_3(g) + CaO(s)$

c. $NO_2(g) + H_2O(l) \rightarrow HNO_3(aq) + NO(g)$

d. $C_6H_6(g) + H_2(g) \rightarrow C_6H_{12}(g)$

10.2 ■ Mole–Mole Relationships

QUESTIONS

7. True or false? For the reaction represented by the chemical equation

$$2H_2(g) + O_2(g) \rightarrow 2H_2O(l)$$

the mole ratio that would be used to convert moles of O_2 reacting to moles of H_2O formed is 2 mol H_2O/2 mol H_2.

8. True or false? For the reaction represented by the balanced chemical equation

$$N_2(g) + 3I_2(s) \rightarrow 2NI_3(s)$$

if you want to prepare 2 mol of $NI_3(s)$, then 1 g of $N_2(g)$ and 3 g of $I_2(s)$ will be needed.

9. Consider the balanced equation

$$CH_4(g) + 2O_2(g) \rightarrow CO_2(g) + 2H_2O(g)$$

What is the mole ratio that would enable you to calculate the number of moles of oxygen needed to react exactly with a given number of moles of $CH_4(g)$? What mole ratios would you use to calculate how many moles of each product form from a given number of moles of CH_4?

10. Consider the unbalanced chemical equation

$$CH_3CH_2OH(l) + O_2(g) \rightarrow CO_2(g) + H_2O(g)$$

Balance the equation. Identify the mole ratios that you would use to calculate the number of moles of each product that would form for a given number of moles of $CH_3CH_2OH(l)$ reacting.

PROBLEMS

11. For each of the following balanced reactions, calculate how many *moles of product* would be produced by complete conversion of 0.15 mol of the reactant indicated in boldface. Write clearly the mole ratio used for the conversion.

a. $\mathbf{2Mg}(s) + O_2(g) \rightarrow 2MgO(s)$

b. $2Mg(s) + \mathbf{O_2}(g) \rightarrow 2MgO(s)$

c. $\mathbf{4Fe}(s) + 3O_2(g) \rightarrow 2Fe_2O_3(s)$

d. $4Fe(s) + \mathbf{3O_2}(g) \rightarrow 2Fe_2O_3(s)$

12. For each of the following balanced chemical equations, calculate how many *moles of each product* would be produced by the complete conversion of 0.25 mol of the reactant indicated in boldface. State clearly the mole ratio used for the conversion.

a. $\mathbf{3PbO}(s) + 2Al(s) \rightarrow 3Pb(s) + Al_2O_3(s)$

b. $\mathbf{C_2H_2}(g) + 2H_2(g) \rightarrow C_2H_6(g)$

c. $BaO_2(s) + \mathbf{2Na}(s) \rightarrow Na_2O_2(s) + Ba(s)$

d. $\mathbf{2CH_4}(g) + 3O_2(g) \rightarrow 2CO(g) + 4H_2O(l)$

13. For each of the balanced reactions below, calculate how many *moles of each product* would be produced by complete conversion of 1.25 mol of the reactant indicated in boldface. State clearly the mole ratio used for the conversion.

a. $\mathbf{C_2H_5OH}(l) + 3O_2(g) \rightarrow 2CO_2(g) + 3H_2O(g)$

b. $\mathbf{N_2}(g) + O_2(g) \rightarrow 2NO(g)$

c. $\mathbf{2NaClO_2}(s) + Cl_2(g) \rightarrow 2ClO_2(g) + 2NaCl(s)$

d. $\mathbf{3H_2}(g) + N_2(g) \rightarrow 2NH_3(g)$

14. For each of the following balanced chemical equations, calculate how many *moles* and how many *grams* of each product would be produced by the complete conversion of 0.50 mol of the reactant indicated in boldface. State clearly the mole ratio used for each conversion.

a. $\mathbf{NH_3}(g) + HCl(g) \rightarrow NH_4Cl(s)$

b. $\mathbf{CH_4}(g) + 4S(s) \rightarrow CS_2(l) + 2H_2S(g)$

c. $\mathbf{PCl_3} + 3H_2O(l) \rightarrow H_3PO_3(aq) + 3HCl(aq)$

d. $\mathbf{NaOH}(s) + CO_2(g) \rightarrow NaHCO_3(s)$

15. For each of the following *unbalanced* equations, indicate how many *moles* of the *second reactant* would be required to react exactly with 0.25 mol of the *first reactant*. State clearly the mole ratio used for the conversion.

a. $CO(g) + O_2(g) \rightarrow CO_2(g)$

b. $AgNO_3(aq) + CuSO_4(aq) \rightarrow Ag_2SO_4(s) + Cu(NO_3)_2(aq)$

c. $PCl_3(l) + H_2O(l) \rightarrow H_3PO_3(l) + HCl(g)$

d. $CH_4(g) + Cl_2(g) \rightarrow CCl_4(l) + HCl(g)$

16. For each of the following *unbalanced* equations, indicate how many *moles* of the *first product* is produced if *0.625 mol* of the *second product* forms. State clearly the mole ratio used for each conversion.

a. $KO_2(s) + H_2O(l) \rightarrow O_2(g) + KOH(s)$

b. $SeO_2(g) + H_2Se(g) \rightarrow Se(s) + H_2O(g)$

c. $CH_3CH_2OH(l) + O_2(g) \rightarrow CH_3CHO(aq) + H_2O(l)$

d. $Fe_2O_3(s) + Al(s) \rightarrow Fe(l) + Al_2O_3(l)$

10.3 ■ *Mass Calculations*

QUESTIONS

17. What quantity serves as the conversion factor between the mass of a sample and how many moles the sample contains?

18. What does it mean to say that the balanced chemical equation for a reaction describes the *stoichiometry* of the reaction?

PROBLEMS

19. Using the average atomic masses given inside the front cover of the text, calculate how many *moles* of each element the following *masses* represent.
    a. 19.5 g of gold
    b. 11.78 g of iron
    c. 2.395 g of carbon dioxide
    d. 1.00 kg of barium chloride
    e. 1.00 mg of magnesium
    f. 86.2 g of sodium acetate
    g. 91.4 g of beryllium

20. Using the average atomic masses given inside the front cover of the text, calculate the number of *moles* of each substance contained in the following *masses*.
    a. 2.01×10^{-2} g of silver
    b. 45.2 mg of ammonium sulfide
    c. 61.7 μg of uranium
    d. 5.23 kg of sulfur dioxide
    e. 272 g of iron(III) nitrate
    f. 12.7 mg of iron(II) sulfate
    g. 6.91×10^3 g of lithium hydroxide

21. Using the average atomic masses given inside the front cover of the text, calculate the *mass in grams* of each of the following samples.
    a. 1.25 mol of platinum(IV) chloride
    b. 0.00255 mol of copper(II) oxide
    c. 1.89×10^{-4} mol of ethane, C_2H_6
    d. 55.56 mol of beryllium
    e. 2.6×10^7 mol of diboron trioxide
    f. 0.45 mol of sodium fluoride
    g. 0.00115 mol of calcium nitrate

22. Using the average atomic masses given inside the front cover of the text, calculate the *mass in grams* of each of the following samples.
    a. 0.00249 mol of diethyl ether, $(C_2H_5)_2O$
    b. 1.37 mol of uranium(VI) fluoride
    c. 3.65×10^{-5} mol of sulfur trioxide
    d. 52.6 mol of potassium carbonate
    e. 2.06×10^4 mol of sodium hydroxide

    f. 71.5 millimol of copper(II) sulfate
    g. 3.37 mol of dichlorobenzene, $C_6H_4Cl_2$

23. For each of the following *unbalanced* equations, indicate how many *moles of each product* could be produced by complete reaction of *1.00 g* of the reactant indicated in boldface. Indicate clearly the mole ratio used for the conversion.
    a. $LiOH(s) + \mathbf{CO_2}(g) \rightarrow Li2CO3(s)\ 1\ H2O(l)$
    b. $\mathbf{Ba(OH)_2}(s) \rightarrow BaO(s) + H_2O(g)$
    c. $C_2H_4(g) + \mathbf{Cl_2}(g) \rightarrow C_2H_4Cl_2(l)$
    d. $H_2SO_4(aq) + \mathbf{NaOH}(aq) \rightarrow Na_2SO_4(aq) + H_2O(l)$

24. For each of the following *unbalanced* equations, calculate how many moles of the *second* reactant would be required to react completely with exactly *25.0 g* of the *first* reactant. Indicate clearly the mole ratio used for each conversion.
    a. $Mg(s) + CuCl_2(aq) \rightarrow MgCl_2(aq) + Cu(s)$
    b. $AgNO_3(aq) + NiCl_2(aq) \rightarrow AgCl(s) + Ni(NO_3)_2(aq)$
    c. $NaHSO_3(aq) + NaOH(aq) \rightarrow Na_2SO_3(aq) + H_2O(l)$
    d. $KHCO_3(aq) + HCl(aq) \rightarrow KCl(aq) + H_2O(l) + CO_2(g)$

25. For each of the following *unbalanced* equations, calculate how many *grams of each product* would be produced by complete reaction of *10.0 g* of the reactant indicated in boldface. Indicate clearly the mole ratio used for the conversion.
    a. $\mathbf{Na}(s) + N_2(g) \rightarrow Na_3N(s)$
    b. $BaO(s) + \mathbf{HCl}(aq) \rightarrow BaCl_2(aq) + H_2O(l)$
    c. $\mathbf{Cl_2}(g) + KI(s) \rightarrow KCl(s) + I_2(s)$
    d. $\mathbf{HgO}(s) \rightarrow Hg(l) + O_2(g)$

26. For each of the following *unbalanced* equations, calculate how many *milligrams of each product* would be produced by complete reaction of *10.0 mg* of the reactant indicated in boldface. Indicate clearly the mole ratio used for the conversion.
    a. $\mathbf{FeSO_4}(aq) + K_2CO_3(aq) \rightarrow FeCO_3(s) + K_2SO_4(aq)$
    b. $\mathbf{Cr}(s) + SnCl_4(l) \rightarrow CrCl_3(s) + Sn(s)$
    c. $Fe(s) + \mathbf{S_8}(s) \rightarrow Fe_2S_3(s)$
    d. $Ag(s) + \mathbf{HNO_3}(aq) \rightarrow AgNO_3(aq) + H_2O(l) + NO(g)$

27. Although mixtures of hydrogen and oxygen are highly explosive, pure elemental hydrogen gas itself burns quietly in air with a pale blue flame, producing water vapor.

    $$2H_2(g) + O_2(g) \rightarrow 2H_2O(g)$$

    Calculate the mass (in grams) of water vapor produced when 56.0 g of pure hydrogen gas burns in air.

28. Given the information in Problem 27, calculate the mass of oxygen gas that would be needed to burn 1.00 g of hydrogen gas.

29. When elemental carbon is burned in the open atmosphere, with plenty of oxygen gas present, the product is carbon dioxide.

$$C(s) + O_2(g) \rightarrow CO_2(g)$$

However, when the amount of oxygen present during the burning of the carbon is restricted, carbon monoxide is more likely to result.

$$2C(s) + O_2(g) \rightarrow 2CO(g)$$

What mass of each product is expected when a 5.00-g sample of pure carbon is burned under each of these conditions?

30. Nitrogen triodide is a very dangerous substance because it decomposes explosively and unpredictably, and with great force. The relative instability of NI_3 is related to the much greater stability of the products of the decomposition. The unbalanced equation is

$$NI_3(s) \rightarrow N_2(g) + I_2(s)$$

Calculate the mass of iodine produced when 1.75 g of NI_3 is completely decomposed.

31. Although we usually think of substances as "burning" only in oxygen gas, the process of rapid oxidation to produce a flame may also take place in other strongly oxidizing gases. For example, when iron is heated and placed in pure chlorine gas, the iron "burns" according to the following (unbalanced) reaction.

$$Fe(s) + Cl_2(g) \rightarrow FeCl_3(s)$$

How many milligrams of iron(III) chloride result when 15.5 mg of iron is reacted with an excess of chlorine gas?

32. Hydrochloric acid will attack and corrode many of the metallic elements, resulting in the generation of hydrogen gas and producing a solution of the metal chloride. Consider the following unbalanced reactions:

$$Zn(s) + HCl(aq) \rightarrow ZnCl_2(aq) + H_2(g)$$

$$Al(s) + HCl(aq) \rightarrow AlCl_3(aq) + H_2(g)$$

$$Mg(s) + HCl(aq) \rightarrow MgCl_2(aq) + H_2(g)$$

Calculate the mass of each metal required to produce 1.00 g of hydrogen by its respective reaction.

33. Small quantities of oxygen gas can be generated in the laboratory by the decomposition of hydrogen peroxide. The unbalanced equation for the reaction is

$$H_2O_2(aq) \rightarrow H_2O(l) + O_2(g)$$

Calculate the mass of oxygen produced when 10.00 g of hydrogen peroxide decomposes.

34. Elemental fluorine and chlorine gases are very reactive. For example, they react with each other to produce an *inter*halogen compound, chlorine monofluoride.

$$Cl_2(g) + F_2(g) \rightarrow 2ClF(g)$$

Calculate how many grams of chlorine gas are required to react completely with 5.00 mg of fluorine gas.

35. With the news that calcium deficiencies in many women's diets may contribute to the development of osteoporosis (bone weakening), the use of dietary calcium supplements has become increasingly common. Many of these calcium supplements consist of nothing more than calcium carbonate, $CaCo_3$. When a calcium carbonate tablet is ingested, it dissolves by reaction with stomach acid, which contains hydrochloric acid, HCl. The unbalanced equation is

$$CaCO_3(s) + HCl(aq) \rightarrow CaCl_2(aq) + H_2O(l) + CO_2(g)$$

What mass of HCl is required to react with a tablet containing 500. mg of calcium carbonate?

36. Sulfur is sometimes used to contain mercury spills in the lab. Sulfur reacts with mercury according to the balanced chemical equation:

$$S(s) + Hg(l) \rightarrow HgS(s)$$

Calculate how many grams of sulfur are required to react exactly with 0.10 g of mercury.

37. Ammonium carbonate has been sold for many years as "smelling salts," which can be used to revive an unconscious person. When ammonium carbonate decomposes, it releases carbon dioxide and ammonia gases, as well as water vapor. The unbalanced equation is

$$(NH_4)_2CO_3(s) \rightarrow NH_3(g) + CO_2(g + H_2O(g)$$

Calculate the mass of each product produced when 125 g of ammonium carbonate decomposes.

38. Solutions of sodium hydroxide cannot be kept for very long because they absorb carbon dioxide rom the air, forming sodium carbonate. The unbalanced equation is

$$NaOH(aq) + CO_2(g) \rightarrow Na_2CO_3(aq) + H_2O(l)$$

Calculate the number of grams of carbon dioxide that can be absorbed by complete reaction with a solution that contains 5.00 g of sodium hydroxide.

39. Thionyl chloride, $SOCl_2$, is used as a very powerful drying agent in many synthetic chemistry experiments in which the presence of even small amounts of water would be detrimental. The unbalanced chemical equation is

$$SOCl_2(l) + H_2O(l) \rightarrow SO_2(g) + HCl(g)$$

Calculate the mass of water consumed by complete reaction of 35.0 g of $SOCl_2$.

40. Magnesium metal, which burns in oxygen with an intensely bright white flame, has been used in photographic flash units. The balanced equation for this reaction is

$$2Mg(s) + O_2(g) \rightarrow 2MgO(s)$$

How many grams of $MgO(s)$ are produced by complete reaction of 1.25 g of magnesium metal?

10.4 ■ *Calculations Involving a Limiting Reactant*

QUESTIONS

41. What is the *limiting reactant* for a process? Why does a reaction stop when the limiting reactant is consumed, even though there may be plenty of the other reactants present?

42. Explain how one determines which reactant in a process is the limiting reactant. Does this depend only on the masses of the reactant present? Is the mole ratio in which the reactants combine involved?

43. What is the *theoretical yield* for a reaction, and how does this quantity depend on the limiting reactant?

44. Can a reactant be present "in excess" in a reaction? Does the presence of an excess of one or more reactants affect the theoretical yield of the reaction?

PROBLEMS

45. For each of the following *unbalanced* synthesis reactions, suppose exactly 1.00 g of *each* reactant is taken. Determine which reactant is limiting, and also determine what mass of the excess reagent will remain after the limiting reactant is consumed.
   a. $K(s) + F_2(g) \rightarrow KF(s)$
   b. $K(s) + O_2(g) \rightarrow K_2O(s)$
   c. $K(s) + N_2(g) \rightarrow K_3N(s)$
   d. $K(s) + C(s) \rightarrow K_4C(s)$

46. For each of the following *unbalanced* chemical equations, suppose that exactly 15.0 g of *each* reactant is taken. Determine which reactant is limiting, and calculate what mass of each product is expected. (Assume that the limiting reactant is completely consumed.)
   a. $Al(s) + HCl(aq) \rightarrow AlCl_3(aq) + H_2(g)$
   b. $NaOH(aq) + CO_2(g) \rightarrow Na_2CO_3(aq) + H_2O(l)$
   c. $Pb(NO_3)_2(aq) + HCl(aq) \rightarrow PbCl_2(s) + HNO_3(aq)$
   d. $K(s) + I_2(s) \rightarrow KI(s)$

47. For each of the following *unbalanced* chemical equations, suppose 10.0 g of *each* reactant is taken. Show by

calculation which reactant is the limiting reagent. Calculate the mass of each product that is expected.
   a. $C_3H_8(g) + O_2(g) \rightarrow CO_2(g) + H_2O(g)$
   b. $Al(s) + Cl_2(g) \rightarrow AlCl_3(s)$
   c. $NaOH(s) + CO_2(g) \rightarrow Na_2CO_3(s) + H_2O(l)$
   d. $NaHCO_3(s) + HCl(aq) \rightarrow$
   $$NaCl(aq) + H_2O(l) + CO_2(g)$$

48. For each of the following *unbalanced* chemical equations, suppose that exactly 50.0 g of *each* reactant is taken. Determine which reactant is limiting, and calculate what mass of the product in boldface is expected. (Assume that the limiting reactant is completely consumed.)
   a. $NH_3(g) + Na(s) \rightarrow \mathbf{NaNH_2}(s) + H_2(g)$
   b. $BaCl_2(aq) + Na_2SO_4(aq) \rightarrow \mathbf{BaSO_4}(s) + H_2O(aq)$
   c. $SO_2(g) + NaOH(s) \rightarrow \mathbf{Na_2SO_3}(s) + H_2O(l)$
   d. $Al(s) + H_2SO_4(aq) \rightarrow \mathbf{Al_2(SO_4)_3}(s) + H_2(g)$

49. For each of the following *unbalanced* chemical equations, suppose 1.00 g of *each* reactant is taken. Show by calculation which reactant is limiting. Calculate the mass of each product that is expected.
   a. $UO_2(s) + HF(aq) \rightarrow UF_4(aq) + H_4O(l)$
   b. $NaNO_3(aq) + H_2SO_4(aq) \rightarrow$
   $$Na_2SO_4(aq) + HNO_3(aq)$$
   c. $Zn(s) + HCl(aq) \rightarrow ZnCl_2(aq) + H_2(g)$
   d. $B(OH)_3(s) + CH_3OH(l) \rightarrow B(OCH_3)_3(s) + H_2O(l)$

50. For each of the following *unbalanced* chemical equations, suppose 10.0 mg of *each* reactant is taken. Show by calculation which reactant is limiting. Calculate the mass of each product that is expected.
   a. $CO(g) + H_2(g) \rightarrow CH_3OH(l)$
   b. $Al(s) + I_2(s) \rightarrow AlI_3(s)$
   c. $Ca(OH)_2(aq) + HBr(aq) \rightarrow CaBr_2(aq) + H_2O(l)$
   d. $Cr(s) + H_3PO_4(aq) \rightarrow CrPO_4(s) + H_2(g)$

51. Elemental bromine, $Br_2(l)$, can be produced by treating a concentrated aqueous sodium bromide solution with gaseous elemental chlorine. The unbalanced chemical equation is

$$Cl_2(g) + NaBr(aq) \rightarrow NaCl(aq) + Br_2(l)$$

If 10.0 g of chlorine gas is reacted with a solution containing 25.00 g of sodium bromide, show which substance is limiting, and calculate the mass of bromine produced.

52. An experiment that led to the formation of the new field of organic chemistry involved the synthesis of urea, CN_2H_4O, by the controlled reaction of ammonia and carbon dioxide:

$$2NH_3(g) + CO_2(g) \rightarrow CN_2H_4O(s) + H_2O(l)$$

What is the theoretical yield of urea when 100. g of ammonia is reacted with 100. g of carbon dioxide?

53. Most general chemistry laboratories contain bottles of several common reagents at each student's desk for ready use. Among these reagents are solutions of ammonia ("ammonium hydroxide") and hydrogen chloride (hydrochloric acid). Because the substances dissolved in these two solutions are normally gaseous, they tend to leave the solutions relatively easily and react leaving a fine dust of ammonium chloride on the lab benches.

$$NH_3(g) + HCl(g) \rightarrow NH_4Cl(s)$$

What is the maximum amount of ammonium chloride that can be deposited when 125 mg of ammonia is evolved from one bottle and 190. mg of HCl is evolved from another?

54. Powdered iron metal reacts spectacularly with elemental chlorine gas, accompanied by much heat and flame.

$$Fe(s) + Cl_2(g) \rightarrow FeCl_3(s)$$

Suppose a 5.00 g sample of iron is added to 10.0 g of chlorine gas. Show which reactant is limiting. Calculate the mass of product produced and the mass of unreacted starting material remaining.

55. One method for chemical analysis involves finding some reagent that will precipitate the species of interest. The mass of the precipitate is then used to determine what mass of the species of interest was present in the original sample. For example, calcium ion can be precipitated from solution by addition of sodium oxalate. The balanced equation is

$$Ca^{2+}(aq) + Na_2C_2O_4(aq) \rightarrow CaC_2O_4(s) + 2Na^+(aq)$$

Suppose a solution is known to contain approximately 15 g of calcium ion. Show by calculation whether the addition of a solution containing 15 g of sodium oxalate will precipitate all of the calcium from the sample.

56. The copper(II) ion in a copper(II) sulfate solution reacts with potassium iodide to produce the triiodide ion, I_3^-. This reaction is commonly used to determine how much copper is present in a given sample.

$$CuSO_4(aq) + KI(aq) \rightarrow CuI(s) + KI_3(aq) + K_2SO_4(aq)$$

If 2.00 g of KI is added to a solution containing 0.525 g of $CuSO_4$, calculate the mass of each product produced.

57. Hydrogen peroxide is used as a cleaning agent in the treatment of cuts and abrasions for several reasons. It is an oxidizing agent that can directly kill many microorganisms; it decomposes upon contact with blood, releasing elemental oxygen gas (which inhibits the growth of anaerobic microorganisms); and it foams upon contact with blood, which provides a cleansing action. In the lab-

oratory, small quantities of hydrogen peroxide can be prepared by the action of an acid on an alkaline earth metal peroxide, such as barium peroxide.

$$BaO_2(s) + 2HCl(aq) \rightarrow H_2O_2(aq) + BaCl_2(aq)$$

What amount of hydrogen peroxide should result when 1.50 g of barium peroxide is treated with 25.0 mL of hydrochloric acid solution containing 0.0272 g of HCl per mL?

58. Silicon carbide, SiC, is one of the hardest materials known. Surpassed in hardness only by diamond, it is sometimes known commercially as carborundum. Silicon carbide is used primarily as an abrasive for sandpaper and is manufactured by heating common sand (silicon dioxide, SiO_2) with carbon in a furnace.

$$SiO_2(s) + C(s) \rightarrow CO(g) + SiC(s)$$

What mass of silicon carbide should result when 1.0 kg of pure sand is heated with an excess of carbon?

10.5 ■ *Percent Yield*

QUESTIONS

59. What is the *actual yield* of a reaction? What is the *percent yield* of a reaction? How do the actual yield and the percent yield differ from the theoretical yield?

60. The text explains that one reason why the actual yield for a reaction may be less than the theoretical yield is side reactions. Suggest some other reasons why the percent yield for a reaction might not be 100%.

61. According to her pre-lab stoichiometric calculation, a student's lab experiment should have produced 5.51 g of NaCl. While actually doing the experiment, this student obtained only 4.32 g of NaCl. What was her percent yield?

62. A student calculated the theoretical yield of $BaSO_4(s)$ in a precipitation experiment to be 1.352 g. When she filtered, dried, and weighed her precipitate, however, her yield was only 1.279 g. Calculate the student's percent yield.

PROBLEMS

63. The compound sodium thiosulfate pentahydrate, $Na_2S_2O_3 \cdot 5H_2O$, is important commercially to the photography business as "hypo," because it has the ability to dissolve unreacted silver salts from photographic film during development. Sodium thiosulfate pentahydrate can be produced by boiling elemental sulfur in an aqueous solution of sodium sulfite.

$$S_8(s) + Na_2SO_3(aq) + H_2O(l) \rightarrow Na_2S_2O_3 \cdot 5H_2O(s)$$
$$\text{(unbalanced)}$$

What is the theoretical yield of sodium thiosulfate pentahydrate when 3.25 g of sulfur is boiled with 13.1 g of sodium sulfite? Sodium thiosulfate pentahydrate is very soluble in water. What is the percent yield of the synthesis if a student doing this experiment is able to isolate (collect) only 5.26 g of the product?

64. Alkali metal hydroxides are sometimes used to "scrub" excess carbon dioxide from the air in closed spaces (such as submarines and spacecraft). For example, lithium hydroxide reacts with carbon dioxide according to the unbalanced chemical equation

$$LiOH(s) + CO_2(g) \rightarrow Li_2CO_3(s) + H_2O(g)$$

Suppose a lithium hydroxide cannister contains 155 g of $LiOH(s)$. What mass of $CO_2(g)$ will the cannister be able to absorb? If it is found that after 24 hours of use the cannister has absorbed 102 g of carbon dioxide, what percentage of its capacity has been reached?

65. Although they were formerly called the inert gases, at least the heavier elements of Group 8 do form relatively stable compounds. For example, xenon combines directly with elemental fluorine at elevated temperatures in the presence of a nickel catalyst.

$$Xe(g) + 2F_2(g) \rightarrow XeF_4(s)$$

What is the theoretical mass of xenon tetrafluoride that should form when 130. g of xenon is reacted with 100. g of F_2? What is the percent yield if only 145 g of XeF_4 is actually isolated?

66. Anhydrous calcium chloride, $CaCl_2$, is frequently used in the laboratory as a drying agent for solvents, because it absorbs 6 mol of water molecules for every mole of $CaCl_2$ used (forming a stable solid hydrated salt, $CaCl_2 \cdot 6H_2O$). Calcium chloride is typically prepared by treating calcium carbonate with hydrogen chloride gas.

$$CaCO_3(s) + 2HCl(g) \rightarrow CaCl_2(s) + CO_2(g) + H_2O(g)$$

A large amount of heat is generated by this reaction, so the water produced from the reaction is usually driven off as steam. Some liquid water may remain, however, and it may dissolve some of the desired calcium chloride. What is the percent yield if 155 g of calcium carbonate is treated with 250. g of anhydrous hydrogen chloride and only 142 g of $CaCl_2$ is obtained?

Additional Problems

67. Natural waters often contain relatively high levels of calcium ion, Ca^{2+}, and hydrogen carbonate ion (bicarbonate), HCO_3^-, from the leaching of minerals into the water. When such water is used commercially or in the home, heating of the water leads to the formation of solid calcium carbonate, $CaCO_3$, which forms a deposit ("scale") on the interior of boilers, pipes, and other plumbing fixtures.

$$Ca(HCO_3)_2(aq) \rightarrow CaCO_3(s) + CO_2(g) + H_2O(l)$$

If a sample of well water contains 2.0×10^{-3} mg of $Ca(HCO_3)_2$ per milliliter, what mass of $CaCO_3$ scale would 1.0 ml of this water be capable of depositing?

68. One process for the commercial production of baking soda (sodium hydrogen carbonate) involves the following reaction, in which the carbon dioxide is used in its solid form ("dry ice") both to serve as a source of reactant and to cool the reaction system to a temperature low enough for the sodium hydrogen carbonate to precipitate:

$$NaCl(aq) + NH_3(aq) + H_2O(l) + CO_2(s) \rightarrow$$
$$NH_4Cl(aq) + NaHCO_3(s)$$

Because they are relatively cheap, sodium chloride and water are typically present in excess. What is the expected yield of $NaHCO_3$ when one performs such a synthesis using 10.0 g of ammonia and 15.0 g of dry ice, with an excess of NaCl and water?

69. When sulfur is burned in air, the noxious, toxic gas sulfur dioxide results.

$$S(s) + O_2(g) \rightarrow SO_2(g)$$

Some hydrocarbon fuels burned for heat and power are "high-sulfur" fuels, which contribute to air pollution in the United States and other countries. When such fuels are burned, the sulfur they contain is converted to sulfur dioxide. Suppose such a fuel is 1.5% sulfur by mass and has a density of 0.82 g/mL. What mass of sulfur dioxide is released when 1000. gal of this fuel is burned?

70. When the sugar glucose, $C_6H_{12}O_6$, is burned in air, carbon dioxide and water vapor are produced. Write the balanced chemical equation for this process, and calculate the theoretical yield of carbon dioxide when 1.00 g of glucose is burned completely.

71. When elemental copper is strongly heated with sulfur, a mixture of CuS and Cu_2S is produced, with CuS predominating.

$$Cu(s) + S(s) \rightarrow CuS(s)$$
$$2Cu(s) + S(s) \rightarrow Cu_2S(s)$$

What is the theoretical yield of CuS when 31.8 g of Cu(s) is heated with 50.0 g of S? (Assume only CuS is produced in the reaction.) What is the percent yield of CuS if only 40.0 g of CuS can be isolated from the mixture?

72. Potassium chromate is used in chemical analysis to precipitate quantitatively lead ion from solution (lead chromate is very insoluble).

$$Pb^{2+}(aq) + CrO_4^{2-}(aq) \rightarrow PbCrO_4(s)$$

Suppose a solution is known to contain no more than 15 mg of lead ion. What mass of potassium chromate should be added to guarantee precipitation of all the lead ion?

73. The traditional method of analysis for the amount of chloride ion present in a sample was to dissolve the sample in water and then slowly to add a solution of silver nitrate. Silver chloride is very insoluble in water, and by adding a slight excess of silver nitrate, it is possible effectively to remove all chloride ion from the sample.

$$Ag^+(aq) + Cl^-(aq) \rightarrow AgCl(s)$$

Suppose a 1.054-g sample is known to contain 10.3% chloride ion by mass. What mass of silver nitrate must be used to completely precipitate the chloride ion from the sample? What mass of silver chloride will be obtained?

74. For each of the following reactions, give the balanced equation for the reaction and state the meaning of the equation in terms of numbers of *individual molecules* and in terms of *moles* of molecules.
    a. $UO_2(s) + HF(aq) \rightarrow UF_4(aq) + H_2O(l)$
    b. $NaC_2H_3O_2(aq) + H_2SO_4(aq) \rightarrow Na_2SO_4(aq) + HC_2H_3O_2(aq)$
    c. $Mg(s) + HCl(aq) \rightarrow MgCl_2(aq) + H_2(g)$
    d. $B_2O_3(s) + H_2O(l) \rightarrow B(OH)_3(aq)$

75. True or false? For the reaction represented by the balanced chemical equation

$$Mg(OH)_2(aq) + 2HCl(aq) \rightarrow 2H_2O(l) + MgCl_2(aq)$$

for 0.40 mol of $Mg(OH)_2$, 0.20 mol of HCl will be needed.

76. Consider the balanced equation

$$C_3H_8(g) + 5O_2(g) \rightarrow 3CO_2(g) + 4H_2O(g)$$

What mole ratio enables you to calculate the number of moles of oxygen needed to react exactly with a given number of moles of $C_3H_8(g)$? What mole ratios enable you to calculate how many moles of each product form from a given number of moles of C_3H_8?

77. For each of the following balanced reactions, calculate how many *moles of each product* would be produced by complete conversion of 0.50 mol of the reactant indicated in boldface. Indicate clearly the mole ratio used for the conversion.
    a. $\mathbf{2H_2O_2}(l) \rightarrow 2H_2O(l) + O_2(g)$
    b. $\mathbf{2KClO_3}(s) \rightarrow 2KCl(s) + 3O_2(g)$
    c. $\mathbf{2Al}(s) + 6HCl(aq) \rightarrow 2AlCl_3(aq) + 3H_2(g)$
    d. $\mathbf{C_3H_8}(g) + 5O_2(g) \rightarrow 3CO_2(g) + 4H_2O(g)$

78. For each of the following balanced equations, indicate how many *moles of the product* could be produced by complete reaction of *1.00 g* of the reactant indicated in boldface. Indicate clearly the mole ratio used for the conversion.
    a. $\mathbf{NH_3}(g) + HCl(g) \rightarrow NH_4Cl(s)$
    b. $\mathbf{CaO}(s) + CO_2(g) \rightarrow CaCO_3(s)$
    c. $\mathbf{4Na}(s) + O_2(g) \rightarrow 2Na_2O(s)$
    d. $\mathbf{2P}(s) + 3Cl_2(g) \rightarrow 2PCl_3(l)$

79. Using the average atomic masses given inside the front cover of the text, calculate how many *moles* of each element the following *masses* represent.
    a. 1.5 mg of lithium
    b. 2.0×10^{-3} g of dinitrogen monoxide
    c. 4.84×10^4 g of phosphorus trichloride
    d. 3.6×10^{-2} μg of uranium(VI) fluoride
    e. 1.0 kg of lead(II) sulfide
    f. 20.4 g of sulfuric acid
    g. 62.8 g of glucose, $C_6H_{12}O_6$

80. Using the average atomic masses given inside the front cover of the text, calculate the *mass in grams* of each of the following samples.
    a. 5.0 mol of nitric acid
    b. 0.000305 mol of mercury
    c. 2.31×10^{-5} mol of potassium chromate
    d. 10.5 mol of aluminum chloride
    e. 4.9×10^4 mol of sulfur hexafluoride
    f. 125 mol of ammonia
    g. 0.01205 mol of sodium peroxide

81. For each of the following *unbalanced* equations, indicate how many *moles* of the *second reactant* would be required for complete reaction of *1.00 g* of the *first reactant*. Indicate clearly the mole ratio used for the conversion.
    a. $CO(g) + O_2(g) \rightarrow CO_2(g)$
    b. $AgNO_3(aq) + CuSO_4(aq) \rightarrow Ag_2SO_4(s) + Cu(NO_3)_2 (aq)$
    c. $Al(s) + HCl(g) \rightarrow AlCl_3(s) + H_2(g)$
    d. $C_3H_8(g) + O_2(g) \rightarrow CO_2(g) + H_2O(g)$

82. One step in the commercial production of sulfuric acid, H_2SO_4, involves the conversion of sulfur dioxide, SO_2, into sulfur trioxide, SO_3.

$$2SO_2(g) + O_2(g) \rightarrow 2SO_3(g)$$

If 150 kg of SO_2 reacts completely, what mass of SO_3 should result?

83. Many metals occur naturally as sulfide compounds; examples include ZnS and CoS. Air pollution often accompanies the processing of these ores, because toxic sulfur dioxide is released as the ore is converted from the sulfide to the oxide by roasting (smelting). For example, consider the unbalanced equation for the roasting reaction for zinc.

$$ZnS(s) + O_2(g) \rightarrow ZnO(s) + SO_2(g)$$

How many kilograms of sulfur dioxide are produced when 1.0×10^2 kg of ZnS are roasted in excess oxygen by this process?

84. Elemental chlorine oxidizes the bromide ion of sodium bromide as follows:

$$Cl_2(g) + 2NaBr(aq) \rightarrow 2NaCl(aq) + Br_2(l)$$

How many grams of elemental bromine are produced when 25.0 g of elemental chlorine gas is pumped slowly into a large excess of sodium bromide solution?

85. When elemental copper is placed in a solution of silver nitrate, the following oxidation–reduction reaction takes place, forming elemental silver.

$$Cu(s) + 2AgNO_3(aq) \rightarrow Cu(NO_3)_2(aq) + Ag(s)$$

What mass of copper is required to remove all the silver from a silver nitrate solution containing 1.95 mg of silver nitrate?

86. When small quantities of elemental hydrogen gas are needed for laboratory work, the hydrogen is often generated by chemical reaction of a metal with acid. For example, zinc reacts with hydrochloric acid, releasing gaseous elemental hydrogen:

$$Zn(s) + 2HCl(aq) \rightarrow ZnCl_2(aq) + H_2(g)$$

What mass of hydrogen gas is produced when 2.50 g of zinc is reacted with excess aqueous hydrochloric acid?

87. The gaseous hydrocarbon acetylene, C_2H_2, is used in welders' torches because of the large amount of heat released when acetylene burns with oxygen.

$$2C_2H_2(g) + 5O_2(g) \rightarrow 4CO_2(g) + 2H_2O(g)$$

How many grams of oxygen gas are needed for the complete combustion of 150 g of acetylene?

88. For each of the following *unbalanced* chemical equations, suppose exactly 5.0 g of each reactant is taken. Determine which reactant is limiting, and calculate what mass of each product is expected, assuming that the limiting reactant is completely consumed.
    a. $Na(s) + Br_2(l) \rightarrow NaBr(s)$
    b. $Zn(s) + CuSO_4(aq) \rightarrow ZnSO_4)(aq) + Cu(s)$

c. $NH_4Cl(aq) + NaOH(aq) \rightarrow NH_3(g) + H_2O(l)$
$$+ NaCl(aq)$$
d. $Fe_2O_3(s) + CO(g) \rightarrow Fe(s) + CO_2(g)$

89. For each of the following *unbalanced* chemical equations, suppose 25.0 g of *each* reactant is taken. Show by calculation which reactant is limiting. Calculate the theoretical yield in grams of the product in boldface.
    a. $C_2H_5OH(l) + O_2(g) \rightarrow \mathbf{CO_2}(g) + H_2O(l)$
    b. $N_2(g) + O_2(g) \rightarrow \mathbf{NO}(g)$
    c. $NaClO_2(aq) + Cl_2(g) \rightarrow ClO_2(g) + \mathbf{NaCl}(aq)$
    d. $H_2(g) + N_2(g) \rightarrow \mathbf{NH_3}(g)$

90. Hydrazine, N_2H_4, emits a large quantity of energy when it reacts with oxygen, which has led to hydrazine's use as a fuel for rockets:

$$N_2H_4(l) + O_2(g) \rightarrow N_2(g) + 2H_2O(g)$$

How many moles of each of the gaseous products are produced when 20.0 g of pure hydrazine is ignited in the presence of 20.0 g of pure oxygen? How many grams of each product are produced?

91. Although elemental chlorine, Cl_2, is added to drinking water supplies primarily to kill microorganisms, another beneficial reaction that also takes place removes sulfides (which would impart unpleasant odors or tastes to the water). For example, the noxious-smelling gas hydrogen sulfide (its odor resembles that of rotten eggs) is removed from water by chlorine by the reaction:

$$H_2S(aq) + Cl_2(aq) \rightarrow HCl(aq) + S_8(s) \quad \text{(unbalanced)}$$

What mass of sulfur is removed from the water when 50. L of water containing 1.5×10^{-5} g of H_2S per liter is treated with 1.0 g of $Cl_2(g)$?

92. Before going to lab, a student read in his lab manual that the percent yield for a difficult reaction to be studied was likely to be only 40.% of the theoretical yield. The student's pre-lab stoichiometric calculations predict that the theoretical yield should be 12.5 g. What is the student's actual yield likely to be?

Cumulative Review for Chapters 9–10

1. What does the average *atomic mass* of an element represent? What unit is used for average atomic mass? Express the atomic mass unit in grams. Why is the average atomic mass for an element typically *not* a whole number?

2. Perhaps the most important concept in introductory chemistry concerns what a *mole* of a substance represents. The mole concept will come up again and again in later chapters in this book. What does one mole of a substance represent on a microscopic, atomic basis? What does one mole of a substance represent on a macroscopic, mass basis? Why have chemists defined the mole in this manner?

3. How do we know that 16.00 g of oxygen contains the same number of atoms as does 12.01 g of carbon, and that 22.99 g of sodium contains the same number of atoms as each of these? How do we know that 106.0 g of Na_2CO_3 contains the same number of carbon atoms as does 12.01 g of carbon, but three times as many oxygen atoms as in 16.00 g of oxygen, and twice as many sodium atoms as in 22.99 g of sodium?

4. Define *molar mass*. Using H_3PO_4 as an example, calculate the molar mass from the atomic masses of the elements.

5. What is meant by the *percentage composition* by mass for a compound? Describe in general terms how this information is obtained by experiment for new compounds. How can this information be calculated for known compounds?

6. Define, compare, and contrast what are meant by the *empirical* and *molecular* formulas for a substance. What does each of these formulas tell us about a compound? What information must be known for a compound before the molecular formula can be determined. Why is the molecular formula an *integer multiple* of the empirical formula?

7. When chemistry teachers prepare an exam question on determining the empirical formula of a compound, they usually take a known compound and calculate the percentage composition of the compound from the formula. They then give students this percentage composition data and have the students calculate the original formula. Using a compound of *your* choice, first use the molecular formula of the compound to calculate the percentage composition of the compound. Then use this percentage composition data to calculate the empirical formula of the compound.

8. Rather than giving students straight percentage composition data for determining the empirical formula of a compound (see Question 7), sometimes chemistry teachers will try to emphasize the experimental nature of formula determination by converting the percentage composition data into actual experimental masses. For example, the compound CH_4 contains 74.87% carbon by mass. Rather than giving students the data in this form, a teacher might instead say "When 1.000 g of a compound was analyzed, it was found to contain 0.7487 g of carbon, with the remainder consisting of hydrogen." Using the compound you chose for Question 7, and the percentage composition data you calculated, reword your data as suggested in this problem in terms of actual "experimental" masses. Then from these masses, calculate the empirical formula of your compound.

9. Balanced chemical equations give us information in terms of individual molecules reacting in the proportions indicated by the coefficients, and also in terms of macroscopic amounts (that is, moles). Write a balanced chemical equation of your choice, and interpret in words the meaning of the equation on the molecular and macroscopic levels.

10. Consider the balanced chemical equation for the combustion of butane (C_4H_{10}):

$$2C_4H_{10}(g) + 13O_2(g) \rightarrow 8CO_2(g) + 10H_2O(g)$$

Write the mole ratios that would permit you, for a given amount of $C_4H_{10}(g)$, to calculate the number of moles of each product that would be produced, as well as the number of moles of $O_2(g)$ that would be consumed. Show how these mole ratios would be used if 0.55 mol of is $C_4H_{10}(g)$ combusted.

11. In the practice of chemistry one of the most important calculations concerns the masses of products expected when particular masses of reactants are used in an experiment. For example, chemists judge the practicality and efficiency of a reaction by seeing how close the amount of product actually obtained is to the expected amount. Using a balanced chemical equation and an amount of starting material of your choice, summarize and illustrate the various steps needed in such a calculation for the expected amount of product.

12. What is meant by a *limiting reactant* in a particular reaction? In what way is the reaction "limited"? What does it mean to say that one or more of the reactants are present *in excess?* What happens to a reaction when the limiting reactant is used up?

13. For a balanced chemical equation of your choice, and using 25.0 g of each of the reactants in your equation, illustrate and explain how you would determine which reactant is the limiting reactant. Indicate *clearly* in your discussion how the choice of limiting reactant follows from your calculations.

14. What do we mean by the *theoretical yield* for a reaction? What is meant by the *actual yield?* Why might the actual yield for an experiment be *less* than the theoretical yield? Can the actual yield be *more* than the theoretical yield?

PROBLEMS

15. For 1.00-g samples of each of the following substances, calculate the number of moles present, as well as the n\ of atoms of each type present in the sample.
    a. $Na(s)$
    b. $H_2O(l)$
    c. $K_2CO_3(s)$
    d. $NO_2(g)$
    e. $C_{12}H_{22}O_{11}(s)$
    f. $Br_2(l)$
    g. $NaOH(s)$
    h. $Na_2O_2(s)$
    i. $O_3(g)$
    j. $NaC_2H_3O_2(s)$

16. For the compounds in Question 15, calculate the percentage by mass of each element present in the compounds.

17. A 151.9-mg sample of a new compound has been analyzed and found to contain the following masses of elements: carbon, 82.80 mg; hydrogen, 13.90 mg; oxygen, 55.15 mg. Calculate the empirical formula of this compound.

18. For each of the following balanced equations, calculate how many grams of each product would be formed if 25.0 g of the reactant listed first reacts completely with the second.
    a. $2AgNO_3(aq) + CaSO_4(aq) \rightarrow$
       $$Ag_2SO_4(s) + Ca(NO_3)_2(aq)$$
    b. $2Al(s) + 6HNO_3(aq) \rightarrow 2Al(NO_3)_3(aq) + 3H_2(g)$
    c. $H_3PO_4(aq) + 3NaOH(aq) \rightarrow$
       $$Na_3PO_4(aq) + 3H_2O(l)$$
    d. $CaO(s) + 2HCl(aq) \rightarrow CaCl_2(aq) + H_2O(l)$

19. For the reactions in Question 18, calculate the mass of each product formed if 12.5 g of the first reactant is combined with 10.0 g of the second reactant. Indicate which substance is the limiting reactant for each case.

20. Chlorine gas is a very reactive substance and will combine with most metals; for example,

    $$2Na(s) + Cl_2(g) \rightarrow 2NaCl(s)$$
    $$Mg(s) + Cl_2(g) \rightarrow MgCl_2(s)$$
    $$2Al(s) + 3Cl2(g) \rightarrow 2AlCl_3(s)$$

    Suppose individual 10.0-g samples of these three metals are reacted with separate 10.0 g samples of $Cl_2(g)$. In each case, determine whether the metal or chlorine is the limiting reactant, and calculate the theoretical yield of metal chloride for each process. If 9.85 g of product were obtained in each case, calculate the percent yield for each reaction.

CHAPTER 11

Modern Atomic Theory

The concept of atoms is a very useful one. It explains many important observations, such as why compounds always have the same composition (a specific compound always contains the same types and numbers of atoms) and how chemical reactions occur (they involve a rearrangement of atoms).

Once chemists came to "believe" in atoms, a logical question followed: what are atoms like? What is the structure of an atom? In Chapter 4 we learned to picture the atom with a positively charged nucleus composed of protons and neutrons at its center and electrons moving around the nucleus in a space very large compared to the size of the nucleus.

In this chapter we will look at atomic structure in more detail. In particular, we will develop a picture of the electron arrangements in atoms—a picture that allows us to account for the chemistry of the various elements. Recall from our discussion of the periodic table in Chapter 4 that, although atoms exhibit a great variety of characteristics, certain elements can be

The brilliant colors in fireworks are due to the light emitted by various types of atoms. Each atom emits a color that is characteristic of that atom (left). Neon, a noble gas, glows when a current is passed through it (right).

Alkali metals Halogens Noble gases

grouped together because they behave similarly. For example, fluorine, chlorine, bromine, and iodine (the halogens) show great chemical similarities. Likewise lithium, sodium, potassium, rubidium, and cesium (the alkali metals) exhibit many similar properties, and the noble gases (helium, neon, argon, krypton, xenon, and radon) are all very nonreactive. Although the members of each of these groups of elements show great similarity *within* the group, the differences in behavior *between* groups are striking. In this chapter we will see that it is the way the electrons are arranged in various atoms that accounts for these facts. However, before we examine atomic structure, we must consider the nature of electromagnetic radiation, which plays a central role in the study of the atom's behavior.

11.1 Electromagnetic Radiation and Energy

AIM: To understand electromagnetic radiation and the concept of quantized energy.

Light from the sun being diffracted by a prism.

One of the ways in which energy travels through space is by **electromagnetic radiation.** The light from the sun, the energy used to cook food in a microwave oven, the X rays used by dentists, and the radiant heat from a fireplace are all examples of electromagnetic radiation. Although these forms of radiant energy seem quite different, they all exhibit the same type of wavelike behavior and travel at the speed of light in a vacuum.

Waves have three primary characteristics: wavelength, frequency, and speed. **Wavelength** (symbolized by the Greek letter lambda, λ) is the *distance between two consecutive peaks or troughs in a wave,* as shown in Figure 11.1. **Frequency** (symbolized by the Greek letter nu, ν) indicates how many waves pass a given point per second. **Speed** indicates how fast a given peak moves through space.

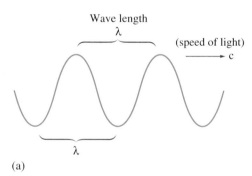

Wave length
λ

(speed of light)
c

λ

(a)

(b)

FIGURE 11.1
(a) A light wave moves through space at a speed of 3×10^8 m/s, which is denoted by the letter *c*. The distance between successive peaks or troughs is the wavelength, denoted by λ. (b) You can picture the wave traveling through space much as a swell (peak) in the ocean approaches the shore. A surfer is propelled toward the beach at the speed at which the wave is traveling.

CHEMISTRY IN FOCUS

Atmospheric Effects

The gaseous atmosphere of the earth is crucial to life in many different ways. One of the most important characteristics of the atmosphere is the way its molecules absorb radiation from the sun.

If it weren't for the protective nature of the atmosphere, the sun would "fry" us with its high-energy radiation. We are protected by the atmospheric ozone, a form of oxygen consisting of O_3 molecules, which absorbs high-energy radiation and thus prevents it from reaching the earth. This explains why we are so concerned that chemicals released into the atmosphere are destroying this high-altitude ozone.

The atmosphere also plays a central role in controlling the earth's temperature, a phenomenon called the *greenhouse effect*. The atmospheric gases CO_2, H_2O, CH_4, N_2O, and others do not absorb light in the visible region. Therefore, the visible light from the sun passes through the atmosphere to warm the earth. In turn, the earth radiates this energy back toward space as infrared radiation. (For example, think of the heat radiated from black asphalt on a hot summer day.) But the gases listed above are strong *absorbers* of *infrared* waves, and they reradiate some of this energy back toward the earth as shown in Figure 11.2. Thus these gases act as an insulating blanket keeping the earth much warmer than it would be without them. (If these gases were not present, all of the heat the earth radiates would be lost into space.)

However, there is a problem. When we burn fossil fuels (coal, petroleum, and natural gas), one of the products is CO_2. Because we use such huge quantities of fossil fuels, the CO_2 content in the atmosphere is increasing gradually but significantly. This should cause the earth to get warmer, eventually changing the weather patterns on the earth's surface and melting the polar ice caps, which would flood many low-lying areas.

Because the natural forces that control the earth's temperature are not very well understood at this point, it is difficult to decide whether the greenhouse warming has already started. But many scientists think it has. For example, the 1980s were among the warmest years the earth experienced since people started keeping records.

The greenhouse effect is something we must watch closely. Controlling it may mean lowering our dependence on fossil fuels and increasing our reliance on nuclear, solar, or other power sources. In recent years, the trend has been in the opposite direction.

FIGURE 11.2
Certain of the gases in the earth's atmosphere reflect back some of the infrared (heat) radiation produced by the earth. This keeps the earth warmer than it would be otherwise.

A composite satellite image of the earth's biomass constructed from the radiation given off by living matter over a multiyear period.

CHEMISTRY IN FOCUS

Solar Polar Bears

The polar bear, a regal beast that has dominated the world's arctic regions for thousands of years, can exist in its incredibly hostile environment partly because its fur is an almost perfect absorber and converter of solar radiation.

What color is a polar bear's fur? White, the obvious answer, is incorrect. The hairs on a polar bear are completely colorless and transparent. The bear *appears* white because of the way the rough inner surfaces of the hollow hairs reflect visible light. The most interesting characteristic of each of these hollow fibers is its ability to act as a solar converter designed to trap ultraviolet light and transmit it to the bear's black skin. In the summer, the sun directly supplies up to 25% of the bear's total energy requirements. This allows the polar bear to be very active in pursuing prey, while still building up the layers of blubber it needs to survive the winter. This fascinating system

also ensures that although the skin of the polar bear is very warm, the outer layers of the fur remain at about the same temperature as the bear's surroundings. Because of the small temperature difference between the outer layers of its fur and the air, the bear loses very little energy through heat leakage to the environment.

Human society could benefit greatly from what we know about polar bear fur as we continue to search for more efficient energy supplies. Clearly, covering our roofs with polar bear pelts is not an option, but polar bear hair provides an excellent model for the possible development of synthetic optical fibers to convert the sun's radiant energy to other energy forms.

A pair of polar bears in the Arctic.

We sometimes use the generic term *light* for electromagnetic radiation.

Electromagnetic radiation, which we often call light, is divided into the various classes according to wavelength, as shown in Figure 11.3. Radiation provides an important means of energy transfer. For example, the energy from the sun reaches the earth mainly in the forms of visible and ultraviolet radiation, and the glowing coals of a fireplace transmit heat energy by infrared radiation. In a microwave oven, the water molecules in food absorb microwave radiation, which increases their motions. This energy is then transferred to other types of molecules by collisions, causing an increase in the food's temperature.

Although we will not go into any details here, scientists have much evidence that a beam of light can also be thought of as a stream of tiny packets of energy called **photons.** So what is the exact nature of light? Does it consist of waves or is it a stream of discrete particles of energy? It seems to be both (Figure 11.4). This situation is often referred to as the wave–particle nature of light.

FIGURE 11.3
The different wavelengths of electromagnetic radiation.

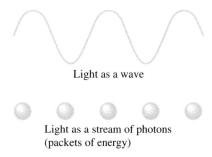

Light as a wave

Light as a stream of photons
(packets of energy)

FIGURE 11.4
Electromagnetic radiation (a beam of light) can be pictured in two ways: as a wave and as a stream of individual packets of energy called photons.

11.2 The Energy Levels of Hydrogen

AIM: To understand how the emission spectrum of hydrogen demonstrates the quantized nature of energy.

An atom can lose energy by *emitting* a photon.

Each photon of blue light carries a larger quantity of energy than a photon of red light.

An atom with excess energy is said to be in an *excited state.* An excited atom can release some or all of its excess energy by emitting a photon (a "particle" of electromagnetic radiation) and thus move to a lower energy state. The lowest possible energy state of an atom is called its *ground state.*

We can learn a great deal about the energy states of hydrogen atoms by observing the photons they emit. To understand the significance of this, you need to know that the *different wavelengths of light carry different amounts of energy per photon.* For example, a beam of red light has lower-energy photons than a beam of blue light.

When a hydrogen atom absorbs energy from some outside source, it uses this energy to enter an excited state. It can release this excess energy (go back to a lower state) by emitting a photon of light (Figure 11.5). We can

FIGURE 11.5
(a) A sample of H atoms receives energy from an external source, which causes some of the atoms to become excited (to possess excess energy). (b) The excited atoms (H) can release the excess energy by emitting photons. The energy of each emitted photon corresponds exactly to the energy lost by each excited atom.

FIGURE 11.6
When an excited H atom returns to a lower energy level, it emits a photon that contains the energy released by the atom. Thus the energy of the photon corresponds to the difference in energy between the two states.

FIGURE 11.7
When excited hydrogen atoms return to lower energy states, they emit photons of certain energies, and thus certain colors. Shown here are the colors and wavelengths (in nanometers) of the photons in the visible region that are emitted by excited hydrogen atoms.

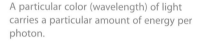

A particular color (wavelength) of light carries a particular amount of energy per photon.

picture this process in terms of the energy-level diagram shown in Figure 11.6. The important point here is that *the energy contained in the photon corresponds to the change in energy that the atom experiences* in going from the excited state to the lower state.

Consider the following experiment. Suppose we take a sample of H atoms and put a lot of energy into the system (as represented in Figure 11.5). When we study the photons of visible light emitted, we see only certain colors (Figure 11.7). That is, *only certain types of photons* are produced. We don't see all colors; we see only selected colors. This is a very significant result. Let's discuss carefully what it means.

Because only certain photons are emitted, we know that only certain energy changes are occurring (Figure 11.8). This means that the hydrogen atom must have *certain discrete energy levels* (Figure 11.9). Excited hydrogen atoms *always* emit photons with the same discrete colors (wavelengths)—those shown in Figure 11.7. They *never* emit photons with energies (colors) in between those shown. So we can conclude that all hydrogen atoms have the same set of discrete energy levels. We say the energy levels of hydrogen are **quantized.** That is, only *certain values are allowed.* Scientists have found that the energy levels of *all* atoms are quantized.

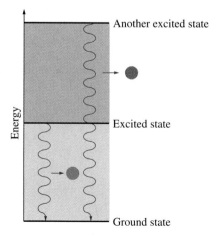

FIGURE 11.8
Hydrogen atoms have several excited-state energy levels. The color of the photon emitted depends on the energy change that produces it. A larger energy change may correspond to a blue photon, whereas a smaller change may produce a red photon.

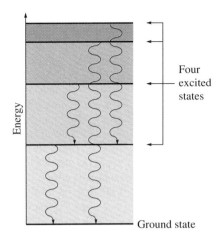

FIGURE 11.9
Each photon emitted by an excited hydrogen atom corresponds to a particular energy change in the hydrogen atom. In this diagram the horizontal lines represent discrete energy levels present in the hydrogen atom. A given H atom can exist in any of these energy states and can undergo energy changes to the ground state as well as to other excited states.

FIGURE 11.10
(a) Continuous energy levels. Any energy value is allowed. (b) Discrete (quantized) energy levels. Only certain energy states are allowed.

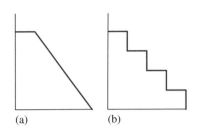

FIGURE 11.11
The difference between continuous and quantized energy levels can be illustrated by comparing a flight of stairs with a ramp. (a) A ramp varies continuously in elevation. (b) A flight of stairs allows only certain elevations; the elevations are quantized.

The quantized nature of the energy levels in atoms was a surprise when scientists discovered it. It had been assumed prior to this that an atom could exist at any energy level. That is, everyone had assumed that atoms could have a continuous set of energy levels rather than only certain discrete values (Figure 11.10). A useful analogy here is the contrast between the elevations allowed by a ramp, which vary continuously, and those allowed by a set of steps, which are discrete (Figure 11.11). The discovery of the quantized nature of energy has radically changed our view of the atom, as we will see in the next few sections.

11.3 *The Bohr Model of the Atom*

AIM: To learn about Bohr's model of the hydrogen atom.

In 1911 at the age of twenty-five, Niels Bohr (Figure 11.12) received his Ph.D. in physics. He was convinced that the atom could be pictured as a small positive nucleus with electrons orbiting around it.

Over the next two years, Bohr constructed a model of the hydrogen atom with quantized energy levels that agreed with the hydrogen emission results we have just discussed. Bohr pictured the electron moving in circular orbits corresponding to the various allowed energy levels. He suggested that the electron could jump to a different orbit by absorbing or emitting a photon of light with exactly the correct energy content. Thus in the Bohr atom, the

FIGURE 11.12
Niels Hendrik David Bohr (1885–1962) as a boy lived in the shadow of his younger brother Harald, who played on the 1908 Danish Olympic Soccer Team and later became a distinguished mathematician. In school, Bohr received his poorest marks in composition and struggled with writing during his entire life. In fact, he wrote so poorly that he was forced to dictate his Ph.D. thesis to his mother. He is one of the very few people who felt the need to write rough drafts of postcards. Nevertheless, Bohr was a brilliant physicist. After receiving his Ph.D. in Denmark, he constructed a quantum model for the hydrogen atom by the time he was 27. Even though his model later proved to be incorrect, Bohr remained a central figure in the drive to understand the atom. He was awarded the Nobel Prize in physics in 1922.

FIGURE 11.13
The Bohr model of the hydrogen atom represented the electron as restricted to certain circular orbits around the nucleus.

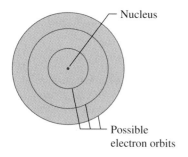

Nucleus

Possible electron orbits

Although Bohr's model is consistent with the energy levels for hydrogen, it is fundamentally incorrect.

energy levels in the hydrogen atom represented certain allowed circular orbits (Figure 11.13).

At first Bohr's model appeared very promising. It fit the hydrogen atom very well. However, when this model was applied to atoms other than hydrogen, it did not work. In fact, further experiments showed that the Bohr model is fundamentally incorrect. Although the Bohr model paved the way for later theories, it is important to realize that the current theory of atomic structure is not the same as the Bohr model. Electrons do *not* move around the nucleus in circular orbits like planets orbiting the sun. Surprisingly, as we shall see later in this chapter, we do not know exactly how the electrons move in an atom.

11.4 The Wave Mechanical Model of the Atom

AIM: To understand how the electron's position is represented in the wave mechanical model.

By the mid-1920s it had become apparent that the Bohr model was incorrect. Scientists needed to pursue a totally new approach. Two young physicists, Louis Victor de Broglie from France and Werner Schrödinger from Austria, suggested that because light seems to have both wave and particle characteristics (it behaves simultaneously as a wave and as a stream of particles), the electron might also exhibit both of these characteristics. Although everyone had assumed that the electron was a tiny particle, these scientists said it might be useful to find out whether it could be described as a wave.

There is now much experimental evidence suggesting that all matter exhibits both wave and particle properties.

Louis Victor de Broglie

FIGURE 11.14
A representation of the photo of the firefly experiment. Remember that a picture is brightest where the film has been exposed to the most light. Thus the intensity of the color reflects how often the firefly visited a given point in the room. Notice that the brightest area is in the center of the room near the source of the sex attractant.

When Schrödinger carried out a mathematical analysis based on this idea, he found that it led to a new model for the hydrogen atom that seemed to apply equally well to other atoms—something Bohr's model failed to do. We will now explore a general picture of this model, which is called the **wave mechanical model** of the atom.

In the Bohr model, the electron was assumed to move in circular orbits. In the wave mechanical model, on the other hand, the electron states are described by orbitals. *Orbitals are nothing like orbits.* To approximate the idea of an orbital, picture a single male firefly in a room in the center of which an open vial of female sex-attractant hormones is suspended. The room is extremely dark and there is a camera in one corner with its shutter open. Every time the firefly "flashes," the camera records a pinpoint of light and thus the firefly's position in the room at that moment. The firefly senses the sex attractant, and as you can imagine, it spends a lot of time at or close to it. However, now and then the insect flies randomly around the room.

When the film is taken out of the camera and developed, the picture will probably look like Figure 11.14. Because a picture is brightest where the film has been exposed to the most light, the color intensity at any given point tells us how often the firefly visited a given point in the room. Notice that, as we might expect, the firefly spent the most time near the room's center.

Now suppose you are watching the firefly in the dark room. You see it flash at a given point far from the center of the room. Where do you expect to see it next? There is really no way to be sure. The firefly's flight path is not precisely predictable. However, if you had seen the time-exposure picture of the firefly's activities (Figure 11.14), you would have some idea where to look next. Your best chance would be to look more toward the center of the room. Figure 11.14 suggests there is the highest probability (the highest odds, the greatest likelihood) of finding the firefly at any particular moment near the center of the room. You *can't be sure* the firefly will fly toward the center of the room, but it *probably* will. So the time-exposure picture is a kind of "probability map" of the firefly's flight pattern.

According to the wave mechanical model, the electron in the hydrogen atom can be pictured as being something like this firefly. Schrödinger found that he could not precisely describe the electron's path. His mathematics enabled him only to predict the probabilities of finding the electron at given points in space around the nucleus. In its ground state the hydrogen electron has a probability map like that shown in Figure 11.15. The more intense the

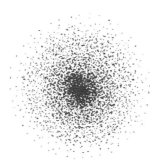

FIGURE 11.15
The probability map, or orbital, that describes the hydrogen electron in its lowest possible energy state. The more intense the color of a given dot, the more likely it is that the electron will be found at that point. We have no information about when the electron will be at a particular point or about how it moves. Note that the probability of the electron's presence is highest closest to the positive nucleus (located at the center of this diagram), as might be expected.

color at a particular point, the more probable it is that the electron will be found at that point at a given instant. The model gives *no information about when* the electron occupies a certain point in space or *how it moves.* In fact, we have good reasons to believe that we can *never know* the details of electron motion, no matter how sophisticated our models may become. But one thing we feel confident about is that the electron *does not* orbit the nucleus in circles as Bohr suggested.

11.5 The Hydrogen Orbitals

AIM: To learn about the shapes of orbitals designated by s, p, and d.

(a)   (b)

FIGURE 11.16
The hydrogen 1s orbital. (a) The size of the orbital is defined by a sphere that contains 90% of the total electron probability. That is, the electron can be found *inside* this sphere 90% of the time. (b) The 1s orbital is often represented simply as a sphere. However, the most accurate picture of the orbital is the probability map represented in (a).

The probability map for the hydrogen electron shown in Figure 11.15 is called an **orbital.** Although the probability of finding the electron decreases at greater distances from the nucleus, the probability of finding it even at great distances from the nucleus never becomes exactly zero. A useful analogy might be the lack of a sharp boundary between the earth's atmosphere and "outer space." The atmosphere fades away gradually, but there are always a few molecules present. Because the edge of an orbital is "fuzzy," an orbital does not have an exactly defined size. So chemists arbitrarily define its size as the sphere that contains 90% of the total electron probability (Figure 11.16a). This means that the electron spends 90% of the time inside this surface and 10% somewhere outside this surface. (Note that we are *not* saying the electron travels only on the *surface* of the sphere.) The orbital represented in Figure 11.16(b) is named the **1s orbital,** and it describes the hydrogen electron's lowest energy state (the ground state).

In Section 11.2 we saw that the hydrogen atom can absorb energy to transfer the electron to a higher energy state (an excited state). In terms of the obsolete Bohr model, this meant the electron was transferred to an orbit with a larger radius. In the wave mechanical model, these higher energy states correspond to different kinds of orbitals with different shapes.

At this point we need to stop and consider how the hydrogen atom is organized. Remember, we showed earlier that the hydrogen atom has discrete energy levels. We call these levels **principal energy levels** and label them with integers (Figure 11.17). Next we find that each of these levels is subdivided into **sublevels.** The following analogy should help you understand this. Picture an inverted triangle (Figure 11.18). We divide the principal levels into

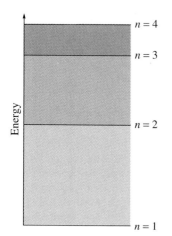

FIGURE 11.17
The first four principal energy levels in the hydrogen atom. Each level is assigned an integer, *n*.

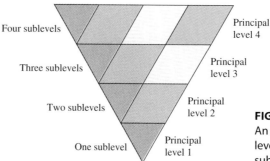

FIGURE 11.18
An illustration of how principal levels can be divided into sublevels.

various numbers of sublevels. Principal level 1 consists of one sublevel, principal level 2 has two sublevels, principal level 3 has three sublevels, and principal level 4 has four sublevels.

Like our triangle, the principal energy levels in the hydrogen atom contain sublevels. As we will see presently, these sublevels contain spaces for the electron that we call orbitals. Principal energy level 1 consists of just one sublevel, or one type of orbital. The spherical shape of this orbital is shown in Figure 11.16. We label this orbital 1*s*. The number 1 is for the principal energy level, and *s* is a shorthand way to label a particular sublevel (type of orbital).

Principal energy level 2 has two sublevels. (Note the correspondence between the principal energy level number and the number of sublevels.) These sublevels are labeled 2*s* and 2*p*. The 2*s* sublevel consists of one orbital (called the 2*s*), and the 2*p* sublevel consists of three orbitals (called $2p_x$, $2p_y$, and $2p_z$). Let's return to the inverted triangle to illustrate this. Figure 11.19 shows principal level 2 divided into the sublevels 2*s* and 2*p* (which is subdivided into $2p_x$, $2p_y$, and $2p_z$). The orbitals have the shapes shown in Figures 11.20 and 11.21. The 2*s* orbital is spherical like the 1*s* orbital but larger in size (see Figure 11.20). The three 2*p* orbitals are not spherical but have two "lobes." These orbitals are shown in Figure 11.21 both as electron probability maps and as surfaces that contain 90% of the total electron probability. Notice that the label *x*, *y*, or *z* on a given 2*p* orbital tells along which axis the lobes of that orbital are directed.

What we have learned so far about the hydrogen atom is summarized in Figure 11.22. Principal energy level 1 has one sublevel, which contains the 1*s* orbital. Principal energy level 2 contains two sublevels, one of which contains the 2*s* orbital and one of which contains the 2*p* orbitals (three of them). Note that each orbital is designated by a symbol or label. We summarize the information given by this label in the box on p. 306.

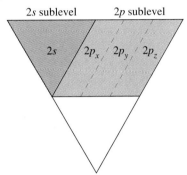

FIGURE 11.19
Principal level 2 shown divided into the 2*s* and 2*p* sublevels.

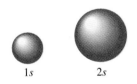

FIGURE 11.20
The relative sizes of the 1*s* and 2*s* orbitals of hydrogen.

FIGURE 11.21
The three 2*p* orbitals: (a) $2p_x$ (b) $2p_z$ (c) $2p_y$. The *x, y,* or *z* label indicates along which axis the two lobes are directed. Each orbital is shown both as a probability map and as a surface that encloses 90% of the electron probability.

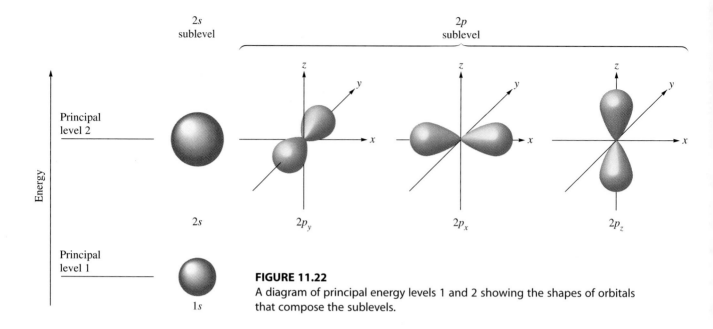

FIGURE 11.22
A diagram of principal energy levels 1 and 2 showing the shapes of orbitals that compose the sublevels.

Orbital Labels

1. The number tells the principal energy level.

2. The letter tells the shape. The letter *s* means a spherical orbital; the lctter *p* means a two-lobed orbital. The *x, y,* or *z* subscript on a *p* orbital label tells along which of the coordinate axes the two lobes lie.

One important characteristic of orbitals is that as the level number increases, the average distance of the electron in that orbital from the nucleus also increases. That is, when the hydrogen electron is in the 1*s* orbital (the ground state), it spends most of its time much closer to the nucleus than when it occupies the 2*s* orbital (an excited state).

You may be wondering at this point why hydrogen, which has only one electron, has more than one orbital. It is best to think of an orbital as a *potential space* for an electron. The hydrogen electron can occupy only a single orbital at a time, but the other orbitals are still available should the electron be transferred into one of them. For example, when a hydrogen atom is in its ground state (lowest possible energy state), the electron is in the 1*s* orbital. By adding the correct amount of energy (for example, a specific photon of light), we can excite the electron to the 2*s* orbital or to one of the 2*p* orbitals.

So far we have discussed only two of hydrogen's energy levels. There are many others. For example, level 3 has three sublevels (see Figure 11.18), which we label 3*s*, 3*p*, and 3*d*. The 3*s* sublevel contains a single 3*s* orbital, a spherical orbital larger than 1*s* and 2*s* (Figure 11.23). Sublevel 3*p* contains

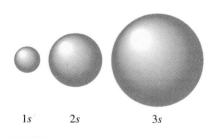

FIGURE 11.23
The relative sizes of the spherical 1*s*, 2*s*, and 3*s* orbitals of hydrogen.

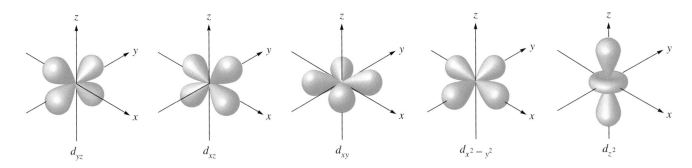

FIGURE 11.24
The shapes and labels of the five 3d orbitals.

three orbitals: $3p_x$, $3p_y$, and $3p_z$, which are shaped like the $2p$ orbitals except that they are larger. The $3d$ sublevel contains five $3d$ orbitals with the shapes and labels shown in Figure 11.24. (You do not need to memorize the $3d$ orbital shapes and labels. They are shown for completeness.)

Notice as you compare levels 1, 2, and 3 that a new type of orbital (sublevel) is added in each principal energy level. (Recall that the p orbitals are added in level 2 and the d orbitals in level 3.) This makes sense because in going farther out from the nucleus, there is more space available and thus room for more orbitals.

Think of orbitals as ways of dividing up the space around a nucleus.

It might help you to understand that the number of orbitals increases with the principal energy level if you think of a theater in the round. Picture a round stage with circular rows of seats surrounding it. The farther from the stage a row of seats is, the more seats it contains because the circle is larger. Orbitals divide up the space around a nucleus somewhat like the seats in this circular theater. The greater the distance from the nucleus, the more space there is and the more orbitals we find.

The pattern of increasing numbers of orbitals continues with level 4. Level 4 has four sublevels labeled $4s$, $4p$, $4d$, and $4f$. The $4s$ sublevel has a single $4s$ orbital. The $4p$ sublevel contains three orbitals ($4p_x$, $4p_y$, and $4p_z$). The $4d$ sublevel has five $4d$ orbitals. The $4f$ sublevel has seven $4f$ orbitals.

The $4s$, $4p$, and $4d$ orbitals have the same shapes as the earlier s, p, and d orbitals, respectively, but are larger. We will not be concerned here with the shapes of the f orbitals.

11.6 *The Wave Mechanical Model: Further Development*

AIMS: To review the energy levels and orbitals of the wave mechanical model of the atom. To learn about electron spin.

A model for the atom is of little use if it does not apply to all atoms. The Bohr model was discarded because it could be applied only to hydrogen. The wave mechanical model can be applied to all atoms in basically the same form as we have just used it for hydrogen. In fact, the major triumph of this model is its ability to explain the periodic table of the elements. Recall that the elements on the periodic table are arranged in vertical groups, which contain elements that typically show similar chemical properties. The wave mechanical model of the atom allows us to explain, based on electron arrangements, why these similarities occur. We will see in due time how this is done.

Remember that an atom has as many electrons as it has protons to give it a zero overall charge. Therefore, all atoms beyond hydrogen have more than one electron. Before we can consider the atoms beyond hydrogen, we must describe one more property of electrons that determines how they can be arranged in an atom's orbitals. This property is spin. Each electron appears to be spinning as a top spins on its axis. Like the top, an electron can spin only in one of two directions. We often represent spin with an arrow: either ↑ or ↓. One arrow represents the electron spinning in the one direction, and the other represents the electron spinning in the opposite direction. For our purposes, what is most important about electron spin is that two electrons must have *opposite* spins to occupy the same orbital. That is, two electrons that have the same spin cannot occupy the same orbital. This leads to the **Pauli exclusion principle:** an atomic orbital can hold a maximum of two electrons, and those two electrons must have opposite spins.

Before we apply the wave mechanical model to atoms beyond hydrogen, we will summarize the model for convenient reference.

Principal Components of the Wave Mechanical Model of the Atom

1. Atoms have a series of energy levels called **principal energy levels,** which are designated by whole numbers symbolized by n; n can equal 1, 2, 3, 4, ... Level 1 corresponds to $n = 1$, level 2 corresponds to $n = 2$, and so on.

2. The energy of the level increases as the value of n increases.

3. Each principal energy level contains one or more *types* of orbitals, called **sublevels.**

4. The number of sublevels present in a given principal energy level equals n. For example, level 1 contains one sublevel ($1s$); level 2 contains two sublevels (two types of orbitals), the $2s$ orbital and the three $2p$ orbitals; and so on. These are summarized in the following table. The number of each type of orbital is shown in parentheses.

n	Sublevels (Types of Orbitals) Present			
1	$1s(1)$			
2	$2s(1)$	$2p(3)$		
3	$3s(1)$	$3p(3)$	$3d(5)$	
4	$4s(1)$	$4p(3)$	$4d(5)$	$4f(7)$

5. The n value is always used to label the orbitals of a given principal level and is followed by a letter that indicates the type (shape) of the

orbital. For example, the designation 3*p* means an orbital in level 3 that has two lobes (a *p* orbital always has two lobes).

6. An orbital can be empty or it can contain one or two electrons, but never more than two. If two electrons occupy the same orbital, they must have opposite spins.

7. The shape of an orbital does not indicate the details of electron movement. It indicates the probability distribution for an electron residing in that orbital.

EXAMPLE 11.1 *Understanding the Wave Mechanical Model of the Atom*

Indicate whether each of the following statements about atomic structure is true or false.

a. An *s* orbital is always spherical in shape.

b. The 2*s* orbital is the same size as the 3*s* orbital.

c. The number of lobes on a *p* orbital increases as *n* increases. That is, a 3*p* orbital has more lobes than a 2*p* orbital.

d. Level 1 has one *s* orbital, level 2 has two *s* orbitals, level 3 has three *s* orbitals, and so on.

e. The electron path is indicated by the surface of the orbital.

Solution

a. True. The size of the sphere increases as *n* increases, but the shape is always spherical.

b. False. The 3*s* orbital is larger (the electron is farther from the nucleus on average) than the 2*s* orbital.

c. False. A *p* orbital always has two lobes.

d. False. Each principal energy level has only one *s* orbital.

e. False. The electron is *somewhere inside* the orbital surface 90% of the time. The electron does not move around *on* this surface.

 Self-Check Exercise 11.1

Define the following terms.

a. Bohr orbits
b. orbitals
c. orbital size
d. sublevel

See Problems 11.33 through 11.40.

11.7 Electron Arrangements in the First Eighteen Atoms on the Periodic Table

AIMS: To understand how the principal energy levels fill with electrons in atoms beyond hydrogen. To learn about valence electrons and core electrons.

H (Z = 1)
He (Z = 2)
Li (Z = 3)
Be (Z = 4)
B (Z = 5)
C (Z = 6)
N (Z = 7)
O (Z = 8)
F (Z = 9)
Ne (Z = 10)

We will now describe the electron arrangements in atoms with $Z = 1$ to $Z = 18$ by placing electrons in the various orbitals in the principal energy levels, starting with $n = 1$, and then continuing with $n = 2$, $n = 3$, and so on. For the first eighteen elements, the individual sublevels fill in the following order: $1s$, then $2s$, then $2p$, then $3s$, then $3p$.

The most attractive orbital to an electron in an atom is always the $1s$, because in this orbital the negatively charged electron is closer to the positively charged nucleus than in any other orbital. That is, the $1s$ orbital involves the space around the nucleus that is closest to the nucleus. As n increases, the orbital becomes larger—the electron, on average, occupies space farther from the nucleus.

So in its ground state hydrogen has its lone electron in the $1s$ orbital. This is commonly represented in two ways. First, we say that hydrogen has the electron arrangement, or **electron configuration, $1s^1$.** This just means there is one electron in the $1s$ orbital. We can also represent this configuration by using an **orbital diagram,** also called a **box diagram,** in which orbitals are represented by boxes grouped by sublevel with small arrows indicating the electrons. For *hydrogen,* the electron configuration and box diagram are

Number of electrons in the orbital

$\rightarrow 1s^1$

Value of n (principal energy level)

Type (shape) of orbital

H: $1s^1$ $1s$
                      ↑

   Configuration   Orbital diagram

The arrow represents an electron spinning in a particular direction. The next element is *helium,* $Z = 2$. It has two protons in its nucleus and so has two electrons. Because the $1s$ orbital is the most desirable, both electrons go there but with opposite spins. For helium, the electron configuration and box diagram are

Two electrons in $1s$ orbital

He: $1s^2$ $1s$
                       ↑↓

The opposite electron spins are shown by the opposing arrows in the box.

Lithium ($Z = 3$) has three electrons, two of which go into the $1s$ orbital. That is, two electrons fill that orbital. The $1s$ orbital is the only orbital for $n = 1$, so the third electron must occupy an orbital with $n = 2$—in this case the $2s$ orbital. This gives a $1s^2 2s^1$ configuration. The electron configuration and box diagram are

Li: $1s^2 2s^1$ $1s$ $2s$
                           ↑↓   ↑

The next element, *beryllium,* has four electrons, which occupy the $1s$ and $2s$ orbitals with opposite spins.

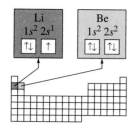

Be: $1s^2 2s^2$

$$\begin{array}{cc} 1s & 2s \\ \boxed{\uparrow\downarrow} & \boxed{\uparrow\downarrow} \end{array}$$

Boron has five electrons, four of which occupy the $1s$ and $2s$ orbitals. The fifth electron goes into the second type of orbital with $n = 2$, one of the $2p$ orbitals.

B: $1s^2 2s^2 2p^1$

$$\begin{array}{ccc} 1s & 2s & 2p \\ \boxed{\uparrow\downarrow} & \boxed{\uparrow\downarrow} & \boxed{\uparrow}\boxed{}\boxed{} \end{array}$$

Because all the $2p$ orbitals have the same energy, it does not matter which $2p$ orbital the electron occupies.

Carbon, the next element, has six electrons: two electrons occupy the $1s$ orbital, two occupy the $2s$ orbital, and two occupy $2p$ orbitals. There are three $2p$ orbitals, so each of the mutually repulsive electrons occupies a different $2p$ orbital. For reasons we will not consider, in the separate $2p$ orbitals the electrons have the same spin.

The configuration for carbon could be written $1s^2 2s^2 2p^1 2p^1$ to indicate that the electrons occupy separate $2p$ orbitals. However, the configuration is usually given as $1s^2 2s^2 2p^2$, and it is understood that the electrons are in different $2p$ orbitals.

Like charges repel.

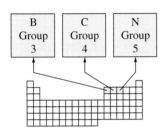

C: $1s^2 2s^2 2p^2$

$$\begin{array}{ccc} 1s & 2s & 2p \\ \boxed{\uparrow\downarrow} & \boxed{\uparrow\downarrow} & \boxed{\uparrow}\boxed{\uparrow}\boxed{} \end{array}$$

Note the like spins for the unpaired electrons in the $2p$ orbitals.

The configuration for *nitrogen,* which has seven electrons, is $1s^2 2s^2 2p^3$. The three electrons in $2p$ orbitals occupy separate orbitals and have like spins.

N: $1s^2 2s^2 2p^3$

$$\begin{array}{ccc} 1s & 2s & 2p \\ \boxed{\uparrow\downarrow} & \boxed{\uparrow\downarrow} & \boxed{\uparrow}\boxed{\uparrow}\boxed{\uparrow} \end{array}$$

The configuration for *oxygen,* which has eight electrons, is $1s^2 2s^2 2p^4$. One of the $2p$ orbitals is now occupied by a pair of electrons with opposite spins, as required by the Pauli exclusion principle.

O: $1s^2 2s^2 2p^4$

$$\begin{array}{ccc} 1s & 2s & 2p \\ \boxed{\uparrow\downarrow} & \boxed{\uparrow\downarrow} & \boxed{\uparrow\downarrow}\boxed{\uparrow}\boxed{\uparrow} \end{array}$$

The electron configurations and orbital diagrams for *fluorine* (nine electrons) and *neon* (ten electrons) are

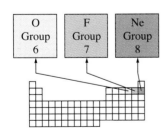

F: $1s^2 2s^2 2p^5$

$$\begin{array}{ccc} 1s & 2s & 2p \\ \boxed{\uparrow\downarrow} & \boxed{\uparrow\downarrow} & \boxed{\uparrow\downarrow}\boxed{\uparrow\downarrow}\boxed{\uparrow} \end{array}$$

Ne: $1s^2 2s^2 2p^6$

$$\begin{array}{ccc} 1s & 2s & 2p \\ \boxed{\uparrow\downarrow} & \boxed{\uparrow\downarrow} & \boxed{\uparrow\downarrow}\boxed{\uparrow\downarrow}\boxed{\uparrow\downarrow} \end{array}$$

With neon, the orbitals with $n = 1$ and $n = 2$ are completely filled.

For *sodium,* which has eleven electrons, the first ten electrons occupy the $1s$, $2s$, and $2p$ orbitals, and the eleventh electron must occupy the first orbital with $n = 3$, the $3s$ orbital. The electron configuration for sodium is $1s^2 2s^2 2p^6 3s^1$. To avoid writing the inner-level electrons, we often abbreviate the configuration $1s^2 2s^2 2p^6 3s^1$ as $[Ne]3s^1$, where $[Ne]$ represents the electron configuration of neon, $1s^2 2s^2 2p^6$.

[Ne] is shorthand for $1s^2 2s^2 2p^6$.

H $1s^1$							He $1s^2$
Li $2s^1$	Be $2s^2$	B $2p^1$	C $2p^2$	N $2p^3$	O $2p^4$	F $2p^5$	Ne $2p^6$
Na $3s^1$	Mg $3s^2$	Al $3p^1$	Si $3p^2$	P $3p^3$	S $3p^4$	Cl $3p^5$	Ar $3p^6$

FIGURE 11.25
The electron configurations in the sublevel last occupied for the first eighteen elements.

The orbital diagram for sodium is

$$\begin{array}{cccc} 1s & 2s & 2p & 3s \\ \boxed{\uparrow\downarrow} & \boxed{\uparrow\downarrow} & \boxed{\uparrow\downarrow}\boxed{\uparrow\downarrow}\boxed{\uparrow\downarrow} & \boxed{\uparrow} \end{array}$$

The next element, *magnesium*, $Z = 12$, has the electron configuration $1s^2 2s^2 2p^6 3s^2$, or $[Ne]3s^2$.

The next six elements, *aluminum* through *argon*, have electron configurations obtained by filling the $3p$ orbitals one electron at a time. Figure 11.25 summarizes the electron configurations of the first eighteen elements by giving the number of electrons in the type of orbital (sublevel) occupied last.

EXAMPLE 11.2 *Writing Orbital Diagrams*

Write the orbital diagram for magnesium.

Solution

Magnesium ($Z = 12$) has twelve electrons that are placed successively in the $1s$, $2s$, $2p$, and $3s$ orbitals to give the electron configuration $1s^2 2s^2 2p^6 3s^2$. The orbital diagram is

$$\begin{array}{cccc} 1s & 2s & 2p & 3s \\ \boxed{\uparrow\downarrow} & \boxed{\uparrow\downarrow} & \boxed{\uparrow\downarrow}\boxed{\uparrow\downarrow}\boxed{\uparrow\downarrow} & \boxed{\uparrow\downarrow} \end{array}$$

Only occupied orbitals are shown here.

 Self-Check Exercise 11.2

Write the complete electron configuration and the orbital diagram for each of the elements aluminum through argon.

See Problems 11.45 through 11.50.

At this point it is useful to introduce the concept of **valence electrons**—that is, *the electrons in the outermost (highest) principal energy level of an atom.* For example, nitrogen, which has the electron configuration $1s^2 2s^2 2p^3$, has electrons in principal levels 1 and 2. Therefore, level 2 (which has $2s$ and $2p$ sublevels) is the valence level of nitrogen, and the $2s$ and $2p$ electrons are the valence electrons. For the sodium atom (electron configuration $1s^2 2s^2 2p^6 3s^1$, or $[Ne]3s^1$) the valence electron is the electron in the $3s$

orbital, because in this case principal energy level 3 is the outermost level that contains an electron. The valence electrons are the most important electrons to chemists because, being the outermost electrons, they are the ones involved when atoms attach to each other (form bonds), as we will see in the next chapter. The inner electrons, which are known as **core electrons,** are not involved in bonding atoms to each other.

Note in Figure 11.25 that a very important pattern is developing: except for helium, *the atoms of elements in the same group (vertical column of the periodic table) have the same number of electrons in a given type of orbital* (sublevel), except that the orbitals are in different principal energy levels. Remember that the elements were originally organized into groups on the periodic table on the basis of similarities in chemical properties. Now we understand the reason behind these groupings. Elements with the same valence electron arrangement show very similar chemical behavior.

11.8 *Electron Configurations and the Periodic Table*

AIM: To learn about the electron configurations of atoms with Z greater than 18.

In the previous section we saw that we can describe the atoms beyond hydrogen by simply filling the atomic orbitals starting with level $n = 1$ and working outward in order. This works fine until we reach the element *potassium* ($Z = 19$), which is the next element after argon. Because the $3p$ orbitals are fully occupied in argon, we might expect the next electron to go into a $3d$ orbital (recall that for $n = 3$ the sublevels are $3s$, $3p$, and $3d$). However, experiments show that the chemical properties of potassium are very similar to those of lithium and sodium. Because we have learned to associate similar chemical properties with similar valence-electron arrangements, we predict that the valence-electron configuration for potassium is $4s^1$, resembling sodium ($3s^1$) and lithium ($2s^1$). That is, we expect the last electron in potassium to occupy the $4s$ orbital instead of one of the $3d$ orbitals. This means that principal energy level 4 begins to fill before level 3 has been completed. This conclusion is confirmed by many types of experiments. So the electron configuration of potassium is

K: $1s^2 2s^2 2p^6 3s^2 3p^6 4s^1$, or [Ar]$4s^1$

The next element is *calcium,* with an additional electron that also occupies the $4s$ orbital.

[Ar] is shorthand for $1s^2 2s^2 2p^6 3s^2 3p^6$.

Ca: $1s^2 2s^2 2p^6 3s^2 3p^6 4s^2$, or [Ar]$4s^2$

The $4s$ orbital is now full.

After calcium the next electrons go into the $3d$ orbitals to complete principal energy level 3. The elements that correspond to filling the $3d$ orbitals are called transition metals. Then the $4p$ orbitals fill. Figure 11.26 gives partial electron configurations for the elements potassium through krypton.

Note from Figure 11.26 that all of the transition metals have the general configuration [Ar]$4s^2 3d^n$ except chromium ($4s^1 3d^5$) and copper ($4s^1 3d^{10}$). The reasons for these exceptions are complex and will not be discussed here.

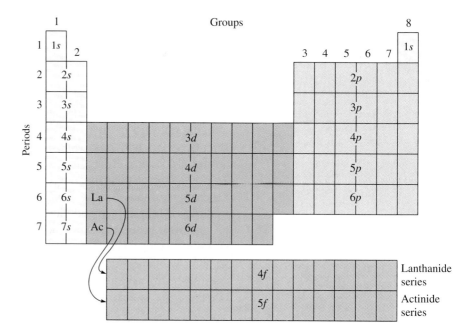

FIGURE 11.26

Partial electron configurations for the elements potassium through krypton. The transition metals shown in green (scandium through zinc) have the general configuration [Ar]$4s^2 3d^n$, except for chromium and copper.

| K $4s^1$ | Ca $4s^2$ | Sc $3d^1$ | Ti $3d^2$ | V $3d^3$ | Cr $4s^1 3d^5$ | Mn $3d^5$ | Fe $3d^6$ | Co $3d^7$ | Ni $3d^8$ | Cu $4s^1 3d^{10}$ | Zn $3d^{10}$ | Ga $4p^1$ | Ge $4p^2$ | As $4p^3$ | Se $4p^4$ | Br $4p^5$ | Kr $4p^6$ |

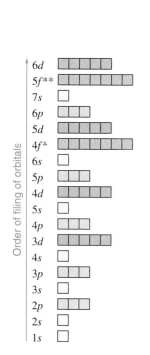

FIGURE 11.28

A box diagram showing the order in which orbitals fill to produce the atoms in the periodic table. Each box can hold two electrons.

*After the 6s orbital is full, one electron goes into a 5d orbital. This corresponds to the element lanthanum ([Xe]$6s^2 5d^1$). After lanthanum, the 4f orbitals fill with electrons.

**After the 7s orbital is full, one electron goes into 6d. This is actinium ([Rn]$7s^2 6d^1$). The 5f orbitals then fill.

FIGURE 11.27

The orbitals being filled for elements in various parts of the periodic table. Note that in going along a horizontal row (a period), the $(n + 1)s$ orbital fills before the nd orbital. The group label indicates the number of valence electrons (the number of s plus the number of p electrons in the highest occupied principal energy level) for the elements in each group.

Instead of continuing to consider the elements individually, we will now look at the overall relationship between the periodic table and orbital filling. Figure 11.27 shows which type of orbital is filling in each area of the periodic table. Note the points in the box on the following page.

To help you further understand the connection between orbital filling and the periodic table, Figure 11.28 shows the orbitals in the order in which they fill.

Orbital Filling

1. In a principal energy level that has *d* orbitals, the *s* orbital from the *next* level fills before the *d* orbitals in the current level. That is, the $(n + 1)s$ orbitals always fill before the *nd* orbitals. For example, the 5*s* orbitals fill for rubidium and strontium before the 4*d* orbitals fill for the second row of transition metals (yttrium through cadmium).

2. After lanthanum, which has the electron configuration $[Xe]6s^2 5d^1$, a group of fourteen elements called the **lanthanide series,** or the lanthanides, occurs. This series of elements corresponds to the filling of the seven 4*f* orbitals.

3. After actinium, which has the configuration $[Rn]7s^2 6d^1$, a group of fourteen elements called the **actinide series,** or the actinides, occurs. This series corresponds to the filling of the seven 5*f* orbitals.

4. Except for helium, the group numbers indicate the sum of electrons in the *ns* and *np* orbitals in the highest principal energy level that contains electrons (where *n* is the number that indicates a particular principal energy level). These electrons are the valence electrons, the electrons in the outermost principal energy level of a given atom.

The $(n + 1)s$ orbital fills before the *nd* orbitals fill.

Lanthanides are elements in which the 4*f* orbitals are being filled.

Actinides are elements in which the 5*f* orbitals are being filled.

A periodic table is almost always available to you. If you understand the relationship between the electron configuration of an element and its position on the periodic table, you can figure out the expected electron configuration of any atom.

EXAMPLE 11.3 *Determining Electron Configurations*

Using the periodic table inside the front cover of the text, give the electron configurations for sulfur (S), gallium (Ga), hafnium (Hf), and radium (Ra).

Solution

Sulfur is element 16 and resides in Period 3, where the 3*p* orbitals are being filled (see Figure 11.29). Because sulfur is the fourth among the "3*p* elements," it must have four 3*p* electrons. Sulfur's electron configuration is

S: $1s^2 2s^2 2p^6 3s^2 3p^4$, or $[Ne]3s^2 3p^4$

FIGURE 11.29
The positions of the elements considered in Example 11.3.

Molten lead being poured into a mold to make toy soldiers.

Gallium is element 31 in Period 4 just after the transition metals (see Figure 11.29). It is the first element in the "4p series" and has a $4p^1$ arrangement. Gallium's electron configuration is

Ga: $1s^2 2s^2 2p^6 3s^2 3p^6 4s^2 3d^{10} 4p^1$, or $[Ar]4s^2 3d^{10} 4p^1$

Hafnium is element 72 and is found in Period 6, as shown in Figure 11.29. Note that it occurs just after the lanthanide series (see Figure 11.27). Thus the 4f orbitals are already filled. Hafnium is the second member of the 5d transition series and has two 5d electrons. Its electron configuration is

Hf: $1s^2 2s^2 2p^6 3s^2 3p^6 4s^2 3d^{10} 4p^6 5s^2 4d^{10} 5p^6 6s^2 4f^{14} 5d^2$, or $[Xe]6s^2 4f^{14} 5d^2$

Radium is element 88 and is in Period 7 (and Group 2), as shown in Figure 11.29. Thus radium has two electrons in the 7s orbital, and its electron configuration is

Ra: $1s^2 2s^2 2p^6 3s^2 3p^6 4s^2 3d^{10} 4p^6 5s^2 4d^{10} 5p^6 6s^2 4f^{14} 5d^{10} 6p^6 7s^2$, or $[Rn]7s^2$

 Self-Check Exercise 11.3

Using the periodic table inside the front cover of the text, predict the electron configurations for fluorine, silicon, cesium, lead, and iodine. If you have trouble, use Figure 11.27.

See Problems 11.55 through 11.64.

Summary of the Wave Mechanical Model and Valence-Electron Configurations

The concepts we have discussed in this chapter are very important. They allow us to make sense of a good deal of chemistry. When it was first observed that elements with similar properties occur periodically as the atomic number increases, chemists wondered why. Now we have an explanation. The wave mechanical model pictures the electrons in an atom as arranged in orbitals, with each orbital capable of holding two electrons. As we build up the atoms, the same types of orbitals recur in going from one principal energy level to another. This means that particular valence-electron configurations recur periodically. For reasons we will explore in the next chapter, elements with a particular type of valence configuration all show very similar chemical behavior. Thus groups of elements, such as the alkali metals, show similar chemistry because all the elements in that group have the same type of valence-electron arrangement. This concept, which explains so much chemistry, is the greatest contribution of the wave mechanical model to modern chemistry.

For reference, the valence-electron configurations for all the elements are shown on the periodic table in Figure 11.30. Note the following points:

The group label gives the total number of valence electrons for that group.

1. The group labels for Groups 1, 2, 3, 4, 5, 6, 7, and 8 indicate the *total number* of valence electrons for the atoms in these groups. For example, all the elements in Group 5 have the configuration $ns^2\ np^3$. (Any d electrons present are always in the next lower principal energy level than the valence electrons and so are not counted as valence electrons.)

Representative Elements — **Transition Elements** — **Representative Elements**

1 ns^1	2 ns^2										3 ns^2np^1	4 ns^2np^2	5 ns^2np^3	6 ns^2np^4	7 ns^2np^5	8 ns^2np^6
1 H $1s^1$																2 He $1s^2$
3 Li $2s^1$	4 Be $2s^2$										5 B $2s^22p^1$	6 C $2s^22p^2$	7 N $2s^22p^3$	8 O $2s^22p^4$	9 F $2s^22p^5$	10 Ne $2s^22p^6$
11 Na $3s^1$	12 Mg $3s^2$										13 Al $3s^23p^1$	14 Si $3s^23p^2$	15 P $3s^23p^3$	16 S $3s^23p^4$	17 Cl $3s^23p^5$	18 Ar $3s^23p^6$
19 K $4s^1$	20 Ca $4s^2$	21 Sc $4s^23d^1$	22 Ti $4s^23d^2$	23 V $4s^23d^3$	24 Cr $4s^13d^5$	25 Mn $4s^23d^5$	26 Fe $4s^23d^6$	27 Co $4s^23d^7$	28 Ni $4s^23d^8$	29 Cu $4s^13d^{10}$	30 Zn $4s^23d^{10}$	31 Ga $4s^24p^1$	32 Ge $4s^24p^2$	33 As $4s^24p^3$	34 Se $4s^24p^4$	35 Br $4s^24p^5$	36 Kr $4s^24p^6$
37 Rb $5s^1$	38 Sr $5s^2$	39 Y $5s^24d^1$	40 Zr $5s^24d^2$	41 Nb $5s^14d^4$	42 Mo $5s^14d^5$	43 Tc $5s^14d^6$	44 Ru $5s^14d^7$	45 Rh $5s^14d^8$	46 Pd $5s^04d^{10}$	47 Ag $5s^14d^{10}$	48 Cd $5s^24d^{10}$	49 In $5s^25p^1$	50 Sn $5s^25p^2$	51 Sb $5s^25p^3$	52 Te $5s^25p^4$	53 I $5s^25p^5$	54 Xe $5s^25p^6$
55 Cs $6s^1$	56 Ba $6s^2$	57 La $6s^25d^1$	72 Hf $6s^25d^2$	73 Ta $6s^25d^3$	74 W $6s^25d^4$	75 Re $6s^25d^5$	76 Os $6s^25d^6$	77 Ir $6s^25d^7$	78 Pt $6s^15d^9$	79 Au $6s^15d^{10}$	80 Hg $6s^25d^{10}$	81 Tl $6s^26p^1$	82 Pb $6s^26p^2$	83 Bi $6s^26p^3$	84 Po $6s^26p^4$	85 At $6s^26p^5$	86 Rn $6s^26p^6$
87 Fr $7s^1$	88 Ra $7s^2$	89 Ac $7s^26d^1$	104 Unq $7s^26d^2$	105 Unp $7s^26d^3$	106 Unh $7s^26d^4$	107 Uns $7s^26d^5$	108 Uno	109 Une $7s^26d^7$	110 Uun	111 Uuu						

(Left axis: Period number, highest occupied electron level)

FIGURE 11.30
The periodic table with atomic symbols, atomic numbers, and partial electron configurations. (The configurations for elements 108, 110, and 111 are not yet known.) We will not discuss the configurations for the *f* transition elements (lanthanides and actinides), so they are not included here.

2. The elements in Groups 1, 2, 3, 4, 5, 6, 7, and 8 are often called the **main-group elements,** or **representative elements.** Remember that every member of a given group (except for helium) has the same valence-electron configuration, except that the electrons are in different principal energy levels.

3. We will not be concerned in this text with the configurations for the *f* transition elements (lanthanides and actinides), so these are not included in Figure 11.30.

11.9 Atomic Properties and the Periodic Table

AIM: To understand the general trends in atomic properties in the periodic table.

With all of this talk about electron probability and orbitals, we must not lose sight of the fact that chemistry is still fundamentally a science based on the observed properties of substances. We know that wood burns, steel rusts, plants grow, sugar tastes sweet, and so on because we *observe* these phenomena. The atomic theory is an attempt to help us understand why these things occur. If we understand why, we can hope to better control the chemical events that are so crucial in our daily lives.

Thin sheets of the metal gold (gold leaf) to be used for decorative purposes.

In the next chapter we will see how our ideas about atomic structure help us understand how and why atoms combine to form compounds. As we explore this, and as we use theories to explain other types of chemical behavior later in the text, it is important that we distinguish the observation (steel rusts) from the attempts to explain why the observed event occurs (theories). The observations remain the same over the decades, but the theories (our explanations) change as we gain a clearer understanding of how nature operates. A good example of this is the replacement of the Bohr model for atoms by the wave mechanical model.

Because the observed behavior of matter lies at the heart of chemistry, you need to understand thoroughly the characteristic properties of the various elements and the trends (systematic variations) that occur in those properties. To that end, we will now consider some especially important properties of atoms and see how they vary, horizontally and vertically, on the periodic table.

Metals and Nonmetals

The most fundamental classification of the chemical elements is into metals and nonmetals. **Metals** typically have the following physical properties: a lustrous appearance, the ability to change shape without breaking (they can be pulled into a wire or pounded into a thin sheet), and excellent conductivity of heat and electricity. **Nonmetals** typically do not have these physical properties, although there are some exceptions. (For example, solid iodine is lustrous; the graphite form of carbon is an excellent conductor of electricity; and the diamond form of carbon is an excellent conductor of heat.) However, it is the *chemical* differences between metals and nonmetals that interest us the most: *metals tend to lose electrons to form positive ions, and nonmetals tend to gain electrons to form negative ions.* When a metal and a nonmetal react, a transfer of one or more electrons from the metal to the nonmetal often occurs.

Most of the elements are classed as metals, as is shown in Figure 11.31. Note that the metals are found on the left-hand side and at the center of the periodic table. The relatively few nonmetals are in the upper right-hand corner of the table. A few elements exhibit both metallic and nonmetallic behavior; they are classed as **metalloids** or semimetals.

FIGURE 11.31
The classification of elements as metals, nonmetals, and metalloids.

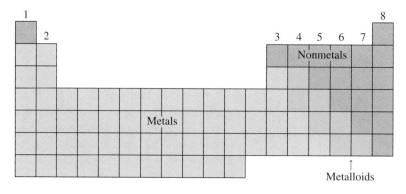

Fireworks

The art of using mixtures of chemicals to produce explosives is an ancient one. Black powder—a mixture of potassium nitrate, charcoal, and sulfur—was being used in China well before A.D. 1000, and it has been used through the centuries in military explosives, in construction blasting, and for fireworks.

Before the nineteenth century, fireworks were confined mainly to rockets and loud bangs. Orange and yellow colors came from the presence of charcoal and iron filings. However, with the great advances in chemistry in the nineteenth century, new compounds found their way into fireworks. Salts of copper, strontium, and barium added brilliant colors. Magnesium and aluminum metals gave a dazzling white light.

How do fireworks produce their brilliant colors and loud bangs? Actually, only a handful of different chemicals are responsible for most of the spectacular effects. To produce the noise and flashes, an oxidizer (something with a strong affinity for

Fireworks over New York City.

electrons) is reacted with a metal such as magnesium or aluminum mixed with sulfur. The resulting reaction produces a brilliant flash, which is due to the aluminum or magnesium burning, and a loud report is pro-

duced by the rapidly expanding gases. For a color effect, an element with a colored flame is included.

Yellow colors in fireworks are due to sodium. Strontium salts give the red color familiar from highway safety flares. Barium salts give a green color.

Although you might think that the chemistry of fireworks is simple, achieving the vivid white flashes and the brilliant colors requires complex combinations of chemicals. For example, because the white flashes produce high flame temperatures, the colors tend to wash out. Another problem arises from the use of sodium salts. Because sodium produces an extremely bright yellow color, sodium salts cannot be used when other colors are desired. In short, the manufacture of fireworks that produce the desired effects and are also safe to handle requires very careful selection of chemicals.*

*The chemical mixtures in fireworks are very dangerous. *Do not* experiment with chemicals on your own.

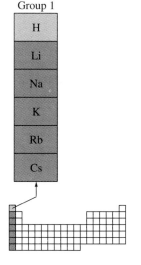

It is important to understand that simply being classified as a metal does not mean that an element behaves exactly like all other metals. For example, some metals can lose one or more electrons much more easily than others. In particular, cesium can give up its outermost electron (a $6s$ electron) more easily than can lithium (a $2s$ electron). In fact, for the alkali metals (Group 1) the ease of giving up an electron varies as follows:

$$Cs \quad > \quad Rb \quad > \quad K \quad > \quad Na \quad > \quad Li$$

Loses an electron most easily   Least likely to lose an electron

Note that as we go down the group, the metals become more likely to lose an electron. This makes sense because as we go down the group, the electron being removed resides, on average, farther and farther from the nucleus. That is, the $6s$ electron lost from Cs is much farther from the attractive positive nucleus—and so is easier to remove—than the $2s$ electron that must be removed from a lithium atom.

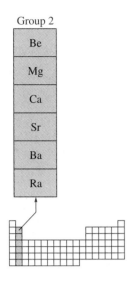

Group 2

The same trend is also seen in the Group 2 metals (alkaline earth metals): the farther down in the group the metal resides, the more likely it is to lose an electron.

Just as metals vary somewhat in their properties, so do nonmetals. In general, the elements that can most effectively pull electrons from metals occur in the upper right-hand corner of the periodic table.

As a general rule, we can say that the most chemically active metals appear in the lower left-hand region of the periodic table, whereas the most chemically active nonmetals appear in the upper right-hand region. The properties of the semimetals, or metalloids, lie between the metals and the nonmetals, as might be expected.

Ionization Energies

The **ionization energy** of an atom is the energy required to remove an electron from an individual atom in the gas phase:

$$M(g) \quad \Longrightarrow \quad M^+(g) + e^-$$

Ionization
energy

As we have noted, the most characteristic chemical property of a metal atom is losing electrons to nonmetals. Another way of saying this is to say that *metals have relatively low ionization energies*—a relatively small amount of energy is needed to remove an electron from a typical metal.

Recall that metals at the bottom of a group lose electrons more easily than those at the top. In other words, ionization energies tend to decrease in going from the top to the bottom of a group.

Group

Ionization
energies
decrease
down a
group.

Energy needed
to remove
an
electron
decreases.

In contrast to metals, nonmetals have relatively large ionization energies. Nonmetals tend to gain, not lose, electrons. Recall that metals appear on the left-hand side of the periodic table and nonmetals appear on the right. Thus it is not surprising that ionization energies tend to increase from left to right across a given period on the periodic table.

Energy required to remove
an electron increases.

Period

Ionization energies generally
increase across a period

In general, the elements that appear in the lower left-hand region of the periodic table have the lowest ionization energies (and are therefore the most chemically active metals). On the other hand, the elements with the highest ionization energies (the most chemically active nonmetals) occur in the upper right-hand region of the periodic table.

Atomic Size

The sizes of atoms vary as shown in Figure 11.32. Notice that atoms get larger as we go down a group on the periodic table and that they get smaller as we go from left to right across a period.

We can understand the increase in size that we observe as we go down a group by remembering that as the principal energy level increases, the average distance of the electrons from the nucleus also increases. So atoms get bigger as electrons are added to larger principal energy levels.

Explaining the decrease in **atomic size** across a period requires a little thought about the atoms in a given row (period) of the periodic table. Recall that the atoms in a particular period all have their outermost electrons in a given principal energy level. That is, the atoms in Period 1 have their outer electrons in the 1s orbital (principal energy level 1), the atoms in Period 2 have their outermost electrons in principal energy level 2 (2s and 2p orbitals), and so on (see Figure 11.27). Because all the orbitals in a given principal energy level are expected to be the same size, we might expect the atoms in a given period to be the same size. However, remember that the number of

FIGURE 11.32
Relative atomic sizes for selected atoms. Note that atomic size increases down a group and decreases across a period.

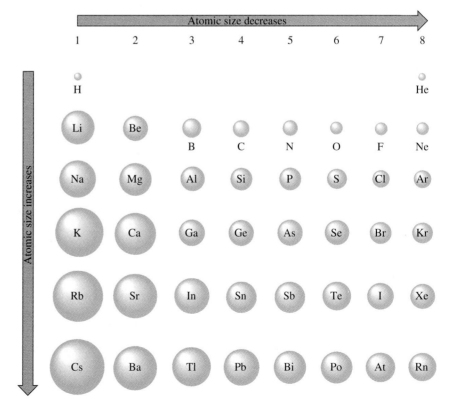

protons in the nucleus increases as we move from atom to atom in the period. The resulting increase in positive charge on the nucleus tends to pull the electrons closer to the nucleus. So instead of remaining the same size across a period as electrons are added in a given principal energy level, the atoms get smaller as the electron "cloud" is drawn in by the increasing nuclear charge.

Chapter Review

Key Terms

electromagnetic radiation *(11.1)*
wavelength *(11.1)*
frequency *(11.1)*
photon *(11.1)*
quantized energy levels *(11.2)*
wave mechanical model *(11.4)*
orbital *(11.5)*
principal energy levels *(11.5)*
sublevels *(11.5)*
Pauli exclusion principle *(11.6)*

electron configuration *(11.7)*
orbital (box) diagram *(11.7)*
valence electrons *(11.7)*
core electrons *(11.7)*
lanthanide series *(11.8)*
actinide series *(11.8)*
main-group (representative) elements *(11.8)*
metals *(11.9)*
nonmetals *(11.9)*
ionization energy *(11.9)*
atomic size *(11.9)*

Summary

1. Energy travels through space by electromagnetic radiation ("light"), which can be characterized by the wavelength and frequency of the waves. Light can also be thought of as packets of energy called photons. Atoms can gain energy by absorbing a photon and can lose energy by emitting a photon.

2. The emissions of energy from hydrogen atoms produce only certain energies as hydrogen changes from a higher to a lower energy. This shows that the energy levels of hydrogen are quantized.

3. The Bohr model of the hydrogen atom postulated that the electron moved in circular orbits corresponding to the various allowed energy levels. Though it worked well for hydrogen, the Bohr model did not work for other atoms.

4. The wave mechanical model explains atoms by postulating that the electron has both wave and particle characteristics. Electron states are described by orbitals,

which are probability maps indicating how likely it is to find the electron at a given point in space. The orbital size can be thought of as a surface containing 90% of the total electron probability.

5. According to the Pauli exclusion principle, an atomic orbital can hold a maximum of two electrons, and those electrons must have opposite spins.

6. Atoms have a series of energy levels, called principal energy levels (*n*), which contain one or more sublevels (types of orbitals). The number of sublevels increases with increasing *n*.

7. Valence electrons are the *s* and *p* electrons in the outermost principal energy level of an atom. Core electrons are the inner electrons of an atom.

8. Metals are found at the left and center of the periodic table. The most chemically active metals are found in the lower left-hand corner of the periodic table. The most chemically active nonmetals are located in the upper right-hand corner.

9. Ionization energy, the energy required to remove an electron from a gaseous atom, decreases going down a group and increases going from left to right across a period.

10. For the representative elements, atomic size increases going down a group but decreases going from left to right across a period.

Questions and Problems

All even-numbered exercises have answers in the back of this book and solutions in the Solutions Guide.

11.1 ■ *Electromagnetic Radiation and Energy*

QUESTIONS

1. Give several examples of *electromagnetic radiation*.

2. How are the different types of electromagnetic radiation similar? How do they differ?

3. What does the *wavelength* of electromagnetic radiation represent? Sketch a representation of a wave indicating the wavelength on your diagram.

4. What is the *frequency* of electromagnetic radiation? How do the *frequency* and *speed* of electromagnetic radiation differ?

5. What is a "packet" of electromagnetic energy called?

6. What is meant by the *wave–particle* nature of light?

11.2 ■ *The Energy Levels of Hydrogen*

QUESTIONS

7. What does it mean to say that an atom is in an "excited state"?

8. How does an atom in an excited state return to its ground state?

9. The longer the wavelength of light, the (larger/smaller) will be the amount of energy carried per photon of the light.

10. The higher the frequency of light, the (larger/smaller) will be the amount of energy carried per photon of the light.

11. Describe briefly why the study of electromagnetic radiation has been important to our understanding of the arrangement of electrons in atoms.

12. What does it mean to say that the hydrogen atom has *discrete energy levels?* How is this fact reflected in the radiation that excited hydrogen atoms emit?

13. Because a given element's atoms emit only certain photons of light, only certain _____ are occurring in those particular atoms.

14. The energy of an emitted photon corresponds to the difference in energy between the excited state of the emitting atom and its _____ state.

15. What does it mean to say that the energy levels of hydrogen are *quantized?* What experimental evidence exists for this?

16. What is meant by the *ground state* of an atom?

11.3 ■ *The Bohr Model of the Atom*

QUESTIONS

17. What are the essential points of Bohr's theory of the structure of the hydrogen atom?

18. According to Bohr, what types of motions do electrons have in an atom, and what happens when energy is applied to the atom?

19. How does the Bohr theory account for the observed phenomenon of the emission of discrete wavelengths of light by excited atoms?

20. Why was Bohr's theory for the hydrogen atom initially accepted, and why was it ultimately discarded?

11.4 ■ *The Wave Mechanical Model of the Atom*

QUESTIONS

21. What major assumption (that was analogous to what had already been demonstrated for electromagnetic radiation) did de Broglie and Schrödinger make about the motion of tiny particles?

22. Discuss briefly the difference between an orbit (as described by Bohr for hydrogen) and an orbital (as described by the more modern, wave mechanical picture of the atom).

23. Why was Schrödinger not able to describe exactly the pathway an electron takes as it moves through the space of an atom?

24. Explain why we cannot *exactly* specify the location of an electron in an atom but can only discuss where an electron is *most likely* to be at any given time.

11.5 ■ *The Hydrogen Orbitals*

QUESTIONS

25. Why are the orbitals of the hydrogen atom described as "probability maps"? Why are the edges of the hydrogen orbitals sometimes drawn to appear "fuzzy"?

26. When we draw a picture of an orbital, we are indicating that the probability of finding the electron within this region of space is greater than 90%. Why is this probability never 100%?

27. What are the differences between the 2s orbital and the 1s orbital of hydrogen? How are they similar?

28. What overall shape do the 2p orbitals have? How are the individual 2p orbitals alike, and how do they differ?

29. As an electron moves from one principal energy level to a higher-number level, the distance of the electron from the nucleus (increases/decreases).

30. If an electron moves from the 1s orbital to the 2s orbital, its energy (increases/decreases).

31. Although a hydrogen atom has only one electron, the hydrogen atom possesses a complete set of available orbitals. What purpose do these additional orbitals serve?

32. Into how many sublevels is the fourth principal energy level of the hydrogen atom divided? What designations are given to these sublevels?

11.6 ■ *The Wave Mechanical Model: Further Development*

QUESTIONS

33. What do we mean when we say that each electron in an atom has its own intrinsic "spin"?

34. What is the *Pauli exclusion principle?* How many electrons can occupy an orbital, according to this principle? Why?

35. The energy of a principal energy level (increases/decreases) as n increases.

36. The number of sublevels in a principal energy level (increases/decreases) as n increases.

37. According to the Pauli exclusion principle, a given orbital can contain only _____ electrons.

38. According to the Pauli exclusion principle, the electrons within a given orbital must have _____ spins.

39. Which of the following orbital designations is (are) not correct?
    a. $1p$ c. $3d$
    b. $2f$ d. $4g$

40. Which of the following orbital designations is (are) not correct?
    a. $1d$ c. $4d$
    b. $2d$ d. $5f$

11.7 ■ *Electron Arrangements in the First Eighteen Atoms on the Periodic Table*

QUESTIONS

41. Why is the $1s$ orbital the first orbital to be filled in any atom?

42. When a hydrogen atom is in its ground state, in which orbital is its electron found? Why?

43. Which electrons of an atom are the *valence* electrons? Why are these electrons especially important?

44. What important feature do the elements in a given group (vertical column) of the periodic table have in common?

PROBLEMS

45. Write the full electron configuration ($1s^2 2s^2$, etc.) for each of the following elements.
    a. silicon, $Z = 14$ c. magnesium, $Z = 12$
    b. argon, $Z = 18$ d. helium, $Z = 2$

46. Write the electron configuration ($1s^2 2s^2$, and so on) for each of the following elements.
    a. strontium, $Z = 38$
    b. zinc, $Z = 30$
    c. helium, $Z = 2$
    d. bromine, $Z = 35$

47. Write the full electron configuration ($1s^2 2s^2$, etc.) for each of the following elements.
    a. sodium, $Z = 11$
    b. cesium, $Z = 55$
    c. nitrogen, $Z = 7$
    d. beryllium, $Z = 4$

48. Write the full electron configuration ($1s^2 2s^2$, etc.) for each of the following elements.
    a. carbon, $Z = 6$
    b. phosphorus, $Z = 15$
    c. sulfur, $Z = 16$
    d. boron, $Z = 5$

49. Write the complete orbital diagram for each of the following elements, using boxes to represent orbitals and arrows to represent electrons.
    a. sodium, $Z = 11$
    b. calcium, $Z = 20$
    c. chlorine, $Z = 17$
    d. argon, $Z = 18$

50. Write the complete orbital diagram for each of the following elements, using boxes to represent orbitals and arrows to represent electrons.
    a. aluminum, $Z = 13$
    b. phosphorus, $Z = 15$
    c. bromine, $Z = 35$
    d. argon, $Z = 18$

51. How many valence electrons does each of the following atoms possess?
    a. lithium, $Z = 3$ c. argon, $Z = 18$
    b. aluminum, $Z = 13$ d. phosphorus, $Z = 15$

52. How many valence electrons does each of the following atoms possess?
    a. magnesium, $Z = 12$ c. bromine, $Z = 35$
    b. carbon, $Z = 6$ d. cesium, $Z = 55$

11.8 ■ *Electron Configurations and the Periodic Table*

QUESTIONS

53. Why do we believe that the valence electrons of calcium and potassium reside in the $4s$ orbital rather than in the $3d$ orbital?

54. Would you expect the valence electrons of rubidium and strontium to reside in the $5s$ or the $4p$ orbitals? Why?

PROBLEMS

55. Using the symbol of the previous noble gas to indicate the core electrons, write the valence shell electron configuration for each of the following elements.
    a. rubidium, $Z = 37$
    b. chlorine, $Z = 17$
    c. phosphorus, $Z = 15$
    d. barium, $Z = 56$

56. Using the symbol of the previous noble gas to indicate the core electrons, write the valence shell electron configuration for each of the following elements.
    a. calcium, $Z = 20$
    b. francium, $Z = 87$
    c. yttrium, $Z = 39$
    d. cerium, $Z = 58$

57. Using the symbol of the previous noble gas to indicate the core electrons, write the electron configuration for each of the following elements.
    a. scandium, $Z = 21$
    b. yttrium, $Z = 39$
    c. lanthanum, $Z = 57$
    d. actinium, $Z = 89$

58. Using the symbol of the previous noble gas to indicate the core electrons, write the valence shell electron configuration for each of the following elements.
    a. silicon, $Z = 14$
    b. gallium, $Z = 31$
    c. vanadium, $Z = 23$
    d. scandium, $Z = 21$

59. How many $3d$ electrons are found in each of the following elements?
    a. nickel, $Z = 28$
    b. iron, $Z = 26$
    c. manganese, $Z = 25$
    d. vanadium, $Z = 23$

60. How many $4d$ electrons are found in each of the following elements?
    a. yttrium, $Z = 39$
    b. zirconium, $Z = 40$
    c. strontium, $Z = 38$
    d. cadmium, $Z = 48$

61. For each of the following elements, indicate which set of orbitals is being filled last.
    a. tungsten, $Z = 74$
    b. iron, $Z = 26$
    c. europium, $Z = 63$
    d. cerium, $Z = 58$

62. For each of the following elements, indicate which set of orbitals is being filled last.
    a. lanthanum, $Z = 57$

b. lutetium, $Z = 71$
    c. osmium, $Z = 76$
    d. zinc, $Z = 30$

63. Write the valence shell electron configuration of each of the following elements, basing your answer on the element's location on the periodic table.
    a. hafnium, $Z = 72$
    b. radium, $Z = 88$
    c. antimony, $Z = 51$
    d. lead, $Z = 82$

64. Write the shorthand valence shell electron configuration of each of the following elements, basing your answer on the element's location on the periodic table.
    a. uranium, $Z = 92$
    b. manganese, $Z = 25$
    c. mercury, $Z = 80$
    d. francium, $Z = 87$

11.9 ■ Atomic Properties and the Periodic Table

QUESTIONS

65. What are some of the physical properties that distinguish the metallic elements from the nonmetals? Are these properties absolute, or do some nonmetallic elements exhibit some metallic properties (and vice versa)?

66. What types of ions do the metals and the nonmetallic elements form? Do the metals lose or gain electrons in doing this? Do the nonmetallic elements gain or lose electrons in doing this?

67. Give some similarities that exist among the elements of Group 1.

68. Give some similarities that exist among the elements of Group 7.

69. Which metallic elements within a given group (vertical column) of the periodic table lose electrons most easily? Why?

70. Which elements in a given period (horizontal row) of the periodic table lose electrons most easily? Why?

71. Where are the most nonmetallic elements located on the periodic table? Why do these elements pull electrons from metallic elements so effectively during a reaction?

72. Why do the metallic elements of a given period (horizontal row) typically have much lower ionization energies than do the nonmetallic elements of the same period?

73. Explain why the atoms of the elements at the bottom of a given group (vertical column) of the periodic table are

larger than the atoms of the elements at the top of the same group.

74. Though all the elements in a given period (horizontal row) of the periodic table have their valence electrons in the same types of orbitals, the sizes of the atoms decrease from left to right within a period. Explain why.

PROBLEMS

75. In each of the following sets of elements, indicate which element shows the most active chemical behavior.
    a. Li, K, Cs
    b. Mg, Sr, Ra
    c. S, Se, Te

76. In each of the following sets of elements, indicate which element would be expected to have the lowest ionization energy.
    a. Li, K, Cs
    b. Li, C, F
    c. F, Cl, I
    d. Rb, Sr, In

77. Arrange the following sets of elements in order of increasing atomic size.
    a. Sn, Xe, Rb, Sr
    b. Rn, He, Xe, Kr
    c. Pb, Ba, Cs, At

78. In each of the following sets of elements, indicate which element has the smallest atomic size.
    a. Na, K, Rb
    b. Na, Si, S
    c. N, P, As
    d. N, O, F

Additional Problems

79. The distance in meters between two consecutive peaks (or troughs) in a wave is called the _____.

80. The speed at which electromagnetic radiation moves through a vacuum is called the _____.

81. The portion of the electromagnetic spectrum between wavelengths of approximately 400 and 700 nanometers is called the _____ region.

82. A beam of light can be thought of as consisting of a stream of light particles called _____.

83. The lowest possible energy state of an atom is called the _____ state.

84. The energy levels of hydrogen (and other atoms) are _____, which means that only certain values of energy are allowed.

85. According to Bohr, the electron in the hydrogen atom moved around the nucleus in circular paths called _____.

86. In the modern theory of the atom, a(n) _____ represents a region of space in which there is a high probability of finding an electron.

87. Electrons found in the outermost principal energy level of an atom are referred to as _____ electrons.

88. An element with partially filled *d* orbitals is called a/an _____.

89. The _____ of electromagnetic radiation represents the number of waves passing a given point in space each second.

90. Only two electrons can occupy a given orbital in an atom, and to be in the same orbital, they must have opposite _____.

91. One bit of evidence that the present theory of atomic structure is "correct" lies in the magnetic properties of matter. Atoms with *unpaired* electrons are attracted by magnetic fields and thus are said to exhibit *paramagnetism*. The degree to which this effect is observed is directly related to the *number* of unpaired electrons present in the atom. On the basis of the electron orbital diagrams for the following elements, indicate which atoms would be expected to be paramagnetic, and tell how many unpaired electrons each atom contains.
    a. phosphorus, $Z = 15$
    b. iodine, $Z = 53$
    c. germanium, $Z = 32$

92. Without referring to your textbook or a periodic table, write the full electron configuration, the orbital box diagram, and the noble gas shorthand configuration for the elements with the following atomic numbers.
    a. $Z = 19$ d. $Z = 26$
    b. $Z = 22$ e. $Z = 30$
    c. $Z = 14$

93. Without referring to your textbook or a periodic table, write the full electron configuration, the orbital box diagram, and the noble gas shorthand configuration for the elements with the following atomic numbers.
    a. $Z = 28$ d. $Z = 37$
    b. $Z = 18$ e. $Z = 23$
    c. $Z = 35$

94. Write the general valence configuration (for example, ns^1 for Group 1) for the group in which each of the following elements is found.
    a. barium, $Z = 56$
    b. bromine, $Z = 35$
    c. tellurium, $Z = 52$
    d. potassium, $Z = 19$
    e. sulfur, $Z = 16$

95. How many valence electrons does each of the following atoms have?
    a. cesium, $Z = 55$
    b. strontium, $Z = 38$
    c. bromine, $Z = 35$
    d. selenium, $Z = 34$

96. In the text (Section 11.4) it was mentioned that current theories of atomic structure suggest that all matter and all energy demonstrate both particle-like and wave-like properties under the appropriate conditions, although the wave-like nature of matter becomes apparent only in very small and very fast-moving particles. The relationship between wavelength (λ) observed for a particle and the mass and velocity of that particle is called the de Broglie relationship. It is

    $$\lambda = h/mv$$

    in which h is Planck's constant (6.63×10^{-34} J s*), m represents the mass of the particle in kilograms, and v represents the velocity of the particle in meters per second. Calculate the "de Broglie wavelength" for each of the following, and use your numerical answers to explain why macroscopic (large) objects are not ordinarily discussed in terms of their "wave-like" properties.
    a. an electron moving at 0.90 times the speed of light
    b. a 150-g ball moving at a speed of 10. m/s
    c. a 75-kg person walking at a speed of 2 km/h

97. Light waves move through space at a speed of _____ meters per second.

98. How do we know that the energy levels of the hydrogen atom are not *continuous,* as physicists originally assumed?

99. As an electron moves from one principal energy level to a higher-number level, the attractive force that the nucleus exerts on the electron (increases/decreases).

100. Into how many sublevels is the third principal energy level of hydrogen divided? What are the names of the orbitals that constitute these sublevels? What are the general shapes of these orbitals?

101. What condition related to spin must be fulfilled for two electrons to occupy the same orbital?

102. Which of the following orbital designations is (are) *not* correct?
    a. 1*p*
    b. 3*d*
    c. 3*f*
    d. 2*p*
    e. 5*f*
    f. 6*s*

103. Why do the two electrons in the 2*p* sublevel of carbon occupy *different* 2*p* orbitals?

104. Write the full electron configuration ($1s^2 2s^2$, etc.) for each of the following elements.
    a. chlorine, $Z = 17$
    b. oxygen, $Z = 8$
    c. aluminum, $Z = 13$
    d. lithium, $Z = 3$

105. Write the complete orbital diagram for each of the following elements, using boxes to represent orbitals and arrows to represent electrons.
    a. scandium, $Z = 21$
    b. sulfur, $Z = 16$
    c. potassium, $Z = 19$
    d. nitrogen, $Z = 7$

106. How many valence electrons does each of the following atoms have?
    a. nitrogen, $Z = 7$
    b. chlorine, $Z = 17$
    c. sodium, $Z = 11$
    d. aluminum, $Z = 13$

107. What name is given to the group of ten elements in which the electrons are filling the 3*d* sublevel?

108. Using the symbol of the previous noble gas to indicate the core electrons, write the valence shell electron configuration for each of the following elements.
    a. zirconium, $Z = 40$
    b. iodine, $Z = 53$
    c. germanium, $Z = 32$
    d. cesium, $Z = 55$

109. Using the symbol of the previous noble gas to indicate core electrons, write the valence shell electron configuration for each of the following elements.
    a. titanium, $Z = 22$
    b. selenium, $Z = 34$
    c. antimony, $Z = 51$
    d. strontium, $Z = 38$

110. For each of the following elements, indicate which set of orbitals is being filled last.
    a. chromium, $Z = 24$
    b. silver, $Z = 47$
    c. uranium, $Z = 92$
    d. germanium, $Z = 32$

111. Write the shorthand valence shell electron configuration of each of the following elements, basing your answer on the element's location on the periodic table.
    a. nickel, $Z = 28$
    b. niobium, $Z = 41$
    c. hafnium, $Z = 72$
    d. astatine, $Z = 85$

112. Metals have relatively (low/high) ionization energies, whereas nonmetals have relatively (high/low) ionization energies.

113. In each of the following sets of elements, indicate which element shows the most active chemical behavior.
    a. B, Al, In   b. Na, Al, S   c. B, C, F

114. In each of the following sets of elements, indicate which element has the largest atomic size.
    a. Be, Ca, Ba
    b. Mg, Si, Cl
    c. Be, N, F

*Note that s is the abbreviation for "seconds."

12

Chemical Bonding

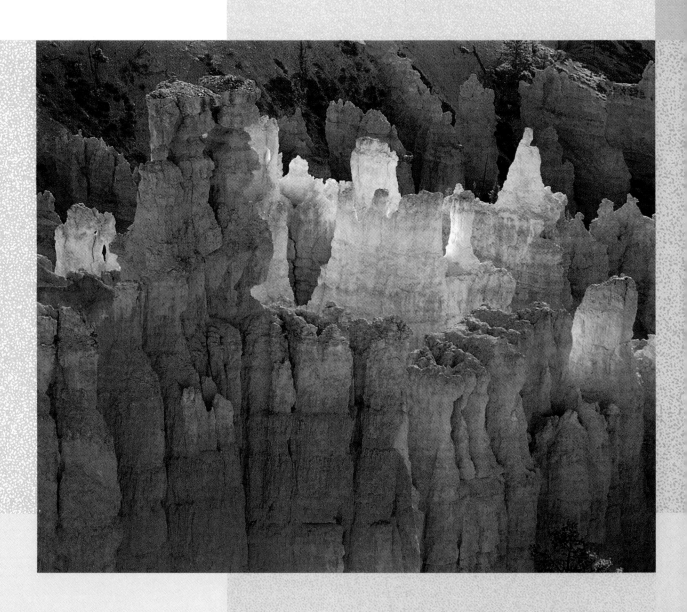

The world around us is composed almost entirely of compounds and mixtures of compounds. Rocks, coal, soil, petroleum, trees, and human beings are all complex mixtures of chemical compounds in which different kinds of atoms are bound together. Most of the pure elements found in the earth's crust also contain many atoms bound together. In a gold nugget each gold atom is bound to many other gold atoms, and in a diamond many carbon atoms are bonded very strongly to each other. Substances composed of unbound atoms do exist in nature, but they are very rare. (Examples include the argon atoms in the atmosphere and the helium atoms found in natural gas reserves.)

The manner in which atoms are bound together has a profound effect on the chemical and physical properties of substances. For example, both graphite and diamond are composed solely of carbon atoms. However, graphite is a soft, slippery material used as a lubricant in locks, and diamond is one of the hardest materials known, valuable both as a gemstone and in industrial cutting tools. Why do

Natural rock formations in Bryce Canyon, Utah (left). Diamond, composed of carbon atoms bonded together to produce one of the hardest materials known, makes a beautiful gemstone (right).

329

these materials, both composed solely of carbon atoms, have such different properties? The answer lies in the different ways in which the carbon atoms are bound to each other in these substances.

Molecular bonding and structure play the central role in determining the course of chemical reactions, many of which are vital to our survival. Most reactions in biological systems are very sensitive to the structures of the participating molecules; in fact, very subtle differences in shape sometimes serve to channel the chemical reaction one way rather than another. Molecules that act as drugs must have exactly the right structure to perform their functions correctly. Structure also plays a central role in our senses of smell and taste. Substances have a particular odor because they fit into the specially shaped receptors in our nasal passages. Taste is also dependent on molecular shape, as we discuss in the "Chemistry in Focus" on page 351.

To understand the behavior of natural materials, we must understand the nature of chemical bonding and the factors that control the structures of compounds. In this chapter, we will present various classes of compounds that illustrate the different types of bonds. We will then develop models to describe the structure and bonding that characterize the materials found in nature.

12.1 Types of Chemical Bonds

AIMS: To learn about ionic and covalent bonds and explain how they are formed. To learn about the polar covalent bond.

A water molecule.

What is a chemical bond? Although there are several possible ways to answer this question, we will define a **bond** as a force that holds groups of two or more atoms together and makes them function as a unit. For example, in water the fundamental unit is the H—O—H molecule, which we describe as being held together by the two O—H bonds. We can obtain information about the strength of a bond by measuring the energy required to break the bond, the **bond energy.**

Atoms can interact with one another in several ways to form aggregates. We will consider specific examples to illustrate the various types of chemical bonds.

In Chapter 7 we saw that when solid sodium chloride is dissolved in water, the resulting solution conducts electricity, a fact that convinces chemists that sodium chloride is composed of Na^+ and Cl^- ions. Thus when sodium and chlorine react to form sodium chloride, electrons are transferred from the sodium atoms to the chlorine atoms to form Na^+ and Cl^- ions, which then aggregate to form solid sodium chloride. The resulting solid sodium chloride is a very sturdy material; it has a melting point of approximately 800 °C. The strong bonding forces present in sodium chloride result from the attractions among the closely packed, oppositely charged ions. This is an example of **ionic bonding.** Ionic substances are formed when an atom that loses electrons relatively easily reacts with an atom that has a high affinity for electrons. In other words, an **ionic compound** results when a metal reacts with

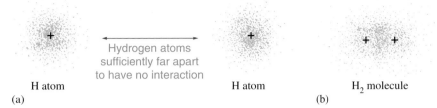

(a) H atom   Hydrogen atoms sufficiently far apart to have no interaction   H atom H_2 molecule (b)

FIGURE 12.1
The formation of a bond between two hydrogen atoms. (a) Two separate hydrogen atoms. (b) When two hydrogen atoms come close together, the two electrons are attracted simultaneously by both nuclei. This produces the bond. Note the relatively large electron probability between the nuclei indicating sharing of the electrons.

a nonmetal.

Metal   Nonmetal   Ionic compound

$$M \; + \; X \; \rightarrow \; M^+, X^-$$

e^-

We have seen that a bonding force develops when two very different types of atoms react to form oppositely charged ions. But how does a bonding force develop between two identical atoms? Let's explore this situation by considering what happens when two hydrogen atoms are brought close together, as shown in Figure 12.1. When hydrogen atoms are close together, the two electrons are simultaneously attracted to both nuclei. Note in Figure 12.1(b) how the electron probability increases between the two nuclei indicating that the electrons are shared by the two nuclei.

The type of bonding we encounter in the hydrogen molecule and in many other molecules where *electrons are shared by nuclei* is called **covalent bonding.** Note that in the H_2 molecule the electrons reside primarily in the space between the two nuclei, where they are attracted simultaneously by both protons. Although we will not go into detail about it here, the increased attractive forces in this area lead to the formation of the H_2 molecule from the two separated hydrogen atoms. When we say that a bond is formed between the hydrogen atoms, we mean that the H_2 molecule is more stable than two separated hydrogen atoms by a certain quantity of energy (the bond energy).

So far we have considered two extreme types of bonding. In ionic bonding, the participating atoms are so different that one or more electrons are transferred to form oppositely charged ions. The bonding results from the attractions between these ions. In covalent bonding, two identical atoms share electrons equally. The bonding results from the mutual attraction of the two nuclei for the shared electrons. Between these extremes are intermediate cases in which the atoms are not so different that electrons are completely transferred but are different enough so that unequal sharing of electrons results, forming what is called a **polar covalent bond.** The hydrogen fluoride (HF) molecule contains this type of bond, which produces the following charge distribution:

H—F
δ^+ δ^-

where δ (delta) is used to indicate a partial or fractional charge.

Ionic and covalent bonds are the extreme bond types.

FIGURE 12.2
Probability representations of the electron sharing in HF. (a) What the probability map would look like if the two electrons in the H—F bond were shared equally. (b) The actual situation, where the shared pair spends more time close to the fluorine atom than to the hydrogen atom. This gives fluorine a slight excess of negative charge and the hydrogen a slight deficit of nega- tive charge (a slight positive charge).

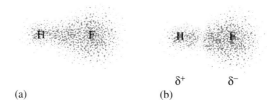

(a)   (b)

The most logical explanation for the development of *bond polarity* (the partial positive and negative charges on the atoms in such molecules as HF) is that the electrons in the bonds are not shared equally. For example, we can account for the polarity of the HF molecule by assuming that the fluorine atom has a stronger attraction than the hydrogen atom for the shared elec- trons (Figure 12.2). Because bond polarity has important chemical implica- tions, we find it useful to assign a number that indicates an atom's ability to attract shared electrons. In the next section we show how this is done.

12.2 Electronegativity

AIM: To understand the nature of bonds and their relationship to electronegativity.

FIGURE 12.3
Electronegativity values for selected elements. Note that electronegativity generally increases across a period and decreases down a group. Note also that metals have relatively low electronega- tivity values and that nonmetals have relatively high values.

We saw in the previous section that when a metal and a nonmetal react, one or more electrons are transferred from the metal to the nonmetal to give ionic bonding. On the other hand, two identical atoms react to form a covalent bond in which electrons are shared equally. When *different* nonmetals react, a bond forms in which electrons are shared *unequally,* giving a polar covalent bond. The unequal sharing of electrons between two atoms is described by a prop- erty called **electronegativity:** *the relative ability of an atom in a molecule to attract shared electrons to itself.*

Chemists determine electronegativity values for the elements (Figure 12.3) by measuring the polarities of the bonds between various atoms. Note that

Increasing electronegativity →

Decreasing electronegativity

												H 2.1					
Li 1.0	Be 1.5											B 2.0	C 2.5	N 3.0	O 3.5	F 4.0
Na 0.9	Mg 1.2											Al 1.5	Si 1.8	P 2.1	S 2.5	Cl 3.0
K 0.8	Ca 1.0	Sc 1.3	Ti 1.5	V 1.6	Cr 1.6	Mn 1.5	Fe 1.8	Co 1.9	Ni 1.9	Cu 1.9	Zn 1.6	Ga 1.6	Ge 1.8	As 2.0	Se 2.4	Br 2.8
Rb 0.8	Sr 1.0	Y 1.2	Zr 1.4	Nb 1.6	Mo 1.8	Tc 1.9	Ru 2.2	Rh 2.2	Pd 2.2	Ag 1.9	Cd 1.7	In 1.7	Sn 1.8	Sb 1.9	Te 2.1	I 2.5
Cs 0.7	Ba 0.9	La-Lu 1.0-1.2	Hf 1.3	Ta 1.5	W 1.7	Re 1.9	Os 2.2	Ir 2.2	Pt 2.2	Au 2.4	Hg 1.9	Tl 1.8	Pb 1.9	Bi 1.9	Po 2.0	At 2.2
Fr 0.7	Ra 0.9	Ac 1.1	Th 1.3	Pa 1.4	U 1.4	Np-No 1.4-1.3										

TABLE 12.1

The Relationship Between Electronegativity and Bond Type

Electronegativity Difference Between the Bonding Atoms	Bond Type	Covalent Character	Ionic Character
Zero	Covalent		
↓	↓	Decreases	Increases
Intermediate	Polar covalent		
↓	↓		
Large	Ionic		

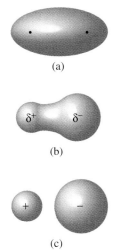

(a)

(b)

(c)

FIGURE 12.4

The three possible types of bonds: (a) a covalent bond formed between identical atoms; (b) a polar covalent bond, with both ionic and covalent components; and (c) an ionic bond, with no electron sharing.

electronegativity generally increases going from left to right across a period and decreases going down a group for the representative elements. The range of electronegativity values is from 4.0 for fluorine to 0.7 for cesium and francium. Remember, the higher the atom's electronegativity value, the closer the shared electrons tend to be to that atom when it forms a bond.

The polarity of a bond depends on the *difference* between the electronegativity values of the atoms forming the bond. If the atoms have very similar electronegativities, the electrons are shared almost equally and the bond shows little polarity. If the atoms have very different electronegativity values, a very polar bond is formed. In extreme cases one or more electrons are actually transferred, forming ions and an ionic bond. For example, when an element from Group 1 (electronegativity values of about 0.8) reacts with an element from Group 7 (electronegativity values of about 3), ions are formed and an ionic substance results. In general, if the *difference* between the electronegativities of two elements is about 1.7 or greater, the bond is considered to be ionic.

The relationship between electronegativity and bond type is shown in Table 12.1. The various types of bonds are summarized in Figure 12.4.

 EXAMPLE 12.1 *Using Electronegativity to Determine Bond Polarity*

Using the electronegativity values given in Figure 12.3, arrange the following bonds in order of increasing polarity: H—H, O—H, Cl—H, S—H, and F—H.

Solution

The polarity of the bond increases as the difference in electronegativity increases. From the electronegativity values in Figure 12.3, the following variation in bond polarity is expected (the electronegativity value appears in parentheses below each element).

Bond	Electronegativity Values	Difference in Electronegativity Values	Bond Type	Polarity
H—H	(2.1)(2.1)	2.1 − 2.1 = 0	Covalent	
S—H	(2.5)(2.1)	2.5 − 2.1 = 0.4	Polar covalent	Increasing
Cl—H	(3.0)(2.1)	3.0 − 2.1 = 0.9	Polar covalent	
O—H	(3.5)(2.1)	3.5 − 2.1 = 1.4	Polar covalent	
F—H	(4.0)(2.1)	4.0 − 2.1 = 1.9	Polar covalent	

Therefore, in order of increasing polarity, we have

H—H   S—H   Cl—H   O—H   F—H

Least polar   Most polar

Self-Check Exercise 12.1

For each of the following pairs of bonds, choose the bond that will be more polar.

a. H—P, H—C

b. O—F, O—I

c. N—O, S—O

d. N—H, Si—H

See Problems 12.17 through 12.20.

12.3 Bond Polarity and Dipole Moments

AIM: To understand bond polarity and how it is related to molecular polarity.

(a)

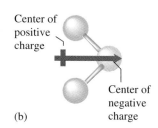

Center of positive charge

Center of negative charge

(b)

FIGURE 12.5
(a) The charge distribution in the water molecule. The oxygen has a charge of $2\delta^-$ because it pulls δ^- of charge from each hydrogen atom ($\delta^- + \delta^- = 2\delta^-$).
(b) The water molecule behaves as if it had a positive end and a negative end, as indicated by the arrow.

We saw in Section 12.1 that hydrogen fluoride has a positive end and a negative end. A molecule such as HF that has a center of positive charge and a center of negative charge is said to have a **dipole moment.** The dipolar character of a molecule is often represented by an arrow. This arrow points toward the negative charge center, and its tail indicates the positive center of charge:

δ^+ δ^-

Any diatomic (two-atom) molecule that has a polar bond has a dipole moment. Some polyatomic (more than two atoms) molecules also have dipole moments. For example, because the oxygen atom in the water molecule has a greater electronegativity than the hydrogen atoms, the electrons are not shared equally. This results in a charge distribution (Figure 12.5a) that causes the molecule to behave as though it had two centers of charge—one positive and one negative. So the water molecule has a dipole moment.

The fact that the water molecule is polar (has a dipole moment) has a profound impact on its properties. In fact, it is not overly dramatic to state that the polarity of the water molecule is crucial to life as we know it on earth. Because water molecules are polar, they can surround and attract both positive and negative ions (Figure 12.6). These attractions allow ionic materials to dissolve in water. Also, the polarity of water molecules causes them to attract each other strongly (Figure 12.7). This means that much energy is

FIGURE 12.6
(a) Polar water molecules are strongly attracted to positive ions by their negative ends. (b) They are also strongly attracted to negative ions by their positive ends.

FIGURE 12.7
Polar water molecules are strongly attracted to each other.

required to change water from a liquid to a gas (the molecules must be separated from each other to undergo this change of state). Therefore, it is the polarity of the water molecule that causes water to remain a liquid at the temperatures on the earth's surface. If it were nonpolar, water would be a gas and the oceans would be empty.

12.4 *Stable Electron Configurations and Charges on Ions*

AIMS: To learn about stable electron configurations. To learn to predict the formulas of ionic compounds.

We have seen many times that when a metal and a nonmetal react to form an ionic compound, the metal atom loses one or more electrons to the nonmetal. In Chapter 5, where binary ionic compounds were introduced, we saw that in these reactions, Group 1 metals always form 1+ cations, Group 2 metals always form 2+ cations, and aluminum in Group 3 always forms a 3+

TABLE 12.2

The Formation of Ions by Metals and Nonmetals

		Electron Configuration	
Group	Ion Formation	Atom	Ion
1	$Na \rightarrow Na^+ + e^-$	$[Ne]3s^1 \xrightarrow{\quad e^-\ lost\quad}$	$[Ne]$
2	$Mg \rightarrow Mg^{2+} + 2e^-$	$[Ne]3s^2 \xrightarrow{\quad 2e^-\ lost\quad}$	$[Ne]$
3	$Al \rightarrow Al^{3+} + 3e^-$	$[Ne]3s^23p^1 \xrightarrow{\quad 3e^-\ lost\quad}$	$[Ne]$
6	$O + 2e^- \rightarrow O^{2-}$	$[He]2s^22p^4 + 2e^- \rightarrow [He]2s^22p^6 = [Ne]$	
7	$F + e^- \rightarrow F^-$	$[He]2s^22p^5 + e^- \rightarrow [He]2s^22p^6 = [Ne]$	

cation. For the nonmetals, the Group 7 elements always form 1− anions, and the Group 6 elements always form 2− anions. This is further illustrated in Table 12.2.

Notice something very interesting about the ions in Table 12.2: they all have the electron configuration of neon, a noble gas. That is, sodium loses its one valence electron (the $3s$) to form Na^+, which has an [Ne] electron configuration. Likewise Mg loses its two valence electrons to form Mg^{2+}, which also has an [Ne] electron configuration. On the other hand, the nonmetal atoms gain just the number of electrons needed for them to achieve the noble gas electron configuration. The O atom gains two electrons and the F atom gains one electron to give O^{2-} and F^-, respectively, both of which have the [Ne] electron configuration. We can summarize these observations as follows:

Electron Configurations of Ions

Now that we know something about the electron configurations of atoms, we can explain why these various ions are formed.

1. Representative (main group) metals form ions by losing enough electrons to achieve the configuration of the previous noble gas (that is, the noble gas that occurs before the metal in question on the periodic table). For example, note from the periodic table inside the front cover of the text that neon is the noble gas previous to sodium and magnesium. Similarly, helium is the noble gas previous to lithium and beryllium.

2. Nonmetals form ions by gaining enough electrons to achieve the configuration of the next noble gas (that is, the noble gas that follows the element in question on the periodic table). For example, note that neon is the noble gas that follows oxygen and fluorine, and argon is the noble gas that follows sulfur and chlorine.

This brings us to an important general principle. In observing millions of stable compounds, chemists have learned that **in almost all stable chemical compounds of the representative elements, all of the atoms have achieved a noble gas electron configuration.** The importance of this observation cannot be overstated. It forms the basis for all of our fundamental ideas about why and how atoms bond to each other.

We have already seen this principle operating in the formation of ions (see Table 12.2). We can summarize this behavior as follows: when representative metals and nonmetals react, they transfer electrons in such a way that both the cation and the anion have noble gas electron configurations.

On the other hand, when nonmetals react with each other, they share electrons in ways that lead to a noble gas electron configuration for each atom in the resulting molecule. For example, oxygen ($[He]2s^22p^4$), which needs two more electrons to achieve an [Ne] configuration, can get these electrons by combining with two H atoms (each of which has one electron):

O: [He]   2s ⇅   2p ⇅ ⇅ ⇅
                                        H   H

to form water, H_2O. This fills the valence orbitals of oxygen.

In addition, each H shares two electrons with the oxygen atom:

H ⇅ O ⇅ H

which fills the H $1s$ orbital, giving it a $1s^2$ or [He] electron configuration. We will have much more to say about covalent bonding in Section 12.6.

At this point let's summarize the ideas we have introduced so far.

Electron Configurations and Bonding

Atoms in stable compounds almost always have a noble gas electron configuration.

1. When a *nonmetal and a Group 1, 2, or 3 metal* react to form a binary ionic compound, the ions form in such a way that the valence electron configuration of the *nonmetal* is *completed* to achieve the configuration of the *next* noble gas, and the valence orbitals of the *metal* are *emptied* to achieve the configuration of the *previous* noble gas. In this way both ions achieve noble gas electron configurations.

2. When *two nonmetals* react to form a covalent bond, they share electrons in a way that completes the valence electron configurations of both atoms. That is, both nonmetals attain noble gas electron configurations by sharing electrons.

Predicting Formulas of Ionic Compounds

To show how to predict what ions form when a metal reacts with a nonmetal, we will consider the formation of an ionic compound from calcium and oxygen. We can predict what compound will form by considering the valence electron configurations of the two atoms.

Ca: $[Ar]4s^2$

O: $[He]2s^22p^4$

Differences in electronegativities greater than 2 lead to ionic bonds.

From Figure 12.3 we see that the electronegativity of oxygen (3.5) is much greater than that of calcium (1.0), giving a difference of 2.5. Because of this large difference, electrons are transferred from calcium to oxygen to form an oxygen anion and a calcium cation. How many electrons are transferred? We can base our prediction on the observation that noble gas configurations are the most stable. Note that oxygen needs two electrons to fill its valence orbitals ($2s$ and $2p$) and achieve the configuration of neon ($1s^2 2s^2 2p^6$), which is the next noble gas.

$$O + 2e^- \rightarrow O^{2-}$$
$$[He]2s^2 2p^4 + 2e^- \rightarrow [He]2s^2 2p^6, \text{ or } [Ne]$$

And by losing two electrons, calcium can achieve the configuration of argon (the previous noble gas).

$$Ca \rightarrow Ca^{2+} + 2e^-$$
$$[Ar]4s^2 \rightarrow [Ar] + 2e^-$$

Two electrons are therefore transferred as follows:

$$Ca + O \rightarrow Ca^{2+} + O^{2-}$$
$$2e^-$$

To predict the formula of the ionic compound, we use the fact that chemical compounds are always electrically neutral—they have the same total quantities of positive and negative charges. In this case we must have equal numbers of Ca^{2+} and O^{2-} ions, and the empirical formula of the compound is CaO.

The same principles can be applied to many other cases. For example, consider the compound formed from aluminum and oxygen. Aluminum has the electron configuration $[Ne]3s^2 3p^1$. To achieve the neon configuration, aluminum must lose three electrons, forming the Al^{3+} ion.

$$Al \rightarrow Al^{3+} + 3e^-$$
$$[Ne]3s^2 3p^1 \rightarrow [Ne] + 3e^-$$

$3 \times (2-)$ balances $2 \times (3+)$

Therefore, the ions will be Al^{3+} and O^{2-}. Because the compound must be electrically neutral, there will be three O^{2-} ions for every two Al^{3+} ions, and the compound has the empirical formula Al_2O_3.

Table 12.3 shows common elements that form ions with noble gas electron configurations in ionic compounds.

TABLE 12.3

Common Ions with Noble Gas Configurations in Ionic Compounds

Group 1	Group 2	Group 3	Group 6	Group 7	Electron Configuration
Li^+	Be^{2+}				[He]
Na^+	Mg^{2+}	Al^{3+}	O^{2-}	F^-	[Ne]
K^+	Ca^{2+}		S^{2-}	Cl^-	[Ar]
Rb^+	Sr^{2+}		Se^{2-}	Br^-	[Kr]
Cs^+	Ba^{2+}		Te^{2-}	I^-	[Xe]

Notice that our discussion in this section refers to metals in Groups 1, 2, and 3 (the representative metals). The transition metals exhibit more complicated behavior (they form a variety of ions), which we will not be concerned with in this text.

12.5 Ionic Bonding and Structures of Ionic Compounds

AIMS: To learn about ionic structures. To understand factors governing ionic size.

When metals and nonmetals react, the resulting ionic compounds are very stable; large amounts of energy are required to "take them apart." For example, the melting point of sodium chloride is approximately 800 °C. The strong bonding in these ionic compounds results from the attractions between the oppositely charged cations and anions.

We write the formula of an ionic compound such as lithium fluoride simply as LiF, but this is really the empirical, or simplest, formula. The actual solid contains huge and equal numbers of Li^+ and F^- ions packed together in a way that maximizes the attractions of the oppositely charged ions. A representative part of the lithium fluoride structure is shown in Figure 12.8(a). In this structure the larger F^- ions are packed together like hard spheres, and the much smaller Li^+ ions are interspersed regularly among the F^- ions. The structure shown in Figure 12.8(b) represents only a tiny part of the actual structure, which continues in all three dimensions with the same pattern as that shown.

The structures of virtually all binary ionic compounds can be explained by a model that involves packing the ions as though they were hard spheres. The larger spheres (usually the anions) are packed together, and the small ions occupy the interstices (spaces or holes) among them.

To understand the packing of ions it helps to realize that *a cation is always smaller than the parent atom, and an anion is always larger than the parent atom.* This makes sense because when a metal loses all of its valence

FIGURE 12.8
The structure of lithium fluoride. (a) This structure represents the ions as packed spheres. (b) This structure shows the positions (centers) of the ions. The spherical ions are packed in the way that maximizes the ionic attractions.

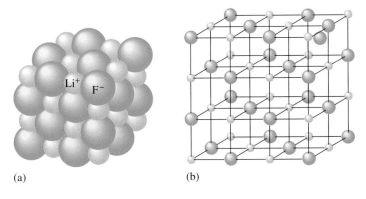

(a)   (b)

FIGURE 12.9
Relative sizes of some ions and their parent atoms. Note that cations are smaller and anions are larger than their parent atoms. The sizes (radii) are given in units of picometers (1 pm = 10^{-12} m).

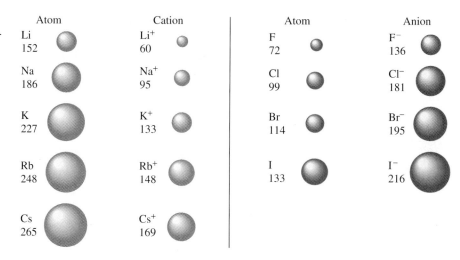

Atom	Cation	Atom	Anion
Li 152	Li$^+$ 60	F 72	F$^-$ 136
Na 186	Na$^+$ 95	Cl 99	Cl$^-$ 181
K 227	K$^+$ 133	Br 114	Br$^-$ 195
Rb 248	Rb$^+$ 148	I 133	I$^-$ 216
Cs 265	Cs$^+$ 169		

electrons to form a cation, it gets much smaller. On the other hand, in forming an anion, a nonmetal gains enough electrons to achieve the next noble gas electron configuration and so becomes much larger. The relative sizes of the Group 1 and Group 7 atoms and their ions are shown in Figure 12.9.

Ionic Compounds Containing Polyatomic Ions

So far in this chapter we have discussed only binary ionic compounds, which contain ions derived from single atoms. However, many compounds contain polyatomic ions: charged species composed of several atoms. For example, ammonium nitrate contains the NH_4^+ and NO_3^- ions. These ions with their opposite charges attract each other in the same way as do the simple ions in binary ionic compounds. However, the *individual* polyatomic ions are held together by covalent bonds, with all of the atoms behaving as a unit. For example, in the ammonium ion, NH_4^+, there are four N—H covalent bonds. Likewise the nitrate ion, NO_3^-, contains three covalent N—O bonds. Thus, although ammonium nitrate is an ionic compound because it contains the NH_4^+ and NO_3^- ions, it also contains covalent bonds in the individual polyatomic ions. When ammonium nitrate is dissolved in water, it behaves as a strong electrolyte like the binary ionic compounds sodium chloride and potassium bromide. As we saw in Chapter 7, this occurs because when an ionic solid dissolves, the ions are freed to move independently and can conduct an electric current.

The common polyatomic ions, which are listed in Table 5.5, are all held together by covalent bonds.

When spheres are packed together, they do not fill up all of the space. The spaces (holes) that are left can be occupied by smaller spheres.

12.6 Lewis Structures

AIM: To learn to write Lewis structures.

Bonding involves just the valence electrons of atoms. Valence electrons are transferred when a metal and a nonmetal react to form an ionic compound. Valence electrons are shared between nonmetals in covalent bonds.

G. N. Lewis in his lab.

Remember that the electrons in the highest principal energy level of an atom are called the valence electrons.

Lewis structures show only valence electrons.

The **Lewis structure** is a representation of a molecule that shows how the valence electrons are arranged among the atoms in the molecule. These representations are named after G. N. Lewis, who conceived the idea while lecturing to a class of general chemistry students in 1902. The rules for writing Lewis structures are based on observations of many molecules from which chemists have learned that the *most important requirement for the formation of a stable compound is that the atoms achieve noble gas electron configurations.*

We have already seen this rule operate in the reaction of metals and nonmetals to form binary ionic compounds. An example is the formation of KBr, where the K^+ ion has the [Ar] electron configuration and the Br^- ion has the [Kr] electron configuration. In writing Lewis structures, *we include only the valence electrons.* Using dots to represent valence electrons, we write the Lewis structure for KBr as follows:

$$K^+ \qquad\qquad [\,:\!\overset{..}{\underset{..}{Br}}\!:\,]^-$$

Noble gas   Noble gas
configuration [Ar]   configuration [Kr]

No dots are shown on the K^+ ion because it has lost its only valence electron (the $4s$ electron). The Br^- ion is shown with eight electrons because it has a filled valence shell.

Next we will consider Lewis structures for molecules with covalent bonds, involving nonmetals in the first and second periods. The principle of achieving a noble gas electron configuration applies to these elements as follows:

1. Hydrogen forms stable molecules where it shares two electrons. That is, it follows a **duet rule.** For example, when two hydrogen atoms, each with one electron, combine to form the H_2 molecule, we have

By sharing electrons, each hydrogen in H_2 has, in effect, two electrons; that is, each hydrogen has a filled valence shell.

2. Helium does not form bonds because its valence orbitals are already filled; it is a noble gas. Helium has the electron configuration $1s^2$ and can be represented by the Lewis structure

He :

[He] configuration

3. The second-row nonmetals carbon through fluorine form stable molecules when they are surrounded by enough electrons to fill the valence orbitals—that is, the one $2s$ and the three $2p$ orbitals. Eight electrons are required

Carbon, nitrogen, oxygen, and fluorine almost always obey the octet rule in stable molecules.

to fill these orbitals, so these elements typically obey the **octet rule;** they are surrounded by eight electrons. An example is the F_2 molecule, which has the following Lewis structure:

$$: \overset{..}{\underset{..}{F}} \cdot \qquad \rightarrow \qquad : \overset{..}{\underset{..}{F}} : \overset{..}{\underset{..}{F}} : \qquad \leftarrow \qquad \cdot \overset{..}{\underset{..}{F}} :$$

F atom with seven F_2 F atom with seven
valence electrons   molecule   valence electrons

Note that each fluorine atom in F_2 is, in effect, surrounded by eight valence electrons, two of which are shared with the other atom. This is a **bonding pair** of electrons, as we discussed earlier. Each fluorine atom also has three pairs of electrons that are not involved in bonding. These are called **lone pairs** or **unshared pairs.**

4. Neon does not form bonds because it already has an octet of valence electrons (it is a noble gas). The Lewis structure is

$$: \overset{..}{\underset{..}{Ne}} :$$

Note that only the valence electrons ($2s^2 2p^6$) of the neon atom are represented by the Lewis structure. The $1s^2$ electrons are core electrons and are not shown.

Next we want to develop some general procedures for writing Lewis structures for molecules. Remember that Lewis structures involve only the valence electrons on atoms, so before we proceed, we will review the relationship of an element's position on the periodic table to the number of valence electrons it has. Recall that the group number gives the total number of valence electrons. For example, all Group 6 elements have six valence electrons (valence configuration $ns^2 np^4$).

Group 6

Group 6
O $2s^2 2p^4$
S $3s^2 3p^4$
Se $4s^2 4p^4$
Te $5s^2 5p^4$

Similarly, all Group 7 elements have seven valence electrons (valence configuration $ns^2 np^5$).

Group 7

Group 7
F $2s^2 2p^5$
Cl $3s^2 3p^5$
Br $4s^2 4p^5$
I $5s^2 5p^5$

In writing the Lewis structure for a molecule, we need to keep the following things in mind:

1. We must include all the valence electrons from all atoms. The total number of electrons available is the sum of all the valence electrons from all the atoms in the molecule.

2. Atoms that are bonded to each other share one or more pairs of electrons.

3. The electrons are arranged so that each atom is surrounded by enough electrons to fill the valence orbitals of that atom. This means two electrons for hydrogen and eight electrons for second-row nonmetals.

The best way to make sure we arrive at the correct Lewis structure for a molecule is to use a systematic approach. We will use the approach summarized by the following rules.

Steps for Writing Lewis Structures

STEP 1 Obtain the sum of the valence electrons from all of the atoms. Do not worry about keeping track of which electrons come from which atoms. It is the *total* number of valence electrons that is important.

STEP 2 Use one pair of electrons to form a bond between each pair of bound atoms. For convenience, a line (instead of a pair of dots) is often used to indicate each pair of bonding electrons.

STEP 3 Arrange the remaining electrons to satisfy the duet rule for hydrogen and the octet rule for each second-row element.

To see how these rules are applied, we will write the Lewis structures of several molecules.

EXAMPLE 12.2   *Writing Lewis Structures: Simple Molecules*

Write the Lewis structure of the water molecule.

Solution

We will follow the steps listed above.

STEP 1 We sum the *valence* electrons for H_2O.

$$\underset{\substack{\uparrow \\ \text{H} \\ \text{(Group 1)}}}{1} + \underset{\substack{\uparrow \\ \text{H} \\ \text{(Group 1)}}}{1} + \underset{\substack{\uparrow \\ \text{O} \\ \text{(Group 6)}}}{6} = 8 \text{ valence electrons}$$

STEP 2 Using a pair of electrons per bond, we draw in the two O—H bonds, using a line to indicate each pair of bonding electrons.

H—O—H

Note that

H—O—H   represents   H : O : H

STEP 3 We arrange the remaining electrons around the atoms to achieve a noble gas electron configuration for each atom. Four electrons have been used in forming the two bonds, so four electrons (8 − 4) remain to be distributed. Each hydrogen is satisfied with two electrons (duet rule), but oxygen needs eight electrons to have a noble gas electron configuration. So the remaining four electrons are added to oxygen as two lone pairs. Dots are used to represent the lone pairs.

H—Ö—H

might also be drawn as

H :Ö: H

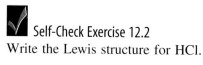

This is the correct Lewis structure for the water molecule. Each hydrogen shares two electrons, and the oxygen has four electrons and shares four to give a total of eight.

$$ \text{H} \ominus \ddot{\text{O}} \ominus \text{H} $$

2e⁻   8e⁻   2e⁻

Note that a line is used to represent a shared pair of electrons (bonding electrons) and dots are used to represent unshared pairs.

 Self-Check Exercise 12.2
Write the Lewis structure for HCl.

See Problems 12.59 through 12.62.

12.7 Lewis Structures of Molecules with Multiple Bonds

AIM: To learn how to write Lewis structures for molecules with multiple bonds.

Now let's write the Lewis structure for carbon dioxide. Summing the valence electrons gives

$$ 4 + 6 + 6 = 16 $$

C   O   O
(Group 4) (Group 6) (Group 6)

O—C—O

represents

O : C : O

After forming a bond between the carbon and each oxygen,

O—C—O

we distribute the remaining electrons to achieve noble gas electron configurations on each atom. In this case twelve electrons (16 − 4) remain after the bonds are drawn. The distribution of these electrons is determined by a trial-and-error process. We have six pairs of electrons to distribute. Suppose we try three pairs on each oxygen to give

:Ö—C—Ö:

represents

:Ö: C :Ö:

:Ö—C—Ö:

Is this correct? To answer this question we need to check two things:

1. The total number of electrons. There are sixteen valence electrons in this structure, which is the correct number.
2. The octet rule for each atom. Each oxygen has eight electrons around it, but the carbon has only four. This cannot be the correct Lewis structure.

How can we arrange the sixteen available electrons to achieve an octet for each atom? Suppose we place two shared pairs between the carbon and each oxygen:

$$\ddot{O}=C=\ddot{O}$$

represents

$$\ddot{O}::C::\ddot{O}$$

Now each atom is surrounded by eight electrons, and the total number of electrons is sixteen, as required. This is the correct Lewis structure for carbon dioxide, which has two *double* bonds. A **single bond** involves two atoms sharing one electron pair. A **double bond** involves two atoms sharing two pairs of electrons.

In considering the Lewis structure for CO_2, you may have come up with

:O≡C—Ö: or   :Ö—C≡O:

Note that both of these structures have the required sixteen electrons and that both have octets of electrons around each atom (verify this for yourself). Both of these structures have a **triple bond** in which three electron pairs are shared. Are these valid Lewis structures for CO_2? Yes. So there really are three Lewis structures for CO_2:

:Ö—C≡O: Ö=C=Ö   :O≡C—Ö:

This brings us to a new term, **resonance.** A molecule shows resonance when *more than one Lewis structure can be drawn for the molecule.* In such a case we call the various Lewis structures **resonance structures.**

Of the three resonance structures for CO_2 shown above, the one in the center with two double bonds most closely fits our experimental information about the CO_2 molecule. In this text we will not be concerned about how to choose which resonance structure for a molecule gives the "best" description of that molecule's properties.

Next let's consider the Lewis structure of the CN^- (cyanide) ion. Summing the valence electrons, we have

CN⁻

$$4 + 5 + 1 = 10$$

Note that the negative charge means an extra electron must be added. After first drawing a single bond (C—N), we distribute the remaining electrons to achieve a noble gas configuration for each atom. Eight electrons remain to be distributed. We can try various possibilities, such as

C̈—N̈   or   :C̈—N: or   :C—N̈:

These structures are incorrect. To show why none is a valid Lewis structure, count the electrons around the C and N atoms. In the left structure, neither

Side notes (left margin):

Ö=C=Ö

represents

Ö::C::Ö

:O≡C—Ö:

represents

:O:::C:Ö:

:C≡N:

represents

:C : : :N:

atom satisfies the octet rule. In the center structure, C has eight electrons but N has only four. In the right structure, the opposite is true. Remember that both atoms must simultaneously satisfy the octet rule. Therefore, the correct arrangement is

$$: C \equiv N :$$

(Satisfy yourself that both carbon and nitrogen have eight electrons.) In this case we have a triple bond between C and N, in which three electron pairs are shared. Because this is an anion, we indicate the charge outside of square brackets around the Lewis structure.

$$[: C \equiv N :]^-$$

In summary, sometimes we need double or triple bonds to satisfy the octet rule. Writing Lewis structures is a trial-and-error process. Start with single bonds between the bonded atoms and add multiple bonds as needed.

We will write the Lewis structure for NO_2^- in Example 12.3 to make sure the procedures for writing Lewis structures are clear.

EXAMPLE 12.3   *Writing Lewis Structures: Resonance Structures*

Write the Lewis structure for the NO_2^- anion.

Solution

STEP 1   Sum the valence electrons for NO_2^-.

$$\text{Valence electrons: } \underset{O}{6} + \underset{N}{5} + \underset{O}{6} + \underset{\substack{-1 \\ \text{charge}}}{1} = 18 \text{ electrons}$$

STEP 2   Put in single bonds.

$$O—N—O$$

STEP 3   Satisfy the octet rule. In placing the electrons, we find there are two Lewis structures that satisfy the octet rule:

$$[\ddot{O}=\ddot{N}—\ddot{O} :]^- \quad \text{and} \quad [: \ddot{O}—\ddot{N}=\ddot{O}]^-$$

Verify that each atom in these structures is surrounded by an octet of electrons. Try some other arrangements to see whether other structures exist in which the eighteen electrons can be used to satisfy the octet rule. It turns out that these are the only two that work. Note that this is another case where resonance occurs; there are two valid Lewis structures.

 Self-Check Exercise 12.3

Ozone is a very important constituent of the atmosphere. At upper levels it protects us by absorbing high-energy radiation from the sun. Near the earth's surface it produces harmful air pollution. Write the Lewis structure for ozone, O_3.

See Problems 12.63 through 12.68.

Now let's consider a few more cases in Example 12.4.

███ **EXAMPLE 12.4** *Writing Lewis Structures: Summary*

Give the Lewis structure for each of the following:

a. HF   e. CF_4
b. N_2 f. NO^+
c. NH_3 g. NO_3^-
d. CH_4

Solution

In each case we apply the three steps for writing Lewis structures. Recall that lines are used to indicate shared electron pairs and that dots are used to indicate nonbonding pairs (lone pairs). The following table summarizes our results.

Molecule or Ion	Total Valence Electrons	Draw Single Bonds	Calculate Number of Electrons Remaining	Use Remaining Electrons to Achieve Noble Gas Configurations	Check Atom	Electrons
a. HF	$1 + 7 = 8$	H — F	$8 - 2 = 6$	H — F:	H	2
					F	8
b. N_2	$5 + 5 = 10$	N — N	$10 - 2 = 8$	:N≡N:	N	8
c. NH_3	$5 + 3(1) = 8$	H—N—N with H below	$8 - 6 = 2$	H—N—N with H below	H	2
					N	8
d. CH_4	$4 + 4(1) = 8$	H—C—H with H above and below	$8 - 8 = 0$	H—C—H with H above and below	H	2
					C	8
e. CF_4	$4 + 4(7) = 32$	F—C—F with F above and below	$32 - 8 = 24$	:F—C—F: with :F: above and below	F	8
					C	8
f. NO^+	$5 + 6 - 1 = 10$	N — O	$10 - 2 = 8$	$[:N≡O:]^+$	N	8
					O	8
g. NO_3^-	$5 + 3(6) + 1 = 24$	[see structure]	$24 - 6 = 18$	[see resonance structures]	N	8
					O	8
				NO_3^- shows resonance.	N	8
					O	8
					N	8
					O	8

You may wonder how to decide which atom is the central atom in molecules of binary compounds. In cases where there is one atom of a given element and several atoms of a second element, the single atom is almost always the central atom of the molecule.

 Self-Check Exercise 12.4

Write the Lewis structures for the following molecules:

a. NF_3 f. SO_4^{2-}
b. O_2 g. NH_4^+
c. CO   h. ClO_3^-
d. PH_3 i. SO_2
e. H_2S

See Problems 12.55 through 12.68.

Remember, when writing Lewis structures, you don't have to worry about which electrons come from which atoms in a molecule. It is best to think of a molecule as a new entity that uses all the available valence electrons from the various atoms to achieve the strongest possible bonds. Think of the valence electrons as belonging to the molecule, rather than to the individual atoms. Simply distribute all the valence electrons so that noble gas electron configurations are obtained for each atom, without regard to the origin of each particular electron.

Some Exceptions to the Octet Rule

The idea that covalent bonding can be predicted by achieving noble gas electron configurations for all atoms is a simple and very successful idea. The rules we have used for Lewis structures describe correctly the bonding in most molecules. However, with such a simple model, some exceptions are inevitable. Boron, for example, tends to form compounds in which the boron atom has fewer than eight electrons around it—that is, it does not have a complete octet. Boron trifluoride, BF_3, a gas at normal temperatures and pressures, reacts very energetically with molecules such as water and ammonia that have unshared electron pairs (lone pairs).

The violent reactivity of BF_3 with electron-rich molecules arises because the boron atom is electron-deficient. The Lewis structure that seems most consistent with the properties of BF_3 (twenty-four valence electrons) is

Note that in this structure the boron atom has only six electrons around it. The octet rule for boron could be satisfied by drawing a structure with a double bond between the boron and one of the flourines. However, experiments indicate that each B—F bond is a single bond in accordance with the above Lewis structure. This structure is also consistent with the reactivity of BF_3 with electron-rich molecules. For example, BF_3 reacts vigorously with NH_3 to form H_3NBF_3.

Note that in the product H_3NBF_3, which is very stable, boron has an octet of electrons.

It is also characteristic of beryllium to form molecules where the beryllium atom is electron-deficient.

The elements carbon, nitrogen, oxygen, and fluorine obey the octet rule in the vast majority of their compounds. However, even these elements show a few exceptions. One important example is the oxygen molecule, O_2. The following Lewis structure that satisfies the octet rule can be drawn for O_2 (see Self-Check Exercise 12.4).

FIGURE 12.10
When liquid oxygen is poured between the poles of a magnet, it "sticks" until it boils away. This shows that the O_2 molecule has unpaired electrons (is paramagnetic).

Paramagnetic substances have unpaired electrons and are drawn toward the space between a magnet's poles.

However, this structure does not agree with the *observed behavior* of oxygen. For example, the photo in Figure 12.10 shows that when liquid oxygen is poured between the poles of a strong magnet, it "sticks" there until it boils away. This provides clear evidence that oxygen is paramagnetic—that is, it contains unpaired electrons. However, the above Lewis structure shows only pairs of electrons. That is, no unpaired electrons are shown. There is no simple Lewis structure that satisfactorily explains the paramagnetism of the O_2 molecule.

Any molecule that contains an odd number of electrons does not conform to our rules for Lewis structures. For example, NO and NO_2 have eleven and seventeen valence electrons, respectively, and conventional Lewis structures cannot be drawn for these cases.

Even though there are exceptions, most molecules can be described by Lewis structures in which all the atoms have noble gas electron configurations, and this is a very useful model for chemists.

12.8 *Molecular Structure*

AIM: To understand molecular structure and bond angles.

So far in this chapter we have considered the Lewis structures of molecules. These structures represent the arrangement of the *valence electrons* in a molecule. We use the word *structure* in another way when we talk about the **molecular structure** or **geometric structure** of a molecule. These terms refer to the three-dimensional arrangement of the *atoms* in a molecule. For example, the water molecule is known to have the molecular structure

$$\underset{H \qquad\quad H}{\overset{O}{\diagdown\diagup}}$$

which is often called "bent" or "V-shaped." To describe the structure more precisely, we often specify the **bond angle.** For the H_2O molecule the bond angle is about $106°$.

(a)

(b)

(c)

Computer graphics of (a) a linear molecule containing three atoms, (b) a trigonal planar molecule, and (c) a tetrahedral molecule.

~105°

On the other hand, some molecules exhibit a **linear structure** (all atoms in a line). An example is the CO_2 molecule.

O—C—O

180°

Note that a linear molecule has a 180° bond angle.

A third type of molecular structure is illustrated by BF_3, which is planar or flat (all four atoms in the same plane) with 120° bond angles.

120°   F   120°
              B
        F   F
           120°

The name usually given to this structure is **trigonal planar structure**, although triangular might seem to make more sense.

Another type of molecular structure is illustrated by methane, CH_4. This molecule has the molecular structure shown in Figure 12.11, which is called a **tetrahedral structure** or a **tetrahedron.** The dashed lines shown connecting the H atoms define the four identical triangular faces of the tetrahedron.

In the next section we will discuss these various molecular structures in more detail. In that section we will learn how to predict the molecular structure of a molecule by looking at the molecule's Lewis structure.

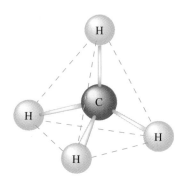

FIGURE 12.11
The tetrahedral molecular structure of methane. This representation is called a ball-and-stick model; the atoms are represented by balls and the bonds by sticks. The dashed line shows the outline of the tetrahedron.

109.5°

12.9 *Molecular Structure: The VSEPR Model*

AIM: To learn to predict molecular geometry from the number of electron pairs.

The structures of molecules play a very important role in determining their properties. For example, as we will see in the "Chemistry in Focus" on page 351, taste is directly related to molecular structure. Structure is particularly

CHEMISTRY IN FOCUS

*T*aste—*It's the Structure That Counts*

Why do certain substances taste sweet, sour, bitter, or salty? Of course, it has to do with the taste buds on our tongues. But how do these taste buds work? For example, why does sugar taste sweet to us? The answer to this question remains elusive, but it does seem clear that sweet taste depends on how certain molecules fit the "sweet receptors" in our taste buds.

One of the mysteries of the sweet taste sensation is the wide variety of molecules that tastes sweet. For example, the many types of sugars include glucose and sucrose (table sugar). The first artificial sweetener was probably the Romans' sapa (see "Chemistry in Focus: Sugar of Lead" in Chapter 5), made by boiling wine in lead vessels to produce a syrup that contained lead acetate, $Pb(C_2H_3O_2)_2$, called sugar of lead because of its sweet taste. Other widely used modern artificial sweeteners include saccharin, cyclamate, and aspartame, whose structures are shown in the accompanying figure. Note the great disparity of structures for these sweet-tasting molecules. It's certainly not obvious which structural features trigger a sweet sensation when these molecules interact with the taste buds.

The pioneers in relating structure to sweet taste were two chemists, Robert S. Shallenberger and Terry E. Acree of Cornell University, who almost thirty years ago suggested that all sweet-tasting substances must contain a common feature they called a glycophore. They postulated that a glycophore always contains an atom or group of atoms that have available electrons located near a hydrogen atom attached to a relatively electronegative atom. Murray Goodman, a chemist at the University of California at San Diego, expanded the definition of a glycophore to include a hydrophobic ("water-hating") region. Goodman finds that a "sweet molecule" tends to be L-shaped with positively and negatively charged regions on the upright of the L and a hydrophobic region on the base of the L. To be sweet the L must be planar. If it is twisted in one direction, it gives a bitter taste. Twisting it in the other direction makes it tasteless. Goodman reports that by using his model he can design sweeteners, but these molecules remain too expensive for commercial use.

So the search goes on for a better artificial sweetener. One thing for sure, it all has to do with molecular structure.

Saccharin

Sodium cyclamate

Aspartame
(Nutra sweet™)

important for biological molecules; a slight change in the structure of a large biomolecule can completely destroy its usefulness to a cell and may even change the cell from a normal one to a cancerous one.

Many experimental methods now exist for determining the molecular structure of a molecule—that is, the three-dimensional arrangement of the atoms. These methods must be used when accurate information about the structure is required. However, it is often useful to be able to predict the *approximate* molecular structure of a molecule. In this section we consider a simple model that allows us to do this. This model, called the **valence shell electron pair repulsion (VSEPR) model,** is useful for predicting the molecular structures of molecules formed from nonmetals. The main idea of this model is that *the structure around a given atom is determined by minimizing repulsions between electron pairs.* This means that the bonding and nonbonding electron pairs (lone pairs) around a given atom are positioned *as far apart as possible.* To see how this model works, we will first consider the molecule $BeCl_2$, which has the following Lewis structure (it is an exception to the octet rule).

$$: \overset{..}{\underset{..}{Cl}} - Be - \overset{..}{\underset{..}{Cl}} :$$

Note that there are two pairs of electrons around the beryllium atom. What arrangement of these electron pairs allows them to be as far apart as possible to minimize the repulsions? The best arrangement places the pairs on opposite sides of the beryllium atom at 180° from each other.

$$- Be -$$
$$180°$$

This is the maximum possible separation for two electron pairs. Now that we have determined the optimal arrangement of the electron pairs around the central atom, we can specify the molecular structure of $BeCl_2$—that is, the positions of the atoms. Because each electron pair on beryllium is shared with a chlorine atom, the molecule has a **linear structure** with a 180° bond angle.

$$: \overset{..}{\underset{..}{Cl}} - Be - \overset{..}{\underset{..}{Cl}} :$$
$$180°$$

Whenever two pairs of electrons are present around an atom, they should always be placed at an angle of 180° to each other to give a linear arrangement.

Next let's consider BF_3, which has the following Lewis structure (it is another exception to the octet rule).

$$\overset{\displaystyle :\overset{..}{F}:}{\underset{\displaystyle : \overset{..}{\underset{..}{F}} - B - \overset{..}{\underset{..}{F}} :}{\big|}}$$

Here the boron atom is surrounded by three pairs of electrons. What arrangement minimizes the repulsions among three pairs of electrons? Here the greatest distance between electron pairs is achieved by angles of 120°.

$$120° \quad \underset{120°}{\overset{|}{B}} \quad 120°$$

Because each of the electron pairs is shared with a fluorine atom, the molecular structure is

This is a planar (flat) molecule with a triangular arrangement of F atoms, commonly described as a trigonal planar structure. *Whenever three pairs of electrons are present around an atom, they should always be placed at the corners of a triangle (in a plane at an angle of 120° to each other).*

Next let's consider the methane molecule, which has the Lewis structure

$$H-\underset{\underset{H}{|}}{\overset{\overset{H}{|}}{C}}-H \quad \text{or} \quad H:\underset{\cdot\cdot}{\overset{\cdot\cdot}{\underset{H}{\overset{H}{C}}}}:H$$

There are four pairs of electrons around the central carbon atom. What arrangement of these electron pairs best minimizes the repulsions? First we try a square planar arrangement:

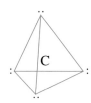

The carbon atom and the electron pairs are all in a plane represented by the surface of the paper, and the angles between the pairs are all 90°.

Is there another arrangement with angles greater than 90° that would put the electron pairs even farther away from each other? The answer is yes. We can get larger angles than 90° by using the following three-dimensional structure, which has angles of approximately 109.5°.

In this drawing the wedge indicates a position above the surface of the paper and the dashed lines indicate positions behind that surface. The regular line indicates a position on the surface of the page. The figure formed by connecting the lines is called a tetrahedron, so we call this arrangement of electron pairs the **tetrahedral arrangement.**

A tetrahedron has four equal triangular faces.

This is the maximum possible separation of four pairs around a given atom. *Whenever four pairs of electrons are present around an atom, they should always be placed at the corners of a tetrahedron (the tetrahedral arrangement).*

Now that we have the arrangement of electron pairs that gives the least repulsion, we can determine the positions of the atoms and thus the molecular structure of CH_4. In methane each of the four electron pairs is shared

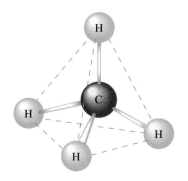

FIGURE 12.12
The molecular structure of methane. The tetrahedral arrangement of electron pairs produces a tetrahedral arrangement of hydrogen atoms.

between the carbon atom and a hydrogen atom. Thus the hydrogen atoms are placed as shown in Figure 12.12, and the molecule has a tetrahedral structure with the carbon atom at the center.

Recall that the main idea of the VSEPR model is to find the arrangement of electron pairs around the central atom which minimizes the repulsions. Then we can determine the *molecular structure* by knowing how the electron pairs are shared with the peripheral atoms. A systematic procedure for using the VSEPR model to predict the structure of a molecule is outlined below.

Steps for Predicting Molecular Structure Using the VSEPR Model

STEP 1 Draw the Lewis structure for the molecule.

STEP 2 Count the electron pairs and arrange them in the way that minimizes repulsion (that is, put the pairs as far apart as possible).

STEP 3 Determine the positions of the atoms from the way the electron pairs are shared.

STEP 4 Determine the name of the molecular structure from the positions of the *atoms*.

EXAMPLE 12.5 *Predicting Molecular Structure Using the VSEPR Model, I*

Ammonia, NH_3, is used as a fertilizer (injected into the soil) and as a household cleaner (in aqueous solution). Predict the structure of ammonia using the VSEPR model.

Solution

STEP 1 Draw the Lewis structure.

$$H-\overset{\cdot\cdot}{N}-H$$
$$|$$
$$H$$

STEP 2 Count the pairs of electrons and arrange them to minimize repulsions. The NH_3 molecule has four pairs of electrons around the N atom: three bonding pairs and one nonbonding pair. From the discussion of the methane molecule, we know that the best arrangement of four electron pairs is the tetrahedral structure shown in Figure 12.13(a).

STEP 3 Determine the positions of the atoms. The three H atoms share electron pairs as shown in Figure 12.13(b).

STEP 4 Name the molecular structure. It is very important to recognize that the name of the molecular structure is always based on the *positions of the atoms. The placement of the electron pairs determines the structure, but the name is based on the positions of the atoms.* Thus it is incorrect to say that the NH_3 molecule is tetrahedral. It has a tetrahedral arrangement of electron

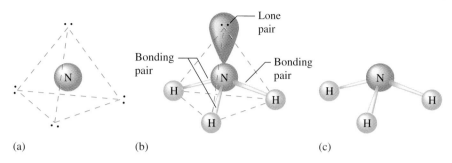

FIGURE 12.13
(a) The tetrahedral arrangement of electron pairs around the nitrogen atom in the ammonia molecule. (b) Three of the electron pairs around nitrogen are shared with hydrogen atoms as shown, and one is a lone pair. Although the arrangement of *electron pairs* is tetrahedral, as in the methane molecule, the hydrogen atoms in the ammonia molecule occupy only three corners of the tetrahedron. A lone pair occupies the fourth corner. (c) The NH$_3$ molecule has the trigonal pyramid structure (a pyramid with a triangle as a base).

pairs but *not* a tetrahedral arrangement of atoms. The molecular structure of ammonia is a **trigonal pyramid** (one side is different from the other three) rather than a tetrahedron.

EXAMPLE 12.6 *Predicting Molecular Structure Using the VSEPR Model, II*

Describe the molecular structure of the water molecule.

Solution

STEP 1 The Lewis structure for water is

H—Ö—H

STEP 2 There are four pairs of electrons: two bonding pairs and two non-bonding pairs. To minimize repulsions, these are best arranged in a tetrahedral structure as shown in Figure 12.14(a).

STEP 3 Although H$_2$O has a tetrahedral arrangement of *electron pairs,* it is *not a tetrahedral molecule.* The *atoms* in the H$_2$O molecule form a V shape, as shown in Figure 12.14(b) and (c).

STEP 4 The molecular structure is called V-shaped or bent.

FIGURE 12.14
(a) The tetrahedral arrangement of the four electron pairs around oxygen in the water molecule. (b) Two of the electron pairs are shared between oxygen and the hydrogen atoms, and two are lone pairs. (c) The V-shaped molecular structure of the water molecule.

Self-Check Exercise 12.5

Predict the arrangement of electron pairs around the central atom. Then sketch and name the molecular structure for each of the following molecules or ions.

a. NH_4^+ d. H_2S
b. SO_4^{2-} e. ClO_3^-
c. NF_3 f. BeF_2

See Problems 12.81 through 12.84.

The various cases we have considered are summarized in Table 12.4. Note the following general rules.

Rules for Predicting
Molecular Structure Using the VSEPR Model

---

1. Two pairs of electrons on a central atom in a molecule are always placed 180° apart. This is a linear arrangement of pairs.

2. Three pairs of electrons on a central atom in a molecule are always placed 120° apart in the same plane as the central atom. This is a trigonal planar (triangular) arrangement of pairs.

3. Four pairs of electrons on a central atom in a molecule are always placed 109.5° apart. This is a tetrahedral arrangement of electron pairs.

4. When *every pair* of electrons on the central atom is *shared* with another atom, the molecular structure has the same name as the arrangement of electron pairs.

Number of Pairs	*Name of Arrangement*
2	linear
3	trigonal planar
4	tetrahedral

5. When one or more of the electron pairs around a central atom are unshared (lone pairs), the name for the molecular structure is *different* from that for the arrangement of electron pairs (see cases 4 and 5 in Table 12.4).

12.10 *Molecular Structure:*
Molecules with Double Bonds

AIM: To learn to apply the VSEPR model to molecules with double bonds.

Up to this point we have applied the VSEPR model only to molecules (and ions) that contain single bonds. In this section we will show that this model applies equally well to species with one or more double bonds. We will

TABLE 12.4

Arrangements of Electron Pairs and the Resulting Molecular Structures for Two, Three, and Four Electron Pairs

Case	Number of Electron Pairs	Bonds	Electron Pair Arrangement	Ball-and-Stick Model	Angle Between Pairs	Molecular Structure	Partial Lewis Structure	Ball-and-Stick Model	Example
1	2	2	Linear		180°	Linear	A — B — A		BeF_2
2	3	3	Trigonal planar (triangular)		120°	Trigonal planar (triangular)	A ⟍ B ⟋ A, A		BF_3
3	4	4	Tetrahedral		109.5°	Tetrahedral	A—B—A with A above and A below		CH_4
4	4	3	Tetrahedral		109.5°	Trigonal pyramid	A—B̈—A with A below		NH_3
5	4	2	Tetrahedral		109.5°	Bent or V-shaped	A—B̈—A		H_2O

develop the procedures for dealing with molecules with double bonds by considering examples whose structures are known.

First we will examine the structure of carbon dioxide, a substance that may be contributing to the warming of the earth. The carbon dioxide molecule has the Lewis structure

$$\ddot{\text{O}}{=}\text{C}{=}\ddot{\text{O}}$$

as discussed in Section 12.7. Carbon dioxide is known by experiment to be a linear molecule. That is, it has a 180° bond angle.

180°

Recall from Section 12.9 that two electron pairs around a central atom can minimize their mutual repulsions by taking positions on opposite sides of the atom (at 180° from each other). This causes a molecule like $BeCl_2$, which has the Lewis structure

$$:\ddot{\text{Cl}}{-}\text{Be}{-}\ddot{\text{Cl}}:$$

to have a linear structure (see Section 12.9). Now recall that CO_2 has two double bonds and is known to be linear, so the double bonds must be at 180°

from each other. Therefore, we conclude that each double bond in this molecule acts *effectively* as one repulsive unit. This conclusion makes sense if we think of a bond in terms of an electron density "cloud" between two atoms. For example, we can picture the single bonds in $BeCl_2$ as follows:

The minimum repulsion between these two electron density clouds occurs when they are on opposite sides of the Be atom (180° angle between them).

Each double bond in CO_2 involves the sharing of four electrons between the carbon atom and an oxygen atom. Thus we might expect the bonding cloud to be "fatter" than for a single bond:

However, the repulsive effects of these two clouds produce the same result as for single bonds; the bonding clouds have minimum repulsions when they are positioned on opposite sides of the carbon. The bond angle is 180°, and so the molecule is linear:

In summary, examination of CO_2 leads us to the conclusion that in using the VSEPR model for molecules with double bonds, each double bond should be treated the same as a single bond. In other words, although a double bond involves four electrons, these electrons are restricted to the space between a given pair of atoms. Therefore, these four electrons do not function as two independent pairs but are "tied together" to form one effective repulsive unit.

We reach this same conclusion by considering the known structures of other molecules, that contain double bonds. For example, consider the ozone molecule, which has eighteen valence electrons and exhibits the resonance structures:

$$:\ddot{O}-\ddot{O}=\ddot{O}: \longleftrightarrow \ddot{O}=\ddot{O}-\ddot{O}:$$

The ozone molecule is known to have a bond angle close to 120°. Recall that 120° angles represent the minimum repulsion for three pairs of electrons.

This indicates that the double bond in the ozone molecule is behaving as one effective repulsive unit:

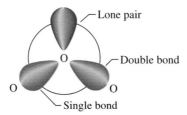

These and other examples lead us to the following rule: *When using the VSEPR model to predict the molecular geometry of a molecule, a double bond is counted the same as a single electron pair.*

Thus CO_2 has two "effective pairs" that lead to its linear structure, whereas O_3 has three "effective pairs" that lead to its bent structure with a 120° bond angle. Therefore, to use the VSEPR model for molecules (or ions) that have double bonds, we use the same steps as those given in Section 12.9, but we count any double bond the same as a single electron pair. Although we have not shown it here, triple bonds also count as one repulsive unit in applying the VSEPR model.

EXAMPLE 12.7 *Predicting Molecular Structure Using the VSEPR Model, III*

Predict the structure of the nitrate ion.

Solution

STEP 1 The Lewis structures for NO_3^- are

STEP 2 In each resonance structure there are effectively three pairs of electrons: the two single bonds and the double bond (which counts as one pair). These three "effective pairs" will require a trigonal planar arrangement (120° angles).

STEP 3 The atoms are all in a plane, with the nitrogen at the center and the three oxygens at the corners of a triangle (trigonal planar arrangement).

STEP 4 The NO_3^- ion has a trigonal planar structure.

Chapter Review

Key Terms

bond *(12.1)*
bond energy *(12.1)*
ionic bonding *(12.1)*
ionic compound *(12.1)*
covalent bonding *(12.1)*
polar covalent bond *(12.1)*
electronegativity *(12.2)*
dipole moment *(12.3)*
Lewis structure *(12.6)*
duet rule *(12.6)*
octet rule *(12.6)*
bonding pair *(12.6)*
lone pair *(12.6)*

single bond *(12.7)*
double bond *(12.7)*
triple bond *(12.7)*
resonance *(12.7)*
molecular (geometric) structure *(12.8)*
linear structure *(12.8)*
trigonal planar structure *(12.8)*
tetrahedral structure *(12.8)*
valence shell electron pair repulsion (VSEPR) model *(12.9)*

Summary

1. Chemical bonds hold groups of atoms together. They can be classified into several types. An ionic bond is formed when a transfer of electrons occurs to form ions; in a purely covalent bond, electrons are shared equally between identical atoms. Between these extremes lies the polar covalent bond, in which electrons are shared unequally between atoms with different electronegativities.

2. Electronegativity is defined as the relative ability of an atom in a molecule to attract the electrons shared in a bond. The difference in electronegativity values between the atoms involved in a bond determines the polarity of that bond.

3. In stable chemical compounds, the atoms tend to achieve a noble gas electron configuration. In the formation of a binary ionic compound involving representative elements, the valence-electron configuration of the nonmetal is completed: it achieves the configuration of the next noble gas. The valence orbitals of the metal are emptied to give the electron configuration of the previous noble gas. Two nonmetals share the valence electrons so that both atoms have completed valence-electron configurations (noble gas configurations).

4. Lewis structures are drawn to represent the arrangement of the valence electrons in a molecule. The rules for drawing Lewis structures are based on the observation that nonmetal atoms tend to achieve noble gas electron configurations by sharing electrons. This leads to a duet rule for hydrogen and to an octet rule for many other atoms.

5. Some molecules have more than one valid Lewis structure, a property called resonance. Although Lewis structures in which the atoms have noble gas electron configurations correctly describe most molecules, there are some notable exceptions, including O_2, NO, NO_2, and the molecules that contain Be and B.

6. The molecular structure of a molecule describes how the atoms are arranged in space.

7. The molecular structure of a molecule can be predicted by using the valence shell electron pair repulsion (VSEPR) model. This model bases its prediction on minimum repulsions among the electron pairs around an atom, which means arranging the electron pairs as far apart as possible.

Questions and Problems

All even-numbered exercises have answers in the back of this book and solutions in the Solutions Guide.

12.1 ■ Types of Chemical Bonds

QUESTIONS

1. Define a chemical bond.

2. In what terms do we describe the strength of chemical bonds?

3. _____ compounds result when a metallic element reacts with a nonmetal.

4. A(n) _____ bond requires the complete transfer of an electron from one atom to another.

5. Describe the type of chemical bonding that exists between the atoms in the hydrogen molecule, H_2.

6. Describe the type of chemical bonding that exists between the atoms in the hydrogen fluoride molecule, HF.

12.2 ■ Electronegativity

QUESTIONS

7. The ability of an atom to attract a shared pair of electrons toward itself is referred to as the atom's _____.

8. If one atom of a covalent bond attracts electrons more strongly toward itself than does the second atom, the bond will be _____.

9. A molecule is said to possess a dipole moment if the centers of positive and negative charge in the molecule are _____.

10. The relative polarity of a bond is determined by the difference in _____ of the atoms forming the bond.

PROBLEMS

11. For each of the following sets of elements, identify the element expected to be most electronegative and that expected to be least electronegative.
    a. Na, Al, Mg
    b. Te, S, O
    c. Na, Cl, P

12. For each of the following sets of elements, identify which element would be expected to be most electronegative and which would be expected to be least electronegative.
    a. K, Sc, Ca
    b. Br, F, At
    c. C, O, N

13. On the basis of the electronegativity values given in Figure 12.3, indicate whether each of the following bonds would be expected to be ionic, covalent, or polar covalent.
    a. H—H   c. H—Na
    b. H—Cl   d. H—O

14. On the basis of the electronegativity values given in Figure 12.3, indicate whether each of the following bonds would be expected to be ionic, covalent, or polar covalent.
    a. N—N   c. N—Cl
    b. N—O   d. N—Na

15. Which of the following molecules contain polar covalent bonds?
    a. dinitrogen, N_2 c. dioxygen, O_2
    b. hydrogen iodide, HI

16. Which of the following molecules contain polar covalent bonds?
    a. sulfur, S_8
    c. hydrogen peroxide, H_2O_2
    b. hydrogen, H_2
    d. chlorine monofluoride, ClF

17. On the basis of the electronegativity values given in Figure 12.3, indicate which is the more polar bond in each of the following pairs.
    a. H—F or H—Cl
    c. H—Br or H—Cl
    b. H—Cl or H—I
    d. H—I or H—Br

18. On the basis of the electronegativity values given in Figure 12.3, indicate which is the more polar bond in each of the following pairs.
    a. H—O or H—N
    c. H—O or H—F
    b. H—N or H—F
    d. H—O or H—Cl

19. On the basis of the electronegativity values given in Figure 12.3, indicate which is the more polar bond in each of the following pairs.
    a. H—N or H—P
    c. H—P or H—S
    b. H—O or H—S
    d. H—S or H—I

20. On the basis of the electronegativity values given in Figure 12.3, indicate which bond of the following pairs has a more ionic character.
    a. Na—O or Na—N
    c. Na—Cl or K—Cl
    b. K—S or K—P
    d. Na—Cl or Mg—Cl

12.3 ■ *Bond Polarity and Dipole Moments*

QUESTIONS

21. What is a *dipole moment?* Give four examples of molecules that possess dipole moments, and draw the direction of the dipole as shown in this section.

22. Why is the presence of a dipole moment in the water molecule so important? What are some properties of water that are determined by its polarity?

PROBLEMS

23. In each of the following diatomic molecules, which end of the molecule is negative relative to the other end?
    a. hydrogen chloride, HCl
    b. carbon monoxide, CO
    c. bromine monofluoride, BrF

24. In each of the following diatomic molecules, which end of the molecule is positive relative to the other end?
    a. hydrogen fluoride, HF
    b. chlorine monofluoride, ClF
    c. iodine monochloride, ICl

25. For each of the following bonds, draw a figure indicating the direction of the bond dipole including which end of the bond is positive and which is negative.

    a. N—Cl
    c. N—I
    b. N—Br
    d. N—F

26. For each of the following bonds, draw a figure indicating the direction of the bond dipole including which end of the bond is positive and which is negative.
    a. Cl—F
    c. Br—Cl
    b. I—Br
    d. Br—F

27. For each of the following bonds, draw a figure indicating the direction of the bond dipole including which end of the bond is positive and which is negative.
    a. Si—H
    c. S—H
    b. P—H
    d. Cl—H

28. For each of the following bonds, draw a figure indicating the direction of the bond dipole including which end of the bond is positive and which is negative.
    a. S—P
    c. S—N
    b. S—O
    d. S—Cl

12.4 ■ *Stable Electron Configurations and Charges on Ions*

QUESTIONS

29. In virtually every stable compound, each of the atoms has achieved an electron configuration analogous to that of the _____ elements.

30. Metals form positive ions by losing enough electrons to achieve the electron configuration of the _____ noble gas.

31. Nonmetals form negative ions by (losing/gaining) enough electrons to achieve the electron configuration of the next noble gas.

32. Explain how the atoms in *covalent* molecules achieve configurations similar to those of the noble gases. How does this differ from the situation in ionic compounds?

PROBLEMS

33. Write the electron configuration for each of the following atoms and for the simple ion that the element most commonly forms. In each case, indicate which noble gas has the same electron configuration as the ion.
    a. magnesium, $Z = 12$
    d. radium, $Z = 88$
    b. lithium, $Z = 3$
    e. nitrogen, $Z = 7$
    c. selenium, $Z = 34$

34. Write the electron configuration for each of the following atoms and for the simple ion that the element most commonly forms. In each case, indicate which noble gas has the same electron configuration as the ion.
    a. rubidium, $Z = 37$
    d. cesium, $Z = 55$
    b. oxygen, $Z = 8$
    e. barium, $Z = 56$
    c. strontium, $Z = 38$

35. What simple ion does each of the following elements most commonly form?
    a. strontium, $Z = 38$
    b. nitrogen, $Z = 7$
    c. radium, $Z = 88$
    d. fluorine, $Z = 9$

36. What simple ion does each of the following elements most commonly form?
    a. calcium, $Z = 20$
    b. nitrogen, $Z = 7$
    c. bromine, $Z = 35$
    d. scandium, $Z = 21$

37. On the basis of their electron configurations, predict the formula of the simple binary ionic compound likely to form when the following pairs of elements react with each other.
    a. aluminum, Al, and oxygen, O
    b. cesium, Cs, and oxygen, O
    c. barium, Ba, and chlorine, Cl
    d. francium, Fr, and oxygen, O
    e. radium, Ra, and chlorine, Cl
    f. barium, Ba, and tellurium, Te

38. On the basis of their electron configurations, predict the formula of the simple binary ionic compound likely to form when the following pairs of elements react with each other.
    a. calcium, Ca, and oxygen, O
    b. strontium, Sr, and fluorine, F
    c. aluminum, Al, and sulfur, S
    d. rubidium, Rb, and nitrogen, N
    e. sodium, Na, and tellurium, Te

39. Which noble gas has the same electron configuration as each of the ions in the following compounds?
    a. calcium sulfide, CaS
    b. magnesium iodide, MgI_2
    c. strontium phosphide, Sr_3P_2
    d. potassium oxide, K_2O

40. Name the noble gas atom that has the same electron configuration as each of the ions in the following compounds.
    a. aluminum sulfide, Al_2S_3
    b. magnesium nitride, Mg_3N_2
    c. rubidium oxide, Rb_2O
    d. cesium iodide, CsI

12.5 ■ Ionic Bonding and Structures of Ionic Compounds

QUESTIONS

41. Why is the formula written for an ionic compound such as NaCl the *empirical* formula, rather than a *molecular* formula?

42. Describe in general terms the structure of ionic solids such as NaCl. How are the ions packed in the crystal?

43. Why are cations always smaller than the atoms from which they are formed?

44. Why are anions always larger than the atoms from which they are formed?

PROBLEMS

45. For each of the following pairs, indicate which species is larger. Explain your reasoning in terms of the electron structure of each species.
    a. K or K^+
    b. Li or I^-
    c. Cl^- or F^-
    d. Br or Br^-

46. For each of the following pairs, indicate which species is larger. Explain your reasoning in terms of the electron structure of each species.
    a. Li^+ or F^-
    b. Na^+ or Cl^-
    c. Ca^{2+} or O^{2-}
    d. Cs^+ or I^-

47. For each of the following pairs, indicate which is smaller.
    a. Fe or Fe^{3+}
    b. Cl or Cl^-
    c. Al^{3+} or Na^+

48. For each of the following pairs, indicate which is smaller.
    a. Cs^+ or I^-
    b. Na^+ or Br^-
    c. Cs or Cs^+
    d. O or O^{2-}

12.6 and 12.7 ■ Lewis Structures

QUESTIONS

49. Why are the *valence* electrons of an atom the only electrons likely to be involved in bonding to other atoms?

50. Explain what the "duet" and "octet" rules are and how they are used to describe the arrangement of electrons in a molecule.

51. What type of structure must each atom in a compound usually exhibit for the compound to be stable?

52. When elements in the second and third periods occur in compounds, what number of electrons in the valence shell represents the most stable electron arrangement? Why?

PROBLEMS

53. How many electrons are involved when two atoms in a molecule are connected by a "double bond"? Write the Lewis structure of a molecule containing a double bond.

54. What does it mean when two atoms in a molecule are connected by a "triple bond"? Write the Lewis structure of a molecule containing a triple bond.

55. Write the Lewis structure for each of the following atoms.
    a. N ($Z = 7$)
    b. Br ($Z = 35$)
    c. Cs ($Z = 55$)
    d. B ($Z = 5$)
    e. Ga ($Z = 31$)
    f. Xe ($Z = 54$)

56. Write the Lewis structure for each of the following atoms.
    a. Rb ($Z = 37$)   d. Ba ($Z = 56$)
    b. Cl ($Z = 17$)   e. P ($Z = 15$)
    c. Kr ($Z = 36$)   f. At ($Z = 85$)

57. What is the *total* number of *valence* electrons in each of the following molecules?
    a. P_4O_{10}
    b. NI_3
    c. H_2SO_4
    d. H_3PO_4

58. Give the *total* number of *valence* electrons in each of the following molecules.
    a. CBr_4
    b. NO_2
    c. C_6H_6

59. Write a Lewis structure for each of the following simple molecules. Show all bonding valence electron pairs as lines and all nonbonding valence electron pairs as dots.
    a. PH_3 c. HBr
    b. SF_2 d. CCl_4

60. Write a Lewis structure for each of the following simple molecules. Show all bonding valence electron pairs as lines and all nonbonding valence electron pairs as dots.
    a. NH_3 c. NCl_3
    b. CI_4 d. $SiBr_4$

61. Write a Lewis structure for each of the following molecules. Show all bonding valence electron pairs as lines and all nonbonding valence electron pairs as dots.
    a. H_3PO_4 c. SiH_4
    b. PBr_3 d. N_2

62. Write a Lewis structure for each of the following simple molecules. Show all bonding valence electron pairs as lines and all nonbonding valence electron pairs as dots.
    a. H_2S c. C_2H_4
    b. SiF_4 d. C_3H_8

63. Write a Lewis structure for each of the following simple molecules. Show all bonding valence electron pairs as lines and all nonbonding valence electron pairs as dots. For those molecules that exhibit resonance, draw the various possible resonance forms.
    a. Cl_2O b. CO_2 c. SO_3

64. Write a Lewis structure for each of the following simple molecules. Show all bonding valence electron pairs as lines and all nonbonding valence electrons as dots. For those molecules that exhibit resonance, draw the various possible resonance forms.
    a. NO_2 b. H_2SO_4 c. N_2O_4

65. Write a Lewis structure for each of the following polyatomic ions. Show all bonding valence electron pairs as lines and all nonbonding valence electron pairs as dots. For those ions that exhibit resonance, draw the various possible resonance forms.
    a. sulfate ion, SO_4^{2-}
    b. phosphate ion, PO_4^{3-}
    c. sulfite ion, SO_3^{2-}

66. Write a Lewis structure for each of the following polyatomic ions. Show all bonding valence electron pairs as lines and all nonbonding valence electrons as dots. For those ions that exhibit resonance, draw the various possible resonance forms.
    a. chlorate ion, ClO_3^-
    b. peroxide ion, O_2^{2-}
    c. acetate ion, $C_2H_3O_2^-$

67. Write a Lewis structure for each of the following polyatomic ions. Show all bonding valence electron pairs as lines and all nonbonding valence electron pairs as dots. For those ions that exhibit resonance, draw the various possible resonance forms.
    a. nitrite ion
    b. hydrogen carbonate ion
    c. hydroxide ion

68. Write a Lewis structure for each of the following polyatomic ions. Show all bonding valence electron pairs as lines and all nonbonding valence electron pairs as dots. For those ions that exhibit resonance, draw the various possible resonance forms.
    a. cyanide ion, CN^-
    b. hydrogen sulfate ion, HSO_4^-
    c. azide ion, N_3^-

12.8 ■ *Molecular Structure*

QUESTIONS

69. What is the geometric structure of the water molecule? How many pairs of valence electrons are there on the oxygen atom in the water molecule? What is the approximate H—O—H bond angle in water?

70. What is the geometric structure of the ammonia molecule? How many pairs of electrons surround the nitrogen atom in NH_3? What is the approximate H—N—H bond angle in ammonia?

71. What is the geometric structure of the boron trifluoride molecule, BF_3? How many pairs of valence electrons are present on the boron atom in BF_3? What are the approximate F—B—F bond angles in BF_3?

72. What is the geometric structure of the CH_4 molecule? How many pairs of valence electrons are present on the carbon atom of CH_4? Refer to Figure 12.11 and estimate the H—C—H bond angles in CH_4.

12.9 ■ *Molecular Structure: The VSEPR Model*

QUESTIONS

73. Why is the geometric structure of a molecule important, especially for biological molecules?

74. What general principles determine the molecular structure (shape) of a molecule?

75. How is the structure around a given atom related to repulsion between valence electron pairs on the atom?

76. Why are all diatomic molecules *linear,* regardless of the number of valence electron pairs on the atoms involved?

77. Although the valence electron pairs in ammonia have a tetrahedral arrangement, the overall geometric structure of the ammonia molecule is *not* described as being tetrahedral. Explain.

78. Although both the BF_3 and NF_3 molecules contain the same number of atoms, the BF_3 molecule is flat, whereas the NF_3 molecule is trigonal pyramidal. Explain.

PROBLEMS

79. For the indicated atom in each of the following molecules, give the number and arrangement of the electron pairs around that atom.
    a. C in CH_4
    b. C in CBr_4
    c. each of the carbon atoms in C_2H_6

80. For the indicated atom in each of the following molecules or ions, give the number and arrangement of the electron pairs around that atom.
    a. P in PH_3
    b. Cl in ClO_4^-
    c. O in H_2O

81. Using the VSEPR theory, predict the molecular structure of each of the following molecules.
    a. NCl_3
    b. H_2Se
    c. $SiCl_4$

82. Using the VSEPR theory, predict the molecular structure of each of the following molecules.
    a. GeH_4 b. PCl_3 c. Cl_2O

83. Using the VSEPR theory, predict the molecular structure of each of the following polyatomic ions.
    a. sulfate ion, SO_4^{2-}
    b. phosphate ion, PO_4^{3-}
    c. ammonium ion, NH_4^+

84. Using the VSEPR theory, predict the molecular structure of each of the following polyatomic ions.
    a. chlorate ion

    b. hydrogen phosphate ion (hydrogen is bonded to oxygen)
    c. sulfite ion

85. For each of the following molecules or ions, indicate the bond angle expected between the central atom and any two adjacent hydrogen atoms.
    a. H_2O c. NH_4^+
    b. NH_3 d. CH_4

86. For each of the following molecules or ions, indicate the bond angle expected between the central atom and any two adjacent chlorine atoms.
    a. Cl_2O c. CCl_4
    b. NCl_3 d. C_2Cl_4

87. Predict the geometric structure of the carbonate ion, CO_3^{2-}. What are the bond angles in this molecule?

88. Predict the geometric structure of the acetylene molecule, C_2H_2. What are the bond angles in this molecule?

Additional Problems

89. What is *resonance?* Give three examples of molecules or ions that exhibit resonance, and draw Lewis structures for each of the possible resonance forms.

90. When two atoms share two pairs of electrons, a _____ bond is said to exist between them.

91. The geometric arrangement of electron pairs around a given atom is determined principally by the tendency to minimize _____ between the electron pairs.

92. In each case, which of the following pairs of bonded elements forms the more polar bond?
    a. S—F or S—Cl
    b. N—O or P—O
    c. C—H or Si—H

93. For each case, which of the following pairs of bonded elements forms the more polar bond?
    a. Br—Cl or Br—F
    b. As—S or As—O
    c. Pb—C or Pb—Si

94. The quantity of energy necessary to _____ a chemical bond is referred to as the bond energy.

95. A _____ chemical bond represents the equal sharing of a pair of electrons between two nuclei.

96. For each of the following pairs of elements, identify which element would be expected to be more electronegative. It should not be necessary to look at a table of actual electronegativity values.

a. Be or Ba
b. N or P
c. F or Cl

97. On the basis of the electronegativity values given in Figure 12.3, indicate whether each of the following bonds would be expected to be ionic, covalent, or polar covalent.
a. H—O
b. O—O
c. H—H
d. H—Cl

98. Which of the following molecules contain polar covalent bonds?
a. carbon monoxide, CO
b. chlorine, Cl_2
c. iodine monochloride, ICl
d. phosphorus, P_4

99. On the basis of the electronegativity values given in Figure 12.3, indicate which is the more polar bond in each of the following pairs.
a. N—P or N—O
b. N—C or N—O
c. N—S or N—C
d. N—F or N—S

100. In each of the following diatomic molecules, which end of the molecule is positive relative to the other end?
a. hydrogen fluoride, HF
b. iodine monochloride, ICl
c. nitrogen monoxide, NO

101. For each of the following bonds, draw a figure indicating the direction of the bond dipole including which end of the bond is positive and which is negative.
a. N—Cl
b. N—P
c. N—S
d. N—C

102. Write the electron configuration for each of the following atoms and for the simple ion that the element most commonly forms. In each case, indicate which noble gas has the same electron configuration as the ion.
a. aluminum, $Z = 13$
b. bromine, $Z = 35$
c. calcium, $Z = 20$
d. lithium, $Z = 3$
e. fluorine, $Z = 9$

103. What simple ion does each of the following elements most commonly form?
a. barium, $Z = 56$
b. rubidium, $Z = 37$
c. aluminum, $Z = 13$
d. oxygen, $Z = 8$

104. On the basis of their electron configurations, predict the formula of the simple binary ionic compound likely to form when the following pairs of elements react with each other.
a. sodium, Na, and selenium, Se
b. rubidium, Rb, and fluorine, F
c. potassium, K, and tellurium, Te
d. barium, Ba, and selenium, Se

e. potassium, K, and astatine, At
f. francium, Fr, and chlorine, Cl

105. Which noble gas has the same electron configuration as each of the ions in the following compounds?
a. calcium bromide, $CaBr_2$
b. aluminum selenide, Al_2Se_3
c. strontium oxide, SrO
d. potassium sulfide, K_2S

106. For each of the following pairs, indicate which is smaller.
a. Rb^+ or Na^+
b. Mg^{2+} or Al^{3+}
c. F^- or I^-
d. Na^+ or K^+

107. Write the Lewis structure for each of the following atoms.
a. He ($Z = 2$)
b. Br ($Z = 35$)
c. Sr ($Z = 38$)
d. Ne ($Z = 10$)
e. I ($Z = 53$)
f. Ra ($Z = 88$)

108. What is the *total* number of valence electrons in each of the following molecules?
a. SiH_4
b. SF_6
c. N_2O_4
d. AsI_3

109. Write a Lewis structure for each of the following simple molecules. Show all bonding valence electron pairs as lines and all nonbonding valence electron pairs as dots.
a. GeH_4
b. ICl
c. NI_3

110. Write a Lewis structure for each of the following simple molecules. Show all bonding valence electron pairs as lines and all nonbonding valence electron pairs as dots.
a. N_2H_4
b. C_2H_6
c. NCl_3
d. $SiCl_4$

111. Write a Lewis structure for each of the following simple molecules. Show all bonding valence electron pairs as lines and all nonbonding valence electron pairs as dots. For those molecules that exhibit resonance, draw the various possible resonance forms.
a. SO_2
b. N_2O (N in center)
c. O_3

112. Write a Lewis structure for each of the following polyatomic ions. Show all bonding valence electron pairs as lines and all nonbonding valence electron pairs as dots. For those ions that exhibit resonance, draw the various possible resonance forms.
a. nitrate ion
b. carbonate ion
c. ammonium ion

113. Why is the molecular structure of H_2O nonlinear, whereas that of BeF_2 is linear, even though both molecules consist of three atoms?

114. For the indicated atom in each of the following molecules, give the number and the arrangement of the electron pairs around that atom.
    a. C in CCl_4
    b. Ge in GeH_4
    c. B in BF_3

115. Using the VSEPR theory, predict the molecular structure of each of the following molecules.
    a. Cl_2O
    b. OF_2
    c. $SiCl_4$

116. Using the VSEPR theory, predict the molecular structure of each of the following polyatomic ions.
    a. chlorate ion
    b. chlorite ion
    c. perchlorate ion

117. For each of the following molecules, indicate the bond angle expected between the central atom and any two adjacent fluorine atoms.
    a. BeF_2
    b. BF_3
    c. NF_3
    d. CF_4

118. Using the VSEPR theory, predict the molecular structure of each of the following molecules or ions containing multiple bonds.
    a. SO_2
    b. SO_3
    c. HCO_3^- (hydrogen is bonded to oxygen)
    d. HCN

119. Using the VSEPR theory, predict the molecular structure of each of the following molecules or ions containing multiple bonds.
    a. CO_3^{2-}
    b. HNO_3 (hydrogen is bonded to oxygen)
    c. NO_2^-
    d. C_2H_2

120. Explain briefly how substances with ionic bonding differ in properties from substances with covalent bonding.

121. Explain the difference between a covalent bond formed between two atoms of the same element and a covalent bond formed between atoms of two different elements.

Cumulative Review for Chapters 11–12

QUESTIONS

1. What is *electromagnetic radiation?* Give some examples of such radiation. Explain what the *wavelength* (λ) and *frequency* (ν) of electromagnetic radiation represent. Sketch a representation of a wave and indicate on your drawing one wavelength of the wave. At what speed does electromagnetic radiation move through space? How is this speed related to λ and ν? What wavelengths correspond approximately to the visible light region of the electromagnetic spectrum?

2. Explain what it means for an atom to be in an *excited state* and what it means for an atom to be in its *ground state.* How does an excited atom *return* to its ground state? What is a *photon?* How is the wavelength (color) of light related to the energy of the photons being emitted by an atom? How is the energy of the photons being *emitted* by an atom related to the energy changes taking place *within* the atom?

3. Do atoms in excited states emit radiation randomly, at any wavelength? Why? What does it mean to say that the hydrogen atom has only certain *discrete energy levels* available? How do we know this? What does it mean to say that the energy levels of an atom are *quantized?* Is it just the energy levels of hydrogen atoms that are quantized, or is this a general phenomenon among all atoms? Why was the quantization of energy levels surprising to scientists when it was first discovered?

4. Describe Bohr's model of the hydrogen atom. How did Bohr envision the relationship between the electron and the nucleus of the hydrogen atom? How did Bohr's model explain the emission of only discrete wavelengths of light by excited hydrogen atoms? Why did Bohr's model not stand up as more experiments were performed using elements other than hydrogen?

5. Schrödinger and de Broglie suggested a "wave–particle duality" for small particles—that is, if electromagnetic radiation showed some particle-like properties, then perhaps small particles might exhibit some wave-like properties. Explain. How does the wave–mechanical picture of the atom fundamentally differ from the Bohr model? How do wave–mechanical *orbitals* differ from Bohr's *orbits?* What does it mean to say that an orbital represents a probability map for an electron?

6. Describe the general characteristics of the first (lowest-energy) hydrogen atomic orbital. How is this orbital designated symbolically? Does this orbital have a sharp "edge"? Does the orbital represent a surface upon which the electron travels at all times?

7. Use the wave–mechanical picture of the hydrogen atom to describe what happens when the atom absorbs energy and moves to an "excited" state. What do the *principal energy levels* and their sublevels represent for a hydrogen atom? How do we designate specific principal energy levels and sublevels in hydrogen? Describe the sublevels and orbitals that constitute the second principal energy level of hydrogen. How are the individual orbitals in these sublevels designated?

8. Describe the sublevels and orbitals that constitute the third and fourth principal energy levels of hydrogen. How are each of the orbitals designated and what are the general shapes of their probability maps? How are the orbitals in the fourth principal energy level similar to the orbitals in the third level, and how do they differ?

9. Describe *electron spin.* How does electron spin affect the total number of electrons that can be accommodated in a given orbital? What does the *Pauli exclusion principle* tell us about electrons and their spins?

10. Summarize the postulates of the wave–mechanical model of the atom.

11. List the *order* in which the orbitals are filled as the atoms beyond hydrogen are built up. How many electrons overall can be accommodated in the first and second principal energy levels? How many electrons can be placed in a given *s* subshell? In a given *p* subshell? In a specific *p* orbital? Why do we assign unpaired electrons in the 2*p* orbitals of carbon, nitrogen, and oxygen?

12. Define the *valence electrons* in an atom. Define the *core electrons* in an atom. Why are the valence electrons more important to the atom's chemical properties than the core electrons? How is the number of valence electrons in an atom related to the atom's position on the periodic table? What evidence convinces us that the 4*s* subshell fills *before* the 3*d* subshell?

13. Sketch the overall shape of the periodic table and indicate the *general regions* of the table that represent the various *s, p, d,* and *f* orbitals being filled. You do not have to include specific elements but your drawing should indicate the number of vertical groups as well as the principal energy levels.

14. Using the general periodic table you developed in Question 13, show how the valence electron configuration of most of the elements can be written just by knowing the relative *location* of the element on the table. Give specific examples.

15. What are the *representative elements?* In what region(s) of the periodic table are these elements found? In what general area of the periodic table are the *metallic* elements found? In what general area of the table are the *nonmetals* found? Where in the table are the *metalloids* located? Are most of the representative elements metals or nonmetals?

16. You have learned how the properties of the elements vary *systematically,* corresponding to the electron structures of the elements being considered. Discuss how the *ionization energies* and *atomic sizes* of elements vary, both within a vertical group (family) of the periodic table and within a horizontal row (period).

17. In general, what do we mean by a *chemical bond?* What does the *bond energy* tell us about the strength of a chemical bond? Name the principal types of chemical bonds.

18. What do we mean by *ionic* bonding? Give an example of a substance whose particles are held together by ionic bonding. What experimental evidence do we have for the existence of ionic bonding? In general, what types of substances react to produce compounds having ionic bonding? Write a balanced chemical equation illustrating the formation of a typical ionic substance from its elements.

19. What do we mean by *covalent* bonding and *polar covalent* bonding? How are these two bonding types similar and how do they differ? What circumstance must exist for a bond to be purely covalent? How does a polar covalent bond differ from an ionic bond?

20. Define *electronegativity.* How does the polarity of a bond depend on the *difference* in electronegativity of the two atoms participating in the bond? If two atoms have exactly the *same* electronegativity, what type of bond will exist between the atoms? If two atoms have vastly different electronegativities, what type of bond will exist between them? If two atoms have moderate differences in electronegativity, what type of bonding results?

21. What does it mean to say that a molecule has a dipole moment? What is the *difference* between a polar bond and a polar molecule (one that has a dipole moment)? Give an example of a molecule that has polar bonds and that has a dipole moment. Give an example of a molecule that has polar bonds, but that does *not* have a dipole moment. What are some implications of the fact that water has a dipole moment?

22. How is the attainment of a noble gas electron configuration important to our ideas of how atoms bond to each other? When atoms of a metal react with atoms of a nonmetal, what type of electron configurations do the resulting ions attain? Explain how the atoms in a covalently

bonded compound can attain noble gas electron configurations.

23. Give evidence that ionic bonds are very strong. Does an ionic substance contain discrete molecules? With what general type of structure do ionic compounds occur? Sketch a representation of a general structure for an ionic compound. Why is a cation always smaller and an anion always larger than the respective parent atom? Describe the bonding in an ionic compound containing polyatomic ions. How are the atoms within a given polyatomic ion held together?

24. Why does a Lewis structure for a molecule show only the valence electrons? What is the most important factor for the formation of a stable compound? How do we use this requirement when writing Lewis structures?

25. In writing Lewis structures for molecules, what is meant by the *duet rule?* To which element does the duet rule apply? What do we mean by the *octet rule?* Why is attaining an octet of electrons important for an atom when it forms bonds to other atoms? What is a bonding *pair* of electrons? What is a nonbonding (or *lone*) pair of electrons?

26. For three simple molecules of your own choice, *apply* the rules for writing Lewis structures. Write your discussion as if you are explaining the method to someone who is *not* familiar with Lewis structures.

27. What does a *double* bond between two atoms represent in terms of the number of electrons shared? What does a *triple* bond represent? When writing a Lewis structure, explain how we recognize when a molecule must contain double or triple bonds. What are *resonance structures?* Under what circumstances does a molecule exhibit resonance?

28. Although many simple molecules fulfill the octet rule, some common molecules are exceptions to this rule. Give three examples of molecules whose Lewis structures are exceptions to the octet rule and explain how each molecule is an exception.

29. What do we mean by the *geometric structure* of a molecule? Draw the geometric structures of at least four simple molecules of your choosing and indicate the bond angles in the structures. Explain the main ideas of the *valence shell electron pair repulsion (VSEPR) theory.* Using several examples, explain how you would *apply* the VSEPR theory to predict their geometric structures. Write your discussion as if you are explaining the method to someone who is not familiar with the VSEPR theory.

30. What bond angle results when there are only two valence electron pairs around an atom? What bond angle results when there are three valence pairs? What bond angle results when there are four pairs of valence electrons around the central atom in a molecule? Give examples of molecules containing these bond angles.

31. How do we predict the geometric structure of a molecule whose Lewis structure indicates that the molecule contains a double or triple bond? Give an example of such a molecule, write its Lewis structure, and show how the geometric shape is derived.

PROBLEMS

32. Sketch representations of the orbitals of the $1s$, $2s$, $2p$, $3s$, $3p$, and $3d$ subshells. Illustrate the shape, directional orientation, and relative size of the orbitals.

33. Without consulting your textbook, write the electron configurations and orbital diagrams for the first twenty elements ($Z = 1$ to $Z = 20$).

34. Without consulting your textbook, write general valence electron configurations for each group of the representative elements. For example, for Group 1 the general configuration would be [noble gas]ns^1.

35. Indicate how many valence electrons the element possesses and write the noble gas shorthand electron configuration for each of the following elements.
    a. K
    b. Mg
    c. Ga
    d. P
    e. Br
    f. Si
    g. Xe
    h. Ge
    i. S
    j. I
    k. Cs
    l. Ra

36. Write Lewis electron structures for each of the following molecules or ions, and use the VSEPR theory to predict their geometric shapes. If resonance is possible for any of the molecules or ions, draw all likely resonance structures.
    a. $GeCl_4$
    b. NO_3^-
    c. SO_4^{2-}
    d. SO_3^{2-}
    e. SO_2
    f. O_2
    g. O_3
    h. CH_3NH_2
    i. C_2H_6
    j. C_2H_4
    k. BF_3
    l. BeF_2
    m. NO_2^-
    n. PF_3
    o. N_2H_4

13

Gases

We live immersed in a gaseous solution. The earth's atmosphere is a mixture of gases that consists mainly of elemental nitrogen, N_2, and oxygen, O_2. The atmosphere both supports life and acts as a waste receptacle for the exhaust gases that accompany many industrial processes. The chemical reactions of these waste gases in the atmosphere lead to various types of pollution, including smog and acid rain. The two main sources of pollution are transportation and the production of electricity. The combustion of fuel in vehicles produces CO, CO_2, NO, and NO_2, along with unburned fragments of the petroleum used as fuel. The combustion of coal and petroleum in power plants produces NO_2 and SO_2 in the exhaust gases. These

mixtures of chemicals can be activated by absorbing light to produce the photochemical smog that afflicts most large cities. The SO_2 in the air reacts with oxygen to produce SO_3 gas, which combines with water in the air to produce droplets of sulfuric acid (H_2SO_4), a major component of acid rain.

The relationship between the temperature of a gas and its volume explains how these hot-air balloons can float safely through the atmosphere (left). The earth's atmosphere contains a mixture of gases (right).

The gases in the atmosphere also shield us from harmful radiation from the sun and keep the earth warm by reflecting heat radiation back toward the earth. In fact, there is now great concern that an increase in atmospheric carbon dioxide, a product of the combustion of fossil fuels, is causing a dangerous warming of the earth. (See "Chemistry in Focus: Atmospheric Effects," in Chapter 11.)

In this chapter we will look carefully at the properties of gases. First we will see how measurements of gas properties lead to various types of laws—statements that show how the properties are related to each other. Then we will construct a model to explain why gases behave as they do. This model will show how the behavior of the individual particles of a gas leads to the observed properties of the gas itself (a collection of many, many particles).

The study of gases provides an excellent example of the scientific method in action. It illustrates how observations lead to natural laws, which in turn can be accounted for by models.

13.1 Pressure

AIMS: To learn about atmospheric pressure and how barometers work. To learn the various units of pressure.

A gas uniformly fills any container, is easily compressed, and mixes completely with any other gas (see Section 3.1). One of the most obvious properties of a gas is that it exerts pressure on its surroundings. For example, when you blow up a balloon, the air inside pushes against the elastic sides of the balloon and keeps it firm.

The gases most familiar to us form the earth's atmosphere. The pressure exerted by this gaseous mixture that we call air can be dramatically demonstrated by the experiment shown in Figure 13.1. A small volume of water is placed in a metal can and the water is boiled, which fills the can with steam. The can is then sealed and allowed to cool. Why does the can collapse as it cools? It is the atmospheric pressure that crumples the can. When the can is cooled after being sealed so that no air can flow in, the water vapor (steam) inside the can condenses to a very small volume of liquid water. As a gas, the water vapor filled the can, but when it is condensed to a liquid, the liquid does

Dry air (air from which the water vapor has been removed) is 78.1% N_2 molecules, 20.9% O_2 molecules, 0.9% Ar atoms, and 0.03% CO_2 molecules, along with smaller amounts of Ne, He, CH_4, Kr, and other trace components.

FIGURE 13.1
The pressure exerted by the gases in the atmosphere can be demonstrated by boiling water in an aluminum beverage can (a), and then turning off the heat and sealing the can. As the can cools, the water vapor condenses, lowering the gas pressure inside the can. This causes the can to crumple (b).

(a)

(b)

FIGURE 13.2
(a) When a glass tube is filled with mercury and inverted in a dish of mercury at sea level, the mercury flows out of the tube until a column approximately 760 mm high remains (the height varies with atmospheric conditions).
(b) A diagram showing how the pressure of the atmosphere balances the weight of the column of mercury in the tube.

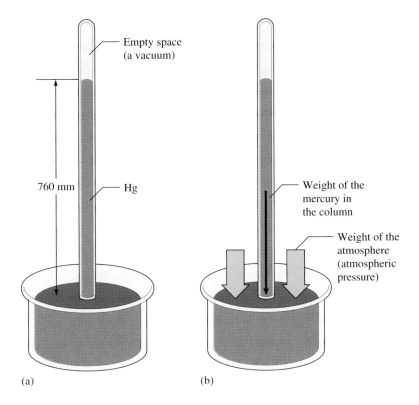

Empty space
(a vacuum)

760 mm

Hg

Weight of the
mercury in
the column

Weight of the
atmosphere
(atmospheric
pressure)

(a)　　　　　(b)

As a gas, water occupies 1200 times as much space as it does as a liquid at 25 °C and atmospheric pressure.

not come close to filling the can. The H_2O molecules formerly present as a gas are now collected in a much smaller volume of liquid, and there are very few molecules of gas left to exert pressure outward and counteract the air pressure. As a result, the pressure exerted by the gas molecules in the atmosphere smashes the can.

A device that measures atmospheric pressure, the **barometer,** was invented in 1643 by an Italian scientist named Evangelista Torricelli (1608–1647), who had been a student of the famous astronomer Galileo. Torricelli's barometer is constructed by filling a glass tube with liquid mercury and inverting it in a dish of mercury, as shown in Figure 13.2(a). Notice that a large quantity of mercury stays in the tube. In fact, at sea level the height of this column of mercury averages 760 mm. Why does this mercury stay in the tube, seemingly in defiance of gravity? Figure 13.2(b) illustrates how the pressure exerted by the atmospheric gases on the surface of mercury in the dish keeps the mercury in the tube.

Atmospheric pressure results from the mass of the air being pulled toward the center of the earth by gravity—in other words, it results from the weight of the air. Changing weather conditions cause the atmospheric pressure to vary, so the height of the column of Hg supported by the atmosphere at sea level varies; it is not always 760 mm. The meteorologist who says a "low" is approaching means that the atmospheric pressure is going to decrease. This condition often occurs in conjunction with a storm.

Atmospheric pressure also varies with altitude. For example, when Torricelli's experiment is done in Breckenridge, Colorado (elevation 9600 feet), the atmosphere supports a column of mercury only about 520 mm high because the air is "thinner." That is, there is less air pushing down on the earth's surface at Breckenridge than at sea level.

Soon after Torricelli died, a German physicist named Otto von Guericke invented an air pump. In a famous demonstration for the King of Prussia in 1683, Guericke placed two hemispheres together, pumped the air out of the resulting sphere through a valve, and showed that teams of horses could not pull the hemispheres apart. Then, after secretly opening the air valve, Guericke easily separated the hemispheres by hand. The King of Prussia was so impressed that he awarded Guericke a lifetime pension!

FIGURE 13.3

A device (called a manometer) for measuring the pressure of a gas in a container. The pressure of the gas is equal to *h* (the difference in mercury levels) in units of torr (equivalent to mm Hg). (a) Gas pressure = atmospheric pressure − *h*. (b) Gas pressure = atmospheric pressure + *h*.

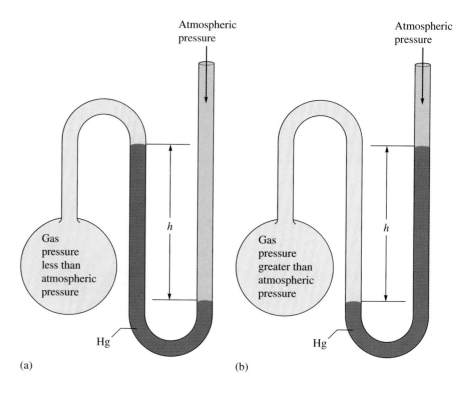

(a)　　　　　　　　(b)

Units of Pressure

Mercury is used to measure pressure because of its high density. By way of comparison, the column of water required to measure a given pressure would be 13.6 times as high as a mercury column used for the same purpose.

Because instruments used for measuring pressure (see Figure 13.3) often contain mercury, the most commonly used units for pressure are based on the height of the mercury column (in millimeters) that the gas pressure can support. The unit **mm Hg** (millimeters of mercury) is often called the **torr** in honor of Torricelli. The terms *torr* and *mm Hg* are used interchangeably by chemists. A related unit for pressure is the **standard atmosphere** (abbreviated atm).

$$1 \text{ standard atmosphere} = 1.000 \text{ atm} = 760.0 \text{ mm Hg} = 760.0 \text{ torr}$$

The SI unit for pressure is the **pascal** (abbreviated Pa).

$$1 \text{ standard atmosphere} = 101{,}325 \text{ Pa}$$

Thus 1 atmosphere is about 100,000 or 10^5 pascals. Because the pascal is so small we will use it sparingly in this book. A unit of pressure that is employed in the engineering sciences and that we use for measuring tire pressure is pounds per square inch, abbreviated psi.

$$1.000 \text{ atm} = 14.69 \text{ psi}$$

1.000 atm

760.0 mm Hg
760.0 torr
14.69 psi
101,325 Pa

Sometimes we need to convert from one unit of pressure to another. We do this by using conversion factors. The process is illustrated in Example 13.1.

EXAMPLE 13.1 *Pressure Unit Conversions*

The pressure of the air in a tire is measured to be 28 psi. Represent this pressure in atmospheres, torr, and pascals.

Checking the air pressure in a tire.

$1.9 \times 760.0 = 1444$
$1444 \implies 1400 = 1.4 \times 10^3$
Round off

$1.9 \times 101{,}325 = 192{,}517.5$
$192{,}517.5 \implies 190{,}000 = 1.9 \times 10^5$
Round off

Solution

To convert from pounds per square inch to atmospheres, we need the equivalence statement

$$1.000 \text{ atm} = 14.69 \text{ psi}$$

which leads to the conversion factor

$$\frac{1.000 \text{ atm}}{14.69 \text{ psi}}$$

$$28 \text{ psi} \times \frac{1.000 \text{ atm}}{14.69 \text{ psi}} = 1.9 \text{ atm}$$

To convert from atmospheres to torr, we use the equivalence statement

$$1.000 \text{ atm} = 760.0 \text{ torr}$$

which leads to the conversion factor

$$\frac{760.0 \text{ torr}}{1.000 \text{ atm}}$$

$$1.9 \text{ atm} \times \frac{760.0 \text{ torr}}{1.000 \text{ atm}} = 1.4 \times 10^3 \text{ torr}$$

To change from torr to pascals, we need the equivalence statement

$$1.000 \text{ atm} = 101{,}325 \text{ Pa}$$

which leads to the conversion factor

$$\frac{101{,}325 \text{ Pa}}{1.000 \text{ atm}}$$

$$1.9 \text{ atm} \times \frac{101{,}325 \text{ Pa}}{1.000 \text{ atm}} = 1.9 \times 10^5 \text{ Pa}$$

Note: The best way to check a problem like this is to make sure the final units are the ones required.

 Self-Check Exercise 13.1

On a summer day in Breckenridge, Colorado, the atmospheric pressure is 525 mm Hg. What is this air pressure in atmospheres?

See Problems 13.7 through 13.12

13.2 *Pressure and Volume: Boyle's Law*

AIMS: To understand the law that relates the pressure and volume of a gas. To do calculations involving this law.

The first careful experiments on gases were performed by the Irish scientist Robert Boyle (1627–1691). Using a J-shaped tube closed at one end (Figure 13.4), which he reportedly set up in the multi-story entryway of his house,

FIGURE 13.4
A J-tube similar to the one used by Boyle. The pressure on the trapped gas can be changed by adding or withdrawing mercury.

Boyle studied the relationship between the pressure of the trapped gas and its volume. Representative values from Boyle's experiments are given in Table 13.1. The units given for the volume (cubic inches) and pressure (inches of mercury) are the ones Boyle used. Keep in mind that the metric system was not in use at this time.

First let's examine Boyle's observations (Table 13.1) for general trends. Note that as the pressure increases, the volume of the trapped gas decreases. In fact, if you compare the data from experiments 1 and 4, you can see that as the pressure is doubled (from 29.1 to 58.2), the volume of the gas is halved (from 48.0 to 24.0). The same relationship can be seen in experiments 2 and 5 and in experiments 3 and 6 (approximately).

We can see the relationship between the volume of a gas and its pressure more clearly by looking at the product of the values of these two properties ($P \times V$) using Boyle's observations. This product is shown in the last column of Table 13.1. Note that for all the experiments,

$$P \times V = 1.4 \times 10^3 \text{ (in Hg)} \times \text{in}^3$$

with only a slight variation due to experimental error. Other similar measurements on gases show the same behavior. This means that the relationship of the pressure and volume of a gas can be expressed in words as

pressure times volume equals a constant

or in terms of an equation as

$$PV = k$$

which is called **Boyle's law,** where k is a constant at a specific temperature for a given amount of gas. For the data we used from Boyle's experiment, $k = 1.41 \times 10^3$(in. Hg) $\times$ in^3.

It is often easier to visualize the relationships between two properties if we make a graph. Figure 13.5 uses the data given in Table 13.1 to show how pressure is related to volume. This relationship, called a plot or a graph, shows

For Boyle's law to hold, the amount of gas (moles) must not be changed. The temperature must also be constant.

The fact that the constant is sometimes 1.40×10^3 instead of 1.41×10^3 is due to experimental error (uncertainties in measuring the values of *P* and *V*).

TABLE 13.1

A Sample of Boyle's Observations
(moles of gas and temperature both constant)

Experiment	Pressure (in Hg)	Volume (in³)	Pressure × Volume (in Hg) × (in³) Actual	Rounded*
1	29.1	48.0	1396.8	1.40 × 10³
2	35.3	40.0	1412.0	1.41 × 10³
3	44.2	32.0	1414.4	1.41 × 10³
4	58.2	24.0	1396.8	1.40 × 10³
5	70.7	20.0	1414.0	1.41 × 10³
6	87.2	16.0	1395.2	1.40 × 10³
7	117.5	12.0	1410.0	1.41 × 10³

*Three significant figures are allowed in the product because both of the numbers that are multiplied together have three significant figures.

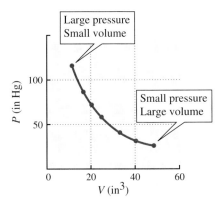

FIGURE 13.5
A plot of *P* versus *V* from Boyle's data in Table 13.1.

that *V* decreases as *P* increases. When this type of relationships exists, we say that volume and pressure are inversely related or *inversely proportional;* when one increases, the other decreases. Boyle's law is illustrated by the gas samples in Figure 13.6.

Boyle's law means that if we know the volume of a gas at a given pressure, we can predict the new volume if the pressure is changed, *provided that neither the temperature nor the amount of gas is changed.* For example, if we represent the original pressure and volumes as P_1 and V_1 and the final values as P_2 and V_2, using Boyle's law we can write

$$P_1V_1 = k$$

and

$$P_2V_2 = k$$

We can also say

$$P_1V_1 = k = P_2V_2$$

or simply

$$P_1V_1 = P_2V_2$$

This is really another way to write Boyle's law. We can solve for the final volume (V_2) by dividing both sides of the equation by P_2.

$$\frac{P_1V_1}{P_2} = \frac{P_2V_2}{P_2}$$

Canceling the P_2 terms on the right gives

$$\frac{P_1}{P_2} \times V_1 = V_2$$

or

$$V_2 = V_1 \times \frac{P_1}{P_2}$$

FIGURE 13.6
Illustration of Boyle's law. These three flasks contain the same number of molecules. At 298K, $P \times V = 1$ L atm in all three flasks.

$P = 1$ atm	$P = 2$ atm	$P = 4$ atm
$V = 1$ L	$V = 0.50$ L	$V = 0.25$ L
$T = 298$ K	$T = 298$ K	$T = 298$ K

This equation tells us that we can calculate the new gas volume (V_2) by multiplying the original volume (V_1) by the ratio of the original pressure to the final pressure (P_1/P_2), as illustrated in Example 13.2.

EXAMPLE 13.2   *Calculating Volume Using Boyle's Law*

Freon-12 (the common name for the compound CCl_2F_2) has been widely used in refrigeration systems, but is now being replaced by other compounds that do not lead to the breakdown of the protective ozone in the upper atmosphere. Consider a 1.5-L sample of gaseous CCl_2F_2 at a pressure of 56 torr. If pressure is changed to 150 torr at a constant temperature.

a. Will the volume of the gas increase or decrease?
b. What will be the new volume of the gas?

Solution

a. As the first step in a gas law problem, always write down the information given, in the form of a table showing the initial and final conditions.

Initial Conditions	*Final Conditions*
$P_1 = 56$ torr	$P_2 = 150$ torr
$V_1 = 1.5$ L	$V_2 = ?$

Drawing a picture also is often helpful. Notice that the pressure is increased from 56 torr to 150 torr, so the volume must decrease:

We can verify this by using Boyle's law in the form

$$V_2 = V_1 \times \frac{P_1}{P_2}$$

Note that V_2 is obtained by "correcting" V_1 using the ratio P_1/P_2. Because P_1 is less than P_2, the ratio P_1/P_2 is a fraction that is less than 1. Thus V_2 must be a fraction of (smaller than) V_1; the volume decreases.

b. We calculate V_2 as follows:

$$V_2 = V_1 \times \frac{P_1}{P_2} = 1.5 \text{ L} \times \frac{56 \text{ torr}}{150 \text{ torr}} = 0.56 \text{ L}$$

The volume of the gas decreases from 1.5 to 0.56 L. This change is in the expected direction.

The fact that the volume decreases in Example 13.2 makes sense because the pressure was increased. *To help catch errors, make it a habit to check whether an answer to a problem makes physical sense.*

A neon sign.

 Self-Check Exercise 13.2

A sample of neon to be used in a neon sign has a volume of 1.51 L at a pressure of 635 torr. Calculate the volume of the gas after it is pumped into the glass tubes of the sign, where it shows a pressure of 785 torr.

See Problems 13.21 and 13.22.

EXAMPLE 13.3   *Calculating Pressure Using Boyle's Law*

In an automobile engine the gaseous fuel–air mixture enters the cylinder and is compressed by a moving piston before it is ignited. In a certain engine the initial cylinder volume is 0.725 L. After the piston moves up, the volume is 0.075 L. The fuel–air mixture initially has a pressure of 1.00 atm. Calculate the pressure of the compressed fuel–air mixture, assuming that both the temperature and the amount of gas remain constant.

Solution

We summarize the given information in the following table:

Initial Conditions	*Final Conditions*
$P_1 = 1.00$ atm	$P_2 = ?$
$V_1 = 0.725$ L	$V_2 = 0.075$ L

Then we solve Boyle's law in the form $P_1V_1 = P_2V_2$ for P_2 by dividing both sides by V_2 to give the equation

$$P_2 = P_1 \times \frac{V_1}{V_2} = 1.00 \text{ atm} \times \frac{0.725 \text{ L}}{0.075 \text{ L}} = 9.7 \text{ atm}$$

Note that the pressure must increase because the volume gets smaller. Pressure and volume are inversely related.

$P_1V_1 = P_2V_2$

$\dfrac{P_1V_1}{V_2} = \dfrac{P_2\cancel{V_2}}{\cancel{V_2}}$

$P_1 \times \dfrac{V_1}{V_2} = P_2$

$\dfrac{0.725}{0.075} = 9.666\ldots$

9.666 ➡ 9.7
Round off

13.3 Volume and Temperature: Charles's Law

AIMS: To learn about absolute zero. To learn about the law relating the volume and temperature of a sample of gas at constant moles and pressure, and to do calculations involving that law.

The air in a balloon expands when it is heated. This means that some of the air escapes from the balloon, lowering the air density inside and thus making the balloon buoyant.

Temperatures such as 0.00000002 K have been obtained in the laboratory, but 0 K has never been reached.

In the century following Boyle's findings, scientists continued to study the properties of gases. The French physicist Jacques Charles (1746–1823), who was the first person to fill a balloon with hydrogen gas and who made the first solo balloon flight, showed that the volume of a given amount of gas (at constant pressure) increases with the temperature of the gas. That is, the volume increases when the temperature increases. A plot of the volume of a given sample of gas (at constant pressure) versus its temperature (in Celsius degrees) gives a straight line. This type of relationship is called *linear,* and this behavior is shown for several gases in Figure 13.7.

The solid lines in Figure 13.7 are based on actual measurements of temperature and volume for the gases listed. As we cool the gases they eventually liquefy, so we cannot determine any experimental points below this temperature. However, when we extend each straight line (which is called *extrapolation* and is shown here by a dashed line), something very interesting happens. *All* of the lines extrapolate to zero volume at the same temperature: −273 °C. This suggests that −273 °C is the lowest possible temperature, because a negative volume is physically impossible. In fact, experiments have shown that matter cannot be cooled to temperatures lower than −273 °C. Therefore, this temperature is defined as **absolute zero** on the Kelvin scale.

When the volumes of the gases shown in Figure 13.7 are plotted against temperature on the Kelvin scale rather than the Celsius scale, the plots shown in Figure 13.8 result. These plots show that the volume of each gas is *directly proportional to the temperature* (in kelvins) and extrapolates to zero when the temperature is 0 K. Let's illustrate this statement with an example. Suppose

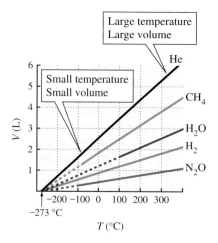

FIGURE 13.7
Plots of V(L) versus T (°C) for several gases.

FIGURE 13.8
Plots of V versus T as in Figure 13.7, except that here the Kelvin scale is used for temperature.

we have 1 L of gas at 300 K. When we double the temperature of this gas to 600 K (without changing its pressure), the volume also doubles, to 2 L. Verify this type of behavior by looking carefully at the lines for various gases shown in Figure 13.8.

The direct proportionality between volume and temperature (in kelvins) is represented by the equation known as **Charles's law:**

$$V = bT$$

where T is in kelvins and b is the proportionality constant. Charles's law holds for a given sample of gas at constant pressure. It tells us that (for a given amount of gas at a given pressure) the volume of the gas is directly proportional to the temperature on the Kelvin scale:

From Figure 13.8 for Helium

$V(L)$	$T(K)$	b
0.7	73	0.01
1.7	173	0.01
2.7	273	0.01
3.7	373	0.01
5.7	573	0.01

$$V = bT \ \text{ or } \ \frac{V}{T} = b = \text{constant}$$

Notice that in the second form, this equation states that the *ratio* of V to T (in kelvins) must be constant. (This is shown for helium in the margin.) Thus when we triple the temperature (in kelvins) of a sample of gas, the volume of the gas triples also.

$$\frac{V}{T} = \frac{3 \times V}{3 \times T} = b = \text{constant}$$

We can also write Charles's law in terms V_1 and T_1 (the initial conditions) and V_2 and T_2 (the final conditions).

$$\frac{V_1}{T_1} = b \ \text{ and } \ \frac{V_2}{T_2} = b$$

Charles's law in the form $V_1/T_1 = V_2/T_2$ applies only when both the amount of gas (moles) and the pressure are constant.

Thus

$$\frac{V_1}{T_1} = \frac{V_2}{T_2}$$

We will illustrate the use of this equation in Examples 13.4 and 13.5.

■■■■ **EXAMPLE 13.4** *Calculating Volume Using Charles's Law, I*

A 2.0-L sample of air is collected at 298 K and then cooled to 278 K. The pressure is held constant at 1.0 atm.

a. Does the volume increase or decrease?
b. Calculate the volume of the air at 278 K.

Solution

a. Because the gas is cooled, the volume of the gas must decrease:

$$\frac{V}{T} = \text{constant}$$

$\dfrac{V_1}{T_1}$ ⟹ $\dfrac{V_2}{T_2}$

Temperature smaller, volume smaller

T is decreased, so V must decrease to maintain a constant ratio.

b. To calculate the new volume, V_2, we will use Charles's law in the form

$$\frac{V_1}{T_1} = \frac{V_2}{T_2}$$

We are given the following information:

Initial Conditions	*Final Conditions*
$T_1 = 298$ K	$T_2 = 278$ K
$V_1 = 2.0$ L	$V_2 = ?$

We want to solve the equation

$$\frac{V_1}{T_1} = \frac{V_2}{T_2}$$

for V_2. We can do this by multiplying both sides by T_2 and canceling.

$$T_2 \times \frac{V_1}{T_1} = \frac{V_2}{\cancel{T_2}} \times \cancel{T_2} = V_2$$

Thus

$$V_2 = T_2 \times \frac{V_1}{T_1} = 278 \ \cancel{K} \times \frac{2.0 \ L}{298 \ \cancel{K}} = 1.9 \ L$$

Note that the volume gets smaller when the temperature decreases, just as we predicted.

EXAMPLE 13.5   *Calculating Volume Using Charles's Law, II*

A sample of gas at 15 °C (at 1 atm) has a volume of 2.58 L. The temperature is then raised to 38 °C (at 1 atm).

a. Does the volume of the gas increase or decrease?
b. Calculate the new volume.

Solution

a. In this case we have a given sample (constant amount) of gas that is heated from 15 °C to 38 °C *while the pressure is held constant.* We know from Charles's law that the volume of a given sample of gas is directly proportional to the temperature (at constant pressure). So the increase in temperature will *increase* the volume; the new volume will be greater than 2.58 L.

b. To calculate the new volume, we use Charles's law in the form

$$\frac{V_1}{T_1} = \frac{V_2}{T_2}$$

We are given the following information:

Initial Conditions	*Final Conditions*
$T_1 = 15$ °C	$T_2 = 38$ °C
$V_1 = 2.58$ L	$V_2 = ?$

As is often the case, the temperatures are given in Celsius degrees. However, in order for us to use Charles's law, the temperature *must be in kelvins.* Thus we must convert by adding 273 to each temperature.

Initial Conditions

$T_1 = 15\ °C = 15 + 273 = 288\ K$

$V_1 = 2.58\ L$

Final Conditions

$T_2 = 38\ °C = 38 + 273$
$= 311\ K$

$V_2 = ?$

Solving for V_2 gives

$$V_2 = V_1 \times \frac{T_2}{T_1} = 2.58\ L \left(\frac{311\ K}{288\ K}\right) = 2.79\ L$$

The new volume (2.79 L) is greater than the initial volume (2.58 L), as we expected.

 Self-Check Exercise 13.3

A child blows a bubble that contains air at 28 °C and has a volume of 23 cm^3 at 1 atm. As the bubble rises, it encounters a pocket of cold air (temperature 18 °C). If there is no change in pressure, will the bubble get larger or smaller as the air inside cools to 18 °C? Calculate the new volume of the bubble.

See Problems 13.29 and 13.30.

Notice from Example 13.5 that we adjust the volume of a gas for a temperature change by multiplying the original volume by the ratio of the kelvin temperatures—final (T_2) over initial (T_1). Remember to check whether your answer makes sense. When the temperature increases (at constant pressure), the volume must increase, and vice versa.

EXAMPLE 13.6 *Calculating Temperature Using Charles's Law*

In former times, gas volume was used as a way to measure temperature using devices called gas thermometers. Consider a gas that has a volume of 0.675 L at 35 °C and 1 atm pressure. What is the temperature (in units of °C) of a room where this gas has a volume of 0.535 L at 1 atm pressure?

Solution

The information given in the problem is

Initial Conditions

$T_1 = 35\ °C = 35 + 27 - 273 = 308\ K$

$V_1 = 0.0675\ L$

$P_1 = 1\ atm$

Final Conditions

$T_2 = ?$

$V_2 = 0.535\ L$

$P_2 = 1\ atm$

The pressure remains constant, so we can use Charles's law in the form

$$\frac{V_1}{T_1} = \frac{V_2}{T_2}$$

and solve for T_2. First we multiply both sides by T_2.

$$T_2 \times \frac{V_1}{T_1} = \frac{V_2}{P_2} \times P_2 = V_2$$

Next we multiply both sides by T_1.

$$\cancel{T_1} \times T_2 \times \frac{V_1}{\cancel{T_1}} = T_1 \times V_2$$

This gives

$$T_2 \times V_1 = T_1 \times V_2$$

Now we divide both sides by V_1 (multiply by $1/V_1$):

$$\frac{1}{\cancel{V_1}} \times T_2 \times \cancel{V_1} = \frac{1}{V_1} \times T_1 \times V_2$$

and obtain

$$T_2 = T_1 \times \frac{V_2}{V_1}$$

We have now isolated T_2 on one side of the equation, and we can do the calculation.

$$T_2 = T_1 \times \frac{V_2}{V_1} = (308 \text{ K}) \times \frac{0.535 \cancel{L}}{0.675 \cancel{L}} = 244 \text{ K}$$

To convert from units of K to units of °C, we subtract 273 from the Kelvin temperature.

$$T_{°C} = T_K - 273 = 244 - 273 = -29 \text{ °C}$$

The room is very cold; the new temperature is -29 °C.

13.4 Volume and Moles: Avogadro's Law

AIM: To understand the law relating the volume and the number of moles of a sample of gas at constant temperature and pressure, and to do calculations involving this law.

What is the relationship between the volume of a gas and the number of molecules present in the gas sample? Experiments show that when the number of moles of gas is doubled (at constant temperature and pressure), the volume doubles. In other words, the volume of a gas is directly proportional to the number of moles if temperature and pressure remain constant. Figure 13.9 illustrates this relationship, which can also be represented by the equation

$$V = an \quad \text{or} \quad \frac{V}{n} = a$$

where V is the volume of the gas, n is the number of moles, and a is the proportionality constant. Note that this equation means that the ratio of V to n is constant as long as the temperature and pressure remain constant. Thus when the number of moles of gas is increased by a factor of 5, the volume

FIGURE 13.9
The relationship between volume V and number of moles n. As the number of moles is increased from 1 to 2 (a to b), the volume doubles. When the number of moles is tripled (c), the volume is also tripled. The temperature and pressure remain the same in these cases.

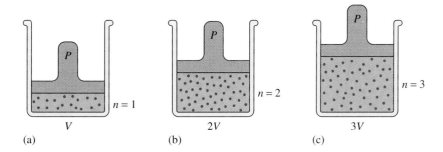

(a) $n = 1$ V

(b) $n = 2$ $2V$

(c) $n = 3$ $3V$

also increases by a factor of 5:

$$\frac{V}{n} = \frac{5 \times V}{5 \times n} = a = \text{constant}$$

and so on. In words, this equation means that *for a gas at constant temperature and pressure, the volume is directly proportional to the number of moles of gas.* This relationship is called **Avogadro's law** after the Italian scientist Amadeo Avogadro, who first postulated it in 1811.

For cases where the number of moles of gas is changed from an initial amount to another amount (at constant T and P), we can represent Avogadro's law as

$$\underset{\substack{\text{Initial} \\ \text{amount}}}{\frac{V_1}{n_1}} = a = \underset{\substack{\text{Final} \\ \text{amount}}}{\frac{V_2}{n_2}}$$

or

$$\frac{V_1}{n_1} = \frac{V_2}{n_2}$$

We will illustrate the use of this equation in Example 13.7.

EXAMPLE 13.7   *Using Avogadro's Law in Calculations*

Suppose we have a 12.2-L sample containing 0.50 mol of oxygen gas, O_2, at a pressure of 1 atm and a temperature of 25 °C. If all of this O_2 is converted to ozone, O_3, at the same temperature and pressure, what will be the volume of the ozone formed?

Solution

To do this problem we need to compare the moles of gas originally present to the moles of gas present after the reaction. We know that 0.50 mol of O_2 is present initially. To find out how many moles of O_3 will be present after the reaction, we need to use the balanced equation for the reaction.

$$3O_2(g) \rightarrow 2O_3(g)$$

We calculate the moles of O_3 produced by using the appropriate mole ratio from the balanced equation.

$$0.50 \, \cancel{\text{mol } O_2} \times \frac{2 \, \text{mol } O_3}{3 \, \cancel{\text{mol } O_2}} = 0.33 \, \text{mol } O_3$$

Avogadro's law states that

$$\frac{V_1}{n_1} = \frac{V_2}{n_2}$$

where V_1 is the volume of n_1 moles of O_2 gas and V_2 is the volume of n_2 moles of O_3 gas. In this case we have

Initial Conditions	*Final Conditions*
$n_1 = 0.50$ mol	$n_2 = 0.33$ mol
$V_1 = 12.2$ L	$V_2 = ?$

$$\frac{V_1}{n_1} = \frac{V_2}{n_2}$$

$$n_2 \times \frac{V_1}{n_1} = \frac{V_2}{\cancel{n_2}} \times \cancel{n_2}$$

$$V_1 \times \frac{n_2}{n_1} = V_2$$

Solving Avogadro's law for V_2 gives

$$V_2 = V_1 \times \frac{n_2}{n_1} = 12.2 \, \text{L} \left(\frac{0.33 \, \cancel{\text{mol}}}{0.50 \, \cancel{\text{mol}}} \right) = 8.1 \, \text{L}$$

Note that the volume decreases, as it should, because fewer molecules are present in the gas after O_2 is converted to O_3.

Self-Check Exercise 13.4

Consider two samples of nitrogen gas (composed of N_2 molecules). Sample 1 contains 1.5 mol of N_2 and has a volume of 36.7 L at 25 °C and 1 atm. Sample 2 has a volume of 16.5 L at 25 °C and 1 atm. Calculate the number of moles of N_2 in Sample 2.

See Problems 13.41 through 13.44.

13.5 The Ideal Gas Law

AIM: To understand the ideal gas law and use it in calculations.

We have considered three laws that describe the behavior of gases as it is revealed by experimental observations.

Constant *n* means a constant number of moles of gas.

Boyle's law: $PV = k$ or $V = \dfrac{k}{P}$ (at constant T and n)

Charles's law: $V = bT$ (at constant P and n)

Avogadro's law: $V = an$ (at constant T and P)

These relationships, which show how the volume of a gas depends on pressure, temperature, and number of moles of gas present, can be combined as follows:

$$V = R \left(\frac{Tn}{P} \right)$$

where R is the combined proportionality constant and is called the **universal gas constant.** When the pressure is expressed in atmospheres and the volume is in liters, R always has the value 0.08206 L atm/K mol. We can rearrange the above equation by multiplying both sides by P:

$$P \times V = \not{P} \times R\left(\frac{Tn}{\not{P}}\right)$$

$$R = 0.08206 \frac{\text{L atm}}{\text{K mol}}$$

to obtain the **ideal gas law** written in its usual form,

$$PV = nRT$$

The ideal gas law involves all the important characteristics of a gas: its pressure (P), volume (V), number of moles (n), and temperature (T). Knowledge of any three of these properties is enough to define completely the condition of the gas, because the fourth property can be determined from the ideal gas law.

It is important to recognize that the ideal gas law is based on experimental measurements of the properties of gases. A gas that obeys this equation is said to behave *ideally*. That is, this equation defines the behavior of an **ideal gas.** Most gases obey this equation closely at pressures of approximately 1 atm or lower, when the temperature is approximately 0 °C or higher. You should assume ideal gas behavior when working problems involving gases in this text.

The ideal gas law can be used to solve a variety of problems. Example 13.8 demonstrates one type, where you are asked to find one property characterizing the condition of a gas given the other three properties.

EXAMPLE 13.8 *Using the Ideal Gas Law in Calculations*

A sample of hydrogen gas, H_2, has a volume of 8.56 L at a temperature of 0 °C and a pressure of 1.5 atm. Calculate the number of moles of H_2 present in this gas sample. (Assume that the gas behaves ideally.)

Solution

In this problem we are given the pressure, volume, and temperature of the gas: $P = 1.5$ atm, $V = 8.56$ L, and $T = 0$ °C. Remember that the temperature must be changed to the Kelvin scale.

$$T = 0 \text{ °C} = 0 + 273 = 273 \text{ K}$$

We can calculate the number of moles of gas present by using the ideal gas law, $PV = nRT$. We solve for n by dividing both sides by RT:

$$\frac{PV}{RT} = n\frac{\not{RT}}{\not{RT}}$$

to give

$$\frac{PV}{RT} = n$$

Thus

$$n = \frac{PV}{RT} = \frac{(1.5 \text{ atm})(8.56 \text{ L})}{\left(0.08206 \frac{\text{L atm}}{\text{K mol}}\right)(273 \text{ K})} = 0.57 \text{ mol}$$

Self-Check Exercise 13.5

A weather balloon contains 1.10×10^5 mol of helium and has a volume of 2.70×10^6 L at 1.00 atm pressure. Calculate the temperature of the helium in the balloon in kelvins and in Celsius degrees.

See Problems 13.53 through 13.60.

EXAMPLE 13.9   *Ideal Gas Law Calculations Involving Conversion of Units*

What volume is occupied by 0.250 mol of carbon dioxide gas at 25 °C and 371 torr?

Solution

We can use the ideal gas law to calculate the volume, but we must first convert pressure to atmospheres and temperature to the Kelvin scale.

$$P = 371 \text{ torr} = 371 \cancel{\text{ torr}} \times \frac{1.000 \text{ atom}}{760.0 \cancel{\text{ torr}}} = 0.488 \text{ atm}$$

$$T = 25 \text{ °C} = 25 + 273 = 298 \text{ K}$$

We solve for V by dividing both sides of the ideal gas law ($PV = nRT$) by P.

$$PV = nRT$$
$$\frac{PV}{\cancel{P}} = \frac{nRT}{P}$$
$$V = \frac{nRT}{P}$$

$$V = \frac{nRT}{P} = \frac{(0.250 \cancel{\text{ mol}})\left(0.08206 \frac{\text{L } \cancel{\text{atm}}}{\text{K } \cancel{\text{mol}}}\right)(298 \cancel{\text{ K}})}{0.488 \cancel{\text{ atm}}} = 12.5 \text{ L}$$

The volume of the sample of CO_2 is 12.5 L.

 Self-Check Exercise 13.6

Radon, a radioactive gas formed naturally in the soil, can cause lung cancer. It can pose a hazard to humans by seeping into houses, and there is concern about this problem in many areas. A 1.5-mol sample of radon gas has a volume of 21.0 L at 33 °C. What is the pressure of the gas?

See Problems 13.53 through 13.60.

Note that R has units of L atm/K mol. Accordingly, whenever we use the ideal gas law, we must express the volume in units of liters, the temperature in kelvins, and the pressure in atmospheres. When we are given data in other units, we must first convert to the appropriate units.

The ideal gas law can also be used to calculate the changes that will occur when the conditions of the gas are changed as illustrated in Example 13.10.

EXAMPLE 13.10   *Using the Ideal Gas Law Under Changing Conditions*

Suppose we have a 0.240-mol sample of ammonia gas at 25 °C with a volume of 3.5 L at a pressure of 1.68 atm. The gas is compressed to a volume of 1.35 L at 25 °C. Use the ideal gas law to calculate the final pressure.

Solution

In this case we have a sample of ammonia gas in which the conditions are changed. We are given the following information:

Initial Conditions	*Final Conditions*
$V_1 = 3.5$ L	$V_2 = 1.35$ L
$P_1 = 1.68$ atm	$P_2 = ?$
$T_1 = 25\ °C = 25 + 273 = 298$ K	$T_2 = 25\ °C = 25 + 273 = 298$ K
$n_1 = 0.240$ mol	$n_2 = 0.240$ mol

Note that both n and T remain constant—only P and V change. Thus we could simply use Boyle's law ($P_1V_1 = P_2V_2$) to solve for P_2. However, we will use the ideal gas law to solve this problem in order to introduce the idea that one equation—the ideal gas equation—can be used to do almost any gas problem. The key idea here is that in using the ideal gas law to describe a change in conditions for a gas, we always *solve the ideal gas equation in such a way that the variables that change are on one side of the equals sign and the constant terms are on the other side.* That is, we start with the ideal gas equation in the conventional form ($PV = nRT$) and rearrange it so that all the terms that change are moved to one side and all the terms that do not change are moved to the other side. In this case the pressure and volume change, and the temperature and number of moles remain constant (as does R, by definition). So we write the ideal gas law as

$$PV = nRT$$

Change   Remain constant

Because n, R, and T remain the same in this case, we can write $P_1V_1 = nRT$ and $P_2V_2 = nRT$. Combining these gives

$$P_1V_1 = nRT = P_2V_2 \text{ or } P_1V_1 = P_2V_2$$

and

$$P_2 = P_1 \times \frac{V_1}{V_2} = (1.68 \text{ atm}) \left(\frac{3.5\text{ L}}{1.35\text{ L}} \right) = 4.4 \text{ atm}$$

Check: Does this answer make sense? The volume was decreased (at constant temperature and constant number of moles), which means that the pressure should increase, as the calculation indicates.

 Self-Check Exercise 13.7

A sample of methane gas that has a volume of 3.8 L at 5 °C is heated to 86 °C at constant pressure. Calculate its new volume.

See Problems 13.61 and 13.62.

Note that in solving Example 13.10, we actually obtained Boyle's law ($P_1V_1 = P_2V_2$) from the ideal gas equation. You might well ask, "Why go to all this trouble?" The idea is to learn to use the ideal gas equation to solve all types of gas law problems. This way you will never have to ask yourself, "Is this a Boyle's law problem or a Charles's law problem?"

We continue to practice using the ideal gas law in Example 13.11. Remember, the key idea is to rearrange the equation so that the quantities that change are moved to one side of the equation and those that remain constant are moved to the other.

EXAMPLE 13.11   *Calculating Volume Changes Using the Ideal Gas Law*

A sample of diborane gas, B_2H_6, a substance that bursts into flames when exposed to air, has a pressure of 0.454 atm at a temperature of -15 °C and a volume of 3.48 L. If conditions are changed so that the temperature is 36 °C and the pressure is 0.616 atm, what will be the new volume of the sample?

Solution

We are given the following information:

Initial Conditions	**Final Conditions**
$P_1 = 0.454$ atm	$P_2 = 0.616$ atm
$V_1 = 3.48$ L	$V_2 = ?$
$T_1 = -15$ °C $= 273 - 15 = 258$ K	$T_2 = 36$ °C $= 273 + 36 = 309$ K

$$PV = nRT$$

$$\frac{PV}{T} = \frac{nR\cancel{T}}{\cancel{T}}$$

$$\frac{PV}{T} = nRT$$

Note that the value of n is not given. However, we know that n is constant (that is, $n_1 = n_2$) because no diborane gas is added or taken away. Thus in this experiment, n is constant and P, V, and T change. Therefore, we rearrange the ideal gas equation ($PV = nRT$) by dividing both sides by T:

$$\underset{\text{Change}}{\frac{PV}{T}} = \underset{\text{Constant}}{nR}$$

which leads to the equation

$$\frac{P_1V_1}{T_1} = nR = \frac{P_2V_2}{T_2}$$

or

$$\frac{P_1V_1}{T_1} = \frac{P_2V_2}{T_2}$$

We can now solve for V_2 by dividing both sides by P_2 and multiplying both sides by T_2.

$$\frac{1}{P_2} \times \frac{P_1V_1}{T_1} = \frac{\cancel{P_2}V_2}{T_2} \times \frac{1}{\cancel{P_2}} = \frac{V_2}{T_2}$$

$$T_2 \times \frac{P_1V_1}{P_2T_1} = \frac{V_2}{\cancel{T_2}} \times \cancel{T_2} = V_2$$

That is,

$$\frac{T_2P_1V_1}{P_2T_1} = V_2$$

It is sometimes convenient to think in terms of the ratios of the initial temperature and pressure and the final temperature and pressure. That is,

Always convert the temperature to the Kelvin scale and the pressure to atmospheres when applying the ideal gas law.

$$V_2 = \frac{T_2P_1V_1}{T_1P_2} = V_1 \times \frac{T_2}{T_1} \times \frac{P_1}{P_2}$$

Substituting the information given yields

$$V_2 = \frac{309 \, \cancel{K}}{258 \, \cancel{K}} \times \frac{0.454 \, \cancel{atm}}{0.616 \, \cancel{atm}} \times 3.48 \, \text{L} = 3.07 \, \text{L}$$

Self-Check Exercise 13.8

A sample of argon gas with a volume of 11.0 L at a temperature of 13 °C and a pressure of 0.747 atm is heated to 56 °C and a pressure of 1.18 atm. Calculate the final volume.

See Problems 13.61 and 13.62.

The equation obtained in Example 13.11,

$$\frac{P_1V_1}{T_1} = \frac{P_2V_2}{T_2}$$

is often called the **combined gas law** equation. It holds when the amount of gas (moles) is held constant. While it may be convenient to remember this equation, it is not necessary because you can always use the ideal gas equation.

CHEMISTRY IN FOCUS

What Does Orville Redenbacher Know About Hot Gas?

Have you ever wondered what makes popcorn pop? The popping is linked with the properties of gases. What happens when a gas is heated? Charles's law tells us that if the pressure is held constant, the volume of the gas must increase as the temperature is increased. But what happens if the gas being heated is trapped at a constant volume? We can see what happens by rearranging the ideal gas law (PV = nRT) as follows:

$$P = \left(\frac{nR}{V}\right)T$$

When *n*, R, and V are held constant, the pressure of a gas is directly proportional to the temperature. Thus as the temperature of the trapped gas increases, its pressure also increases. This is exactly what happens inside a kernel of popcorn as it is heated. The moisture inside the kernal vaporized by the heat produces increasing pressure. The pressure finally becomes so great that the kernal breaks open, allowing the starch inside to expand to about 40 times its original size.

What's special about popcorn? Why does it pop while "regular" corn doesn't? William da Silva, a biologist at the University of Campinas in Brazil, has traced the "popability" of popcorn to its outer casing, called the pericarp. The molecules in the pericarp of popcorn, which are packed in a much more orderly way than in regular corn, transfer heat unusually quickly, producing a very fast pressure jump that pops the kernel. In addition, because the pericarp of popcorn is much thicker and stronger than that of regular corn, it can withstand more pressure, leading to a more explosive pop when the moment finally comes.

Popcorn popping.

13.6 Dalton's Law of Partial Pressures

AIM: To understand the relationship between the partial and total pressures of a gas mixture, and to use this relationship in calculations.

Many important gases contain a mixture of components. One notable example is air. Scuba divers who are going deeper than 150 feet use another important mixture, helium and oxygen. Normal air is not used because the nitrogen present dissolves in the blood in large quantities as a result of the high pressures experienced by the diver under several hundred feet of water. When the diver returns too quickly to the surface, the nitrogen bubbles out of the blood just as soda fizzes when it's opened, and the diver gets "the bends"— a very painful and potentially fatal condition. Because helium gas is only sparingly soluble in blood, it does not cause this problem.

Studies of gaseous mixtures show that each component behaves independently of the others. In other words, a given amount of oxygen exerts the same pressure in a 1.0-L vessel whether it is alone or in the presence of nitrogen (as in the air) or helium.

Among the first scientists to study mixtures of gases was John Dalton. In 1803 Dalton summarized his observations in this statement: *For a mixture of gases in a container, the total pressure exerted is the sum of the partial pressures of the gases present. The* **partial pressure** *of a gas is the pressure that the gas would exert if it were alone in the container.* This statement, known as **Dalton's law of partial pressures,** can be expressed as follows for a mixture containing three gases:

$$P_{\text{total}} = P_1 + P_2 + P_3$$

where the subscripts refer to the individual gases (gas 1, gas 2, and gas 3). The pressures P_1, P_2, and P_3 are the partial pressures; that is, each gas is responsible for only part of the total pressure (Figure 13.10).

Assuming that each gas behaves ideally, we can calculate the partial pressure of each gas from the ideal gas law:

$$PV = nRT$$

$$\frac{P\cancel{V}}{\cancel{V}} = \frac{nRT}{V}$$

$$P = \frac{nRT}{V}$$

$$P_1 = \frac{n_1 RT}{V}, \; P_2 = \frac{n_2 RT}{V}, \; P_3 = \frac{n_3 RT}{V}$$

FIGURE 13.10
When two gases are present, the total pressure is the sum of the partial pressures of the gases.

2.4 atm

0.50 mol H_2

5.0 L at 20 °C
P_{H_2} = 2.4 atm

6.0 atm

1.25 mol He

5.0 L at 20 °C
P_{He} = 6.0 atm

8.4 atm

1.25 mol He
+ 0.50 mol H_2
―――――――
1.75 mol gas

5.0 L at 20 °C
P_{Total} = 8.4 atm
= 6.0 atm + 2.4 atm
= $P_{H_2} + P_{He}$

The total pressure of the mixture, P_{total}, can be represented as

$$P_{total} = P_1 + P_2 + P_3 = \frac{n_1 RT}{V} + \frac{n_2 RT}{V} + \frac{n_3 RT}{V}$$

$$= n_1 \left(\frac{RT}{V}\right) + n_2 \left(\frac{RT}{V}\right) + n_3 \left(\frac{RT}{V}\right)$$

$$= (n_1 + n_2 + n_3)\left(\frac{RT}{V}\right)$$

$$= n_{total}\left(\frac{RT}{V}\right)$$

where n_{total} is the sum of the numbers of moles of the gases in the mixture. Thus for a mixture of ideal gases, it is the *total number of moles of particles* that is important, not the *identity* of the individual gas particles. This idea is illustrated in Figure 13.11.

The fact that the pressure exerted by an ideal gas is affected by the *number* of gas particles and is independent of the *nature* of the gas particles tells us two important things about ideal gases.

1. The volume of the individual gas particle (atom or molecule) must not be very important.

2. The forces among the particles must not be very important.

If these factors were important, the pressure of the gas would depend on the nature of the individual particles. For example, an argon atom is much larger than a helium atom. Yet 1.75 mol of argon gas in a 5.0-L container at 20 °C exerts the same pressure as 1.75 mol of helium gas in a 5.0-L container at 20 °C.

The same idea applies to the forces among the particles. Although the forces among gas particles depend on the nature of the particles, this seems to have little influence on the behavior of an ideal gas. We will see that these observations strongly influence the model that we will construct to explain ideal gas behavior.

FIGURE 13.11
The total pressure of a mixture of gases depends on the number of moles of gas particles (atoms or molecules) present, not on the identities of the particles. Note that these three samples show the same total pressure because each contains 1.75 mol of gas. The detailed nature of the mixture is unimportant.

EXAMPLE 13.12 *Using Dalton's Law of Partial Pressures, I*

Mixtures of helium and oxygen are used in the "air" tanks of underwater divers for deep dives. For a particular dive, 12 L of O_2 at 25 °C and 1.0 atm and 46 L of He at 25 °C and 1.0 atm were both pumped into a 5.0-L tank. Calculate the partial pressure of each gas and the total pressure in the tank at 25 °C.

Solution

$PV = nRT$

$\dfrac{PV}{RT} = \dfrac{nRT}{RT}$

$\dfrac{PV}{RT} = n$

Because the partial pressure of each gas depends on the moles of that gas present, we must first calculate the number of moles of each gas by using the ideal gas law in the form

$$n = \frac{PV}{RT}$$

From the above description we know that $P = 1.0$ atm, $V = 12$ L for O_2 and 46 L for He, and $T = 25 + 273 = 298$ K. Also, $R = 0.08206$ L atm/K mol (as always).

$$\text{Moles of } O_2 = n_{O_2} = \frac{(1.0 \text{ atm})(12 \text{ L})}{(0.08206 \text{ L atm/K mol})(298 \text{ K})} = 0.49 \text{ mol}$$

$$\text{Moles of He} = n_{He} = \frac{(1.0 \text{ atm})(46 \text{ L})}{(0.08206 \text{ L atm/K mol})(298 \text{ K})} = 1.9 \text{ mol}$$

The tank containing the mixture has a volume of 5.0 L, and the temperature is 25 °C (298 K). We can use these data and the ideal gas law to calculate the partial pressure of each gas.

$$P = \frac{nRT}{V}$$

$$P_{O_2} = \frac{(0.49 \text{ mol})(0.08206 \text{ L atm/K mol})(298 \text{ K})}{5.0 \text{ L}} = 2.4 \text{ atm}$$

$$P_{He} = \frac{(1.9 \text{ mol})(0.08206 \text{ L atm/K mol})(298 \text{ K})}{5.0 \text{ L}} = 9.3 \text{ atm}$$

The total pressure is the sum of the partial pressures.

$$P_{total} = O_2 + P_{He} = 2.4 \text{ atm} + 9.3 \text{ atm} = 11.7 \text{ atm}$$

Divers use a mixture of oxygen and helium in their breathing tanks for dives to depths greater than 150 feet.

Self-Check Exercise 13.9

A 2.0-L flask contains a mixture of nitrogen gas and oxygen gas at 25 °C. The total pressure of the gaseous mixture is 0.91 atm, and the mixture is known to contain 0.050 mol of N_2. Calculate the partial pressure of oxygen and the moles of oxygen present.

See Problems 13.67 through 13.70.

A mixture of gases occurs whenever a gas is collected by displacement of water. For example, Figure 13.12 shows the collection of the oxygen gas that was produced by the decomposition of solid potassium chlorate. The

FIGURE 13.12
The production of oxygen by thermal decomposition of $KClO_3$. MnO_2 is mixed with the $KClO_3$ to make the reaction proceed at a more rapid rate.

TABLE 13.2

The Vapor Pressure of Water as a Function of Temperature

T (°C)	P (torr)
0.0	4.579
10.0	9.209
20.0	17.535
25.0	23.756
30.0	31.824
40.0	55.324
60.0	149.4
70.0	233.7
90.0	525.8

gas is collected by bubbling it into a bottle that is initially filled with water. Thus the gas in the bottle is really a mixture of water vapor and oxygen. (Water vapor is present because molecules of water escape from the surface of the liquid and collect as a gas in the space above the liquid.) Therefore, the total pressure exerted by this mixture is the sum of the partial pressure of the gas being collected and the partial pressure of the water vapor. The partial pressure of the water vapor is called the vapor pressure of water. Because water molecules are more likely to escape from hot water than from cold water, the *vapor pressure* of water increases with temperature. This is shown by the values of vapor pressure at various temperatures shown in Table 13.2.

EXAMPLE 13.13   *Using Dalton's Law of Partial Pressures, II*

A sample of solid potassium chlorate, $KClO_3$, was heated in a test tube (see Figure 13.12) and decomposed according to the reaction

$$2KClO_3(s) \rightarrow 2KCl(s) + 3O_2(g)$$

The oxygen produced was collected by displacement of water at 22 °C. The resulting mixture of O_2 and H_2O vapor had a total pressure of 754 torr and a volume of 0.650 L. Calculate the partial pressure of O_2 in the gas collected and the number of moles of O_2 present. The vapor pressure of water at 22 °C is 21 torr.

Solution

We know the total pressure (754 torr) and the partial pressure of water (vapor pressure = 21 torr). We can find the partial pressure of O_2 from Dalton's law of partial pressures:

$$P_{total} = P_{O_2} + P_{H_2O} = P_{O_2} + 21 \text{ torr} = 754 \text{ torr}$$

or

$$P_{O_2} + 21 \text{ torr} = 754 \text{ torr}$$

$$PV = nRT$$

$$\frac{PV}{RT} = \frac{n\cancel{RT}}{\cancel{RT}}$$

$$\frac{PV}{RT} = n$$

We can solve for P_{O_2} by subtracting 21 torr from both sides of the equation.

$$P_{O_2} = 754 \text{ torr} - 21 \text{ torr} = 733 \text{ torr}$$

Next we solve the ideal gas law for the number of moles of O_2.

$$n_{O_2} = \frac{P_{O_2}V}{RT}$$

In this case, $P_{O_2} = 733$ torr. We change the pressure to atmospheres as follows:

$$\frac{733 \cancel{\text{ torr}}}{760 \cancel{\text{ torr}}/\text{atm}} = 0.964 \text{ atm}$$

Then,

$$V = 0.650 \text{ L}$$
$$T = 22 \text{ °C} = 22 + 273 = 295 \text{ K}$$
$$R = 0.08206 \text{ L atm/K mol}$$

so

$$n_{O_2} = \frac{(0.964 \cancel{\text{ atm}})(0.650 \cancel{\text{ L}})}{(0.08206 \cancel{\text{ L}} \cancel{\text{ atm}}/\cancel{\text{K}} \text{ mol})(29\,5 \cancel{\text{ K}})} = 2.59 \times 10^{-2} \text{ mol}$$

 Self-Check Exercise 13.10

Consider a sample of hydrogen gas collected over water at 25 °C where the vapor pressure of water is 24 torr. The volume occupied by the gaseous mixture is 0.500 L, and the total pressure is 0.950 atm. Calculate the partial pressure of H_2 and the number of moles of H_2 present.

See Problems 13.71 through 13.74.

13.7 Laws and Models: A Review

AIM: To understand the relationship between laws and models (theories).

In this chapter we have considered several properties of gases and have seen how the relationships among these properties can be expressed by various laws written in the form of mathematical equations. The most useful of these is the ideal gas equation, which relates all the important gas properties. However, under certain conditions gases do not obey the ideal gas equation. For example, at high pressures and/or low temperatures, the properties of gases deviate significantly from the predictions of the ideal gas equation. On the other hand, as the pressure is lowered and/or the temperature is increased, almost all gases show close agreement with the ideal gas equation. This means that an ideal gas is really a hypothetical substance. At low pressures and/or high temperatures, real gases *approach* the behavior expected for an ideal gas.

At this point we want to build a model (a theory) to explain *why* a gas behaves as it does. We want to answer the question *What are the characteristics of the individual gas particles that cause a gas to behave as it does?* However, before we do this let's briefly review the scientific method. Recall that a law is a generalization about behavior that has been observed in many experiments. Laws are very useful; they allow us to predict the behavior of similar systems. For example, a chemist who prepares a new gaseous compound can assume that that substance will obey the ideal gas equation (at least at low *P* and/or high *T*).

However, laws do not tell us *why* nature behaves the way it does. Scientists try to answer this question by constructing theories (building models). The models in chemistry are speculations about how individual atoms or molecules (microscopic particles) cause the behavior of macroscopic systems (collections of atoms and molecules in large enough numbers so that we can observe them).

A model is considered successful if it explains known behavior and predicts correctly the results of future experiments. But a model can never be proved absolutely true. In fact, by its very nature *any model is an approximation* and is destined to be modified, at least in part. Models range from the simple (to predict approximate behavior) to the extraordinarily complex (to account precisely for observed behavior). In this text, we use relatively simple models that fit most experimental results.

13.8 The Kinetic Molecular Theory of Gases

AIM: To understand the basic postulates of the kinetic molecular theory.

A relatively simple model that attempts to explain the behavior of an ideal gas is the **kinetic molecular theory.** This model is based on speculations about the behavior of the individual particles (atoms or molecules) in a gas. The assumptions (postulates) of the kinetic molecular theory can be stated as follows:

Postulates of the Kinetic Molecular Theory of Gases

1. Gases consist of tiny particles (atoms or molecules).

2. These particles are so small, compared with the distances between them, that the volume (size) of the individual particles can be assumed to be negligible (zero).

3. The particles are in constant random motion, colliding with the walls of the container. These collisions with the walls cause the pressure exerted by the gas.

4. The particles are assumed not to attract or to repel each other.

5. The average kinetic energy of the gas particles is directly proportional to the Kelvin temperature of the gas.

The kinetic energy referred to in postulate 5 is the energy associated with the motion of a particle. Kinetic energy (*KE*) is given by the equation $KE = \frac{1}{2}mv^2$, where *m* is the mass of the particle and *v* is the velocity (speed) of the particle. The greater the mass or velocity of a particle, the greater its kinetic energy. Postulate 5 means that if a gas is heated to higher temperatures, the average speed of the particles increases; therefore, their kinetic energy increases.

Although real gases do not conform exactly to the five assumptions listed above, we will see in the next section that these postulates do indeed explain *ideal* gas behavior—behavior shown by real gases at high temperatures and/or low pressures.

13.9 The Implications of the Kinetic Molecular Theory

AIMS: To understand the term temperature. To learn how the kinetic molecular theory explains the gas laws.

In this section we will discuss the *qualitative* relationships between the kinetic molecular (KM) theory and the properties of gases. That is, without going into the mathematical details, we will show how the kinetic molecular theory explains some of the observed properties of gases.

The Meaning of Temperature

In Chapter 2 we introduced temperature very practically as something we measure with a thermometer. We know that as the temperature of an object increases, the object feels "hotter" to the touch. But what does temperature really mean? How does matter change when it gets "hotter"? The kinetic molecular theory allows us to answer this very important question. As postulate 5 of the KM theory states, the temperature of a gas reflects how rapidly, on average, its individual gas particles are moving. At high temperatures the particles move very fast and hit the walls of the container frequently, whereas at low temperatures the particles' motions are more sluggish and they collide with the walls of the container much less often. Therefore, temperature really is a measure of the motions of the gas particles. In fact, the Kelvin temperature of a gas is directly proportional to the average kinetic energy of the gas particles.

The Relationship Between Pressure and Temperature

To see how the meaning of temperature given above helps to explain gas behavior, picture a gas in a rigid container. As the gas is heated to a higher temperature, the particles move faster, hitting the walls more often. And, of course, the impacts become more forceful as the particles move faster. If the pressure is due to collisions with the walls, the gas pressure should increase as temperature is increased.

Is this what we observe when we measure the pressure of a gas as it is heated? Yes. A given sample of gas in a rigid container (if the volume is not changed) shows an increase in pressure as its temperature is increased.

FIGURE 13.13
(a) A gas confined in a cylinder with a movable piston. The gas pressure P_{gas} is just balanced by the external pressure P_{ext}. That is, $P_{gas} = P_{ext}$. (b) The temperature of the gas is increased at constant pressure P_{ext}. The increased particle motions at the higher temperature push back the piston, increasing the volume of the gas.

The Relationship Between Volume and Temperature

Now picture the gas in a container with a movable piston. As shown in Figure 13.13(a), the gas pressure P_{gas} is just balanced by an external pressure P_{ext}. What happens when we heat the gas to a higher temperature? As the temperature increases, the particles move faster, causing the gas pressure to increase. As soon as the gas pressure P_{gas} becomes greater than P_{ext} (the pressure holding the piston), the piston moves up until $P_{gas} = P_{ext}$. Therefore, the KM model predicts that the volume of the gas will increase as we raise its temperature at a constant pressure. This agrees with experimental observations (as summarized by Charles's law).

EXAMPLE 13.14 *Using the Kinetic Molecular Theory to Explain Gas Law Observations*

Use the KM theory to predict what will happen to the pressure of a gas when its volume is decreased (n and T constant). Does this prediction agree with the experimental observations?

Solution

When we decrease the gas's volume (make the container smaller), the particles hit the walls more often because they do not have to travel so far between the walls. This would suggest an increase in pressure. This prediction on the basis of the model is in agreement with experimental observations of gas behavior (as summarized by Boyle's law).

In this section we have seen that the predictions of the kinetic molecular theory generally fit the behavior observed for gases. This makes it a useful and successful model.

13.10 *Gas Stoichiometry*

AIMS: To understand the molar volume of an ideal gas. To learn the definition of STP. To use these concepts and the ideal gas equation.

We have seen repeatedly in this chapter just how useful the ideal gas equation is. For example, if we know the pressure, volume, and temperature for a given sample of gas, we can calculate the number of moles present: $n = PV/RT$. This fact makes it possible to do stoichiometric calculations for reactions involving gases. We will illustrate this process in Example 13.15.

EXAMPLE 13.15   *Gas Stoichiometry: Calculating Volume*

Calculate the volume of oxygen gas produced at 1.00 atm and 25 °C by the complete decomposition of 10.5 g of potassium chlorate. The balanced equation for the reaction is

$$2KClO_3(s) \rightarrow 2KCl(s) + 3O_2(g)$$

Solution

This is a stoichiometry problem very much like the type we considered in Chapter 10. The only difference is that in this case, we want to calculate the volume of a gaseous product rather than the number of grams. To do so, we can use the relationship between moles and volume given by the ideal gas law.

We'll summarize the steps required to do this problem in the following schematic:

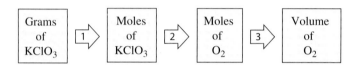

STEP 1.   To find the moles of $KClO_3$ in 10.5 g, we use the molar mass of $KClO_3$ (122.6 g).

$$10.5 \text{ g } KClO_3 \times \frac{1 \text{ mol } KClO_3}{122.6 \text{ g } KClO_3} = 8.56 \times 10^{-2} \text{ mol } KClO_3$$

STEP 2.   To find the moles of O_2 produced, we use the mole ratio of O_2 to $KClO_3$ derived from the balanced equation.

$$8.56 \times 10^{-2} \text{ mol } KClO_3 \times \frac{3 \text{ mol } O_2}{2 \text{ mol } KClO_3} = 1.28 \times 10^{-1} \text{ mol } O_2$$

STEP 3.   To find the volume of oxygen produced, we use the ideal gas law $PV = nRT$, where

$$P = 1.00 \text{ atm}$$
$$V = ?$$
$$n = 1.28 \times 10^{-1} \text{ mol, the moles of } O_2 \text{ we calculated}$$
$$R = 0.08206 \text{ L atm/K mol}$$
$$T = 25 \text{ °C} = 25 + 273 = 298 \text{ K}$$

Solving the ideal gas law for V gives

$$V = \frac{nRT}{P} = \frac{(1.28 \times 10^{-1} \text{ mol})\left(0.08206 \frac{\text{L atm}}{\text{K mol}}\right)(298 \text{ K})}{1.00 \text{ atm}} = 3.13 \text{ L}$$

Thus 3.13 L of O_2 will be produced.

 Self-Check Exercise 13.11

Calculate the volume of hydrogen produced at 1.50 atm and 19 °C by the reaction of 26.5 g of zinc with excess hydrochloric acid according to the balanced

equation

$$Zn(s) + 2HCl(aq) \rightarrow ZnCl_2(aq) + H_2(g)$$

See Problems 13.85 through 13.92

In dealing with the stoichiometry of reactions involving gases, it is useful to define the volume occupied by 1 mol of a gas under certain specified conditions. For 1 mol of an ideal gas at 0 °C (273 K) and 1 atm, the volume of the gas given by the ideal gas law is

$$V = \frac{nRT}{P} = \frac{(1.00 \text{ mol})(0.08206 \text{ L atm/K mol})(273 \text{ K})}{1.00 \text{ atm}} = 22.4 \text{ L}$$

This volume of 22.4 L is called the **molar volume** of an ideal gas.

STP: 0 °C and 1 atm

The conditions 0 °C and 1 atm are called **standard temperature and pressure** (abbreviated **STP**). Properties of gases are often given under these conditions. Remember, the molar volume of an ideal gas is 22.4 L *at STP.* That is, 22.4 L contains 1 mol of an ideal gas at STP.

EXAMPLE 13.16   *Gas Stoichiometry: Calculations Involving Gases at STP*

A sample of nitrogen gas has a volume of 1.75 L at STP. How many moles of N_2 are present?

Solution

We could solve this problem by using the ideal gas equation, but we can take a shortcut by using the molar volume of an ideal gas at STP. Because 1 mol of an ideal gas at STP has a volume of 22.4 L, a 1.75-L sample of N_2 at STP contains considerably less than 1 mol. We can find how many moles by using the equivalence statement

$$1.000 \text{ mol} = 22.4 \text{ L (STP)}$$

which leads to the conversion factor we need:

$$1.75 \text{ L } N_2 \times \frac{1.000 \text{ mol } N_2}{22.4 \text{ L } N_2} = 7.81 \times 10^{-2} \text{ mol } N_2$$

 Self-Check Exercise 13.12

Ammonia is commonly used as a fertilizer to provide a source of nitrogen for plants. A sample of $NH_3(g)$ occupies 5.00 L at 25 °C and 15.0 atm. What volume will this sample occupy at STP?

See Problems 13.95 through 13.98

Standard conditions (STP) and molar volume are also useful in carrying out stoichiometric calculations on reactions involving gases, as shown in Example 13.17.

EXAMPLE 13.17   *Gas Stoichiometry: Reactions Involving Gases at STP*

Quicklime, CaO, is produced by heating calcium carbonate, $CaCO_3$. Calculate the volume of CO_2 produced at STP from the decomposition of 152 g

of $CaCO_3$ according to the reaction

$$CaCO_3(s) \rightarrow CaO(s) + CO_2(g)$$

Solution

The strategy for solving this problem is summarized by the following schematic:

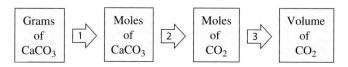

STEP 1. Using the molar mass of $CaCO_3$ (100.1 g), we calculate the number of moles of $CaCO_3$.

$$152 \text{ g CaCO}_3 \times \frac{1 \text{ mol CaCO}_3}{100.0 \text{ g CaCO}_3} = 1.52 \text{ mol CaCO}_3$$

STEP 2. Each mole of $CaCO_3$ produces 1 mol of CO_2, so 1.52 mol of CO_2 will be formed.

STEP 3. We can convert the moles of CO_2 to volume by using the molar volume of an ideal gas, because the conditions are STP.

$$1.52 \text{ mol CO}_2 \times \frac{22.4 \text{ L CO}_2}{1 \text{ mol CO}_2} = 34.1 \text{ L CO}_2$$

Thus the decomposition of 152 g of $CaCO_3$ produces 34.1 L of CO_2 at STP.

Remember that the molar volume of an ideal gas is 22.4 L at STP.

Note that the final step in Example 13.17 involves calculating the volume of gas from the number of moles. Because the conditions were specified as STP, we were able to use the molar volume of a gas at STP. If the conditions of a problem are different from STP, we must use the ideal gas law to compute the volume, as we did in Section 13.5.

Chapter Review

Key Terms

barometer *(13.1)*
mm Hg *(13.1)*
torr *(13.1)*
standard atmosphere *(13.1)*
pascal *(13.1)*
Boyle's law *(13.2)*
absolute zero *(13.2)*
Charles's law *(13.3)*
Avogadro's law *(13.4)*
universal gas constant *(13.5)*
ideal gas law *(13.5)*

ideal gas *(13.5)*
combined gas law *(13.5)*
partial pressures *(13.6)*
Dalton's law of partial
  pressures *(13.6)*
kinetic molecular theory
  (13.8)
molar volume *(13.10)*
standard temperature and
  pressure (STP) *(13.10)*

Summary

1. Atmospheric pressure is measured with a barometer. The most commonly used units of pressure are mm Hg (torr), atmospheres, and pascals (the SI unit).

2. Boyle's law states that the volume of a given amount of gas is inversely proportional to its pressure (at constant temperature): $PV = k$ or $P = k/V$. That is, as pressure increases, volume decreases.

3. Charles's law states that, for a given amount of gas at constant pressure, the volume is directly proportional to the temperature (in kelvins): $V = bT$. At -273 °C (0 K),

the volume of a gas extrapolates to zero, and this temperature is called absolute zero.

4. Avogadro's law states that for a gas at constant temperature and pressure, the volume is directly proportional to the number of moles of gas: $V = an$.

5. These three laws can be combined into the ideal gas law, $PV = nRT$, where R is called the universal gas constant. This equation makes it possible to calculate any one of the properties—volume, pressure, temperature, or moles of gas present—given the other three. A gas that obeys this equation is said to behave ideally.

6. From the ideal gas equation we can derive the combined gas law,

$$\frac{P_1V_1}{T_1} = \frac{P_2V_2}{T_2}$$

which holds when the amount of gas (moles) remains constant.

7. The pressure of a gas mixture is described by Dalton's law of partial pressures, which states that the total pressure of the mixture of gases in a container is the sum of the partial pressures of the gases that make up the mixture.

8. The kinetic molecular theory of gases is a model that accounts for ideal gas behavior. This model assumes that a gas consists of tiny particles with negligible volumes, that there are no interactions among particles, and that the particles are in constant motion, colliding with the container walls to produce pressure.

Questions and Problems

All even-numbered exercises have answers in the back of this book and solutions in the Solutions Guide.

13.1 ■ *Pressure*

QUESTIONS

1. What are the three physical states of matter? Summarize the properties of each of these states.

2. How are the three states of matter similar, and how do they differ?

3. What is meant by "the pressure of the atmosphere"? What causes this pressure?

4. How do we measure atmospheric pressure? Is the atmospheric pressure constant everywhere on the surface of the earth?

5. One *standard atmosphere* of pressure is equivalent to _____ pascals.

6. One *standard atmosphere* of pressure is equivalent to _____ mm Hg.

PROBLEMS

7. Convert the following pressures into atmospheres.
   a. 724 torr
   b. 127 kPa
   c. 744 mm Hg
   d. 135,400 Pa

8. Convert the following pressures to units of atmospheres.
   a. 110.2 kPa
   b. 74.2 cm Hg
   c. 441 mm Hg
   d. 921 torr

9. Convert the following pressures into mm Hg.
   a. 0.989 atm
   b. 102.4 kPa
   c. 924 torr
   d. 1.03 atm

10. Convert the following pressures to units of mm Hg.
    a. 1.02 atm
    b. 121.4 kPa
    c. 792 torr
    d. 1.09×10^4 Pa

11. Convert the following pressures into pascals.
    a. 774 torr
    b. 0.965 atm
    c. 112.5 kPa
    d. 801 mm Hg

12. Convert the following pressures to units of kilopascals.
    a. 2.07×10^6 Pa
    b. 795 mm Hg
    c. 10.9 atm
    d. 659 torr

13.2 ■ *Pressure and Volume: Boyle's Law*

QUESTIONS

13. When the pressure on a sample of gas is increased (at constant temperature), the volume of the sample _____.

14. When the volume of a sample of gas is decreased, the pressure of the sample of gas _____.

15. The volume of a sample of ideal gas is _____ proportional to the pressure on it at constant temperature.

16. A mathematical expression that summarizes Boyle's law is _____.

PROBLEMS

17. For each of the following sets of pressure/volume data, calculate the missing quantity. Assume that the temperature and the amount of gas remain constant.
    a. $V = 1.05$ L at 989 mm Hg; $V = ?$ at 761 mm Hg
    b. $V = 255$ mL at 1.31 atm; $V = 211$ mL at ? atm
    c. $V = 11.2$ L at 761 mm Hg; $V = ?$ at 1.15 atm

18. For each of the following sets of pressure/volume data, calculate the missing quantity. Assume that the temperature and the mass of gas remain constant.
    a. $V = 541$ mL at 1.00 atm; $V = ?$ at 699 torr
    b. $V = 2.32$ L at 110.2 kPa; $V = ?$ at 0.995 atm
    c. $V = 4.15$ mL at 135 atm; $V = 10.0$ mL at ? mm Hg

19. For each of the following sets of pressure/volume data, calculate the missing quantity. Assume that the temperature and the amount of gas remain constant.
    a. $V = 19.3$ L at 102.1 kPa; $V = 10.0$ L at ? kPa
    b. $V = 25.7$ mL at 755 torr; $V = ?$ at 761 mm Hg
    c. $V = 51.2$ L at 1.05 atm; $V = ?$ at 112.2 kPa

20. For each of the following sets of pressure/volume data, calculate the missing quantity. Assume that the temperature and the mass of gas remain constant.
    a. $V = 561$ mL at 1.82 atm; $V = ?$ at 245 mm Hg
    b. $V = 561$ mL at 1.82 atm; $V = ?$ at 1.82 kPa
    c. $V = 561$ mL at 1.82 atm; $V = ?$ at 2.45×10^4 Pa

21. The pressure on a 6.24-L sample of gas is increased from 1.04 atm to 2.18 atm. What will be the new volume of the gas (at constant temperature)?

22. If the pressure exerted on the gas in a weather balloon decreases from 1.01 atm to 0.562 atm as it rises, by what factor will the volume of the gas in the balloon increase as it rises?

23. A 1.04-L sample of gas at 759 mm Hg pressure is expanded until its volume is 2.24 L. What will be the pressure in the expanded gas sample (at constant temperature)?

24. What pressure (in atmospheres) is required to compress 1.00 L of gas at 760. mm Hg pressure to a volume of 50.0 mL?

13.3 ■ Volume and Temperature: Charles's Law

QUESTIONS

25. What is meant by the *absolute zero* of temperature?

26. How can Charles's law be used to determine absolute zero?

27. The volume of a sample of ideal gas is _____ proportional to its temperature (K) at constant pressure.

28. A mathematical expression that summarizes Charles's law is _____.

PROBLEMS

29. If a 25.0-mL sample of nitrogen gas at 26.2 °C is cooled to 15.4 °C, what is the new volume of the gas?

30. If 525 mL of gas at 25 °C is heated to 50. °C, at constant pressure, calculate the new volume of the sample.

31. For each of the following sets of volume/temperature data, calculate the missing quantity. Assume that the pressure and the amount of gas remain constant.
    a. V455 mL at 19 °C; $V = ?$ at 45 °C
    b. $V = 5.51$ L at 297 K; $V = 1.75$ L at ? °C
    c. $V = 227$ L at 359 K; $V = 541$ mL at ? °C

32. For each of the following sets of volume/temperature data, calculate the missing quantity. Assume that the pressure and the mass of gas remain constant.
    a. $V = 25.0$ L at 0 °C; $V = 50.0$ L at ? °C
    b. $V = 247$ mL at 25 °C; $V = 255$ mL at ? °C.
    c. $V = 1.00$ mL at -272 °C; $V = ?$ at 25 °C

33. For each of the following sets of volume/temperature data, calculate the missing quantity. Assume that the pressure and the amount of gas remain constant.
    a. $V = 25$ mL at 25 °C; $V = ?$ at 0 °C
    b. $V = 10.2$ L at 100. °C; $V = ?$ at 100 K
    c. $V = 551$ mL at 75 °C; $V = 1.00$ mL at ? °C

34. For each of the following sets of volume/temperature data, calculate the missing quantity. Assume that the pressure and the mass of gas remain constant.
    a. $V = 2.01 \times 10^2$ L at 1150 °C; $V = 5.00$ L at ? °C
    b. $V = 44.2$ mL at 298 K; $V = ?$ at 0 K
    c. $V = 44.2$ mL at 298 K; $V = ?$ at 0 °C

35. To what temperature must 500. mL of gas at 22 °C be cooled, at constant pressure, so that the volume of the gas is reduced to 1.00 mL?

36. A sample of neon gas occupies 266 mL at 25.2 °C. At what temperature would the volume of this sample of neon be reduced to half its initial size (at constant pressure)? At what temperature would the volume of this sample of neon be doubled (at constant pressure)?

37. The label on an aerosol spray can contains a warning that the can should not be heated to over 130 °F because of the danger of explosion due to the pressure increase as it is heated. Calculate the potential volume of the gas contained in a 500.-mL aerosol can when it is heated from 25 °C to 54 °C (approximately 130 °F), assuming a constant pressure.

38. As we noted in Example 13.6, gas volume was formerly used as a way to measure temperature by applying Charles's law. Suppose a sample in a gas thermometer has a volume of 135 mL at 11 °C. Indicate what temperature would correspond to each of the following volumes, assuming that the pressure remains constant: 113 mL, 142 mL, 155 mL, 127 mL.

13.4 ■ Volume and Moles: Avogadro's Law

QUESTIONS

39. At conditions of constant temperature and pressure, the volume of a sample of ideal gas is _____ proportional to the number of moles of gas present.

40. A mathematical expression that summarizes Avogadro's law is _____.

PROBLEMS

41. If 0.214 mol of argon gas occupies a volume of 652 mL at a particular temperature and pressure, what vol-

ume would 0.375 mol of argon have under the same conditions?

42. If 0.500 mol of nitrogen gas occupies a volume of 11.2 L at 0 °C, what volume will 2.00 mol of nitrogen occupy under the same conditions?

43. If 3.25 mol of argon gas occupies a volume of 100. L at a particular temperature and pressure, what volume does 14.15 mol of argon occupy under the same conditions?

44. If 46.2 g of oxygen gas occupies a volume of 100. L at a particular temperature and pressure, what volume will 5.00 g of oxygen gas occupy under the same conditions?

13.5 ■ *The Ideal Gas Law*

QUESTIONS

45. What do we mean by an *ideal* gas?

46. Under what conditions do *real* gases behave most ideally?

47. Show how Boyle's gas law can be derived from the ideal gas law.

48. Show how Charles's gas law can be derived from the ideal gas law.

PROBLEMS

49. Given each of the following sets of values for three of the gas variables, calculate the unknown quantity.
    a. $P = 1.024$ atm; $V = ?$; $n = 0.0104$ mol; $T = 279$ K
    b. $P = 755$ mm Hg; $V = 255$ mL; $n = ?$; $T = 27$ °C
    c. $P = 12.2$ atm; $V = 34.1$ mL; $n = 0.000104$ mol; $T = ?$

50. Given each of the following sets of values for an ideal gas, calculate the unknown quantity.
    a. $P = 782$ mm Hg; $V = ?$; $n = 0.210$ mol; $T = 27$ °C
    b. $P = ?$ mm Hg; $V = 644$ mL; $n = 0.0921$ mol; $T = 303$ K
    c. $P = 745$ mm Hg; $V = 11.2$ L; $n = 0.401$ mol; $T = ?$ K

51. Given each of the following sets of values for three of the gas variables, calculate the unknown quantity.
    a. $P = 7.74 \times 10^3$ Pa; $V = 12.2$ mL; $n = ?$ mol; $T = 298$ K
    b. $P = ?$ mm Hg; $V = 43.0$ mL; $n = 0.421$ mol; $T = 223$ K
    c. $P = 455$ mm Hg; $V = ?$ mL; $n = 4.4 \times 10^{-2}$ mol; $T = 331$ °C

52. Given each of the following sets of values for an ideal gas, calculate the unknown quantity.
    a. $P = 1.01$ atm; $V = ?$; $n = 0.00831$ mol; $T = 25$ °C
    b. $P = ?$ atm; $V = 602$ mL; $n = 8.01 \times 10^{-3}$ mol; $T = 310$ K
    c. $P = 0.998$ atm; $V = 629$ mL; $n = ?$ mol; $T = 35$ °C

53. At what temperature does 5.25 g of helium occupy a volume of 10.0 L at a pressure of 1.02 atm?

54. What volume is occupied by 5.03 g of O_2 at 28 °C and a pressure of 0.998 atm?

55. Suppose two 200.0-L tanks are to be filled separately with the gases helium and hydrogen. What mass of each gas is needed to produce a pressure of 135 atm in its respective tank at 24 °C?

56. Suppose two 200.0-L tanks are to be filled separately with the gases helium and hydrogen. What mass of each gas is needed to produce a pressure of 135 atm in its respective tank at 24 °C?

57. At what temperature will a 1.0-g sample of neon gas exert a pressure of 500. torr in a 5.0-L container?

58. At what temperature does 16.3 g of nitrogen gas have a pressure of 1.25 atm in a 25.0-L tank?

59. What is the pressure in a 25-L vessel containing 1.0 kg of oxygen gas at 300. K?

60. Calculate the pressure in a 212-L tank containing 51.3 lb of argon gas at 25 °C.

61. When 500. mL of O_2 gas at 25 °C and 1.045 atm is cooled to −40. °C and the pressure is increased to 2.00 atm, what is the new volume of the gas sample?

62. What will be the new volume if 125 mL of He gas at 100 °C and 0.981 atm is cooled to 25 °C and the pressure is increased to 1.15 atm?

63. What is the final pressure for a sample of gas when 500. mL of the gas is cooled from 25 °C and 1.00 atm to −272 °C with no change in the volume of the sample?

64. At what temperature does 5.00 g of H_2 occupy a volume of 50.0 L at a pressure of 761 mm Hg?

13.6 ■ *Dalton's Law of Partial Pressures*

QUESTIONS

65. Explain why the measured properties of a mixture of gases depend only on the total number of moles of particles, not on the identity of the individual gas particles. How is this observation summarized as a law?

66. We often collect small samples of gases in the laboratory by bubbling the gas into a bottle or flask containing water. Explain why the gas becomes saturated with water vapor and how we must take the presence of water vapor into account when calculating the properties of the gas sample.

PROBLEMS

67. If 4.0 g of $O_2(g)$ and 4.0 g of $He(g)$ are placed in a 5.0-L vessel at 65 °C, what will be the partial pressure of each gas and the total pressure in the vessel?

68. A gaseous mixture contains 5.23 g of N_2 and 4.41 g of O_2. What volume does this mixture occupy at 25 °C and 1.00 atm pressure?

69. A tank contains a mixture of 3.0 mol of N_2, 2.0 mol of O_2, and 1.0 mol of CO_2 at 25 °C and a total pressure of 10.0 atm. Calculate the partial pressure (in torr) of each gas in the mixture.

70. What pressure exists in a 25.0-L tank containing 50.1 g of O_2 and 26.3 g of N_2 at 27 °C?

71. A sample of oxygen gas is saturated with water vapor at 27 °C. The total pressure of the mixture is 772 torr, and the vapor pressure of water is 26.7 torr at 27 °C. What is the partial pressure of the oxygen gas?

72. A sample of oxygen gas is collected by displacement of water at 25 °C and 1.02 atm total pressure. If the vapor pressure of water is 23.756 mm Hg at 25 °C, what is the partial pressure of the oxygen gas in the sample?

73. A 500.-mL sample of O_2 gas at 24 °C was prepared by decomposing a 3% aqueous solution of hydrogen peroxide, H_2O_2, in the presence of a small amount of manganese catalyst by the reaction

$$2H_2O_2(aq) \rightarrow 2H_2O(g) + O_2(g)$$

The oxygen thus prepared was collected by displacement of water. The total pressure of gas collected was 755 mm Hg. What is the partial pressure of O_2 in the mixture? How many moles of O_2 are in the mixture? (The vapor pressure of water at 24 °C is 23 mm Hg.)

74. Small quantities of hydrogen gas can be prepared in the laboratory by the addition of aqueous hydrochloric acid to metallic zinc.

$$Zn(s) + 2HCl(aq) \rightarrow ZnCl_2(aq) + H_2(g)$$

Typically, the hydrogen gas is bubbled through water for collection and becomes saturated with water vapor. Suppose 240. mL of hydrogen gas is collected at 30. °C and has a total pressure of 1.032 atm by this process. What is the partial pressure of hydrogen gas in the sample? How many moles of hydrogen gas are present in the sample? How many grams of zinc must have reacted to produce this quantity of hydrogen? (The vapor pressure of water is 32 torr at 30 °C.)

13.7 ■ *Laws and Models: A Review*

QUESTIONS

75. What is a scientific *law*? What is a *theory*? How do these concepts differ? Does a law explain a theory, or does a theory attempt to explain a law?

76. When is a scientific theory considered to be successful? Are all theories successful? Will a theory that has

been successful in the past necessarily be successful in the future?

13.8 ■ *The Kinetic Molecular Theory of Gases*

QUESTIONS

77. The observed behavior of gases indicates that the volumes of the actual molecules present are _____ compared to the bulk volume of the gas sample.

78. The kinetic molecular theory of gases proposes that the observed pressure of the gas arises from _____ of the gas molecules with the walls of their container.

79. Temperature is a measure of the average _____ of the molecules in a sample of gas.

80. The kinetic molecular theory of gases suggests that gas particles exert _____ attractive or repulsive forces on each other.

13.9 ■ *The Implications of the Kinetic Molecular Theory*

QUESTIONS

81. How is the phenomenon of temperature explained on the basis of the kinetic molecular theory? What microscopic property of gas molecules is reflected in the temperature measured?

82. Explain, in terms of the kinetic molecular theory, how an increase in the temperature of a gas confined to a rigid container causes an increase in the pressure of the gas.

13.10 ■ *Gas Stoichiometry*

QUESTIONS

83. What is the *molar volume* of a gas? Do all gases that behave ideally have the same molar volume?

84. What conditions are considered "standard temperature and pressure" (STP) for gases? Suggest a reason why these particular conditions might have been chosen for STP.

PROBLEMS

85. Consider the following *unbalanced* chemical equation for the decomposition of nitrogen triiodide.

$$NI_3(s) \rightarrow N_2(g) + I_2(s)$$

What volume of nitrogen gas is produced at 27 °C and 755 mm Hg if 1.24 g of nitrogen triiodide decomposes?

86. Consider the following reaction:

$$P_4(s) + 6H_2(g) \rightarrow 4PH_3(g)$$

What volume of hydrogen gas, at 25 °C and 753 mm Hg, is required to react exactly with 2.51 g of phosphorus?

87. Consider the following *unbalanced* chemical equation for the combustion of propane.

$$C_3H_8(g) + O_2(g) \rightarrow CO_2(g) + H_2O(g)$$

What volume of oxygen gas at 25 °C and 1.04 atm is needed for the complete combustion of 5.53 g of propane?

88. Zinc Metal reacts vigorously with chlorine gas to form zinc chloride:

$$Zn(s) + Cl_2(g) \rightarrow ZnCl_2(s)$$

What volume of chlorine gas at 35 °C and 1.01 atm is required to react completely with 1.13 g of zinc?

89. Consider the following *unbalanced* chemical equation.

$$Si(s) + N_2(g) \rightarrow Si_3N_4(s)$$

What volume of nitrogen gas, measured at 100. °C and 802 torr, is required to react with 115 g of Si?

90. When calcium carbonate is heated strongly, carbon dioxide gas is evolved:

$$CaCO_3(s) \rightarrow CaO(s) + CO_2(g)$$

If 4.74 g of calcium carbonate is heated, what volume of $CO_2(g)$ would be produced when collected at 26 °C and 0.997 atm?

91. Many transition metal salts are hydrates: they contain a fixed number of water molecules bound per formula unit of the salt. For example, copper(II) sulfate most commonly exists as the pentahydrate, $CuSO_4 \cdot 5H_2O$. If 5.00 g of $CuSO_4 \cdot 5H_2O$ is heated strongly so as to drive off all of the waters of hydration as water vapor, what volume will this water vapor occupy at 350. °C and a pressure of 1.04 atm?

92. If water is added to magnesium nitride, ammonia gas is produced when the mixture is heated.

$$Mg_3N_2(s) + 3H_2O(l) \rightarrow 3MgO(s) + 2NH_3(g)$$

If 10.3 g of magnesium nitride is treated with water, what volume of ammonia gas would be collected at 24 °C and 752 mm Hg?

93. What volume does 16.0 g of O_2 occupy at STP?

94. What volume does a mixture of 2.01 g He(g) and 4.14 g $N_2(g)$ occupy at 45 °C and 1.02 atm?

95. An ideal gas has a volume of 50. mL at 100. °C and a pressure of 690 torr. Calculate the volume of his sample of gas at STP.

96. A sample of hydrogen gas has a volume of 145 mL when measured at 44 °C and 1.47 atm. What volume would the hydrogen sample occupy at STP?

97. A mixture contains 5.00 g *each* of O_2, N_2, CO_2, and Ne

gas. Calculate the volume of this mixture at STP. Calculate the partial pressure of each gas in the mixture at STP.

98. A gaseous mixture contains 6.25 g of He and 4.97 g of Ne. What volume does the mixture occupy at STP? Calculate the partial pressure of each gas in the mixture at STP.

99. Given the following *unbalanced* chemical equation for the combination reaction of sodium metal and chlorine gas

$$Na(s) + Cl_2(g) \rightarrow NaCl(s)$$

what volume of chlorine gas, measured at STP, is necessary for the complete reaction of 4.81 g of sodium metal?

100. What volume of chlorine gas at STP is required for the complete reaction with 10.2 g of nitrogen in the following reaction?

$$N_2(g) + 3Cl_2(g) \rightarrow 2NCl_3(g)$$

101. During the making of steel, iron(II) oxide is reduced to metallic iron by treatment with carbon monoxide gas.

$$FeO(s) + CO(g) \rightarrow Fe(s) + CO_2(g)$$

102. Potassium permanganate, $KMnO_4$, is produced commercially by oxidizing aqueous potassium manganate, K_2MnO_4, with chlorine gas. The *unbalanced* chemical equation is

$$K_2MnO_4(aq) + Cl_2(g) \rightarrow KMnO_4(s) + KCl(aq)$$

What volume of $Cl_2(g)$, measured at STP, is needed to produce 10.0 g of $KMnO_4$?

Additional Problems

103. When doing any calculation involving gas samples, we must express the temperature in terms of the _____ temperature scale.

104. Two moles of ideal gas occupy a volume that is _____ the volume of 1 mol of ideal gas under the same temperature and pressure conditions.

105. Summarize the postulates of the kinetic molecular theory for gases. How does the kinetic molecular theory account for the observed properties of temperature and pressure?

106. Give a formula or equation that represents each of the following gas laws.
a. Boyle's law   d. the ideal gas law
b. Charles's law   e. the combined gas law
c. Avogadro's law

107. For a mixture of gases in the same container, the total pressure exerted by the mixture of gases is the _____ of the pressures that those gases would exert if

they were alone in the container under the same conditions.

108. A helium tank contains 25.2 L of helium at 8.40 atm pressure. Determine how many 1.50-L balloons at 755 mm Hg can be inflated with the gas in the tank, assuming that the tank will also have to contain He at 755 mm Hg after the balloons are filled (that is, it is not possible to empty the tank completely). The temperature is 25 °C in all cases.

109. As weather balloons rise from the earth's surface, the pressure of the atmosphere becomes less, tending to cause the volume of the balloon to expand. However, the temperature is much lower in the upper atmosphere than at sea level. Would this temperature effect tend to make such a balloon expand or contract? Weather balloons do, in fact, expand as they rise. What does this tell you?

110. Consider the following chemical equation.

$$2NO_2(g) \rightarrow N_2O_4(g)$$

If 25.0 mL of NO_2 gas is completely converted to N_2O_4 gas under the same conditions, what volume will the N_2O_4 occupy?

111. Carbon dioxide gas, in the dry state, may be produced by heating calcium carbonate.

$$CaCO_3(s) \rightarrow CaO(s) + CO_2(g)$$

What volume of CO_2, collected dry at 55 °C and a pressure of 774 torr, is produced by complete thermal decomposition of 10.0 g of $CaCO_3$?

112. Carbon dioxide gas, saturated with water vapor, can be produced by the addition of aqueous acid to calcium carbonate.

$$CaCO_3(s) + 2H^+(aq) \rightarrow Ca^{2+}(aq) + H_2O(l) + CO_2(g)$$

How many moles of $CO_2(g)$, collected at 60. °C and 774 torr total pressure, are produced by the complete reaction of 10.0 g of $CaCO_3$ with acid? What volume does this wet CO_2 occupy? What volume would the CO_2 occupy at 774 torr if a desiccant (a chemical drying agent) were added to remove the water? (The vapor pressure of water at 60. °C is 149.4 mm Hg.)

113. Sulfur trioxide, SO_3, is produced in enormous quantities each year for use in the synthesis of sulfuric acid.

$$S(s) + O_2(g) \rightarrow SO_2(g)$$
$$2SO_2(g) + O_2(g) \rightarrow 2SO_3(g)$$

What volume of $O_2(g)$ at 350. °C and a pressure of 5.25 atm is needed to completely convert 5.00 g of sulfur to sulfur trioxide?

114. Calculate the volume of $O_2(g)$ produced at 25 °C and 630. torr when 50.0 g of $KClO_3(s)$ is heated in the presence of a small amount of MnO_2 catalyst.

115. If 10.0 g of liquid helium at 1.7 K is completely vaporized, what volume does the helium occupy at STP?

116. Convert the following pressures into atmospheres.
    a. 665 mm Hg
    b. 124 kPa
    c. 2.540×10^6 Pa
    d. 803 torr

117. Convert the following pressures into mm Hg.
    a. 0.903 atm
    b. 2.1240×10^6 Pa
    c. 445 kPa
    d. 342 torr

118. Convert the following pressures into pascals.
    a. 645 mm Hg
    b. 221 kPa
    c. 0.876 atm
    d. 32 torr

119. For each of the following sets of pressure/volume data, calculate the missing quantity. Assume that the temperature and the amount of gas remain constant.
    a. $V = 123$ L at 4.56 atm; $V = ?$ at 1002 mm Hg
    b. $V = 634$ mL at 25.2 mm Hg; $V = 166$ mL at ? atm
    c. $V = 443$ L at 511 torr; $V = ?$ at 1.05 kPa

120. For each of the following sets of pressure/volume data, calculate the missing quantity. Assume that the temperature and the amount of gas remain constant.
    a. $V = 255$ mL at 1.00 mm Hg; $V = ?$ at 2.00 torr
    b. $V = 1.3$ L at 1.0 kPa; $V = ?$ at 1.0 atm
    c. $V = 1.3$ L at 1.0 kPa; $V = ?$ at 1.0 mm Hg

121. A particular balloon is designed by its manufacturer to be inflated to a volume of no more than 2.5 L. If the balloon is filled with 2.0 L of helium at sea level, is released, and rises to an altitude at which the atmospheric pressure is only 500. mm Hg, will the balloon burst?

122. What pressure is needed to compress the air in a 1.105-L cylinder at 755 torr to a volume of 1.00 mL?

123. An expandable vessel contains 729 mL of gas at 22 °C. What volume will the gas sample in the vessel have if it is placed in a boiling water bath (100. °C)?

124. For each of the following sets of volume/temperature data, calculate the missing quantity. Assume that the pressure and the amount of gas remain constant.
    a. $V = 100.$ mL at 74 °C; $V = ?$ at -74 °C
    b. $V = 500.$ mL at 100 °C; $V = 600.$ mL at ? °C
    c. $V = 10,000$ L at 25 °C; $V = ?$ at 0 K

125. For each of the following sets of volume/temperature data, calculate the missing quantity. Assume that the pressure and the amount of gas remain constant.
    a. $V = 22.4$ L at 0 °C; $V = 44.4$ L at ? K
    b. $V = 1.0 \times 10^{-3}$ mL at -272 °C; $V = ?$ at 25 °C
    c. $V = 32.3$ L at -40 °C; $V = 1000.$ L at ? °C

126. A 25-L sample of nitrogen gas is cooled from 25 °C to a final temperature of $-100.$ °C. What is the new volume of the gas?

127. If 4.0 g of helium gas occupies a volume of 22.4 L at 0 °C and a pressure of 1.0 atm, what volume does 3.0 g of He occupy under the same conditions?

128. If 23.2 g of a given gas occupies a volume of 93.2 L at a particular temperature and pressure, what mass of the gas occupies a volume of 10.4 L under the same conditions?

129. Given each of the following sets of values for three of the gas variables, calculate the unknown quantity.
    a. $P = 21.2$ atm; $V = 142$ mL; $n = 0.432$ mol; $T = ?$ K
    b. $P = ?$ atm: $V = 1.23$ mL; $n = 0.000115$ mol; $T = 293$ K
    c. $P = 755$ mm Hg; $V = ?$ mL; $n = 0.473$ mol; $T = 131$ °C

130. Given each of the following sets of values for three of the gas variables, calculate the unknown quantity.
    a. $P = 1.034$ atm; $V = 21.2$ mL; $n = 0.00432$ mol; $T = ?$ K
    b. $P = ?$ atm; $V = 1.73$ mL; $n = 0.000115$ mol; $T = 182$ K
    c. $P = 1.23$ mm Hg; $V = ?$ L; $n = 0.773$ mol; $T = 152$ °C

131. What volume is occupied by 32.0 g of SO_2 at 22 °C and a pressure of 1.054 atm?

132. Suppose three 100.-L tanks are to be filled separately with the gases CH_4, N_2, and CO_2, respectively. What mass of each gas is needed to produce a pressure of 120. atm in its tank at 27 °C?

133. At what temperature does 4.00 g of helium gas have a pressure of 1.00 atm in a 22.4-L vessel?

134. What is the pressure in a 100.-mL flask containing 55 mg of oxygen gas at 26 °C?

135. A weather balloon is filled with 1.0 L of helium at 23 °C and 1.0 atm. What volume does the balloon have when it has risen to a point in the atmosphere where the pressure is 220 torr and the temperature is -31 °C?

136. At what temperature does 100. mL of N_2 at 300. K and 1.13 atm occupy a volume of 500. mL at a pressure of 1.89 atm?

137. If 1.0 mol of $N_2(g)$ is injected into a 5.0-L tank already containing 50. g of O_2 at 25 °C, what will be the total pressure in the tank?

138. A mixture contains 5.0 g *each* of O_2, N_2, CO_2, and Ne gas. Calculate the volume of this mixture at 29 °C and a pressure of 755 mm Hg.

139. A flask of hydrogen gas is collected at 1.023 atm and 35 °C by displacement of water from the flask. The vapor pressure of water at 35 °C is 42.2 mm Hg. What is the partial pressure of hydrogen gas in the flask?

140. Consider the following chemical equation.

$$N_2(g) + 3H_2(g) \rightarrow 2NH_3(g)$$

What volumes of nitrogen gas and hydrogen gas, each measured at 11 °C and 0.998 atm, are needed to produce 5.00 g of ammonia?

141. Consider the following *unbalanced* chemical equation.

$$C_6H_{12}O_6(s) + O_2(g) \rightarrow CO_2(g) + H_2O(g)$$

What volume of oxygen gas, measured at 28 °C and 0.976 atm, is needed to react with 5.00 g of $C_6H_{12}O_6$? What volume of each product is produced under the same conditions?

142. Consider the following *unbalanced* chemical equation.

$$Cu_2S(s) + O_2(g) \rightarrow Cu_2O(s) + SO_2(g)$$

What volume of oxygen gas, measured at 27.5 °C and 0.998 atm, is required to react with 25 g of copper(I) sulfide? What volume of sulfur dioxide gas is produced under the same conditions?

143. When sodium bicarbonate, $NaHCO_3(s)$, is heated, sodium carbonate is produced, with the evolution of water vapor and carbon dioxide gas.

$$2NaHCO_3(s) \rightarrow Na_2CO_3(s) + H_2O(g) + CO_2(g)$$

What total volume of gas, measured at 29 °C and 769 torr, is produced when 1.00 g of $NaHCO_3(s)$ is completely converted to $Na_2CO_3(s)$?

144. What volume does 35 moles of N_2 occupy at STP?

145. A sample of oxygen gas has a volume of 125 L at 25 °C and a pressure of 0.987 atm. Calculate the volume of this oxygen sample at STP.

146. A mixture contains 5.0 g of He, 1.0 g of Ar, and 3.5 g of Ne. Calculate the volume of this mixture at STP. Calculate the partial pressure of each gas in the mixture at STP.

147. What volume of hydrogen gas at STP is required for the complete reaction of 10.0 g of nitrogen in the following reaction?

$$N_2(g) + 3H_2(g) \rightarrow 2NH_3(g)$$

148. Concentrated hydrogen peroxide solutions are explosively decomposed by traces of transition metal ions (such as Mn or Fe):

$$2H_2O_2(aq) \rightarrow 2H_2O(l) + O_2(g)$$

What volume of pure $O_2(g)$, collected at 27 °C and 764 torr, would be generated by decomposition of 125 g of a 50.0% by mass hydrogen peroxide solution?

14

Liquids and Solids

You have only to think about water to appreciate how different the three states of matter are. Flying, swimming, and ice skating are all done in contact with water in its various states. We swim in liquid water and skate on water in its solid form (ice). Airplanes fly in an atmosphere containing water in the gaseous state (water vapor). To allow these various activities, the arrangements of the water molecules must be significantly different in their gas, liquid, and solid forms.

In Chapter 13 we saw that the particles of a gas are far apart, are in rapid random motion, and have little effect on each other. Solids are obviously very different from gases. Gases have low densities, have high compressibilities, and completely fill a container. Solids have much greater densities than gases, are compressible only to a very slight extent, and are rigid; a solid maintains its shape regardless of its container. These properties indicate that the components of a solid are close together and exert large attractive forces on each other.

Ice from the Columbia Glacier floats in Prince William Sound (left). *A swimmer in water* (right).

TABLE 14.1

Densities of the Three States of Water

State	Density (g/cm³)
solid (0 °C, 1 atm)	0.9168
liquid (25 °C, 1 atm)	0.9971
gas (400 °C, 1 atm)	3.26×10^{-4}

The properties of liquids lie somewhere between those of solids and of gases—but not midway between, as can be seen from some of the properties of the three states of water. For example, it takes about seven times more energy to change liquid water to steam (a gas) at 100 °C than to melt ice to form liquid water at 0 °C.

$$H_2O(s) \rightarrow H_2O(l) \qquad \text{energy required} \cong 6 \text{ kJ/mol}$$
$$H_2O(l) \rightarrow H_2O(g) \qquad \text{energy required} \cong 41 \text{ kJ/mol}$$

These values indicate that going from the liquid to the gaseous state involves a much greater change than going from the solid to the liquid. Therefore, we can conclude that the solid and liquid states are more similar than the liquid and gaseous states. This is also demonstrated by the densities of the three states of water (Table 14.1). Note that water in its gaseous state is about 3000 times less dense than in the solid and liquid states and that the latter two states have very similar densities.

We find in general that the liquid and solid states show many similarities and are strikingly different from the gaseous state (see Figure 14.1). The best way to picture the solid state is in terms of closely packed, highly ordered particles in contrast to the widely spaced, randomly arranged particles of a gas. The liquid state lies in between, but its properties indicate that it much more closely resembles the solid than the gaseous state. It is useful to picture a liquid in terms of particles that are generally quite close together, but with a more disordered arrangement than for the solid state and with some empty spaces. For most substances, the solid state has a higher density than the liquid, as Figure 14.1 suggests. However, water is an exception to this rule. Ice has an unusual amount of empty space and so is less dense than liquid water, as indicated in Table 14.1.

In this chapter we will explore the important properties of liquids and solids. We will illustrate many of these properties by considering one of the earth's most important substances: water.

FIGURE 14.1
Representations of the gas, liquid, and solid states.

Gas   Liquid   Solid

14.1 Water and Its Phase Changes

AIM: To learn some of the important features of water.

In the world around us we see many solids (soil, rocks, trees, concrete, and so on), and we are immersed in the gases of the atmosphere. But the liquid we most commonly see is water; it is virtually everywhere, covering about 70% of the earth's surface. Approximately 97% of the earth's water is found in the oceans, which are actually mixtures of water and huge quantities of dissolved salts.

Water is one of the most important substances on earth. It is crucial for sustaining the reactions within our bodies that keep us alive, but it also affects our lives in many indirect ways. The oceans help moderate the earth's temperature. Water cools automobile engines and nuclear power plants. Water provides a means of transportation on the earth's surface and acts as a medium for the growth of the myriads of creatures we use as food, and much more.

Pure water is a colorless, tasteless substance that at 1 atm pressure freezes to form a solid at 0 °C and vaporizes completely to form a gas at 100 °C. This means that (at 1 atm pressure) the liquid range of water occurs between the temperatures 0 °C and 100 °C.

What happens when we heat liquid water? First the temperature of the water rises. Just as with gas molecules, the motions of the water molecules increase as it is heated. Eventually the temperature of the water reaches 100 °C; now bubbles develop in the interior of the liquid, float to the surface, and burst—the boiling point has been reached. An interesting thing happens at the boiling point: even though heating continues, the temperature stays at 100 °C until all the water has changed to vapor. Only when all of the water has changed to the gaseous state does the temperature begin to rise again. (We are now heating the vapor.) At 1 atm pressure, liquid water always changes to gaseous water at 100 °C, the **normal boiling point** for water.

The experiment just described is represented in Figure 14.2, which is called the **heating/cooling curve** for water. Going from left to right on this graph means energy is being added (heating). Going from right to left on the graph means that energy is being removed (cooling).

The water we drink often has a taste because of the substances dissolved in it.

FIGURE 14.2
The heating/cooling curve for water heated or cooled at a constant rate. The plateau at the boiling point is longer than the plateau at the melting point, because it takes almost seven times as much energy (and thus seven times the heating time) to vaporize liquid water than to melt ice.

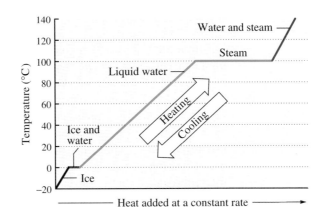

When liquid water is cooled, the temperature decreases until it reaches 0 °C, where the liquid begins to freeze (see Figure 14.2). The temperature remains at 0 °C until all the liquid water has changed to ice and then begins to drop again as cooling continues. At 1 atm pressure, water freezes (or, in the opposite process, ice melts) at 0 °C. This is called the **normal freezing point** of water. Liquid and solid water can coexist indefinitely if the temperature is held at 0 °C. However, at temperatures below 0 °C liquid water freezes, while at temperatures above 0 °C ice melts.

Interestingly, water expands when it freezes. That is, one gram of ice at 0 °C has a greater volume than one gram of liquid water at 0 °C. This has very important practical implications. For instance, water in a confined space can break its container when it freezes and expands. This accounts for the bursting of water pipes and engine blocks that are left unprotected in freezing weather.

The expansion of water when it freezes also explains why ice cubes float. Recall that density is defined as mass/volume. When one gram of liquid water freezes, its volume becomes greater (it expands). Therefore, the *density* of one gram of ice is less than the density of one gram of water, because in the case of ice we divide by a slightly larger volume. For example, at 0 °C the density of liquid water is

$$\frac{1.00 \text{ g}}{1.00 \text{ mL}} = 1.00 \text{ g/mL}$$

and the density of ice is

$$\frac{1.00 \text{ g}}{1.09 \text{ mL}} = 0.917 \text{ g/mL}.$$

The lower density of ice also means that ice floats on the surface of lakes as they freeze, providing a layer of insulation that helps to prevent lakes and rivers from freezing solid in the winter. This means that aquatic life continues to have liquid water available through the winter.

14.2 *Energy Requirements for the Changes of State*

AIMS: To learn about interactions among water molecules. To understand and use heat of fusion and heat of vaporization.

It is important to recognize that changes of state from solid to liquid and from liquid to gas are *physical* changes. No *chemical* bonds are broken in these processes. Ice, water, and steam all contain H_2O molecules. When water is boiled to form steam, water molecules are separated from each other (see Figure 14.3) but the individual molecules remain intact.

The bonding forces that hold the atoms of a molecule together are called **intramolecular** (within the molecule) **forces.** The forces that occur among molecules that cause them to aggregate to form a solid or a liquid are called **intermolecular** (between the molecules) **forces**. These two types of forces are illustrated in Figure 14.4.

FIGURE 14.3
Both liquid water and gaseous water contain H_2O molecules. In liquid water the H_2O molecules are close together, whereas in the gaseous state the molecules are widely separated. The bubbles contain gaseous water.

— Intramolecular forces

— Intermolecular forces

FIGURE 14.4
Intramolecular (bonding) forces exist between the atoms in a molecule and hold the molecule together. Intermolecular forces exist between molecules. These are the forces that cause water to condense to a liquid or form a solid at low enough temperatures. Intermolecular forces are typically much weaker than intramolecular forces.

Remember that temperature is a measure of the random motions (average kinetic energy) of the particles in a substance.

It takes energy to melt ice and to vaporize water, because intermolecular forces between water molecules must be overcome. In ice the molecules are virtually locked in place, although they can vibrate about their positions. When energy is added, the vibrational motions increase, and the molecules eventually achieve the greater movement and disorder characteristic of liquid water. The ice has melted. As still more energy is added, the gaseous state is eventually reached, in which the individual molecules are far apart and interact relatively little. However, the gas still consists of water molecules. It would take *much* more energy to overcome the covalent bonds and decompose the water molecules into their component atoms.

The energy required to melt 1 mol of a substance is called the **molar heat of fusion.** For ice, the molar heat of fusion is 6.02 kJ/mol. The energy required to change 1 mol of liquid to its vapor is called the **molar heat of vaporization.** For water, the molar heat of vaporization is 40.6 kJ/mol at 100 °C. Notice in Figure 14.2 that the plateau that corresponds to the vaporization of water is much longer than that for the melting of ice. This occurs because it takes much more energy (almost seven times as much) to vaporize a mole of water than to melt a mole of ice. This is consistent with our models of solids, liquids, and gases (see Figure 14.1). In liquids, the particles (molecules) are relatively close together, so most of the intermolecular forces are still present. However, when the molecules go from the liquid to the gaseous state, they must be moved far apart. To separate the molecules enough to form a gas, virtually all of the intermolecular forces must be overcome, and this requires large quantities of energy.

Whales Need Changes of State

A sperm whale.

Sperm whales are prodigious divers. They commonly dive a mile or more into the ocean, hovering at that depth in search of schools of squid or fish. To remain motionless at a given depth, the whale must have the same density as the surrounding water. Because the density of seawater increases with depth, the sperm whale has a system that automatically increases its density as it dives. This system involves the spermaceti organ found in the whale's head. Spermaceti is a waxy substance with the formula

$$CH_3\text{--}(CH_2)_{15}\text{--}O\text{--}\underset{\displaystyle \|}{\underset{\displaystyle O}{C}}\text{--}(CH_2)_{14}CH_3$$

which is a liquid above 30 °C. At the ocean surface the spermaceti in the whale's head is a liquid, warmed by the flow of blood through the spermaceti organ. When the whale dives, this blood flow decreases and the colder water causes the spermaceti to begin freezing. Because solid spermaceti is more dense than the liquid state, the sperm whale's density increases as it dives, matching the increase in the water's density.* When the whale wants to resurface, blood flow through the spermaceti organ increases, remelting the spermaceti and making the whale more buoyant. So the sperm whale's sophisticated density-regulating mechanism is based on a simple change of state.

*For most substances, the solid state is more dense than the liquid state. Water is an important exception.

EXAMPLE 14.1   Calculating Energy Changes: Solid to Liquid

Calculate the energy required to melt 8.5 g of ice at 0 °C. The molar heat of fusion for ice is 6.02 kJ/mol.

Solution

The molar heat of fusion is the energy required to melt *1 mol* of ice. In this problem we have 8.5 g of solid water. We must find out how many moles of ice this mass represents. Because the molar mass of water is $16 + 2(1) = 18$, we know that 1 mol of water has a mass of 18 g, so we can convert 8.5 g of H_2O to moles of H_2O.

$$8.5 \text{ g } H_2O \times \frac{1 \text{ mol } H_2O}{18 \text{ g } H_2O} = 0.47 \text{ mol } H_2O$$

Because 6.02 kJ of energy is required to melt a mole of solid water, our sample will take about half this amount (we have approximately half a mole of ice). To calculate the exact amount of energy required, we will use the equivalence statement

6.02 kJ required for 1 mol of H_2O

which leads to the conversion factor we need:

$$0.47 \text{ mol } H_2O \times \frac{6.02 \text{ kJ}}{\text{mol } H_2O} = 2.8 \text{ kJ}$$

This can be represented symbolically as

| 0.47 mol ice | → $\frac{6.02 \text{ kJ}}{\text{mol}}$ | 2.8 kJ required |

EXAMPLE 14.2 *Calculating Energy Changes: Liquid to Gas*

Specific heat capacity was discussed in Section 3.6.

Calculate the energy (in kJ) required to heat 25 g of liquid water from 25 °C to 100. °C and change it to steam at 100. °C. The specific heat capacity of liquid water is 4.18 J/g °C, and the molar heat of vaporization of water is 40.6 kJ/mol.

Solution

This problem can be split into two parts: (1) heating the water to its boiling point and (2) converting the liquid water to vapor at the boiling point.

STEP 1: HEATING TO BOILING We must first supply energy to heat the liquid water from 25 °C to 100. °C. Because 4.18 J is required to heat *one* gram of water by *one* Celsius degree, we must multiply by both the mass of water (25 g) and the temperature change (100. °C − 25 °C = 75 °C):

| Energy required (Q) | = | Specific heat capacity (s) | × | Mass of water (m) | × | Temperature change (ΔT) |

which we can represent by the equation

$$Q = s \times m \times \Delta T$$

Thus

$$Q = 4.18 \, \frac{\text{J}}{\text{g °C}} \times 25 \text{ g} \times 75 \text{ °C} = 7.8 \times 10^3 \text{ J}$$

Energy required to heat 25 g of water from 25 °C to 100. °C — Specific heat capacity — Mass of water — Temperature change

$$= 7.8 \times 10^3 \text{ J} \times \frac{1 \text{ kJ}}{1000 \text{ J}} = 7.8 \text{ kJ}$$

STEP 2: VAPORIZATION Now we must use the molar heat of vaporization to calculate the energy required to vaporize the 25 g of water at 100. °C. The heat of vaporization is given *per mole* rather than per gram, so we must first convert the 25 g of water to moles.

$$25 \text{ g H}_2\text{O} \times \frac{1 \text{ mol H}_2\text{O}}{18 \text{ g H}_2\text{O}} = 1.4 \text{ mol H}_2\text{O}$$

We can now calculate the energy required to vaporize the water.

$$\frac{40.6 \text{ kJ}}{\text{mol H}_2\text{O}} \times 1.4 \text{ mol H}_2\text{O} = 57 \text{ kJ}$$

Molar heat of vaporization — Moles of water

The total energy is the sum of the two steps.

$$7.8 \text{ kJ} \quad + \quad 57 \text{ kJ} \quad = \quad 65 \text{ kJ}$$

Heat from   Change to
25 °C to   vapor
100. °C

 Self-Check Exercise 14.1

Calculate the total energy required to melt 15 g of ice at 0 °C, heat the water to 100. °C, and vaporize it to steam at 100. °C.

Hint: Break the process into three steps and then take the sum.

See Problems 14.15 through 14.18.

CHEMISTRY IN FOCUS

Boiling Points

One very interesting fact about water is that its boiling point changes with elevation. Although water boils at 100 °C in Champaign, Illinois, its boiling point is only 90 °C in Breckenridge, Colorado. The reason for this difference is that Champaign is very near sea level and Breckenridge is nearly 10,000 ft above sea level. The variation of water's boiling point with elevation is illustrated in the accompanying table.

Because of this phenomenon, cooking in the mountains is very different from cooking at sea level. It takes much longer to cook an egg or a potato in boiling water at high elevations, because the cooking is taking place at a much lower temperature. For example, because liquid water cannot be heated to a temperature higher than its boiling point, potatoes boil in Breckenridge, Colorado, at 90 °C instead of 100 °C, as they would in Champaign, Illinois.

These campers in the mountains of Pakistan will find that their cooking water boils at a temperature significantly lower than 100 °C.

Boiling Point of Water at Various Locations

Location	Feet Above Sea Level	Boiling Point (°C)
top of Mt. Everest, Tibet	29,028	70
top of Mt. McKinley, Alaska	20,320	79
top of Mt. Whitney, California	14,494	85
Leadville, Colorado	10,150	89
Boulder, Colorado	5,430	94
New York City, New York	10	100
Death Valley, California	−282	100.3

14.3 Intermolecular Forces

AIMS: To learn about dipole–dipole attraction, hydrogen bonding, and London dispersion forces. To understand the effect of these forces on the properties of liquids.

The polarity of a molecule was discussed in Section 12.3.

We have seen that covalent bonding forces within molecules arise from the sharing of electrons, but how do intermolecular forces arise? Actually several types of intermolecular forces exist. To illustrate one type, we will consider the forces that exist among water molecules.

As we saw in Chapter 12, water is a polar molecule—it has a dipole moment. When molecules with dipole moments are put together, they orient themselves to take advantage of their charge distributions. Molecules with dipole moments can attract each other by lining up so that the positive and negative ends are close to each other, as shown in Figure 14.5(a). This is called a **dipole–dipole attraction.** In the liquid, the dipoles find the best compromise between attraction and repulsion, as shown in Figure 14.5(b).

Dipole–dipole forces are typically only about 1% as strong as covalent or ionic bonds, and they become weaker as the distance between the dipoles increases. In the gas phase, where the molecules are usually very far apart, these forces are relatively unimportant.

See Section 12.2 for a discussion of electronegativity.

Particularly strong dipole–dipole forces occur between molecules in which hydrogen is bound to a highly electronegative atom, such as nitrogen, oxygen, or fluorine. Two factors account for the strengths of these interactions: the great polarity of the bond and the close approach of the dipoles, which is made possible by the very small size of the hydrogen atom. Because dipole–dipole attractions of this type are so unusually strong, they are given a special name—**hydrogen bonding.** Figure 14.6 illustrates hydrogen bonding among water molecules.

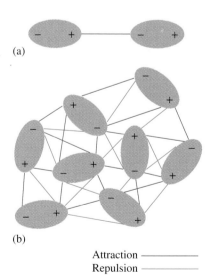

FIGURE 14.5
(a) The interaction of two polar molecules. (b) The interaction of many dipoles in a liquid.

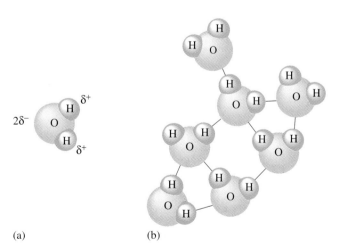

FIGURE 14.6
(a) The polar water molecule. (b) Hydrogen bonding among water molecules. The small size of the hydrogen atoms allows the molecules to get very close and thus to produce strong interactions.

FIGURE 14.7

The boiling points of the covalent hydrides of elements in Group 6.

Hydrogen bonding has a very important effect on various physical properties. For example, the boiling points for the covalent compounds of hydrogen with the elements in Group 6 are given in Figure 14.7. Note that the boiling point of water is much higher than would be expected from the trend shown by the other members of the series. Why? Because the especially large electronegativity value of the oxygen atom compared with that of the other group members causes the O—H bonds to be much more polar than the S—H, Se—H, or Te—H bonds. This leads to very strong hydrogen bonding forces among the water molecules. An unusually large quantity of energy is required to overcome these interactions and separate the molecules to produce the gaseous state. That is, water molecules tend to remain together in the liquid state even at relatively high temperatures, hence the very high boiling point of water.

However, even molecules without dipole moments must exert forces on each other. We know this because all substances—even the noble gases—exist in the liquid and solid states at very low temperatures. There must be forces to hold the atoms or molecules as close together as they are in these condensed states. The forces that exist among noble gas atoms and nonpolar molecules are called **London dispersion forces.** To understand the origin of these forces, consider a pair of noble gas atoms. Although we usually assume that the electrons of an atom are uniformly distributed about the nucleus (see Figure 14.8a), this is apparently not true at every instant. Atoms can develop a temporary dipolar arrangement of charge as the electrons move around the nucleus (see Figure 14.8b). This *instantaneous dipole* can then *induce* a similar dipole in a neighboring atom, as shown in Figure 14.8(c). The interatomic attraction thus formed is both weak and short-lived, but it can be very significant for large atoms and large molecules, as we will see.

FIGURE 14.8

(a) Two atoms with spherical electron probability. These atoms have no polarity. (b) The atom on the left develops an instantaneous dipole when more electrons happen to congregate on the left than on the right. (c) The dipole in the atom on the left induces a dipole in the atom on the right. (d) Nonpolar molecules such as H_2 can also develop instantaneous and induced dipoles.

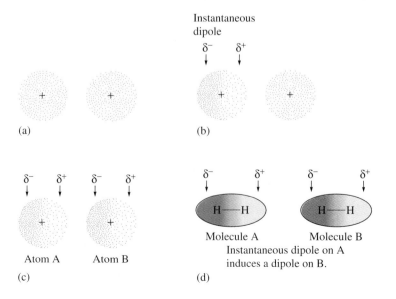

TABLE 14.2

The Freezing Points of the Group 8 Elements

Element	Freezing Point (°C)
helium*	− 272.0 (25 atm)
neon	− 248.6
argon	− 189.4
krypton	− 157.3
xenon	− 111.9

*Helium will not freeze unless the pressure is increased above 1 atm.

The motions of the atoms must be greatly slowed down before the weak London dispersion forces can lock the atoms into place to produce a solid. This explains, for instance, why the noble gas elements have such low freezing points (see Table 14.2).

Nonpolar molecules such as H_2, N_2, and I_2, none of which has a permanent dipole moment, also attract each other by London dispersion forces (see Figure 14.8d).

14.4 Evaporation and Vapor Pressure

AIM: To understand the relationship among vaporization, condensation, and vapor pressure.

Water is used to absorb heat from nuclear reactors. The water is then cooled in cooling towers before it is returned to the environment.

Vapor, not *gas,* is the term we customarily use for the gaseous state of a substance that exists naturally as a solid or liquid at 25 °C and 1 atm.

We all know that a liquid can evaporate from an open container. This is clear evidence that the molecules of a liquid can escape the liquid's surface and form a gas. This process, which is called **vaporization** or **evaporation,** requires energy to overcome the relatively strong intermolecular forces in the liquid.

The fact that vaporization requires energy has great practical significance; in fact, one of the most important roles that water plays in our world is to act as a coolant. Because of the strong hydrogen bonding among its molecules in the liquid state, water has an unusually large heat of vaporization (41 kJ/mol). A significant portion of the sun's energy is spent evaporating water from the oceans, lakes, and rivers rather than warming the earth. The vaporization of water is also crucial to our body's temperature-control system, which relies on the evaporation of perspiration.

Vapor Pressure

When we place a given amount of liquid in a container and then close it, we observe that the amount of liquid at first decreases slightly but eventually becomes constant. The decrease occurs because there is a transfer of molecules from the liquid to the vapor phase (Figure 14.9). However, as the number of vapor molecules increases, it becomes more and more likely that some of them will return to the liquid. The process by which vapor molecules form a liquid is called **condensation.** Eventually, the same number of molecules are leaving the liquid as are returning to it: the rate of condensation equals

FIGURE 14.9

Behavior of a liquid in a closed container. (a) Net evaporation occurs at first, so the amount of liquid decreases slightly. (b) As the number of vapor molecules increases, the rate of condensation increases. (c) Finally the rate of condensation equals the rate of evaporation. The system is at equilibrium.

(a)   (b)   (c)

A system at equilibrium is dynamic on the molecular level, but shows no visible changes.

the rate of evaporation. *At this point no further change occurs in the amounts of liquid or vapor, because the two opposite processes exactly balance each other;* the system is at *equilibrium.* Note that this system is highly *dynamic* on the molecular level—molecules are constantly escaping from and entering the liquid. However, there is no *net* change because the two opposite processes just *balance* each other. As an analogy, consider two island cities connected by a bridge. Suppose the traffic flow on the bridge is the same in both directions. There is motion—we can see the cars traveling across the bridge—but the number of cars in each city is not changing because an equal number enter and leave each one. The result is no *net* change in the number of autos in each city: an equilibrium exists.

The pressure of the vapor present at equilibrium with its liquid is called the *equilibrium vapor pressure* or, more commonly, the **vapor pressure** of the liquid. A simple barometer can be used to measure the vapor pressure of a liquid, as shown in Figure 14.10. Because mercury is so dense, any common liquid injected at the bottom of the column of mercury floats to the top, where it produces a vapor, and the pressure of this vapor pushes some mercury out of the tube. When the system reaches equilibrium, the vapor pressure can be determined from the change in the height of the mercury column.

FIGURE 14.10

(a) It is easy to measure the vapor pressure of a liquid by using a simple barometer of the type shown here.
(b) The water vapor pushed the mercury level down 24 mm (760 − 736), so the vapor pressure of water is 24 mm Hg at this temperature. (c) Diethyl ether is much more volatile than water and thus shows a higher vapor pressure. In this case, the mercury level has been pushed down 545 mm (760 − 215), so the vapor pressure of diethyl ether is 545 mm Hg at this temperature.

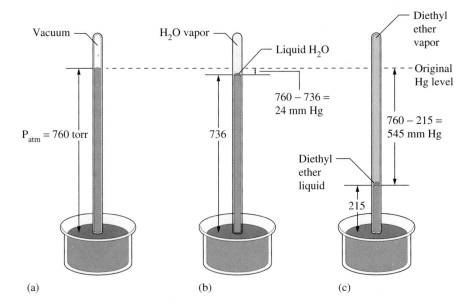

In effect, we are using the space above the mercury in the tube as a closed container for each liquid. However, in this case as the liquid vaporizes, the vapor formed creates a pressure that pushes some mercury out of the tube and lowers the mercury level. The mercury level stops changing when the excess liquid floating on the mercury comes to equilibrium with the vapor. The change in the mercury level (in millimeters) from its initial position (before the liquid was injected) to its final position is equal to the vapor pressure of the liquid.

The vapor pressures of liquids vary widely (see Figure 14.10). Liquids with high vapor pressures are said to be *volatile*—they evaporate rapidly.

Heavy molecules move at lower speeds than light ones and so produce a lower vapor pressure.

The vapor pressure of a liquid at a given temperature is determined by the *intermolecular forces* that act among the molecules. Liquids in which the intermolecular forces are large have relatively low vapor pressures, because such molecules need high energies to escape to the vapor phase. For example, although water is a much smaller molecule than diethyl ether, C_2H_5—O—C_2H_5, the strong hydrogen-bonding forces in water cause its vapor pressure to be much lower than that of ether (see Figure 14.10).

EXAMPLE 14.3 *Using Knowledge of Intermolecular Forces to Predict Vapor Pressure*

Predict which substance in each of the following pairs will show the largest vapor pressure at a given temperature.

a. $H_2O(l)$, $CH_3OH(l)$

b. $CH_3OH(l)$, $CH_3CH_2CH_2CH_2OH(l)$

Solution

a. Water contains two polar O—H bonds; methanol (CH_3OH) has only one. Therefore, the hydrogen bonding among H_2O molecules is expected to be much stronger than that among CH_3OH molecules. This gives water a lower vapor pressure than methanol.

b. Each of these molecules has one polar O—H bond. However, because $CH_3CH_2CH_2CH_2OH$ is a much larger molecule than CH_3OH, it is much less likely to escape from its liquid. Thus $CH_3CH_2CH_2CH_2OH(l)$ has a lower vapor pressure than $CH_3OH(l)$.

14.5 The Solid State: Types of Solids

AIM: To learn about the various types of crystalline solids.

Solids play a very important role in our lives. The concrete we drive on, the trees that shade us, the windows we look through, the paper that holds this print, the diamond in an engagement ring, and the plastic lenses in eyeglasses are all important solids. Most solids, such as wood, paper, and glass, contain mixtures of various components. However, some natural solids, such as diamonds and table salt, are nearly pure substances.

(a)   (b)   (c)

FIGURE 14.12
Several crystalline solids: (a) quartz, SiO_2; (b) rock salt, NaCl; and (c) iron pyrite, FeS_2.

Cl⁻   Na⁺

FIGURE 14.11
The regular arrangement of sodium and chloride ions in sodium chloride, a crystalline solid.

Many substances form **crystalline solids**—those with a regular arrangement of their components. This is illustrated by the partial structure of sodium chloride shown in Figure 14.11. The highly ordered arrangement of the components in a crystalline solid produces beautiful, regularly shaped crystals such as those shown in Figure 14.12.

There are many different types of crystalline solids. For example, both sugar and salt have beautiful crystals that we can easily see. However, although both dissolve readily in water, the properties of the resulting solutions are quite different. The salt solution readily conducts an electric current; the sugar solution does not. This behavior arises from the different natures of the components in these two solids. Common salt, NaCl, is an ionic solid that contains Na^+ and Cl^- ions. When solid sodium chloride dissolves in water, sodium ions and chloride ions are distributed throughout the resulting solution. These ions are free to move through the solution to conduct an electric current. Table sugar (sucrose), on the other hand, is composed of neutral molecules that are dispersed throughout the water when the solid dissolves. No ions are present, and the resulting solution does not conduct electricity. These examples illustrate two important types of crystalline solids: **ionic solids,** represented by sodium chloride; and **molecular solids,** represented by sucrose.

A third type of crystalline solid is represented by elements such as graphite and diamond (both pure carbon), boron, silicon, and all metals. These substances, which contain atoms of only one element covalently bonded to each other, are called **atomic solids.**

We have seen that crystalline solids can be grouped conveniently into three classes as shown in Figure 14.13. Notice that the names of the three classes come from the components of the solid. An ionic solid contains ions,

FIGURE 14.13
The classes of crystaline solids.

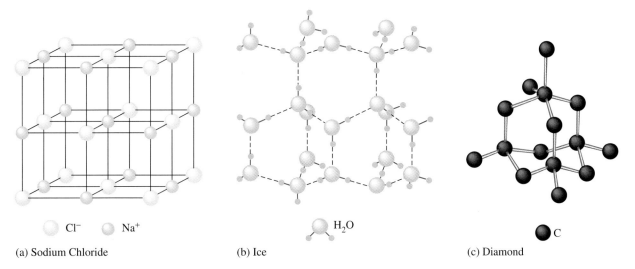

(a) Sodium Chloride   (b) Ice   (c) Diamond

FIGURE 14.14

Examples of three types of crystalline solids. Only part of the structure is shown in each case. The structures continue in three dimensions with the same patterns. (a) An ionic solid. The spheres represent alternating Na^+ and Cl^- ions in solid sodium chloride. (b) A molecular solid. Each unit of three spheres represents an H_2O molecule in ice. The dashed lines show the hydrogen bonding among the polar water molecules. (c) An atomic solid. Each sphere represents a carbon atom in diamond.

a molecular solid contains molecules, and an atomic solid contains atoms. Examples of the three types of solids are shown in Figure 14.14.

The properties of a solid are determined primarily by the nature of the forces that hold the solid together. For example, although argon, copper, and diamond are all atomic solids (their components are atoms), they have strikingly different properties. Argon has a very low melting point (-189 °C), whereas diamond and copper melt at high temperatures (about 3500 °C and 1083 °C, respectively). Copper is an excellent conductor of electricity (it is widely used for electrical wires), whereas both argon and diamond are insulators. The shape of copper can easily be changed; it is both malleable (will form thin sheets) and ductile (can be pulled into a wire). Diamond, on the other hand, is the hardest natural substance known. The marked differences in properties among these three atomic solids are due to differences in bonding. We will explore the bonding in solids in the next section.

The internal forces in a solid determine many of the properties of the solid.

14.6 *Bonding in Solids*

AIMS: To understand the interparticle forces in crystalline solids. To learn about how the bonding in metals determines metallic properties.

We have seen that crystalline solids can be divided into three classes, depending on the fundamental particle or unit of the solid. Ionic solids consist of oppositely charged ions packed together, molecular solids contain molecules, and atomic solids have atoms as their fundamental particles. Examples of the various types of solids are given in Table 14.3 (p.426).

TABLE 14.3

Examples of the Various Types of Solids

Type of Solid	Examples	Fundamental Unit(s)
ionic	sodium chloride, $NaCl(s)$	Na^+, Cl^- ions
ionic	ammonium nitrate, $NH_4NO_3(s)$	NH_4^+, NO_3^- ions
molecular	dry ice, $CO_2(s)$	CO_2 molecules
molecular	ice, $H_2O(s)$	H_2O molecules
atomic	diamond, $C(s)$	C atoms
atomic	iron, $Fe(s)$	Fe atoms
atomic	argon, $Ar(s)$	Ar atoms

Ionic solids were also discussed in Section 12.5.

When spheres are packed together, there are many small empty spaces (holes) left among the spheres.

FIGURE 14.15
The packing of Cl^- and Na^+ ions in solid sodium chloride.

Ionic Solids

Ionic solids are stable substances with high melting points that are held together by the strong forces that exist between oppositely charged ions. The structures of ionic solids can be visualized best by thinking of the ions as spheres packed together as efficiently as possible. For example, in NaCl the larger Cl^- ions are packed together much like one would pack balls in a box. The smaller Na^+ ions occupy the small spaces ("holes") left among the spherical Cl^- ions, as represented in Figure 14.15.

Molecular Solids

In a molecular solid the fundamental particle is a molecule. Examples of molecular solids include ice (contains H_2O molecules), dry ice (contains CO_2 molecules), sulfur (contains S_8 molecules), and white phosphorus (contains P_4 molecules). The latter two substances are shown in Figure 14.16.

Molecular solids tend to melt at relatively low temperatures because the intermolecular forces that exist among the molecules are relatively weak. If the molecule has a dipole moment, dipole–dipole forces hold the solid together. In solids with nonpolar molecules, London dispersion forces hold the solid together.

FIGURE 14.16
(Left) Sulfur crystals contain S_8 molecules. (Right) White phosphorus contains P_4 molecules. It is so reactive with the oxygen in air that it must be stored under water.

FIGURE 14.17
A representation of part of the structure of solid phosphorus, a molecular solid that contains P_4 molecules.

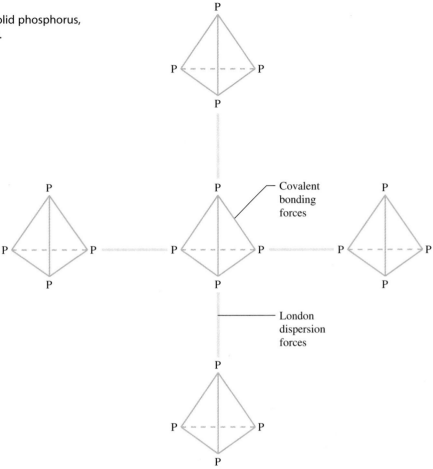

Part of the structure of solid phosphorus is represented in Figure 14.17. Note that the distances between P atoms in a given molecule are much shorter than the distances between the P_4 molecules. This is because the covalent bonds *between atoms* in the molecule are so much stronger than the London dispersion forces *between molecules*.

Atomic Solids

The properties of atomic solids vary greatly because of the different ways in which the fundamental particles, the atoms, can interact with each other. For example, the solids of the Group 8 elements have very low melting points (see Table 14.2), because these atoms, having filled valence orbitals, cannot form covalent bonds with each other. So the forces in these solids are the relatively weak London dispersion forces.

On the other hand, diamond, a form of solid carbon, is one of the hardest substances known and has an extremely high melting point (about 3500 °C). The incredible hardness of diamond arises from the very strong covalent carbon–carbon bonds in the crystal, which lead to a giant molecule. In fact, the entire crystal can be viewed as one huge molecule. A small part

CHEMISTRY IN FOCUS

Metal with a Memory

A distraught mother walks into the optical shop carrying her mangled pair of $400 eyeglasses. Her child had gotten into her purse, found her glasses, and twisted them into a pretzel. She hands them to the optometrist with little hope that they can be salvaged. The optometrist says not to worry and drops the glasses into a dish of warm water where the glasses magically spring back to their original shape. The optometrist hands the restored glasses to the woman and says there is no charge for repairing them.

How can the frames "remember" their original shape when placed in hot water? The answer is a nickel–titanium alloy called Nitinol that was developed in the late 1950s and early 1960s at the Naval Ordnance Laboratory in White Oak, Maryland, by William J. Buehler. (The name Nitinol comes from *Ni*ckel *Ti*tanium *N*aval *O*rdnance *L*aboratory.)

Nitinol has the amazing ability to remember a shape originally impressed in it. For example, note the accompanying photos. What causes Nitinol to behave this way? Although the details are too complicated to describe here, this phenomenon results from two different forms of solid Nitinol. When Nitinol is heated to a sufficiently high temperature, the Ni and Ti atoms arrange themselves in a way that leads to the most compact and regular pattern of the atoms—a form called austenite (A). When the alloy is cooled its atoms rearrange slightly to a form called martensite (M). The shape desired (for example, the word *ICE*) is set into the alloy at a high temperature (A form), then the metal is cooled, causing it to assume the M form. In this process no visible change is noted. Then, if the image is deformed, it will magically return if the alloy is heated (hot water works

fine) to a temperature that changes it back to the A form.

Nitinol has many medical applications, including hooks used by orthopedic surgeons to attach ligaments and tendons to bone, braces to straighten teeth, and "baskets" to catch blood clots. In the latter case a length of Nitinol wire is shaped into a tiny basket and this shape is set at a high temperature. The wires forming the basket are then straightened so they can be inserted as a small bundle through a catheter. When the wires warm up in the blood, the basket shape springs back and acts as a filter to stop blood clots from moving to the heart.

The most promising consumer use of Nitinol is for eyeglasses frames. It's handy to have frames that remember their original shape.

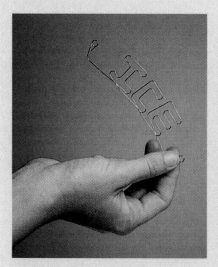

The word ICE is formed from Nitinol wire.

The wire is stretched to obliterate the word ICE.

The wire pops back to ICE when immersed in warm water.

of the diamond structure is represented in Figure 14.14. In diamond each carbon atom is bound covalently to four other carbon atoms to produce a very stable solid. Several other elements also form solids whereby the atoms join together covalently to form giant molecules. Silicon and boron are examples.

At this point you might be asking yourself, "Why aren't solids such as a crystal of diamond, which is a 'giant molecule,' classed as molecular solids?" The answer is that, by convention, a solid is classed as a molecular solid only if (like ice, dry ice, sulfur, and phosphorus) it contains small molecules. Substances like diamond that contain giant molecules are called network solids.

Bonding in Metals

Metals represent another type of atomic solid. Metals have familiar physical properties: they can be pulled into wires, can be hammered into sheets, and are efficient conductors of heat and electricity. However, although the shapes of most pure metals can be changed relatively easily, metals are also durable and have high melting points. These facts indicate that it is difficult to separate metal atoms but relatively easy to slide them past each other. In other words, the bonding in most metals is *strong* but *nondirectional.*

The simplest picture that explains these observations is the **electron sea model,** which pictures a regular array of metal atoms in a "sea" of valence electrons that are shared among the atoms in a nondirectional way and that are quite mobile in the metal crystal. The mobile electrons can conduct heat and electricity, and the atoms can be moved rather easily, as, for example, when the metal is hammered into a sheet or pulled into a wire.

Because of the nature of the metallic crystal, other elements can be introduced relatively easily to produce substances called alloys. An **alloy** is best defined as *a substance that contains a mixture of elements and has metallic properties.* There are two common types of alloys.

In a **substitutional alloy** some of the host metal atoms are *replaced* by other metal atoms of similar sizes. For example, in brass approximately one-third of the atoms in the host copper metal have been replaced by zinc atoms, as shown in Figure 14.18(a). Sterling silver (93% silver and 7% copper) and pewter (85% tin, 7% copper, 6% bismuth, and 2% antimony) are other examples of substitutional alloys.

An **interstitial alloy** is formed when some of the interstices (holes) among the closely packed metal atoms are occupied by atoms much smaller than the host atoms, as shown in Figure 14.18(b). Steel, the best-known interstitial

FIGURE 14.18

Two types of alloys. (a) Brass is a substitutional alloy in which copper atoms in the host crystal are replaced by the similarly sized zinc atoms. (b) Steel is an interstitial alloy in which carbon atoms occupy interstices (holes) among the closely packed iron atoms.

○ Cu ○ Zn

(a) Brass

○ Fe ● C

(b) Steel

A steel sculpture in Chicago.

alloy, contains carbon atoms in the "holes" of an iron crystal. The presence of interstitial atoms changes the properties of the host metal. Pure iron is relatively soft, ductile, and malleable because of the absence of strong directional bonding. The spherical metal atoms can be moved rather easily with respect to each other. However, when carbon, which forms strong directional bonds, is introduced into an iron crystal, the presence of the directional carbon–iron bonds makes the resulting alloy harder, stronger, and less ductile than pure iron. The amount of carbon directly affects the properties of steel. *Mild steels* (containing less than 0.2% carbon) are still ductile and malleable and are used for nails, cables, and chains. *Medium steels* (containing 0.2–0.6% carbon) are harder than mild steels and are used in rails and structural steel beams. *High-carbon steels* (containing 0.6–1.5% carbon) are tough and hard and are used for springs, tools, and cutlery.

Many types of steel also contain elements in addition to iron and carbon. Such steels are often called *alloy steels* and can be viewed as being mixed interstitial (carbon) and substitutional (other metals) alloys. An example is stainless steel, which has chromium and nickel atoms substituted for some of the iron atoms. The addition of these metals greatly increases the steel's resistance to corrosion.

EXAMPLE 14.4 *Identifying Types of Crystalline Solids*

Name the type of crystalline solid formed by each of the following substances:

a. ammonia
b. iron
c. cesium fluoride
d. argon
e. sulfur

Solution

a. Solid ammonia contains NH_3 molecules, so it is a molecular solid.

b. Solid iron contains iron atoms as the fundamental particles. This is an atomic solid.

c. Solid cesium fluoride contains the Cs^+ and F^- ions. It is an ionic solid.

d. Solid argon contains argon atoms, which cannot form covalent bonds to each other. This is an atomic solid.

e. Sulfur contains S_8 molecules, so it is a molecular solid.

 Self-Check Exercise 14.2

Name the type of crystalline solid formed by each of the following substances:

a. sulfur trioxide
b. barium oxide
c. gold

See Problems 14.41 and 14.42.

Chapter Review

Key Terms

normal boiling point *(14.1)*
heating/cooling curve *(14.1)*
normal freezing point *(14.1)*
intramolecular forces *(14.2)*
intermolecular forces *(14.2)*
molar heat of fusion *(14.2)*
molar heat of vaporization *(14.2)*
dipole–dipole attraction *(14.3)*
hydrogen bonding *(14.3)*
London dispersion forces *(14.3)*
vaporization (evaporation) *(14.4)*
condensation *(14.4)*

vapor pressure *(14.4)*
crystalline solid *(14.5)*
ionic solid *(14.5)*
molecular solid *(14.5)*
atomic solid *(14.5)*
alloy *(14.6)*

Summary

1. Liquids and solids exhibit some similarities and are very different from the gaseous state.

2. The temperature at which a liquid changes its state to a gas (at 1 atm pressure) is called the normal boiling point of that liquid. Similarly, the temperature at which a liquid freezes (at 1 atm pressure) is the normal freezing point. Changes of state are physical changes, not chemical changes.

3. To convert a substance from the solid to the liquid and then to the gaseous state requires the addition of energy. Forces among the molecules in a solid or a liquid must be overcome by the input of energy. The energy required to melt 1 mol of a substance is called the molar heat of fusion, and the energy required to change 1 mol of liquid to the gaseous state is called the molar heat of vaporization.

4. There are several types of intermolecular forces. Dipole–dipole interactions occur when molecules with dipole moments attract each other. A particularly strong dipole–dipole interaction called hydrogen bonding occurs in molecules that contain hydrogen bonded to a very electronegative element such as N, O, or F. London dispersion forces occur when instantaneous dipoles in atoms or nonpolar molecules lead to relatively weak attractions.

5. The change of a liquid to its vapor is called vaporization or evaporation. The process whereby vapor molecules form a liquid is called condensation. In a closed container, the pressure of the vapor over its liquid reaches a constant value called the vapor pressure of the liquid.

6. Many solids are crystalline (contain highly regular arrangements of their components). The three types of crystalline solids are ionic, molecular, and atomic solids. In ionic solids, the ions are packed together in a way that maximizes the attractions of oppositely charged ions and minimizes the repulsions among identically charged ions. Molecular solids are held together by dipole–dipole attractions if the molecules are polar and by London dispersion forces if the molecules are nonpolar. Atomic solids are held together by covalent bonding forces or London dispersion forces, depending on the atoms present.

Questions and Problems

All even-numbered exercises have answers in the back of this book and solutions in the Solutions Guide.

14.1 ■ *Water and Its Phase Changes*

QUESTIONS

1. How does water help to moderate the environment of the earth?

2. Describe some uses, both in nature and in industry, of water as a *cooling* agent.

3. How does the density of water in the solid state compare with its density in the liquid state?

4. Discuss some implications of the fact that, unlike most substances, water *expands* in volume when it freezes.

5. Describe, on both a microscopic and a macroscopic basis, what happens to a sample of water as it is heated from room temperature to 50 °C above its normal boiling point.

6. Figure 14.2 presents the *cooling curve* for water. Discuss the meaning of the different portions of this curve (for example, explain what each flat section and each sloping section represents).

14.2 ■ *Energy Requirements for the Changes of State*

QUESTIONS

7. Describe what happens on a microscopic basis when a solid melts.

8. Describe what happens on a microscopic basis when a liquid is boiled.

9. Explain the difference between *intra*molecular forces and *inter*molecular forces. Which forces must be overcome in order to melt a solid or to vaporize a liquid?

10. Energy must be applied to a liquid to make it boil. Where does this energy finally reside?

11. Discuss the similarities and differences between the arrangements of molecules and the forces between molecules in liquid water versus stream, and in liquid water versus ice.

12. The energy required to melt 1 mol of ice is ≈6 kJ/mol, whereas the energy required to vaporize 1 mol of water is ≈41 kJ/mol. Why is nearly seven times more energy needed to vaporize a given amount of water as to melt it?

PROBLEMS

13. The following data have been collected for substance X. Construct a heating curve for substance X. (The drawing does not need to be absolutely to scale, but it should clearly show relative differences.)

normal melting point	−15 °C
molar heat of fusion	2.5 kJ/mol
normal boiling point	134 °C
molar heat of vaporization	55.3 kJ/mol

14. Consider the data for substance X given in Problem 13. If the molar mass of substance X is 52 g/mol, what quantity of heat is required to melt 10.0 g of substance X at −15 °C? What quantity of heat is required to vaporize 25.0 g of substance X at 134 °C?

15. The molar heat of fusion of chloroform ($CHCl_3$) is 8.80 kJ/mol at its normal melting point of −63.6 °C. The molar heat of vaporization of chloroform is 31.4 kJ/mol at its normal boiling point of 61.7 °C. Calculate the heat required to melt 11.5 g of chloroform at its normal melting point. Calculate the heat required to vaporize 11.5 g of chloroform at its normal boiling point.

16. The molar heats of fusion and vaporization for water are 6.02 kJ/mol and 40.6 kJ/mol, respectively, and the specific heat capacity of liquid water is 4.18 J/g °C. What total quantity of heat energy is required to melt 5.0 g of ice at 0 °C, to heat the liquid water from 0 °C to 100 °C, and to vaporize the liquid water at 100 °C?

17. Given that the specific heat capacities of ice and steam are 2.06 J/g °C and 2.03 J/g °C, respectively, and considering the information about water given in Problem 16, calculate the total quantity of heat evolved when 10.0 g of steam at 200. °C is condensed, cooled, and frozen to ice at −50. °C.

18. The heat of fusion of aluminum is 3.95 kJ/g. What is the *molar* heat of fusion of aluminum? What quantity of energy is needed to melt 10.0 g of aluminum? What quantity of energy is required to melt 10.0 mol of aluminum?

14.3 ■ *Intermolecular Forces*

QUESTIONS

19. What is a *dipole–dipole* attraction? Give three examples of liquid substances in which you would expect dipole–dipole attractions to be large.

20. How is the strength of dipole–dipole interactions related to the *distance* between polar molecules? Are dipole–dipole forces short-range or long-range forces?

21. What is meant by *hydrogen bonding*? Give three examples of substances that would be expected to exhibit hydrogen bonding in the liquid state.

22. Explain why the existence of hydrogen bonding causes water to have an unusually high boiling point.

23. Why are the dipole–dipole interactions between polar molecules *not* important in the vapor phase?

24. Although the noble gas elements are monatomic and could not give rise to dipole–dipole forces or hydrogen bonding, these elements still can be liquefied and solidified. Explain.

PROBLEMS

25. Discuss the types of intermolecular forces acting in the liquid state of each of the following substances.
   a. N_2 c. NH_3
   b. HBr   d. He

26. Discuss the types of intermolecular forces acting in the liquid state of each of the following substances.
   a. Kr   c. NF_3
   b. S_8 d. H_2O

27. The boiling points of the noble gas elements are listed below. Comment on the trend in the boiling points. Why do the boiling points vary in this manner?

He	−272 °C	Kr	−152.3 °C
Ne	−245.9 °C	Xe	−107.1 °C
Ar	−185.7 °C	Rn	−61.8 °C

28. The heats of fusion of three substances are listed below. Explain the trend this list reflects.

HI	2.87 kJ/mol
HBr	2.41 kJ/mol
HCl	1.99 kJ/mol

29. When dry ammonia gas (NH_3) is bubbled into a 125-mL sample of water, the volume of the sample (initially, at least) *decreases* slightly. Suggest a reason for this.

30. When 50 mL of liquid water at 25 °C is added to 50 mL of ethanol (ethyl alcohol), also at 25 °C, the combined volume of the mixture is considerably *less* than 100 mL. Give a possible explanation.

14.4 ■ *Evaporation and Vapor Pressure*

QUESTIONS

31. Describe, on a microscopic basis, the processes of *evaporation* and *condensation*. Which process requires the input of energy?

32. What is *vapor pressure?* On a microscopic basis, how does a vapor pressure develop in a closed flask containing a small amount of liquid? What processes are going on in the flask?

33. What do we mean by a *dynamic equilibrium?* Describe how the development of a vapor pressure above a liquid represents such an equilibrium.

34. Describe an experimental method that could be used to determine the vapor pressure of a volatile liquid.

PROBLEMS

35. Which substance in each pair would be expected to be more volatile at a particular temperature? Explain your reasoning.
    a. $H_2O(l)$ or $H_2S(l)$
    b. $H_2O(l)$ or $CH_3OH(l)$
    c. $CH_3OH(l)$ or $CH_3CH_2OH(l)$

36. Which substance in each pair would be expected to show the largest vapor pressure at a given temperature? Explain your reasoning.
    a. $H_2O(l)$ or $HF(l)$
    b. $CH_3OCH_3(l)$ or $CH_3CH_2OH(l)$
    c. $CH_3OH(l)$ or $CH_3SH(l)$

37. Although water and ammonia differ in molar mass by only one unit, the boiling point of water is over 100 °C higher than that of ammonia. Explain.

38. Two molecules that contain the same number of each kind of atom but that have different molecular structures are said to be *isomers* of each other. For example, both ethyl alcohol and dimethyl ether (shown below) have the formula C_2H_6O and are isomers. Based on considerations of intermolecular forces, which substance would you expect to be more volatile? Which would you expect to have the higher boiling point? Explain.

dimethyl ether	ethyl alcohol
CH_3—O—CH_3	CH_3—CH_2—OH

14.5 ■ *The Solid State: Types of Solids*

QUESTIONS

39. What are crystalline solids? What kind of microscopic structure do such solids have? How is this microscopic structure reflected in the macroscopic appearance of such solids?

40. On the basis of the smaller units that make up the crystals, cite three types of crystalline solids. For each type of crystalline solid, give an example of a substance that forms that type of solid.

14.6 ■ *Bonding in Solids*

QUESTIONS

41. What are the fundamental particles in ionic solids? Give two examples of ionic solids, and tell what individual particles make them up.

42. What are the fundamental particles in molecular solids? Give two examples of molecular solids, and tell what individual particles make them up.

43. Ionic solids are generally considerably harder than most molecular solids. Explain.

44. Ionic solids typically have melting points hundreds of degrees higher than the melting points of molecular solids. Explain.

45. What types of forces exist between the individual particles in an ionic solid? Are these forces relatively strong or relatively weak?

46. Ordinary ice (solid water) melts at 0 °C, whereas dry ice (solid carbon dioxide) melts at a much lower temperature. Explain the differences in the melting points of these two substances on the basis of the intermolecular forces involved.

47. Explain and compare the intermolecular forces that exist in a sample of solid krypton, Kr, with those that exist in diamond, C.

48. How do we explain that a metal (such as copper) conducts electricity well in the solid state, whereas an ionic substance (such as copper sulfate) does *not* conduct electricity in the solid state even though the ionic substance consists of electrically charged particles.

49. What is an *alloy?* Explain the differences in structure between substitutional and interstitial alloys. Give an example of each type.

50. Explain how the properties of a metal may be modified by alloying the metal with some other substance. Discuss, in particular, how the properties of iron are modified in producing the various types of steel.

Additional Problems

MATCHING

For Exercises 51–60 choose one of the following terms to match the definition or description given.

   a. alloy
   b. specific heat
   c. crystalline solid
   d. dipole–dipole attraction
   e. equilibrium vapor pressure
   f. intermolecular
   g. intramolecular
   h. ionic solids
   i. London dispersion forces
   j. molar heat of fusion
   k. molar heat of vaporization
   l. molecular solids
   m. normal boiling point
   n. semiconductor

51. boiling point at pressure of 1 atm

52. energy required to melt 1 mol of a substance

53. forces between atoms in a molecule

54. forces between molecules in a solid

55. instantaneous dipole forces for nonpolar molecules

56. lining up of opposite charges on adjacent polar molecules

57. maximum pressure of vapor that builds up in a closed container

58. mixture of elements having metallic properties overall

59. repeating arrangement of component species in a solid

60. solids that melt at relatively low temperatures

61. Given the densities and conditions of ice, liquid water, and steam listed in Table 14.1, calculate the volume of 1.0 g of water under each of these circumstances.

62. As you will see in Chapter 20, in carbon compounds a given group of atoms can often be arranged in more than one way. This means that more than one structure may be possible for the same atoms. For example, both the molecules dimethyl ether and ethanol have the same number of each type of atom, but they have different structures and are said to be isomers of one another.

   dimethyl ether $CH_3—O—CH_3$
   ethanol $CH_3—CH_2—OH$

Which substance would you expect to have the larger vapor pressure? Why?

63. Which of the substances in each of the following sets would be expected to have the highest boiling point? Explain why.
   a. Ga, KBr, O_2
   b. Hg, NaCl, He
   c. H_2, O_2, H_2O

64. Which of the substances in each of the following sets would be expected to have the lowest melting point. Explain why.
   a. H_2, N_2, O_2
   b. Xe, NaCl, C(diamond)
   c. Cl_2, Br_2, I_2

65. When a person has a severe fever, one therapy to reduce the fever is an "alcohol rub." Explain how the evaporation of alcohol from the person's skin removes heat energy from the body.

66. What is steel? How do the properties of steel differ from the properties of its constituents?

67. Some properties of aluminum are summarized in the following list.

normal melting point	658 °C
heat of fusion	3.95 kJ/g
normal boiling point	2467 °C
heat of vaporization	10.52 kJ/g
specific heat of the solid	0.902 J/g °C

   a. Calculate the quantity of energy required to heat 1.00 mol of aluminum from 25 °C to its normal melting point.
   b. Calculate the quantity of energy required to melt 1.00 mol of aluminum at 658 °C.
   c. Calculate the amount of energy required to vaporize 1.00 mol of aluminum at 2467 °C.

68. What are some important uses of water, both in nature and in industry? What is the liquid range for water?

69. Describe, on both a microscopic and a macroscopic basis, what happens to a sample of water as it is cooled from room temperature to 50 °C below its normal freezing point.

70. Cake mixes and other packaged foods that require cooking often contain special directions for use at high elevations. Typically these directions indicate that the food

should be cooked longer above 5000 ft. Explain why it takes longer to cook something at higher elevations.

71. Why is there no change in *intra*molecular forces when a solid is melted? Are intramolecular forces stronger or weaker than intermolecular forces?

72. What do we call the energies required, respectively, to melt and to vaporize 1 mol of a substance? Which of these energies is always larger for a given substance? Why?

73. The molar heat of vaporization of carbon disulfide, CS_2, is 28.4 kJ/mol at its normal boiling point of 46 °C. How much energy (heat) is required to vaporize 1.0 g of CS_2 at 46 °C? How much heat is evolved when 50. g of CS_2 is condensed from the vapor to the liquid form at 46 °C?

74. Which is stronger, a dipole–dipole attraction between two molecules or a covalent bond between two atoms within the same molecule? Explain.

75. What is *hydrogen bonding* and how does it arise? Give three examples of substances in which you would expect hydrogen bonding to be important in the liquid state of the substance.

76. What are *London dispersion forces* and how do they arise in a nonpolar molecule? Are London forces typically stronger or weaker than dipole–dipole attractions between polar molecules? Are London forces stronger or weaker than covalent bonds? Explain.

77. Discuss the types of intermolecular forces acting in the liquid state of each of the following substances.
    a. N_2
    b. NH_3
    c. He
    d. CO_2 (linear, nonpolar)

78. Explain how the evaporation of water acts as a coolant for the earth.

79. What do we mean when we say a liquid is *volatile?* Do volatile liquids have large or small vapor pressures? What types of intermolecular forces occur in highly volatile liquids?

80. Although methane, CH_4, and ammonia, NH_3, differ in molar mass by only one unit, the boiling point of ammonia is over 100 °C higher than that of methane (a nonpolar molecule). Explain.

81. Which type of solid is likely to have the highest melting point—an ionic solid, a molecular solid, or an atomic solid? Explain.

82. What types of intermolecular forces exist in a crystal of ice? How do these forces differ from the types of intermolecular forces that exist in a crystal of solid oxygen?

83. Discuss the *electron sea* model for metals. How does this model account for the fact that metals are very good conductors of electricity?

CHAPTER

15

Solutions

436

Most of the important chemistry that keeps plants, animals, and humans functioning occurs in aqueous solutions. Even the water that comes out of a tap is not pure water but a solution of various materials in water. For example, tap water may contain dissolved chlorine to disinfect it, dissolved minerals that make it "hard," and traces of many other substances that result from natural and human-initiated pollution. We encounter many other chemical solutions in our daily lives: air, shampoo, orange soda, coffee, gasoline, cough syrup, and many others.

A **solution** is a homogeneous mixture, a mixture in which the components are uniformly intermingled. This means that a sample from one part is the same as a sample from any other part. For example, the first sip of coffee is the same as the last sip.

The atmosphere that surrounds us is a gaseous solution containing $O_2(g)$, $N_2(g)$, and other gases randomly dispersed. Solutions can also be solids. For example, brass is a homogeneous mixture—a solution—of copper and zinc.

Seawater is a chemical solution (left). *Brass, a solid solution of copper and zinc, is used to make musical instruments and many other objects* (right).

437

TABLE 15.1

Various Types of Solutions

Example	State of Solution	Original State of Solute	State of Solvent
air, natural gas	gas	gas	gas
vodka in water, antifreeze in water	liquid	liquid	liquid
brass	solid	solid	solid
carbonated water (soda)	liquid	gas	liquid
seawater, sugar solution	liquid	solid	liquid

These examples illustrate that a solution can be a gas, a liquid, or a solid (see Table 15.1). The substance present in the largest amount is called the **solvent,** and the other substance or substances are called **solutes.** For example, when we dissolve a teaspoon of sugar in a glass of water, the sugar is the solute and the water is the solvent.

Aqueous solutions are solutions with water as the solvent. Because they are so important, in this chapter we will concentrate on the properties of aqueous solutions.

15.1 *Solubility*

AIMS: To understand the process of dissolving. To learn why certain components dissolve in water.

FIGURE 15.1
When solid sodium chloride dissolves, the ions are dispersed randomly throughout the solution.

Cations are positive ions. Anions are negative ions.

What happens when you put a teaspoon of sugar in your iced tea and stir it, or when you add salt to water for cooking vegetables? Why do the sugar and salt "disappear" into the water? What does it mean when something dissolves—that is, when a solution forms?

We saw in Chapter 7 that when sodium chloride dissolves in water, the resulting solution conducts an electric current. This convinces us that the solution contains *ions* that can move (this is how the electric current is conducted). The dissolving of solid sodium chloride in water is represented in Figure 15.1. Notice that in the solid state the ions are packed closely together. However, when the solid dissolves, the ions are separated and dispersed throughout the solution. The strong ionic forces that hold the sodium chloride crystal together are overcome by the strong attractions between the ions and the polar water molecules. This process is represented in Figure 15.2. Notice that each polar water molecule orients itself in a way to maximize its attraction with a Cl^- or Na^+ ion. The negative end of a water molecule is attracted to a Na^+ ion, while the positive end is attracted to a Cl^- ion. The strong forces holding the positive and negative ions in the solid are replaced by strong water–ion interactions, and the solid dissolves (the ions disperse).

It is important to remember that when an ionic substance (such as a salt) dissolves in water, it breaks up into *individual* cations and anions, which are dispersed in the water. For instance, when ammonium nitrate, NH_4NO_3, dissolves in water, the resulting solution contains NH_4^+ and NO_3^- ions, which

FIGURE 15.2
Polar water molecules interact with the positive and negative ions of a salt. These interactions replace the strong ionic forces holding the ions together in the undissolved solid, thus assisting in the dissolving process.

move around independently. This process can be represented as

$$NH_4NO_3(s) \xrightarrow{H_2O(l)} NH_4^+(aq) + NO_3^-(aq)$$

where (*aq*) indicates that the ions are surrounded by water molecules.

Water also dissolves many nonionic substances. Sugar is one example of a nonionic solute that is very soluble in water. Another example is ethanol, C_2H_5OH. Wine, beer, and mixed drinks are aqueous solutions of ethanol (and other substances). Why is ethanol so soluble in water? The answer lies in the structure of the ethanol molecule (Figure 15.3a). The molecule contains a polar O—H bond like those in water, which makes it very compatible with water. Just as hydrogen bonds form among water molecules in pure water (see Figure 14.6), ethanol molecules can form hydrogen bonds with water molecules in a solution of the two. This is shown in Figure 15.3(b).

FIGURE 15.3
(a) The ethanol molecule contains a polar O—H bond similar to those in the water molecule. (b) The polar water molecule interacts strongly with the polar O—H bond in ethanol.

FIGURE 15.4

The structure of common table sugar (called sucrose). The large number of polar O—H groups in the molecule causes sucrose to be very soluble in water.

FIGURE 15.5

A molecule typical of those found in petroleum. The bonds are not polar.

Oil floats on the water as it is released from a damaged oil tanker in Alaska.

The sugar molecule (common table sugar has the chemical name sucrose) is shown in Figure 15.4. Notice that this molecule has many polar O—H groups, each of which can hydrogen-bond to a water molecule. Because of the attractions between sucrose and water molecules, solid sucrose is quite soluble in water.

Many substances do not dissolve in water. For example, when petroleum leaks from a damaged tanker, it does not disperse uniformly in the water (does not dissolve) but rather floats on the surface because its density is less than that of water. Petroleum is a mixture of molecules like the one shown in Figure 15.5. Since carbon and hydrogen have very similar electronegativities, the bonding electrons are shared almost equally and the bonds are essentially nonpolar. The resulting molecule with its nonpolar bonds cannot form attractions to the polar water molecules and this prevents it from being soluble in water. This situation is represented in Figure 15.6.

Notice in Figure 15.6 that the water molecules in liquid water are associated with each other by hydrogen-bonding interactions. In order for a solute to dissolve in water, a "hole" must be made in the water structure for each

FIGURE 15.6

An oil layer floating on water. For a substance to dissolve, the water–water hydrogen bonds must be broken to make a "hole" for each solute particle. However, the water–water interactions will break only if they are replaced by similar strong interactions with the solute.

solute particle. This will occur only if the lost water–water interactions are replaced by similar water–solute interactions. In the case of sodium chloride, strong interactions occur between the polar water molecules and the Na^+ and Cl^- ions. This allows the sodium chloride to dissolve. In the case of ethanol or sucrose, hydrogen-bonding interactions can occur between the O—H groups on these molecules and water molecules, making these substances soluble as well. But oil molecules are not soluble in water, because the many water–water interactions that would have to be broken to make "holes" for these large molecules are not replaced by favorable water–solute interactions.

CHEMISTRY IN FOCUS

*I*nk—*An Interesting Suspension*

Ink is everywhere in our world—in textbooks, on posters, on potato chip bags, and even on soda cans. The use of ink has a long history. Four thousand years ago the Egyptians used ink to write official documents. Although the Egyptian system was crude, it contained the essential components: a pigment, a vehicle, and a substrate. The substrate is the surface to which the ink is applied—the Egyptians used papyrus. The pigment (coloring agent) used by the Egyptians was soot (carbon dust), which was dispersed in a vehicle consisting of water and plant gum.

Although modern ink appears to be a solution, it is not. It is really a suspension of very finely ground pigment particles ($\sim10^{-5}$ mm in diameter) in a liquid. If ink were a true solution, the coloring agent would soak into the paper producing fuzzy, indistinct letters. Since it is a dispersion, the pigment settles on the surface of the paper, where it sticks after the liquid vehicle has evaporated.

More than half of the ink used in the United States is black and contains—just like the Egyptian ink—tiny particles of carbon. Colored pigments often contain metal ions; examples are lead chromate ($PbCrO_4$, yellow), cadmium selenide (CdSe, red), and iron(III) ferrocyanide

An ink drawing.

($Fe_4[Fe(CN)_6]_3$, blue). White ink usually contains the pigment titanium (IV) oxide (TiO_2).

The liquid vehicle in ink must perform a difficult task. It must be able to flow from the pen or printing press to the substrate, but then must evaporate or solidify almost immediately if the pigment is to stay in place.

Early inks were water-based, but water evaporates relatively slowly (especially when the humidity is high) and thus can "run," smearing the printing. To avoid these problems ink producers turned to natural oils, such as linseed oil and tung oil, for vehicles. These oils solidify by reacting with the oxygen in the air—oxidation produces links among the molecules. The very large molecules produced by this reaction yield a solid. In the past, solvents such as alcohols were added to oil-based inks to make them more fluid, allowing for better transfer from printing press to substrate. However, the evaporation of these solvents led to significant air pollution. In response to this problem the Federal Clean Air Act (1970) specified that ink can contain no more than 20% of its mass as volatile solvents unless special equipment is installed around the printing presses to recapture the solvent.

To combat air quality problems ink makers are again turning to water. Modern inks usually contain vehicles consisting of polymer–water mixtures. Polymers are synthetic molecules made by putting small molecules (monomers) together to form very large molecules. When these polymers are exposed to air, they form even larger molecules and solidify (heat is often used to speed the process). These new inks are both more environmentally sound and more efficient, proving once again that we can use more sophisticated technology and protect the environment at the same time.

These considerations account for the observed behavior *"like dissolves like."* In other words, we observe that a given solvent usually dissolves solutes that have polarities similar to itself. For example, water dissolves most polar solutes, because the solute–solvent interactions formed in the solution are similar to the water–water interactions present in the pure solvent. Likewise, nonpolar solvents dissolve nonpolar solutes. For example, dry cleaning solvents used for removing grease stains from clothes are nonpolar liquids. "Grease" is composed of nonpolar molecules, so a nonpolar solvent is needed to remove a grease stain.

15.2 Solution Composition: An Introduction

AIM: To learn qualitative terms associated with the concentration of a solution.

Even for very soluble substances, there is a limit to how much solute can be dissolved in a given amount of solvent. For example, when you add sugar to a glass of water, the sugar rapidly disappears at first. However, as you continue to add more sugar, at some point the solid no longer dissolves but collects at the bottom of the glass. When a solution contains as much solute as will dissolve at that temperature, we say it is **saturated.** If a solid solute is added to a solution already saturated with that solute, the added solid does not dissolve. A solution that has *not* reached the limit of solute that will dissolve in it is said to be **unsaturated.** When more solute is added to an unsaturated solution, it dissolves.

Although a chemical compound always has the same composition, a solution is a mixture and the amounts of the substances present can vary in different solutions. For example, coffee can be strong or weak. Strong coffee has more coffee dissolved in a given amount of water than weak coffee. To describe a solution completely, we must specify the amounts of solvent and solute. We sometimes use the qualitative terms *concentrated* and *dilute* to describe a solution. A relatively large amount of solute is dissolved in a **concentrated** solution (strong coffee is concentrated). A relatively small amount of solute is dissolved in a **dilute** solution (weak coffee is dilute).

Although these qualitative terms serve a useful purpose, we often need to know the exact amount of solute present in a given amount of solution. In the next several sections, we will consider various ways to describe the composition of a solution.

15.3 Solution Composition: Mass Percent

AIM: To understand the concentration term mass percent *and learn how to calculate it.*

Describing the composition of a solution means specifying the amount of solute present in a given quantity of the solution. We typically give the amount of solute in terms of mass (number of grams) or in terms of moles. The quantity of solution is defined in terms of mass or volume.

One common way of describing a solution's composition is **mass percent** (sometimes called *weight percent*), which expresses the mass of solute present in a given mass of solution. The definition of mass percent is:

$$\text{Mass percent} = \frac{\text{mass of solute}}{\text{mass of solution}} \times 100\%$$

$$= \frac{\text{grams of solute}}{\text{grams of solute} + \text{grams of solvent}} \times 100\%$$

The mass of the solution is the sum of the masses of the solute and the solvent.

For example, suppose a solution is prepared by dissolving 1.0 g of sodium chloride in 48 g of water. The solution has a mass of 49 g (48 g of H_2O plus 1.0 g of NaCl), and there is 1.0 g of solute (NaCl) present. The mass percent of solute, then, is

$$\frac{1.0 \text{ g solute}}{49 \text{ g solution}} \times 100\% = 0.020 \times 100\% = 2.0\% \text{ NaCl}$$

EXAMPLE 15.1 *Solution Composition: Calculating Mass Percent*

A solution is prepared by mixing 1.00 g of ethanol, C_2H_5OH, with 100.0 g of water. Calculate the mass percent of ethanol in this solution.

Solution

In this case we have 1.00 g of solute (ethanol) and 100.0 g of solvent (water). We now apply the definition of mass percent.

$$\text{Mass percent } C_2H_5OH = \left(\frac{\text{grams of } C_2H_5OH}{\text{grams of solution}} \right) \times 100\%$$

$$= \left(\frac{1.00 \text{ g } C_2H_5OH}{100.0 \text{ g } H_2O + 1.00 \text{ g } C_2H_5OH} \right) \times 100\%$$

$$= \frac{1.00 \text{ g}}{101.0 \text{ g}} \times 100\%$$

$$= 0.990\% \text{ } C_2H_5OH$$

 Self-Check Exercise 15.1

A 135-g sample of seawater is evaporated to dryness, leaving 4.73 g of solid residue (the salts formerly dissolved in the seawater). Calculate the mass percent of solute present in the original seawater.

See Problems 15.17 and 15.18.

EXAMPLE 15.2 *Solution Composition: Determining Mass of Solute*

Although milk is not a true solution (it is really a suspension of tiny globules of fat, protein, and other substrates in water), it does contain a dissolved sugar called lactose. Cow's milk typically contains 4.5% by mass of lactose, $C_{12}H_{22}O_{11}$. Calculate the mass of lactose present in 175 g of milk.

Solution

We are given the following information:

Mass of solution (milk) = 175 g
Mass percent of solute (lactose) = 4.5%

We need to calculate the mass of solute (lactose) present in 175 g of milk. Using the definition of mass percent, we have

$$\text{Mass percent} = \frac{\text{grams of solute}}{\text{grams of solution}} \times 100\%$$

We now substitute the quantities we know:

Mass of lactose   Mass percent

$$\text{Mass percent} = \frac{\text{grams of solute}}{175\ \text{g}} \times 100\% = 4.5\%$$

Mass of milk

We now solve for grams of solute by multiplying both sides by 175 g:

$$\cancel{175\ \text{g}} \times \frac{\text{grams of solute}}{\cancel{175\ \text{g}}} \times 100\% = 4.5\% \times 175\ \text{g}$$

and then dividing both sides by 100%:

$$\text{Grams of solute} \times \frac{\cancel{100\%}}{\cancel{100\%}} = \frac{4.5\%}{100\%} \times 175\ \text{g}$$

to give

$$\text{Grams of solute} = 0.045 \times 175\ \text{g} = 7.9\ \text{g lactose}$$

 Self-Check Exercise 15.2

What mass of water must be added to 425 g of formaldehyde to prepare a 40.0% (by mass) solution of formaldehyde? This solution, called formalin, is used to preserve biological specimens.

Hint: Substitute the known quantities into the definition for mass percent, and then solve for the unknown quantity (mass of solvent).

See Problems 15.15 and 15.16.

15.4 Solution Composition: Molarity

AIMS: To understand molarity. To learn to use molarity to calculate the number of moles of solute present.

When a solution is described in terms of mass percent, the amount of solution is given in terms of its mass. However, it is often more convenient to measure the volume of a solution than to measure its mass. Because of this, chemists often describe a solution in terms of concentration. We define the *concentration* of a solution as the amount of solute in a *given volume* of solution. The most commonly used expression of concentration is **molarity (*M*).**

Molarity describes the amount of solute in moles and the volume of the solution in liters. Molarity is *the number of moles of solute per volume of solution in liters.* That is

$$M = \text{molarity} = \frac{\text{moles of solute}}{\text{liters of solution}} = \frac{\text{mol}}{\text{L}}$$

A solution that is 1.0 molar (written as 1.0 *M*) contains 1.0 mol of solute per liter of solution.

EXAMPLE 15.3 *Solution Composition: Calculating Molarity, I*

Calculate the molarity of a solution prepared by dissolving 11.5 g of solid NaOH in enough water to make 1.50 L of solution.

Solution

We are given the following information:

Mass of solute $= 11.5$ g NaOH
Volume of solution $= 1.50$ L

Because we are asked to calculate the molarity of the solution, we start by writing the definition of molarity.

$$M = \frac{\text{moles of solute}}{\text{liters of solution}}$$

We have the mass (in grams) of solute, so we need to convert the mass of solute to moles (using the molar mass of NaOH). Then we can divide the number of moles by the volume in liters.

We compute the number of moles of solute, using the molar mass of NaOH (40.0 g).

$$11.5 \text{ g NaOH} \times \frac{1 \text{ mol NaOH}}{40.0 \text{ g NaOH}} = 0.288 \text{ mol NaOH}$$

Then we divide by the volume of the solution in liters.

$$\text{Molarity} = \frac{\text{moles of solute}}{\text{liters of solution}} = \frac{0.288 \text{ mol NaOH}}{1.50 \text{ L solution}} = 0.192 \text{ } M \text{ NaOH}$$

EXAMPLE 15.4 *Solution Composition: Calculating Molarity, II*

Calculate the molarity of a solution prepared by dissolving 1.56 g of gaseous HCl into enough water to make 26.8 mL of solution.

Solution

We are given

Mass of solute (HCl) $= 1.56$ g
Volume of solution $= 26.8$ mL

Molarity is defined as

$$\frac{\text{Moles of solute}}{\text{Liters of solution}}$$

so we must change 1.56 g of HCl to moles of HCl, and then we must change 26.8 mL to liters (because molarity is defined in terms of liters). First we calculate the number of moles of HCl (molar mass = 36.5 g).

$$1.56 \text{ g } \cancel{\text{HCl}} \times \frac{1 \text{ mol HCl}}{36.5 \text{ g } \cancel{\text{HCl}}} = 0.0427 \text{ mol HCl}$$

$$= 4.27 \times 10^{-2} \text{ mol HCl}$$

Next we change the volume of the solution from milliliters to liters, using the equivalence statement 1 L = 1000 mL, which gives the appropriate conversion factor.

$$26.8 \text{ mL} \times \frac{1 \text{ L}}{1000 \text{ mL}} = 0.0268 \text{ L}$$

$$= 2.68 \times 10^{-2} \text{ L}$$

Finally, we divide the moles of solute by the liters of solution.

$$\text{Molarity} = \frac{4.27 \times 10^{-2} \text{ mol HCl}}{2.68 \times 10^{-2} \text{ L solution}} = 1.59 \text{ } M \text{ HCl}$$

 Self-Check Exercise 15.3

Calculate the molarity of a solution prepared by dissolving 1.00 g of ethanol, C_2H_5OH, in enough water to give a final volume of 101 mL.

See Problems 15.37 through 15.42.

It is important to realize that the description of a solution's composition may not accurately reflect the true chemical nature of the solute as it is present in the dissolved state. Solute concentration is always written in terms of the form of the solute *before* it dissolves. For example, describing a solution as 1.0 M NaCl means that the solution was prepared by dissolving 1.0 mol of solid NaCl in enough water to make 1.0 L of solution; it does not mean that the solution contains 1.0 mol of NaCl units. Actually the solution contains 1.0 mol of Na^+ ions and 1.0 mol of Cl^- ions. That is, it contains 1.0 M Na^+ and 1.0 M Cl^-.

EXAMPLE 15.5   *Solution Composition: Calculating Ion Concentration from Molarity*

Give the concentrations of all the ions in each of the following solutions:

a. 0.50 M $Co(NO_3)_2$
b. 1 M $FeCl_3$

Solution

Remember, ionic compounds separate into the component ions when they dissolve in water.

a. When solid $Co(NO_3)_2$ dissolves, it produces ions as follows:

$$Co(NO_3)_2(s) \xrightarrow{H_2O(l)} Co^{2+}(aq) + 2NO_3^-(aq)$$

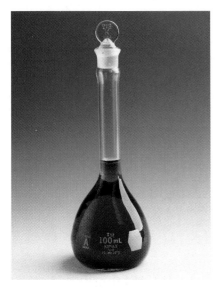

which we can represent as

$$1 \text{ mol } Co(NO_3)_2(s) \xrightarrow{H_2O(l)} 1 \text{ mol } Co^{2+}(aq) + 2 \text{ mol } NO_3^-(aq)$$

Therefore, a solution that is 0.50 M $Co(NO_3)_2$ contains 0.50 M Co^{2+} and (2×0.50) M NO_3^-, or 1.0 M NO_3^-.

b. When solid $FeCl_3$ dissolves, it produces ions as follows:

$$FeCl_3(s) \xrightarrow{H_2O(l)} Fe^{3+}(aq) + 3Cl^-(aq)$$

or

$$1 \text{ mol } FeCl_3(s) \xrightarrow{H_2O(l)} 1 \text{ mol } Fe^{3+}(aq) + 3 \text{ mol } Cl^-(aq)$$

A solution that is 1 M $FeCl_3$ contains 1 M Fe^{3+} ions and 3 M Cl^- ions.

✓ Self-Check Exercise 15.4

Give the concentrations of the ions in each of the following solutions:

a. 0.10 M Na_2CO_3

b. 0.010 M $Al_2(SO_4)_3$

See Problems 15.49 and 15.50.

Often we need to determine the number of moles of solute present in a given volume of a solution of known molarity. To do this, we use the definition of molarity. When we multiply the molarity of a solution by the volume (in liters), we get the moles of solute present in that sample:

$$\text{Liters of solution} \times \text{molarity} = \text{liters of solution} \times \frac{\text{moles of solute}}{\text{liters of solution}}$$

$$= \text{moles of solute}$$

EXAMPLE 15.6 *Solution Composition: Calculating Number of Moles from Molarity*

How many moles of Ag^+ ions are present in 25 mL of a 0.75 M $AgNO_3$ solution?

Solution

In this problem we know

Molarity of the solution = 0.75 M

Volume of the solution = 25 mL

We need to calculate the moles of Ag^+ present. To solve this problem, we must first recognize that a 0.75 M $AgNO_3$ solution contains 0.75 M Ag^+ ions and 0.75 M NO_3^- ions. Next we must express the volume in liters. That is, we must convert from mL to L.

$$25 \text{ mL} \times \frac{1 \text{ L}}{1000 \text{ mL}} = 0.025 \text{ L} = 2.5 \times 10^{-2} \text{ L}$$

Caption (left column):

A solution of cobalt (II) nitrate.

$M = \frac{\text{moles of solute}}{\text{liters of solution}}$

Liters $\times$ M ⟹ Moles of solute

FIGURE 15.7
Steps involved in the preparation of a standard aqueous solution. (a) Put a weighed amount of a substance (the solute) into the volumetric flask, and add a small quantity of water. (b) Dissolve the solid in the water by gently swirling the flask (*with the stopper in place*). (c) Add more water (with gentle swirling) until the level of the solution just reaches the mark etched on the neck of the flask. Then mix the solution thoroughly by inverting the flask several times.

(a)   (b)   (c)

Now we multiply the volume times the molarity.

$$2.5 \times 10^{-2} \text{ L solution} \times \frac{0.75 \text{ mol Ag}^+}{\text{L solution}} = 1.9 \times 10^{-2} \text{ mol Ag}^+$$

 Self-Check Exercise 15.5

Calculate the number of moles of Cl^- ions in 1.75 L of 1.0×10^{-3} *M* $AlCl_3$.

See Problems 15.49 and 15.50.

A **standard solution** is a solution whose *concentration is accurately known*. When the appropriate solute is available in pure form, a standard solution can be prepared by weighing out a sample of solute, transferring it completely to a *volumetric flask* (a flask of accurately known volume), and adding enough solvent to bring the volume up to the mark on the neck of the flask. This procedure is illustrated in Figure 15.7.

EXAMPLE 15.7 *Solution Composition: Calculating Mass from Molarity*

To analyze the alcohol content of a certain wine, a chemist needs 1.00 L of an aqueous 0.200 *M* $K_2Cr_2O_7$ (potassium dichromate) solution. How much solid $K_2Cr_2O_7$ (molar mass = 294.2 g) must be weighed out to make this solution?

Solution

We know the following:

> Molarity of the solution = 0.200 *M*
> Volume of the solution = 1.00 L

We need to calculate the number of grams of solute ($K_2Cr_2O_7$) present (and thus the mass needed to make the solution). First we determine the number of moles of $K_2Cr_2O_7$ present by multiplying the volume (in liters) by the molarity.

Liters × M ⟹ Moles of solute

$$1.00 \ \cancel{L \ solution} \times \frac{0.200 \ mol \ K_2Cr_2O_7}{\cancel{L \ solution}} = 0.200 \ mol \ K_2Cr_2O_7$$

Then we convert the moles of $K_2Cr_2O_7$ to grams, using the molar mass of $K_2Cr_2O_7$ (294.2 g).

$$0.200 \ \cancel{mol \ K_2Cr_2O_7} \times \frac{294.2 \ g \ K_2Cr_2O_7}{\cancel{mol \ K_2Cr_2O_7}} = 58.8 \ g \ K_2Cr_2O_7$$

Therefore, to make 1.00 L of 0.200 *M* $K_2Cr_2O_7$, the chemist must weigh out 58.8 g of $K_2Cr_2O_7$ and dissolve it in enough water to make 1.00 L of solution. This is most easily done by using a 1.00-L volumetric flask (see Figure 15.7).

 Self-Check Exercise 15.6

Formalin is an aqueous solution of formaldehyde, HCHO, used as a preservative for biological specimens. How many grams of formaldehyde must be used to prepare 2.5 L of 12.3 *M* formalin?

See Problems 15.51 and 15.52.

15.5 Dilution

AIM: To learn to calculate the concentration of a solution made by diluting a stock solution.

The molarities of stock solutions of the common concentrated acids are:

Sulfuric (H_2SO_4)	18 *M*
Nitric (HNO_3)	16 *M*
Hydrochloric (HCl)	12 *M*

To save time and space in the laboratory, solutions that are routinely used are often purchased or prepared in concentrated form (called *stock solutions*). Water (or another solvent) is then added to achieve the molarity desired for a particular solution. The process of adding more solvent to a solution is called **dilution.** For example, the common laboratory acids are purchased as concentrated solutions and diluted with water as they are needed. A typical dilution calculation involves determining how much water must be added to an amount of stock solution to achieve a solution of the desired concentration. The key to doing these calculations is to remember that *only water is added in the dilution.* The amount of solute in the final, more dilute, solution is the *same* as the amount of solute in the original concentrated stock solution. That is,

Dilution with water doesn't alter the number of moles of solute present.

Moles of solute after dilution = moles of solute before dilution

The number of moles of solute stays the same but more water is added, increasing the volume, so the molarity decreases.

$$M = \frac{\overset{\text{Remains constant}}{\text{moles of solute}}}{\underset{\text{Increases}}{\text{volume (L)}}}$$

Decreases   Increases
(water added)

For example, suppose we want to prepare 500. mL of 1.00 *M* acetic acid, $HC_2H_3O_2$, from a 17.5 *M* stock solution of acetic acid. What volume of the stock solution is required?

The first step is to determine the number of moles of acetic acid needed in the final solution. We do this by multiplying the volume of the solution by its molarity.

$$\begin{matrix} \text{Volume of dilute} \\ \text{solution (liters)} \end{matrix} \times \begin{matrix} \text{molarity of} \\ \text{dilute solution} \end{matrix} = \begin{matrix} \text{moles of solute} \\ \text{present} \end{matrix}$$

The number of moles of solute present in the more dilute solution equals the number of moles of solute that must be present in the more concentrated (stock) solution, because this is the only source of acetic acid.

Because molarity is defined in terms of liters, we must first change 500. mL to liters and then multiply the volume (in liters) by the molarity.

$$\underset{\substack{V_{\text{dilute solution}} \\ \text{(in mL)}}}{500.\ \text{mL solution}} \times \underset{\text{Convert mL to L}}{\frac{1\ \text{L solution}}{1000\ \text{mL solution}}} = 0.500\ \text{L solution}$$

Liters $\times$ M ⟹ Moles of solute

$$0.500\ \text{L solution} \times \underset{M_{\text{dilute solution}}}{\frac{1.00\ \text{mol HC}_2\text{H}_3\text{O}_2}{\text{L solution}}} = 0.500\ \text{mol HC}_2\text{H}_3\text{O}_2$$

Now we need to find the volume of 17.5 M acetic acid that contains 0.500 mol of $HC_2H_3O_2$. We will call this unknown volume V. Because volume $\times$ molarity = moles, we have

$$V\ (\text{in liters}) \times \frac{17.5\ \text{mol HC}_2\text{H}_3\text{O}_2}{\text{L solution}} = 0.500\ \text{mol HC}_2\text{H}_3\text{O}_2$$

Solving for V $\left(\text{by dividing both sides by } \dfrac{17.5\ \text{mol}}{\text{L solution}}\right)$ gives

$$V = \frac{0.500\ \text{mol HC}_2\text{H}_3\text{O}_2}{\dfrac{17.5\ \text{mol HC}_2\text{H}_3\text{O}_2}{\text{L solution}}} = 0.0286\ \text{L, or 28.6 mL, of solution}$$

Therefore, to make 500. mL of a 1.00 M acetic acid solution, we take 28.6 mL of 17.5 M acetic acid and dilute it to a total volume of 500. mL. This process is illustrated in Figure 15.8. Because the moles of solute remain the same before and after dilution, we can write

$$\underset{\substack{\text{Molarity} \quad \text{Volume} \\ \text{before} \quad \text{before} \\ \text{dilution} \quad \text{dilution}}}{\overset{\text{Initial Conditions}}{M_1 \times V_1}} = \text{moles of solute} = \underset{\substack{\text{Molarity} \quad \text{Volume} \\ \text{after} \quad \text{after} \\ \text{dilution} \quad \text{dilution}}}{\overset{\text{Final Conditions}}{M_2 \times V_2}}$$

We can check our calculations on acetic acid by showing that $M_1 \times V_1 = M_2 \times V_2$. In the above example, $M_1 = 17.5$ M, $V_1 = 0.0286$ L, $V_2 = 0.500$ L, and $M_2 = 1.00$ M, so

$$M_1 \times V_1 = 17.5\ \frac{\text{mol}}{\text{L}} \times 0.0286\ \text{L} = 0.500\ \text{mol}$$

$$M_2 \times V_2 = 1.00\ \frac{\text{mol}}{\text{L}} \times 0.500\ \text{L} = 0.500\ \text{mol}$$

(a)   (b)   (c)

FIGURE 15.8
(a) 28.6 mL of 17.5 *M* acetic acid solution are transferred to a volumetric flask that already contains some water. (b) Water is added to the flask (with swirling) to bring the volume to the calibration mark, and the solution is mixed by inverting the flask several times. (c) The resulting solution is 1.00 *M* acetic acid.

and therefore

$$M_1 \times V_1 = M_2 \times V_2$$

This shows that the volume (V_2) we calculated is correct.

EXAMPLE 15.8 *Calculating Concentrations of Diluted Solutions*

What volume of 16 *M* sulfuric acid must be used to prepare 1.5 L of a 0.10 *M* H_2SO_4 solution?

Solution

We can summarize what we are given as follows:

Initial Conditions (concentrated)	*Final Conditions (dilute)*
$M_1 = 16 \dfrac{\text{mol}}{\text{L}}$	$M_2 = 0.10 \dfrac{\text{mol}}{\text{L}}$
$V_1 = ?$	$V_2 = 1.5 \text{ L}$

We know that

$$\text{Moles of solute} = M_1 \times V_1 = M_2 \times V_2$$

and we can solve the equation

$$M_1 \times V_1 = M_2 \times V_2$$

for V_1 by dividing both sides by M_1:

$$\frac{\cancel{M_1} \times V_1}{\cancel{M_1}} = \frac{M_2 \times V_2}{M_1}$$

Approximate dilutions can be carried out using a calibrated beaker. Here concentrated sulfuric acid is being added to water to make a dilute solution.

to give

$$V_1 = \frac{M_2 \times V_2}{M_1}$$

Now we substitute the known values of M_2, V_2, and M_1.

$$V_1 = \frac{\left(0.10 \ \frac{\cancel{mol}}{\cancel{L}}\right)(1.5 \ L)}{16 \ \frac{\cancel{mol}}{\cancel{L}}} = 9.4 \times 10^{-3} L$$

$$9.4 \times 10^{-3} \cancel{L} \times \frac{1000 \ mL}{1 \cancel{L}} = 9.4 \ mL$$

It is always best to add concentrated acid to water, not water to the acid. That way, if any splashing occurs accidentally, it is dilute acid that splashes.

Therefore, $V_1 = 9.4 \times 10^{-3}$ L, or 9.4 mL. To make 1.5 L of 0.10 M H_2SO_4 using 16 M H_2SO_4, we must take 9.4 mL of the concentrated acid and dilute it with water to a final volume of 1.5 L. The correct way to do this is to add the 9.4 mL of acid to about 1 L of water and then dilute to 1.5 L by adding more water.

Self-Check Exercise 15.7

What volume of 12 M HCl must be taken to prepare 0.75 L of 0.25 M HCl?

See Problems 15.57 and 15.58.

15.6 Stoichiometry of Solution Reactions

AIM: To understand the strategy for solving stoichiometric problems for solution reactions.

Because so many important reactions occur in solution, it is important to be able to do stoichiometric calculations for solution reactions. The principles needed to perform these calculations are very similar to those developed in Chapter 10. It is helpful to think in terms of the following steps:

Steps for Solving Stoichiometric Problems Involving Solutions

See Section 7.3 for a discussion of net ionic equations.

STEP 1 Write the balanced equation for the reaction. For reactions involving ions, it is best to write the net ionic equation.

STEP 2 Calculate the moles of reactants.

STEP 3 Determine which reactant is limiting.

STEP 4 Calculate the moles of other reactants or products, as required.

STEP 5 Convert to grams or other units, if required.

EXAMPLE 15.9 *Solution Stoichiometry:*
Calculating Mass of Reactants and Products

Calculate the mass of solid NaCl that must be added to 1.50 L of a 0.100 *M* AgNO$_3$ solution to precipitate all of the Ag$^+$ ions in the form of AgCl. Calculate the mass of AgCl formed.

Solution

STEP 1 *Write the balanced equation for the reaction.*
When added to the AgNO$_3$ solution (which contains Ag$^+$ and NO$_3^-$ ions), the solid NaCl dissolves to yield Na$^+$ and Cl$^-$ ions. Solid AgCl forms according to the following balanced net ionic reaction:

This reaction was discussed in Section 7.2.

$$\text{Ag}^+(aq) + \text{Cl}^-(aq) \rightarrow \text{AgCl}(s)$$

STEP 2 *Calculate the moles of reactants.*
In this case we must add enough Cl$^-$ ions to just react with all the Ag$^+$ ions present, so we must calculate the moles of Ag$^+$ ions present in 1.50 L of a 0.100 *M* AgNO$_3$ solution. (Remember that a 0.100 *M* AgNO$_3$ solution contains 0.100 *M* Ag$^+$ ions and 0.100 *M* NO$_3^-$ ions.)

Liters × *M* ⇨ Moles of solute

$$1.50 \, \cancel{L} \times \frac{0.100 \text{ mol Ag}^+}{\cancel{L}} = 0.150 \text{ mol Ag}^+$$

Moles of Ag$^+$ present
in 1.5 L of 0.100 *M* AgNO$_3$

STEP 3 *Determine which reactant is limiting.*
In this situation we want to add just enough Cl$^-$ to react with the Ag$^+$ present. That is, we want to precipitate *all* the Ag$^+$ in the solution. Thus the Ag$^+$ present determines the amount of Cl$^-$ needed.

STEP 4 *Calculate the moles of Cl— required.*
We have 0.150 mol of Ag$^+$ ions and, because one Ag$^+$ ion reacts with one Cl$^-$ ion, we need 0.150 mol of Cl$^-$:

$$0.150 \, \cancel{\text{mol Ag}^+} \times \frac{1 \text{ mol Cl}^-}{1 \, \cancel{\text{mol Ag}^+}} = 0.150 \text{ mol Cl}^-$$

so 0.150 mol of AgCl will be formed.

$$0.150 \text{ mol Ag}^+ + 0.150 \text{ mol Cl}^- \rightarrow 0.150 \text{ mol AgCl}$$

STEP 5. *Convert to grams of NaCl required.*
To produce 0.150 mol Cl$^-$, we need 0.150 mol NaCl. We calculate the mass of NaCl required as follows:

When aqueous sodium chloride is added to a solution of silver nitrate, a white silver chloride precipitate forms.

$$0.150 \, \cancel{\text{mol NaCl}} \times \frac{58.4 \text{ g NaCl}}{\cancel{\text{mol NaCl}}} = 8.76 \text{ g NaCl}$$

Moles	⇨	Mass

Times molar mass

The mass of AgCl formed is

$$0.150 \, \cancel{\text{mol AgCl}} \times \frac{143.3 \text{ g AgCl}}{\cancel{\text{mol AgCl}}} = 21.5 \text{ g AgCl}$$

See Section 7.2 for a discussion of this reaction.

EXAMPLE 15.10 *Solution Stoichiometry: Determining Limiting Reactants and Calculating Mass of Products*

When $Ba(NO_3)_2$ and K_2CrO_4 react in aqueous solution, the yellow solid $BaCrO_4$ is formed. Calculate the mass of $BaCrO_4$ that forms when 3.50×10^{-3} mol of solid $Ba(NO_3)_2$ is dissolved in 265 mL of 0.0100 M K_2CrO_4 solution.

Solution

STEP 1 The original K_2CrO_4 solution contains the ions K^+ and CrO_4^{2-}. When the $Ba(NO_3)_2$ is dissolved in this solution, Ba^{2+} and NO_3^- ions are added. The Ba^{2+} and CrO_4^{2-} ions react to form solid $BaCrO_4$. The balanced net ionic equation is

$$Ba^{2+}(aq) + CrO_4^{2-}(aq) \rightarrow BaCrO_4(s)$$

STEP 2 Next we determine the moles of reactants. We are told that 3.50×10^{-3} mol of $Ba(NO_3)_2$ is added to the K_2CrO_4 solution. Each formula unit of $Ba(NO_3)_2$ contains one Ba^{2+} ion, so 3.50×10^{-3} mol of $Ba(NO_3)_2$ gives 3.50×10^{-3} mol of Ba^{2+} ions in solution.

3.50×10^{-3} mol $Ba(NO_3)_2$	dissolves to give	3.50×10^{-3} mol Ba^{2+}

Barium chromate precipitating.

Because $V \times M$ = moles of solute, we can compute the moles of K_2CrO_4 in the solution from the volume and molarity of the original solution. First we must convert the volume of the solution (265 mL) to liters.

$$265 \text{ mL} \times \frac{1 \text{ L}}{1000 \text{ mL}} = 0.265 \text{ L}$$

Next we determine the number of moles of K_2CrO_4, using the molarity of the K_2CrO_4 solution (0.0100 M).

$$0.265 \text{ L} \times \frac{0.0100 \text{ mol } K_2CrO_4}{\text{L}} = 2.65 \times 10^{-3} \text{ mol } K_2CrO_4$$

We know that

2.65×10^{-3} mol K_2CrO_4	dissolves to give	2.65×10^{-3} mol CrO_4^{2-}

so the solution contains 2.65×10^{-3} mol of CrO_4^{2-} ions.

STEP 3 The balanced equation tells us that one Ba^{2+} ion reacts with one CrO_4^{2-}. Because the number of moles of CrO_4^{2-} ions (2.65×10^{-3}) is smaller than the number of moles of Ba^{2+} ions (3.50×10^{-3}), the CrO_4^{2-} will run out first.

$$Ba^{2+}(aq) + CrO_4^{2-}(aq) \rightarrow BaCrO_4(s)$$

3.50×10^{-3} mol	2.65×10^{-3} mol

Smaller (runs out first)

Therefore, the CrO_4^{2-} is limiting.

STEP 4   The 2.65×10^{-3} mol of CrO_4^{2-} ions will react with 2.65×10^{-3} mol of Ba^{2+} ions to form 2.65×10^{-3} mol of $BaCrO_4$.

STEP 5   The mass of $BaCrO_4$ formed is obtained from its molar mass (253.3 g) as follows:

$$2.65 \times 10^{-3} \text{ mol BaCrO}_4 \times \frac{253.3 \text{ g BaCrO}_4}{\text{mol BaCrO}_4} = 0.671 \text{ g BaCrO}_4$$

Self-Check Exercise 15.8

When aqueous solutions of Na_2SO_4 and $Pb(NO_3)_2$ are mixed, $PbSO_4$ precipitates. Calculate the mass of $PbSO_4$ formed when 1.25 L of 0.0500 *M* $Pb(NO_3)_2$ and 2.00 L of 0.0250 *M* Na_2SO_4 are mixed.

Hint: Calculate the moles of Pb^{2+} and SO_4^{2-} in the mixed solution, decide which ion is limiting, and calculate the moles of $PbSO_4$ formed.

See Problems 15.65 through 15.68.

15.7 Neutralization Reactions

AIM: To learn how to do calculations involved in acid–base reactions.

So far we have considered the stoichiometry of reactions in solution that result in the formation of a precipitate. Another common type of solution reaction occurs between an acid and a base. We introduced these reactions in Section 7.4. Recall from that discussion that an acid is a substance that furnishes H^+ ions. A strong acid, such as hydrochloric acid, HCl, dissociates (ionizes) completely in water.

$$HCl(aq) \;\rightarrow\; H^+(aq) + Cl^-(aq)$$

Strong bases are water-soluble metal hydroxides, which are completely dissociated in water. An example is NaOH, which dissolves in water to give Na^+ and OH^- ions.

$$NaOH(s) \xrightarrow{\text{H}_2\text{O}(l)} Na^+(aq) + OH^-(aq)$$

When a strong acid and strong base react, the net ionic reaction is

$$H^+(aq) + OH^-(aq) \;\rightarrow\; H_2O(l)$$

An acid–base reaction is often called a **neutralization reaction.** When just enough strong base is added to react exactly with the strong acid in a solution, we say the acid has been *neutralized.* One product of this reaction is always water. The steps in dealing with the stoichiometry of any neutralization reaction are the same as those we followed in the previous section.

EXAMPLE 15.11 *Solution Stoichiometry: Calculating Volume in Neutralization Reactions*

What volume of a 0.100 *M* HCl solution is needed to neutralize 25.0 mL of a 0.350 *M* NaOH solution?

Solution

STEP 1 *Write the balanced equation for the reaction.*
Hydrochloric acid is a strong acid, so all the HCl molecules dissociate to produce H^+ and Cl^- ions. Also, when the strong base NaOH dissolves, the solution contains Na^+ and OH^- ions. When these two solutions are mixed, the H^+ ions from the hydrochloric acid react with the OH^- ions from the sodium hydroxide solution to form water. The balanced net ionic equation for the reaction is

$$H^+(aq) \; + \; OH^-(aq) \; \rightarrow \; H_2O(l)$$

STEP 2 *Calculate the moles of reactants.*
In this problem we are given a volume (25.0 mL) of 0.350 *M* NaOH, and we want to add just enough 0.100 *M* HCl to provide just enough H^+ ions to react with all the OH^-. Therefore, we must calculate the number of moles of OH^- ions in the 25.0-mL sample of 0.350 *M* NaOH. To do this, we first change the volume to liters and multiply by the molarity.

$$25.0 \; \cancel{mL \; NaOH} \times \frac{1 \, \cancel{L}}{1000 \; \cancel{mL}} \times \frac{0.350 \; mol \; OH^-}{\cancel{L \; NaOH}} = 8.75 \times 10^{-3} \; mol \; OH^-$$

Moles of OH^- present
in 25.0 mL of
0.350 *M* NaOH

STEP 3 *Determine which reactant is limiting.*
This problem requires the addition of just enough H^+ ions to react exactly with the OH^- ions present, so the number of moles of OH^- ions present determines the number of moles of H^+ that must be added. The OH^- ions are limiting.

STEP 4 *Calculate the moles of H+ required.*
The balanced equation tells us that the H^+ and OH^- ions react in a 1:1 ratio, so 8.75×10^{-3} mol of H^+ ions is required to neutralize (exactly react with) the 8.75×10^{-3} mol of OH^- ions present.

STEP 5 *Calculate the volume of 0.100 M HCl required.*
Next we must find the volume (V) of 0.100 *M* HCl required to furnish this amount of H^+ ions. Because the volume (in liters) times the molarity gives

the number of moles, we have

$$V \times \frac{0.100 \text{ mol H}^+}{\text{L}} = 8.75 \times 10^{-3} \text{ mol H}^+$$

Unknown
volume
(in liters)   Moles of
H$^+$ needed

Now we must solve for V by dividing both sides of the equation by 0.100.

$$V \times \frac{0.100 \text{ mol H}^+}{0.100 \text{ L}} = \frac{8.75 \times 10^{-3} \text{ mol H}^+}{0.100}$$

$$V = 8.75 \times 10^{-2} \text{ L}$$

Changing liters to milliliters, we have

$$V = 8.75 \times 10^{-2} \text{ L} \times \frac{1000 \text{ ml}}{\text{L}} = 87.5 \text{ mL}$$

Therefore, 87.5 mL of 0.100 M HCl are required to neutralize 25.0 mL of 0.350 M NaOH.

 Self-Check Exercise 15.9

Calculate the volume of 0.10 M HNO$_3$ needed to neutralize 125 mL of 0.050 M KOH.

See Problems 15.69 through 15.74.

15.8 *Solution Composition: Normality*

AIMS: To learn about normality and equivalent weight. To learn to use these concepts in stoichiometric calculations.

Normality is another unit of concentration that is sometimes used, especially when dealing with acids and bases. The use of normality focuses mainly on the H$^+$ and OH$^-$ available in an acid–base reaction. Before we discuss normality, however, we need to define some terms. One **equivalent of an acid** is the *amount of that acid that can furnish 1 mol of H+ ions.* Similarly, one **equivalent of a base** is defined as the *amount of that base that can furnish 1 mol of OH− ions.* The **equivalent weight** of an acid or base is the mass in grams of 1 equivalent (equiv) of that acid or base.

The common strong acids are HCl, HNO$_3$, and H$_2$SO$_4$. For HCl and HNO$_3$ each molecule of acid furnishes one H$^+$ ion, so 1 mol of HCl can furnish 1 mol of H$^+$ ions. This means that

Furnishes 1 mol of H$^+$
↓

$$1 \text{ mol HCl} = 1 \text{ equiv HCl}$$
$$\text{Molar mass (HCl)} = \text{equivalent weight (HCl)}$$

Likewise, for HNO_3,

$$1 \text{ mol } HNO_3 = 1 \text{ equiv } HNO_3$$
$$\text{Molar mass } (HNO_3) = \text{equivalent weight } (HNO_3)$$

However, H_2SO_4 can furnish *two* H^+ ions per molecule, so 1 mol of H_2SO_4 can furnish *two* mol of H^+. This means that

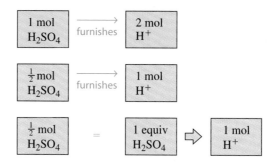

Because each mole of H_2SO_4 can furnish 2 mol of H^+, we need only to take $\frac{1}{2}$ mol of H_2SO_4 to get 1 equiv of H_2SO_4. Therefore,

$$\frac{1}{2} \text{ mol } H_2SO_4 = 1 \text{ equiv } H_2SO_4$$

and

$$\text{Equivalent weight } (H_2SO_4) = \frac{1}{2} \text{ molar mass } (H_2SO_4)$$
$$= \frac{1}{2} (98 \text{ g}) = 49 \text{ g}$$

The equivalent weight of H_2SO_4 is 49 g.

The common strong bases are NaOH and KOH. For NaOH and KOH, each formula unit furnishes one OH^- ion, so we can say

$$1 \text{ mol } NaOH = 1 \text{ equiv } NaOH$$
$$\text{Molar mass } (NaOH) = \text{equivalent weight } (NaOH)$$

$$1 \text{ mol } KOH = 1 \text{ equiv } KOH$$
$$\text{Molar mass } (KOH) = \text{equivalent weight } (KOH)$$

These ideas are summarized in Table 15.2.

TABLE 15.2

The Molar Masses and Equivalent Weights of the Common Strong Acids and Bases

	Molar Mass (g)	Equivalent Weight (g)
Acid		
HCl	36.5	36.5
HNO_3	63.0	63.0
H_2SO_4	98.0	$49.0 = \dfrac{98.0}{2}$
Base		
NaOH	40.0	40.0
KOH	56.1	56.1

EXAMPLE 15.12 *Solution Stoichiometry: Calculating Equivalent Weight*

Phosphoric acid, H_3PO_4, can furnish three H^+ ions per molecule. Calculate the equivalent weight of H_3PO_4.

Solution

The key point here involves how many protons (H^+ ions) each molecule of H_3PO_4 can furnish.

$$\boxed{H_3PO_4} \Rightarrow_{\text{furnishes}} \boxed{?\ H^+}$$

Because each H_3PO_4 can furnish three H^+ ions, 1 mol of H_3PO_4 can furnish 3 mol of H^+ ions:

$$\boxed{\begin{array}{c}1\ \text{mol}\\ H_3PO_4\end{array}} \Rightarrow_{\text{furnishes}} \boxed{\begin{array}{c}3\ \text{mol}\\ H^+\end{array}}$$

so 1 equiv of H_3PO_4 (the amount that can furnish 1 mol of H^+) is one-third of a mole.

$$\boxed{\begin{array}{c}\frac{1}{3}\text{mol}\\ H_3PO_4\end{array}} \Rightarrow_{\text{furnishes}} \boxed{\begin{array}{c}1\ \text{mol}\\ H^+\end{array}}$$

This means the equivalent weight of H_3PO_4 is one-third its molar mass.

$$\boxed{\begin{array}{c}\text{Equivalent}\\ \text{weight}\end{array}} = \boxed{\begin{array}{c}\text{Molar mass}\\ \hline 3\end{array}}$$

$$\text{Equivalent weight } (H_3PO_4) = \frac{\text{molar mass } (H_3PO_4)}{3}$$

$$= \frac{98.0\ \text{g}}{3} = 32.7\ \text{g}$$

Normality (N) is defined as the number of equivalents of solute per liter of solution.

$$\text{Normality} = N = \frac{\text{number of equivalents}}{1\ \text{liter of solution}} = \frac{\text{equivalents}}{\text{liter}} = \frac{\text{equiv}}{L}$$

This means that a 1 N solution contains 1 equivalent of solute per liter of solution. Notice that when we multiply the volume of a solution in liters by the normality, we get the number of equivalents.

 L × Normality ⇨ Equiv

$$N \times V = \frac{\text{equiv}}{\cancel{L}} \times \cancel{L} = \text{equiv}$$

EXAMPLE 15.13 *Solution Stoichiometry: Calculating Normality*

A solution of sulfuric acid contains 86 g of H_2SO_4 per liter of solution. Calculate the normality of this solution.

Whenever you need to calculate the concentration of a solution, first write the appropriate definition. Then decide how to calculate the quantities shown in the definition.

Solution

We want to calculate the normality of this solution, so we focus on the definition of normality, the number of equivalents per liter:

$$N = \frac{\text{equiv}}{\text{L}}$$

This definition leads to two questions we need to answer:

1. What is the number of equivalents?

2. What is the volume?

We know the volume; it is 1.0 L. To find the number of equivalents present, we must calculate the number of equivalents represented by 86 g of H_2SO_4. To do this calculation, we focus on the definition of the equivalent: it is the amount of acid that furnishes 1 mol of H^+. Because H_2SO_4 can furnish two H^+ ions per molecule, 1 equiv of H_2SO_4 is $\frac{1}{2}$ mol of H_2SO_4, so

$$\text{Equivalent weight (H}_2\text{SO}_4) = \frac{\text{molar mass (H}_2\text{SO}_4)}{2}$$

$$= \frac{98.0 \text{ g}}{2} = 49.0 \text{ g}$$

We have 86 g of H_2SO_4.

$$86 \text{ g H}_2\text{SO}_4 \times \frac{1 \text{ equiv H}_2\text{SO}_4}{49.0 \text{ g H}_2\text{SO}_4} = 1.8 \text{ equiv H}_2\text{SO}_4$$

$$N = \frac{\text{equiv}}{\text{L}} = \frac{1.8 \text{ equiv H}_2\text{SO}_4}{1.0 \text{ L}} = 1.8 \text{ N H}_2\text{SO}_4$$

We know that 86 g is more than 1 equiv of H_2SO_4 (49 g), so this answer makes sense.

 Self-Check Exercise 15.10

Calculate the normality of a solution containing 23.6 g of KOH in 755 mL of solution.

See Problems 15.79 and 15.80.

The main advantage of using equivalents is that 1 equiv of acid contains the same number of available H^+ ions as the number of OH^- ions present in 1 equiv of base. That is,

0.75 equiv (base) will react exactly with 0.75 equiv (acid).

0.23 equiv (base) will react exactly with 0.23 equiv (acid).

And so on.

In each of these cases, the *number of* H^+ ions furnished by the sample of acid is the same as the *number of* OH^- ions furnished by the sample of base. The point is that n *equivalents of any acid will exactly neutralize* n *equivalents of any base.*

$$\boxed{\begin{array}{c} \text{n equiv} \\ \text{acid} \end{array}} \quad \leftarrow \text{ reacts exactly with } \rightarrow \quad \boxed{\begin{array}{c} \text{n equiv} \\ \text{base} \end{array}}$$

Because we know that equal equivalents of acid and base are required for neutralization, we can say that

$$\text{equiv (acid)} = \text{equiv (base)}$$

That is,

$$N_{\text{acid}} \times V_{\text{acid}} = \text{equiv (acid)} = \text{equiv (base)} = N_{\text{base}} \times V_{\text{base}}$$

Therefore, for any neutralization reaction, the following relationship holds:

$$N_{\text{acid}} \times V_{\text{acid}} = N_{\text{base}} \times V_{\text{base}}$$

EXAMPLE 15.14 *Solution Stoichiometry: Using Normality in Calculations*

What volume of a 0.075 N KOH solution is required to react exactly with 0.135 L of 0.45 N H_3PO_4?

Solution

We know that for neutralization, equiv (acid) = equiv (base), or

$$N_{\text{acid}} \times V_{\text{acid}} = N_{\text{base}} \times V_{\text{base}}$$

We want to calculate for the volume of base, V_{base}, so we solve for V_{base} by dividing both sides by N_{base}.

$$\frac{N_{\text{acid}} \times V_{\text{acid}}}{N_{\text{base}}} = \frac{\cancel{N_{\text{base}}} \times V_{\text{base}}}{\cancel{N_{\text{base}}}} = V_{\text{base}}$$

Now we can substitute the given values $N_{\text{acid}} = 0.45\ N$, $V_{\text{acid}} = 0.135$ L, and $N_{\text{base}} = 0.075\ N$ into the equation.

$$V_{\text{base}} = \frac{N_{\text{acid}} \times V_{\text{acid}}}{N_{\text{base}}} = \frac{\left(0.45\ \dfrac{\text{equiv}}{\cancel{L}}\right)(0.135\ \text{L})}{0.075\ \dfrac{\text{equiv}}{\cancel{L}}} = 0.81\ \text{L}$$

This gives $V_{\text{base}} = 0.81$ L, so 0.81 L of 0.075 N KOH is required to react exactly with 0.135 L of 0.45 N H_3PO_4.

 Self-Check Exercise 15.11

What volume of 0.50 N H_2SO_4 is required to react exactly with 0.250 L of 0.80 N KOH?

See Problems 15.85 and 15.86.

Chapter Review

Key Terms

solution *(p. 437)*
solvent *(p. 438)*
solute *(p. 438)*
aqueous solution *(p. 438)*
saturated *(15.2)*
unsaturated *(15.2)*
concentrated *(15.2)*
dilute *(15.2)*
mass percent *(15.3)*
molarity (*M*) *(15.4)*
standard solution *(15.4)*
dilution *(15.5)*
neutralization reaction *(15.7)*
equivalent of an acid *(15.8)*

equivalent of a base *(15.8)*
equivalent weight *(15.8)*
normality *(15.8)*

Summary

1. A solution is a homogeneous mixture. The solubility of a solute in a given solvent depends on the interactions between the solvent and solute particles. Water dissolves many ionic compounds and compounds with polar molecules, because strong forces occur between the solute and the polar water molecules. Nonpolar solvents tend to dissolve nonpolar solutes. "Like dissolves like."

2. Solution composition can be described in many ways. Two of the most important are in terms of mass percent of solute:

$$\text{Mass percent} = \frac{\text{mass of solute}}{\text{mass of solution}} \times 100\%$$

and molarity:

$$\text{Molarity} = \frac{\text{moles of solute}}{\text{liters of solution}}$$

3. A standard solution is one whose concentration is accurately known. Solutions are often made from a stock solution by dilution. When a solution is diluted, only solvent is added, which means that

Moles of solute after dilution = moles of solute before dilution

4. Normality is defined as the number of equivalents per liter of solution. One equivalent of acid is the amount of acid that furnishes 1 mol of H^+ ions. One equivalent of base is the amount of base that furnishes 1 mol of OH^- ions.

Questions and Problems

All even-numbered exercises have answers in the back of this book and solutions in the Solutions Guide.

15.1 ■ *Solubility*

QUESTIONS

1. What does it mean that a solution is a *homogeneous* mixture? Give two examples of homogeneous mixtures.

2. How do the properties of a *non*homogeneous (heterogeneous) mixture differ from those of a solution? Give two examples of *non*homogeneous mixtures.

3. In a solution, the substance present in the largest amount is called the _____, whereas the other substances present are called the _____.

4. A metallic alloy, such as brass, is an example of a _____ solution.

5. Discuss how an *ionic* solute dissolves in water. How are the strong interionic forces in the solid overcome to permit the solid to dissolve? How are the dissolved positive and negative ions shielded from one another, preventing them from recombining to form the solid?

6. Why are some molecular solids (such as sugar or ethyl alcohol) soluble in water, while other molecular solids (such as petroleum) are insoluble in water? What structural feature(s) of *some* molecular solids may tend to make them soluble in water?

7. A substance such as NaCl dissolves in water because the strong ionic forces that exist in solid NaCl can be overcome by, and replaced by, forces between _____ and the ions.

8. When an ionic substance such as potassium bromide, KBr, dissolves, the resulting solution contains separate, hydrated ions that behave _____ of one another.

15.2 ■ *Solution Composition: An Introduction*

QUESTIONS

9. A solution that contains as much solute as will dissolve at a given temperature is said to be _____.

10. A solution that has not reached its limit of dissolved solute is said to be _____.

11. A solution is a homogeneous mixture and, unlike a compound, has _____ composition.

12. The label "concentrated H_2SO_4" on a bottle means that there is a relatively _____ amount of H_2SO_4 present in the solution.

15.3 ■ Solution Composition: Mass Percent

QUESTIONS

13. A solution that is 5% by mass NaCl contains 5 g of NaCl per _____ g of solution.

14. A solution has been prepared to be 9% (by mass) glucose. For every 100.0 g of solution present there are _____ g glucose.

PROBLEMS

15. Calculate the mass percent of KNO_3 in each of the following solutions.
    a. 12 g of KNO_3 in 100. g of water
    b. 12 g of KNO_3 in 88 g of water
    c. 152 mg of KNO_3 in 786 mg of water
    d. 152 mg of KNO_3 in 786 g of water

16. Calculate the mass percent of NH_4NO_3 in each of the following solutions.
    a. 1.0 g NH_4NO_3 in 10 g water
    b. 1.0 g NH_4NO_3 in 25 g water
    c. 1.0 g NH_4NO_3 in 75 g water
    d. 1.0 g NH_4NO_3 in 100 g water

17. Calculate the mass, in grams, of NaCl present in each of the following solutions.
    a. 11.5 g of 6.25% NaCl solution
    b. 6.25 g of 11.5% NaCl solution
    c. 54.3 g of 0.91% NaCl solution
    d. 452 g of 12.3% NaCl solution

18. For a 15.0% (by mass) NaCl solution, calculate the indicated quantity.
    a. the mass of NaCl in 150. g of the solution
    b. the amount of solution needed to obtain 35.0 g NaCl
    c. the mass of NaCl needed to make 1000. g of the solution
    d. the mass of NaCl contained in 1000. g of the solution

19. In general chemistry laboratories, a sodium hydrogen carbonate solution is typically available for neutralizing spills of acid. If 50. g of $NaHCO_3$ is mixed with 950. g of water, what is the mass percent of the solution?

20. A certain alloy is made by dissolving 5.31 g of copper and 4.03 g of zinc in 145 g of iron. Calculate the percent of each component in the alloy.

21. The label of a brand of household insecticide spray lists the ingredients as "pyrethrums, 5.4%; inert ingredients, 44.2%; propellant, 50.4%." If the total net mass of the contents of the spray can is 24.0 oz, what is the total mass of pyrethrums present?

22. A 151-g portion of a sodium chloride solution is evaporated, producing 5.35 g of dry solid NaCl. Calculate the percentage of NaCl in the original solution.

23. If 45 g of a 2.2% (by mass) $NaHCO_3$ solution is to be prepared, how many grams of $NaHCO_3$ are needed?

24. How many grams of KBr are contained in 125 g of a 6.25% (by mass) KBr solution?

25. How many grams of sugar are contained in 250. g of an aqueous mixture that contains (by mass) 10.% sugar and 5.0% alcohol?

26. How many grams of $CuCl_2$ are required to prepare 1250. g of a 1.25% (by mass) $CuCl_2$ solution?

27. Concentrated hydrochloric acid solution contains 37.2% (by mass) HCl and has a density of 1.19 g/mL. How many grams of hydrogen chloride are contained in 255 mL of concentrated HCl solution?

28. A hexane solution contains as impurities 5.2% (by mass) heptane and 2.9% (by mass) pentane. Calculate the mass of each component present in 93 g of the solution.

15.4 ■ Solution Composition: Molarity

QUESTIONS

29. A solution that is labeled "1 *M* HCl" contains 1 mol of dissolved HCl per _____ of the solution.

30. A solution that is 0.50 *M* in $CuCl_2$ contains _____ mol of Cu^{2+} and _____ mol of Cl^- per liter.

31. What is a *standard* solution? Describe the steps involved in preparing a standard solution.

32. If you were to prepare exactly 1.00 L of a 5 *M* NaCl solution, you would *not* need exactly 1.00 L of water. Explain.

PROBLEMS

33. For each of the following solutions, the number of moles of solute is given, followed by the total volume of solution prepared. Calculate the molarity.
    a. 0.50 mol of NaCl; 0.200 L
    b. 0.50 mol of NaCl; 0.125 L
    c. 0.25 mol of NaCl; 100. mL
    d. 0.75 mol of NaCl; 300. mL

34. For each of the following solutions, the number of moles of solute is given, followed by the total volume of solution prepared. Calculate the molarity.
    a. 0.50 mol KBr; 250 mL
    b. 0.50 mol KBr; 500. mL
    c. 0.50 mol KBr; 750 mL
    d. 0.50 mol KBr; 1.0 L

35. For each of the following solutions, the mass of solute is given, followed by the total volume of solution prepared. Calculate the molarity.
    a. 521 g of KBr; 4.25 L
    b. 49.3 g of $NaNO_3$; 151 mL
    c. 6.25 mg of NH_4Cl; 1.75 mL
    d. 58.5 g of NaCl; 2.01 L

36. For each of the following solutions the mass of the solute is given, followed by the total volume of the solution prepared. Calculate the molarity.
    a. 4.25 g $CuCl_2$; 125 mL
    b. 0.101 g $NaHCO_3$; 11.3 mL
    c. 52.9 g Na_2CO_3; 1.15 L
    d. 0.14 mg KOH; 1.5 mL

37. If a 45.3-g sample of potassium nitrate is dissolved in enough water to make 225 mL of solution, what will be the molarity?

38. If 275 g of $CuSO_4$ is dissolved in enough water to make 4.25 L, what is the molarity of the solution?

39. Standard solutions of calcium ion used to test for water hardness are prepared by dissolving pure calcium carbonate, $CaCO_3$, in dilute hydrochloric acid. A 1.745-g sample of $CaCO_3$ is placed in a 250.0-mL volumetric flask and dissolved in HCl. Then the solution is diluted to the calibration mark of the volumetric flask. Calculate the resulting molarity of calcium ion.

40. An alcoholic iodine solution ("tincture" of iodine) is prepared by dissolving 5.15 g of iodine crystals in enough alcohol to make a volume of 225 mL. Calculate the molarity of iodine in the solution.

41. A 1.5 mg sample of NaCl is dissolved in enough water to make 1.0 mL of solution. What is the molarity of NaCl in the solution?

42. If 495 g of NaOH is dissolved to a final total volume of 20.0 L, what is the molarity of the solution?

43. How many *moles* of the indicated solute does each of the following solutions contain?
    a. 10.0 L of 0.550 *M* $NaHCO_3$ solution
    b. 5.0 L of 12 *M* HCl solution
    c. 250. mL of 19.4 *M* NaOH solution
    d. 125 mL of 17.0 *M* acetic acid, $HC_2H_3O_2$

44. Calculate the number of *moles* and number of *grams* of the indicated solutes contained in each of the following solution samples.
    a. 1.29 L of 0.411 *M* HCl
    b. 145 mL of 0.215 *M* $CaCl_2$
    c. 24.9 mL of 1.15 *M* HNO_3
    d. 1.01 L of 5.41 *M* NaCl

45. How many *grams* of the indicated solute does each of the following solutions contain?
    a. 2.00 L of 1.33 *M* NaCl solution
    b. 0.050 mL (approximately 1 drop) of 6.0 *M* HCl solution
    c. 125 mL of 3.05 *M* HNO_3 solution
    d. 1.25 L of 0.503 *M* NaBr solution

46. What mass in *grams* of the indicated solute does each of the following solutions contain?
    a. 145 mL of 0.0221 M EDTA solution (Molar mass for EDTA =292.2 g)
    b. 2.25 L of 0.135 *M* $CuSO_4$ solution
    c. 1.02 mL of 0.452 *M* H_3PO_4 solution
    d. 24 mL of 1.0 *M* HCl solution

47. What mass (in grams) of NH_4Cl is needed to prepare 450. mL of 0.251 *M* NH_4Cl solution?

48. What volume of 0.25 *M* NaCl solution can be prepared from 5.2 g NaCl(s)?

49. Calculate the number of moles of the indicated ion present in each of the following solutions.
    a. Na^+ ion in 1.00 L of 0.251 *M* Na_2SO_4 solution
    b. Cl^- ion in 5.50 L of 0.10 *M* $FeCl_3$ solution
    c. NO_3^- ion in 100. mL of 0.55 *M* $Ba(NO_3)_2$ solution
    d. NH_4^+ ion in 250. mL of 0.350 *M* $(NH_4)_2SO_4$ solution

50. Calculate the number of moles of *each* ion present in each of the following solutions.
    a. 10.2 mL of 0.451 *M* $AlCl_3$ solution
    b. 5.51 L of 0.103 *M* Na_3PO_4 solution
    c. 1.75 mL of 1.25 *M* $CuCl_2$ solution
    d. 25.2 mL of 0.00157 *M* $Ca(OH)_2$ solution

51. Standard silver nitrate solutions are used in the titration analysis of samples containing chloride ion. How many grams of silver nitrate are needed to prepare 250. mL of standard 0.100 *M* $AgNO_3$ solution?

52. The substance Na_2H_2EDTA ($Na_2H_2C_{10}H_{12}N_2O_8$) is used in the titration analysis of samples containing "hard water." How many grams of Na_2H_2EDTA are needed to prepare 250 mL of 0.0200 *M* "EDTA" solution?

15.5 ■ *Dilution*

QUESTIONS

53. When a concentrated stock solution is diluted to prepare a less concentrated reagent, the number of _____ is the same both before and after the dilution.

54. When the volume of a given solution is doubled (by adding water), the new concentration of solute is _____ the original concentration.

55. Calculate the new molarity that results when each of the following solutions is diluted to a final total volume of 500.0 mL.
    a. 250.0 mL of 0.1015 *M* HCl
    b. 10.1 mL of 5.41 *M* NaCl
    c. 50.0 mL of 1.21 *M* HNO$_3$
    d. 125.1 mL of 0.5514 *M* NaOH

56. Calculate the new molarity that results when 250. mL of water is added to each of the following solutions.
    a. 125 mL of 0.251 *M* HCl
    b. 445 mL of 0.499 *M* H$_2$SO$_4$
    c. 5.25 L of 0.101 *M* HNO$_3$
    d. 11.2 mL of 14.5 *M* HC$_2$H$_3$O$_2$

57. How many mL of 3.0 *M* H$_2$SO$_4$ solution can be prepared by using 100. mL of 18.0 *M* H$_2$SO$_4$?

58. Concentrated sulfuric acid is typically 18.1 *M* H$_2$SO$_4$. Calculate the volume (in mL) of concentrated sulfuric acid needed to prepare 125 mL of a 0.100 *M* H$_2$SO$_4$ solution?

59. A chemistry student needs 125 mL of 0.150 *M* NaOH solution for her experiment, but the only solution available in the laboratory is 3.02 *M*. Describe how the student could prepare the solution she needs.

60. If 75 mL of 0.211 *M* NaOH is diluted to a final volume of 125 mL, what is the concentration of NaOH in the diluted solution?

61. How much *water* must be added to 500. mL of 0.200 *M* HCl to produce a 0.150 *M* solution? (Assume that the volumes are additive.)

62. When 5.0 L of water is added to 1.0 L of 6.0 *M* HCl, what is the molarity of the resulting solution? (Assume that the volumes are additive.)

15.6 ■ *Stoichiometry of Solution Reactions*

63. One way to determine the amount of chloride ion in a water sample is to titrate the sample with standard AgNO$_3$ solution to produce solid AgCl.

$$Ag^+(aq) + Cl^-(aq) \rightarrow AgCl(s)$$

If a 25.0-mL water sample requires 27.2 mL of 0.104 *M* AgNO$_3$ in such a titration, what is the concentration of Cl$^-$ in the sample?

64. What volume (in mL) of 0.25 *M* Na$_2$SO$_4$ solution is needed to precipitate all the barium, as BaSO$_4$(*s*), from 12.5 mL of 0.15 *M* Ba(NO$_3$)$_2$ solution?

$$Ba(NO_3)_2 \, (aq) + Na_2SO_4 \, (aq) \rightarrow BaSO_4 \, (s) + 2NaNO_3 \, (aq)$$

65. If 36.2 mL of 0.158 *M* CaCl$_2$ solution is added to 37.5 mL of 0.149 *M* Na$_2$CO$_3$, what mass of calcium carbonate, CaCO$_3$, will be precipitated? The reaction is

$$CaCl_2 \, (aq) + Na_2CO_3 \, (aq) \rightarrow CaCO_3 \, (s) + 2NaCl \, (aq)$$

66. What mass (in grams) of AgNO$_3$ is required to precipitate all of the chloride ion, as AgCl, from 135 mL of 0.101 *M* NaCl solution?

$$AgNO_3(aq) + NaCl(aq) \rightarrow AgCl(s) + NaNO_3(aq)$$

67. When aqueous solutions of lead(II) ion are treated with potassium chromate solution, a bright yellow precipitate of lead(II) chromate, PbCrO$_4$, forms. How many grams of lead chromate form when a 1.00-g sample of Pb(NO$_3$)$_2$ is added to 25.0 mL of 1.00 *M* K$_2$CrO$_4$ solution?

68. Aluminum ion may be precipitated from aqueous solution by addition of hydroxide ion, forming Al(OH)$_3$. A large excess of hydroxide ion must not be added, however, because the precipitate of Al(OH)$_3$ will redissolve to form a soluble aluminum/hydroxide complex. How many grams of solid NaOH should be added to 10.0 mL of 0.250 *M* AlCl$_3$ to just precipitate all the aluminum?

15.7 ■ *Neutralization Reactions*

69. What volume of 0.200 *M* HCl solution is needed to exactly neutralize 25.0 mL of 0.150 *M* NaOH solution?

70. What volume of 0.175 *M* HCl solution is needed to exactly neutralize 24.9 mL of 0.451 *M* NaOH solution?

71. A 25.0-mL sample of HNO$_3$ solution of unknown molarity is exactly neutralized by titration with 22.7 mL of 0.204 *M* NaOH solution. Calculate the molarity of the HNO$_3$ solution.

72. The total acidity in water samples can be determined by neutralization with standard sodium hydroxide solution. What is the total concentration of hydrogen ion, H$^+$, present in a water sample if 100. mL of the sample requires 7.2 mL of 2.5×10^{-3} *M* NaOH to be neutralized?

73. What volume of 1.00 *M* NaOH is required to neutralize each of the following solutions?
    a. 25.0 mL of 0.154 *M* acetic acid, HC$_2$H$_3$O$_2$
    b. 35.0 mL of 0.102 *M* hydrofluoric acid, HF
    c. 10.0 mL of 0.143 *M* phosphoric acid, H$_3$PO$_4$
    d. 35.0 mL of 0.220 *M* sulfuric acid, H$_2$SO$_4$

74. What volume of 0.101 *M* HNO$_3$ is required to neutralize each of the following solutions?
    a. 12.7 mL of 0.501 *M* NaOH
    b. 24.9 mL of 0.00491 *M* Ba(OH)$_2$
    c. 49.1 mL of 0.103 *M* NH$_3$
    d. 1.21 L of 0.102 *M* KOH

15.8 ■ *Solution Composition: Normality*

QUESTIONS

75. One _____ of an acid (or base) is the amount of the acid (or base) required to provide 1 mol of hydrogen ion (or hydroxide ion).

76. A solution that contains 1 equivalent of acid or base per liter is said to be a _____ solution.

77. Explain why the equivalent weight of H_2SO_4 is half the molar mass of this substance. How many hydrogen ions are produced when each H_2SO_4 molecule reacts with excess OH^- ions?

78. How many equivalents of hydroxide ion are needed to react with 1.53 equivalents of hydrogen ion? How did you know this when no balanced chemical equation was provided for the reaction?

PROBLEMS

79. For each of the following solutions, calculate the mass of solute that would be needed to prepare 125 mL of solution.
    a. 0.151 *N* HNO_3
    b. 0.215 *N* H_2SO_4
    c. 0.0751 *N* H_3PO_4

80. For each of the following solutions, the mass of solute taken is indicated, along with the total volume of solution prepared. Calculate the normality of each solution.
    a. 0.113 g NaOH; 10.2 mL
    b. 12.5 mg $Ca(OH)_2$; 100. mL
    c. 12.4 g H_2SO_4; 155 mL

81. Calculate the normality of each of the following solutions.
    a. 0.250 *M* HCl
    b. 0.105 *M* H_2SO_4
    c. 5.3×10^{-2} *M* H_3PO_4

82. Calculate the normality of each of the following solutions.
    a. 4.01×10^{-3} *M* H_3PO_4
    b. 0.000101 *M* $Ba(OH)_2$
    c. 0.101 *M* $HC_2H_3O_2$

83. A solution of phosphoric acid, H_3PO_4, is found to contain 35.2 g of H_3PO_4 per liter of solution. Calculate the molarity and normality of the solution.

84. A solution of the sparingly soluble base $Ca(OH)_2$ is prepared in a volumetric flask by dissolving 5.21 mg of $Ca(OH)_2$ to a total volume of 1000. mL. Calculate the molarity and normality of the solution.

85. How many milliliters of 0.50 *N* NaOH are required to neutralize exactly 15.0 mL of 0.35 *N* H_2SO_4?

86. How many milliliters of 0.103 *M* H_2SO_4 are required to neutralize exactly 4.25 L of 0.104 *M* NaOH?

87. What volume of 0.151 *N* NaOH is required to neutralize 24.2 mL of 0.125 *N* H_2SO_4? What volume of 0.151 *N* NaOH is required to neutralize 24.1 mL of 0.125 *M* H_2SO_4?

88. Suppose that 27.34 mL of standard 0.1021 *M* NaOH is required to neutralize 25.00 mL of unknown H_2SO_4 solution. Calculate the molarity and the normality of the unknown solution.

Additional Problems

89. A mixture is prepared by mixing 50.0 g of ethanol, 50.0 g of water, and 5.0 g of sugar. What is the mass percent of each component in the mixture? How many grams of the mixture should one take in order to have 1.5 g of sugar? How many grams of the mixture should one take in order to have 10.0 g of alcohol?

90. Explain the difference in meaning between the following two solutions: "50. g of NaCl dissolved in 1.0 L of water" and "50. g of NaCl dissolved in enough water to make 1.0 L of solution." For which solution can the molarity be calculated directly (using the molar mass of NaCl)?

91. Suppose 50.0 mL of 0.250 *M* $CoCl_2$ solution is added to 25.0 mL of 0.350 *M* $NiCl_2$ solution. Calculate the concentration, in moles per liter, of each of the ions present after mixing. Assume that the volumes are additive.

92. How many grams of 5.0% by mass NaCl solution can be prepared by dilution of 75 g of 25% NaCl solution?

93. Calculate the mass of AgCl formed, and the concentration of silver ion remaining in solution, when 10.0 g of solid $AgNO_3$ is added to 50. mL of 1.0×10^{-2} *M* NaCl solution. Assume there is no volume change upon addition of the solid.

94. Calculate the mass of solid $BaSO_4$ formed, and the concentration of barium ion remaining in solution, when 10. mL of 0.50 *M* $Ba(NO_3)_2$ is added to 10. mL of 0.20 *M* H_2SO_4 solution. Assume the volumes are additive.

95. Many metal ions form insoluble sulfide compounds when a solution of the metal ion is treated with hydrogen sulfide gas. For example, nickel(II) precipitates nearly quantitatively as NiS when H_2S gas is bubbled through a nickel ion solution. How many milliliters of gaseous H_2S at STP are needed to precipitate all the nickel ion present in 10. mL of 0.050 *M* $NiCl_2$ solution?

96. Strictly speaking, the solvent is the component of a solution that is present in the largest amount on a *mole* basis. For solutions involving water, water is almost always the solvent because there tend to be many more water molecules present than molecules of any conceivable solute. To see why this is so, calculate the number of moles of water present in 1.0 L of water. Recall that the density of water is very nearly 1.0 g/mL under most conditions.

97. Aqueous ammonia is typically sold by chemical supply houses as the saturated solution, which has a concentration of 14.5 mol/L. What volume of NH_3 at STP is required to prepare 100. mL of concentrated ammonia solution?

98. What volume of hydrogen chloride gas at STP is required to prepare 500. mL of 0.100 M HCl solution?

99. What do we mean when we say that "like dissolves like"? Do two molecules have to be identical to be able to form a solution in one another?

100. The concentration of a solution of HCl is 33.1% by mass, and its density was measured to be 1.147 g/mL. How many milliliters of the HCl solution are required to obtain 10.0 g of HCl?

101. An experiment calls for 1.00 g of silver nitrate, but all that is available in the laboratory is a 0.50% solution of $AgNO_3$. Assuming the density of the silver nitrate solution to be very nearly that of water because it is so dilute, determine how many milliliters of the solution should be used.

102. What is the molarity of NaCl in the solution that results when 10.0 g of NaCl is placed in a calibrated flask and dissolved and then water is added to the 100. mL mark?

103. A solution is 0.1% by mass calcium chloride. Therefore, 100. g of the solution contains _____ g of calcium chloride.

104. Calculate the mass percent of KNO_3 in each of the following solutions.
    a. 5.0 g of KNO_3 in 75 g of water
    b. 2.5 mg of KNO_3 in 1.0 g of water
    c. 11 g of KNO_3 in 89 g of water
    d. 11 g of KNO_3 in 49 g of water

105. Calculate the total mass of 25% (by mass) sugar solution that one should take in order to obtain the quantity of sugar listed.
    a. 25 g of sugar
    b. 5.0 g of sugar
    c. 100. g of sugar
    d. 1.0 kg of sugar

106. A certain grade of steel is made by dissolving 5.0 g of carbon and 1.5 g of nickel per 100. g of molten iron. What is the mass percent of each component in the finished steel?

107. A sugar solution is prepared in such a way that it contains 10.% dextrose by mass. What quantity of this solution do we need to obtain 25 g of dextrose?

108. How many grams of Na_2CO_3 are contained in 500. g of a 5.5% by mass Na_2CO_3 solution?

109. How many grams of $AgNO_3$ are required to prepare 100. g of a 1% $AgNO_3$ solution?

110. A solution contains 7.5% by mass NaCl and 2.5% by mass KBr. What mass of *each* solute is contained in 125 g of the solution?

111. A solution that is 1.0 M in Na_2SO_4 contains _____ mol of sodium ion and _____ mol of sulfate ion per liter.

112. For each of the following solutions, the number of moles of solute is given, followed by the total volume of solution prepared. Calculate the molarity.
    a. 0.10 mol of $CaCl_2$; 25 mL
    b. 2.5 mol of KBr; 2.5 L
    c. 0.55 mol of $NaNO_3$; 755 mL
    d. 4.5 mol of Na_2SO_4; 1.25 L

113. For each of the following solutions, the mass of the solute is given, followed by the total volume of solution prepared. Calculate the molarity.
    a. 5.0 g of $BaCl_2$; 2.5 L
    b. 3.5 g of KBr; 75 mL
    c. 21.5 g of Na_2CO_3; 175 mL
    d. 55 g of $CaCl_2$; 1.2 L

114. If 125 g of sucrose, $C_{12}H_{22}O_{11}$, is dissolved in enough water to make 450. mL of solution, calculate the molarity.

115. Concentrated hydrochloric acid is made by pumping hydrogen chloride gas into distilled water. If concentrated HCl contains 439 g of HCl per liter, what is the molarity?

116. If 1.5 g of NaCl is dissolved in enough water to make 1.0 L of solution, what is the molarity of NaCl in the solution?

117. How many *moles* of the indicated solute does each of the following solutions contain?
    a. 1.5 L of 3.0 M H_2SO_4 solution
    b. 35 mL of 5.4 M NaCl solution
    c. 5.2 L of 18 M H_2SO_4 solution
    d. 0.050 L of 1.1×10^{-3} M NaF solution

118. How many *grams* of the indicated solute does each of the following solutions contain?
    a. 3.8 L of 1.5 *M* KCl solution
    b. 15 mL of 5.4 *M* NaCl solution
    c. 20. L of 12.1 *M* HCl solution
    d. 25 mL of 0.100 *M* HClO$_4$ solution

119. If 10. g of AgNO$_3$ is available, what volume of 0.25 *M* AgNO$_3$ solution can be prepared?

120. Calculate the number of moles of *each* ion present in each of the following solutions.
    a. 1.25 L of 0.250 *M* Na$_3$PO$_4$ solution
    b. 3.5 mL of 6.0 *M* H$_2$SO$_4$ solution
    c. 25 mL of 0.15 *M* AlCl$_3$ solution
    d. 1.50 L of 1.25 *M* BaCl$_2$ solution

121. Calcium carbonate, CaCO$_3$, can be obtained in a very pure state. Standard solutions of calcium ion are usually prepared by dissolving calcium carbonate in acid. What mass of CaCO$_3$ should be taken to prepare 500. mL of 0.0200 *M* calcium ion solution?

122. Calculate the new molarity when 150. mL of water is added to each of the following solutions.
    a. 125 mL of 0.200 *M* HBr
    b. 155 mL of 0.250 *M* Ca(C$_2$H$_3$O$_2$)$_2$
    c. 0.500 L of 0.250 *M* H$_3$PO$_4$
    d. 15 mL of 18.0 *M* H$_2$SO$_4$

123. How many mL of 12.1 *M* HCl are needed to prepare 100. mL of 0.100 *M* HCl solution?

124. When 50. mL of 5.4 *M* NaCl is diluted to a final volume of 300. mL, what is the concentration of NaCl in the diluted solution?

125. When 10. L of water is added to 3.0 L of 6.0 *M* H$_2$SO$_4$, what is the molarity of the resulting solution? Assume the volumes are additive.

126. How many milliliters of 0.10 *M* Na$_2$S solution are required to precipitate all the nickel, as NiS, from 25.0 mL of 0.20 *M* NiCl$_2$ solution?

$$NiCl_2(aq) + Na_2S(aq) \rightarrow NiS(s) + 2NaCl(aq)$$

127. How many grams of Ba(NO$_3$)$_2$ are required to precipitate all the sulfate ion present in 15.3 mL of 0.139 *M* H$_2$SO$_4$ solution?

$$Ba(NO_3)_2(aq) + H_2SO_4(aq) \rightarrow BaSO_4(s) + 2HNO_3(aq)$$

128. What volume of 0.150 *M* HNO$_3$ solution is needed to exactly neutralize 35.0 mL of 0.150 *M* NaOH solution?

129. What volume of 0.250 *M* HCl is required to neutralize each of the following solutions?
    a. 25.0 mL of 0.103 *M* sodium hydroxide, NaOH
    b. 50.0 mL of 0.00501 *M* calcium hydroxide, Ca(OH)$_2$
    c. 20.0 mL of 0.226 *M* ammonia, NH$_3$
    d. 15.0 mL of 0.0991 *M* potassium hydroxide, KOH

130. For each of the following solutions, the mass of solute taken is indicated, as well as the total volume of solution prepared. Calculate the normality of each solution.
    a. 15.0 g of HCl; 500. mL
    b. 49.0 g of H$_2$SO$_4$; 250. mL
    c. 10.0 g of H$_3$PO$_4$; 100. mL

131. Calculate the normality of each of the following solutions.
    a. 0.50 *M* acetic acid, HC$_2$H$_3$O$_2$
    b. 0.00250 *M* sulfuric acid, H$_2$SO$_4$
    c. 0.10 *M* potassium hydroxide, KOH

132. A sodium dihydrogen phosphate solution was prepared by dissolving 5.0 g of NaH$_2$PO$_4$ in enough water to make 500. mL of solution. What are the molarity and normality of the resulting solution?

133. How many milliliters of 0.50 *M* NaOH are needed to neutralize exactly 15.0 mL of 0.35 *M* H$_2$SO$_4$?

134. If 27.5 mL of 3.5×10^{-2} *N* Ca(OH)$_2$ solution are needed to neutralize 10.0 mL of nitric acid solution of unknown concentration, what is the normality of the nitric acid?

Cumulative Review for Chapters 13–15

1. What are some of the general properties of gases that distinguish them from liquids and solids?

2. One of the most obvious property of gaseous materials is the pressure they exert on their surroundings. In particular, the pressure exerted by the atmospheric gases is important. How does the pressure of the atmosphere arise, and how is this pressure commonly measured?

3. What is the *SI* unit of pressure? What units of pressure are commonly used in the United States? Why are these common units more convenient to use than the *SI* unit? Describe a *manometer* and explain how such a device can be used to measure the pressure of gas samples.

4. Your textbook gives several definitions and formulas for Boyle's law for gases. Write, in your *own* words, what this law really tells us about gases. Now write two mathematical expressions that describe Boyle's law. Do these two expressions tell us different things, or are they different representations of the same phenomena? Sketch the general shape of a graph of pressure *versus* volume for an ideal gas.

5. When using Boyle's law in solving problems in the textbook, you may have noticed that questions were often qualified by stating that "the temperature and amount of gas remain the same." Why was this qualification necessary?

6. What does Charles's law tell us about how the volume of a gas sample varies as the temperature of the sample is changed? How does this volume–temperature relationship *differ* from the volume–pressure relationship of Boyle's law? Give two mathematical expressions that describe Charles's law. For Charles's law to hold true, why must the pressure and amount of gas remain the same?

7. Explain how the concept of absolute zero came about through Charles's studies of gases. Hint: What would happen to the volume of a gas sample at absolute zero (if the gas did not liquefy first)? What temperature scale is defined with its lowest point as the absolute zero of temperature? What is absolute zero in Celsius degrees?

8. What does Avogadro's law tell us about the relationship between the volume of a sample of gas and the number of molecules the gas contains? Why must the temperature and pressure be held constant for valid comparisons using Avogadro's law? Does Avogadro's law describe a direct or an inverse relationship between the volume and the number of moles of gas?

9. What do we mean specifically by an *ideal* gas? Explain why the *ideal gas law* ($PV = nRT$) is actually a combination of Boyle's, Charles's, and Avogadro's gas laws. What is the numerical value and what are the specific units of the universal gas constant, R? Why is close attention to *units* especially important when doing ideal gas law calculations?

10. Dalton's law of partial pressures concerns the properties of mixtures of gases. What is meant by the *partial pressure* of an individual gas in a mixture? How does the *total pressure* of a gaseous mixture depend on the partial pressures of the individual gases in the mixture? How does Dalton's law help us realize that in an ideal gas sample, the volume of the individual molecules is insignificant compared with the bulk volume of the sample?

11. Many common laboratory preparations of gaseous substances involve collecting the gas produced by displacement of water from a receiving container (see Figure 13.11). What happens to a gas sample when it is collected by displacement of water? How is Dalton's law of partial pressures used in determining the partial pressure of the prepared gas in such an experiment?

12. Without consulting your textbook, list and explain the main postulates of the kinetic molecular theory for gases. How do these postulates help us account for the following bulk properties of a gas: the pressure of the gas and why the pressure of the gas increases with increased temperature; the fact that a gas fills its entire container; and that the volume of a given sample of gas increases as its temperature is increased.

13. What does "STP" stand for? What conditions correspond to STP? What is the volume occupied by one mole of an ideal gas at STP?

14. In general, how do we envision the structures of solids and liquids? Explain how the densities and compressibilities of solids and liquids contrast with those properties of gaseous substances. How do we know that the structures of the solid and liquid states of a substance are more comparable to each other than to the properties of the substance in the gaseous state?

15. Describe some of the physical properties of water. Why is water one of the most important substances on earth?

16. Define the *normal* boiling point of water. Why does a sample of boiling water remain at the same temperature until all the water has been boiled? Define the normal freezing point of water. Sketch a representation of a heating/cooling

curve for water, marking clearly the normal freezing and boiling points.

17. Are changes in state physical or chemical changes? Explain. What type of forces must be overcome to melt or vaporize a substance (are these forces *intra*molecular or *inter*molecular)? Define the *molar heat of fusion* and *molar heat of vaporization*. Why is the molar heat of vaporization of water so much larger than its molar heat of fusion? Why does the boiling point of a liquid vary with altitude?

18. What is a *dipole–dipole attraction?* How do the strengths of dipole–dipole forces compare with the strengths of typical covalent bonds? What is *hydrogen bonding?* What conditions are necessary for hydrogen bonding to exist in a substance or mixture? What experimental evidence do we have for hydrogen bonding?

19. Define *London dispersion forces.* Draw a picture showing how London forces arise. Are London forces relatively strong or relatively weak? Explain. Although London forces exist among all molecules, for what type of molecule are they the *only* major intermolecular force?

20. Why does the process of *vaporization* require an input of energy? Why is it so important that water has a large heat of vaporization? What is *condensation?* Explain how the processes of vaporization and condensation represent an *equilibrium* in a closed container. Define the *equilibrium vapor pressure* of a liquid. Describe how this pressure arises in a closed container. Describe an experiment that demonstrates vapor pressure and enables us to measure the magnitude of that pressure. How is the magnitude of a liquid's vapor pressure related to the intermolecular forces in the liquid?

21. Define a *crystalline solid.* Describe in detail some important types of crystalline solids and name a substance that is an example of each type of solid. Explain how the particles are held together in each type of solid (the interparticle forces that exist). How do the interparticle forces in a solid influence the bulk physical properties of the solid?

22. Define the bonding that exists in metals and how this model explains some of the unique physical properties of metals. What are metal *alloys?* Identify the two main types of alloys, and describe how their structures differ. Give several examples of each type of alloy.

23. Define a *solution.* Describe how an ionic solute such as NaCl dissolves in water to form a solution. How are the strong bonding forces in a crystal of ionic solute overcome? Why do the ions in a solution not attract each other so strongly as to reconstitute the ionic solute? How does

a molecular solid such as sugar dissolve in water? What forces between water molecules and the molecules of a molecular solid may help the solute dissolve? Why do some substances *not* dissolve in water at all?

24. Define a *saturated* solution. Does saturated mean the same thing as saying the solution is *concentrated?* Explain. Why does a solute dissolve only to a particular extent in water? How does formation of a saturated solution represent an equilibrium?

25. The concentration of a solution may be expressed in various ways. Two means of expressing concentration were introduced in Chapter 15—mass percent and molarity. How are these two concentration expressions the same, and how do they differ? Suppose 5.0 g of NaCl is dissolved in 15.0 g of water to give a solution volume of 16.1 mL. Explain how you would calculate the mass percent of NaCl and the molarity of NaCl in this solution. Which number did you *not* use for the mass percent calculation? Which number did you *not* use for the molarity calculation? Suppose instead of being given the volume of the solution after mixing, you had been given the density of the solution. Explain how you would calculate the molarity of this solution with this information.

26. When a solution is diluted by adding additional solvent, the *concentration* of solute changes but the *amount* of solute present does not change. Explain. Suppose 250. mL of water is added to 125 mL of 0.551 *M* NaCl solution. Explain *how* you would calculate the concentration of the solution after dilution.

27. What is one *equivalent* of an acid? What does an equivalent of a base represent? How is the equivalent weight of an acid or base related to the substance's molar mass? Give an example of an acid and a base that have equivalent weights *equal* to their molar masses. Give an example of an acid and a base that have equivalent weights that are *not equal* to their molar masses. What is a *normal* solution of an acid or base? How is the *normality* of an acid or base solution related to its *molarity?* Give an example of a solution whose normality is equal to its molarity, and an example of a solution whose normality is *not* the same as its molarity.

PROBLEMS

28. Suppose each of the following gas samples is expanded from the volume given and an initial pressure of 761 mm Hg to the indicated pressures (at constant temperature). Calculate the new volume of each of the gas samples.
   a. 24.5 mL, 701 torr
   b. 5.41 L, 0.549 atm
   c. 221 mL, 55.1 kPa

29. Suppose each of the following gas samples is heated from an initial temperature of 26.2 °C to the indicated temperature at constant pressure. Calculate the final volume for each of the gas samples.
    a. 41.7 mL, 289 K
    b. 7.81 L, 455 °F
    c. 541 mL, 76.1 °C

30. Calculate the volume of each of the following gas samples at *STP.*
    a. 45.1 mL, 24.1 °C, 775 mm Hg
    b. 4.31 L, 72.1 °C, 0.890 atm
    c. 5.12 mL, 289 K, 91.2 kPa
    d. 91.3 L, 451 °C, 1.45 atm

31. A 1.35-g sample of impure $KClO_3$ was heated and decomposed according to the following equation:

$$2KClO_3(s) \rightarrow 2KCl(s) + 3O_2(g)$$

The oxygen gas produced was collected by displacement of water at 775 mm Hg total pressure and 24 °C. The volume of gas collected was 158 mL. Calculate the partial pressure of oxygen gas in the sample (see your textbook for the saturation vapor pressure of water at various temperatures). Calculate the number of moles of oxygen gas collected. Calculate the number of moles of $KClO_3$ that must have decomposed to produce this amount of oxygen. Calculate the mass of $KClO_3$ that must have been originally present in the sample. Calculate the percent $KClO_3$ (by mass) in the original sample.

32. Hydrogen peroxide decomposes as follows:

$$2H_2O_2(aq) \rightarrow 2H_2O(l) + O_2(g)$$

Assuming the oxygen is collected and dried (water vapor removed), calculate the volume of oxygen gas produced at *STP* if 100. g of 3.11% (by mass) H_2O_2 solution decomposes. What volume would this amount of dry gas have if it were collected at 24 °C and 771 mm Hg instead of *STP*?

33. Calculate the total energy required to melt 55.1 g of ice at 0 °C, to warm the resulting liquid water from 0 °C to 100 °C, and to boil the water at 100 °C.

34. If 5.51 g of NaCl is dissolved in each of the following amounts of water, calculate the percent NaCl in each solution.
    a. 25.0 g
    b. 45.1 g
    c. 100. g
    d. 995 g
    e. 5034 g

35. It is desired to prepare some common standard solutions for use in the lab using 500.0-mL volumetric flasks (see Figure 15.7) to contain the solutions. If the following masses of solutes are used, calculate the resulting molarity of each solution.
    a. 4.865 g NaCl
    b. 78.91 g $AgNO_3$
    c. 121.1 g Na_2CO_3

36. Suppose each of the following solutions is diluted by adding the indicated amount of water. Calculate the new concentration of the solutions.
    a. 125 mL of 0.751 *M* HCl; 150. mL water added
    b. 155 g of 9.76% $AgNO_3$; 125 g water added
    c. 2.75 mL of 18.1 *M* H_2SO_4; 951 mL water added

37. Calculate the volume (in mL) of each of the following acid solutions that would be required to neutralize 36.2 mL of 0.259 *M* NaOH solution.
    a. 0.271 *M* HCl
    b. 0.119 *M* H_2SO_4
    c. 0.171 *M* H_3PO_4

38. What volume of 0.242 *M* H_2SO_4 produces the same number of moles of H^+ ions as each of the following?
    a. 41.5 mL of 0.118 *M* HCl
    b. 27.1 mL of 0.121 *M* H_3PO_4

Appendix

USING YOUR CALCULATOR

In this section we will review how to use your calculator to perform common mathematical operations. This discussion assumes that your calculator uses the algebraic operating system, the system used by most brands.

One very important principle to keep in mind as you use your calculator is that it is not a substitute for your brain. Keep thinking as you do the calculations. Keep asking yourself, "Does the answer make sense?"

Addition, Subtraction, Multiplication, and Division

Performing these operations on a pair of numbers always involves the following steps:

1. Enter the first number, using the numbered keys and the decimal (.) key if needed.

2. Enter the operation to be performed.

3. Enter the second number.

4. Press the "equals" key to display the answer.

For example, the operation

$$15.1 + 0.32$$

is carried out as follows:

Press	Display
15.1	15.1
+	15.1
.32	0.32
=	15.42

The answer given by the display is 15.42. If this is the final result of a calculation, you should round it off to the correct number of significant figures (15.4), as discussed in Section 2.5. If this number is to be used in further calculations, use it exactly as it appears on the display. Round off only the final answer in the calculation.

Do the following operations for practice. The detailed procedures are given below.

   a. $1.5 + 32.86$ c. 0.33×153

   b. $23.5 - 0.41$ d. $\dfrac{9.3}{0.56}$ or $9.3 \div 0.56$

PROCEDURES

a. **Press**	**Display**		b. **Press**	**Display**
1.5	1.5		23.5	23.5
+	1.5		−	23.5
32.86	32.86		.41	0.41
=	34.36		=	23.09
Rounded:	34.4		Rounded:	23.1

c. **Press**	**Display**		d. **Press**	**Display**
.33	0.33		9.3	9.3
×	0.33		÷	9.3
153	153		.56	0.56
=	50.49		=	16.607143
Rounded:	50.		Rounded:	17

Squares, Square Roots, Reciprocals, and Logs

Now we will consider four additional operations that we often need to solve chemistry problems.

The *squaring* of a number is done with a key labeled X^2. The *square root* key is usually labeled $\sqrt{X}$. To take the *reciprocal* of a number, you need the 1/X key. The *logarithm* of a number is determined by using a key labeled log or logX.

To perform these operations, take the following steps:

1. Enter the number.

2. Press the appropriate function key.

3. The answer is displayed automatically.

For example, let's calculate the square root of 235.

Press	Display
235	235
$\sqrt{X}$	15.32971
Rounded:	15.3

We can obtain the log of 23 as follows:

Press	Display
23	23
log	1.3617278
Rounded:	1.36

Often a key on a calculator serves two functions. In this case, the first function is listed on the key and the second is shown on the calculator just above the key. For example, on some calculators the top row of keys appears as follows:

1/X   X²

[2nd] [R/S] [√X] [off] [on/C]

To make the calculator square a number, we must use 2nd and then √X; pressing 2nd tells the calculator we want the function that is listed *above* the key. Thus we can obtain the square of 11.56 on this calculator as follows:

Press	*Display*
11.56	11.56
2nd then √X	133.6336
Rounded:	133.6

We obtain the reciprocal of 384 (1/384) on this calculator as follows:

Press	*Display*
384	384
2nd then R/S	0.0026042
Rounded:	0.00260

Your calculator may be different! See the user's manual if you are having trouble with these operations.

Chain Calculations

In solving problems you often have to perform a series of calculations—a calculation chain. This is generally quite easy if you key in the chain as you read the numbers and operations in order. For example, to perform the calculation

$$\frac{14.68 + 1.58 - 0.87}{0.0850}$$

you should use the appropriate keys as you read it to yourself:

14.68 plus 1.58 equals; minus .87 equals; divided by 0.0850 equals

The details follow.

Press	*Display*
14.68	14.68
+	14.68
1.58	1.58
=	16.26
−	16.26
.87	0.87
=	15.39
÷	15.39
.0850	0.0850
=	181.05882
Rounded:	181

Note that you must press [=] after every operation to keep the calculation "up to date."

For more practice, consider the calculation

$$(0.360)(298) + \frac{(14.8)(16.0)}{1.50}$$

Here you are adding two numbers, but each must be obtained by the indicated calculations. One procedure is to calculate each number first and then add them. The first term is

$$(0.360)(298) = 107.28$$

The second term,

$$\frac{(14.8)(16.0)}{1.50}$$

can be computed easily by reading it to yourself. It "reads"

14.8 times 16.0 equals; divided by 1.50 equals;

and is summarized as follows:

Press	*Display*
14.8	14.8
×	14.8
16.0	16.0
=	236.8
÷	236.8
1.50	1.50
=	157.86667

Now we can keep this last number on the calculator and add it to 107.28 from the first calculation.

Press	*Display*
+	157.86667
107.28	107.28
=	265.14667
Rounded:	265

To summarize,

$$(0.360)(298) + \frac{(14.8)(16.0)}{1.50}$$

becomes

107.28 + 157.86667

and the sum is 265.14667 or, rounded to the correct number of significant figures, 265. There are other ways to do this calculation, but this is the safest way (assuming you are careful).

A common type of chain calculation involves a number of terms multiplied together in the numerator and the denominator, as in

$$\frac{(323)(.0821)(1.46)}{(4.05)(76)}$$

There are many possible sequences by which this calculation can be carried out, but the following seems the most natural.

323 times .0821 equals; times 1.46 equals; divided by 4.05 equals; divided by 76 equals

This sequence is summarized as follows:

Press	Display
323	323
$\times$	323
.0821	0.0821
$=$	26.5183
$\times$	26.5183
1.46	1.46
$=$	38.716718
$\div$	38.716718
4.05	4.05
$=$	9.5596835
$\div$	9.5596835
76	76
$=$	0.1257853

The answer is 0.1257853, which, when rounded to the correct number of significant figures, is 0.13. Note that when two or more numbers are multiplied in the denominator, you must divide by *each* one.

Here are some additional chain calculations (with solutions) to give you more practice.

a. $15 - (0.750)(243)$ b. $\dfrac{(13.1)(43.5)}{(1.8)(63)}$

c. $\dfrac{(85.8)(0.142)}{(16.46)(18.0)} + \dfrac{(131)(0.0156)}{10.17}$

d. $(18.1)(0.051) - \dfrac{(325)(1.87)}{(14.0)(3.81)} + \dfrac{1.56 - 0.43}{1.33}$

SOLUTIONS

a. $15 - 182 = -167$ b. 5.0

c. $0.0411 + 0.201 = 0.242$

d. $0.92 - 11.4 + 0.850 = -9.6$

In performing chain calculations, take the following steps in the order listed.
1. Perform any additions and subtractions that appear inside parentheses.
2. Complete the multiplications and divisions of individual terms.
3. Add and subtract individual terms as required.

BASIC ALGEBRA

In solving chemistry problems you will use, over and over again, relatively few mathematical procedures. In this section we review the few algebraic manipulations that you will need.

Solving an Equation
In the course of solving a chemistry problem, we often construct an algebraic equation that includes the unknown quantity (the thing we want to calculate). An example is

$(1.5)V = (0.23)(0.08206)(298)$

We need to "solve this equation for V." That is, we need to isolate V on one side of the equals sign with all the numbers on the other side. How can we do this? The key idea in solving an algebraic equation is that *doing the same thing on both sides of the equals sign* does not change the equality. That is, it is always "legal" to do the same thing to both sides of the equation. Here we want to solve for V, so we must get the number 1.5 on the other side of the equals sign. We can do this by dividing *both sides* by 1.5.

$\dfrac{(1.5)V}{1.5} = \dfrac{(0.23)(0.08206)(298)}{1.5}$

Now the 1.5 in the denominator on the left cancels the 1.5 in the numerator:

$\dfrac{(\cancel{1.5})V}{\cancel{1.5}} = \dfrac{(0.23)(0.08206)(298)}{1.5}$

to give

$V = \dfrac{(0.23)(0.08206)(298)}{1.5}$

Using the procedures in "Using Your Calculator" for chain calculations, we can now obtain the value for V with a calculator.

$V = 3.7$

Sometimes it is necessary to solve an equation that consists of symbols. For example, consider the equation

$\dfrac{P_1V_1}{T_1} = \dfrac{P_2V_2}{T_2}$

Let's assume we want to solve for T_2. That is, we want to isolate T_2 on one side of the equation. There are several possible ways to proceed, keeping in mind that we always do the same thing on both sides of the equals sign. First we multiply both sides by T_2.

$T_2 \times \dfrac{P_1V_1}{T_1} = \dfrac{P_2V_2}{\cancel{T_2}} \times \cancel{T_2}$

This cancels T_2 on the right. Next we multiply both sides by T_1.

$T_2 \times \dfrac{P_1V_1}{\cancel{T_1}} \times \cancel{T_1} = P_2V_2T_1$

This cancels T_1 on the left. Now we divide both sides by P_1V_1.

$$T_2 \times \frac{\cancel{P_1V_1}}{\cancel{P_1V_1}} = \frac{P_2V_2T_1}{P_1V_1}$$

This yields the desired equation,

$$T_2 = \frac{P_2V_2T_1}{P_1V_1}$$

For practice, solve each of the following equations for the variable indicated.

a. $PV = k$; solve for P

b. $1.5x + 6 = 3$; solve for x

c. $PV = nRT$; solve for n

d. $\dfrac{P_1V_1}{T_1} = \dfrac{P_2V_2}{T_2}$; solve for V_2

e. $\dfrac{°F - 32}{°C} = \dfrac{9}{5}$; solve for $°C$

f. $\dfrac{°F - 32}{°C} = \dfrac{9}{5}$; solve for $°F$

SOLUTIONS

a. $\dfrac{P\cancel{V}}{\cancel{V}} = \dfrac{k}{V}$

$P = \dfrac{k}{V}$

b. $1.5x + 6 - 6 = 3 - 6$

$1.5x = -3$

$\dfrac{\cancel{1.5}x}{\cancel{1.5}} = \dfrac{-3}{1.5}$

$x = -\dfrac{3}{1.5} = -2$

c. $\dfrac{PV}{RT} = \dfrac{nR\cancel{T}}{\cancel{RT}}$

$\dfrac{PV}{RT} = n$

d. $\dfrac{P_1V_1}{T_1} \times T_2 = \dfrac{P_2V_2}{\cancel{T_2}} \times \cancel{T_2}$

$\dfrac{P_1V_1T_2}{T_1P_2} = \dfrac{P_2V_2}{\cancel{P_2}}$

$\dfrac{P_1V_1T_2}{T_1P_2} = V_2$

e. $\dfrac{°F - 32}{°\cancel{C}} \times °\cancel{C} = \dfrac{9}{5}\ °C$

$\dfrac{5}{9}(°F - 32) = \dfrac{\cancel{5}}{\cancel{9}} \times \dfrac{\cancel{9}}{\cancel{5}}\ °C$

$\dfrac{5}{9}(°F - 32) = °C$

f. $\dfrac{°F - 32}{°\cancel{C}} \times °\cancel{C} = \dfrac{9}{5}\ °C$

$°F - \cancel{32} + \cancel{32} = \dfrac{9}{5}\ °C + 32$

$°F = \dfrac{9}{5}\ °C + 32$

SCIENTIFIC (EXPONENTIAL) NOTATION

The numbers we must work with in scientific measurements are often very large or very small; thus it is convenient to express them using powers of 10. For example, the number 1,300,000 can be expressed as 1.3×10^6, which means multiply 1.3 by 10 six times, or

$$1.3 \times 10^6 = 1.3 \times \underbrace{10 \times 10 \times 10 \times 10 \times 10 \times 10}_{10^6\ =\ 1\ \text{million}}$$

A number written in scientific notation always has the form:

A number (between 1 and 10) times
the appropriate power of ten

To represent a large number such as 20,500 in scientific notation, we must move the decimal point in such a way as to achieve a number between 1 and 10 and then multiply the result by a power of 10 to compensate for moving the decimal

point. In this case, we must move the decimal point four places to the left.

$$2\underset{4}{\underbrace{\ 0}}\ \underset{3}{\underbrace{5}}\ \underset{2}{\underbrace{0}}\ \underset{1}{\underbrace{0}}$$

to give a number between 1 and 10:

2.05

where we retain only the significant figures (the number 20,500 has three significant figures). To compensate for moving the decimal point four places to the left, we must multiply by 10^4. Thus

$$20{,}500 = 2.05 \times 10^4$$

As another example, the number 1985 can be expressed as 1.985×10^3. To end up with the number 1.985, which is between 1 and 10, we had to move the decimal point three places to the left. To compensate for that, we must multiply by 10^3. Some other examples are given in the accompanying list.

Number	Exponential Notation
5.6	5.6×10^0 or 5.6×1
39	3.9×10^1
943	9.43×10^2
1126	1.126×10^3

So far, we have considered numbers greater than 1. How do we represent a number such as 0.0034 in exponential notation? First, to achieve a number between 1 and 10, we start with 0.0034 and move the decimal point three places to the right.

$$0 . \underset{1\ \ 2\ \ 3}{0\ \ 0\ \ 3}\ 4$$

This yields 3.4. Then, to compensate for moving the decimal point to the right, we must multiply by a power of 10 with a negative exponent—in this case, 10^{-3}. Thus

$$0.0034 = 3.4 \times 10^{-3}$$

In a similar way, the number 0.00000014 can be written as 1.4×10^{-7}, because going from 0.00000014 to 1.4 requires that we move the decimal point seven places to the right.

Mathematical Operations with Exponentials

We next consider how various mathematical operations are performed using exponential numbers. First we cover the various rules for these operations; then we consider how to perform them on your calculator.

Multiplication and Division

When two numbers expressed in exponential notation are multiplied, the initial numbers are multiplied and the exponents of 10 are *added*.

$$(M \times 10^m)(N \times 10^n) = (MN) \times 10^{m+n}$$

For example (to two significant figures, as required),

$$(3.2 \times 10^4)(2.8 \times 10^3) = 9.0 \times 10^7$$

When the numbers are multiplied, if a result greater than 10 is obtained for the initial number, the decimal point is moved one place to the left and the exponent of 10 is increased by 1.

$$(5.8 \times 10^2)(4.3 \times 10^8) = 24.9 \times 10^{10}$$
$$= 2.49 \times 10^{11}$$
$$= 2.5 \times 10^{11} \text{ (two significant figures)}$$

Division of two numbers expressed in exponential notation involves normal division of the initial numbers and *subtraction* of the exponent of the divisor from that of the dividend. For example,

$$\underset{\text{Divisor}}{\frac{4.8 \times 10^8}{\underline{2.1 \times 10^3}}} = \frac{4.8}{2.1} \times 10^{(8-3)} = 2.3 \times 10^5$$

If the initial number resulting from the division is less than 1, the decimal point is moved one place to the right and the exponent of 10 is decreased by 1. For example,

$$\frac{6.4 \times 10^3}{8.3 \times 10^5} = \frac{6.4}{8.3} \times 10^{(3-5)} = 0.77 \times 10^{-2}$$
$$= 7.7 \times 10^{-3}$$

Addition and Subtraction

In order for us to add or subtract numbers expressed in exponential notation, *the exponents of the numbers must be the same.* For example, to add 1.31×10^5 and 4.2×10^4, we must rewrite one number so that the exponents of both are the same. The number 1.31×10^5 can be written 13.1×10^4: decreasing the exponent by 1 compensates for moving the decimal point one place to the right. Now we can add the numbers.

$$\begin{array}{r} 13.1 \times 10^4 \\ + \ 4.2 \times 10^4 \\ \hline 17.3 \times 10^4 \end{array}$$

In correct exponential notation, the result is expressed as 1.73×10^5.

To perform addition or subtraction with numbers expressed in exponential notation, we add or subtract only the initial numbers. The exponent of the result is the same as the exponents of the numbers being added or subtracted. To subtract 1.8×10^2 from 8.99×10^3, we first convert 1.8×10^2 to 0.18×10^3 so that both numbers have the same exponent. Then we subtract.

$$\begin{array}{r} 8.99 \times 10^3 \\ -0.18 \times 10^3 \\ \hline 8.81 \times 10^3 \end{array}$$

Powers and Roots

When a number expressed in exponential notation is taken to some power, the initial number is taken to the appropriate power and the exponent of 10 is *multiplied* by that power.

$$(N \times 10^n)^m = N^m \times 10^{m \times n}$$

For example,

$$(7.5 \times 10^2)^2 = (7.5)^2 \times 10^{2 \times 2}$$
$$= 56. \times 10^4$$
$$= 5.6 \times 10^5$$

When a root is taken of a number expressed in exponential notation, the root of the initial number is taken and the exponent of 10 is divided by the number representing the root. For example, we take the square root of a number as follows:

$$\sqrt{N \times 10^n} = (N \times 10^n)^{1/2} = \sqrt{N} \times 10^{n/2}$$

For example,

$$(2.9 \times 10^6)^{1/2} = \sqrt{2.9} \times 10^{6/2}$$
$$= 1.7 \times 10^3$$

Using a Calculator to Perform Mathematical Operations on Exponentials

In dealing with exponential numbers, you must first learn to enter them into your calculator. First the number is keyed in and then the exponent. There is a special key that must be pressed just before the exponent is entered. This key is often labeled $\boxed{\text{EE}}$ or $\boxed{\text{exp}}$. For example, the number 1.56×10^6 is entered as follows:

Press	Display
1.56	1.56
EE or exp	1.56 00
6	1.56 06

To enter a number with a negative exponent, use the change-of-sign key $\boxed{+/-}$ after entering the exponent number. For example, the number 7.54×10^{-3} is entered as follows:

Press	Display
7.54	7.54
EE or exp	7.54 00
3	7.54 03
+/-	7.54 −03

Once a number with an exponent is entered into your calculator, the mathematical operations are performed exactly the same as with a "regular" number. For example, the numbers 1.0×10^3 and 1.0×10^2 are multiplied as follows:

Press	Display
1.0	1.0
EE or exp	1.0 00
3	1.0 03
×	1 03
1.0	1.0
EE or exp	1.0 00
2	1.0 02
=	1 05

The answer is correctly represented as 1.0×10^5.

The numbers 1.50×10^5 and 1.1×10^4 are added as follows:

Press	Display
1.5	1.50
EE or exp	1.50 00
5	1.50 05
+	1.5 05
1.1	1.1
EE or exp	1.1 00
4	1.1 04
=	1.61 05

The answer is correctly represented as 1.61×10^5. Note that when exponential numbers are added, the calculator automatically takes into account any difference in exponents.

To take the power, root, or reciprocal of an exponential number, enter the number first, then press the appropriate key or keys. For example, the square root of 5.6×10^3 is obtained as follows:

Press	Display
5.6	5.6
EE or exp	5.6 00
3	5.6 03
$\sqrt{X}$	7.4833148 01

The answer is correctly represented as 7.5×10^1.

Practice by performing the following operations that involve exponential numbers. The answers follow the exercises.

a. $7.9 \times 10^2 \times 4.3 \times 10^4$ f. $\dfrac{1}{8.3 \times 10^2}$

b. $\dfrac{5.4 \times 10^3}{4.6 \times 10^5}$ g. $\log(1.0 \times 10^{-7})$

c. $1.7 \times 10^2 + 1.63 \times 10^3$ h. $-\log(1.3 \times 10^{-5})$

d. $4.3 \times 10^{-3} + 1 \times 10^{-4}$ i. $\sqrt{6.7 \times 10^9}$

e. $(8.6 \times 10^{-6})^2$

SOLUTIONS

a. 3.4×10^7 f. 1.2×10^{-3}

b. 1.2×10^{-2} g. -7.00

c. 1.80×10^3 h. 4.89

d. 4.4×10^{-3} i. 8.2×10^4

e. 7.4×10^{-11}

GRAPHING FUNCTIONS

In interpreting the results of a scientific experiment, it is often useful to make a graph. If possible, the function to be graphed should be in a form that gives a straight line. The equation for a straight line (a *linear equation*) can be represented in the general form

$$y = mx + b$$

where y is the *dependent variable*, x is the *independent variable*, m is the *slope*, and b is the *intercept* with the y axis.

To illustrate the characteristics of a linear equation, the function $y = 3x + 4$ is plotted in Figure A.1. For this equation $m = 3$ and $b = 4$. Note that the y intercept occurs when $x = 0$. In this case the y intercept is 4, as can be seen from the equation ($b = 4$).

The slope of a straight line is defined as the ratio of the rate of change in y to that in x:

$$m = \text{slope} = \frac{\Delta y}{\Delta x}$$

For the equation $y = 3x + 4$, y changes three times as fast as x (because x has a coefficient of 3). Thus the slope in this case is 3. This can be verified from the graph. For the triangle shown in Figure A.1,

$$\Delta y = 15 - 16 = 36 \qquad \text{and} \qquad \Delta x = 15 - 3 = 12$$

Thus

$$\text{Slope} = \frac{\Delta y}{\Delta x} = \frac{36}{12} = 3$$

The above example illustrates a general method for obtaining the slope of a line from the graph of that line. Simply draw a triangle with one side parallel to the y axis and the other side parallel to the x axis, as shown in Figure A.1. Then determine the lengths of the sides to get Δy and Δx, respectively, and compute the ratio $\Delta y/\Delta x$.

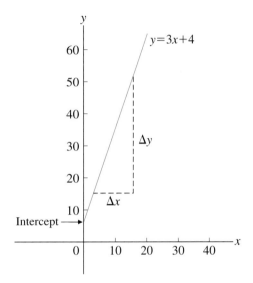

FIGURE A.1
Graph of the linear equation $y = 3x + 4$.

SI UNITS AND CONVERSION FACTORS

These conversion factors are given with more significant figures than those typically used in the body of the text.

LENGTH
SI Unit: Meter (m)

1 meter	= 1.0936 yards
1 centimeter	= 0.39370 inch
1 inch	= 2.54 centimeters
	(exactly)
1 kilometer	= 0.62137 mile
1 mile	= 5280. feet
	= 1.6093 kilometers

VOLUME
SI Unit: Cubic Meter (m³)

1 liter	= 10^{-3} m^3
	= 1 dm^3
	= 1.0567 quarts
1 gallon	= 4 quarts
	= 8 pints
	= 3.7854 liters
1 quart	= 32 fluid ounces
	= 0.94635 liter

MASS
SI Unit: Kilogram (kg)

1 kilogram	= 1000 grams
	= 2.2046 pounds
1 pound	= 453.59 grams
	= 0.45359 kilogram
	= 16 ounces
1 atomic mass unit	= 1.66057×10^{-27} kilograms

PRESSURE
SI Unit: Pascal (Pa)

1 atmosphere	= 101.325 kilopascals
	= 760. torr (mm Hg)
	= 14.70 pounds per square inch

ENERGY
SI Unit: Joule (J)

1 joule	= 0.23901 calorie
1 calorie	= 4.184 joules

PHOTO CREDITS

Photographs by Sean Brady were arranged with the assistance of Professor Doug Sawyer.

CHAPTER 1

p. xxvi, Alan Becker / The Image Bank; p. 1, Addison Geary / Stock Boston; p. 3, Bart Eklund; p.4, Sean Brady / 24th Street Group, A Division of American Color; p.5, NASA; p.7, Ken O'Donoghue; p.9, Robert Harding Associates; p.11, Claude Charlier / Photo Researchers, Inc.

CHAPTER 2

p.14, David M. Dennis / Tom Stack & Associates; p.15, Sean Brady / 24th Street Group, A Division of American Color; p.16, Ray Simons / Photo Researchers, Inc.; p.22, Diane Schiumo / Fundamental Photographs; p.23, David J. Sams / Stock Boston; p.24, Sean Brady / 24th Street Group, A Division of American Color; p.46, Dan McCoy / Rainbow; p.47, Thomas Pantages.

CHAPTER 3

p. 56, Greg Vaughn / Tom Stack & Associates; p. 57, Sean Brady / 24th Street Group, A Division of American Color; p. 58 (top), Brian Parker / Tom Stack & Associates; p. 58 (bottom), Richard Megna / Fundamental Photographs; p. 59 (top), Richard Megna / Fundamental Photographs; p. 59 (bottom), Sean Brady / 24th Street Group, A Division of American Color; p. 62, Jim Pickerell / TSW / Click Chicago; p. 63, Grant Heilman/ Grant Heilman Photography; p. 64, John Deeks / Photo Researchers, Inc.; p. 65, Richard Megna / Fundamental Photographs; p. 65, Richard Megna / Fundamental Photographs; p. 68, Jim Richardson / West Light; p. 71, Robert E. Lyons / Photo Nats, Inc.; p. 74, Jack Fields / Photo Researchers, Inc.

CHAPTER 4

p. 84, Al Tielemans / Duomo; p. 85, Sean Brady / 24th Street Group, A Division of American Color; p. 86, The Granger Collection; p. 87, Mark Heifner / Science Stock America; p. 89, Walter Urie / West Light; p. 91, The Granger Collection ; p. 94, The Bettmann Archive; p. 96, Dr. E. R. Degginger; p. 100, Sean Brady / 24th Street Group, A Division of American Color; p. 103, Tom Flynn / Taurus Photos / Science Photo Library International; p. 104, Dr. E. R. Degginger; p. 107, Dr. E.R. Degginger; p. 107, Sean Brady / 24th Street Group, A Division of American Color; p. 107, Sean Brady / 24th Street Group, A Division of American Color; p. 107, Dr. E.R. Degginger; p. 107, Sean Brady / 24th Street Group; p. 108, Paul Silverman / Fundamental Photographs; p. 109, Robert Landau / West Light; p. 113, Dr. E. R. Degginger.

CHAPTER 5

p. 124, John Gerlach / Tom; p. 125, Bob Daemmrich / The Image Works; p. 126, Art Resource; p. 131, Sean Brady / 24th Street Group, A Division of American Color; p. 136, Sean Brady / 24th Street Group, A Division of American Color; p. 136, Sean Brady / 24th Street Group, A Division of American Color.

CHAPTER 6

p. 156, Richard Megna / Fundamental Photographs; p. 157, C. J. Allen / Stock Boston; p. 158 (top right), Dr. E. R. Degginger; p. 158 (bottom), Sean Brady / 24th Street Group, A Division of American Color; p. 159 (top a, b), Adam J. Stoltman / Duomo; p. 159 (bottom a-d), Ken O'Donoghue; p. 159, Richard Megna / Fundamental Photographs; p. 159, Sean Brady / 24th Street Group, A Division of American Color; p. 159, Sean Brady / 24th Street Group, A Division of American Color; p. 159, Sean Brady / 24th Street Group, A Division of American Color; p. 162 (all), Richard Megna / Fundamental Photographs; p. 166, Dr. E. R. Degginger; p. 168, Dr. E. R. Degginger; p. 169, Richard Megna / Fundamental Photographs.

CHAPTER 7

p. 176, Runk / Schoenberger / Grant Heilman; p. 177, Dan McCoy / Rainbow; p. 179, Dr. E. R. Degginger; p. 184, Courtesy, Dr. Featherstone / Eastman Dental Center; p. 186, Ken O'Donoghue; p. 192, Sean Brady / 24th Street Group, A Division of American Color; p. 194, Dr. E.R. Degginger.

CHAPTER 8

p. 200, NASA; p. 201, John Mead / Science Photo Library / Photo Researchers, Inc.; 203, Richard Megna / Fundamental Photographs; p. 204, Richard Megna / Fundamental Photographs; p. 206, Dan McCoy / Rainbow; p. 208, Courtesy, Morton Thiokol; p. 211, Gary Gladstone / The Image Bank.

CHAPTER 9

p. 220, Richard Megna / Fundamental Photographs; p. 221, Williamson / Edwards / The Image Bank; p. 222, Dr. E. R. Degginger; p. 228 (all), Ken O'Donoghue; p. 229 (top), Ken O'Donoghue; p. 229 (bottom), Sean Brady / 24th Street Group, A Division of American Color; p. 231, Sean Brady / 24th Street Group, A Division of American Color; p. 232, David Parker / Science Photo Library / Photo Researchers, Inc.; p. 235, James Carmichael / Bruce Coleman, Inc.

CHAPTER 10

p. 260, Sean Brady / 24th Street Group, A Division of American Color; p. 261, Dan McCoy / Rainbow; p. 263, Tom Stack / Tom Stack & Associates; p. 271, NASA; p. 272, George Olson / The Photo File; p. 275, Grant Heilman / Grant Heilman Photography; p. 280, Ken O'Donoghue; p. 294, Craig Newbauer / Peter Arnold, Inc.

CHAPTER 11

p. 295, Sohm / Chromosohm / The Image Works; p. 296, Alfred Paseika / Taurus Photos, Inc. / Science Photo Library International; p. 296, S. Cazenave / Vandystadt / Photo Researchers, Inc.; p. 297, Goddard Space Flight Center / NASA; p. 298, Rod Allin / Tom Stack & Associates; p. 302, The Granger Collection; p. 303, The Granger Collection; p. 316, Dan McCoy / Rainbow; p. 318, Tom Tracy / The Photo File; p. 319, Jim Zuckerman / West Light.

CHAPTER 12

p. 328, M.L. Sinibaldi / The Stock Market; p. 329, Tino Hammid; p. 341, The Bancroft Library; p. 349 (both), Donald Clegg; p. 350 (all), Digital Art / West Light.

CHAPTER 13

p. 370, Grant Heilman / Grant Heilman Photography; p. 371, Bob Daemmrich / The Image Works; p. 372 (both), Ken O'Donoghue; p. 373, The Granger Collection; p. 375, Ken O'Donoghue; p. 379, Sean Brady / 24th Street Group, A Division of American Color; p. 380, Duomo; p. 391, Sean Brady / 24th Street Group, A Division of American Color; p. 394, Tom Stack / Tom Stack & Associates.

CHAPTER 14

p. 410 Don Klumpp / The Image Bank; p. 411, David Madison / Duomo; p. 416, Flip Nicklin / Nicklin Associates; p. 418, Galen Rowell / After Image; p. 421, David Bartruff / The Photo File; p. 424 (all), Sean Brady / 24th Street Group, A Division of American Color; p. 426 (left), Dr. E. R. Degginger; p. 426 (right), Richard Megna / Fundamental Photographs; p. 428 (all), Sean Brady / 24th Street Group, A Division of American Color; p. 430, T. J. Florian / Rainbow.

CHAPTER 15

p. 436, William Johnson / Stock Boston; p. 437, Lawrence Migdale / Stock Boston; p. 440, Michelle Barnes / The Photo File; p. 441, Sean Brady / 24th Street Group, A Division of American Color; p. 447, Thomas Pantages; p. 451, Thomas Pantages; p. 453, Richard Megna / Fundamental Photographs; p. 454, Ken O'Donoghue.

Glossary

Acid a substance that produces hydrogen ions in aqueous solution; a proton donor.

Acid–base indicator a substance that marks the end point of an acid–base titration by changing color.

Acid rain rainwater with an acidic pH, a result of air pollution by sulfur dioxide and nitrogen oxides.

Acidic oxide a covalent oxide that dissolves in water to give an acidic solution.

Actinide series a group of fourteen elements following actinium on the periodic table, in which the $5f$ orbitals are being filled.

Activation energy the threshold energy that must be overcome to produce a chemical reaction.

Air pollution contamination of the atmosphere, mainly by the gaseous products of transportation and the production of electricity.

Alcohol an organic compound in which the hydroxyl group is a substituent on a hydrocarbon.

Aldehyde an organic compound containing the carbonyl group bonded to at least one hydrogen atom.

Alkali metal a Group 1 metal.

Alkaline earth metal a Group 2 metal.

Alkane a saturated hydrocarbon with the general formula C_nH_{2n+2}.

Alkene an unsaturated hydrocarbon containing a carbon–carbon double bond. The general formula is C_nH_{2n}.

Alkyne an unsaturated hydrocarbon containing a carbon–carbon triple bond. The general formula is C_nH_{2n-2}.

Alloy a substance that contains a mixture of elements and has metallic properties.

Alloy steel a form of steel containing carbon plus metals such as chromium, cobalt, manganese, and molybdenum.

Alpha (α) particle a helium nucleus produced in radioactive decay.

Alpha-particle production a common mode of decay for radioactive nuclides in which the mass number changes.

Amine an organic base derived from ammonia in which one or more of the hydrogen atoms are replaced by organic groups.

α-Amino acid an organic acid in which an amino group, a hydrogen atom and an R group are attached to the carbon atom next to the carboxyl group.

Ampere the unit of measurement for electric current; 1 ampere is equal to 1 coulomb of charge per second.

Amphoteric substance a substance that can behave either as an acid or as a base.

Anion a negative ion.

Anode in a galvanic cell, the electrode at which oxidation occurs.

Aqueous solution a solution in which water is the dissolving medium, or solvent.

Aromatic hydrocarbon one of a special class of cyclic unsaturated hydrocarbons, the simplest of which is benzene.

Arrhenius concept a concept postulating that acids produce hydrogen ions in aqueous solution, whereas bases produce hydroxide ions.

Atmosphere the mixture of gases that surrounds the earth's surface.

Atom the fundamental unit of which elements are composed.

Atomic mass (weight) the weighted average mass of the atoms in a naturally occurring element.

Atomic number the number of protons in the nucleus of an atom; each element has a unique atomic number.

Atomic radius half the distance between the atomic nuclei in a molecule consisting of identical atoms.

Atomic solid a solid that contains atoms at the lattice points.

Aufbau principle a principle stating that as protons are added one by one to the nucleus to build up the elements, electrons are similarly added to hydrogen-like orbitals.

Autoionization the transfer of a proton from one molecule to another of the same substance.

Avogadro's law equal volumes of gases at the same temperature and pressure contain the same number of particles (atoms or molecules).

Avogadro's number the number of atoms in exactly 12 grams of pure ^{12}C, equal to 6.022×10^{23}.

Angular momentum quantum number (l) the quantum number relating to the shape of an atomic orbital; it can assume any integral value from 0 to $n - 1$ for each value of n.

Ball-and-stick model a molecular model that distorts the sizes of atoms but shows bond relationships clearly.

Barometer a device for measuring atmospheric pressure.

Base a substance that produces hydroxide ions in aqueous solution; a proton acceptor.

Basic oxide an ionic oxide that dissolves in water to produce a basic solution.

Battery a group of galvanic cells connected in series.

Beta (β) particle an electron produced in radioactive decay.

Beta-particle production a decay process for radioactive nuclides in which the mass number remains constant and the atomic number increases by one. The net effect is to change a neutron to a proton.

Binary compound a two-element compound.

Binding energy (nuclear) the energy required to decompose a nucleus into its component nucleons.

Biochemistry the study of the chemistry of living systems.

Biomolecule a molecule that functions in maintaining and/or reproducing life.

Bond (chemical bond) the force that holds two atoms together in a compound.

Bond energy the energy required to break a given chemical bond.

Bond length the distance between the nuclei of the two atoms that are connected by a bond.

Bonding pair an electron pair found in the space between two atoms.

Boyle's law   the volume of a given sample of gas at constant temperature varies inversely with the pressure.

Breeder reactor   a nuclear reactor in which fissionable fuel is produced while the reactor runs.

Brønsted–Lowry model   a model proposing that an acid is a proton donor and that a base is a proton acceptor.

Buffer capacity   the ability of a buffered solution to absorb protons or hydroxide ions without a significant change in pH.

Buffered solution   a solution that resists a change in its pH when either hydroxide ions or protons are added.

Calorie   a unit of measurement for energy; 1 calorie is the quantity of energy required to heat 1 gram of water by one Celsius degree.

Calorimetry   the science of measuring heat flow.

Carbohydrate   a polyhydroxyl ketone or polyhydroxyl aldehyde or a polymer composed of these.

Carbon steel   an alloy of iron containing up to about 1.5% carbon.

Carboxyl group   the —COOH group in an organic acid.

Carboxylic acid   an organic compound containing the carboxyl group.

Catalyst   a substance that speeds up a reaction without being consumed.

Cathode   in a galvanic cell, the electrode at which reduction occurs.

Cathode rays   the "rays" emanating from the negative electrode (cathode) in a partially evacuated tube; a stream of electrons.

Cathodic protection   the connection of an active metal, such as magnesium, to steel in order to protect the steel from corrosion.

Cation   a positive ion.

Cell potential (electromotive force)   the driving force in a galvanic cell that pushes electrons from the reducing agent in one compartment to the oxidizing agent in the other.

Chain reaction (nuclear)   a self-sustaining fission process caused by the production of neutrons that proceed to split other nuclei.

Charles's law   the volume of a given sample of gas at constant pressure is directly proportional to the temperature in kelvins.

Chemical change   the change of substances into other substances through a reorganization of the atoms; a chemical reaction.

Chemical equation   a representation of a chemical reaction showing the relative numbers of reactant and product molecules.

Chemical equilibrium   a dynamic reaction system in which the concentrations of all reactants and products remain constant as a function of time.

Chemical formula   a representation of a molecule in which the symbols for the elements are used to indicate the types of atoms present and subscripts are used to show the relative numbers of atoms.

Chemical kinetics   the area of chemistry that concerns reaction rates.

Chemical property   the ability of a substance to change to a different substance.

Chemical stoichiometry   the quantities of materials consumed and produced in a chemical reaction.

Collision model   a model based on the idea that molecules must collide in order to react; used to account for the observed characteristics of reaction rates.

Combustion reaction   the vigorous and exothermic oxidation–reduction reaction that takes place between certain substances (particularly organic compounds) and oxygen.

Complete ionic equation   an equation that shows as ions all substances that are strong electrolytes.

Compound   a substance with constant composition that can be broken down into elements by chemical processes.

Condensation   the process by which vapor molecules re-form a liquid.

Condensed states of matter   liquids and solids.

Conjugate acid   the species formed when a proton is added to a base.

Conjugate acid–base pair   two species related to each other by the donating and accepting of a single proton.

Conjugate base   what remains of an acid molecule after a proton is lost.

Continuous spectrum   a spectrum that exhibits all the wavelengths of visible light.

Control rods   in a nuclear reactor, rods composed of substances that absorb neutrons. These rods regulate the power level of the reactor.

Core electron   an inner electron in an atom; one that is not in the outermost (valence) principal quantum level.

Corrosion   the process by which metals are oxidized in the atmosphere.

Covalent bonding   a type of bonding in which atoms share electrons.

Critical mass   the mass of fissionable material required to produce a self-sustaining chain reaction.

Critical reaction (nuclear)   a reaction in which exactly one neutron from each fission event causes another fission event, thus sustaining the chain reaction.

Crystalline solid   a solid characterized by the regular arrangement of its components.

Dalton's law of partial pressures   for a mixture of gases in a container, the total pressure exerted is the sum of the pressures that each gas would exert if it were alone.

Denaturation   the breaking down of the three-dimensional structure of a protein, resulting in the loss of its function.

Density   a property of matter representing the mass per unit volume.

Deoxyribonucleic acid (DNA)   a huge nucleotide polymer having a double-helical structure with complementary bases on the two strands. Its major functions are protein synthesis and the storage and transport of genetic information.

Diatomic molecule   a molecule composed of two atoms.

Dilution   the process of adding solvent to lower the concentration of solute in a solution.

Dipole–dipole attraction   the attractive force resulting when polar molecules line up such that the positive and negative ends are close to each other.

Dipole moment   a property of a molecule whereby the charge distribution can be represented by a center of positive charge and a center of negative charge.

Disaccharide   a sugar formed from two monosaccharides joined by a glycoside linkage.

Distillation   a method for separating the components of a liquid mixture that depends on differences in the ease of vaporization of the components.

Double bond   a bond in which two atoms share two pairs of electrons.

Dry cell battery   a common battery used in calculators, watches, radios, and tape players.

Electrical conductivity   the ability to conduct an electric current.

Electrochemistry   the study of the interchange of chemical and electrical energy.

Electrolysis   a process that involves forcing a current through a cell to cause a nonspontaneous chemical reaction to occur.

Electrolyte   a material that dissolves in water to give a solution that conducts an electric current.

Electrolytic cell   a cell that uses electrical energy to produce a chemical change that would not otherwise occur.

Electromagnetic radiation   radiant energy that exhibits wave-like behavior and travels through space at the speed of light in a vacuum.

Electron   a negatively charged particle that occupies the space around the nucleus of an atom.

Electronegativity   the tendency of an atom in a molecule to attract shared electrons to itself.

Element   a substance that cannot be decomposed into simpler substances by chemical or physical means. It consists of atoms all having the same atomic number.

Empirical formula   the simplest whole-number ratio of atoms in a compound.

End point   the point in a titration at which the indicator changes color.

Endothermic   refers to a reaction in which energy (as heat) flows into the system.

Energy   the capacity to do work or to cause the flow of heat.

Enthalpy   at constant pressure, the change in enthalpy equals the energy flow as heat.

Enzyme   a large molecule, usually a protein, that catalyzes biological reactions.

Equilibrium constant   the value obtained when equilibrium concentrations of the chemical species are substituted into the equilibrium expression.

Equilibrium expression   the expression (from the law of mass action) equal to the product of the product concentrations divided by the product of the reactant concentrations, each concentration having first been raised to a power represented by the coefficient in the balanced equation.

Equilibrium position   a particular set of equilibrium concentrations.

Equivalence point (stoichiometric point)   the point in a titration when enough titrant has been added to react exactly with the substance in solution that is being titrated.

Essential elements   the elements known to be essential to human life.

Ester   an organic compound produced by the reaction between a carboxylic acid and an alcohol.

Exothermic   refers to a reaction in which energy (as heat) flows out of the system.

Exponential notation   expresses a number in the form $N \times 10^M$; a convenient method for representing a very large or very small number and for easily indicating the number of significant figures.

Fat (glyceride)   an ester composed of glycerol and fatty acids.

Fatty acid   a long-chain carboxylic acid.

Filtration   a method for separating the components of a mixture containing a solid and a liquid.

Fission   the process of using a neutron to split a heavy nucleus into two nuclei with smaller mass numbers.

Fossil fuel   a fuel that consists of carbon-based molecules derived from decomposition of once-living organisms; coal, petroleum, or natural gas.

Frequency   the number of waves (cycles) per second that pass a given point in space.

Fuel cell   a galvanic cell for which the reactants are continuously supplied.

Functional group   an atom or group of atoms in hydrocarbon derivatives that contains elements in addition to carbon and hydrogen.

Fusion   the process of combining two light nuclei to form a heavier, more stable nucleus.

Galvanic cell   a device in which chemical energy from a spontaneous oxidation-reduction reaction is changed to electrical energy that can be used to do work.

Galvanizing   a process in which steel is coated with zinc to prevent corrosion.

Gamma (γ) ray   a high-energy photon produced in radioactive decay.

Gas   one of the three states of matter; has neither fixed shape nor fixed volume.

Geiger–Müller counter (Geiger counter)   an instrument that measures the rate of radioactive decay by registering the ions and electrons produced as a radioactive particle passes through a gas-filled chamber.

Gene   a given segment of the DNA molecule that contains the code for a specific protein.

Greenhouse effect   a warming effect exerted by certain molecules in the earth's atmosphere (particularly carbon dioxide and water).

Ground state   the lowest possible energy state of an atom or molecule.

Group (of the periodic table)   a vertical column of elements having the same valence electron configuration and similar chemical properties.

Haber process   the manufacture of ammonia from nitrogen and hydrogen, carried out at high pressure and high temperature with the aid of a catalyst.

Half-life (of a radioactive sample)   the time required for the number of nuclides in a radioactive sample to reach half the original number of nuclides.

Half-reactions   the two parts of an oxidation–reduction reaction, one representing oxidation, the other reduction.

Halogen   a Group 7 element.

Hard water   water from natural sources that contains relatively large concentrations of calcium and magnesium ions.

Heat   energy transferred between two objects because of a temperature difference between them.

Heating curve   a plot of temperature versus time for a substance, where energy is added at a constant rate.

Heisenberg uncertainty principle   a principle stating that there is a fundamental limitation to how precisely we can know both the position and the momentum of a particle at a given time.

Herbicide   a pesticide applied to kill weeds.

Heterogeneous equilibrium   an equilibrium involving reactants and/or products in more than one state.

Heterogeneous mixture   a mixture that has different properties in different regions of the mixture.

Homogeneous equilibrium   an equilibrium system in which all reactants and products are in the same state.

Homogeneous mixture   a mixture that is the same throughout; a solution.

Hydration   the interaction between solute particles and water molecules.

Hydride   a binary compound containing hydrogen.

Hydrocarbon   a compound of carbon and hydrogen.

Hydrocarbon derivative   an organic molecule that contains one or more elements in addition to carbon and hydrogen.

Hydrogen bonding   unusually strong dipole–dipole attractions that occur among molecules in which hydrogen is bonded to a highly electronegative atom.

Hydrohalic acid   an aqueous solution of a hydrogen halide.

Hydronium ion   the H_3O^+ ion; a hydrated proton.

Hypothesis   one or more assumptions put forth to explain observed phenomena.

Ideal gas   a hypothetical gas that exactly obeys the ideal gas law. A real gas approaches ideal behavior at high temperature and/or low pressure.

Ideal gas law   an equation relating the properties of an ideal gas, expressed as $PV = nRT$, where P = pressure, V = volume, n = moles of the gas, R = the universal gas constant, and T = temperature on the Kelvin scale. This equation expresses behavior closely approached by real gases at high temperature and/or low pressure.

Indicator   a chemical that changes color and is used to mark the end point of a titration.

Intermolecular forces   relatively weak interactions that occur between molecules.

Intramolecular forces   interactions that occur within a given molecule.

Ion   an atom or a group of atoms that has a net positive or negative charge.

Ionic bonding   the attraction between oppositely charged ions.

Ionic compound   a compound that results when a metal reacts with a nonmetal to form cations and anions.

Ionic solid   a solid containing cations and anions that dissolves in water to give a solution containing the separated ions, which are mobile and thus free to conduct an electric current.

Ionization energy   the quantity of energy required to remove an electron from a gaseous atom or ion.

Ion-product constant (K_w)   the equilibrium constant for the autoionization of water; $K_w = [H^+][OH^-]$. At 25 °C, K_w equals 1.0×10^{-14}.

Isomers   species that have the same chemical formula but different properties.

Isotopes   atoms of the same element (the same number of protons) that have different numbers of neutrons. They have identical atomic numbers but different mass numbers.

Joule   a unit of measurement for energy; 1 calorie = 4.184 joules.

Ketone   an organic compound containing the carbonyl group bonded to two carbon atoms.

Kinetic energy $\left(\frac{1}{2}mv^2\right)$ energy due to the motion of an object; dependent on the mass of the object and the square of its velocity.

Kinetic molecular theory   a model that assumes that an ideal gas is composed of tiny particles (molecules) in constant motion.

Lanthanide series   a group of fourteen elements following lanthanum on the periodic table, in which the $4f$ orbitals are being filled.

Lattice   a three-dimensional system of points designating the positions of the centers of the components of a solid (atoms, ions, or molecules).

Law of chemical equilibrium   a general description of the equilibrium condition; it defines the equilibrium expression.

Law of conservation of energy   energy can be converted from one form to another but can be neither created nor destroyed.

Law of conservation of mass   mass is neither created nor destroyed.

Law of constant composition   a given compound always contains elements in exactly the same proportion by mass.

Law of mass action   (also called the law of chemical equilibrium) a general description of the equilibrium condition; it defines the equilibrium expression.

Law of multiple proportions   a law stating that when two elements form a series of compounds, the ratios of the masses of the second element that combine with one gram of the first element can always be reduced to small whole numbers.

Lead storage battery   a battery (used in cars) in which the anode is lead, the cathode is lead coated with lead dioxide, and the electrolyte is a sulfuric acid solution.

Le Châtelier's principle   if a change is imposed on a system at equilibrium, the position of the equilibrium will shift in a direction that tends to reduce the effect of that change.

Lewis structure a diagram of a molecule showing how the valence electrons are arranged among the atoms in the molecule.

Limiting reactant (limiting reagent) the reactant that is completely consumed when a reaction is run to completion.

Line spectrum a spectrum showing only certain discrete wavelengths.

Linear accelerator a type of particle accelerator in which a changing electrical field is used to accelerate a beam of charged particles along a linear path.

Lipids water-insoluble substances that can be extracted from cells by nonpolar organic solvents.

Liquid one of the three states of matter; has a fixed volume but takes the shape of its container.

London dispersion forces the relatively weak forces, which exist among noble gas atoms and nonpolar molecules, that involve an accidental dipole that induces a momentary dipole in a neighbor.

Lone pair an electron pair that is localized on a given atom; an electron pair not involved in bonding.

Magnetic quantum number m_l, the quantum number reflecting the orientation of an orbital in space relative to the other orbitals with the same l quantum number. It can have integral values between l and $-l$, including zero.

Main-group (representative) elements elements in the groups labeled 1, 2, 3, 4, 5, 6, 7, and 8 on the periodic table. The group number gives the sum of the valence s and p electrons.

Mass the quantity of matter in an object.

Mass number the total number of protons and neutrons in the atomic nucleus of an atom.

Mass percent the percent by mass of a component of a mixture or of a given element in a compound.

Matter the material of the universe.

Metal an element that gives up electrons relatively easily and is typically lustrous, malleable, and a good conductor of heat and electricity.

Metalloid an element that has both metallic and nonmetallic properties.

Metallurgy the process of separating a metal from its ore and preparing it for use.

Millimeters of mercury (mm Hg) a unit of measurement for pressure, also called a torr; 760 mm Hg = 760 torr = 101,325 Pa = 1 standard atmosphere.

Mixture a material of variable composition that contains two or more substances.

Model (theory) a set of assumptions put forth to explain the observed behavior of matter. The models of chemistry usually involve assumptions about the behavior of individual atoms or molecules.

Moderator a substance used in a nuclear reactor to slow down the neutrons.

Molar heat of fusion the energy required to melt 1 mol of a solid.

Molar heat of vaporization the energy required to vaporize 1 mol of a liquid.

Molar mass the mass in grams of one mole of a compound.

Molar volume the volume of one mole of an ideal gas; equal to 22.42 liters at standard temperature and pressure.

Molarity moles of solute per volume of solution in liters.

Mole (mol) the number equal to the number of carbon atoms in exactly 12 grams of pure ^{12}C: Avogadro's number. One mole represents 6.022×10^{23} units.

Mole ratio (stoichiometry) the ratio of moles of one substance to moles of another substance in a balanced chemical equation.

Molecular equation an equation representing a reaction in solution and showing the reactants and products in undissociated form, whether they are strong or weak electrolytes.

Molecular formula the exact formula of a molecule, giving the types of atoms and the number of each type.

Molecular solid a solid composed of small molecules.

Molecular structure the three-dimensional arrangement of atoms in a molecule.

Molecular weight (molar mass) the mass in grams of one mole of a substance.

Molecule a bonded collection of two or more atoms of the same element or different elements.

Monoprotic acid an acid with one acidic proton.

Natural law a statement that expresses generally observed behavior

Net ionic equation an equation for a reaction in solution, representing strong electrolytes as ions and showing only those components that are directly involved in the chemical change.

Network solid an atomic solid containing strong directional covalent bonds.

Neutralization reaction an acid–base reaction.

Neutron a particle in the atomic nucleus with a mass approximately equal to that of the proton but with no charge.

Noble gas a Group 8 element.

Nonelectrolyte a substance that, when dissolved in water, gives a nonconducting solution.

Nonmetal an element that does not exhibit metallic characteristics. Chemically, a typical nonmetal accepts electrons from a metal.

Normal boiling point the temperature at which the vapor pressure of a liquid is exactly one atmosphere; the boiling temperature under one atmosphere of pressure.

Normal melting/freezing point the melting/freezing point of a solid at a total pressure of one atmosphere.

Normality the number of equivalents of a substance dissolved in a liter of solution.

Nuclear atom the modern concept of the atom as having a dense center of positive charge (the nucleus) and electrons moving around the outside.

Nuclear transformation the change of one element into another.

Nucleon a particle in an atomic nucleus, either a neutron or a proton.

Nucleus the small, dense center of positive charge in an atom.

Nuclide   the general term applied to each unique atom; represented by $^A_Z X$, where X is the symbol for a particular element.

Octet rule   the observation that atoms of nonmetals form the most stable molecules when they are surrounded by eight electrons (to fill their valence orbitals).

Orbital   a representation of the space occupied by an electron in an atom; the probability distribution for the electron.

Organic acid   an acid with a carbon-atom backbone and a carboxyl group.

Organic chemistry   the study of carbon-containing compounds (typically containing chains of carbon atoms) and their properties.

Oxidation   an increase in oxidation state (a loss of electrons).

Oxidation–reduction (redox) reaction   a reaction in which one or more electrons are transferred.

Oxidation states   a concept that provides a way to keep track of electrons in oxidation–reduction reactions according to certain rules.

Oxidizing agent (electron acceptor)   a reactant that accepts electrons from another reactant.

Oxyacid   an acid in which the acidic proton is attached to an oxygen atom.

Ozone O_3, a form of elemental oxygen much less common than O_2 in the atmosphere near the earth.

Partial pressures   the independent pressures exerted by different gases in a mixture.

Particle accelerator   a device used to accelerate nuclear particles to very high speeds.

Pascal   the SI unit of measurement for pressure; equal to one newton per square meter.

Percent yield   the actual yield of a product as a percentage of the theoretical yield.

Periodic table   a chart showing all the elements arranged in columns in such a way that all the elements in a given column exhibit similar chemical properties.

pH scale   a log scale based on 10 and equal to $-\log[H^+]$; a convenient way to represent solution acidity.

Phenyl group   the benzene molecule minus one hydrogen atom.

Photochemical smog   air pollution produced by the action of light on oxygen, nitrogen oxides, and unburned fuel from auto exhaust to form ozone and other pollutants.

Photon   a "particle" of electromagnetic radiation.

Physical change   a change in the form of a substance, but not in its chemical nature; chemical bonds are not broken in a physical change.

Physical property   a characteristic of a substance that can change without the substance becoming a different substance.

Polar covalent bond   a covalent bond in which the electrons are not shared equally because one atom attracts them more strongly than the other.

Polar molecule   a molecule that has a permanent dipole moment.

Polyatomic ion   an ion containing a number of atoms.

Polyelectronic atom   an atom with more than one electron.

Polymer   a large, usually chain-like molecule built from many small molecules (monomers).

Polymerization   a process in which many small molecules (monomers) are joined together to form a large molecule.

Polyprotic acid   an acid with more than one acidic proton. It dissociates in a stepwise manner, one proton at a time.

Porous disk   a disk in a tube connecting two different solutions in a galvanic cell; it allows ion flow without extensive mixing of the solutions.

Positron production   a mode of nuclear decay in which a particle is formed that has the same mass as an electron but opposite charge. The net effect is to change a proton to a neutron.

Potential energy   energy due to position or composition.

Precipitation reaction   a reaction in which an insoluble substance forms and separates from the solution as a solid.

Precision   the degree of agreement among several measurements of the same quantity; the reproducibility of a measurement.

Primary structure (of a protein)   the order (sequence) of amino acids in the protein chain.

Principal quantum number   the quantum number reflecting the size and energy of an orbital; it can have any positive integer value.

Probability distribution (orbital)   a representation indicating the probabilities of finding an electron at various points in space.

Product   a substance resulting from a chemical reaction. It is shown to the right of the arrow in a chemical equation.

Protein   a natural polymer formed by condensation reactions between amino acids.

Proton   a positively charged particle in an atomic nucleus.

Pure substance   a substance with constant composition.

Radioactive decay (radioactivity)   the spontaneous decomposition of a nucleus to form a different nucleus.

Radiocarbon dating (carbon-14 dating)   a method for dating ancient wood or cloth on the basis of the radioactive decay of the nuclide $^{14}_6 C$.

Radiotracer   a radioactive nuclide, introduced into an organism for diagnostic purposes, whose pathway can be traced by monitoring its radioactivity.

Random error   an error that has an equal probability of being high or low.

Rate of decay   the change per unit time in the number of radioactive nuclides in a sample.

Reactant   a starting substance in a chemical reaction. It appears to the left of the arrow in a chemical equation.

Reactor core   the part of a nuclear reactor where the fission reaction takes place.

Reducing agent (electron donor)   a reactant that donates electrons to another substance, reducing the oxidation state of one of its atoms.

Reduction   a decrease in oxidation state (a gain of electrons).

Rem a unit of radiation dosage that accounts for both the energy of the dose and its effectiveness in causing biological damage (from *r*oentgen *e*quivalent for *m*an).

Resonance a condition occurring when more than one valid Lewis structure can be written for a particular molecule. The actual electronic structure is represented not by any one of the Lewis structures but by the average of all of them.

Salt an ionic compound.

Salt bridge a U-tube containing an electrolyte that connects the two compartments of a galvanic cell, allowing ion flow without extensive mixing of the different solutions.

Saturated solution a solution that contains as much solute as can be dissolved in that solution.

Scientific method a process of studying natural phenomena that involves making observations, forming laws and theories, and testing theories by experimentation.

Scientific notation see *Exponential notation*.

Scintillation counter an instrument that measures radioactive decay by sensing the flashes of light that the radiation produces in a detector.

Secondary structure (of a protein) the three-dimensional structure of the protein chain (for example, α-helix, random coil, or pleated sheet).

SI units International System of units based on the metric system and on units derived from the metric system.

Sigma (σ) bond a covalent bond in which the electron pair is shared in an area centered on a line running between the atoms.

Significant figures the certain digits and the first uncertain digit of a measurement.

Silica the fundamental silicon–oxygen compound, which has the empirical formula SiO_2 and forms the basis of quartz and certain types of sand.

Silicates salts that contain metal cations and polyatomic silicon–oxygen anions that are usually polymeric.

Single bond a bond in which two atoms share one pair of electrons.

Solid one of the three states of matter; has a fixed shape and volume.

Solubility the amount of a substance that dissolves in a given volume of solvent or solution at a given temperature.

Solubility product the constant for the equilibrium expression representing the dissolving of an ionic solid in water.

Solute a substance dissolved in a solvent to form a solution.

Solution a homogeneous mixture.

Solvent the dissolving medium in a solution.

Somatic damage radioactive damage to an organism resulting in its sickness or death.

Specific heat another name for specific heat capacity.

Specific heat capacity the amount of energy required to raise the temperature of one gram of a substance by one Celsius degree.

Spectator ions ions present in solution that do not participate directly in a reaction.

Standard atmosphere a unit of measurement for pressure equal to 760 mm Hg.

Standard solution a solution the concentration of which is accurately known.

Standard temperature and pressure (STP) the condition 0 °C and 1 atmosphere of pressure.

States of matter the three different forms in which matter can exist: solid, liquid, and gas.

Stoichiometric quantities quantities of reactants mixed in exactly the amounts that result in their all being used up at the same time.

Stoichiometry of a reaction the relative quantities of reactants and products involved in the reaction.

Strong acid an acid that completely dissociates (ionizes) to produce H^+ ion and the conjugate base.

Strong base a metal hydroxide compound that completely dissociates into its ions in water.

Strong electrolyte a material that, when dissolved in water, gives a solution that conducts an electric current very efficiently.

Structural formula the representation of a molecule in which the relative positions of the atoms are shown and the bonds are indicated by lines.

Subcritical reaction (nuclear) a reaction in which fewer than one of the neutrons from each fission event causes another fission event and the process dies out.

Sublimation the process by which a substance goes directly from the solid state to the gaseous state without passing through the liquid state.

Substitution reaction (hydrocarbons) a reaction in which an atom, usually a halogen, replaces a hydrogen atom in a hydrocarbon.

Supercooling the process of cooling a liquid to a temperature below its freezing point without its changing to a solid.

Supercritical reaction (nuclear) a reaction in which more than one of the neutrons from each fission event causes another fission event. The process rapidly escalates to a violent explosion.

Superheating the process of heating a liquid to a temperature above its boiling point without its boiling.

Systematic error an error that always occurs in the same direction.

Tertiary structure (of a protein) the overall shape of a protein, long and narrow or globular, maintained by different types of intramolecular interactions.

Theoretical yield the maximum amount of a given product that can be formed when the limiting reactant is completely consumed.

Theory (model) a set of assumptions put forth to explain some aspect of the observed behavior of matter.

Titration a technique in which one solution is used to analyze another.

Torr another name for millimeter of mercury (mm Hg).

Trace elements   metals present only in trace amounts in the human body.

Transition metals   several series of elements in which inner orbitals (*d* or *f* orbitals) are being filled.

Transuranium elements   the elements beyond uranium that are made artificially by particle bombardment.

Triple bond   a bond in which two atoms share three pairs of electrons.

Uncertainty (in measurement)   the characteristic reflecting the fact that any measurement involves estimates and cannot be exactly reproduced.

Unit factor   an equivalence statement between units that is used for converting from one set of units to another.

Universal gas constant   the combined proportionality constant in the ideal gas law; 0.08206 L atm/K mol, or 8.314 J/K mol.

Unsaturated solution   a solution in which more solute can be dissolved than is dissolved already.

Valence electrons   the electrons in the outermost occupied principal quantum level of an atom.

Valence shell electron pair repulsion (VSEPR) model   a model the main postulate of which is that the structure around a given atom in a molecule is determined principally by the tendency to minimize electron-pair repulsions.

Vapor pressure   the pressure of the vapor over a liquid at equilibrium in a closed container.

Vaporization (evaporation)   the change in state that occurs when a liquid evaporates to form a gas.

Viscosity   the resistance of a liquid to flow.

Volt   the unit of measurement for electric potential; it is defined as one joule of work per coulomb of charge transferred.

Wavelength   the distance between two consecutive peaks or troughs in a wave.

Weak acid   an acid that dissociates only to a slight extent in aqueous solution.

Weak base   a base that reacts with water to produce hydroxide ions to only a slight extent in aqueous solution.

Weak electrolyte   a material that, when dissolved in water, gives a solution that conducts only a small electric current.

Weight   the force exerted on an object by gravity.

Solutions

TO SELF-CHECK EXERCISES

Chapter 2

SELF-CHECK EXERCISE 2.1

$357 = 3.57 \times 10^2$

$0.0055 = 5.5 \times 10^{-3}$

SELF-CHECK EXERCISE 2.2

a. Three significant figures. The leading zeros (to the left of the 1) do not count, but the trailing zeros do.

b. Five significant figures. The one captive zero and the two trailing zeros all count.

c. This is an exact number obtained by counting the cars. It has an unlimited number of significant figures.

SELF-CHECK EXERCISE 2.3

a. $12.6 \times 0.53 = 6.678 = 6.7$
   Limiting

b. $12.6 \times 0.53 = 6.7$;   6.7   Limiting
   Limiting -4.59
                    $2.11 = 2.1$

c.   25.36
   $- 4.15$ $\dfrac{21.21}{2.317} = 9.15408 = 9.154$
   ___
   21.21

SELF-CHECK EXERCISE 2.4

$0.750\ \cancel{L} \times \dfrac{1.06\ \text{qt}}{1\ \cancel{L}} = 0.795\ \text{qt}$

SELF-CHECK EXERCISE 2.5

$225\ \dfrac{\cancel{mi}}{h} \times \dfrac{1760\ \cancel{yd}}{1\ \cancel{mi}} \times \dfrac{1\ \cancel{m}}{1.094\ \cancel{yd}} \times \dfrac{1\ \text{km}}{1000\ \cancel{m}} = 362\ \dfrac{\text{km}}{h}$

SELF-CHECK EXERCISE 2.6

The best way to solve this problem is to convert 172 K to Celsius degrees. To do this we will use the formula $T_{\circ C} = T_K - 273$.
In this case

$$T_{\circ C} = T_K - 273 = 172 - 273 = -101$$

So 172 K = -101 °C, which is a lower temperature than -75 °C. Thus 172 K is colder than -75 °C.

SELF-CHECK EXERCISE 2.7

The problem is 41 °C = ? °F.
   Using the formula

$$T_{\circ F} = 1.80(T_{\circ C}) + 32$$

we have

$$T_{\circ F} = ?\ °F = 1.80(41) + 32 = 74 + 32 = 106$$

That is, 41 °C = 106 °F.

SELF-CHECK EXERCISE 2.8

This problem can be stated as 239 °F = ? °C.
   Using the formula

$$T_{\circ C} = \dfrac{T_{\circ F} - 32}{1.80}$$

we have in this case

$$T_{\circ C} = ?\ °C = \dfrac{239 - 32}{1.80} = \dfrac{207}{1.80} = 115$$

That is, 239 °F = 115 °C.

SELF-CHECK EXERCISE 2.9

We obtain the density of the cleaner by dividing its mass by its volume.

$$\text{Density} = \dfrac{\text{mass}}{\text{volume}} = \dfrac{28.1\ \text{g}}{35.8\ \text{mL}} = 0.785\ \text{g/mL}$$

This density identifies the liquid as isopropyl alcohol.

Chapter 3

SELF-CHECK EXERCISE 3.1

Items (a) and (c) are physical properties. When the solid gallium melts, it forms liquid gallium. There is no change in composition. Items (b) and (d) reflect the ability to change composition and are thus chemical properties. Statement (b) means that platinum does not react with oxygen to form some new substance. Statement (d) means that copper does react in the air to form a new substance, which is green.

SELF-CHECK EXERCISE 3.2

a. Milk turns sour because new substances are formed. This is a chemical change.

b. Melting the wax is a physical change (a change of state). When the wax burns, new substances are formed. This is a chemical change.

SELF-CHECK EXERCISE 3.3

a. Wine is a homogeneous mixture of alcohol and other dissolved substances dispersed uniformly in water.

b. Helium and oxygen form a homogeneous mixture.

c. Oil and vinegar salad dressing is a heterogeneous mixture. (Note the two distinct layers the next time you look at a bottle of dressing.)

d. Common salt is a pure substance (sodium chloride), so it always has the same composition. (Note that other substances such as iodine are often added to commercial preparations of table salt, which is mostly sodium chloride. Thus commercial table salt is a homogeneous mixture.)

SELF-CHECK EXERCISE 3.4

The conversion factor needed is $\dfrac{1 \text{ cal}}{4.184 \text{ J}}$, and the conversion is

$$28.4 \text{ J} \times \frac{1 \text{ cal}}{4.184 \text{ J}} = 6.79 \text{ cal}$$

SELF-CHECK EXERCISE 3.5

We know that it takes 4.184 J of energy to change the temperature of each gram of water by 1 °C, so we must multiply 4.184 by the mass of water (454 g) and the temperature change (98.6 °C − 5.4 °C = 93.2 °C).

$$4.184 \ \frac{\text{J}}{\text{g} \, °\text{C}} \times 454 \text{ g} \times 93.2 \ °\text{C} = 1.77 \times 10^5 \text{ J}$$

SELF-CHECK EXERCISE 3.6

From Table 3.2, the specific heat capacity for solid gold is 0.13 J/g °C. Because it takes 0.13 J to change the temperature of *one* gram of gold by *one* Celsius degree, we must multiply 0.13 by the sample size (5.63 g) and the change in temperature (32 °C − 21 °C = 11 °C).

$$0.13 \ \frac{\text{J}}{\text{g} \, °\text{C}} \times 5.63 \text{ g} \times 11 \ °\text{C} = 8.1 \text{ J}$$

We can change this energy to units of calories as follows:

$$8.1 \text{ J} \times \frac{1 \text{ cal}}{4.184 \text{ J}} = 1.9 \text{ cal}$$

SELF-CHECK EXERCISE 3.7

Table 3.2 lists the specific heat capacities of several metals. We want to calculate the specific heat capacity (s) for this metal and then use Table 3.2 to identify the metal. Using the equation

$$Q = s \times m \times \Delta T$$

We can solve for s by dividing both sides by m (the mass of the sample) and by ΔT:

$$\frac{Q}{m \times \Delta T} = s$$

In this case,

Q = energy (heat) required = 10.1 J
m = 2.8 g
ΔT = temperature change = 36 °C − 21 °C = 15 °C

so

$$s = \frac{Q}{m \times \Delta T} = \frac{10.1 \text{ J}}{(2.8 \text{ g}) (15 \ °\text{C})} = 0.24 \text{ J/g} \ °\text{C}$$

Table 3.2 shows that silver has a specific heat capacity of 0.24 J/g °C. The metal is silver.

Chapter 4

SELF-CHECK EXERCISE 4.1

a. P_4O_{10} b. UF_6 c. $AlCl_3$

SELF-CHECK EXERCISE 4.2

In the symbol $^{90}_{38}\text{Sr}$, the number 38 is the atomic number, which represents the number of protons in the nucleus of a strontium atom. Because the atom is neutral overall, it must also have 38 electrons. The number 90 (the mass number) represents the number of protons plus the number of neutrons. Thus the number of neutrons is $A - Z = 90 - 38 = 52$.

SELF-CHECK EXERCISE 4.3

The atom $^{201}_{80}\text{Hg}$ has 80 protons, 80 electrons, and $201 - 80 = 121$ neutrons.

SELF-CHECK EXERCISE 4.4

The atomic number for phosphorus is 15 and the mass number is $15 + 17 = 32$. Thus the symbol for the atom is $^{32}_{15}\text{P}$.

SELF-CHECK EXERCISE 4.5

Element	Symbol	Atomic Number	Metal or Nonmetal	Family Name
a. argon	Ar	18	nonmetal	noble gas
b. chlorine	Cl	17	nonmetal	halogen
c. barium	Ba	56	metal	alkaline earth metals
d. cesium	Cs	55	metal	alkali metals

SELF-CHECK EXERCISE 4.6

a. KI
   $(1+) + (1-) = 0$

b. Mg_3N_2
   $3(2+) + 2(3-) = (6+) + (6-) = 0$

c. Al_2O_3
   $2(3+) + 3(2-) = 0$

Chapter 5

SELF-CHECK EXERCISE 5.1

a. rubidium oxide   b. strontium iodide   c. potassium sulfide

SELF-CHECK EXERCISE 5.2

a. The compound $PbBr_2$ must contain Pb^{2+}—named lead(II)—to balance the charges of the two Br^- ions. Thus the name is lead(II) bromide. The compound $PbBr_4$ must contain Pb^{4+}—named lead(IV)—to balance the charges of the four Br^- ions. The name is therefore lead(IV) bromide.

b. The compound FeS contains the S^{2-} ion (sulfide) and thus the iron cation present must be Fe^{2+}, iron(II). The name is iron(II) sulfide. The compound Fe_2S_3 contains three S^{2-} ions and two iron cations of unknown charge. We can determine the iron charge from the following:

$$2(?+) + 3(2-) = 0$$

$\uparrow$ Iron charge $\uparrow$ S^{2-} charge

In this case, ? must represent 3 because

$$2(3+) + 3(2-) = 0$$

Thus Fe_2S_3 contains Fe^{3+} and S^{2-}, and its name is iron(III) sulfide.

c. The compound $AlBr_3$ contains Al^{3+} and Br^-. Because aluminum forms only one ion (Al^{3+}), no Roman numeral is required. The name is aluminum bromide.

d. The compound Na_2S contains Na^+ and S^{2-} ions. The name is sodium sulfide. (Because sodium forms only Na^+, no Roman numeral is needed.)

e. The compound $CoCl_3$ contains three Cl^- ions. Thus the cobalt cation must be Co^{3+}, which is named cobalt(III) because cobalt is a transition metal and can form more than one type of cation. Thus the name of $CoCl_3$ is cobalt(III) chloride.

SELF-CHECK EXERCISE 5.3

Compound	Individual Names	Prefixes	Name
a. CCl_4	carbon chloride	none tetra-	carbon tetrachloride
b. NO_2	nitrogen oxide	none di-	nitrogen dioxide
c. IF_5	iodine fluoride	none penta-	iodine pentafluoride

SELF-CHECK EXERCISE 5.4

a. silicon dioxide

b. dioxygen difluoride

c. xenon hexafluoride

SELF-CHECK EXERCISE 5.5

a. chlorine trifluoride

b. vanadium(V) fluoride

c. copper(I) chloride

d. manganese(IV) oxide

e. magnesium oxide

f. water

SELF-CHECK EXERCISE 5.6

a. calcium hydroxide

b. sodium phosphate

c. potassium permanganate

d. ammonium dichromate

e. cobalt(II) perchlorate (Perchlorate has a 1− charge, so the cation must be Co^{2+} to balance the two ClO_4^- ions.)

f. potassium chlorate

g. copper(II) nitrite (This compound contains two NO_2^- (nitrite) ions and thus must contain a Cu^{2+} cation.)

SELF-CHECK EXERCISE 5.7

Compound	Name
a. $NaHCO_3$	sodium hydrogen carbonate
	Contains Na^+ and HCO_3^-; often called sodium bicarbonate (common name).
b. $BaSO_4$	barium sulfate
	Contains Ba^{2+} and SO_4^{2-}.
c. $CsClO_4$	cesium perchlorate
	Contains Cs^+ and ClO_4^-.
d. BrF_5	bromine pentafluoride
	Both nonmetals (Type III binary).
e. NaBr	sodium bromide
	Contains Na^+ and Br^- (Type I binary).
f. KOCl	potassium hypochlorite
	Contains K^+ and OCl^-.
g. $Zn_3(PO_4)_2$	zinc(II) phosphate
	Contains Zn^{2+} and PO_4^{3-}; Zn is a transition metal and officially requires a Roman numeral. However, because Zn forms only the Zn^{2+} cation, the II is usually left out. Thus the name of the compound is usually given as zinc phosphate.

SELF-CHECK EXERCISE 5.8

Name	Chemical Formula
a. ammonium sulfate	$(NH_4)_2SO_4$
	Two ammonium ions (NH_4^+) are required for each sulfate ion (SO_4^{2-}) to achieve charge balance.
b. vanadium(V) fluoride	VF_5
	The compound contains V^{5+} ions and requires five F^- ions for charge balance.

c. disulfur dichloride S_2Cl_2
  The prefix *di-* indicates two of each atom.

d. rubidium peroxide Rb_2O_2
  Because rubidium is in Group 1, it forms only $1+$ ions. Thus two Rb^+ ions are needed to balance the $2-$ charge on the peroxide ion (O_2^{2-}).

e. aluminum oxide Al_2O_3
  Aluminum forms only $3+$ ions. Two Al^{3+} ions are required to balance the charge on three O^{2-} ions.

Chapter 6

SELF-CHECK EXERCISE 6.1

a. $Mg(s) + H_2O(l) \rightarrow Mg(OH)_2(s) + H_2(g)$
  Note that magnesium (which is in Group 2) always forms the Mg^{2+} cation and thus requires two OH^- anions for a zero net charge.

b. Ammonium dichromate contains the polyatomic ions NH_4^+ and $Cr_2O_7^{2-}$ (you should have these memorized). Because NH_4^+ has a $1+$ charge, two NH_4^+ cations are required for each $Cr_2O_7^{2-}$, with its $2-$ charge, to give the formula $(NH_4)_2Cr_2O_7$. Chromium(III) oxide contains Cr^{3+} ions—signified by chromium(III)— and O^{2-} (the oxide ion). To achieve a net charge of zero, the solid must contain two Cr^{3+} ions for every three O^{2-} ions, so the formula is Cr_2O_3. Nitrogen gas contains diatomic molecules and is written $N_2(g)$, and gaseous water is written $H_2O(g)$. Thus the unbalanced equation for the decomposition of ammonium dichromate is

$$(NH_4)_2Cr_2O_7(s) \rightarrow Cr_2O_3(s) + N_2(g) + H_2O(g)$$

c. Gaseous ammonia, $NH_3(g)$, and gaseous oxygen, $O_2(g)$, react to form nitrogen monoxide gas, $NO(g)$, plus gaseous water, $H_2O(g)$. The unbalanced equation is

$$NH_3(g) + O_2(g) \rightarrow NO(g) + H_2O(g)$$

SELF-CHECK EXERCISE 6.2

Step 1 The reactants are propane, $C_3H_8(g)$, and oxygen, $O_2(g)$; the products are carbon dioxide, $CO_2(g)$, and water, $H_2O(g)$. All are in the gaseous state.

Step 2 The unbalanced equation for the reaction is

$$C_3H_8(g) + O_2(g) \rightarrow CO_2(g) + H_2O(g)$$

Step 3 We start with C_3H_8 because it is the most complicated molecule. C_3H_8 contains three carbon atoms per molecule, so a coefficient of 3 is needed for CO_2.

$$C_3H_8(g) + O_2(g) \rightarrow 3CO_2(g) + H_2O(g)$$

Also, each C_3H_8 molecule contains eight hydrogen atoms, so a coefficient of 4 is required for H_2O.

$$C_3H_8(g) + O_2(g) \rightarrow 3CO_2(g) + 4H_2O(g)$$

The final element to be balanced is oxygen. Note that the left side of the equation now has two oxygen atoms, and the right side has ten. We can balance the oxygen by using a coefficient of 5 for O_2.

$$C_3H_8(g) + 5O_2(g) \rightarrow 3CO_2(g) + 4H_2O(g)$$

Step 4 *Check:*

$$3 \text{ C, 8 H, 10 O} \rightarrow 3 \text{ C, 8 H, 10 O}$$

Reactant	Product
atoms	atoms

We cannot divide all coefficients by a given integer to give smaller integer coefficients.

SELF-CHECK EXERCISE 6.3

a. $NH_4NO_2(s) \rightarrow N_2(g) + H_2O(g)$ (unbalanced)
  $NH_4NO_2(s) \rightarrow N_2(g) + 2H_2O(g)$ (balanced)

b. $NO(g) \rightarrow N_2O(g) + NO_2(g)$ (unbalanced)
  $3NO(g) \rightarrow N_2O(g) + NO_2(g)$ (balanced)

c. $HNO_3(l) \rightarrow NO_2(g) + H_2O(l) + O_2(g)$ (unbalanced)
  $4HNO_3(l) \rightarrow 4NO_2(g) + 2H_2O(l) + O_2(g)$ (balanced)

Chapter 7

SELF-CHECK EXERCISE 7.1

a. The ions present are

$$Ba^{2+}(aq) + 2NO_3^-(aq) + Na^+(aq) + Cl^-(aq) \rightarrow$$

Ions in   Ions in
Ba(NO₃)₂(aq)   NaCl(aq)

Exchanging the anions gives the possible solid products $BaCl_2$ and $NaNO_3$. Using Table 7.1, we see that both substances are very soluble (rules 1, 2, and 3). Thus no solid forms.

b. The ions present in the mixed solution before any reaction occurs are

$$2Na^+(aq) + S^{2-}(aq) + Cu^{2+}(aq) + 2NO_3^-(aq) \rightarrow$$

Ions in   Ions in
Na₂S(aq)   Cu(NO₃)₂(aq)

Exchanging the anions gives the possible solid products CuS and $NaNO_3$. According to rules 1 and 2 in Table 7.1, $NaNO_3$ is soluble, and by rule 6, CuS should be insoluble. Thus CuS will precipitate. The balanced equation is

$$Na_2S(aq) + Cu(NO_3)_2(aq) \rightarrow CuS(s) + 2NaNO_3(aq)$$

c. The ions present are

$$NH_4^+(aq) + Cl^-(aq) + Pb^{2+}(aq) + 2NO_3^-(aq) \rightarrow$$

Ions in   Ions in
NH₄Cl(aq)   Pb(NO₃)₂(aq)

Exchanging the anions gives the possible solid products

NH_4NO_3 and $PbCl_2$. NH_4NO_3 is soluble (rules 1 and 2) and $PbCl_2$ is insoluble (rule 3). Thus $PbCl_2$ will precipitate. The balanced equation is

$$2NH_4Cl(aq) + Pb(NO_3)_2(aq) \rightarrow PbCl_2(s) + 2NH_4NO_3(aq)$$

SELF-CHECK EXERCISE 7.2

a. *Molecular equation:*

$$Na_2S(aq) + Cu(NO_3)_2(aq) \rightarrow CuS(s) + 2NaNO_3(aq)$$

Complete ionic equation:

$$2Na^+(aq) + S^{2-}(aq) + Cu^{2+}(aq) + 2NO_3^-(aq)$$
$$\rightarrow CuS(s) + 2Na^+(aq) + 2NO_3^-(aq)$$

Net ionic equation:

$$S^{2-}(aq) + Cu^{2+}(aq) \rightarrow CuS(s)$$

b. *Molecular equation:*

$$2NH_4Cl(aq) + Pb(NO_3)_2(aq) \rightarrow PbCl_2(s) + 2NH_4NO_3(aq)$$

Complete ionic equation:

$$2NH_4^+(aq) + 2Cl^-(aq) + Pb^{2+}(aq) + 2NO_3^-(aq)$$
$$\rightarrow PbCl_2(s) + 2NH_4^+(aq) + 2NO_3^-(aq)$$

Net ionic equation:

$$2Cl^-(aq) + Pb^{2+}(aq) \rightarrow PbCl_2(s)$$

Chapter 8

SELF-CHECK EXERCISE 8.1

a. The compound NaBr contains the ions Na^+ and Br^-. Thus each sodium atom loses one electron ($Na \rightarrow Na^+ + e^-$), and each bromine atom gains one electron ($Br + e^- \rightarrow Br^-$).

$$Na + Na + Br - Br \rightarrow (Na^+Br^-) + (Na^+Br-)$$

b. The compound CaO contains the Ca^{2+} and O^{2-} ions. Thus each calcium atom loses two electrons ($Ca \rightarrow Ca^{2+} + 2e^-$), and each oxygen atom gains two electrons ($O + 2e^- \rightarrow O^{2-}$).

$$Ca + Ca + O - O \rightarrow (Ca^{2+}\ O^{2-}) + (Ca^{2+}\ O^{2-})$$

SELF-CHECK EXERCISE 8.2

a. oxidation–reduction reaction; combustion reaction

b. synthesis reaction; oxidation–reduction reaction; combustion reaction

c. synthesis reaction; oxidation–reduction reaction

d. decomposition reaction; oxidation–reduction reaction

e. precipitation reaction; (and double displacement)

f. synthesis reaction; oxidation–reduction reaction

g. acid–base reaction; (and double displacement)

h. combustion reaction; oxidation–reduction reaction

Chapter 9

SELF-CHECK EXERCISE 9.1

The average mass of nitrogen is 14.01 amu. The appropriate equivalence statement is 1 N atom = 14.01 amu, which yields the conversion factor we need:

$$23\ \text{N atoms} \times \frac{14.01\ \text{amu}}{\text{N atom}} = 322.2\ \text{amu}$$

(exact)

SELF-CHECK EXERCISE 9.2

The average mass of oxygen is 16.00 amu, which gives the equivalence statement 1 O atom = 16.00 amu. The number of oxygen atoms present is

$$288\ \text{amu} \times \frac{1\ \text{O atom}}{16.00\ \text{amu}} = 18.0\ \text{O atoms}$$

SELF-CHECK EXERCISE 9.3

Note that the sample of 5.00×10^{20} atoms of chromium is less than 1 mol (6.022×10^{23} atoms) of chromium. What fraction of a mole it represents can be determined as follows:

$$5.00 \times 10^{20}\ \text{atoms Cr} \times \frac{1\ \text{mol Cr}}{6.022 \times 10^{23}\ \text{atoms Cr}} =$$
$$8.30 \times 10^{-4}\ \text{mol Cr}$$

Because the mass of 1 mol of chromium atoms is 52.00 g, the mass of 5.00×10^{20} atoms can be determined as follows:

$$8.30 \times 10^{-4}\ \text{mol Cr} \times \frac{52.00\ \text{g Cr}}{1\ \text{mol Cr}} = 4.32 \times 10^{-2}\ \text{g Cr}$$

SELF-CHECK EXERCISE 9.4

Each molecule of C_2H_3Cl contains two carbon atoms, three hydrogen atoms, and one chlorine atom, so 1 mol of C_2H_3Cl molecules contains 2 mol of C atoms, 3 mol of H atoms, and 1 mol of Cl atoms.

Mass of 2 mol of C atoms: $2 \times 12.01 = 24.02$ g
Mass of 3 mol of H atoms: $3 \times 1.008 = 3.024$ g
Mass of 1 mol of Cl atoms: $1 \times 35.45 = 35.45$ g
$\overline{\hspace{3cm}62.494\ \text{g}}$

The molar mass of C_2H_3Cl is 62.49 g (rounding to the correct number of significant figures).

SELF-CHECK EXERCISE 9.5

The formula for sodium sulfate is Na_2SO_4. One mole of Na_2SO_4 contains 2 mol of sodium ions and 1 mol of sulfate ions.

1 mol of $Na_2SO_4 \rightarrow$ 1 mol of

Na^+
SO_4^{2-}
Na^+

2 mol Na^+

1 mol SO_4^{2-}

Mass of 2 mol of Na^+ = 2×22.99 = 45.98 g
Mass of 1 mol of SO_4^{2-} = $32.07 + 4(16.00)$ = 96.07 g
Mass of 1 mol of Na_2SO_4 = 142.05 g

The molar mass for sodium sulfate is 142.05 g.

A sample of sodium sulfate with a mass of 300.0 g represents more than 1 mol. (Compare 300.0 g to the molar mass of Na_2SO_4.) We calculate the number of moles of Na_2SO_4 present in 300.0 g as follows:

$$300.0 \text{ g Na}_2\text{SO}_4 \times \frac{1 \text{ mol Na}_2\text{SO}_4}{142.05 \text{ g Na}_2\text{SO}_4} = 2.112 \text{ mol Na}_2\text{SO}_4$$

SELF-CHECK EXERCISE 9.6

First we must compute the mass of 1 mol of C_2F_4 molecules (the molar mass). Because 1 mol of C_2F_4 contains 2 mol of C atoms and 4 mol of F atoms, we have:

$$2 \text{ mol C} \times \frac{12.01 \text{ g}}{\text{mol}} = 24.02 \text{ g C}$$

$$4 \text{ mol F} \times \frac{19.00 \text{ g}}{\text{mol}} = 76.00 \text{ g F}$$

Mass of 1 mol of C_2F_4: 100.02 g = molar mass

Using the equivalence statement 100.02 g C_2F_4 = 1 mol C_2F_4, we calculate the moles of C_2F_4 units in 135 g of Teflon.

$$135 \text{ g C}_2\text{F}_4 \text{ units} \times \frac{1 \text{ mol C}_2\text{F}_4}{100.02 \text{ g C}_2\text{F}_4} = 1.35 \text{ mol C}_2\text{F}_4 \text{ units}$$

Next, using the equivalence statement 1 mol = 6.022×10^{23} units, we calculate the number in C_2F_4 units in 135 g of Teflon.

$$1.35 \text{ mol C}_2\text{F}_4 \times \frac{6.022 \times 10^{23} \text{ units}}{1 \text{ mol}} = 8.13 \times 10^{23} \text{ C}_2\text{F}_4 \text{ units}$$

SELF-CHECK EXERCISE 9.7

The molar mass of penicillin F is computed as follows:

$$\text{C: } 14 \text{ mol} \times 12.01 \frac{\text{g}}{\text{mol}} = 168.1 \text{ g}$$

$$\text{H: } 20 \text{ mol} \times 1.008 \frac{\text{g}}{\text{mol}} = 20.16 \text{ g}$$

$$\text{N: } 2 \text{ mol} \times 14.01 \frac{\text{g}}{\text{mol}} = 28.02 \text{ g}$$

$$\text{S: } 1 \text{ mol} \times 32.07 \frac{\text{g}}{\text{mol}} = 32.07 \text{ g}$$

$$\text{O: } 4 \text{ mol} \times 16.00 \frac{\text{g}}{\text{mol}} = 64.00 \text{ g}$$

Mass of 1 mol of $C_{14}H_{20}N_2SO_4$ = 312.39 g = 312.4 g

$$\text{Mass percent of C} = \frac{168.1 \text{ g C}}{312.4 \text{ g C}_{14}\text{H}_{20}\text{N}_2\text{SO}_4} \times 100\% = 53.81\%$$

$$\text{Mass percent of H} = \frac{20.16 \text{ g H}}{312.4 \text{ g C}_{14}\text{H}_{20}\text{N}_2\text{SO}_4} \times 100\% = 6.453\%$$

$$\text{Mass percent of N} = \frac{28.02 \text{ g N}}{312.4 \text{ g C}_{14}\text{H}_{20}\text{N}_2\text{SO}_4} \times 100\% = 8.969\%$$

$$\text{Mass percent of S} = \frac{32.07 \text{ g S}}{312.4 \text{ g C}_{14}\text{H}_{20}\text{N}_2\text{SO}_4} \times 100\% = 10.27\%$$

$$\text{Mass percent of O} = \frac{64.00 \text{ g O}}{312.4 \text{ g C}_{14}\text{H}_{20}\text{N}_2\text{SO}_4} \times 100\% = 20.49\%$$

Check: The percentages add up to 99.99%.

SELF-CHECK EXERCISE 9.8

Step 1 0.6884 g lead and 0.2356 g chlorine

Step 2 $0.6884 \text{ g Pb} \times \dfrac{1 \text{ mol Pb}}{207.2 \text{ g Pb}} = 0.003322 \text{ mol Pb}$

$0.2356 \text{ g Cl} \times \dfrac{1 \text{ mol Cl}}{35.45 \text{ g Cl}} = 0.006646 \text{ mol Cl}$

Step 3 $\dfrac{0.003322 \text{ mol Pb}}{0.003322} = 1.000 \text{ mol Pb}$

$\dfrac{0.006646 \text{ mol Cl}}{0.003322} = 2.001 \text{ mol Cl}$

These numbers are very close to integers, so step 4 is unnecessary. The empirical formula is $PbCl_2$.

SELF-CHECK EXERCISE 9.9

Step 1 0.8007 g C, 0.9333 g N, 0.2016 g H, and 2.133 g O

Step 2 $0.8007 \text{ g C} \times \dfrac{1 \text{ mol C}}{12.01 \text{ g C}} = 0.06667 \text{ mol C}$

$0.9333 \text{ g N} \times \dfrac{1 \text{ mol N}}{14.01 \text{ g N}} = 0.06662 \text{ mol N}$

$0.2016 \text{ g H} \times \dfrac{1 \text{ mol H}}{1.008 \text{ g H}} = 0.2000 \text{ mol H}$

$2.133 \text{ g O} \times \dfrac{1 \text{ mol O}}{16.00 \text{ g O}} = 0.1333 \text{ mol O}$

Step 3 $\dfrac{0.06667 \text{ mol C}}{0.06667} = 1.001 \text{ mol C}$

$\dfrac{0.06662 \text{ mol N}}{0.06667} = 1.000 \text{ mol N}$

$\dfrac{0.2000 \text{ mol H}}{0.06662} = 3.002 \text{ mol H}$

$\dfrac{0.1333 \text{ mol O}}{0.06662} = 2.001 \text{ mol O}$

The empirical formula is CNH_3O_2.

SELF-CHECK EXERCISE 9.10

Step 1 In 100.00 g of Nylon-6 the masses of elements present are 63.68 g C, 12.38 g N, 9.80 g H, and 14.14 g O.

Step 2 $63.68 \text{ g C} \times \dfrac{1 \text{ mol C}}{12.01 \text{ g C}} = 5.302 \text{ mol C}$

$12.38 \text{ g N} \times \dfrac{1 \text{ mol N}}{14.01 \text{ g N}} = 0.8837 \text{ mol N}$

$9.80 \text{ g H} \times \dfrac{1 \text{ mol H}}{1.008 \text{ g H}} = 9.72 \text{ mol H}$

$14.14 \text{ g O} \times \dfrac{1 \text{ mol O}}{16.00 \text{ g O}} = 0.8838 \text{ mol O}$

Step 3 $\dfrac{5.302 \text{ mol C}}{0.8836} = 6.000 \text{ mol C}$

$\dfrac{0.8837 \text{ mol N}}{0.8837} = 1.000 \text{ mol N}$

$\dfrac{9.72 \text{ mol H}}{0.8837} = 11.0 \text{ mol H}$

$\dfrac{0.8838 \text{ mol O}}{0.8837} = 1.000 \text{ mol O}$

The empirical formula for Nylon-6 is $C_6NH_{11}O$.

SELF-CHECK EXERCISE 9.11

Step 1 First we convert the mass percents to mass in grams. In 100.0 g of the compound, there are 71.65 g of chlorine, 24.27 g of carbon, and 4.07 g of hydrogen.

Step 2 We use these masses to compute the moles of atoms present.

$71.65 \text{ g Cl} \times \dfrac{1 \text{ mol Cl}}{35.45 \text{ g Cl}} = 2.021 \text{ mol Cl}$

$24.27 \text{ g C} \times \dfrac{1 \text{ mol C}}{12.01 \text{ g C}} = 2.021 \text{ mol C}$

$4.07 \text{ g H} \times \dfrac{1 \text{ mol H}}{1.008 \text{ g H}} = 4.04 \text{ mol H}$

Step 3 Dividing each mole value by 2.021 (the smallest number of moles present), we obtain the empirical formula $ClCH_2$.

To determine the molecular formula, we must compare the empirical formula mass to the molar mass. The empirical formula mass is 49.48.

Cl:	35.45
C:	12.01
2 H:	2 × (1.008)
$ClCH_2$:	49.48 = empirical formula mass

The molar mass is known to be 98.96. We know that

Molar mass = $n \times$ (empirical formula mass)

So we can obtain the value of n as follows:

$$\frac{\text{Molar mass}}{\text{Empirical formula mass}} = \frac{98.96}{49.48} = 2$$

Molecular formula = $(ClCH_2)_2 = Cl_2C_2H_4$

This substance is composed of molecules with the formula $Cl_2C_2H_4$.

Chapter 10

SELF-CHECK EXERCISE 10.1

The problem can be stated as follows:

$$4.30 \text{ mol } C_3H_8 \xrightarrow{\text{yields}} ? \text{ mol } CO_2$$

From the balanced equation

$$C_3H_8(g) + 5O_2(g) \rightarrow 3CO_2(g) + 4H_2O(g)$$

we derive the equivalence statement

$$1 \text{ mol } C_3H_8 = 3 \text{ mol } CO_2$$

The appropriate conversion factor (moles of C_3H_8 must cancel) is 3 mol CO_2/1 mol C_3H_8, and the calculation is

$$4.30 \text{ mol } C_3H_8 \times \frac{3 \text{ mol } CO_2}{1 \text{ mol } C_3H_8} = 12.9 \text{ mol } CO_2$$

Thus we can say

$$4.30 \text{ mol } C_3H_8 \text{ yields } 12.9 \text{ mol } CO_2$$

SELF-CHECK EXERCISE 10.2

The problem can be sketched as follows:

$$C_3H_8(g) \quad + \quad 5O_2(g) \quad \rightarrow \quad 3CO_2(g) \quad + \quad 4H_2O(g)$$

96.1 g C_3H_8			Grams of CO_2
↓			↑
Use molar mass of C_3H_8			Use molar mass of CO_2
↓			↑
Moles of C_3H_8	→ Use mole ratio → between CO_2 and C_3H_8		Moles of CO_2

We have already done the first step in Example 10.4.

$$\boxed{\begin{array}{c}96.1 \text{ g}\\C_3H_8\end{array}} \rightarrow \frac{1 \text{ mol}}{44.09 \text{ g}} \rightarrow \boxed{\begin{array}{c}2.18 \text{ mol}\\C_3H_8\end{array}}$$

To find out how many moles of CO_2 can be produced from 2.18 mol of C_3H_8, we see from the balanced equation that 3 mol of CO_2 is produced for each mole of C_3H_8 reacted. The mole ratio we need is 3 mol CO_2/1 mol C_3H_8. The conversion is therefore

$$2.18 \text{ mol } C_3H_8 \times \frac{3 \text{ mol } CO_2}{1 \text{ mol } C_3H_8} = 6.54 \text{ mol } CO_2$$

Next, using the molar mass of CO_2, which is $12.01 + 32.00 = 44.01$ g, we calculate the mass of CO_2 produced.

$$6.54 \text{ mol } CO_2 \times \frac{44.01 \text{ g } CO_2}{1 \text{ mol } CO_2} = 288 \text{ g } CO_2$$

The sequence of steps we took to find the mass of carbon dioxide produced from 96.1 g of propane is summarized in the following diagram.

SELF-CHECK EXERCISE 10.3

We sketch the problem as follows:

$$C_3H_8(g) + 5O_2(g) \rightarrow 3CO_2(g) + 4H_2O(g)$$

96.1 g C_3H_8		Grams of H_2O
↓		↑
$\dfrac{1 \text{ mol } C_3H_8}{44.09 \text{ g}}$		$\dfrac{18.02 \text{ g}}{\text{mol } H_2O}$
↓		↑
Moles of C_3H_8	$\rightarrow \dfrac{4 \text{ mol } H_2O}{1 \text{ mol } C_3H_8} \rightarrow$	Moles of H_2O

Then we do the calculations.

$$96.1 \text{ g } C_3H_8 \rightarrow \frac{1 \text{ mol } C_3H_8}{44.09 \text{ g}} \rightarrow 2.18 \text{ mol } C_3H_8$$

$$2.18 \text{ mol } C_3H_8 \rightarrow \frac{4 \text{ mol } H_2O}{1 \text{ mol } C_3H_8} \rightarrow 8.72 \text{ mol } H_2O$$

$$8.72 \text{ mol } H_2O \rightarrow \frac{18.02 \text{ g}}{\text{mol } H_2O} \rightarrow 157 \text{ g } H_2O$$

Therefore, 157 g of H_2O is produced from 96.1 g C_3H_8.

SELF-CHECK EXERCISE 10.4

a. We first write the balanced equation.

$$SiO_2(s) + 4HF(aq) \rightarrow SiF_4(g) + 2H_2O(l)$$

The map of the steps required is

We convert 5.68 g of SiO_2 to moles as follows:

$$5.68 \text{ g } SiO_2 \times \frac{1 \text{ mol } SiO_2}{60.09 \text{ g } SiO_2} = 9.45 \times 10^{-2} \text{ mol } SiO_2$$

Using the balanced equation, we obtain the appropriate mole ratio and convert to moles of HF.

$$9.45 \times 10^{-2} \text{ mol } SiO_2 \times \frac{4 \text{ mol } HF}{1 \text{ mol } SiO_2} = 3.78 \times 10^{-1} \text{ mol } HF$$

Finally, we calculate the mass of HF by using its molar mass.

$$3.78 \times 10^{-1} \text{ mol } HF \times \frac{20.01 \text{ g } HF}{\text{mol } HF} = 7.56 \text{ g } HF$$

b. The map for this problem is

$$SiO_2(s) + 4HF(aq) \rightarrow SiF_4(g) + 2H_2O(l)$$

5.68 g SiO_2		Grams of H_2O
↓		↑
Use molar mass of SiO_2		Use molar mass of H_2O
↓		↑
Moles of SiO_2	Use mole ratio between H_2O and SiO_2	Moles of H_2O

We have already accomplished the first conversion in part a. Using the balanced equation, we obtain moles of H_2O as follows:

$$9.45 \times 10^{-2} \text{ mol } SiO_2 \times \frac{2 \text{ mol } H_2O}{1 \text{ mol } SiO_2} = 1.89 \times 10^{-1} \text{ mol } H_2O$$

The mass of water formed is

$$1.89 \times 10^{-1} \text{ mol } H_2O \times \frac{18.02 \text{ g } H_2O}{\text{mol } H_2O} = 3.41 \text{ g } H_2O$$

SELF-CHECK EXERCISE 10.5

In this problem, we know the mass of the product to be formed by the reaction

$$CO(g) + 2H_2(g) \rightarrow CH_3OH(l)$$

and we want to find the masses of reactants needed. The procedure is the same one we have been following. We must first convert the mass of CH_3OH to moles, then use the balanced equation to obtain moles of H_2 and CO needed, and then convert these moles to masses. Using the molar mass of CH_3OH (32.04 g/mol), we convert to moles of CH_3OH.

First we convert kilograms to grams.

$$6.0 \text{ kg CH}_3\text{OH} \times \frac{1000 \text{ g}}{\text{kg}} = 6.0 \times 10^3 \text{ g CH}_3\text{OH}$$

Next we convert 6.0×10^3 g CH_3OH to moles of CH_3OH, using the conversion factor 1 mol CH_3OH/32.04 g CH_3OH.

$$6.0 \times 10^3 \text{ g CH}_3\text{OH} \times \frac{1 \text{ mol CH}_3\text{OH}}{32.04 \text{ g CH}_3\text{OH}}$$
$$= 1.9 \times 10^2 \text{ mol CH}_3\text{OH}$$

Then we have two questions to answer:

| ? mol of H_2 | $\longrightarrow$ | 1.9×10^2 mol CH_3OH |
| | required to produce | |

| ? mol of CO | $\longrightarrow$ | 1.9×10^2 mol CH_3OH |
| | required to produce | |

To answer these questions, we use the balanced equation

$$CO(g) + 2H_2(g) \rightarrow CH_3OH(l)$$

to obtain mole ratios between the reactants and the products. In the balanced equation the coefficients for both CO and CH_3OH are 1, so we can write the equivalence statement

$$1 \text{ mol CO} = 1 \text{ mol CH}_3\text{OH}$$

Using the mole ratio 1 mol CO/1 mol CH_3OH, we can now convert from moles of CH_3OH to moles of CO.

$$1.9 \times 10^2 \text{ mol CH}_3\text{OH} \times \frac{1 \text{ mol CO}}{1 \text{ mol CH}_3\text{OH}} = 1.9 \times 10^2 \text{ mol CO}$$

To calculate the moles of H_2 required, we construct the equivalence statement between CH_3OH and H_2, using the coefficients in the balanced equation.

$$2 \text{ mol H}_2 = 1 \text{ mol CH}_3\text{OH}$$

Using the mole ratio 2 mol H_2/1 mol CH_3OH, we can convert moles of CH_3OH to moles of H_2.

$$1.9 \times 10^2 \text{ mol CH}_3\text{OH} \times \frac{2 \text{ mol H}_2}{1 \text{ mol CH}_3\text{OH}} = 3.8 \times 10^2 \text{ mol H}_2$$

We now have the moles of reactants required to produce 6.0 kg of CH_3OH. Since we need the masses of reactants, we must use the molar masses to convert from moles to mass.

$$1.9 \times 10^2 \text{ mol CO} \times \frac{28.01 \text{ g CO}}{1 \text{ mol CO}} = 5.3 \times 10^3 \text{ g CO}$$

$$3.8 \times 10^2 \text{ mol H}_2 \times \frac{2.016 \text{ g H}_2}{1 \text{ mol H}_2} = 7.7 \times 10^2 \text{ H}_2$$

Therefore, we need 5.3×10^3 g CO to react with 7.7×10^2 g H_2 to form 6.0×10^3 g (6.0 kg) of CH_3OH. This whole process is mapped in the following diagram.

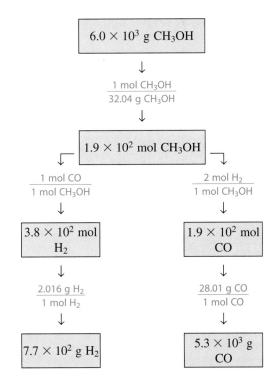

SELF-CHECK EXERCISE 10.6

Step 1 The balanced equation for the reaction is

$$6Li(s) + N_2(g) \rightarrow 2Li_3N(s)$$

Step 2 To determine the limiting reactant, we must convert the masses of lithium (atomic mass = 6.941 g) and nitrogen (molar mass = 28.02 g) to moles.

$$56.0 \text{ g Li} \times \frac{1 \text{ mol Li}}{6.941 \text{ g Li}} = 8.07 \text{ mol Li}$$

$$56.0 \text{ g N}_2 \times \frac{1 \text{ mol N}_2}{28.02 \text{ g N}_2} = 2.00 \text{ mol N}_2$$

Step 3 Using the mole ratio from the balanced equation, we can calculate the moles of lithium required to react with 2.00 mol of nitrogen.

$$2.00 \ \text{mol N}_2 \times \frac{6 \ \text{mol Li}}{1 \ \text{mol N}_2} = 12.0 \ \text{mol Li}$$

Therefore, 12.0 mol of Li is required to react with 2.00 mol of N_2. However, we have only 8.07 mol of Li, so lithium is limiting. It will be consumed before the nitrogen runs out.

Step 4 Because lithium is the limiting reactant, we must use the 8.07 mol of Li to determine how many moles of Li_3N can be formed.

$$8.07 \ \text{mol Li} \times \frac{2 \ \text{mol Li}_3\text{N}}{6 \ \text{mol Li}} = 2.69 \ \text{mol Li}_3\text{N}$$

Step 5 We can now use the molar mass of Li_3N (34.83g) to calculate the mass of Li_3N formed.

$$2.69 \ \text{mol Li}_3\text{N} \times \frac{34.83 \ \text{g Li}_3\text{N}}{1 \ \text{mol Li}_3\text{N}} = 93.7 \ \text{g Li}_3\text{N}$$

SELF-CHECK EXERCISE 10.7

a. **Step 1** The balanced equation is

$$TiCl_4(g) + O_2(g) \rightarrow TiO_2(s) + 2Cl_2(g)$$

Step 2 The numbers of moles of reactants are

$$6.71 \times 10^3 \ \text{g TiCl}_4 \times \frac{1 \ \text{mol TiCl}_4}{189.68 \ \text{g TiCl}_4} = 3.54 \times 10^1 \ \text{mol TiCl}_4$$

$$2.45 \times 10^3 \ \text{g O}_2 \times \frac{1 \ \text{mol O}_2}{32.00 \ \text{g O}_2} = 7.66 \times 10^1 \ \text{mol O}_2$$

Step 3 In the balanced equation both $TiCl_4$ and O_2 have coefficients of 1, so

$$1 \ \text{mol TiCl}_4 = 1 \ \text{mol O}_2$$

and

$$3.54 \times 10^1 \ \text{mol TiCl}_4 \times \frac{1 \ \text{mol O}_2}{1 \ \text{mol TiCl}_4}$$

$$= 3.54 \times 10^1 \ \text{mol O}_2 \ \text{required}$$

We have 7.66×10^1 mol of O_2, so the O_2 is in excess and the $TiCl_4$ is limiting. This makes sense. $TiCl_4$ and O_2 react in a 1:1 mole ratio, so the $TiCl_4$ is limiting because fewer moles of $TiCl_4$ are present than moles of O_2.

Step 4 We will now use the moles of $TiCl_4$ (the limiting reactant) to determine the moles of TiO_2 that would form if the reaction produced 100% of the expected yield (the theoretical yield).

$$3.54 \times 10^1 \ \text{mol TiCl}_4 \times \frac{1 \ \text{mol TiO}_2}{1 \ \text{mol TiCl}_4} = 3.54 \times 10^1 \ \text{mol TiO}_2$$

The mass of TiO_2 expected for 100% yield is

$$3.54 \times 10^1 \ \text{mol TiO}_2 \times \frac{79.88 \ \text{g TiO}_2}{\text{mol TiO}_2} = 2.83 \times 10^3 \ \text{g TiO}_2$$

This amount represents the theoretical yield.

b. Because the reaction is said to give only a 75.0% yield of TiO_2, we use the definition of percent yield,

$$\frac{\text{Actual yield}}{\text{Theoretical yield}} \times 100\% = \% \ \text{yield}$$

to write the equation

$$\frac{\text{Actual yield}}{2.83 \times 10^3 \ \text{g TiO}_2} \times 100\% = 75.0\% \ \text{yield}$$

We now want to solve for the actual yield. First we divide both sides by 100%.

$$\frac{\text{Actual yield}}{2.83 \times 10^3 \ \text{g TiO}_2} \times \frac{100\%}{100\%} = \frac{75.0}{100} = 0.750$$

Then we multiply both sides by 2.83×10^3 g TiO_2.

$$2.83 \times 10^3 \ \text{g TiO}_2 \times \frac{\text{Actual yield}}{2.83 \times 10^3 \ \text{g TiO}_2}$$

$$= 0.750 \times 2.83 \times 10^3 \ \text{g TiO}_2$$

$$\text{Actual yield} = 0.750 \times 2.83 \times 10^3 \ \text{g TiO}_2$$
$$= 2.12 \times 10^3 \ \text{g TiO}_2$$

Thus 2.12×10^3 g of $TiO_2(s)$ is actually obtained in this reaction.

Chapter 11

SELF-CHECK EXERCISE 11.1

a. Circular pathways for electrons in the Bohr model.

b. Three dimensional probability maps that represent the likelihood that the electron will occupy a given point in space. The details of electron motion are not described by an orbital.

c. The surface that contains 90% of the total electron probability. That is, the electron is found somewhere inside this surface 90% of the time.

d. A sublevel is a set of orbitals of given type of orbital within a principal energy level. For example, there are three sublevels in principal level 3; they consist of the $3s$ orbital, the three $3p$ orbitals, and the five $3d$ orbitals.

SELF-CHECK EXERCISE 11.2

Element	Electron Configuration	Orbital Diagram
		$1s$ $2s$ $2p$ $3s$ $3p$
Al	$1s^2 2s^2 2p^6 3s^2 3p^1$ [Ne]$3s^2 3p^1$	⇅ ⇅ ⇅ ⇅ ⇅ ⇅ ↑
Si	[Ne]$3s^2 3p^2$	⇅ ⇅ ⇅ ⇅ ⇅ ⇅ ↑ ↑

Element	Electron Configuration	Orbital Diagram

(Orbital diagram columns labeled: 1s 2s 2p 3s 3p)

Element	Electron Configuration
P	[Ne]$3s^23p^3$
S	[Ne]$3s^23p^4$
Cl	[Ne]$3s^23p^5$
Ar	[Ne]$3s^23p^6$

SELF-CHECK EXERCISE 11.3

Fluorine (F): In Group 7 and Period 2, it is the fifth "2p element." The configuration is $1s^22s^22p^5$, or [He]$2s^22p^5$.

Silicon (Si): In Group 4 and Period 3, it is the second of the "3p elements." The configuration is $1s^22s^22p^63s^23p^2$, or [Ne]$3s^23p^2$.

Cesium (Cs): In Group 1 and Period 6, it is the first of the "6s elements." The configuration is $1s^22s^22p^63s^23p^64s^23d^{10}4p^6 5s^24d^{10}5p^66s^1$, or [Xe]$6s^1$.

Lead (Pb): In Group 4 and Period 6, it is the second of the "6p elements." The configuration is [Xe]$6s^24f^{14}5d^{10}6p^2$.

Iodine (I): In Group 7 and Period 5, it is the fifth of the "5p elements." The configuration is [Kr]$5s^24d^{10}5p^5$.

Chapter 12

SELF-CHECK EXERCISE 12.1

Using the electronegativity values given in Figure 12.3, we choose the bond in which the atoms exhibit the largest difference in electronegativity. (Electronegativity values are shown in parentheses.)

a. H—C > H—P
    (2.1)(2.5)   (2.1)(2.1)

b. O—I > O—F
    (3.5)(2.5)   (3.5)(4.0)

c. S—O > N—O
    (2.5)(3.5)   (3.0)(3.5)

d. N—H > Si—H
    (3.0)(2.1)   (1.8)(2.1)

SELF-CHECK EXERCISE 12.2

H has one electron, and Cl has seven valence electrons. This gives a total of eight valence electrons. We first draw in the bonding pair:

H—Cl, which could be drawn as H : Cl

We have six electrons yet to place. The H already has two electrons, so we place three lone pairs around the chlorine to satisfy the octet rule.

H—C̈l̈ :   or   H : C̈l̈ :

SELF-CHECK EXERCISE 12.3

Step 1 O_3 : 3(6) = 18 valence electrons

Step 2 O—O—O

Step 3 Ö=Ö—Ö̈ :   and   : Ö̈—Ö=Ö̈

This molecule shows resonance (it has two valid Lewis structures).

SELF-CHECK EXERCISE 12.4

See table on top of page A30.

SELF-CHECK EXERCISE 12.5

a. NH_4^+
   The Lewis structure is

   $$\left[\begin{array}{c} H \\ | \\ H-N-H \\ | \\ H \end{array} \right]^+$$

(See Self-Check Exercise 12.4.) There are four pairs of electrons around the nitrogen. This requires a tetrahedral arrangement of electron pairs. The NH_4^+ ion has a tetrahedral molecular structure (case 3 in Table 12.4), because all electron pairs are shared.

b. SO_4^{2-}
   The Lewis structure is

   $$\left[\begin{array}{c} :\ddot{O}: \\ | \\ :\ddot{O}-S-\ddot{O}: \\ | \\ :\ddot{O}: \end{array} \right]^{2-}$$

(See Self-Check Exercise 12.4.) The four electron pairs around the sulfur require a tetrahedral arrangement. The SO_4^{2-} has a tetrahedral molecular structure (case 3 in Table 12.4).

c. NF_3
   The Lewis structure is

   $$\begin{array}{c} \ddot{N} \\ :\ddot{F}\diagup | \diagdown\ddot{F}: \\ :\ddot{F}: \end{array}$$

(See Self-Check Exercise 12.4.) The four pairs of electrons on the nitrogen require a tetrahedral arrangement. In this case only three of the pairs are shared with the fluorine atoms, leaving one lone pair. Thus the molecular structure is a trigonal pyramid (case 4 in Table 12.4).

d. H_2S
   The Lewis structure is   H—S̈—H

(See Self-Check Exercise 12.4.) The four pairs of electrons around the sulfur require a tetrahedral arrangement. In this case two pairs are shared with hydrogen atoms, leaving two lone pairs. Thus the molecular structure is bent or V-shaped (case 5 in Table 12.4).

e. ClO_3^-
   The Lewis structure is

   $$\left[\begin{array}{c} :\ddot{O}-\ddot{Cl}-\ddot{O}: \\ | \\ :\ddot{O}: \end{array} \right]^-$$

(See Self-Check Exercise 12.4.) The four pairs of electrons require a tetrahedral arrangement. In this case, three pairs are shared with oxygen atoms, leaving one lone pair. Thus the molecular structure is a trigonal pyramid (case 4 in Table 12.4).

Answer to Self-Check Exercise 12.4.

Molecule or Ion	Total Valence Electrons	Draw Single Bonds	Calculate Number of Electrons Remaining	Use Remaining Electrons to Achieve Noble Gas Configurations	Check	
					Atom	Electrons
a. NF_3	$5 + 3(7) = 26$	F—N with two F	$26 - 6 = 20$	:F—N—F: with :F:	N	8
					F	8
b. O_2	$2(6) = 12$	O—O	$12 - 2 = 10$	:O=O:	O	8
c. CO	$4 + 6 = 10$	C—O	$10 - 2 = 8$	:C≡O:	C	8
					O	8
d. PH_3	$5 + 3(1) = 8$	P with three H	$8 - 6 = 2$	H—P—H with H	P	8
					H	2
e. H_2S	$2(1) + 6 = 8$	H—S—H	$8 - 4 = 4$	H—S—H	S	8
					H	2
f. SO_4^{2-}	$6 + 4(6) + 2 = 32$	O—S—O (with O above and below)	$32 - 8 = 24$	$\left[:O—S—O: \text{ with } :O:, :O: \right]^{2-}$	S	8
					O	8
g. NH_4^+	$5 + 4(1) - 1 = 8$	H—N—H with H above and below	$8 - 8 = 0$	$\left[H—N—H \text{ with } H, H \right]^{+}$	N	8
					H	2
h. ClO_3^-	$7 + 3(6) + 1 = 26$	Cl with three O	$26 - 6 = 20$	$\left[:O—Cl—O: \text{ with } :O: \right]^{-}$	Cl	8
					O	8
i. SO_2	$6 + 2(6) = 18$	O—S—O	$18 - 4 = 14$	O=S—O: and :O—S=O	S	8
					O	8

f. BeF_2

The Lewis structure is　:F—Be—F:

The two electron pairs on beryllium require a linear arrangement. Because both pairs are shared by fluorine atoms, the molecular structure is also linear (case 1 in Table 12.4).

Chapter 13

SELF-CHECK EXERCISE 13.1

We know that 1.000 atm = 760.0 mm Hg. So

$$525 \text{ mm Hg} \times \frac{1.000 \text{ atm}}{760.0 \text{ mm Hg}} = 0.691 \text{ atm}$$

SELF-CHECK EXERCISE 13.2

Initial Conditions	Final Conditions
$P_1 = 635$ torr	$P_2 = 785$ torr
$V_1 = 1.51$ L	$V_2 = ?$

Solving Boyle's law ($P_1V_1 = P_2V_2$) for V_2 gives

$$V_2 = V_1 \times \frac{P_1}{P_2}$$

$$= 1.51 \text{ L} \times \frac{635 \text{ torr}}{785 \text{ torr}} = 1.22 \text{ L}$$

Note that the volume decreased, as the increase in pressure led us to expect.

SELF-CHECK EXERCISE 13.3

Because the temperature of the gas inside the bubble decreases (at constant pressure), the bubble gets smaller. The conditions are

Initial Conditions
$T_1 = 28\ °C = 28 + 273 = 301$ K
$V_1 = 23$ cm^3

Final Conditions
$T_2 = 18\ °C = 18 + 273 = 291$ K
$V_2 = $?

Solving Charles's law,

$$\frac{V_1}{T_1} = \frac{V_2}{T_2}$$

for V_2 gives

$$V_2 = V_1 \times \frac{T_2}{T_1} = 23\ \text{cm}^3 \times \frac{291\ \cancel{K}}{301\ \cancel{K}} = 22\ \text{cm}^3$$

SELF-CHECK EXERCISE 13.4

Because the temperature and pressure of the two samples are the same, we can use Avogadro's law in the form

$$\frac{V_1}{n_1} = \frac{V_2}{n_2}$$

The following information is given:

Sample 1   *Sample 2*
$V_1 = 36.7$ L $V_2 = 16.5$ L
$n_1 = 1.5$ mol $n_2 = $?

We can now solve Avogadro's law for the value of n_2 (the moles of N_2 in Sample 2):

$$n_2 = n_1 \times \frac{V_2}{V_1} = 1.5\ \text{mol} \times \frac{16.5\ \cancel{L}}{36.7\ \cancel{L}} = 0.67\ \text{mol}$$

Here n_2 is smaller than n_1, which makes sense in view of the fact that V_2 is smaller than V_1.

Note: We isolate n_2 from Avogadro's law as given above by multiplying both sides of the equation by n_2 and then by n_1/V_1:

$$\left(n_2 \times \frac{n_1}{V_1}\right)\frac{V_1}{n_1} = \left(n_2 \times \frac{n_1}{V_1}\right)\frac{V_2}{n_2}$$

to give $n_2 = n_1 \times V_2/V_1$.

SELF-CHECK EXERCISE 13.5

We are given the following information:

$$P = 1.00\ \text{atm}$$
$$V = 2.70 \times 10^6\ \text{L}$$
$$n = 1.10 \times 10^5\ \text{mol}$$

We solve for T by dividing both sides of the ideal gas law by nR:

$$\frac{PV}{nR} = \frac{\cancel{n}R T}{\cancel{n}\cancel{R}} = T$$

to give

$$T = \frac{PV}{nR} = \frac{(1.00\ \cancel{\text{atm}})(2.70 \times 10^6\ \cancel{L})}{(1.10 \times 10^5\ \cancel{\text{mol}})\left(0.08206\ \dfrac{\cancel{L}\ \cancel{\text{atm}}}{\text{K}\ \cancel{\text{mol}}}\right)}$$

$$= 299\ \text{K}$$

The temperature of the helium is 299 K, or $299 - 273 = 26\ °C$.

SELF-CHECK EXERCISE 13.6

We are given the following information about the radon sample:

$$n = 1.5\ \text{mol}$$
$$V = 21.0\ \text{L}$$
$$T = 33\ °C = 33 + 273 = 306\ \text{K}$$
$$P = ?$$

We solve the ideal gas law ($PV = nRT$) for P by dividing both sides of the equation by V:

$$P = \frac{nRT}{V} = \frac{(1.5\ \cancel{\text{mol}})\left(0.08206\ \dfrac{L\ \text{atm}}{\cancel{K}\ \cancel{\text{mol}}}\right)(306\ \cancel{K})}{21.0\ \text{L}}$$

$$= 1.8\ \text{atm}$$

SELF-CHECK EXERCISE 13.7

To solve this problem we take the ideal gas law and separate those quantities that change from those that remain constant (on opposite sides of the equation). In this case volume and temperature change, and number of moles and pressure (and of course R) remain constant. So $PV = nRT$ becomes $V/T = nR/P$, which leads to

$$\frac{V_1}{T_1} = \frac{nR}{P} \quad \text{and} \quad \frac{V_2}{T_2} = \frac{nR}{P}$$

Combining these gives

$$\frac{V_1}{T_1} = \frac{nR}{P} = \frac{V_2}{T_2} \quad \text{or} \quad \frac{V_1}{T_1} = \frac{V_2}{T_2}$$

We are given

Initial Conditions
$T_1 = 5\ °C = 5 + 273 = 278$ K
$V_1 = 3.8$ L

Final Conditions
$T_2 = 86\ °C = 86 + 273 = 359$ K
$V_2 = $?

Thus

$$V_2 = \frac{T_2 V_1}{T_1} = \frac{(359 \text{ K})(3.8 \text{ L})}{278 \text{ K}} = 4.9 \text{ L}$$

Check: Is the answer sensible? In this case the temperature was increased (at constant pressure), so the volume should increase. The answer makes sense.

Note that this problem could be described as a "Charles's law problem." The real advantage of using the ideal gas law is that you need to remember only *one* equation to do virtually any problem involving gases.

SELF-CHECK EXERCISE 13.8

We are given the following information:

Initial Conditions
$P_1 = 0.747$ atm
$T_1 = 13 \,°C = 13 + 273 = 286$ K
$V_1 = 11.0$ L

Final Conditions
$P_2 = 1.18$ atm
$T_2 = 56 \,°C = 56 + 273 = 329$ K
$V_2 = ?$

In this case the number of moles remains constant. Thus we can say

$$\frac{P_1 V_1}{T_1} = nR \quad \text{and} \quad \frac{P_2 V_2}{T_2} = nR$$

or

$$\frac{P_1 V_1}{T_1} = \frac{P_2 V_2}{T_2}$$

Solving for V_2 gives

$$V_2 = V_1 \times \frac{T_2}{T_1} \times \frac{P_1}{P_2} = (11.0 \text{ L})\left(\frac{329 \text{ K}}{286 \text{ K}}\right)\left(\frac{0.747 \text{ atm}}{1.18 \text{ atm}}\right)$$

$$= 8.01 \text{ L}$$

SELF-CHECK EXERCISE 13.9

As usual when dealing with gases, we can use the ideal gas equation $PV = nRT$. First consider the information given:

$$P = 0.91 \text{ atm} = P_{\text{total}}$$
$$V = 2.0 \text{ L}$$
$$T = 25 \,°C = 25 + 273 = 298 \text{ K}$$

Given this information, we can calculate the number of moles of gas in the mixture:
$n_{\text{total}} = n_{N_2} + n_{O_2}$. Solving for n in the ideal gas equation gives

$$n_{\text{total}} = \frac{P_{\text{total}} V}{RT} = \frac{(0.91 \text{ atm})(2.0 \text{ L})}{\left(0.08206 \dfrac{\text{L atm}}{\text{K mol}}\right)(298 \text{ K})} = 0.074 \text{ mol}$$

We also know that 0.050 mol of N_2 is present. Because

$$n_{\text{total}} = \underset{\underset{(0.050 \text{ mol})}{\uparrow}}{n_{N_2}} + n_{O_2} = 0.074 \text{ mol}$$

we can calculate the moles of O_2 present.

$$0.050 \text{ mol} + n_{O_2} = 0.074 \text{ mol}$$
$$n_{O_2} = 0.074 \text{ mol} - 0.050 \text{ mol} = 0.024 \text{ mol}$$

Now that we know the moles of oxygen present, we can calculate the partial pressure of oxygen from the ideal gas equation.

$$P_{O_2} = \frac{n_{O_2} RT}{V} = \frac{(0.024 \text{ mol})\left(0.08206 \dfrac{\text{L atm}}{\text{K mol}}\right)(298 \text{ K})}{2.0 \text{ L}}$$

$$= 0.29 \text{ atm}$$

Although it is not requested, note that the partial pressure of the N_2 must be 0.62 atm, because

$$\underset{P_{N_2}}{\underbrace{0.62 \text{ atm}}} + \underset{P_{O_2}}{\underbrace{0.29 \text{ atm}}} = \underset{P_{\text{total}}}{\underbrace{0.91 \text{ atm}}}$$

SELF-CHECK EXERCISE 13.10

The volume is 0.500 L, the temperature is 25 °C (or 25 + 273 = 298 K), and the total pressure is given as 0.950 atm. Of this total pressure, 24 torr is due to the water vapor. We can calculate the partial pressure of the H_2 because we know that

$$P_{\text{total}} = P_{H_2} + \underset{\underset{24 \text{ torr}}{\uparrow}}{P_{H_2O}} = 0.950 \text{ atm}$$

Before we carry out the calculation, however, we must convert the pressures to the same units. Converting P_{H_2O} to atmospheres gives

$$24 \text{ torr} \times \frac{1.000 \text{ atm}}{760.0 \text{ torr}} = 0.032 \text{ atm}$$

Thus

$$P_{\text{total}} = P_{H_2} + P_{H_2O} = 0.950 \text{ atm} = P_{H_2} + 0.032 \text{ atm}$$

and

$$P_{H_2} = 0.950 \text{ atm} - 0.032 \text{ atm} = 0.918 \text{ atm}$$

Now that we know the partial pressure of the hydrogen gas, we can use the ideal gas equation to calculate the moles of H_2.

$$n_{H_2} = \frac{P_{H_2} V}{RT} = \frac{(0.918 \text{ atm})(0.500 \text{ L})}{\left(0.08206 \dfrac{\text{L atm}}{\text{K mol}}\right)(298 \text{ K})}$$

$$= 0.0188 \text{ mol} = 1.88 \times 10^{-2} \text{ mol}$$

The sample of gas contains 1.88×10^{-2} mol of H_2, which exerts a partial pressure of 0.918 atm.

SELF-CHECK EXERCISE 13.11

We will solve this problem by taking the following steps:

Step 1 Using the atomic mass of zinc (65.38), we calculate the moles of zinc in 26.5 g.

$$26.5 \text{ g Zn} \times \frac{1 \text{ mol Zn}}{65.38 \text{ g Zn}} = 0.405 \text{ mol Zn}$$

Step 2 Using the balanced equation, we next calculate the moles of H_2 produced.

$$0.405 \text{ mol Zn} \times \frac{1 \text{ mol } H_2}{1 \text{ mol Zn}} = 0.405 \text{ mol } H_2$$

Step 3 Now that we know the moles of H_2, we can compute the volume of H_2 by using the ideal gas law, where

$P = 1.50$ atm
$V = ?$
$n = 0.405$ mol
$R = 0.08206$ L atm/K mol
$T = 19 \text{ °C} = 19 + 273 = 292$ K

$$V = \frac{nRT}{P} = \frac{(0.405 \text{ mol})\left(0.08206 \frac{\text{L atm}}{\text{K mol}}\right)(292 \text{ K})}{1.50 \text{ atm}}$$

$$= 6.47 \text{ L of } H_2$$

SELF-CHECK EXERCISE 13.12

Although there are several possible ways to do this problem, the most convenient method involves using the molar volume at STP. First we use the ideal gas equation to calculate the moles of NH_3 present:

$$n = \frac{PV}{RT}$$

where $P = 15.0$ atm, $V = 5.00$ L, and $T = 25 \text{ °C} + 273 = 298$ K.

$$n = \frac{(15.0 \text{ atm})(5.00 \text{ L})}{\left(0.08206 \frac{\text{L atm}}{\text{K mol}}\right)(298 \text{ K})} = 3.07 \text{ mol}$$

We know that at STP each mole of gas occupies 22.4 L. Therefore, 3.07 mol have the volume

$$3.07 \text{ mol} \times \frac{22.4 \text{ L}}{1 \text{ mol}} = 68.8 \text{ L}$$

The volume of the ammonia at STP is 68.8 L.

Chapter 14

SELF-CHECK EXERCISE 14.1

Energy to melt the ice:

$$15 \text{ g } H_2O \times \frac{1 \text{ mol } H_2O}{18 \text{ g } H_2O} = 0.83 \text{ mol } H_2O$$

$$0.83 \text{ mol } H_2O \times 6.02\frac{\text{kJ}}{\text{mol } H_2O} = 5.0 \text{ kJ}$$

Energy to heat the water from 0 °C to 100 °C:

$$4.18 \frac{\text{J}}{\text{g °C}} \times 15 \text{ g} \times 100 \text{ °C} = 6300 \text{ J}$$

$$6300 \text{ J} \times \frac{1 \text{ kJ}}{1000 \text{ J}} = 6.3 \text{ kJ}$$

Energy to vaporize the water at 100 °C:

$$0.83 \text{ mol } H_2O \times 40.6 \frac{\text{kJ}}{\text{mol } H_2O} = 34 \text{ kJ}$$

Total energy required:

$$5.0 \text{ kJ} + 6.3 \text{ kJ} + 34 \text{ kJ} = 45 \text{ kJ}$$

SELF-CHECK EXERCISE 14.2

a. Contains SO_3 molecules—a molecular solid.

b. Contains Ba^{2+} and O^{2-} ions—an ionic solid.

c. Contains Au atoms—an atomic solid.

Chapter 15

SELF-CHECK EXERCISE 15.1

$$\text{Mass percent} = \frac{\text{mass of solute}}{\text{mass of solution}} \times 100\%$$

For this sample, the mass of solution is 135 g and the mass of the solute is 4.73 g, so

$$\text{Mass percent} = \frac{4.73 \text{ g solute}}{135 \text{ g solution}} \times 100\%$$

$$= 3.50\%$$

SELF-CHECK EXERCISE 15.2

Using the definition of mass percent, we have

$$\frac{\text{Mass of solute}}{\text{Mass of solution}} =$$

$$\frac{\text{grams of solute}}{\text{grams of solute} + \text{grams of solvent}} \times 100\% = 40.0\%$$

There are 425 grams of solute (formaldehyde). Substituting, we have

$$\frac{425 \text{ g}}{425 \text{ g} + \text{grams of solvent}} \times 100\% = 40.0\%$$

We must now solve for grams of solvent (water). This will take some patience, but we can do it if we proceed step by step. First we divide both sides by 100%.

$$\frac{425 \text{ g}}{425 \text{ g} + \text{grams of solvent}} \times \frac{\cancel{100\%}}{\cancel{100\%}} = \frac{40.0\%}{100\%} = 0.400$$

Now we have

$$\frac{425 \text{ g}}{425 \text{ g} + \text{grams of solvent}} = 0.400$$

Next we multiply both sides by (425 g + grams of solvent).

$$\cancel{(425 \text{ g} + \text{grams of solvent})} \times \frac{425 \text{ g}}{\cancel{425 \text{ g} + \text{grams of solvent}}}$$

$$= 0.400 \times (425 \text{ g} + \text{grams of solvent})$$

This gives

$$425 \text{ g} = 0.400 \times (425 \text{ g} + \text{grams of solvent})$$

Carrying out the multiplication gives

$$425 \text{ g} = 170. \text{ g} + 0.400 \text{ (grams of solvent)}$$

Now we subtract 170. g from both sides:

$$425 \text{ g} - 170. \text{ g} = \cancel{170. \text{ g}} - \cancel{170. \text{ g}} + 0.400 \text{ (grams of solvent)}$$

$$255 \text{ g} = 0.400 \text{ (grams of solvent)}$$

and divide both sides by 0.400.

$$\frac{255 \text{ g}}{0.400} = \frac{\cancel{0.400}}{\cancel{0.400}} \text{(grams of solvent)}$$

We finally have the answer:

$$\frac{255 \text{ g}}{0.400} = 638 \text{ g} = \text{grams of solvent}$$

$$= \text{mass of water needed}$$

SELF-CHECK EXERCISE 15.3

The moles of ethanol can be obtained from its molar mass (46.1).

$$1.00 \text{ \cancel{g C}}_2\cancel{H_5OH} \times \frac{1 \text{ mol C}_2H_5OH}{46.1 \text{ \cancel{g C}}_2\cancel{H_5OH}}$$

$$= 2.17 \times 10^{-2} \text{ mol C}_2H_5OH$$

$$\text{Volume in liters} = 101 \text{ \cancel{mL}} \times \frac{1 \text{ L}}{1000 \text{ \cancel{mL}}} = 0.101 \text{ L}$$

$$\text{Molarity of C}_2H_5OH = \frac{\text{moles of C}_2H_5OH}{\text{liters of solution}}$$

$$= \frac{2.17 \times 10^{-2} \text{ mol}}{0.101 \text{ L}}$$

$$= 0.215 \ M$$

SELF-CHECK EXERCISE 15.4

When Na_2CO_3 and $Al_2(SO_4)_3$ dissolve in water, they produce ions as follows:

$$Na_2CO_3(s) \xrightarrow{H_2O(l)} 2Na^+(aq) + CO_3^{2-}(aq)$$

$$Al_2(SO_4)_3(s) \xrightarrow{H_2O(l)} 2Al^{3+}(aq) + 3SO_4^{2-}(aq)$$

Therefore, in a 0.10 M Na_2CO_3 solution, the concentration of Na^+ ions is $2 \times 0.10 \ M = 0.20 \ M$ and the concentration of CO_3^{2-} ions is 0.10 M. In a 0.010 M $Al_2(SO_4)_3$ solution, the concentration of Al^{3+} ions is $2 \times 0.010 \ M = 0.020 \ M$ and the concentration of SO_4^{2-} ions is $3 \times 0.010 \ M = 0.030 \ M$.

SELF-CHECK EXERCISE 15.5

When solid $AlCl_3$ dissolves, it produces ions as follows:

$$AlCl_3(s) \xrightarrow{H_2O(l)} Al^{3+}(aq) + 3Cl^-(aq)$$

so a $1.0 \times 10^{-3} \ M$ $AlCl_3$ solution contains $1.0 \times 10^{-3} \ M$ Al^{3+} ions and $3.0 \times 10^{-3} \ M$ Cl^- ions.

To calculate the moles of Cl^- ions in 1.75 L of the $1.0 \times 10^{-3} \ M$ $AlCl_3$ solution, we must multiply the volume by the molarity.

$$1.75 \text{ L solution} \times 3.0 \times 10^{-3} \ M \ Cl^- =$$

$$1.75 \text{ \cancel{L solution}} \times \frac{3.0 \times 10^{-3} \text{ mol Cl}^-}{\cancel{\text{L solution}}}$$

$$= 5.25 \times 10^{-3} \text{ mol Cl}^- = 5.3 \times 10^{-3} \text{ mol Cl}^-$$

SELF-CHECK EXERCISE 15.6

We must first determine the number of moles of formaldehyde in 2.5 L of 12.3 M formalin. Remember that volume of solution (in liters) times molarity gives moles of solute. In this case, the volume of solution is 2.5 L and the molarity is 12.3 mol of HCHO per liter of solution.

$$2.5 \text{ \cancel{L solution}} \times \frac{12.3 \text{ mol HCHO}}{\cancel{\text{L solution}}} = 31 \text{ mol HCHO}$$

Next, using the molar mass of HCHO (30.0 g), we convert 31 mol of HCHO to grams.

$$31 \text{ \cancel{mol HCHO}} \times \frac{30.0 \text{ g HCHO}}{1 \text{ \cancel{mol HCHO}}} = 9.3 \times 10^2 \text{ g HCHO}$$

Therefore, 2.5 L of 12.3 M formalin contains 9.3×10^2 g of formaldehyde. We must weigh out 930 g of formaldehyde and dissolve it in enough water to make 2.5 L of solution.

SELF-CHECK EXERCISE 15.7

We are given the following information:

$$M_1 = 12 \frac{\text{mol}}{\text{L}} \qquad M_2 = 0.25 \frac{\text{mol}}{\text{L}}$$

$$V_1 = ? \text{ (what we need to find)} \qquad V_2 = 0.75 \text{ L}$$

Using the fact that the moles of solute do not change upon dilution, we know that

$$M_1 \times V_1 = M_2 \times V_2$$

Solving for V_1 by dividing both sides by M_1 gives

$$V_1 = \frac{M_2 \times V_2}{M_1} = \frac{0.25 \frac{\text{mol}}{\text{L}} \times 0.75 \text{ L}}{12 \frac{\text{mol}}{\text{L}}}$$

and

$$V_1 = 0.016 \text{ L} = 16 \text{ mL}$$

SELF-CHECK EXERCISE 15.8

Step 1 When the aqueous solutions of Na_2SO_4 (containing Na^+ and SO_4^{2-} ions) and $Pb(NO_3)_2$ (containing Pb^{2+} and NO_3^- ions) are mixed, solid $PbSO_4$ is formed.

$$Pb^{2+}(aq) + SO_4^{2-}(aq) \rightarrow PbSO_4(s)$$

Step 2 We must first determine whether Pb^{2+} or SO_4^{2-} is the limiting reactant by calculating the moles of Pb^{2+} and SO_4^{2-} ions present. Because 0.0500 M $Pb(NO_3)_2$ contains 0.0500 M Pb^{2+} ions, we can calculate the moles of Pb^{2+} ions in 1.25 L of this solution as follows:

$$1.25 \text{ L} \times \frac{0.0500 \text{ mol } Pb^{2+}}{\text{L}} = 0.0625 \text{ mol } Pb^{2+}$$

The 0.0250 M Na_2SO_4 solution contains 0.0250 M SO_4^{2-} ions, and the number of moles of SO_4^{2-} ions in 2.00 L of this solution is

$$2.00 \text{ L} \times \frac{0.0250 \text{ mol } SO_4^{2-}}{\text{L}} = 0.0500 \text{ mol } SO_4^{2-}$$

Step 3 Pb^{2+} and SO_4^{2-} react in a 1:1 ratio, so the amount of SO_4^{2-} ions is limiting because SO_4^{2-} is present in the smaller number of moles.
Step 4 The Pb^{2+} ions are present in excess, and only 0.0500 mol of solid $PbSO_4$ will be formed.
Step 5 We calculate the mass of $PbSO_4$ by using the molar mass of $PbSO_4$ (303.3 g).

$$0.0500 \text{ mol } PbSO_4 \times \frac{303.3 \text{ g } PbSO_4}{1 \text{ mol } PbSO_4} = 15.2 \text{ g } PbSO_4$$

SELF-CHECK EXERCISE 15.9

Step 1 Because nitric acid is a strong acid, the nitric acid solution contains H^+ and NO_3^- ions. The KOH solution contains K^+ and OH^- ions. When these solutions are mixed, the H^+ and OH^- react to form water.

$$H^+(aq) + OH^-(aq) \rightarrow H_2O(l)$$

Step 2 The number of moles of OH^- present in 125 mL of 0.050 M KOH is

$$125 \text{ mL} \times \frac{1 \text{ L}}{1000 \text{ mL}} \times \frac{0.050 \text{ mol } OH^-}{\text{L}} =$$

$$6.3 \times 10^{-3} \text{ mol } OH^-$$

Step 3 H^+ and OH^- react in a 1:1 ratio, so we need 6.3×10^{-3} mol of H^+ from the 0.100 M HNO_3.

Step 4 6.3×10^{-3} mol of OH^- requires 6.3×10^{-3} mol of H^+ to form 6.3×10^{-3} mol of H_2O.

Therefore,

$$V \times \frac{0.100 \text{ mol } H^+}{\text{L}} = 6.3 \times 10^{-3} \text{ mol } H^+$$

where V represents the volume in liters of 0.100 M HNO_3 required. Solving for V, we have

$$V = \frac{6.3 \times 10^{-3} \text{ mol } H^+}{0.100 \frac{\text{mol } H^+}{\text{L}}} = 6.3 \times 10^{-2} \text{ L}$$

$$= 6.3 \times 10^{-2} \text{ L} \times \frac{1000 \text{ mL}}{\text{L}} = 63 \text{ mL}$$

SELF-CHECK EXERCISE 15.10

From the definition of normality, $N = \text{equiv/L}$, we need to calculate (1) the equivalents of KOH and (2) the volume of the solution in liters. To find the number of equivalents, we use the equivalent weight of KOH, which is 56.1 g (see Table 15.2).

$$23.6 \text{ g KOH} \times \frac{1 \text{ equiv KOH}}{56.1 \text{ g KOH}} = 0.421 \text{ equiv KOH}$$

Next we convert the volume to liters.

$$755 \text{ mL} \times \frac{1 \text{ L}}{1000 \text{ mL}} = 0.755 \text{ L}$$

Finally, we substitute these values into the equation that defines normality.

$$\text{Normality} = \frac{\text{equiv}}{\text{L}} = \frac{0.421 \text{ equiv}}{0.755 \text{ L}} = 0.558 \text{ } N$$

To solve this problem, we use the relationship

$$N_{acid} \times V_{acid} = N_{base} \times V_{base}$$

where

$$N_{acid} = 0.50 \frac{equiv}{L}$$

$$V_{acid} = ?$$

$$N_{base} = 0.80 \frac{equiv}{L}$$

$$V_{base} = 0.250 \text{ L}$$

We solve the equation

$$N_{acid} \times V_{acid} = N_{base} \times V_{base}$$

for V_{acid} by dividing both sides by N_{acid}.

$$\frac{N_{acid} \times V_{acid}}{N_{acid}} = \frac{N_{base} \times V_{base}}{N_{acid}}$$

$$V_{acid} = \frac{N_{base} \times V_{base}}{N_{acid}} = \frac{\left(0.80 \, \frac{\cancel{equiv}}{\cancel{L}}\right) \times \left(0.250 \, \text{L}\right)}{0.50 \, \frac{\cancel{equiv}}{\cancel{L}}}$$

$$V_{acid} = 0.40 \text{ L}$$

Therefore, 0.40 L of 0.50 N H_2SO_4 is required to neutralize 0.250 L of 0.80 N KOH.

Answers

TO EVEN-NUMBERED EXERCISES

Chapter 1

2. Examples: physician (understanding cellular processes, understanding how drugs and blood tests work); farmer (understanding which pesticide or fertilizer is needed and how these chemicals work); photographer (understanding how the film exposure and developing chemical processes occur and how they can be controlled and modified).

4. Unfortunately, many examples exist. Chemical and biological weapons are produced in some countries. Although the development of new plastics has been a boon in many endeavors, their use also depletes fossil fuel reserves and increases our solid waste problems. Although biotechnology has produced many exciting new drugs and treatments, the testing procedures which have been developed for determining whether a person has a genetic *likelihood* of developing a particular disease may also be used to make it impossible or difficult for that person to obtain health or life insurance.

6. This answer depends on your own experience, but consider this example. I got a "ding" in the side of my car a few months ago. Although the paint did not appear badly damaged, apparently it was. This part of the car is made of steel (basically iron), and a rust (iron oxide) stain is now appearing where the ding is. This story involves a *chemical substance* (iron) and how it is *chemically changing*.

8. Answer will depend on the student's experience.

10. (a) quantitative—a number (measurement) is indicated explicitly; (b) qualitative—only a qualitative description is given; (c) quantitative—a numerical measurement is indicated; (d) qualitative—only a qualitative description is given; (e) quantitative—a number (measurement) is implied; (f) qualitative—a qualitative judgment is given; (g) quantitative—a numerical quantity is indicated

12. A natural law is a *summary of observed, measurable behavior* that occurs repeatedly and consistently. A theory is an attempt to *explain* such behavior.

14. Most applications of chemistry are oriented toward the interpretation of observations and the solving of problems. Although memorization of some facts may *aid* in these endeavors, it is the ability to combine, relate, and synthesize information that is most important in the study of chemistry.

16. In real-life situations, the problems and applications likely to be encountered are not simple textbook examples. You must be able to observe an event, hypothesize a cause, and then test this hypothesis. You must be able to carry what has been learned in class forward to new, different situations.

Chapter 2

2. three

4. negative; positive

6. (a) -5; (b) 6; (c) -4; (d) 4

8. (a) 4.731×10^{-2}; (b) 4.284×10^3; (c) $4.201 \times 10^0 = 4.201$; (d) 1.41×10^{-10}; (e) 5.23×10^1; (f) 4.909×10^{-2}; (g) 5.4331×10^7; (h) 9.81×10^{-1}

10. (a) 483; (b) 0.0007221; (c) 6.1; (d) 0.0000000911; (e) 4,221,000; (f) 0.00122; (g) 9,999; (h) 0.00001016; (i) 101,600; (j) 0.411; (k) 97,100; (l) 0.000971

12. (a) 1.312×10^{-1}; (b) 1.472×10^3; (c) 1.201×10^{-3}; (d) 4.43×10^5; (e) 7.21×10^0; (f) 9.14×10^{-6}; (g) 1.29×10^1; (h) 1.901×10^{-11}

14. (a) 3.1×10^3; (b) 1×10^6; (c) 1 or 1×10^0; (d) 1.8×10^{-5}; (e) 1×10^7; (f) 1.00×10^6; (g) 1.00×10^{-7}

16. grams

18. (a) mega; (b) milli; (c) nano; (d) mega; (e) centi; (f) micro

20. 100 mi (1 km is less than 1 mi)

22. quart   **24.** kilogram

26. the man is taller (5 ft 9 in)

28. d   **30.** d

32. 40 quarters   **34.** uncertainty

36. The scale of the ruler is marked to the nearest tenth of a centimeter. Writing 2.850 would imply that the scale was marked to the nearest hundredth of a centimeter (and that the zero in the thousandths place had been estimated).

38. (a) infinite, a definition; (b) one; (c) infinite, a definition; (d) one; (e) infinite, a definition

40. final

42. (a) 3.13×10^2; (b) 3.13×10^{-4}; (c) 3.13×10^7; (d) 3.13×10^{-1}; (e) 3.13×10^{-2}

44. (a) 3.42×10^{-4}; (b) 1.034×10^4; (c) 1.7992×10^1; (d) 3.37×10^5

46. decimal   **48.** 3

50. none

52. (a) 641.0; (b) 1.327; (c) 77.34; (d) 3215

54. (a) 124; (b) 1.995×10^{-23}; (c) 1.14×10^{-2}; (d) 5.3×10^{-4}

56. (a) 2.045; (b) 3.8×10^3; (c) 5.19×10^{-5}; (d) 3.8418×10^{-7}

58. an infinite number, a definition

60. 1 ft/12 in.; 12 in./1 ft

62. 1 lb/$0.79

64. (a) 2.44 yd; (b) 42.2 m; (c) 115 in.; (d) 2238 cm; (e) 648.3 mi; (f) 716.7 km; (g) 0.0362 km; (h) 5.01×10^4 cm

66. (a) 0.2543 kg; (b) 2.75×10^3 g; (c) 6.06 lb; (d) 97.0 oz; (e) 1.177 lb; (f) 794 g; (g) 2.5×10^2 g; (h) 1.62 oz

68. 3.1×10^2 km; 3.1×10^5 m; 1.0×10^6 ft

70. 1×10^{-8} cm; 4×10^{-9} in.; 0.1 nm

72. Celsius   **74.** 273

76. Fahrenheit (F)

78. (a) 2 °C; (b) 172 °C; (c) -273 °C; (d) -196 °C; (e) 9727 °C; (f) -271 °C

80. (a) 173 °F; (b) 104 °F; (c) −459 °F; (d) 90. °F

82. (a) −121 °C; (b) approximately 0 °F (−0.4 °F); (c) 673 K; (d) 255 K

84. g/cm^3 (g/mL)   **86.** volume

88. same   **90.** copper

92. (a) 22 g/cm^3; (b) 0.034 g/cm^3; (c) 0.962 g/cm^3; (d) 2.1 × 10^{-5} g/cm^3

94. 0.823 g/mL (g/cm^3)   **96.** float

98. 11.7 mL

100. (a) 1.13 × 10^4 g; 1.13 × 10^7 g; (b) 2.16 × 10^3 g; 2.16 × 10^6 g; (c) 8.80 × 10^2 g; 8.80 × 10^5 g; (d) 7.87 × 10^3 g; 7.87 × 10^6 g

102. (a) 301,100,000,000,000,000,000,000; (b) 5,091,000,000; (c) 720; (d) 123,400; (e) 0.000432002; (f) 0.03001; (g) 0.00000029901; (h) 0.42

104. (a) centimeters or millimeters; (b) kilometers; (c) micrometers; (d) millimeters or micrometers

106. (a) 5.07 × 10^4 kryll; (b) 0.12 blim; (c) 3.70 × 10^{-5} $blim^2$

108. 20. in.   **110.** $1

112. °X = 1.26 °C + 14

114. 3.50 g/L (3.50 × 10^{-3} g/cm^3)

116. 959 g

118. (a) negative; (b) zero; (c) positive; (d) negative

120. (a) 2, positive; (b) 11, negative; (c) 3, positive; (d) 5, negative; (e) 5, positive; (f) zero, zero; (g) 1, negative; (h) 7, negative

122. (a) 2, positive; (b) 3, negative; (c) 1, positive; (d) 8, negative; (e) 4, positive; (f) 1, positive; (g) 6, negative; (h) 1, negative

124. (a) 0.0000298; (b) 4,358,000,000; (c) 0.0000019928; (d) 602,000,000,000,000,000,000,000; (e) 0.101; (f) 0.00787; (g) 98,700,000; (h) 378.99; (i) 0.1093; (j) 2.9004; (k) 0.00039; (l) 0.00000001904

126. (a) 1 × 10^{-2}; (b) 1 × 10^2; (c) 5.5 × 10^{-2}; (d) 3.1 × 10^9; (e) 1 × 10^3; (f) 1 × 10^8; (g) 2.9 × 10^2; (h) 3.453 × 10^4

128. kelvin, K   **130.** centimeter

132. 0.105 m   **134.** 1 kg

136. 10

138. 2.8 (the hundredths place is estimated)

140. (a) 0.0000324; (b) 7,210,000; (c) 2.10 × 10^{-7}; (d) 550,000 (better as 5.50 × 10^5 to show the first zero is significant); (e) 200. (the decimal point shows the zeros are significant)

142. (a) 2149.6; (b) 5.37 × 10^3; (c) 3.83 × 10^{-2}; (d) −8.64 × 10^5

144. (a) 7.6166 × 10^6; (b) 7.25 × 10^3; (c) 1.92 × 10^{-5}; (d) 2.4482 × 10^{-3}

146. 1 yr/12 mo; 12 mo/1 yr

148. (a) 25.7 kg; (b) 3.38 gal; (c) 0.132 qt; (d) 1.09 × 10^4 mL; (e) 2.03 × 10^3 g; (f) 0.58 qt

150. for exactly 6 gross, 864 pencils

152. (a) 352 K; (b) −18 °C; (c) −43 °C; (d) 257 °F

154. 45 g

156. 0.59 g/cm^3

158. (a) 23 °F; (b) 32 °F; (c) −321 °F; (d) −459 °F; (e) 187 °F; (f) −459 °F

Chapter 3

2. states   **4.** container

6. gaseous   **8.** stronger

10. Because gases are mostly empty space, they can be *compressed* easily to smaller volumes. In solids and liquids, most of the sample's bulk volume is filled with the molecules, leaving little empty space.

12. chemical   **14.** chemical

16. When an electric current is transferred through water, the current causes the water molecules to break down into their constituent elements (hydrogen gas and oxygen gas). A chemical change occurs whenever one substance is converted into other substances.

18. Parts g, h, and j represent physical changes. All the other sections represent chemical changes.

20. element   **22.** elements

24. different from   **26.** a variable

28. heterogeneous

30. (a) although the cotton may have been treated with various other substances, it is basically pure cellulose; (b) pure substance; (c) mixture; (d) pure substance

32. (a) homogeneous; (b) heterogeneous; (c) heterogeneous; (d) homogeneous; (e) the paper itself is basically homogeneous

34. filtration

36. The solution is heated to vaporize (boil) the water. The water vapor is then cooled so that it condenses back to the liquid state, and the liquid is collected. After all the water is vaporized from the original sample, pure sodium chloride remains. The process consists of physical changes.

38. the calorie

40. As liquid water is heated, the kinetic energy of the molecules increases: the molecules move more quickly and more randomly. As heating continues, the kinetic energy of the molecules becomes so large that the attractive forces that hold the molecules together in the volume of the liquid are overcome. The liquid is then "boiling," as molecules with high kinetic energies are incorporated into bubbles in the liquid and float to the surface, where they burst and release gaseous water.

42. temperature   **44.** 14.8 g

46. (a) 110.5 kcal; (b) 4.369 kcal; (c) 0.2424 kcal; (d) 45.53 kcal

48. (a) 1.230 × 10^4 cal; (b) 2.904 × 10^5 cal; (c) 9.4 × 10^8 cal; (d) 4.201 × 10^6 cal

50. (a) 1.799 × 10^4 cal; (b) 557.3 kJ; (c) 9.724 × 10^5 J; (d) 154.2 kcal

52. 4.60 J/g°C   **54.** 1.6 × 10^3 g silver

56. 13.55 °C = 14 °C (since the specific heat capacity of iron is given to only two significant figures)

58. 0.031 cal/g°C; 26 J/mol°C

60. gold, 65 J; mercury, 70. J; carbon, 360 J

62. 1.42 J/g°C   **64.** compound

66. physical   **68.** 380,000 J (3.8 × 10^5 J)

70. Aluminum will lose more heat because it has the higher specific heat capacity.

72. 24.2 °C   **74.** 22 °C

76. far apart   **78.** chemical

80. chemical   **82.** electrolysis

84. all except (b) are mixtures   **86.** 9.0 J

88. (a) 627.6 J; (b) 1.867 × 10^4 J; (c) 41.8 J; (d) 17.51 J

90. (a) 12.5 kJ; (b) 2.99 kcal; (c) 2.143 kJ; (d) 3.39 kcal

92. 4.4 × 10^3 J

94. $H_2O(l)$, 7.03 × 10^3 J; $H_2O(s)$, 3.41 × 10^3 J; $H_2O(g)$, 3.4 × 10^3 J; Al, 1.5 × 10^3 J; Fe, 7.6 × 10^2 J; Hg, 2.4 × 10^2 J; C, 1.2 × 10^3 J; Ag, 4.0 × 10^2 J; Au, 2.2 × 10^2 J

96. 0.13 J/g°C

Chapter 4

2. Alchemists discovered several previously unknown elements (mercury, sulfur, antimony) and were the first to prepare several common acids.

4. 111 elements are known; 88 occur naturally; 23 are manmade. Table 4.1 lists the most common elements on the earth.

6. The four most abundant elements in living creatures are oxygen, carbon, hydrogen, and nitrogen (see Table 4.2). In the nonliving world, the most abundant elements are oxygen, silicon, aluminum, and iron (see Table 4.1).

8. Sb (antimony); Cu (copper); Au (gold); Pb (lead); Hg (mercury); K (potassium); Ag (silver); Na (sodium); Sn (tin); W (tungsten)

10. (a) H; (b) Fe; (c) Mg; (d) Ca; (e) Au; (f) He

12. Ir (iridium); Ta (tantalum); Bi (bismuth); Pu (plutonium); Fr (francium); At (astatine)

14. (a) cobalt; (b) silver; (c) chlorine; (d) aluminum; (e) zinc; (f) platinum; (g) chromium; (h) sodium

16. According to Dalton, a given compound always consists of the same number and type of atoms; thus, the composition of the compound on a mass percentage basis is always the same. For example, water molecules from the Atlantic Ocean and the Pacific Ocean all contain two hydrogen atoms bound with one oxygen atom.

18. According to Dalton, all atoms of the same element are *identical;* in particular, every atom of a given element has the same *mass* as every other atom of that element. If a given compound always contains the *same relative numbers* of atoms of each kind, and those atoms always have the same *masses,* then the compound made from those elements always contains the same relative masses of its elements.

20. (a)

(b)

(c)

(d)

(e)

(f)

22. (a) False; Rutherford's bombardment experiments with metal foil suggested that the alpha particles were being deflected by coming near a *dense, positively charged* atomic nucleus. (b) False; The proton and the electron have opposite charges, but the mass of the electron is *much smaller* than the mass of the proton. (c) True

24. neutrons

26. neutron; electron

28. electrons

30. false

32. mass

34. Atoms of the same element (atoms with the same number of protons in the nucleus) may have different numbers of neutrons, and so will have different masses.

36. (a) 37; (b) 23; (c) 46; (d) 30; (e) 53; (f) 95; (g) 83; (h) 42

38. (a) $^{55}_{25}$Mn; (b) $^{25}_{12}$Mg; (c) $^{41}_{20}$Ca; (d) $^{56}_{26}$Fe; (e) $^{238}_{92}$U; (f) $^{244}_{94}$Pu

40.

	Protons	Neutrons	Electrons
(a)	27	33	27
(b)	16	17	16
(c)	4	6	4
(d)	18	22	18
(e)	11	12	11
(f)	36	48	36

42

Name	# of Neutrons	Atomic Number	Mass Number	Symbol
nitrogen	6	7	13	$^{13}_{7}$N
nitrogen	7	7	14	$^{14}_{7}$N
lead	124	82	206	$^{206}_{82}$Pb
iron	31	26	57	$^{57}_{26}$Fe
krypton	48	36	84	$^{84}_{36}$Kr

44. False; The *vertical* columns in the periodic table are called groups or families.

46. Metallic elements are found toward the *left* and *bottom* of the periodic table; there are far more metallic elements than nonmetals.

48. hydrogen, nitrogen, oxygen, fluorine, chlorine, plus all the Group 8 elements (noble gases)

50. The metalloids are found on either side of and next to the "stairstep" region marked on most periodic tables that divides the metallic elements from the nonmetallic elements. Silicon and germanium are metalloids that are used frequently in the electronics industry.

52. (a) 8, noble gases; (b) 7, halogens; (c) 1, alkali metals; (d) 3; (e) 1, alkali metals; (f) 2, alkaline earth elements; (g) 8, noble gases; (h) 7, halogens

54.

Name	Symbol	Atomic Number	Group Number	Metal/Nonmetal
rubidium	Rb	37	1	metal
germanium	Ge	32	4	metalloid
magnesium	Mg	12	2	metal
titanium	Ti	22	—	metal
iodine	I	53	7	nonmetal

56. Most elements are too reactive to be found in the uncombined form in nature and are found only in compounds.

58. These elements are found uncombined in nature and do not readily react with other elements. Although these elements were once thought to form no compounds, this now has been shown to be untrue.

60. diatomic gases: H_2, N_2, O_2, F_2, Cl_2; monatomic gases: He, Ne, Kr, Xe, Rn

62. chlorine

64. diamond

66. electrons

68. 2+

70. -ide

72. nonmetallic

74. (a) Fe^{2+}, 26 protons, 24 electrons, $FeCl_2$; (b) Fe^{3+}, 26 protons, 23 electrons, $FeCl_3$; (c) Ba^{2+}, 56 protons, 54 electrons, $BaCl_2$; (d) Cs^+, 55 protons, 54 electrons, CsCl; (e) S^{2-}, 16 protons, 18 electrons, Na_2S; (f) P^{3-}, 15 protons, 18 electrons, Na_3P; (g) Br^-, 35 protons, 36 electrons, NaBr; (h) O^{2-}, 8 protons, 10 electrons, Na_2O

76. (a) $2e^-$; (b) $2e^-$; (c) $2e^-$; (d) $3e^-$; (e) $1e^-$; (f) $3e^-$

78. (a) Ra^{2+}; (b) Te^{2-}; (c) I^-; (d) Fr^+; (e) At^-; (f) no ion is likely

80. Sodium chloride is an *ionic* compound, consisting of Na^+ and Cl^- *ions*. When NaCl is dissolved in water, these ions are *set free* and can move independently to conduct the electric current. Sugar crystals, although they may *appear* similar visually, contain *no* ions. When sugar is dissolved in water, it dissolves as uncharged *molecules*. No electrically charged species are present in a sugar solution to carry the electric current.

82. The total number of positive charges must equal the total number of negative charges so that the crystals of an ionic compound have *no net charge*. A macroscopic sample of compound ordinarily has no net charge.

84. (a) BaSe; (b) CaI_2; (c) K_2S; (d) SnO_2; (e) SnO; (f) Pb_3P_4; (g) Pb_3N_2; (h) AlI_3

86. (a) 6; (b) 1, alkali metals; (c) transition metals; (d) 2, alkaline earth elements; (e) transition metals; (f) transition metals; (g) 8, noble gases; (h) 2, alkaline earth elements

88. Group 3: boron, B, 5; aluminum, Al, 13; gallium, Ga, 31; indium, In, 49; Group 5: nitrogen, N, 7; phosphorus, P, 15; arsenic, As, 33; antimony, Sb, 51; Group 8: helium, He, 2; neon, Ne, 10; argon, Ar, 18; krypton, Kr, 36

90. Most of an atom's mass is concentrated in the nucleus: the *protons* and *neutrons* that constitute the nucleus have similar masses and are each nearly two thousand times more massive than electrons. The chemical properties of an atom depend on the number and location of the *electrons* it possesses. Electrons are found in the outer regions of the atom and are involved in interactions between atoms.

92. $C_6H_{12}O_6$

94. (a) 29 electrons, 34 neutrons, 29 electrons; (b) 35 protons, 45 neutrons, 35 electrons; (c) 12 protons, 12 neutrons, 12 electrons

96. The chief use of gold in ancient times was as *ornamentation*, whether in statuary or in jewelry. Gold possesses an especially beautiful luster; since it is relatively soft and malleable, it can be worked finely by artisans. Among the metals, gold is inert to attack by most substances in the environment.

98. (a) Ba; (b) Br; (c) Bi; (d) B; (e) K; (f) P

100. (a) Zn; (b) U; (c) W

102. (a) boron; (b) radium; (c) arsenic; (d) calcium; (e) mercury; (f) bromine; (g) fluorine; (h) phosphorus

104. (a) CO_2; (b) $AlCl_3$; (c) $HClO_4$; (d) SCl_6

106. (a) $^{13}_6C$; (b) $^{13}_6C$; (c) $^{13}_6C$; (d) $^{44}_{19}K$; (e) $^{41}_{20}Ca$; (f) $^{35}_{19}K$

108. (a) $^{41}_{20}Ca$, 20, 21, 41; (b) $^{55}_{25}Mn$, 25, 30, 55; (c) $^{109}_{47}Ag$, 47, 62, 109; (d) $^{45}_{21}Sc$, 21, 24, 45

Chapter 5

2. compounds containing a metal and a nonmetal; compounds containing two nonmetals

4. cation (positive ion)

6. sodium ions, Na^+, and chloride ions, Cl^-

8. Roman numeral

10. (a) sodium nitride; (b) potassium oxide; (c) silver bromide [silver(I) bromide]; (d) magnesium iodide; (e) strontium oxide; (f) calcium hydride; (g) barium chloride; (h) aluminum iodide

12. a, c, and d are incorrect

14. (a) lead(II) chloride; (b) iron(III) oxide; (c) tin(II) iodide; (d) mercury(I) oxide; (e) mercury(II) sulfide; (f) copper(I) iodide

16. (a) plumbic oxide; (b) stannous bromide; (c) cuprous sulfide; (d) cuprous iodide; (e) mercurous iodide; (f) chromic fluoride

18. (a) germanium tetrahydride; (b) dinitrogen tetrabromide; (c) diphosphorus pentasulfide; (d) selenium dioxide; (e) ammonia (nitrogen trihydride); (f) silicon dioxide

20. (a) diboron hexahydride, nonionic; (b) calcium nitride, ionic; (c) carbon tetrabromide, nonionic; (d) silver sulfide [silver(I) sulfide], ionic; (e) copper(II) chloride (cupric chloride), ionic; (f) chlorine monofluoride, nonionic

22. (a) aluminum oxide, ionic; (b) diboron trioxide, nonionic; (c) dinitrogen tetroxide, nonionic; (d) cobalt(III) sulfide (cobaltic sulfide), ionic; (e) dinitrogen pentoxide, nonionic; (f) aluminum sulfide, ionic

24. oxygen　　　　　　**26.** perchlorate

28. hypobromite; IO_3^-; periodate; IO^-

30. (a) NO_3^-; (b) NO_2^-; (c) NH_4^+; (d) CN^-

32. (a) PO_4^{3-}; (b) P^{3-}; (c) $H_2PO_4^-$; (d) HPO_4^{2-}

34. (a) hydrogen carbonate, bicarbonate; (b) nitrite; (c) hydrogen sulfate, bisulfate; (d) dihydrogen phosphate; (e) acetate; (f) chlorite

36. (a) ammonium nitrate; (b) potassium chlorate; (c) lead(II) sulfate (plumbous sulfate); (d) calcium phosphate; (e) sodium perchlorate; (f) copper(II) hydroxide (cupric hydroxide)

38. oxygen

40. (a) hypobromous acid; (b) periodic acid (pronounced "per iodic"); (c) phosphorous acid; (d) chlorous acid; (e) selenic acid; (f) hypoiodous acid; (g) iodous acid; (h) hydrotelluric acid

42. (a) PbO_2; (b) $SnBr_2$; (c) CuS; (d) CuI; (e) Hg_2Cl_2; (f) CrF_3

44. (a) CO_2; (b) SO_2; (c) N_2Cl_4; (d) CI_4; (e) PF_5; (f) P_2O_5

46. (a) $Ca_3(PO_4)_2$; (b) NH_4NO_3; (c) $Al(HSO_4)_3$; (d) $BaSO_4$; (e) $Fe(NO_3)_3$; (f) CuOH

48. (a) HCN; (b) HNO_3; (c) H_2SO_4; (d) H_3PO_4; (e) HClO or HOCl; (f) HF; (g) $HBrO_2$; (h) HF

50. (a) Na_2HPO_4; (b) $Mg(C_2H_3O_2)_2$; (c) SrI_2; (d) H_2Se; (e) Ca_3P_2; (f) $AgClO_4$; (g) $Fe(OH)_3$; (h) SnF_2; (i) PbO; (j) B_2O_3; (k) NaH_2PO_4; (l) H_3PO_3

52. A moist paste of NaCl would contain Na^+ and Cl^- ions in solution and would serve as a *conductor* of electrical impulses.

54. $H \rightarrow H^+$ (hydrogen ion) $+ e^-$; $H + e^- \rightarrow H^-$ (hydride ion)

56. oxyanions: IO_3^-, ClO_2^-; oxyacids: $HClO_4$, HClO, $HBrO_2$

58. (a) gold(III) bromide (auric bromide); (b) cobalt(III) cyanide (cobaltic cyanide); (c) magnesium hydrogen phosphate; (d) diboron hexahydride (common name diborane); (e) ammonia; (f) silver(I) sulfate (usually called silver sulfate); (g) beryllium hydroxide

60. (a) ammonium carbonate; (b) ammonium hydrogen carbonate, ammonium bicarbonate; (c) calcium phosphate; (d) sulfurous acid; (e) manganese(IV) oxide; (f) iodic acid; (g) potassium hydride

62. (a) MCl_4; (b) $M(NO_3)_4$; (c) MO_2; (d) $M_3(PO_4)_4$; (e) $M(CN)_4$; (f) $M(SO_4)_2$; (g) $M(Cr_2O_7)_2$

64. M^+ compounds: MD, M_2E, M_3F; M^{2+} compounds: MD_2, ME, M_3F_2; M^{3+} compounds: MD_3, M_2E_3, MF

66. $CaBr_2$, $Ca(HCO_3)_2$, CaH_2, $Ca(C_2H_3O_2)_2$, $Ca(HSO_4)_2$, $Ca_3(PO_4)_2$; $SrBr_2$, $Sr(HCO_3)_2$, SrH_2, $Sr(C_2H_3O_2)_2$, $Sr(HSO_4)_2$, $Sr_3(PO_4)_2$; NH_4Br, NH_4HCO_3, NH_4H, $NH_4C_2H_3O_2$, NH_4HSO_4, $(NH_4)_3PO_4$; $AlBr_3$, $Al(HCO_3)_3$, AlH_3, $Al(C_2H_3O_2)_3$, $Al(HSO_4)_3$, $AlPO_4$; $FeBr_3$, $Fe(HCO_3)_3$, FeH_3, $Fe(C_2H_3O_2)_3$, $Fe(HSO_4)_3$, $FePO_4$; $NiBr_2$, $Ni(HCO_3)_2$, NiH_2, $Ni(C_2H_3O_2)_2$, $Ni(HSO_4)_2$, $Ni_3(PO_4)_2$; AgBr, $AgHCO_3$, AgH, $AgC_2H_3O_2$, $AgHSO_4$, Ag_3PO_4; $AuBr_3$, $Au(HCO_3)_3$,

AuH_3, $Au(C_2H_3O_2)_3$, $Au(HSO_4)_3$, $AuPO_4$; KBr, $KHCO_3$, KH, $KC_2H_3O_2$, $KHSO_4$, K_3PO_4; $HgBr_2$, $Hg(HCO_3)_2$, HgH_2, $Hg(C_2H_3O_2)_2$, $Hg(HSO_4)_2$, $Hg_3(PO_4)_2$; $BaBr_2$, $Ba(HCO_3)_2$, BaH_2, $Ba(C_2H_3O_2)_2$, $Ba(HSO_4)_2$, $Ba_3(PO_4)_2$

68. helium   **70.** iodine

72. $1-$ **74.** $1-$

76. (a) Mn (manganese), atomic number 25, Mn^{2+} (25 protons, 23 electrons), Mn (25 protons, 25 electrons); (b) Ni (nickel), atomic number 28, Ni^{2+} (28 protons, 26 electrons), Ni (28 protons, 28 electrons); (c) N (nitrogen), atomic number 7, N^{3-} (7 protons, 10 electrons), N (7 protons, 7 electrons); (d) Co (cobalt), atomic number 27, Co^{3+} (27 protons, 24 electrons), Co (27 protons, 27 electrons); (e) Fe (iron), atomic number 26, Fe^{2+} (26 protons, 24 electrons), Fe (26 protons, 26 electrons); (f) P (phosphorus), atomic number 15, P^{3-} (15 protons, 18 electrons), P (15 protons, 15 electrons)

78. (a) Na_2S; (b) KCl; (c) BaO; (d) $MgSe$; (e) $CuBr_2$; (f) AlI_3; (g) Al_2O_3; (h) Ca_3N_2

80. b, d, and e are incorrect

82. (a) cobaltic bromide; (b) plumbic iodide; (c) ferric oxide; (d) ferrous sulfide; (e) stannic chloride; (f) stannous oxide

84. (a) iron(III) sulfide (ferric sulfide), ionic; (b) gold(III) chloride (auric chloride), ionic; (c) arsenic trihydride (arsine), nonionic; (d) chlorine monofluoride, nonionic; (e) potassium oxide, ionic; (f) carbon dioxide, nonionic

86. (a) CO_3^{2-}; (b) HCO_3^-; (c) $C_2H_3O_2^-$; (d) CN^-

88. (a) carbonate; (b) chlorate; (c) sulfate; (d) phosphate; (e) perchlorate; (f) permanganate

90. (a) $CaCl_2$; (b) Ag_2O; (c) Al_2S_3; (d) $BeBr_2$; (e) H_2S; (f) KH; (g) MgI_2; (h) CsF

92. (a) Mg_3P_2; (b) CaF_2; (c) $CoBr_3$; (d) FeI_2; (e) BaO; (f) K_2S

Chapter 6

2. Hydrogen peroxide *bubbles* when it is applied to a wound. The bubbling represents the decomposition of the hydrogen peroxide into oxygen gas (the bubbles) and water.

4. The oils and greases deposited on the walls of the oven are converted by the sodium hydroxide into soap, which is water soluble and can be washed away. The formation of soap represents the chemical breakdown of greases and oils.

6. A gas is evolved during fermentation. The odor of the product (alcohol or vinegar) will be noticeable.

8. atoms   **10.** the same

12. water

14. $Zn(s) + S(s) \rightarrow ZnS(s)$

16. $(NH_4)_2CO_3(s) \rightarrow NH_3(g) + CO_2(g) + H_2O(g)$

18. $Cl_2(g) + KI(aq) \rightarrow KCl(aq) + I_2(s)$

20. $Ca(s) + H_2O(l) \rightarrow Ca(OH)_2(s) + H_2(g)$

22. $CaC_2(s) + H_2O(l) \rightarrow C_2H_2(g) + Ca(OH)_2(s)$

24. $H_2S(g) + O_2(g) \rightarrow SO_2(g) + H_2O(g)$

26. $NaCl(aq) + H_2O(l) \rightarrow NaOH(aq) + Cl_2(g) + H_2(g)$

28. $O_2(g) \rightarrow O_3(g)$

30. $SiO_2(s) + C(s) \rightarrow Si(s) + CO(g)$

32. $Xe(g) + F_2(g) \rightarrow XeF_4(s)$

34. $C_{12}H_{22}O_{11}(s) + O_2(g) \rightarrow CO_2(g) + H_2O(g)$

36. whole numbers

38. (a) $Br_2(l) + 2KI(aq) \rightarrow 2KBr(aq) + I_2(s)$; (b) $4Co(s) + 3O_2(g) \rightarrow 2Co_2O_3(s)$; (c) $P_4(s) + 5O_2(g) \rightarrow P_4O_{10}(s)$; (d) $2Al(s) + 6HNO_3(aq) \rightarrow 2Al(NO_3)_3(aq) + 3H_2(g)$; (e) $PBr_3(l) + 3H_2O(l) \rightarrow H_3PO_3(aq) + 3HBr(aq)$; (f) $2NO(g) + O_2(g) \rightarrow 2NO_2(g)$; (g) $2C_2H_6(g) + 7O_2(g) \rightarrow 4CO_2(g) + 6H_2O(g)$; (h) $CuO(s) + H_2SO_4(aq) \rightarrow CuSO_4(aq) + H_2O(l)$

40. (a) $CaF_2(s) + H_2SO_4(l) \rightarrow CaSO_4(s) + 2HF(g)$; (b) $3KBr(s) + H_3PO_4(aq) \rightarrow K_3PO_4(aq) + 3HBr(g)$; (c) $TiCl_4(l) + 4Na(s) \rightarrow 4NaCl(s) + Ti(s)$; (d) $K_2CO_3(s) \rightarrow K_2O(s) + CO_2(g)$; (e) $4KO_2(s) + 2H_2O(l) \rightarrow 4KOH(aq) + 3O_2(g)$; (f) $2Na_2O_2(s) + 2H_2O(g) + 4CO_2(g) \rightarrow 4NaHCO_3(s) + O_2(g)$; (g) $2KNO_2(s) + 2C(s) \rightarrow K_2CO_3(s) + CO(g) + N_2(g)$; (h) $3BaO(s) + 2Al(s) \rightarrow Al_2O_3(s) + 3Ba(s)$

42. (a) $SiI_4(s) + 2Mg(s) \rightarrow Si(s) + 2MgI_2(s)$; (b) $MnO_2(s) + 2Mg(s) \rightarrow Mn(s) + 2MgO(s)$; (c) $8Ba(s) + S_8(s) \rightarrow 8BaS(s)$; (d) $4NH_3(g) + 3Cl_2(g) \rightarrow 3NH_4Cl(s) + NCl_3(g)$; (e) $8Cu_2S(s) + S_8(s) \rightarrow 16CuS(s)$; (f) $2Al(s) + 3H_2SO_4(aq) \rightarrow Al_2(SO_4)_3(aq) + 3H_2(g)$; (g) $2NaCl(s) + H_2SO_4(l) \rightarrow 2HCl(g) + Na_2SO_4(s)$; (h) $2CO(g) + O_2(g) \rightarrow 2CO_2(g)$

44. (a) $Ba(NO_3)_2(aq) + Na_2CrO_4(aq) \rightarrow BaCrO_4(s) + 2NaNO_3(aq)$; (b) $PbCl_2(aq) + K_2SO_4(aq) \rightarrow PbSO_4(s) + 2KCl(aq)$; (c) $C_2H_5OH(l) + 3O_2(g) \rightarrow 2CO_2(g) + 3H_2O(l)$; (d) $CaC_2(s) + 2H_2O(l) \rightarrow Ca(OH)_2(s) + H_2C_2(g)$; (e) $Sr(s) + 2HNO_3(aq) \rightarrow Sr(NO_3)_2(aq) + H_2(g)$; (f) $BaO_2(s) + H_2SO_4(aq) \rightarrow BaSO_4(s) + H_2O_2(aq)$; (g) $2AsI_3(s) \rightarrow 2As(s) + 3I_2(s)$; (h) $2CuSO_4(aq) + 4KI(s) \rightarrow 2CuI(s) + I_2(s) + 2K_2SO_4(aq)$

46. $2Li(s) + 2H_2O(l) \rightarrow 2LiOH(aq) + H_2(g)$; $2Na(s) + 2H_2O(l) \rightarrow 2NaOH(aq) + H_2(g)$; $2K(s) + 2H_2O(l) \rightarrow 2KOH(aq) + H_2(g)$; $2Rb(s) + 2H_2O(l) \rightarrow 2RbOH(aq) + H_2(g)$; $2Cs(s) + 2H_2O(l) \rightarrow 2CsOH(aq) + H_2(g)$; $2Fr(s) + 2H_2O(l) \rightarrow 2FrOH(aq) + H_2(g)$

48. $C_{12}H_{22}O_{11}(aq) + H_2O(l) \rightarrow 4C_2H_6O(aq) + 4CO_2(g)$

50. $2Al_2O_3(s) + 3C(s) \rightarrow 4Al(s) + 3CO_2(g)$

52. $Be(s) + F_2(g) \rightarrow BeF_2(s)$; $Be(s) + Cl_2(g) \rightarrow BeCl_2(s)$; $Mg(s) + F_2(g) \rightarrow MgF_2(s)$; $Mg(s) + Cl_2(g) \rightarrow MgCl_2(s)$; $Ca(s) + F_2(g) \rightarrow CaF_2(s)$; $Ca(s) + Cl_2(g) \rightarrow CaCl_2(s)$; $Sr(s) + F_2(g) \rightarrow SrF_2(s)$; $Sr(s) + Cl_2(g) \rightarrow SrCl_2(s)$; $Ba(s) + F_2(g) \rightarrow BaF_2(s)$; $Ba(s) + Cl_2(g) \rightarrow BaCl_2(s)$; $Ra(s) + F_2(g) \rightarrow RaF_2(s)$; $Ra(s) + Cl_2(g) \rightarrow RaCl_2(s)$

54. $(NH_4)_2Cr_2O_7(s) \rightarrow Cr_2O_3(s) + N_2(g) + 4H_2O(g)$

56. $2KClO_3(s) \rightarrow 2KCl(s) + 3O_2(g)$

58. $NH_3(g) + HCl(g) \rightarrow NH_4Cl(s)$

60. Most oils *decompose* at high temperatures, producing a foul-smelling chemical called acrolein associated with the smell and taste of burned food. Oil that has been heated to too high a temperature for an extended period "turns rancid" and is unfit for use. Also, at high enough temperatures, the oil might ignite.

62. $Fe(s) + S(s) \rightarrow FeS(s)$

64. $C_3H_8(g) + O_2(g) \rightarrow CO_2(g) + H_2O(g)$

66. $KI(aq) + H_2O(l) \rightarrow KOH(aq) + H_2(g) + I_2(s)$

68. $Mg(s) + H_2O(g) \rightarrow Mg(OH)_2(s) + H_2(g)$

70. $CuO(s) + H_2SO_4(aq) \rightarrow CuSO_4(aq) + H_2O(l)$

72. $Na_2SO_3(aq) + S(s) \rightarrow Na_2S_2O_3(aq)$

74. (a) $Ba(NO_3)_2(aq) + 2KF(aq) \rightarrow BaF_2(aq) + 2KNO_3(aq)$; (b) $Zn(s) + 2HCl(aq) \rightarrow ZnCl_2(aq) + H_2(g)$; (c) $2Fe(s) + 3S(s) \rightarrow Fe_2S_3(s)$; (d) $C_6H_{12}O_6(s) + 6O_2(g) \rightarrow 6CO_2(g) + 6H_2O(g)$; (e) $H_2O(l) + Cl_2(g) \rightarrow HCl(aq) + HOCl(aq)$; (f) $2ZnS(s) + 3O_2(g) \rightarrow 2ZnO(s) + 2SO_2(g)$; (g) $PbSO_4(s) + 4NaCl(aq) \rightarrow$

$Na_2SO_4(aq) + Na_2PbCl_4(aq)$; (h) $3Fe_2O_3(s) + C(s) \rightarrow$
$2Fe_3O_4(s) + CO(g)$

76. (a)$Pb(NO_3)_2(aq) + K_2CrO_4(aq) \rightarrow PbCrO_4(s) + 2KNO_3(aq)$;
(b)$BaCl_2(aq) + Na_2SO_4(aq) \rightarrow BaSO_4(s) + 2NaCl(aq)$;
(c)$2CH_3OH(l) + 3O_2(g) \rightarrow 2CO_2(g) + 4H_2O(g)$; (d) $Na_2CO_3(aq) +$
$S(s) + SO_2(g) \rightarrow CO_2(g) + Na_2S_2O_3(aq)$; (e) $Cu(s) + 2H_2SO_4(aq) \rightarrow$
$CuSO_4(aq) + SO_2(g) + 2H_2O(l)$; (f) $MnO_2(s) + 4HCl(aq) \rightarrow$
$MnCl_2(aq) + Cl_2(g) + 2H_2O(l)$; (g) $As_2O_3(s) + 6KI(aq) +$
$6HCl(aq) \rightarrow 2AsI_3(s) + 6KCl(aq) + 3H_2O(l)$; (h) $2Na_2S_2O_3(aq) +$
$I_2(aq) \rightarrow Na_2S_4O_6(aq) + 2NaI(aq)$

Chapter 7

2. Driving forces are types of *changes* in a system that pull a reaction
in the *direction of product formation;* driving forces include formation of a *solid,* formation of *water,* formation of a *gas,* and transfer
of electrons.

4. The net charge of a precipitate must be *zero.* The total number of
positive charges equals the total number of negative charges.

6. ions

8. Consider the two new possible combinations of ions (when two ionic
compounds are mixed, the ions may "switch partners"); if one of
these new possible combinations is insoluble in water, it will form
a precipitate having zero net charge (indicating the proportions in
which the ions must be combined). No foolproof method exists for
predicting by inspection what precipitate may form: we rely on in-
tuition, experience from similar reactions, and "rules of thumb"
based on the results of experiments (such as the general solubility
rules from Table 7.1).

10. "Insoluble" and "slightly" soluble have roughly the same meanings.
However, if a substance is highly toxic and is found in a water supply, for example, the difference between "insoluble" and "slightly
soluble" could be crucial.

12. (a) soluble (most nitrate salts are soluble); (b) soluble (most potassium salts are soluble); (c) soluble (most sodium salts are soluble);
(d) insoluble (most hydroxide compounds are only slightly soluble);
(e) insoluble (exception for chloride salts); (f) soluble (most ammonium salts are soluble); (g) insoluble (most sulfide salts are only
slightly soluble); (h) insoluble (exception for sulfate salts)

14. (a) Rule 6: most sulfide salts are only slightly soluble; (b) Rule 5:
most hydroxide compounds are only slightly soluble; (c) Rule 4: exception; (d) Rule 6: most carbonate salts are only slightly soluble

16. (a) HgS; (b) CaSO_4; (c) AgCl; (d) Ba(CO)_3: Rule 6: most carbonate
compounds are only slightly soluble; (e) Ni_3(PO_4)_2; (f) CuCO_3

18. (a) no precipitate: both $Ba(NO_3)_2$ and HCl are soluble;
(b) $(NH_4)_2S(aq) + CoCl_2(aq) \rightarrow CoS(s) + 2NH_4Cl(aq)$;
(c) $H_2SO_4(aq) + Pb(NO_3)_2 (aq) \rightarrow PbSO_4(s) + 2HNO_3(aq)$;
(d) $CaCl_2(aq) + H_2CO_3(aq) \rightarrow CaCO_3(s) + 2HCl(aq)$; (e) no precipitate: $NH_4C_2H_3O_2$ and $NaNO_3$ are each soluble; (f) $Na_3PO_4(aq) +$
$CrCl_3(aq) \rightarrow 3NaCl(aq) + CrPO_4(s)$

20. (a) $2AgNO_3(aq) + H_2SO_4(aq) \rightarrow Ag_2SO_4(s) + 2HNO_3(aq)$;
(b) $Ca(NO_3)_2(aq) + H_2SO_4(aq) \rightarrow CaSO_4(s) + 2HNO_3(aq)$;
(c) $Pb(NO_3)_2(aq) + H_2SO_4(aq) \rightarrow PbSO_4(s) + 2HNO_3(aq)$

22. (a) $NiCl_2(aq) + H_2S(aq) \rightarrow NiS(s) + 2HCl(aq)$; (b) $CuSO_4(aq) +$
$2NaOH(aq) \rightarrow Na_2SO_4(aq) + Cu(OH)_2(s)$;   (c) $Ba(NO_3)_2(aq) +$
$Na_2CO_3(aq) \rightarrow 2NaNO_3(aq) + BaCO_3(s)$

24. spectator

26. (a) $Fe^{3+}(aq) + 3OH^-(aq) \rightarrow Fe(OH)_3(s)$; (b) $Ni^{2+}(aq) + S^{2-}(aq) \rightarrow$
$NiS(s)$: Rule 6: most sulfide salts are only slightly soluble.
(c) $Ag^+(aq) + Cl^-(aq) \rightarrow AgCl(s)$; (d) $Ba^{2+}(aq) + SO_4^{2-}(aq) \rightarrow$
$BaSO_4(s)$; (e) $Hg_2^{2+}(aq) + 2Br^-(aq) \rightarrow Hg_2Br_2(s)$; (f) $Ba^{2+}(aq) +$
$SO_4^{2-}(aq) \rightarrow BaSO_4(s)$

28. $Ag^+(aq) + Cl^-(aq) \rightarrow AgCl(s)$; $Pb^{2+}(aq) + 2Cl^-(aq) \rightarrow PbCl_2(s)$;
$Hg_2^{2+}(aq) + 2Cl^-(aq) \rightarrow Hg_2Cl_2(s)$

30. $Co^{2+}(aq) + S^{2-}(aq) \rightarrow CoS(s)$; $2Co^{3+}(aq) + 3S^{2-}(aq) \rightarrow Co_2S_3(s)$;
$Fe^{2+}(aq) + S^{2-}(aq) \rightarrow FeS(s)$; $2Fe^{3+}(aq) + 3S^{2-}(aq) \rightarrow Fe_2S_3(s)$

32. Acids have long been noted for their sour taste (for example, the
acetic acid in vinegar and the citric acid in lemon juice). Bases were
noted because of their bitter taste and slippery feel on the skin.

34. HCl

36. salt

38. $RbOH(s) \rightarrow Rb^+(aq) + OH^-(aq)$; $CsOH(s) \rightarrow Cs^+(aq) + OH^-(aq)$

40. (a) $NaOH(aq) + HNO_3(aq) \rightarrow NaNO_3(aq) + H_2O(l)$; (b) $2KOH(aq) +$
$H_2SO_4(aq) \rightarrow K_2SO_4(aq) + 2H_2O(l)$; (c) $RbOH(aq) + HCl(aq) \rightarrow$
$RbCl(aq) + H_2O(l)$; (d) $NaOH(aq) + HClO_4(aq) \rightarrow NaClO_4(aq) +$
$H_2O(l)$

42. A *molecular equation* uses the normal, uncharged formulas for the
compounds involved. The *complete ionic equation* shows the compounds broken up into their respective ions (*all* ions present are
shown). The *net ionic equation* shows only those ions that combine
to form a precipitate, a gas, or a nonionic product such as water. The
net ionic equation shows most clearly the species that combine with
each other.

44. $Pb^{2+}(aq) + 2Cl^-(aq) \rightarrow PbCl_2(s)$; $Pb^{2+}(aq) + CrO_4^{2-}(aq) \rightarrow$
$PbCrO_4(s)$

46. (a) Rule 5: $Co^{3+}(aq) + 3OH^-(aq) \rightarrow Co(OH)_3(s)$; (b) Rule 6:
$2Ag^+(aq) + CO_3^{2-}(aq) \rightarrow Ag_2CO_3(s)$; (c) no reaction (all combinations of ions are soluble); (d) Rule 4: $Ba^{2+}(aq) + SO_4^{2-}(aq) \rightarrow$
$BaSO_4(s)$; (e) no reaction (all combinations of ions are soluble); (f)
Rule 6: $3Ca^{2+}(aq) + 2PO_4^{3-}(aq) \rightarrow Ca_3(PO_4)_2(s)$; (g) Rule 5:
$Al^{3+}(aq) + 3OH^-(aq) \rightarrow Al(OH)_3(s)$

48. $Ca(OH)_2(s) \rightarrow Ca^{2+}(aq) + 2OH^-(aq)$; $Mg(OH)_2(s) \rightarrow$
$Mg^{2+}(aq) + 2OH^-(aq)$; $Sr(OH)_2(s) \rightarrow Sr^{2+}(aq) + 2OH^-(aq)$;
$Ba(OH)_2(s) \rightarrow Ba^{2+}(aq) + 2OH^-(aq)$

50. When *any* strong acid reacts with *any* strong base, the net ionic reaction is the *same*: $H^+(aq) + OH^-(aq) \rightarrow H_2O(l)$. Since the net
ionic reaction is the same for any strong acid, the amount of heat
liberated is also the same.

52. (a) soluble (Rule 2: most potassium salts are soluble); (b) soluble
(Rule 2: most ammonium salts are soluble); (c) insoluble (Rule 6:
most carbonate salts are only slightly soluble); (d) insoluble (Rule
6: most phosphate salts are only slightly soluble); (e) soluble (Rule
2: most sodium salts are soluble); (f) insoluble (Rule 6: most carbonate salts are only slightly soluble); (g) soluble (Rule 3: most chloride salts are soluble)

54. (a) iron(III) hydroxide, $Fe(OH)_3$ (Rule 5: most hydroxide salts are
only slightly soluble); (b) nickel(II) sulfide, NiS (Rule 6: most sulfide salts are only slightly soluble); (c) silver chloride, AgCl (Rule
3: Although most chloride salts are soluble, AgCl is an exception);
(d) barium carbonate, $BaCO_3$ (Rule 6: most carbonate salts are only
slightly soluble); (e) mercury(I) chloride or mercurous chloride,
Hg_2Cl_2 (Rule 3: Although most chloride salts are soluble, Hg_2Cl_2 is

an exception); (f) barium sulfate, $BaSO_4$ (Rule 4: Although most sulfate salts are soluble, $BaSO_4$ is an exception)

56. (a) $Co(NO_3)_2(aq) + (NH_4)_2S(aq) \rightarrow CoS(s) + 2NH_4NO_3(aq)$; (b) $CaCl_2(aq) + H_2SO_4(aq) \rightarrow CaSO_4(s) + 2HCl(aq)$; (c) $FeCl_3(aq) + Na_3PO_4(aq) \rightarrow FePO_4(s) + 3NaCl(aq)$

58. (a)$Ag^+(aq) + Cl^-(aq) \rightarrow AgCl(s)$; (b) $3Ca^{2+}(aq) + 2PO_4^{3-}(aq) \rightarrow Ca_3(PO_4)_2(s)$; (c) $Pb^{2+}(aq) + 2Cl^-(aq) \rightarrow PbCl_2(s)$; (d) $Fe^{3+}(aq) + 3OH^-(aq) \rightarrow Fe(OH)_3(s)$

60. $Fe^{2+}(aq) + S^{2-}(aq) \rightarrow FeS(s)$; $2Cr^{3+}(aq) + 3S^{2-}(aq) \rightarrow Cr_2S_3(s)$; $Ni^{2+}(aq) + S^{2-}(aq) \rightarrow NiS(s)$

62. hydroxide

64. (a) $HClO_4(aq) + RbOH(aq) \rightarrow H_2O(l) + RbClO_4(aq)$; (b) $HNO_3(aq) + KOH(aq) \rightarrow H_2O(l) + KNO_3(aq)$; (c) $H_2SO_4(aq) + 2NaOH(aq) \rightarrow 2H_2O(l) + Na_2SO_4(aq)$; (d) $HBr(aq) + CsOH(aq) \rightarrow H_2O(l) + CsBr(aq)$

66. These anions tend to form insoluble precipitates with many metal ions. The following are illustrative for cobalt (II) chloride, tin (II) chloride, and copper (II) nitrate reacting with sodium salts of the given anions.

a. $CoCl_2(aq) + Na_2S(aq) \rightarrow CoS(s) + 2NaCl(aq)$
$SnCl_2(aq) + Na_2S(aq) \rightarrow SnS(s) + 2NaCl(aq)$
$Cu(NO_3)_2(aq) + Na_2S(aq) \rightarrow CuS(s) + 2NaNO_3(aq)$

b. $CoCl_2(aq) + Na_2CO_3(aq) \rightarrow CoCO_3(s) + 2NaCl(aq)$
$SnCl_2(aq) + Na_2CO_3(aq) \rightarrow SnCO_3(s) + 2NaCl(aq)$
$Cu(NO_3)_2(aq) + Na_2CO_3(aq) \rightarrow CuCO_3(s) + 2NaNO_3(aq)$

c. $CoCl_2(aq) + 2NaOH(aq) \rightarrow Co(OH)_2(s) + 2NaCl(aq)$
$SnCl_2(aq) + 2NaOH(aq) \rightarrow Sn(OH)_2(s) + 2NaCl(aq)$
$Cu(NO_3)_2(aq) + 2NaOH(aq) \rightarrow Cu(OH)_2(s) + 2NaNO_3(aq)$

d. $3CoCl_2(aq) + 2Na_3PO_4(aq) \rightarrow Co_3(PO_4)_2(s) + 6NaCl(aq)$
$3SnCl_2(aq) + 2Na_3PO_4(aq) \rightarrow Sn_3(PO_4)_2(s) + 6NaCl(aq)$
$3Cu(NO_3)_2(aq) + 2Na_3PO_4(aq) \rightarrow Cu_3(PO_4)_2(s) + 6NaNO_3(aq)$

Chapter 8

2. transfer

4. Metal atoms *lose* electrons and form *cations;* nonmetal atoms *gain* electrons and become *anions.*

6. $1-$; one; two

8. $AlBr_3$ is made up of Al^{3+} ions and Br^- ions. Aluminum atoms each lose 3 electrons to become Al^{3+} ions. Bromine atoms each gain 1 electron to become Br^- ions (so each Br_2 molecule gains 2 electrons to become 2 Br^- ions).

10. (a) $2Na(s) + S(s) \rightarrow Na_2S(s)$; (b) $Cu(s) + 2AgNO_3(aq) \rightarrow Cu(NO_3)_2(aq) + 2Ag(s)$; (c) $Mg(s) + 2HCl(aq) \rightarrow MgCl_2(aq) + H_2(g)$; (d) $Pb(s) + 2S(s) \rightarrow PbS_2(s)$; (e) $2Li(s) + 2H_2O(l) \rightarrow 2LiOH(aq) + H_2(g)$.

12. Examples of formation of water: $HCl(aq) + NaOH(aq) \rightarrow H_2O(l) + NaCl(aq)$; $H_2SO_4(aq) + 2KOH(aq) \rightarrow 2H_2O(l) + K_2SO_4(aq)$. Examples of formation of a gaseous product: $Mg(s) + 2HCl(aq) \rightarrow MgCl_2(aq) + H_2(g)$; $2KClO_3(s) \rightarrow 2KCl(s) + 3O_2(g)$.

14. (a) oxidation–reduction; (b) oxidation–reduction; (c) acid–base; (d) acid–base, precipitation; (e) precipitation; (f) precipitation; (g) oxidation–reduction; (h) oxidation–reduction; (i) acid–base

16. oxidation–reduction

18. A decomposition reaction is one in which a given compound is broken down into simpler compounds or constituent elements. The re-

actions $CaCO_3(s) \rightarrow CaO(s) + CO_2(g)$ and $2HgO(s) \rightarrow 2Hg(l) + O_2(g)$ represent decomposition reactions. Such reactions often may be classified in other ways. For example, the reaction of $HgO(s)$ is also an oxidation–reduction reaction.

20. (a) $C_3H_8(l) + 5O_2(g) \rightarrow 3CO_2(g) + 4H_2O(g)$; (b) $2C_4H_{10}(l) + 13O_2(g) \rightarrow 8CO_2(g) + 10H_2O(g)$; (c) $C_5H_{12}(l) + 8O_2(g) \rightarrow 5CO_2(g) + 6H_2O(g)$

22. (a) $C_{19}H_{40}(s) + 29O_2(g) \rightarrow 19CO_2(g) + 20H_2O(g)$; (b) $C_6H_{12}O_6(s) + 6O_2(g) \rightarrow 6CO_2(g) + 6H_2O(g)$; (c) $C_{12}H_{22}O_{11}(s) + 12O_2(g) \rightarrow 12CO_2(g) + 11H_2O(g)$

24. (a) $2Co(s) + 3S(s) \rightarrow Co_2S_3(s)$; (b) $2NO(g) + O_2(g) \rightarrow 2NO_2(g)$; (c) $FeO(s) + CO_2(g) \rightarrow FeCO_3(s)$; (d) $2Al(s) + 3F_2(g) \rightarrow 2AlF_3(s)$; (e) $2NH_3(g) + H_2CO_3(aq) \rightarrow (NH_4)_2CO_3(s)$

26. (a) $2NI_3(s) \rightarrow N_2(g) + 3I_2(g)$; (b) $BaCO_3(s) \rightarrow BaO(s) + CO_2(g)$; (c) $C_6H_{12}O_6(s) \rightarrow 6C(s) + 6H_2O(g)$; (d) $Cu(NH_3)_4SO_4(s) \rightarrow CuSO_4(s) + 4NH_3(g)$; (e) $3NaN_3(s) \rightarrow Na_3N(s) + 4N_2(g)$

28. (a) two, $O + 2e^- \rightarrow O^{2-}$; (b) one, $F + e^- \rightarrow F^-$; (c) three, $N + 3e^- \rightarrow N^{3-}$; (d) one, $Cl + e^- \rightarrow Cl^-$; (e) two, $S + 2e^- \rightarrow S^{2-}$; (f) one, $Br + e^- \rightarrow Br^-$; (g) one, $I + e^- \rightarrow I^-$

30. carbon dioxide gas and water vapor

32. (a) $2C_3H_8O(l) + 9O_2(g) \rightarrow 6CO_2(g) + 8H_2O(g)$; oxidation–reduction, combustion; (b) $HCl(aq) + AgC_2H_3O_2(aq) \rightarrow AgCl(s) + HC_2H_3O_2(aq)$, precipitation, double displacement; (c) $3HCl(aq) + Al(OH)_3(s) \rightarrow AlCl_3(aq) + 3H_2O(l)$, acid–base, double displacement; (d) $2H_2O_2(aq) \rightarrow 2H_2O(l) + O_2(g)$, oxidation–reduction, decomposition; (e) $N_2H_4(l) + O_2(g) \rightarrow N_2(g) + 2H_2O(g)$, oxidation–reduction, combustion

34. $2Zn(s) + O_2(g) \rightarrow 2ZnO(s)$; $4Al(s) + 3O_2(g) \rightarrow 2Al_2O_3(s)$; $2Fe(s) + O_2(g) \rightarrow 2FeO(s)$, $4Fe(s) + 3O_2(g) \rightarrow 2Fe_2O_3(s)$; $2Cr(s) + O_2(g) \rightarrow 2CrO(s)$, $4Cr(s) + 3O_2(g) \rightarrow 2Cr_2O_3(s)$; $2Ni(s) + O_2(g) \rightarrow 2NiO(s)$

36. Al, $3+$; Br, $1-$; Ca, $2+$; Cl, $1-$; Cs, $1+$; I, $1-$; K, $1+$; Li, $1+$; Mg, $2+$; Na, $1+$; O, $2-$; Rb, $1+$; S, $2-$; Sr, $2+$

38. K^+, Ca^{2+}

40. (a) $2Na(s) + O_2(g) \rightarrow Na_2O_2(s)$; (b) $Fe(s) + H_2SO_4(aq) \rightarrow FeSO_4(aq) + H_2(g)$; (c) $2Al_2O_3(s) \rightarrow 4Al(s) + 3O_2(g)$; (d) $2Fe(s) + 3Br_2(l) \rightarrow 2FeBr_3(s)$; (e) $Zn(s) + 2HNO_3(aq) \rightarrow Zn(NO_3)_2(aq) + H_2(g)$

42. (a) $C_5H_{12}(l) + 8O_2(g) \rightarrow 5CO_2(g) + 6H_2O(g)$; (b) $C_2H_6O(l) + 3O_2(g) \rightarrow 2CO_2(g) + 3H_2O(g)$; (c) $2C_6H_6(l) + 15O_2(g) \rightarrow 12CO_2(g) + 6H_2O(g)$

44. (a) $4FeO(s) + O_2(g) \rightarrow 2Fe_2O_3(s)$; (b) $2CO(g) + O_2(g) \rightarrow 2CO_2(g)$; (c) $H_2(g) + Cl_2(g) \rightarrow 2HCl(g)$; (d) $16K(s) + S_8(s) \rightarrow 8K_2S(s)$; (e) $6Na(s) + N_2(g) \rightarrow 2Na_3N(s)$

46. For simplicity, the physical states of the substances are omitted. $2Ba + O_2 \rightarrow 2BaO$; $Ba + S \rightarrow BaS$; $Ba + Cl_2 \rightarrow BaCl_2$; $3Ba + N_2 \rightarrow Ba_3N_2$; $Ba + Br_2 \rightarrow BaBr_2$; $4K + O_2 \rightarrow 2K_2O$; $2K + S \rightarrow K_2S$; $2K + Cl_2 \rightarrow 2KCl$; $6K + N_2 \rightarrow 2K_3N$; $2K + Br_2 \rightarrow 2KBr$; $2Mg + O_2 \rightarrow 2MgO$; $Mg + S \rightarrow MgS$; $Mg + Cl_2 \rightarrow MgCl_2$; $3Mg + N_2 \rightarrow Mg_3N_2$; $Mg + Br_2 \rightarrow MgBr_2$; $4Rb + O_2 \rightarrow 2Rb_2O$; $2Rb + S \rightarrow Rb_2S$; $2Rb + Cl_2 \rightarrow 2RbCl$; $6Rb + N_2 \rightarrow 2Rb_3N$; $2Rb + Br_2 \rightarrow 2RbBr$; $2Ca + O_2 \rightarrow 2CaO$; $Ca + S \rightarrow CaS$; $Ca + Cl_2 \rightarrow CaCl_2$; $3Ca + N_2 \rightarrow Ca_3N_2$; $Ca + Br_2 \rightarrow CaBr_2$; $4Li + O_2 \rightarrow 2Li_2O$; $2Li + S \rightarrow Li_2S$; $2Li + Cl_2 \rightarrow 2LiCl$; $6Li + N_2 \rightarrow 2Li_3N$; $2Li + Br_2 \rightarrow 2LiBr$

48. $Fe(s) + H_2SO_4(aq) \rightarrow FeSO_4(aq) + H_2(g)$; $Zn(s) + H_2SO_4(aq) \rightarrow$

$ZnSO_4(aq) + H_2(g)$; $Mg(s) + H_2SO_4(aq) \rightarrow MgSO_4(aq) + H_2(g)$; $Co(s) + H_2SO_4(aq) \rightarrow CoSO_4(aq) + H_2(g)$; $Ni(s) + H_2SO_4(aq) \rightarrow NiSO_4(aq) + H_2(g)$

50. For simplicity, the physical states of the substances are omitted. $16Na + S_8 \rightarrow 8Na_2S$; $8Ba + S_8 \rightarrow 8BaS$; $16Al + 3S_8 \rightarrow 8Al_2S_3$; $8Fe + S_8 \rightarrow 8FeS$; $16K + S_8 \rightarrow 8K_2S$; $8Ca + S_8 \rightarrow 8CaS$; $8Mg + S_8 \rightarrow 8MgS$

Chapter 9

2. 307 corks; 116 stoppers; 2640 g (2.64×10^2 g)

4. the same

6. (a) one; (b) ten; (c) 100; (d) 150; (e) 133

8. 1.97×10^6 amu; 1500. Au atoms

10. Avogadro's number (6.022×10^{23})

12. 12.01 g carbon

14. 42 g nitrogen

16. 2.66×10^{-23} g

18. 0.50 mol O

20. (a) 0.133 mol Au; (b) 1.04 mol Ca; (c) 2.44×10^{-3} mol Ba; (d) 1.33×10^{-5} mol Pd; (e) 5.20×10^{-13} mol Ni; (f) 8.12 mol Fe; (g) 1.00 mol C

22. (a) 112 g Fe; (b) 30.6 g Ni; (c) 0.240 g Pt; (d) 1.50×10^4 g Pb; (e) 0.0248 g Mg; (f) 1.31×10^5 g Al; (g) 1468 g Li; (h) 3.95×10^{-5} g Na

24. (a) 0.740 g Li; (b) 3.82 g Li; (c) 6.20×10^{20} Li atoms; (d) 1.15×10^{-23} g; (e) 0.0720 mol Li; (f) 4.53×10^{23} Li atoms; (g) 7.89 mol Li

26. adding (summing)

28. (a) 82.98 g; (b) 76.15 g; (c) 97.94 g; (d) 46.07 g; (e) 82.09 g; (f) 98.09 g

30. (a) 68.15 g; (b) 162.99 g; (c) 139.3 g; (d) 136.09 g; (e) 174.18 g; (f) 212.27 g

32. (a) 6.14×10^{-4} mol SO_3; (b) 3.11×10^5 mol PbO_2; (c) 0.495 mol $CHCl_3$; (d) 2.45×10^{-8} mol $C_2H_3Cl_3$; (e) 0.167 mol LiOH

34. (a) 2.36×10^{-6} mol $AlCl_3$; (b) 11.3 mol NaOH; (c) 1.6×10^{-8} mol AsI_3; (d) 526 mol $NaHCO_3$; (e) 0.0357 mol K_2HPO_4

36. (a) 612 g AlI_3; (b) 0.149 g C_6H_6; (c) 721 g $C_6H_{12}O_6$; (d) 2.10×10^7 g C_2H_5OH; (e) 373 g $Ca(NO_3)_2$

38. (a) 0.0559 g CO_2; (b) 4.96×10^5 g NCl_3; (c) 0.361 g NH_4NO_3; (d) 324 g H_2O; (e) 1.00×10^4 g $CuSO_4$

40. (a) 2.58×10^{24} molecules NO_2; (b) 5.61×10^{22} molecules NO_2; (c) 1.17×10^{14} molecules HF; (d) 5.87×10^{12} molecules HF; (e) 1.63×10^{23} molecules NH_3

42. (a) 0.0141 mol S; (b) 0.0159 mol S; (c) 0.0258 mol S; (d) 0.0254 mol S

44. less

46. (a) 32.36% Na, 22.57% S, 45.04% O; (b) 36.46% Na, 25.43% S, 38.07% O; (c) 58.91% Na, 41.09% S; (d) 29.08% Na, 40.56% S, 30.36% O; (e) 55.26% K, 14.59% P, 30.15% O; (f) 44.90% K, 0.5787% H, 17.78% P, 36.74% O; (g) 28.73% K, 1.481% H, 22.76% P, 47.03% O; (h) 79.11% K, 20.89% P

48. (a) 81.10% Ca; (b) 24.74% K; (c) 42.62% Sn; (d) 35.93% Al; (e) 92.26% C; (f) 49.39% N; (g) 12.79% Fe; (h) 43.64% P

50. (a) 34.43% Fe; (b) 29.63% O; (c) 92.25% C; (d) 11.92% N; (e) 93.10% Ag; (f) 45.39% Co; (g) 30.45% N; (h) 43.66% Mn

52. (a) 61.2% PO_4^{3-}; (b) 46.08% SO_4^{2-}; (c) 72.1% SO_4^{2-}; (d) 56.3% Cl^-

54. The empirical formula represents the smallest whole number ratio of the elements present in a compound. The molecular formula indicates the actual number of atoms of each element found in a molecule of the substance.

56. a, c

58. BaO

60. $BaSO_4$

62. $N_2H_8CO_3$ [actually $(NH_4)_2CO_3$]

64. Co_2S_3

66. CuO

68. AlF_3

70. Li_3N

72. $Al_2S_3O_{12}$ [actually $Al_2(SO_4)_3$] **74.** $NaClO_3$

76. molar mass

78. C_6H_6

80. N_2O_4

82. empirical formula, C_3H_3O; molecular formula, $C_6H_6O_2$

84. 5.00 g Al, 0.185 mol, 1.12×10^{23} atoms; 0.140 g Fe, 0.00250 mol, 1.51×10^{21} atoms; 2.7×10^2 g Cu, 4.3 mol, 2.6×10^{24} atoms; 0.00250 g Mg, 1.03×10^{-4} mol, 6.19×10^{19} atoms; 0.062 g Na, 2.7×10^{-3} mol, 1.6×10^{21} atoms; 3.95×10^{-18} g U, 1.66×10^{-20} mol, 1.00×10^4 atoms

86. 24.8% X, 17.4% Y, 57.8% Z. If the molecular formula were actually $X_4Y_2Z_6$, the percentage composition would be the same: the *relative* mass of each element present would not change. The molecular formula is always a whole number multiple of the empirical formula.

88. Cu_2O, CuO

90. (a) 4.31×10^{21} Pb, 8.62×10^{21} N, 2.59×10^{22} O atoms; (b) 8.43×10^{23} O atoms; (c) 1.913×10^{21} S atoms; (d) 7.47×10^{16} U, 4.48×10^{17} F atoms

92. (a) 4.141 g C, 52.96% C, 2.076×10^{23} atoms C; (b) 0.0305 g C, 42.9% C, 1.53×10^{21} atoms C; (c) 14.4 g C, 76.6% C, 7.23×10^{23} atoms C

94. 10.3 g Pb

96. 7.86 g Hg

98. 2.554×10^{-22} g

100. (a) 0.9331 g N; (b) 1.388 g N; (c) 0.8537 g N; (d) 1.522 g N

102. MgN_2O_6 [$Mg(NO_3)_2$]   **104.** average

106. 8.61×10^{11} sodium atoms; 6.92×10^{24} amu

108. (a) 2.0×10^2 g K; (b) 0.0612 g Hg; (c) 1.27×10^{-3} g Mn; (d) 325 g P; (e) 2.7×10^6 g Fe; (f) 868 g Li; (g) 0.2290 g F

110. (a) 44.09 g; (b) 399.9 g; (c) 108.0 g; (d) 342.3 g; (e) 96.09 g; (f) 208.2 g

112. (a) 0.311 mol; (b) 0.270 mol; (c) 0.0501 mol; (d) 2.8 mol; (e) 6.2 mol

114. (a) 4.2 g; (b) 3.05×10^5 g; (c) 0.533 g; (d) 1.99×10^3 g; (e) 4.18×10^3 g

116. (a) 1.15×10^{22} molecules; (b) 2.08×10^{24} molecules; (c) 4.95×10^{22} molecules; (d) 2.18×10^{22} molecules; (e) 6.32×10^{20} formula units (substance is ionic)

118. (a) 38.8% Ca, 20.0% P, 41.3% O; (b) 53.9% Cd, 15.4% S, 30.7% O; (c) 27.9% Fe, 24.06% S, 48.0% O; (d) 43.7% Mn, 56.3% Cl; (e) 29.2% N, 8.39% H, 12.5% C, 50.0% O; (f) 27.4% Na, 1.20% H, 14.3% C, 57.1% O; (g) 27.3% C, 72.7% O; (h) 63.5% Ag, 8.25% N, 28.3% O

120. (a) 36.8% Fe; (b) 93.1% Ag; (c) 55.3% Sr; (d) 55.8% C; (e) 37.5% C; (f) 52.9% Al; (g) 36.7% K; (h) 52.5% K

122. $C_3H_7N_2O$ **124.** HgO

126. $BaCl_2$

Chapter 10

2. The coefficients of the balanced chemical equation indicate the *relative numbers of molecules* (or moles) of each reactant that combine, as well as the number of molecules (or moles) of each product formed.

4. Balanced chemical equations tell us in what proportions *on a mole basis* substances combine; since the molar masses of $C(s)$ and $O_2(g)$ are different, 1 g of O_2 could not represent the same number of moles as 1 g of C.

6. (a) $3MnO_2(s) + 4Al(s) \rightarrow 3Mn(s) + 2Al_2O_3(s)$. Three formula units of manganese(IV) oxide react with four aluminum atoms, producing three manganese atoms and two formula units of aluminum oxide. Three moles of solid manganese(IV) oxide react with four moles of solid aluminum, to produce three moles of solid manganese and two moles of solid aluminum oxide. (b) $B_2O_3(s) + 3CaF_2(s) \rightarrow 2BF_3(g) + 3CaO(s)$. One diboron trioxide molecule reacts with three formula units of calcium fluoride, producing two molecules of boron trifluoride and three formula units of calcium oxide. One mole of solid diboron trioxide reacts with three moles of solid calcium fluoride, to give two moles of gaseous boron trifluoride and three moles of solid calcium oxide. (c) $3NO_2(g) + H_2O(l) \rightarrow 2HNO_3(aq) + NO(g)$. Three molecules of nitrogen dioxide react with one molecule of water, to produce two molecules of nitric acid and one molecule of nitrogen monoxide. Three moles of gaseous nitrogen dioxide react with one mole of liquid water, to produce two moles of aqueous nitric acid and one mole of nitrogen monoxide gas. (d) $C_6H_6(g) + 3H_2(g) \rightarrow C_6H_{12}(g)$. One molecule of C_6H_6 (*benzene*) reacts with three molecules of hydrogen, producing just one molecule of C_6H_{12} (*cyclohexane*). One mole of gaseous benzene reacts with three moles of hydrogen gas, giving one mole of gaseous cyclohexane.

8. false; the amounts of reactants must be on a *mole* basis

10. $CH_3CH_2OH(l) + 3O_2(g) \rightarrow 2CO_2(g) + 3H_2O(g)$; 2 mol CO_2/1 mol CH_3CH_2OH; 3 mol H_2O/1 mol CH_3CH_2OH

12. (a) 0.25 mol Pb; 0.083 mol Al_2O_3; (b) 0.25 mol C_2H_6; (c) 0.13 mol Na_2O_2; 0.13 mol Ba; (d) 0.25 mol CO; 0.50 mol H_2O

14. (a) 0.50 mol NH_4Cl (27 g); (b) 0.13 mol CS_2 (9.5 g); 0.25 mol H_2S (8.5 g); (c) 0.50 mol H_3PO_3 (41 g); 1.5 mol HCl (55 g); (d) 0.50 mol $NaHCO_3$ (42 g)

16. (a) 0.469 mol O_2; (b) 0.938 mol Se; (c) 0.625 mol CH_3CHO; (d) 1.25 mol Fe

18. Stoichiometry is the process of using a chemical equation to calculate the relative masses of reactants and products involved in a reaction.

20. (a) 1.86×10^{-4} mol Ag; (b) 6.63×10^{-4} mol $(NH_4)_2S$; (c) 2.59×10^{-7} mol U; (d) 81.6 mol SO_2; (e) 1.12 mol $Fe(NO_3)_3$; (f) 8.36×10^{-5} mol $FeSO_4$; (g) 289 mol LiOH

22. (a) 0.185 g $(C_2H_5)_2O$; (b) 482 g UF_6; (c) 2.92×10^{-3} g SO_3; (d) 7.27×10^3 g K_2CO_3; (e) 8.24×10^5 g NaOH; (f) 11.4 g $CuSO_4$; (g) 495 g $C_6H_4Cl_2$

24. (a) 1.03 mol $CuCl_2$; (b) 0.0736 mol $NiCl_2$; (c) 0.240 mol NaOH; (d) 0.250 mol HCl

26. (a) 7.63 mg $FeCO_3$; 11.5 mg K_2SO_4; (b) 30.5 mg $CrCl_3$; 17.1 mg Sn; (c) 21.6 mg Fe_2S_3; (d) 20.2 mg $AgNO_3$; 1.43 mg H_2O; 1.19 mg NO

28. 7.94 g O_2

30. 1.69 g I_2

32. 32.4 g Zn; 8.92 g Al; 12.1 g Mg

34. 9.33×10^{-3} g Cl_2

36. 1.6×10^{-2} g S

38. 2.75 g CO_2

40. 2.07 g MgO

42. To determine the limiting reactant, first calculate the number of moles of each reactant present. Then determine how these numbers of moles correspond to the stoichiometric ratio indicated by the balanced chemical equation for the reaction.

44. A reactant is present *in excess* if there is more of it present than is needed to combine with the limiting reactant for the process. An excess of any reactant does not affect the theoretical yield for a process: the theoretical yield is determined by the limiting reactant.

46. (a) HCl is limiting reactant; 18.3 g $AlCl_3$; 0.415 g H_2; (b) NaOH is limiting reactant; 19.9 g Na_2CO_3; 3.38 g H_2O; (c) $Pb(NO_3)_2$ is limiting reactant; 12.6 g $PbCl_2$; 5.71 g HNO_3; (d) I_2 is limiting reactant; 19.6 g KI

48. (a) Na is limiting reactant; 84.9 g $NaNH_2$; (b) $BaCl_2$ is limiting reactant; 56.0 g $BaSO_4$; (c) NaOH is limiting reactant; 78.8 g Na_2SO_3; (d) H_2SO_4 is limiting reactant; 58.1 g $Al_2(SO_4)_3$

50. (a) CO is limiting reactant; 11.4 mg CH_3OH; (b) I_2 is limiting reactant; 10.7 mg AlI_3; (c) HBr is limiting reactant; 12.4 mg $CaBr_2$; 2.23 mg H_2O; (d) H_3PO_4 is limiting reactant; 15.0 mg $CrPO_4$; 0.309 mg H_2

52. 136 g urea

54. 14.5 g $FeCl_3$ produced; 0.5 g Cl_2 remains. Fe is limiting.

56. 0.626 g CuI; 0.690 g KI_3; 0.573 g K_2SO_4

58. 0.67 kg SiC

60. If the reaction occurs in a solvent, the product may have a substantial solubility in the solvent; the reaction may come to equilibrium before the full yield of product is achieved (see Chapter 16); loss of product may occur through operator error.

62. 94.60% yield

64. $2LiOH(s) + CO_2(g) \rightarrow Li_2CO_3(s) + H_2O(g)$. 142 g of CO_2 can be ultimately absorbed; 102 g is 71.8% of the cannister's capacity.

66. 82.6%

68. 28.6 g $NaHCO_3$

70. $C_6H_{12}O_6 + 6O_2 \rightarrow 6CO_2 + 6H_2O$; 1.47 g CO_2

72. 14 mg K_2CrO_4

74. (a) $UO_2(s) + 4HF(aq) \rightarrow UF_4(aq) + 2H_2O(l)$. One formula unit of uranium(IV) oxide combines with four molecules of hydrofluoric acid, producing one uranium(IV) fluoride molecule and two water molecules. One mole of uranium(IV) oxide combines with four moles of hydrofluoric acid to produce one mole of uranium(IV) fluoride and two moles of water. (b) $2NaC_2H_3O_2(aq) + H_2SO_4(aq) \rightarrow Na_2SO_4(aq) + 2HC_2H_3O_2(aq)$. Two molecules (formula units) of sodium acetate react exactly with one molecule of sulfuric acid, producing one molecule (formula unit) of sodium acetate and two molecules of acetic acid. Two moles of sodium acetate combine with one mole of sulfuric acid, producing one mole of sodium sulfate and two moles of acetic acid. (c) $Mg(s) + 2HCl(aq) \rightarrow MgCl_2(aq) + H_2(g)$. One magnesium atom reacts with two hydrochloric acid molecules (formula units) to produce one molecule (formula unit) of magnesium chloride and one molecule of hydrogen gas. One mole of magnesium combines with two moles of hydrochloric acid, producing one mole of magnesium chloride and one mole of gaseous hydrogen. (d) $B_2O_3(s) + 3H_2O(l) \rightarrow 2B(OH)_3(s)$. One molecule (formula unit) of diboron trioxide reacts exactly with three molecules of water, producing two molecules of boron trihydroxide (boric acid). One mole of diboron trioxide combines with three moles of water to produce two moles of boron trihydroxide (boric acid).

76. for O_2, 5 mol O_2/1 mol C_3H_8; for CO_2, 3 mol CO_2/1 mol C_3H_8; for H_2O, 4 mol H_2O/1 mol C_3H_8

78. (a) 0.0587 mol NH_4Cl; (b) 0.0178 mol $CaCO_3$; (c) 0.0217 mol Na_2O; (d) 0.0323 mol PCl_3

80. (a) 3.2×10^2 g HNO_3; (b) 0.0612 g Hg; (c) 4.49×10^{-3} g K_2CrO_4; (d) 1.40×10^3 g $AlCl_3$; (e) 7.2×10^6 g SF_6; (f) 2.13×10^3 g NH_3; (g) 0.9397 g Na_2O_2

82. 1.9×10^2 kg SO_2 **84.** 56.3 g Br_2

86. 0.0771 g H_2

88. (a) Br_2 is limiting reactant, 6.4 g NaBr; (b) $CuSO_4$ is limiting reactant, 5.1 g $ZnSO_4$, 2.0 g Cu; (c) NH_4Cl is limiting reactant, 1.6 g NH_3, 1.7 g H_2O, 5.5 g NaCl; (d) Fe_2O_3 is limiting reactant, 3.5 g Fe, 4.1 g CO_2

90. 0.624 mol N_2, 17.5 g N_2; 1.25 mol H_2O, 22.5 g H_2O

92. 5 g

Chapter 11

2. The different forms of electromagnetic radiation all exhibit the same wavelike behavior and are propagated through space at the same speed (the "speed of light"). The types of electromagnetic radiation differ in their frequency (and wavelength) and in the resulting amount of energy carried per photon.

4. The *frequency* (ν) of electromagnetic radiation represents *how many waves* pass a given point per second along the propagation direction of the wave; it contrasts with the *speed* at which a given wave moves through space.

6. The *wave–particle* nature of light refers to the fact that a beam of electromagnetic energy can be considered not only as a continuous wave but also as a stream of discrete packets of energy moving through space.

8. An atom in an excited state returns to its lowest energy state (ground state) by emitting a photon of energy.

10. larger

12. When excited hydrogen atoms emit their excess energy, the photons of radiation emitted always have exactly the same wavelength and energy. This means that the hydrogen atom possesses only certain allowed energy states, and that the photons emitted correspond to the electron changing from one of these allowed energy states to another allowed energy state. The energy of the photon emitted corresponds to the energy difference between the allowed states. If the hydrogen atom did *not* possess discrete energy levels, then the photons emitted would have random wavelengths and energies.

14. lower energy state (often the ground [lowest energy] state)

16. The ground state of an atom is its lowest possible energy state.

18. According to Bohr, electrons move in discrete, fixed circular orbits around the nucleus. If photons of the applied energy equal the difference in energy between the two orbits, the atom absorbs a photon and the electron moves to a larger orbit.

20. Bohr's theory explained the experimentally observed line spectrum of hydrogen exactly. The theory was discarded because the calculated properties did not correspond closely to experimental measurements for atoms other than hydrogen.

22. An orbit refers to a definite, exact circular pathway around the nucleus, in which Bohr postulated that an electron would be found. An orbital represents a region of space in which there is a high probability of finding the electron.

24. Any experiment to measure the exact location of an electron (such as shooting a beam of light at it) would cause the electron to move. Any measurement would involve the application or removal of energy, which would disturb the electron.

26. Pictures that represent orbitals should be interpreted as probability maps. They do *not* mean that the electron moves only on the surface of, or within, the region in the picture. Since the mathematical probability of finding the electron never becomes zero on moving outward from the nucleus, scientists have decided that pictures of orbitals should represent a 90% probability that the electron will be found inside the region depicted in the drawing.

28. The $2p$ orbitals have two lobes and are sometimes described as having a "dumbbell" shape. The individual $2p$ orbitals ($2p_x$, $2p_y$, $2p_z$) are alike in shape and energy; they differ only in the direction in which the lobes of the orbital are oriented.

30. increases

32. four: $4s$, $4p$, $4d$, and $4f$

34. The Pauli exclusion principle states that an orbital can hold a maximum of two electrons, and those two electrons must have opposite spin.

36. increases

38. paired (opposite spin)

40. a and b are incorrect

42. For a hydrogen atom in its ground state, the electron is in the $1s$ orbital. The $1s$ orbital has the lowest energy of all hydrogen orbitals.

44. The elements in a given vertical column of the periodic table have the same valence electron configuration.

46. (a) $1s^22s^22p^63s^23p^64s^23d^{10}4p^65s^2$
(b) $1s^22s^22p^63s^23p^64s^23d^{10}$
(c) $1s^2$
(d) $1s^22s^22p^63s^23p^64s^23d^{10}4p^5$

48. (a) $1s^22s^22p^2$
(b) $1s^22s^22p^63s^23p^3$
(c) $1s^22s^22p^63s^23p^4$
(d) $1s^22s^22p^1$

50. (a) $(\uparrow\downarrow)$ $(\uparrow\downarrow)$ $(\uparrow\downarrow)$ $(\uparrow\downarrow)$ $(\uparrow\downarrow)$ $(\uparrow\downarrow)$ $(\uparrow)$ $(\,)$ $(\,)$
　　　 $1s$　　 $2s$　　　 $2p$　　　 $3s$　　 $3p$
(b) $(\uparrow\downarrow)$ $(\uparrow\downarrow)$ $(\uparrow\downarrow)(\uparrow\downarrow)(\uparrow\downarrow)$ $(\uparrow\downarrow)$ $(\uparrow)(\uparrow)(\uparrow)$
　　　 $1s$　　 $2s$　　　 $2p$　　　 $3s$　　 $3p$
(c) $(\uparrow\downarrow)$ $(\uparrow\downarrow)$ $(\uparrow\downarrow)(\uparrow\downarrow)(\uparrow\downarrow)$ $(\uparrow\downarrow)$ $(\uparrow\downarrow)(\uparrow\downarrow)(\uparrow\downarrow)$ $(\uparrow\downarrow)$ $(\uparrow\downarrow)(\uparrow\downarrow)(\uparrow\downarrow)(\uparrow\downarrow)(\uparrow\downarrow)$
　　　 $1s$　 $2s$　　　 $2p$　　　 $3s$　　 $3p$　　 $4s$　　　 $3d$
　　　 $(\uparrow\downarrow)$ $(\uparrow\downarrow)(\uparrow)$
　　　　　 $4p$
(d) $(\uparrow\downarrow)$ $(\uparrow\downarrow)$ $(\uparrow\downarrow)(\uparrow\downarrow)(\uparrow\downarrow)$ $(\uparrow\downarrow)$ $(\uparrow\downarrow)(\uparrow\downarrow)(\uparrow\downarrow)$
　　　 $1s$　　 $2s$　　　 $2p$　　　 $3s$　　 $3p$

52. (a) two; (b) four; (c) seven; (d) one

54. The properties of Rb and Sr suggest that they are members of Groups 1 and 2, respectively, and so must be filling the $5s$ orbital. The $5s$ orbital is lower in energy than (and fills before) the $4d$ orbitals.

56. (a) $[Ar]4s^2$; (b) $[Rn]7s^1$; (c) $[Kr]5s^24d^1$; (d) $[Xe]6s^24f^{1}5d^1$

58. (a) $[Ne]3s^23p^2$; (b) $[Ar]4s^23d^{10}4p^1$; (c) $[Ar]4s^23d^3$; (d) $[Ar]4s^23d^1$

60. (a) one; (b) two; (c) zero; (d) 10

62. (a) $5d$; (b) $4f$; (c) $5d$; (d) $3d$

64. (a) $[Rn]7s^25f^36d^1$; (b) $[Ar]4s^23d^5$; (c) $[Xe]6s^24f^{14}5d^{10}$; (d) $[Rn]7s^1$

66. The metallic elements lose electrons and form positive ions (cations); the nonmetallic elements gain electrons and form negative ions (anions).

68. All exist as diatomic molecules (F_2, Cl_2, Br_2, I_2); are nonmetals; have relatively high electronegativities; and form $1-$ ions in reacting with metallic elements.

70. Elements at the left of a period (horizontal row) lose electrons most readily; at the left of a period (given principal energy level) the nuclear charge is the smallest and the electrons are least tightly held.

72. The elements of a given period (horizontal row) have valence electrons in the same subshells, but nuclear charge increases across a period going from left to right. Atoms at the left side have smaller nuclear charges and bind their valence electrons less tightly.

74. The nuclear charge increases from left to right within a period, pulling progressively more tightly on the valence electrons.

76. (a) Cs; (b) Li; (c) I; (d) Rb

78. (a) Na; (b) S; (c) N; (d) F

80. speed of light   **82.** photons

84. quantized   **86.** orbital

88. transition metal

90. spins (different m_s quantum numbers)

92. (a) $1s^22s^22p^63s^23p^64s^1$; $[Ar]4s^1$;

(↑↓) (↑↓) (↑↓)(↑↓)(↑↓) (↑↓) (↑↓)(↑↓)(↑↓) (↑)
 1s   2s   2p   3s   3p   4s

(b) $1s^22s^22p^63s^23p^64s^23d^2$; $[Ar]4s^23d^2$;

(↑↓) (↑↓) (↑↓)(↑↓)(↑↓) (↑↓) (↑↓)(↑↓)(↑↓) (↑↓)
 1s   2s   2p   3s   3p   4s

(↑)(↑)( )( )( )
        3d

(c) $1s^22s^22p^63s^23p^2$; $[Ne]3s^23p^2$;

(↑↓) (↑↓) (↑↓)(↑↓)(↑↓) (↑↓) (↑)(↑)( )
 1s   2s   2p   3s   3p

(d) $1s^22s^22p^63s^23p^64s^23d^6$; $[Ar]4s^23d^6$;

(↑↓) (↑↓) (↑↓)(↑↓)(↑↓) (↑↓) (↑↓)(↑↓)(↑↓) (↑↓)
 1s   2s   2p   3s   3p   4s

(↑↓)(↑)(↑)(↑)(↑)
        3d

(e) $1s^22s^22p^63s^23p^64s^23d^{10}$; $[Ar]4s^23d^{10}$;

(↑↓) (↑↓) (↑↓)(↑↓)(↑↓) (↑↓) (↑↓)(↑↓)(↑↓) (↑↓)
 1s   2s   2p   3s   3p   4s

(↑↓) (↑↓) (↑↓)(↑↓)(↑↓)
        3d

94. (a) ns^2; (b) ns^2np^5; (c) ns^2np^4; (d) ns^1; (e) ns^2np^4

96. (a) 2.7×10^{-12} m; (b) 4.4×10^{-34} m; (c) 2×10^{-35} m. The wavelengths for the ball and the person are infinitesimally small; the wavelength for the electron is nearly the same order of magnitude as the diameter of an atom.

98. Light is emitted from the hydrogen atom only at certain fixed wavelengths. If the energy levels of hydrogen were continuous, a hydrogen atom would emit energy at all possible wavelengths.

100. The third principal energy level of hydrogen is divided into three sublevels (3s, 3p, and 3d); there is a single 3s orbital, a set of three 3p orbitals, and a set of five 3d orbitals. See Figures 11.21–11.24 for the shapes of these orbitals.

102. a, c

104. (a) $1s^22s^22p^63s^23p^5$; (b) $1s^22s^22p^4$; (c) $1s^22s^22p^63s^23p^1$; (d) $1s^22s^1$

106. (a) five (2s, 2p); (b) seven (3s, 3p); (c) one (3s); (d) three (3s, 3p)

108. (a) $[Kr]5s^24d^2$; (b) $[Kr]5s^24d^{10}5p^5$; (c) $[Ar]4s^23d^{10}4p^2$; (d) $[Xe]6s^1$

110. The position of the element (in terms of both the vertical column and the horizontal row) indicates which set of orbitals is being filled last (Fig. 11.27). (a) 3d; (b) 4d; (c) 5f; (d) 4p

112. metals, low; nonmetals, high

114. (a) Ba; (b) Mg; (c) Be

Chapter 12

2. The strength of a chemical bond is characterized by the *bond energy*—the amount of energy required to *break* the bond.

4. ionic

6. The HF molecule contains atoms of two *different elements*. In bonding with each other, these atoms share a pair of valence electrons, but they do *not* share them equally. The bonding in HF is *polar covalent*: although valence electron pairs are shared between atoms, the electron pair is attracted more strongly by one of the atoms than the other. Nonetheless, an HF molecule is more stable in energy than are separated H and F atoms.

8. polar

10. electronegativity

12. In each case, the element *higher up* within a group or to the right in a period of the periodic table has the higher electronegativity. (a) K < Ca < Sc; (b) At < Br < F; (c) C < N < O

14. (a) covalent; (b) polar covalent; (c) polar covalent; (d) ionic

16. c and d

18. The difference in electronegativities is given in parentheses.
(a) H—O (1.4), H—N (0.9), H—O bond is more polar; (b) H—N (0.9), H—F (1.9), H—F bond is more polar; (c) H—O (1.4), H—F (1.9), H—F bond is more polar; (d) H—O (1.4), H—Cl (0.9), H—O bond is more polar.

20. (a) Na—O; (b) K—S; (c) K—Cl; (d) Na—Cl

22. The presence of strong bond dipoles and a large overall dipole moment make water a very polar substance. Properties of water that are dependent on its dipole moment involve its freezing point, melting point, vapor pressure, and its ability to dissolve many substances.

24. (a) H; (b) Cl; (c) I

26. The arrow points toward the more electronegative atom.
(a) $\delta+$ Cl → F $\delta-$; (b) $\delta+$ I → Br $\delta-$; (c) $\delta+$ Br → Cl $\delta-$; (d) $\delta+$ Br → F $\delta-$

28. The arrow points toward the more electronegative atom. (a) $\delta+$ P → S $\delta-$; (b) $\delta+$ S → O $\delta-$; (c) $\delta+$ S → N $\delta-$; (d) $\delta+$ S → Cl $\delta-$

30. previous

32. Atoms in covalent molecules gain a configuration like that of a noble gas by sharing one or more pairs of electrons between atoms: such shared pairs of electrons "belong" to each of the bonding atoms at the same time. In ionic bonding, one atom completely donates one or more electrons to another atom, and then the resulting ions behave independently of one another (they are not "attached" to one another, although they are mutually attracted).

34. (a) Rb: $1s^22s^22p^63s^23p^64s^23d^{10}4p^65s^1$; Rb$^+$: $1s^22s^22p^63s^23p^64s^23d^{10}4p^6$; Kr has the same configuration as Rb$^+$.
(b) O: $1s^22s^22p^4$; O^{2-}: $1s^22s^22p^6$; Ne has the same configuration as O^{2-}. (c) Sr: $1s^22s^22p^63s^23p^64s^23d^{10}4p^65s^2$; Sr^{2+}: $1s^22s^22p^63s^23p^64s^23d^{10}4p^6$; Kr has the same configuration as Sr^{2+}.

(d) Cs: $1s^2 2s^2 2p^6 3s^2 3p^6 4s^2 3d^{10} 4p^6 5s^2 4d^{10} 5p^6 6s^1$; Cs$^+$: $1s^2 2s^2 2p^6 3s^2 3p^6 4s^2 3d^{10} 4p^6 5s^2 4d^{10} 5p^6$; Xe has the same configuration as Cs$^+$. (e) Ba: $1s^2 2s^2 2p^6 3s^2 3p^6 4s^2 3d^{10} 4p^6 5s^2 4d^{10} 5p^6 6s^2$; Ba^{2+}: $1s^2 2s^2 2p^6 3s^2 3p^6 4s^2 3d^{10} 4p^6 5s^2 4d^{10} 5p^6$; Xe has the same configuration as Ba^{2+}.

36. (a) Ca^{2+} ; (b) N^{3-}; (c) Br$^-$; (d) Sc^{3+}

38. (a) CaO; (b) SrF$_2$; (c) Al$_2$S$_3$; (d) Rb$_3$N; (e) Na$_2$Te

40. (a) Al^{3+}, [Ne]; S^{2-}, [Ar]; (b) Mg^{2+}, [Ne]; N^{3-}, [Ne]; (c) Rb$^+$, [Kr]; O^{2-}, [Ne]; (d) Cs$^+$, [Xe]; I$^-$, [Xe]

42. An ionic solid such as NaCl consists of an array of alternating positively and negatively charged ions: that is, each positive ion has as its nearest neighbors a group of negative ions, and each negative ion has a group of positive ions surrounding it. In most ionic solids, the ions are packed as tightly as possible.

44. In forming an anion, an atom gains additional electrons in its outermost (valence) shell. Having additional electrons in the valence shell increases the repulsive forces between electrons, and the outermost shell becomes larger to accommodate this.

46. (a) F$^-$ is larger than Li$^+$. The F$^-$ ion has a filled $n = 2$ shell. A lithium atom has *lost* the electron from its $n = 2$ shell, leaving the $n = 1$ shell as its outermost. (b) Cl$^-$ is larger than Na$^+$, since its valence electrons are in the $n = 3$ shell (Na$^+$ has lost its 3s electron). (c) O^{2-} is larger than Ca^{2+} even though Ca is a member of the fourth period: the increase in size of a negative ion relative to the atom from which it is derived is a large effect. (d) I$^-$ is larger. Both Cs$^+$ and I$^-$ have the same electron configuration (isoelectronic with Xe) and have their valence electrons in the same shell. However, Cs$^+$ has two more positive charges in its nucleus than does I$^-$; this charge causes the $n = 5$ shell of Cs$^+$ to be smaller than that of I$^-$ (the electrons are pulled in closer to the nucleus by the positive charge).

48. (a) Cs$^+$; (b) Na$^+$; (c) Cs$^+$; (d) O^{2-}

50. When atoms form covalent bonds, they try to attain a valence electron configuration similar to that of the following noble gas element. When the elements in the first few horizontal rows of the periodic table form covalent bonds, they attempt to achieve the configurations of the noble gases helium (2 valence electrons, duet rule) and neon and argon (8 valence electrons, octet rule).

52. These elements attain a total of eight valence electrons, giving the valence electron configurations of the noble gases Ne and Ar.

54. Two atoms in a molecule are connected by a triple bond if the atoms share three pairs of electrons (6 electrons) to complete their outermost shells. A simple molecule containing a triple bond is acetylene, C$_2$H$_2$ (H : C : : : C : H).

56. (a) Rb·   (b) : Cl̈ ·   (c) : K̈r :

(d) Ba :   (e) · P̈ ·   (f) : Ät ·

58. (a) 32; (b) 17; (c) 30

60. (a) NH$_3$

62. (b) CI$_4$

(c) NCl$_3$

(d) SiBr$_4$

62. (a) H$_2$S   H—S̈—H

(b) SiF$_4$

(c) C$_2$H$_4$

(d) C$_3$H$_8$

64. (a) NO$_2$

(b) H$_2$SO$_4$

(c) N$_2$O$_4$

66. (a) ClO$_3^-$

(b) O$_2^{2-}$

(c) $C_2H_3O_2^-$

$$\left(\begin{array}{c} H \quad :O: \\ H-C-C-O: \\ H \end{array} \right)^- \leftrightarrow$$

$$\left(H-\overset{H}{\underset{H}{C}}-C=\overset{:O:}{O} \right)^-$$

68. (a) CN^- $(:C\equiv N:)^-$

(b) HSO_4^-

$$\left(H-\overset{..}{\underset{..}{O}}-\overset{:O:}{\underset{:O:}{S}}-\overset{..}{O}: \right)^-$$

(c) N_3^- $\left(\overset{..}{N}=N=\overset{..}{N} \right)^-$

70. The geometric structure of NH_3 is that of a trigonal pyramid. The nitrogen atom of NH_3 is surrounded by four electron pairs (three are bonding, one is a lone pair). The $H-N-H$ bond angle is somewhat less than $109.5°$ (because of the presence of the lone pair).

72. The geometric structure of CH_4 is that of a tetrahedron. The carbon atom of CH_4 is surrounded by four bonding electron pairs. The $H-C-H$ bond angle is the characteristic angle of the tetrahedron, $109.5°$.

74. The general molecular structure of a molecule is determined by how many electron pairs surround the central atom in the molecule, and by which of those pairs are used for bonding to the other atoms of the molecule.

76. Geometry shows that only two points in space are needed to indicate a straight line. A diatomic molecule represents two points in space.

78. In NF_3, the nitrogen atom has *four* pairs of valence electrons; in BF_3, only *three* pairs of valence electrons surround the boron atom. The nonbonding pair on nitrogen in NF_3 pushes the three F atoms out of the plane of the N atom.

80. Each of the indicated atoms is surrounded by four pairs of electrons arranged tetrahedrally. Although the electron pairs are tetrahedral, the overall geometric shape of the molecules may *not* be tetrahedral.

82. (a) tetrahedral; (b) trigonal pyramid; (c) nonlinear (bent)

84. (a) trigonal pyramid; (b) basically tetrahedral around P (distorted somewhat by the H atom); (c) trigonal pyramid

86. (a) approximately tetrahedral (a little less than $109.5°$); (b) approximately tetrahedral (a little less than $109.5°$); (c) tetrahedral ($109.5°$); (d) trigonal planar ($120°$) because of the double bond

88. The acetylene molecule would be linear, with bond angles of $180°$, because of the presence of the triple bond between the carbon atoms.

90. double

92. (a) S—F; (b) P—O; (c) C—H

94. break

96. (a) Be; (b) N; (c) F

98. a, c

100. (a) hydrogen; (b) iodine; (c) nitrogen

102. (a) Al: $1s^22s^22p^63s^23p^1$; Al^{3+}: $1s^22s^22p^6$; Ne has the same configuration as Al^{3+}. (b) Br: $1s^22s^22p^63s^23p^64s^23d^{10}4p^5$; Br^-: $1s^22s^22p^63s^23p^64s^23d^{10}4p^6$; Kr has the same configuration as Br^-. (c) Ca: $1s^22s^22p^63s^23p^64s^2$; Ca^{2+}: $1s^22s^22p^63s^23p^6$; Ar has the same configuration as Ca^{2+}. (d) Li: $1s^22s^1$; Li^+: $1s^2$; He has the same configuration as Li^+. (e) F: $1s^22s^22p^5$; F^-: $1s^22s^22p^6$; Ne has the same configuration as F^-.

104. (a) Na_2Se; (b) RbF; (c) K_2Te; (d) BaSe; (e) KAt; (f) FrCl

106. (a) Na^+; (b) Al^{3+}; (c) F^-; (d) Na^+

108. (a) 8; (b) 48; (c) 34; (d) 26

110. (a) N_2H_4

$$H-\overset{H}{\underset{H}{N}}-\overset{H}{\underset{H}{N}}-H$$

(b) C_2H_6

$$H-\overset{H}{\underset{H}{C}}-\overset{H}{\underset{H}{C}}-H$$

(c) NCl_3

$$:\overset{..}{C}l-\overset{..}{N}-\overset{..}{C}l:$$
$$:\overset{..}{C}l:$$

(d) $SiCl_4$

$$:\overset{..}{C}l:$$
$$:\overset{..}{C}l-Si-\overset{..}{C}l:$$
$$:\overset{..}{C}l:$$

112. (a) NO_3^-

$$\left[\overset{..}{O}=N-\overset{..}{O}: \atop :O: \right]^- \leftrightarrow \left[:\overset{..}{O}-N=\overset{..}{O} \atop :O: \right]^-$$

$$\leftrightarrow \left[:\overset{..}{O}-N-\overset{..}{O}: \atop :O: \right]^-$$

(b) CO_3^{2-}

$$\left[\overset{..}{O}=C-\overset{..}{O}: \atop :O: \right]^{2-} \leftrightarrow \left[:\overset{..}{O}-C=\overset{..}{O} \atop :O: \right]^{2-}$$

$$\leftrightarrow \left[:\overset{..}{O}-C-\overset{..}{O}: \atop :O: \right]^{2-}$$

(c) NH_4^+

$$\left[H-\overset{H}{\underset{H}{N}}-H \right]^+$$

114. (a) four pairs arranged tetrahedrally; (b) four pairs arranged tetrahedrally; (c) three pairs arranged trigonally (planar)

116. (a) trigonal pyramid; (b) nonlinear (V-shaped); (c) tetrahedral

118. (a) nonlinear (V-shaped); (b) trigonal planar; (c) basically trigonal planar around C, distorted somewhat by H; (d) linear

120. Ionic compounds tend to be hard, crystalline substances with relatively high melting and boiling points. Covalently bonded substances tend to be gases, liquids, or relatively soft solids, with much lower melting and boiling points.

Chapter 13

2. Solids are rigid and incompressible and have definite shapes and volumes. Liquids are less rigid than solids; although they have definite volumes, liquids take the shape of their containers. Gases have no fixed volume or shape; they take the volume and shape of their container, and are affected more by changes in their pressure and temperature than are solids or liquids.

4. Atmospheric pressure is measured with a *barometer*. A barometer typically consists of a glass tube several feet long that is sealed at one end. The tube is then filled with mercury and inverted over a reservoir of mercury. The mercury in the tube is supported by the atmospheric pressure on the surface of the mercury in the reservoir. As the atmospheric pressure changes, the mercury moves up or down in the tube depending on whether the atmospheric pressure increases or decreases. For convenience, a millimeter scale is usually mounted behind the glass tube, and the height of the mercury column in the tube is read in millimeters. The atmospheric pressure differs across the earth according to local weather conditions and the height above or below sea level of the reporting station.

6. 760.0 mm Hg

8. (a) 1.088 atm; (b) 0.976 atm; (c) 0.580 atm; (d) 1.21 atm

10. (a) 775 mm Hg; (b) 911 mm Hg; (c) 792 mm Hg; (d) 81.8 mm Hg

12. (a) 2.07×10^3 kPa; (b) 106 kPa; (c) 1.10×10^3 kPa; (d) 87.9 kPa

14. increases

16. $PV = k$; $P_1V_1 = P_2V_2$

18. (a) 588 mL; (b) 2.54 L; (c) 4.26×10^4 mm Hg

20. (a) 3.17×10^3 mL; (b) 5.68×10^4 mL; (c) 4.22×10^3 mL

22. factor $(1.01/0.562) = 1.80$

24. 20.0 atm

26. Absolute zero can be determined using Charles's law, which states that the volume of an ideal gas sample is directly proportional to its temperature. If we measure the volume of a gas sample at several different temperatures and then plot these data, it is possible to extrapolate a straight line mathematically. At the point on the extrapolated line where the volume of the gas sample would be zero, the temperature is absolute zero.

28. $V = bT$; $V_1/T_1 = V_2/T_2$ **30.** 569 mL

32. (a) 546 K = 273 °C; (b) 308 K = 35 °C; (c) 298 mL (3×10^2 mL)

34. (a) 35.4 K = −238 °C; (b) 0 mL (absolute zero; a real gas would condense to a solid or liquid); (c) 40.5 mL

36. The neon's volume would become half the initial value at 149 K (−124 °C). The neon's volume would be doubled at 596 K (323 °C).

38. 113 mL (238 K, −35 °C); 142 mL (299 K, 26 °C); 155 mL (326 K, 53 °C); 127 mL (267 K, −6 °C)

40. $V = an$; $V_1/n_1 = V_2/n_2$ **42.** 44.8 L

44. 10.8 L

46. Real gases behave most ideally at relatively high temperatures and relatively low pressures. We usually assume that a real gas's behavior approaches ideal behavior if the temperature is over 0 °C (273 K) and the pressure is 1 atm or lower.

48. For an ideal gas, $PV = nRT$ is true under any conditions. Consider a particular sample of gas (n remains constant) at a particular fixed pressure (P remains constant). Suppose that at temperature T_1 the volume of the gas sample is V_1. For this set of conditions, the ideal gas equation would be given by $PV_1 = nRT_1$. If the temperature of the gas sample changes to a new temperature, T_2, then the volume of the gas sample changes to a new volume, V_2. For this new set of conditions, the ideal gas equation would be given by $PV_2 = nRT_2$. If we make a *ratio* of these two expressions for the ideal gas equation for this gas sample, and cancel out terms that are constant for this situation (P, n, and R), we get $\dfrac{PV_1}{PV_2} = \dfrac{nRT_1}{nRT_2}$, or $\dfrac{V_1}{V_2} = \dfrac{T_1}{T_2}$, which can be rearranged to the familiar form of Charles's law, $\dfrac{V_1}{T_1} = \dfrac{V_2}{T_2}$.

50. (a) 5.02 L; (b) 3.56 atm = 2.70×10^3 mm Hg; (c) 334 K

52. (a) 0.201 L; (b) 0.338 atm; (c) 2.48×10^{-2} mol

54. 3.89 L

56. 4.43×10^3 g He; 2.23×10^3 g H_2

58. 655 K = 382 °C   **60.** 67.2 atm

62. 85.2 mL   **64.** 246 K = −27 °C

66. As a gas is bubbled through water, the bubbles of gas become saturated with water vapor, thus forming a gaseous mixture. The total pressure for a sample of gas that has been collected by bubbling through water is made up of two components: the pressure of the sample gas and the pressure of water vapor. The partial pressure of the gas equals the total pressure of the sample minus the vapor pressure of water.

68. 7.93 L   **70.** 2.47 atm

72. 751 mm Hg

74. $P_{hydrogen} = 0.990$ atm; 9.55×10^{-3} mol H_2; 0.625 g Zn

76. A theory is successful if it explains known experimental observations. Theories that have been successful in the past may not be successful in the future (for example, as technology evolves, more sophisticated experiments may be possible in the future).

78. collisions   **80.** no

82. If the temperature of a sample of gas is increased, the average kinetic energy of the particles of gas increases. This means that the speeds of the particles increase. If the particles have a higher speed, they hit the walls of the container more frequently and with greater force, thereby increasing the pressure.

84. STP = 0 °C, 1 atm pressure. These conditions were chosen because they are easy to attain and reproduce *experimentally*. The barometric pressure within a laboratory will usually be near 1 atm, and 0 °C can be attained with a simple ice bath.

86. 3.00 L   **88.** 0.432 L

90. 1.17 L   **92.** 5.03 L (dry volume)

94. 16.6 L   **96.** 184 mL

98. 40.5 L; $P_{He} = 0.864$ atm; $P_{Ne} = 0.136$ atm

100. 24.5 L Cl_2 **102.** 0.709 L Cl_2

104. twice

106. (a) $PV = k$; $P_1V_1 = P_2V_2$; (b) $V = bT$; $V_1/T_1 = V_2/T_2$; (c) $V = an$; $V_1/n_1 = V_2/n_2$; (d) $PV = nRT$; (e) $P_1V_1/T_1 = P_2V_2/T_2$

108. 125 balloons   **110.** 12.5 mL

112. 0.0999 mol CO_2; 3.32 L wet; 2.68 L dry

114. 18.1 L O_2

116. (a) 0.875 atm; (b) 1.22 atm; (c) 25.07 atm; (d) 1.06 atm

118. (a) 8.60×10^4 Pa; (b) 2.21×10^5 Pa; (c) 8.88×10^4 Pa; (d) 4.3×10^3 Pa

120. (a) 128 mL; (b) 1.3×10^{-2} L; (c) 9.8 L
122. 8.34×10^5 mm Hg (1.10×10^3 atm)
124. (a) 56.9 mL; (b) 448 K = 175 °C; (c) zero (absolute zero; a real gas would condense to a solid or liquid)
126. 15 L   **128.** 2.59 g
130. (a) 61.8 K; (b) 0.993 atm; (c) 1.67×10^4 L
132. 487 mol gas needed; 7.82 kg CH_4; 13.7 kg N_2; 21.5 kg CO_2
134. 0.42 atm   **136.** 2.51×10^3 K
138. 17 L   **140.** 3.43 L N_2; 10.3 L H_2
142. 5.8 L O_2; 3.9 L SO_2 **144.** 7.8×10^2 L
146. 32 L; P_{He} = 0.86 atm; P_{Ar} = 0.017 atm; P_{Ne} = 0.12 atm
148. 22.5 L O_2

Chapter 14

2. Water, as perspiration, helps cool the human body; on a hot day, you might take an extra shower to cool off. Large bodies of water (e.g., oceans) have a cooling effect on nearby land masses. Water is used as a coolant in *many* commercial situations: for example, some nuclear power plants use water to cool the reactor core; many office buildings are air-conditioned by circulating cold water combined with fan systems.

4. The expansion of water when it freezes often results in broken water pipes during cold weather. This expansion also makes ice float on liquid water. Aquatic life, and probably all life as we know it, would not be possible if ice sank in water.

6. Sloped portions of a heating/cooling curve represent *changes in temperature* as heat is applied or removed; flat portions of such curves represent equilibrium transitions between states.

8. As a sample of liquid water is heated, the motion of the molecules increases as the temperature rises. As the liquid reaches its boiling point, bubbles of vapor begin to form in the liquid; they rise to the surface of the liquid and burst. While the liquid remains at its boiling point, the additional heat energy being supplied is used to overcome attractive forces among the molecules. As heat energy continues to be applied, increasing numbers of molecules will be moving in the right direction and with sufficient energy to escape from the liquid's surface.

10. The additional energy is used to overcome attractive forces among the molecules in the liquid.

12. In a vapor, the molecules are so far apart that intermolecular forces become negligible; in a liquid, the intermolecular forces are still quite strong. It takes more heat to vaporize a liquid than to melt the same amount of solid because of the greater degree to which the intermolecular forces must be overcome in going from the liquid to the gaseous state.

14. 0.48 kJ; 27 kJ   **16.** 15 kJ
18. 107 kJ/mol; 39.5 kJ; 1.07×10^3 kJ
20. Dipole–dipole forces are stronger at shorter distances; they are relatively short-range forces.

22. The boiling point of water, compared with those of the hydrogen compounds of the other Group 6 elements, is unusually high. In water, hydrogen is bonded to a very strongly electronegative element (compared with Se, Te, or S). This causes the O—H bond to be much more polar than the bonds between hydrogen and the other Group 6 elements. This stronger polarity leads to additional forces between molecules that must be overcome to boil the substance.

24. The fact that such nonpolar, monatomic molecules *can* be liquefied and solidified indicates that *some* kind of intermolecular forces are possible between atoms in these substances. London dispersion forces arise when a temporary (instantaneous) dipolar arrangement of charge develops as the electrons of an atom move around its nucleus. This instantaneous dipole can induce a similar dipole in a neighboring atom, leading to a momentary attraction.

26. (a) London dispersion forces; (b) London dispersion forces; (c) dipole–dipole forces and London dispersion forces; (d) dipole–dipole (hydrogen bonding) and London dispersion forces

28. An increase in the heat of fusion is observed for an increase in the size of the halogen atom (the electron cloud of a larger atom is more easily polarized by a neighboring dipole, thus giving larger London dispersion forces).

30. For a homogeneous mixture to form, the forces between molecules of the two substances being mixed must be at least *comparable in magnitude* to the intermolecular forces within each separate substance. In the case of a water–ethanol mixture, the forces that exist when water and ethanol are mixed are stronger than water–water or ethanol–ethanol forces in the separate substances. Ethanol and water molecules can approach one another more closely in the mixture than either substance's molecules could approach a like molecule in the separate substances. Strong hydrogen bonding occurs in both ethanol and water.

32. Vapor pressure is the pressure of vapor present *at equilibrium* above a liquid in a sealed container at a given temperature. When a liquid is placed in a closed container, molecules of the liquid evaporate freely into the empty space above the liquid. As the number of molecules present in the vapor state increases with time, vapor molecules begin to rejoin the liquid state (condense). Eventually a dynamic equilibrium is reached between evaporation and condensation in which the net number of molecules present in the vapor phase becomes *constant* with time.

34. A method is shown in Figure 14.10. The apparatus consists of a barometer into which a volatile liquid may be injected. Because mercury is more dense than other liquids, the injected volatile liquid rises to the top of the mercury column in the tube and floats on top of the mercury. The volatile liquid evaporates into the empty space above the mercury (a virtual vacuum). As the liquid is converted to the gaseous state, the level of the mercury column drops as the pressure of vapor builds up.

36. (a) HF: Although both substances are capable of hydrogen bonding, water has two O—H bonds that can be involved in hydrogen bonding versus only one F—H bond in HF. (b) CH_3OCH_3: Because no H is attached to the O atom, no hydrogen bonding can exist. Thus, the molecule should be relatively more volatile than CH_3CH_2OH even though it contains the same number of atoms of each element; (c) CH_3SH: Hydrogen bonding is not as important for an S—H bond (because S has a lower electronegativity than O). Since there is relatively little hydrogen bonding, CH_3SH is more volatile than CH_3OH.

38. Both substances have the same molar mass. Ethyl alcohol contains a hydrogen atom directly bonded to an oxygen atom, however. Therefore, hydrogen bonding can exist in ethyl alcohol, whereas only weak dipole–dipole forces exist in dimethyl ether. Dimethyl ether is more volatile; ethyl alcohol has a higher boiling point.

40. *Ionic* solids have positive and negative ions as their fundamental particles; a simple example is sodium chloride, in which Na^+ and Cl^- ions are held together by strong electrostatic forces. *Molecular* solids have molecules as their fundamental particles, with the molecules being held together in the crystal by dipole–dipole forces, hydrogen bonding forces, or London dispersion forces (depending on the identity of the substance); simple examples of molecular solids include ice (H_2O) and ordinary table sugar (sucrose). *Atomic* solids have simple atoms as their fundamental particles, with the atoms being held together in the crystal by either covalent bonding (as in graphite or diamond) or metallic bonding (as in copper or other metals).

42. The fundamental particles in molecular solids are individual *molecules;* ice (individual water molecules), table sugar (individual sucrose molecules).

44. Ionic solids consist of a crystal lattice of positively and negatively charged ions. A given ion is surrounded by several ions of the opposite charge, all of which electrostatically attract it strongly. This pattern repeats itself throughout the crystal.

46. Ice contains nonlinear, highly polar water molecules, with extensive, strong hydrogen bonding. Dry ice consists of linear, nonpolar molecules, and only very weak intermolecular forces are possible.

48. In a metal, the valence electrons are mobile and can move throughout the entire metal lattice. In ionic solids, each positive and negative ion is held rigidly in place by several ions of the opposite charge.

50. Alloys may be of two types: *substitutional* (in which one metal is substituted for another in the regular positions of the crystal lattice) and *interstitial* (in which a second metal's atoms fit into the empty spaces [interstices] in a given metal's lattice). The presence of a second metal's atoms in a metal's lattice changes the first metal's properties: frequently the alloy is stronger than either of the original metals because the irregularities introduced into the crystal lattice by the presence of a second metal's atoms prevent the crystal from being deformed as easily. The properties of iron may be modified by alloying with many different substances—particularly with carbon, nickel, chromium, and cobalt. Steels with relatively high carbon content are exceptionally strong, whereas steels with low carbon content are softer, more malleable, and more ductile. Steels produced by alloying iron with nickel, chromium, and cobalt are more resistant to corrosion than iron itself.

52. j   **54.** f

56. d   **58.** a

60. l

62. Dimethyl ether has the larger vapor pressure. No hydrogen bonding is possible because the O atom does not have a hydrogen atom attached. Hydrogen bonding can occur *only* when a hydrogen atom is *directly* attached to a strongly electronegative atom (such as N, O, or F). Hydrogen bonding is possible in ethanol (ethanol contains an —OH group).

64. (a) H_2. London dispersion forces are the only intermolecular forces present in these nonpolar molecules; typically these forces become larger with increasing atomic size (as the atoms become bigger, the edge of the electron cloud lies farther from the nucleus and becomes more easily distorted). (b) Xe. Only the relatively weak London forces exist in a crystal of Xe atoms, whereas in NaCl strong ionic forces exist, and in diamond strong covalent bonding exists between carbon atoms. (c) Cl_2. Only London forces exist among such nonpolar molecules.

66. *Steel* is a general term applied to alloys consisting primarily of iron, but with small amounts of other substances added. Whereas pure iron itself is relatively soft, malleable, and ductile, steels are typically much stronger and harder and much less subject to damage.

68. Water is the solvent in which cellular processes take place in living creatures. Water in the oceans moderates the earth's temperature. Water is used in industry as a cooling agent, and it serves as a means of transportation. The liquid range is 0 °C to 100 °C at 1 atm pressure.

70. At higher altitudes, the boiling points of liquids are lower because there is a lower atmospheric pressure above the liquid. The temperature at which food cooks is determined by the temperature to which the water in the food can be heated before it escapes as steam. Thus, food cooks at a lower temperature at high elevations where the boiling point of water is lowered.

72. Heat of fusion (melt); heat of vaporization (boil). The heat of vaporization is always larger, because virtually all of the intermolecular forces must be overcome to form a gas. In a liquid, considerable intermolecular forces remain. Going from a solid to a liquid requires less energy than going from a liquid to a gas.

74. Dipole–dipole interactions are typically 1% as strong as a covalent bond. Dipole–dipole interactions represent electrostatic attractions between portions of molecules that carry only a *partial* positive or negative charge, and such forces require the molecules that are interacting to come *near* each other.

76. London dispersion forces are relatively weak forces that arise among noble gas atoms and in nonpolar molecules. London forces arise from *instantaneous dipoles* that develop when one atom (or molecule) momentarily distorts the electron cloud of another atom (or molecule). London forces are typically weaker than either permanent dipole–dipole forces or covalent bonds.

78. For each mole of liquid water that evaporates, several kilojoules of heat must be absorbed by the water from its surroundings to overcome attractive forces among the molecules.

80. In NH_3, strong hydrogen bonding can exist. Because CH_4 molecules are nonpolar, only the relatively weak London dispersion forces exist.

82. Strong *hydrogen bonding* forces are present in an ice crystal, while only the much weaker *London forces* exist in the crystal of a nonpolar substance like oxygen.

Chapter 15

2. A *non*homogeneous mixture may differ in composition in various places in the mixture, whereas a solution (a homogeneous mixture) has the same composition throughout. Examples of nonhomogeneous mixtures include spaghetti sauce, a jar of jelly beans, and a mixture of salt and sugar.

4. solid

6. One substance will mix with and dissolve in another substance if the intermolecular forces are similar in the two substances. When the mixture forms, the forces between particles in the mixture will be similar to the forces present in the separate substances. Both sugar and ethyl alcohol molecules contain polar —OH groups, which are comparable to the polar —OH structure in water. Sugar or ethyl alcohol molecules can hydrogen-bond with water molecules and intermingle with them freely to form a solution. Substances like petroleum (whose molecules contain only carbon and hydrogen) are very nonpolar and cannot form interactions with polar water molecules.

8. independently

10. unsaturated

12. large

14. nine

16. (a) 9.1% NH_4NO_3; (b) 3.8% NH_4NO_3; (c) 1.3% NH_4NO_3; (d) 0.99% NH_4NO_3

18. (a) 22.5 g (23 g) NaCl; (b) 233 g solution; (c) 150. g NaCl; (d) 150. g NaCl

20. 3.44% Cu; 2.61% Zn; 93.9% Fe

22. 3.54% NaCl

24. 7.81 g KBr

26. 15.6 g $CuCl_2$

28. 4.8 g heptane; 2.7 g pentane; 85.5 g (86 g) hexane

30. 0.50; 1.0

32. If a solution has a concentration of 5 *M*, then 1 L of solution (*not* solvent) contains 5 mol of solute. To prepare such a solution, place 5 mol of NaCl in a 1-L flask, and then add the amount of water that is necessary to yield a *total* volume of 1L after mixing. The NaCl will occupy some space, so the amount of water will be less than 1.00 L.

34. (a) 2.0 *M*; (b) 1.0 *M*; (c) 0.67 *M*; (d) 0.50 *M*

36. (a) 0.253 *M*; (b) 0.106 *M*; (c) 0.434 *M*; (d) 1.7×10^{-3} *M*

38. 0.405 *M*

40. 0.0902 *M*

42. 0.619 *M*

44. (a) 0.530 mol HCl, 19.3 g HCl; (b) 0.0312 mol $CaCl_2$, 3.46 g $CaCl_2$; (c) 0.0286 mol HNO_3, 1.80 g HNO_3; (d) 5.46 mol NaCl, 319 g NaCl

46. (a) 0.936 g EDTA; (b) 48.5 g $CuSO_4$; (c) 0.0452 g H_3PO_4; (d) 0.87 g HCl

48. 0.36 L

50. (a) 4.60×10^{-3} mol Al^{3+}; 1.38×10^{-2} mol Cl^-; (b) 1.70 mol Na^+; 0.568 mol PO_4^{3-}; (c) 2.19×10^{-3} mol Cu^{2+}; 4.38×10^{-3} mol Cl^-; (d) 3.96×10^{-5} mol Ca^{2+}; 7.91×10^{-5} mol OH^-

52. 1.68 g

54. half

56. (a) 0.0837 *M*; (b) 0.320 *M*; (c) 0.0964 *M*; (d) 0.622 *M*

58. 0.691 mL

60. 0.127 *M* (0.13 *M*)

62. 1.0 *M*

64. 7.5 mL

66. 2.32 g

68. 0.300 g

70. 64.2 mL

72. 1.8×10^{-4} *M*

74. (a) 63.0 mL; (b) 2.42 mL; (c) 50.1 mL; (d) 1.22 L

76. 1 normal

78. 1.53 equivalents OH^- ion. By definition, one equivalent of OH^- ion exactly neutralizes one equivalent of H^+ ion.

80. (a) 0.277 *N*; (b) 3.37×10^{-3} *N*; (c) 1.63 *N*

82. (a) 1.20×10^{-2} *N*; (b) 2.02×10^{-4} *N*; (c) 0.101 *N*

84. 7.03×10^{-5} *M*; 1.41×10^{-4} *N*

86. 2.15×10^3 mL (2.15 L)

88. 0.05583 *M*; 0.1117 *N*

90. Molarity is defined as the number of moles of solute contained in 1 liter of *total* solution volume (solute plus solvent after mixing). In the first example, the total volume after mixing is *not* known and the molarity cannot be calculated. In the second example, the final volume after mixing is known and the molarity can be calculated simply.

92. 3.8×10^2 g 5% NaCl solution

94. 0.47 g $BaSO_4$ forms; concentration of remaining Ba^{2+} ion = 0.15 *M*

96. 56 mol

98. 1.12 L HCl at STP

100. 26.3 mL

102. 1.71 *M* NaCl

104. (a) 6.3% KNO_3; (b) 0.25% KNO_3; (c) 11% KNO_3; (d) 18% KNO_3

106. 4.7% C; 1.4% Ni; 93.9% Fe

108. 28 g Na_2CO_3

110. 9.4 g NaCl; 3.1 g KBr

112. (a) 4.0 *M*; (b) 1.0 *M*; (c) 0.73 *M*; (d) 3.6 *M*

114. 0.812 *M*

116. 0.026 *M*

118. (a) 4.2×10^2 g KCl; (b) 4.7 g NaCl; (c) 8.8×10^3 g HCl; (d) 0.25 g $HClO_4$

120. (a) 0.938 mol Na^+; 0.313 mol PO_4^{3-}; (b) 0.042 mol H^+; 0.021 mol SO_4^{2-}; (c) 0.0038 mol Al^{3+}; 0.011 mol Cl^-; (d) 1.88 mol Ba^{2+}; 3.75 mol Cl^-

122. (a) 0.0909 *M*; (b) 0.127 *M*; (c) 0.192 *M*; (d) 1.6 *M*

124. 0.90 *M*

126. 50. mL

128. 35.0 mL

130. (a) 0.823 *N* HCl; (b) 4.00 *N* H_2SO_4; (c) 3.06 *N* H_3PO_4

132. 0.083 *M* NaH_2PO_4; 0.17 *N* NaH_2PO_4

134. 9.6×10^{-2} *N* HNO_3

Answers

TO EVEN-NUMBERED CUMULATIVE REVIEW EXERCISES

Chapters 1–3

2. After having covered three chapters in this book, you should have adopted an "active" approach to your study of chemistry. You can't just sit and take notes in class, or just review the solved examples in the textbook. You must learn to *interpret* problems and reduce them to simple mathematical relationships. In chemistry you must extend and synthesize what has been discussed, and then apply the material to new situations. Don't become discouraged if this initially proves difficult: it's challenging for every student at first.

4. Sometimes students find it difficult to understand why certain subjects are required for a given college major. The faculty of your major department, however, collectively have many years of experience in the subject in which you have chosen to specialize. They may have experienced problems with the same courses that now give you trouble, but they realize that all the work will be worth the effort in the end. Some courses, particularly those in your major field, have obvious and immediate utility. Other courses—chemistry included—provide general *background* knowledge that will prove useful in understanding your own major, or other subjects related to your major.

6. Whenever a scientific measurement is made, we always employ the instrument or measuring device to the limits of its precision. This usually means that we *estimate* the last significant figure of the measurement. An example of the uncertainty in the last significant figure is given for measuring the length of a pin in the text in figure 2.5. Scientists appreciate the limits of experimental techniques and instruments and always *assume* that the last digit in a number representing a measurement has been estimated. Because instruments or measuring devises always have a limit to their precision, uncertainty cannot be completely excluded from measurements.

8. Dimensional analysis is a method of problem solving that pays particular attention to the units of measurements and uses these units as if they were algebraic symbols that multiply, divide, and cancel. Consider the following example: One dozen eggs costs $1.25. Suppose we want to know how much one egg costs, and also how much three dozen eggs will cost. To solve these problems, we need two equivalence statements:

  1 dozen eggs = 12 eggs
  1 dozen eggs = $1.25

The calculations are: $\frac{\$1.25}{12\ eggs} = \$0.104 = \$0.10$ as the cost of one egg and $\frac{\$1.25}{1\ dozen} \times 3\ dozen = \$3.75$ as the cost of three dozen eggs. See Section 2.6 of the text for how we construct conversion factors from equivalence statements.

10. Scientists say that matter is anything that "has mass and occupies space." Matter is the "stuff" of which everything is made. It can be classified and subdivided in many ways, depending on what we are trying to demonstrate. All the types of matter we have studied are made of atoms. They differ in whether these atoms are all of one element, or are of more than one element, and also in whether these atoms are in physical mixtures or chemical combinations.

Matter can also be classified according to its physical state (solid, liquid, or gas). In addition, it can be classified as a pure substance (one type of molecule) or a mixture (more than one type of molecule).

12. An element is a fundamental substance that cannot be broken down into simpler substances by chemical methods. An element consists of atoms of only one type. Compounds, on the other hand, *can* be broken down into simpler substances. For example, both sulfur and oxygen are *elements*. When sulfur and oxygen are placed together and heated, the *compound* sulfur dioxide (SO_2) forms. Each molecule of sulfur dioxide contains one sulfur atom and two oxygen atoms. On a mass basis, SO_2 always consists of 50% each, by mass, of sulfur and oxygen—that is, sulfur dioxide has a constant composition. Sulfur dioxide from any source would have the same composition (or it wouldn't be sulfur dioxide!).

14. Scientists define energy as "the capacity to do work." Energy is commonly expressed in units of *calories* or *joules* (the SI unit). One calorie is the amount of heat required to raise the temperature of one gram of water by one Celsius degree. Because 1 calorie = 4.184 joules, it takes 4.184 J to raise the temperature of one gram of water by one Celsius degree. The specific heat capacity of a particular substance is the amount of energy required to raise the temperature of one gram of that substance by one Celsius degree (e.g., the specific heat capacity of water is 1.000 cal/g °C, or 4.184 J/g °C). When energy (as heat) is added to or removed from a pure substance, the total heat flow (Q) is given by $Q = s \times m \times \Delta T$, where m is the mass of substance, s is the specific heat capacity of the substance, and ΔT is the temperature change undergone by the substance.

16. (a) 12.1 km; (b) 15.2 lb; (c) 5.55 L; (d) 2.22 qt; (e) 0.555 gal; (f) 1,315 mm; (g) 0.318 m; (h) 0.47 L; (i) 3.84L; (j) 3.83 L

18. (a) -58.2 °F; (b) -34.8 °C; (c) 268 °C; (d) 494 K; (e) 172 °F (1.7×10^2 °F); (f) 295 K

20. (a) 110. cal; (b) 29.42 kJ; (c) 5.531×10^4 J; (d) 328 kJ; (e) 4.541 kcal; (f) 20.1 kcal

Chapters 4–5

2. Although you don't have to memorize all the elements, you should at least be able to give the symbol or name for the most common elements (listed in Table 4.3).

4. The main postulates of Dalton's theory are: (1) Elements are made up of tiny particles called atoms; (2) all atoms of a given element are identical; (3) although all atoms of a given element are identical, these atoms are different from the atoms of all other elements; (4) atoms of one element can combine with atoms of another element to form a compound that will always have the same relative numbers and types of atoms for its composition; and (5) atoms are merely rearranged into new groupings during an ordinary chemical reaction, and no atom is ever destroyed and no new atom is ever created during such a reaction.

6. The expression "nuclear" atom indicates that the atom has a dense center of positive charge (nucleus) around which the electrons move through primarily empty space. Rutherford's experiment involved shooting a beam of α particles at a thin sheet of metal foil. According to the "plum pudding" model of the atom, these positively charged α particles should have passed through the foil. Rutherford detected that a small number of α particles bounced backward to the source of α particles or were deflected from the foil at large angles. Rutherford realized that his observations could be explained if the atoms of the metal foil had a small, dense, positively charged nucleus, with a significant amount of empty space between nuclei. The empty space between nuclei would allow most of the α particles to pass through the foil. If an α particle were to hit a nucleus head-on, it would be deflected backward. If a positively charged α particle passed *near* a positively charged nucleus, then the α particle would be deflected by the repulsive forces. Rutherford's experiment disproved the "plum pudding" model, which envisioned the atom as a uniform sphere of positive charge, with enough negatively charged electrons scattered throughout to balance out the positive charge.

8. Isotopes represent atoms of the same element that have different atomic masses. Isotopes result from the different numbers of neutrons in the nuclei of atoms of a given element. They have the same atomic number (number of protons in the nucleus) but have different mass numbers (total number of protons and neutrons in the nucleus). The different isotopes of an atom are indicated by the form $_{Z}^{A}X$, in which Z represents the atomic number and A the mass number of element X. For example, $_{6}^{13}C$ represents a nuclide of carbon with atomic number 6 (6 protons in the nucleus) and mass number 13 (6 protons plus 7 neutrons in the nucleus). The various isotopes of an element have identical *chemical* properties. The *physical* properties of the isotopes of an element may differ slightly because of the small difference in mass.

10. Most elements are too reactive to be found in nature in other than the combined form. Gold, silver, and platinum, and some of the gaseous elements (such as O_2, N_2, He, and Ar) are found in the elemental form.

12. Ionic compounds typically are hard, crystalline solids with high melting and boiling points. The ability of aqueous solutions of ionic substances to conduct electricity means that ionic substances consist of positively and negatively charged particles (ions). A sample of an ionic substance has no net electrical charge because the total number of positive charges is *balanced* by an equal number of negative charges. An ionic compound could not consist of only cations or only anions because a net charge of zero cannot be obtained when all ions have the same charge. Also, ions of like charge will repel each other.

14. When naming ionic compounds, the positive ion (cation) is named first. For simple binary Type I ionic compounds, the ending *-ide* is added to the root name of the negative ion (anion). For example, the name for K_2S would be "potassium sulf*ide*"—potassium is the cation, sulfide is the anion. Type II compounds, which involve elements that form more than one stable ion, are named by either of two systems: the "Roman numeral" system (which is preferred by

most chemists) and the "*ous-ic*" system. For example, iron can react with oxygen to form either of two stable oxides, FeO or Fe_2O_3. Under the Roman numeral system, FeO would be named iron(II) oxide to show that it contains Fe^{2+} ions; Fe_2O_3 would be named iron(III) oxide to indicate that it contains Fe^{3+} ions. Under the "*ous-ic*" system, FeO is named ferr*ous* oxide and Fe_2O_3 is called ferr*ic* oxide. Type II compounds usually involve transition metals and non-metals.

16. A polyatomic ion is an ion containing more than one atom. Some common polyatomic ions are listed in Table 5.5. Parentheses are used in writing formulas containing polyatomic ions to indicate how many polyatomic ions are present. For example, the correct formula for calcium phosphate is $Ca_3(PO_4)_2$, which indicates that three calcium ions are combined for every two phosphate ions. If we did *not* write the parentheses around the formula for the phosphate ion (that is, if we wrote Ca_3PO_{42}), people might think that 42 oxygen atoms were present!

18. Acids are substances that produce protons (H^+ ions) when dissolved in water. For acids that do *not* contain oxygen, the prefix *hydro-* and the suffix *-ic* are used with the root name of the element present in the acid (for example: HCl, *hydro*chloric acid; H_2S, *hydro*sulfuric acid; HF, *hydro*fluoric acid). For acids whose anions contain oxygen, a series of prefixes and suffixes is used with the name of the central atom in the anion: these prefixes and suffixes indicate the relative (not actual) number of oxygen atoms present in the anion. Most elements that form oxyanions form *two* such anions—for example, sulfur forms sulf*ite* ion (SO_3^{2-}) and sulf*ate* ion (SO_4^{2-}). For an element that forms two oxyanions, the acid containing the anions will have the ending *-ous* if the *-ite* anion is involved and the ending *-ic* if the *-ate* anion is present. For example, H_2SO_3 is sulfur*ous* acid and H_2SO_4 is sulfur*ic* acid. The Group 7 elements each form *four* oxyanions/oxyacids. The prefix *hypo-* is used for the oxyacid that contains fewer oxygen atoms than the *-ite* anion, and the prefix *per-* is used for the oxyacid that contains more oxygen atoms than the *-ate* anion. For example,

Acid Name	Name	Anion	Anion
HBrO	*hypo*brom*ous* acid	BrO^-	hypo-bromite
$HBrO_2$	brom*ous* acid	BrO_2^-	bromite
$HBrO_3$	brom*ic* acid	BrO_3^-	bromate
$HBrO_4$	*per*brom*ic* acid	BrO_4^-	perbromate

20. (a) He, helium, 2; (b) B, boron, 5; (c) C, carbon, 6; (d) F, fluorine, 9; (e) S, sulfur, 16; (f) Ba, barium, 56; (g) Be, beryllium, 4; (h) O, oxygen, 8; (i) P, phosphorus, 15; (j) Si, silicon, 14

22.

trons	Protons	Neutrons	Elec-
(a) $_{2}^{4}He$	2	2	2
(b) $_{17}^{37}Cl$	17	20	17
(c) $_{35}^{79}Br$	35	44	35
(d) $_{20}^{41}Ca$	20	21	20
(e) $_{20}^{40}Ca$	20	20	20
(f) $_{92}^{238}U$	92	146	92
(g) $_{92}^{235}U$	92	143	92
(h) $_{1}^{1}H$	1	0	1

24. (a) K^+, 19 protons, 18 electrons; (b) Ca^{2+}, 20 protons, 18 electrons; (c) N^{3-}, 7 protons, 10 electrons; (d) Br^-, 35 protons, 36 electrons; (e) Al^{3+}, 13 protons, 10 electrons; (f) Ag^+, 47 protons, 46 electrons; (g) Cl^-, 17 protons, 18 electrons; (h) H^+, 1 proton, 0 electrons; (i) H^-, 1 proton, 2 electrons; (j) Na^+, 11 protons, 10 electrons; (k) O^{2-}, 8 protons, 10 electrons; (l) I^-, 53 protons, 54 electrons

26. (a) $FeCl_3$, iron(III) chloride (ferric chloride); (b) Cu_2S, copper(I) sulfide (cuprous sulfide); (c) $CoBr_2$, cobalt(II) bromide (cobaltous bromide); (d) Fe_2O_3, iron(III) oxide (ferric oxide); (e) AuI_3, gold(III) iodide, auric iodide; (f) Cr_2S_3, chromium(III) sulfide, chromic sulfide; (g) MnO_2, manganese(IV) oxide; (h) CuO, copper(II) oxide, cupric oxide; (i) NiS, nickel(II) sulfide, nickelous sulfide

28. (a) NH_4^+, ammonium ion; (b) SO_3^{2-}, sulfite ion; (c) NO_3^-, nitrate ion; (d) SO_4^{2-}, sulfate ion; (e) NO_2^-, nitrite ion; (f) CN^-, cyanide ion; (g) OH^-, hydroxide ion; (h) ClO_4^-, perchlorate ion; (i) ClO^-, hypochlorite ion; (j) PO_4^{3-}, phosphate ion

30. (a) B_2O_3, diboron trioxide; (b) NO_2, nitrogen dioxide; (c) PCl_5, phosphorus pentachloride; (d) N_2O_4, dinitrogen tetroxide; (e) P_2O_5, diphosphorus pentoxide; (f) ICl, iodine monochloride; (g) SF_6, sulfur hexafluoride; (h) N_2O_3, dinitrogen trioxide

Chapters 6–8

2. A chemical equation indicates the substances necessary for a given chemical reaction, and the substances produced by that chemical reaction. The substances to the left of the arrow are called the *reactants;* those to the right of the arrow are called the *products.* A *balanced* equation indicates the relative numbers of molecules in the reaction.

4. Never change the *subscripts* of a *formula:* changing the subscripts changes the *identity* of a substance and makes the equation invalid.

   When balancing a chemical equation, we adjust only the *coefficients* in front of a formula: changing a coefficient changes the *number* of molecules being used in the reaction, *without* changing the *identity* of the substance.

6. In a precipitation reaction, a *solid* (precipitate) forms when the reactants are combined. In such a reaction, the mixture turns *cloudy* as the reactants are combined and a solid settles out on standing. For example, if you mixed solutions of barium nitrate and sodium carbonate, a precipitate of barium carbonate would form. $Ba(NO_3)_2(aq) + Na_2CO_3(aq) \rightarrow BaCO_3(s) + 2NaNO_3(aq)$

8. Nearly all compounds containing the nitrate, sodium, potassium, and ammonium ions are soluble in water. Most salts containing the chloride and sulfate ions are soluble in water, with specific exceptions (see Table 7.1). Most compounds containing the hydroxide, sulfide, carbonate, and phosphate ions are *not* soluble in water (unless the compound also contains Na^+, K^+, or NH_4^+). For example, suppose we combine barium chloride and sulfuric acid solutions
$$BaCl_2(aq) + H_2SO_4(aq) \rightarrow BaSO_4(s) + 2HCl(aq)$$
$$Ba^{2+}(aq) + SO_4^{2-}(aq) \rightarrow BaSO_4(s) \text{ [net ionic reaction]}$$
Because barium sulfate is not soluble in water, a precipitate of $BaSO_4(s)$ forms.

10. Acids (such as the acetic acid found in vinegar) were first noted primarily because of their sour taste, whereas bases were first charactererized by their bitter taste and slippery feel on the skin. Acids and bases neutralize each other, forming water: $H^+(aq) + OH^-(aq) \rightarrow H_2O(l)$. Strong acids and bases ionize *fully* when dissolved in water, which means they are also strong electrolytes.
Strong acids: HCl, HNO_3, H_2SO_4, and $HClO_4$
Strong bases: Group 1 hydroxides (for example, $NaOH$ and KOH)

12. Oxidation–reduction reactions are *electron-transfer* reactions. Oxidation represents a loss of electrons by an atom, molecule, or ion; reduction represents the gain of electrons. Oxidation and reduction always occur together: the electrons lost by one species must be gained by another species. For example, $Mg(s) + F_2(g) \rightarrow MgF_2(s)$ shows a simple oxidation–reduction reaction between a metal and a nonmetal. In this process, Mg atoms lose two electrons each to become Mg^{2+} ions in MgF_2: Mg is oxidized. Each atom of F_2 gains one electron to become an F^- ion, for a total of two electrons gained for each F_2 molecule: F_2 is reduced. $Mg \rightarrow Mg^{2+} + 2e^-$; $2(F + e^- \rightarrow F^-)$

14. In a synthesis reaction, elements or simple compounds react to produce more complex substances. For example,
$$N_2(g) + 3H_2(g) \rightarrow 2NH_3(g)$$
$$NaOH(aq) + CO_2(g) \rightarrow NaHCO_3(s)$$
Decomposition reactions represent the breakdown of complex substances into simpler substances. For example, $2H_2O_2(aq) \rightarrow 2H_2O(l) + O_2(g)$. Synthesis and decomposition reactions are often oxidation–reduction reactions, although not always. For example, the synthesis reaction between $NaOH$ and CO_2 does *not* represent oxidation–reduction.

16. (a) $2Na(s) + 2H_2O(l) \rightarrow 2NaOH(aq) + H_2(g)$
   $Ca(s) + 2H_2O(l) \rightarrow Ca(OH)_2(aq) + H_2(g)$
   (b) $2Na(s) + Br_2(l) \rightarrow 2NaBr(s)$
   $Ca(s) + Br_2(l) \rightarrow CaBr_2(s)$
   (c) $6Na(s) + N_2(g) \rightarrow 2Na_3N(s)$
   $3Ca(s) + N_2(g) \rightarrow Ca_3N_2(s)$
   (d) $2Na(s) + O_2(g) \rightarrow Na_2O_2(s)$
   $2Ca(s) + O_2(g) \rightarrow 2CaO(s)$
   (e) $2Na(s) + S(s) \rightarrow Na_2S(s)$
   $Ca(s) + S(s) \rightarrow CaS(s)$

18. (a) $Ba(NO_3)_2(aq) + K_2CrO_4(aq) \rightarrow BaCrO_4(s) + 2KNO_3(aq)$
   (b) $NaOH(aq) + HC_2H_3O_2(aq) \rightarrow H_2O(l) + NaC_2H_3O_2(aq)$
   (then evaporate the water from the solution)
   (c) $AgNO_3(aq) + NaCl(aq) \rightarrow AgCl(s) + NaNO_3(aq)$
   (d) $Pb(NO_3)_2(aq) + H_2SO_4(aq) \rightarrow PbSO_4(s) + 2HNO_3(aq)$
   (e) $2NaOH(aq) + H_2SO_4(aq) \rightarrow Na_2SO_4(aq) + 2H_2O(l)$
   (then evaporate the water from the solution)
   (f) $Ba(NO_3)_2(aq) + 2Na_2CO_3(aq) \rightarrow BaCO_3(s) + 2NaNO_3(aq)$

20. (a) $FeO(s) + 2HNO_3(aq) \rightarrow Fe(NO_3)_2(aq) + H_2O(l)$
   acid–base; double displacement
   (b) $2Mg(s) + 2CO_2(g) + O_2(g) \rightarrow 2MgCO_3(s)$
   synthesis; oxidation–reduction
   (c) $2NaOH(s) + CuSO_4(aq) \rightarrow Cu(OH)_2(s) + Na_2SO_4(aq)$
   precipitation; double displacement
   (d) $HI(aq) + KOH(aq) \rightarrow KI(aq) + H_2O(l)$
   acid–base; double displacement
   (e) $C_3H_8(g) + 5O_2(g) \rightarrow 3CO_2(g) + 4H_2O(g)$
   combustion; oxidation–reduction
   (f) $Co(NH_3)_6Cl_2(s) \rightarrow CoCl_2(s) + 6NH_3(g)$
   decomposition
   (g) $2HCl(aq) + Pb(C_2H_3O_2)_2(aq) \rightarrow 2HC_2H_3O_2(aq) + PbCl_2(s)$
   precipitation; acid-base; double displacement

(h) $C_{12}H_{22}O_{11}(s) \rightarrow 12C(s) + 11H_2O(g)$
decomposition; oxidation–reduction

(i) $2Al(s) + 6HNO_3(aq) \rightarrow 2Al(NO_3)_3(aq) + 3H_2(g)$
oxidation–reduction

(j) $4B(s) + 3O_2(g) \rightarrow 2B_2O_3(s)$
synthesis; oxidation–reduction

Chapters 9–10

2. On a microscopic basis, one mole of a substance represents Avogadro's number (6.022×10^{23}) of individual units (atoms or molecules) of the substance. On a macroscopic basis, one mole of a substance represents the amount of substance present when the molar mass of the substance in grams is taken. Chemists have chosen these definitions so that a simple relationship will exist between measurable amounts of substances (grams) and the actual number of atoms or molecules present, and so that the number of particles present in samples of *different* substances can easily be compared.

4. The molar mass of a compound is the mass in grams of one mole of the compound and is calculated by summing the average atomic masses of all the atoms present in a molecule of the compound. For example, for H_3PO_4: molar mass $H_3PO_4 = 3(1.008 \text{ g}) + 1(30.97 \text{ g}) + 4(16.00 \text{ g}) = 97.99$ g

6. The *empirical* formula of a compound represents the *relative* number of atoms of each type present in a molecule of the compound, whereas the *molecular* formula represents the *actual* number of atoms of each type present in a real molecule. For example, both acetylene (molecular formula C_2H_2) and benzene (molecular formula C_6H_6) have the same relative number of carbon and hydrogen atoms, and thus have the same empirical formula (CH). The molar mass of the compound must be determined before calculating the actual molecular formula. Since real molecules cannot contain fractional *parts* of atoms, the molecular formula is always a *whole-number multiple* of the empirical formula.

8. In question 7, we chose to calculate the percentage composition of phosphoric acid, H_3PO_4: 3.085% H, 31.60% P, 65.31% O. Using these percentages, and choosing a 2.417-g sample of the compound, our new problem would be worded as follows: "A 2.417-g sample of a compound has been analyzed and was found to contain 0.07456 g H, 0.7638 g of P, and 1.579 g of O. Calculate the empirical formula of the compound."

10. For a given amount of C_4H_{10}, the following mole ratios could be constructed:

To calculate mol CO_2 produced: $\left(\dfrac{8 \text{ mol } CO_2}{2 \text{ mol } C_4H_{10}} \right)$

To calculate mol H_2O produced: $\left(\dfrac{10 \text{ mol } H_2O}{2 \text{ mol } C_4H_{10}} \right)$

To calculate mol O_2 required: $\left(\dfrac{13 \text{ mol } O_2}{2 \text{ mol } C_4H_{10}} \right)$

Using these mole ratios, we could then calculate the numbers of moles of the other substances if 0.55 mol of C_4H_{10} were to be combusted: 2.2 mol CO_2, 2.8 mol H_2O, and 3.6 mol O_2.

12. When arbitrary amounts of reactants are used, one reactant will be present, stoichiometrically, in the least amount: this substance is called the *limiting reactant*. It *limits* the amount of product that can

form in the experiment, because once this substance has reacted completely, the reaction must *stop*. The other reactants in the experiment are present *in excess*, which means that a portion of these reactants will be present *unchanged* after the reaction ends.

14. The *theoretical yield* for an experiment is the mass of product calculated assuming the limiting reactant for the experiment is completely consumed. The *actual yield* for an experiment is the mass of product actually collected by the experimenter. Any experiment is restricted by the skills of the experimenter and by the inherent limitations of the experimental method: for these reasons, the actual yield is often less than the theoretical yield. Although one would expect that the actual yield should never exceed the theoretical yield, in real experiments, sometimes this happens. However, an actual yield greater than a theoretical yield usually means that something is *wrong* in either the experiment (for example, impurities may be present) or the calculations.

16. H_2O: 11.19% H, 88.81% O; K_2CO_3: 56.58% K, 8.690% C, 34.73% O; NO_2: 30.45% N, 69.55% O; $C_{12}H_{22}O_{11}$: 42.10% C, 6.479% H, 51.42% O; NaOH: 57.48% Na, 40.00% O, 2.520% H; Na_2O_2: 58.96% Na, 41.04% O; $NaC_2H_3O_2$: 28.02% Na, 29.28% C, 3.686% H, 39.01% O

18. (a) 22.9 g Ag_2SO_4, 12.1 g $Ca(NO_3)_2$; (b) 197 g $Al(NO_3)_3$, 2.80 g H_2; (c) 41.8 g Na_3PO_4, 13.8 g H_2O; (d) 49.5 g $CaCl_2$, 8.03 g H_2O

20. Na: Cl_2 limiting reactant; 16.5 g theory; 59.7% yield
Mg: Cl_2 limiting reactant; 13.4 g theory; 73.59% yield
Al: Cl_2 limiting reactant; 12.5 g theory; 78.8% yield

Chapters 11–12

2. An atom in its *ground state* is in its lowest possible energy state. When an atom possesses more energy than in its ground state, the atom is in an *excited state*. An atom is promoted from its ground state to an excited state by absorbing energy; when the atom returns from an excited state to its ground state it emits the excess energy as electromagnetic radiation. Atoms do not gain or emit radiation randomly, but rather do so only in discrete bundles of radiation called *photons*. The photons of radiation emitted by atoms are characterized by the wavelength (color) of the radiation: longer-wavelength photons carry less energy than shorter-wavelength photons. The energy of a photon emitted by an atom corresponds *exactly* to the difference in energy between two allowed energy states in an atom.

4. Bohr pictured the electron moving in certain circular orbits around the nucleus, with each orbit being associated with a specific energy (resulting from the attraction between the nucleus and the electron and from the kinetic energy of the electron). Bohr assumed that when an atom absorbs energy, the electron moves from its ground state $(n = 1)$ to an orbit farther away from the nucleus $(n = 2, 3, 4, \ldots)$. Bohr postulated that when an excited atom returns to its ground state, the atom emits the excess energy as radiation. Because the Bohr orbits are located at fixed distances from the nucleus and from each other, when an electron moves from one fixed orbit to another, the energy change is of a definite amount, which corresponds to the emission of a photon with a particular characteristic wavelength and energy. When the simple Bohr model for the atom was applied to the emission spectra of other elements, however, the theory could

not predict or explain the observed emission spectra of these elements.

6. The lowest-energy hydrogen atomic orbital is called the $1s$ orbital. The $1s$ orbital is spherical in shape (the electron density around the nucleus is uniform in all directions). The orbital does *not* have a sharp edge (it appears fuzzy) because the probability of finding the electron gradually decreases as distance from the nucleus increases. The orbital does *not* represent just a spherical surface on which the electron moves (this would be similar to Bohr's original theory)—instead, the $1s$ orbital represents a probability map of electron density around the nucleus for the first principal energy level.

8. The third principal energy level of hydrogen is divided into three sublevels: the $3s$, $3p$, and $3d$ sublevels. The $3s$ subshell consists of the single $3s$ orbital, which is spherical in shape. The $3p$ subshell consists of a set of three equal-energy $3p$ orbitals: each of these $3p$ orbitals has the same shape ("dumbbell"), but each of the $3p$ orbitals is oriented in a different direction in space. The $3d$ subshell consists of a set of five $3d$ orbitals with shapes as indicated in Figure 11.24, which are oriented in different directions around the nucleus. The fourth principal energy level of hydrogen is divided into four sublevels: the $4s$, $4p$, $4d$, and $4f$ orbitals. The $4s$ subshell consists of the single $4s$ orbital. The $4p$ subshell consists of a set of three $4p$ orbitals. The $4d$ subshell consists of a set of five $4d$ orbitals. The shapes of the $4s$, $4p$, and $4d$ orbitals are the *same* as the shapes of the orbitals of the third principal energy level—the orbitals of the fourth principal energy level are *larger* and *further from the nucleus* than the orbitals of the third level, however. The fourth principal energy level also contains a $4f$ subshell consisting of seven $4f$ orbitals (the shapes of the $4f$ orbitals are beyond the scope of this text).

10. Atoms have a series of *principal energy levels* indexed by the letter n. The $n = 1$ level is closest to the nucleus, and the energies of the levels increase as the value of n (and distance from the nucleus) increases. Each principal energy level is divided into *sublevels* (sets of orbitals) of different characteristic shapes designated by the letters *s, p, d,* and *f*. Each s subshell consists of a single *s* orbital; each *p* subshell consists of a set of three *p* orbitals; each *d* subshell consists of a set of five *d* orbitals; and so on. An orbital can be empty or it can contain one or two electrons, but never more than two electrons (if an orbital contains two electrons, then the electrons must have opposite spins). The shape of an orbital represents a probability map for finding electrons—it does not represent a trajectory or pathway for electron movements.

12. The valence electrons of an atom are found in the outermost shell of the atom that contains electrons. The core electrons are those in principal energy levels closer to the nucleus than the outermost shell. The valence electrons are the electrons gained, lost, or shared with other atoms. The arrangement of the elements on the periodic table corresponds to their valence electron configurations (elements in the same vertical group have similar configurations). The evidence that the $4s$ subshell fills *before* the $3d$ subshell is that the elements K and Ca have properties very similar to those of the other Group 1 and Group 2 elements.

14. The general periodic table you drew for Question 13 should resemble that found in Figure 11.27. From the column and row location of an element, you should be able to determine its valence config-

uration. For example, the element in the third horizontal row of the second vertical column has $3s^2$ as its valence configuration. The element in the seventh vertical column of the second horizontal row has valence configuration $2s^2 2p^5$.

16. The ionization energy of an atom represents the energy required to remove an electron from the atom in the gas phase. Moving from top to bottom in a vertical group on the periodic table, the ionization energies decrease. The ionization energies increase when going from left to right within a horizontal row within the periodic table. The relative sizes of atoms also vary systematically with the location of an element on the periodic table. Within a given vertical group, the atoms become progressively larger when going from the top of the group to the bottom. Moving from left to right within a horizontal row on the periodic table, the atoms become progressively smaller.

18. To form an ionic compound, a metallic element reacts with a nonmetallic element, with the metallic element losing electrons to form a positive ion and the nonmetallic element gaining electrons to form a negative ion. The aggregate form of such a compound consists of a crystal lattice of alternating positively and negatively charged ions: a given positive ion is attracted by surrounding negatively charged ions, and a given negative ion is attracted by surrounding positively charged ions. Similar electrostatic attractions exist in three dimensions throughout the crystal of the ionic solid, leading to a very stable system (with very high melting and boiling points, for example). As evidence for the existence of ionic bonding, ionic solids do not conduct electricity (the ions are rigidly held), but melts or solutions of such substances do conduct electric current. For example, when sodium metal and chlorine gas react, a typical ionic substance (sodium chloride) results: $2Na(s) + Cl_2(g) \rightarrow 2Na^+Cl^-(s)$.

20. Electronegativity represents the relative ability of an atom in a molecule to attract shared electrons toward itself. For a bond to be polar, one of the atoms in the bond must attract the shared electron pair toward itself and away from the other atom of the bond—this happens if one atom of the bond is more electronegative than the other. If two atoms in a bond have the same electronegativity, then the two atoms pull the electron pair equally and the bond is nonpolar and covalent. If two atoms sharing a pair of electrons have *vastly* different electronegativities, the electron pair will be pulled so strongly by the more electronegative atom that a negative *ion* may be formed (as well as a positive ion for the other atom) and ionic bonding will result. If the difference in electronegativity between two atoms sharing an electron pair lies somewhere between these two extremes, then a polar covalent bond results.

22. It has been observed over many, many experiments that when an active metal like sodium or magnesium reacts with a nonmetal, the sodium atoms always form Na^+ ions and the magnesium atoms always form Mg^{2+} ions. It has also been observed that when nonmetallic elements like nitrogen, oxygen, or fluorine form simple ions, the ions are always N^{3-}, O^{2-}, and F^-, respectively. Observing that these elements always form the same ions and those ions all contain eight electrons in the outermost shell, scientists speculated that a species that has an octet of electrons (like the noble gas neon) must be very fundamentally stable. The *repeated* observation that so many elements, when reacting, tend to attain an electron

configuration that is isoelectronic with a noble gas led chemists to speculate that *all* elements try to attain such a configuration for their outermost shells. Covalently and polar covalently bonded molecules also strive to attain pseudo-noble gas electron configurations. For a covalently bonded molecule like F_2, each F atom provides one electron of the pair of electrons that constitutes the covalent bond. Each F atom feels also the influence of the other F atom's electron in the shared pair, and each F atom effectively fills its outermost shell.

24. Bonding between atoms to form a molecule involves only the outermost electrons of the atoms, so only these *valence* electrons are shown in the Lewis structures of molecules. The most important requisite for the formation of a stable compound is that each atom of a molecule attain a noble gas electron configuration. In Lewis structures, arrange the bonding and nonbonding valence electrons to try to complete the octet (or duet) for as many atoms as possible.

26. You could choose practically any molecules for your discussion. Let's illustrate the method for ammonia, NH_3. First, count the total number of valence electrons available in the molecule (without regard to their source). For NH_3, since nitrogen is in Group 5, one nitrogen atom would contribute five valence electrons. Since hydrogen atoms have only one electron each, the three hydrogen atoms provide an additional three valence electrons, for a total of eight valence electrons overall. Next, write down the symbols for the atoms in the molecule, and use one pair of electrons (represented by a line) to form a bond between each pair of bound atoms.

$$H-\underset{\underset{H}{|}}{N}-H$$

These three bonds use six of the eight valence electrons. Because each hydrogen already has its duet and the nitrogen atom has only six electrons around it so far, the final two valence electrons must represent a lone pair on the nitrogen.

$$H-\underset{\underset{H}{|}}{\overset{\cdot\cdot}{N}}-H$$

28. Boron and beryllium compounds sometimes do not fit the octet rule. For example, in BF_3, the boron atom has only six valence electrons in its outermost shell, whereas in BeF_2, the beryllium atom has only four electrons in its outermost shell. Other exceptions to the octet rule include any molecule with an odd number of valence electrons (such as NO or NO_2). Even the oxygen gas we breathe is an exception to the octet rule: although we can write a Lewis structure for O_2 satisfying the octet rule for each oxygen, experiments show that O_2 contains *unpaired* electrons (which would not be consistent with a structure in which all the electrons are paired up).

30.

Number of Valence Pairs	Bond Angle	Examples
2	180°	BeF_2, BeH_2
3	120°	BCl_3
4	109.5°	CH_4, CCl_4, GeF_4

32. The shapes of *s, p,* and *d* orbitals are shown in Figures 11.21, 11.22, 11.23, and 11.24.

34. Group 1, [noble gas]ns^1; Group 2, [noble gas]ns^2; Group 3, [noble gas]ns^2np^1; Group 4, [noble gas]ns^2np^2; Group 5, [noble gas]ns^2np^3;

Group 6, [noble gas]ns^2np^4; Group 7, [noble gas]ns^2np^5; Group 8, [noble gas]ns^2np^6 (itself a noble gas)

36. (a) $GeCl_4$

$$\overset{\displaystyle :\ddot{C}l:}{\underset{\displaystyle :\ddot{C}l:}{:\ddot{C}l-Ge-\ddot{C}l:}}$$

(b) NO_3^-

$$\left[\begin{array}{c}\ddot{O}=\underset{\underset{\ddot{O}}{|}}{N}-\ddot{O}:\end{array}\right]^- \leftrightarrow \left[\begin{array}{c}:\ddot{O}-\underset{\underset{\ddot{O}}{|}}{N}=\ddot{O}\end{array}\right]^- \leftrightarrow \left[\begin{array}{c}:\ddot{O}-\underset{\underset{\ddot{O}}{\|}}{N}-\ddot{O}:\end{array}\right]^-$$

(c) SO_4^{2-}

$$\left[\begin{array}{c}:\ddot{O}:\\ :\ddot{O}-\underset{\underset{:\ddot{O}:}{|}}{\overset{|}{S}}-\ddot{O}:\end{array}\right]^{2-}$$

(d) SO_3^{2-}

$$\left[\begin{array}{c}:\ddot{O}-\underset{\underset{:\ddot{O}:}{|}}{S}-\ddot{O}:\end{array}\right]^{2-}$$

(e) SO_2

$$\ddot{O}=\overset{\cdot\cdot}{S}-\ddot{O}: \leftrightarrow :\ddot{O}-\overset{\cdot\cdot}{S}=\ddot{O}$$

(f) O_2

$$\ddot{O}=\ddot{O}$$

(g) O_3

$$\ddot{O}=\overset{\cdot\cdot}{O}-\ddot{O}: \leftrightarrow :\ddot{O}-\overset{\cdot\cdot}{O}=\ddot{O}$$

(h) CH_3NH_2

$$H-\underset{\underset{H}{|}}{\overset{\overset{H}{|}}{C}}-\underset{\underset{H}{|}}{\overset{\cdot\cdot}{N}}-H$$

(i) C_2H_6

$$H-\underset{\underset{H}{|}}{\overset{\overset{H}{|}}{C}}-\underset{\underset{H}{|}}{\overset{\overset{H}{|}}{C}}-H$$

(j) C_2H_4

$$\underset{\underset{H}{|}}{\overset{\overset{H}{|}}{C}}=\underset{\underset{H}{|}}{\overset{\overset{H}{|}}{C}}$$

(k) BF_3

$$:\ddot{F}-\underset{\underset{:\ddot{F}:}{|}}{B}-\ddot{F}:$$

(l) BeF_2

$$:\ddot{F}-Be-\ddot{F}:$$

(m) NO_2^-

$$\left[:\ddot{O}-\overset{\cdot\cdot}{N}=\ddot{O}\right]^- \leftrightarrow \left[\ddot{O}=\overset{\cdot\cdot}{N}-\ddot{O}:\right]^-$$

(n) PF_3

$$:\ddot{F}-\underset{\underset{:\ddot{F}:}{|}}{\overset{\cdot\cdot}{P}}-\ddot{F}:$$

(o) N_2H_4

$$H-\underset{\underset{H}{|}}{\overset{\cdot\cdot}{N}}-\underset{\underset{H}{|}}{\overset{\cdot\cdot}{N}}-H$$

Chapters 13–15

2. The pressure exerted by the atmosphere results from the thick layer of gases above the surface of the earth pressing downward. Atmospheric pressure has traditionally been measured with a mercury barometer (see Figure 13.2).

4. Boyle's law says that the volume of a gas sample will decrease if you squeeze it harder (at constant temperature, for a fixed amount of gas). Two mathematical statements of Boyle's law are

$$P \times V = \text{constant}$$
$$P_1 \times V_1 = P_2 \times V_2$$

These two mathematical formulas say the same thing: if the pressure on a sample of gas is increased, the volume of the sample will decrease. A graph of Boyle's law data is given as Figure 13.5: this type of graph ($xy = k$) is known to mathematicians as a *hyperbola*.

6. Charles's law says that if you heat a sample of gas, the volume of the sample will increase (assuming the pressure and amount of gas remain the same). When the temperature is given in kelvins, Charles's law expresses a *direct* proportionality (if you *in*crease T, then V *in*creases), whereas Boyle's law expresses an *inverse* proportionality (if you *in*crease P, then V *de*creases). Two mathematical statements of Charles's law are $V = bT$ and $(V_1/T_1) = (V_2/T_2)$. With this second formulation, we can determine volume–temperature information for a given gas sample under two sets of conditions. Charles's law holds true only if the amount of gas remains the same (the volume of a gas sample would increase if more gas were present) and also if the pressure remains the same (a change in pressure also changes the volume of a gas sample).

8. Avogadro's law says that the volume of a sample of gas is directly proportional to the number of moles (or molecules) of gas present (at constant temperature and pressure). Avogadro's law holds true only for gas samples compared under the same conditions of temperature and pressure. Avogadro's law expresses a direct proportionality: the more gas in a sample, the larger the sample's volume.

10. The "partial" pressure of an individual gas in a mixture of gases represents the pressure the gas would exert in the same container at the same temperature if it were the *only* gas present. The *total* pressure in a mixture of gases is the sum of the individual partial pressures of the gases present in the mixture. The fact that the partial pressures of the gases in a mixture are additive suggests that the total pressure in a container is a function of the *number* of molecules present, and not of the identity of the molecules or of any other property (such as the molecules' inherent atomic size).

12. The main postulates of the kinetic-molecular theory for gases are: (a) gases consist of tiny particles (atoms or molecules), and the size of these particles themselves is negligible compared with the bulk volume of a gas sample; (b) the particles in a gas are in constant random motion, colliding with each other and with the walls of the container; (c) the particles in a gas sample do not assert any attractive or repulsive forces on one another; and (d) the average kinetic energy of the gas particles is directly related to the absolute temperature of the gas sample. The pressure exerted by a gas results from the molecules colliding with (and pushing on) the walls of the container; the pressure increases with temperature because, at a higher temperature, the molecules move faster and hit the walls of the container with greater force. A gas fills the volume available to it because the molecules in a gas are in constant *random*

motion: the randomness of the molecules' motion means that they eventually will move out into the available volume until the distribution of molecules is uniform; at constant pressure, the volume of a gas sample increases as the temperature is increased because with each collision having greater force, the container must expand so that the molecules are farther apart if the pressure is to remain constant.

14. The molecules are much closer together in solids and liquids than in gaseous substances and interact with each other to a much greater extent. Solids and liquids have much greater densities than do gases, and are much less compressible, because so little room exists between the molecules in the solid and liquid states (the volume of a solid or liquid is not affected very much by temperature or pressure). We know that the solid and liquid states of a substance are similar to each other in structure, since it typically takes only a few kilojoules of energy to melt 1 mol of a solid, whereas it may take 10 times more energy to convert a liquid to the vapor state.

16. The *normal* boiling point of water—that is, water's boiling point at a pressure of exactly 760 mm Hg—is 100 °C. Water remains at 100 °C while boiling, because the additional energy added to the sample is used to overcome attractive forces among the water molecules as they go from the condensed, liquid state to the gaseous state. The normal (760 mm Hg) freezing point of water is exactly 0 °C. A cooling curve for water is given in Figure 14.2.

18. Dipole–dipole forces arise when molecules with permanent dipole moments try to orient themselves so that the positive end of one polar molecule can attract the negative end of another polar molecule. Dipole–dipole forces are not nearly as strong as ionic or covalent bonding forces (only about 1% as strong as covalent bonding forces) since electrostatic attraction is related to the *magnitude* of the charges of the attracting species and drops off rapidly with distance. Hydrogen bonding is an especially strong dipole–dipole attractive force that can exist when hydrogen atoms are directly bonded to the most electronegative atoms (N, O, and F). Because the hydrogen atom is so small, dipoles involving N—H, O—H, and F—H bonds can approach each other much more closely than can other dipoles; because the magnitude of dipole–dipole forces is related to distance, unusually strong attractive forces can exist. The much higher boiling point of water than that of the other covalent hydrogen compounds of the Group 6 elements is evidence for the special strength of hydrogen bonding.

20. The vaporization of a liquid requires an input of energy to overcome the intermolecular forces that exist between the molecules in the liquid state. The large heat of vaporization of water is essential to life since much of the excess energy striking the earth from the sun is dissipated in vaporizing water. Condensation refers to the process by which molecules in the vapor state form a liquid. In a closed container containing a liquid with some empty space above the liquid, an equilibrium occurs between vaporization and condensation. When the liquid is first placed in the container, the liquid phase begins to evaporate into the empty space. As the number of molecules in the vapor phase increases, however, some of these molecules begin to reenter the liquid phase. Eventually, each time a molecule of liquid somewhere in the container enters the vapor phase, another molecule of vapor reenters the liquid phase. No further net change occurs in the amount of liquid phase. The pressure of the vapor in such an equilibrium situation is characteristic for the liquid at each temperature. A simple experiment to determine the vapor pressure of a liquid is shown in Figure 14.10. Typically, liquids with strong intermolecular forces have smaller vapor pressures (they have more difficulty in evaporating) than do liquids with very weak intermolecular forces.

22. The *electron sea* model explains many properties of metallic elements. This model pictures a regular array of metal atoms set in a "sea" of mobile valence electrons. The electrons can move easily throughout the metal to conduct heat or electricity, and the lattice of atoms cations can be deformed with little effort, allowing the metal to be hammered into a sheet or stretched into wire. An alloy is a material that contains a mixture of elements that overall has metallic properties. *Substitutional* alloys consist of a host metal in which some of the atoms in the metal's crystalline structure are replaced by atoms of other metallic elements. For example, sterling silver is an alloy in which some silver atoms have been replaced by copper atoms. An *interstitial alloy* is formed when other, smaller atoms enter the interstices (holes) between atoms in the host metal's crystal structure. Steel is an interstitial alloy in which carbon atoms enter the interstices of a crystal of iron atoms.

24. A saturated solution contains as much solute as can dissolve at a particular temperature. Saying that a solution is *saturated* does not *necessarily* mean that the solute is present at a high concentration—for example, magnesium hydroxide dissolves only to a very small extent before the solution is saturated. A saturated solution is in

equilibrium with undissolved solute: as molecules of solute dissolve from the solid in one place in the solution, dissolved molecules rejoin the solid phase in another part of the solution. Once the rates of dissolving and solid formation become equal, no further net change occurs in the concentration of the solution and the solution is saturated.

26. Adding more solvent to a solution to dilute the solution does *not* change the number of moles of solute present, but changes only the *volume* in which the solute is dispersed. If molarity is used to describe the solution's concentration, then the number of *liters* is changed when solvent is added and the number of *moles per liter* (the molarity) changes, but the actual number of *moles* of solute does *not* change. For example, 125 mL of 0.551 M NaCl contains 0.0689 mol of NaCl. The solution will *still* contain 0.0689 mol of NaCl after the 250 mL of water is added to it. The volume and the concentration will change, but the number of moles of solute in the solution will *not* change. The 0.0689 mol of NaCl, divided by the total volume of the diluted solution in liters, gives the new molarity (0.184 M).

28. (a) 26.6 mL; (b) 9.87 L; (c) 407 mL
30. (a) 42.3 mL; (b) 3.03 L; (c) 4.35 mL; (d) 49.9 L
32. 1.02 L O_2 at STP; 1.10 L O_2 at 24 °C, 771 mm Hg
34. (a) 18.1%; (b) 10.9%; (c) 5.22%; (d) 0.551%; (e) 0.109% NaCl
36. (a) 0.341 M; (b) 5.40%; (c) 0.0522 M
38. (a) 10.1 mL H_2SO_4; (b) 20.3 mL H_2SO_4

Index

TABLE 5.1

Common Simple Cations and Anions

Cation	Name	Anion	Name*
H^+	hydrogen	H^-	hydride
Li^+	lithium	F^-	fluoride
Na^+	sodium	Cl^-	chloride
K^+	potassium	Br^-	bromide
Cs^+	cesium	I^-	iodide
Be^{2+}	beryllium	O^{2-}	oxide
Mg^{2+}	magnesium	S^{2-}	sulfide
Ca^{2+}	calcium		
Ba^{2+}	barium		
Al^{3+}	aluminum		
Ag^+	silver		

*The root is given in color.

TABLE 5.2

Common Type II Cations

Ion	Systematic Name	Older Name
Fe^{3+}	iron(III)	ferric
Fe^{2+}	iron(II)	ferrous
Cu^{2+}	copper(II)	cupric
Cu^+	copper(I)	cuprous
Co^{3+}	cobalt(III)	cobaltic
Co^{2+}	cobalt(II)	cobaltous
Sn^{4+}	tin(IV)	stannic
Sn^{2+}	tin(II)	stannous
Pb^{4+}	lead(IV)	plumbic
Pb^{2+}	lead(II)	plumbous
Hg^{2+}	mercury(II)	mercuric
Hg_2^{2+}*	mercury(I)	mercurous

*Mercury(I) ions always occur bound together in pairs to form Hg_2^{2+}.

TABLE 5.4

Names of Common Polyatomic Ions

Ion	Name	Ion	Name
NH_4^+	ammonium	CO_3^{2-}	carbonate
NO_2^-	nitrite	HCO_3^-	hydrogen carbonate
NO_3^-	nitrate		(bicarbonate is a widely
SO_3^{2-}	sulfite		used common name)
SO_4^{2-}	sulfate	ClO^-	hypochlorite
HSO_4^-	hydrogen sulfate	ClO_2^-	chlorite
	(bisulfate is a widely	ClO_3^-	chlorate
	used common name)	ClO_4^-	perchlorate
OH^-	hydroxide	$C_2H_3O_2^-$	acetate
CN^-	cyanide	MnO_4^-	permanganate
PO_4^{3-}	phosphate	$Cr_2O_7^{2-}$	dichromate
HPO_4^{2-}	hydrogen phosphate	CrO_4^{2-}	chromate
$H_2PO_4^-$	dihydrogen phosphate	O_2^{2-}	peroxide